A Course in Phonology is truly comprehensive ~~covering phonetics,~~ all areas of linear phonology, lexical phonology, and optimality theory. It is unique in that it can serve as both a text for a basic introductory course in phonology and for a more advanced course. The book is pedagogically solid. Phenomena are first exemplified for English, then other languages are discussed. The focus on English builds on what students are familiar with. The integration of phonetics and phonology in the first part of the book and the introduction to optimality theory are particularly valuable. The book stands as a *remarkable achievement* in presenting the current state of the field in a pedagogically-friendly way.

Stuart Davis, Indiana University

Andrew Linn
Sheffield 1999

THE INTERNATIONAL PHONETIC ALPHABET

(revised to 1993, corrected 1996)

Consonants (Pulmonic)

	Bilabial	Labiodental	Dental	Alveolar	Postalveolar	Retroflex	Palatal	Velar	Uvular	Pharyngeal	Glottal
Plosive	p b			t d		ʈ ɖ	c ɟ	k g	q ɢ		ʔ
Nasal	m	ɱ		n		ɳ	ɲ	ŋ	N		
Trill	ʙ			r					R		
Tap or flap				ɾ		ɽ					
Fricative	ɸ β	f v	θ ð	s z	ʃ ʒ	ʂ ʐ	ç ʝ	x ɣ	χ ʁ	ħ ʕ	h ɦ
Lateral fricative				ɬ ɮ							
Approximant		ʋ		ɹ		ɻ	j	ɰ			
Lateral approximant				l		ɭ	ʎ	ʟ			

Where symbols appear in pairs, the one to the right represents a voiced consonant. Shaded areas denote articulations judged impossible.

Consonants (Non-Pulmonic)

Clicks		Voiced implosives		Ejectives	
ʘ	Bilabial	ɓ	Bilabial	ʼ	Examples:
ǀ	Dental	ɗ	Dental/alveolar	pʼ	Bilabial
ǃ	(Post)alveolar	ʄ	Palatal	tʼ	Dental/alveolar
ǂ	Palatoalveolar	ɠ	Velar	kʼ	Velar
ǁ	Alveolar lateral	ʛ	Uvular	sʼ	Alveolar fricative

Other Symbols

ʍ Voiceless labial-velar fricative

w Voiced labial-velar approximant

ɥ Voiced labial-palatal approximant

ʜ Voiceless epiglottal fricative

ʢ Voiced epiglottal fricative

ʡ Epiglottal plosive

ɕ ʑ Alveolo-palatal fricatives

ɺ Alveolar lateral flap

ɧ Simultaneous ʃ and x

Affricates and double articulations can be represented by two symbols joined by a tie bar if necessary.

k͡p t͡s

Vowels

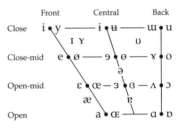

Front Central Back

Close: i•y — ɨ•ʉ — ɯ•u

ɪ ʏ ʊ

Close-mid: e•ø — ɘ•ɵ — ɤ•o

ə

Open-mid: ɛ•œ — ɜ•ɞ — ʌ•ɔ

æ ɐ

Open: a•ɶ — ɑ•ɒ

Where symbols appear in pairs, the one to the right represents a rounded vowel.

Diacritics

Diacritics may be placed above a symbol with a descender, e.g. ŋ̊

̥	Voiceless	n̥ d̥	̤	Breathy voiced	b̤ a̤	̪	Dental	t̪ d̪
̬	Voiced	s̬ t̬	̰	Creaky voiced	b̰ a̰	̺	Apical	t̺ d̺
ʰ	Aspirated	tʰ dʰ	̼	Linguolabial	t̼ d̼	̻	Laminal	t̻ d̻
̹	More rounded	ɔ̹	ʷ	Labialized	tʷ dʷ	̃	Nasalized	ẽ
̜	Less rounded	ɔ̜	ʲ	Palatalized	tʲ dʲ	ⁿ	Nasal release	dⁿ
̟	Advanced	u̟	ˠ	Velarized	tˠ dˠ	ˡ	Lateral release	dˡ
̠	Retracted	e̠	ˤ	Pharyngealized	tˤ dˤ	̚	No audible release	d̚
̈	Centralized	ë	̴	Velarized or pharyngealized ɫ				
̽	Mid-centralized	e̽	̝	Raised	e̝ (ɹ̝ = voiced alveolar fricative)			
̩	Syllabic	n̩	̞	Lowered	e̞ (β̞ = voiced bilabial approximant)			
̯	Non-syllabic	e̯	̘	Advanced tongue root	e̘			
˞	Rhoticity	ɚ a˞	̙	Retracted tongue root	e̙			

Suprasegmentals

ˈ Primary stress

ˌ Secondary stress

ˌfoʊnəˈtɪʃən

ː Long   eː

ˑ Half-long   eˑ

̆ Extra-short   ĕ

| Minor (foot) group

‖ Major (intonation) group

. Syllable break   ɹi.ækt

‿ Linking (absence of a break)

Tones and Word Accents

Level		Contour	
e̋ or ˥	Extra high	ě or ˄	Rising
é or ˦	High	ê or ˅	Falling
ē or ˧	Mid	e᷄ or ˄	High rising
è or ˨	Low	e᷅ or ˅	Low rising
ȅ or ˩	Extra low	e᷈	Rising-falling
↓ Downstep		↗ Global rise	
↑ Upstep		↘ Global fall	

A COURSE IN PHONOLOGY

Iggy Roca and Wyn Johnson
University of Essex

BLACKWELL
Publishers

Copyright © Iggy Roca and Wyn Johnson 1999

The right of Iggy Roca and Wyn Johnson to be identified as the authors
of this work has been asserted in accordance with the Copyright,
Designs and Patents Act 1988

First published 1999

2 4 6 8 10 9 7 5 3 1

Blackwell Publishers Ltd
108 Cowley Road
Oxford OX4 1JF
UK

Blackwell Publishers Inc.
350 Main Street
Malden, Massachusetts 02148
USA

British Library Cataloguing in Publication Data

A CIP catalogue record for this book is available from the British Library.

Library of Congress Cataloging-in-Publication Data

Roca, Iggy.
A course in phonology/Iggy Roca and Wyn Johnson.
p.   cm.
Includes bibliographical references (p.) and index.
ISBN 0–631–21345–7 (alk. paper)
ISBN 0–631–21346–5 (pbk. : alk. paper)
1. Grammar, Comparative and general—Phonology.   2. English
language—Phonology.   I. Johnson, Wyn.   II. Title.
P217.R58   1999
414—dc21   98–51941
                                    CIP

Typeset in 10 on 13 pt Palatino
by Graphicraft Limited, Hong Kong
Printed in Great Britain by T. J. International, Padstow, Cornwall

This book is printed on acid-free paper

Unless it grows out of yourself
no knowledge is really yours,
it is only a borrowed plumage.

D. T. Suzuki, *An Introduction to Zen Buddhism*

To Morris and Noam,
who created generative phonology.

CONTENTS

PREFACE

The field of phonology finds itself in the heat of a revolution. The 1950s and 1960s saw the triumph of generative phonology over its taxonomic predecessor, and with it the establishment of a new way of doing phonology, consolidated through the 1970s and 1980s. The 1990s have witnessed the emergence of Optimality Theory.

Writing a textbook in the midst of revolutionary turmoil would seem like bad timing: aren't textbooks distillations of what philosophers of science have referred to as "normal science"? While accepting the truthfulness of this proposition, we would like to argue that the present state of phonology resembles more a ripple in the ocean (perhaps a rather deep ripple) than an earthquake. In particular, we contend that Optimality Theory is still very much generative phonology. Indeed, the basic constituent elements of Optimality Theory are identical to those of classical generative phonology: a collection of paradigmatic data, a modelling of such data into levels of representation (perhaps only two in OT), and a procedure to effect the mapping between these levels. It is here, of course, that the two theories appear most strikingly to part company: classical generative phonology has rules and Optimality Theory constraints. However, the forms that these constraints evaluate (the "candidates") evidently need to have been composed in the first place, by procedures which, more likely than not, resemble rules.

In the pages that follow we guide the beginner step by step through the wonders of phonology, endeavouring at all times to remain non-doctrinaire: theories provide the mould, but the dough is obviously theory-independent, a foundation the learner needs to become fully conversant with before diving into deep theoretical waters. The presentation of facts in a formal vacuum is, however, ultimately counterproductive, if not simply impracticable. Accordingly, we have largely relied on the familiar rule format, always keeping sight of the current appetite for constraints. Our goal has been to write a text which is sufficiently clear for learning to take place, and sufficiently complete to be worthy of the title "A Course in Phonology". In order to achieve this aim, we survey all the major building blocks of phonology, which, by their very nature, are shared by classical generative phonology and Optimality Theory, and we also supply a preliminary foundation in articulatory phonetics. We have striven for clarity of style and have left the text free of the usual reference clutter, providing instead the fabric of the underlying scholarship in chapter 20. We interact with the reader as we go along and use constant quizzing in the shape of grey boxes. We have a strong belief that learning grows best out of the learner's experience, past and present. As a consequence, we have shied away from potentially mystifying exoticism, and structured the presentation around readily accessible facts of English, while still catering for the exotic through references to foreign data where appropriate. We dispense advice on how to approach the text with maximum efficiency in the "Reading Logistics" section that follows this preface and the acknowledgements.

We have deliberately taken sides with the learner, against the expert phonologist, whenever we felt a conflict. The expert's vista of the field, the result of many years' hard work, is unavailable to the beginner, whose needs are necessarily at variance with the needs of the expert. Indeed, the greatest challenge to teachers and textbook writers alike involves abandoning our vantage point and trying to sit inside the mind of the average learner. This is not an easy undertaking, but we have endeavoured to carry it through to the best of our ability. The result may at times be slightly irritating to the expert, from whom we beg forbearance. Hopefully, however, it will genuinely meet the needs of the learner and induce true understanding.

The book contains three interrelated but clearly distinct parts, of approximately equal length. Part I presents the foundations of both phonology and articulatory phonetics, and explains the differences between these two disciplines. It also supplies the basic tools of the phonological trade as we have known it for almost half a century now: features, rules and derivations, all couched autosegmentally. Part II deals with the familiar suprasegmental aspects of phonology: syllables, stress, and tone and intonation. Part I is appropriate for a short introductory phonology course, by itself or as part of a phonetics component. Parts I and II together provide a solid foundation in phonology at an intermediate level. Part III takes the reader to a substantially more advanced level of both phonological awareness and theoretical sophistication, dealing with such matters as the cycle, multilevel phonology, prosodic phonology, markedness, underspecification, feature geometry, and Optimality Theory. Many of the issues we raise are given practical treatment in the companion volume *A Workbook in Phonology*, which includes a large section on Optimality Theory to complement the exercises in the present book.

Having invested much time and energy in the book, we have high hopes that readers will not need to look back, metaphorically or literally, but will be empowered to take the leap into full enjoyment, both passive and active, of the marvels of phonology. If this aim is achieved, we will feel modestly proud of having provided the soil in which a true and durable knowledge of this exciting field of inquiry has taken root.

ACKNOWLEDGEMENTS

A book of this kind inevitably owes an incommensurable debt to many more than memory or paper availability can realistically account for, and therefore we shall limit ourselves to mentioning those who have had a direct major part in its elaboration. First among these are Bernard Tranel, Kevin Varden and other Blackwell's anonymous readers, all of whom made an invaluable contribution to the shaping of the book through the several years of writing. For phonetic information, we are particularly grateful to Judith Broadbent, Dick and Katrina Hayward, Paul Kerswill and Linda Shockey. Of our own students, we must single out Nick Sherrard and, in particular, Paula Reimers, who carefully read through the whole final draft and offered us most valuable painstaking comments. Finally, Philip Carpenter skilfully, if not always painlessly, steered the project to success through its various phases, and was eventually joined by Simon Eckley, Jack Messenger, Fiona Sewell, and the remainder of the Blackwell team. To all these, and to the many others who contributed to the project in a variety of ways and capacities, our deepest gratitude. It goes without saying that any errors or infelicities that may have escaped scrutiny are of our sole making.

Reading Logistics

This book has been written with you, the reader, in mind. Our aim has been to present phonology in a way that is both comprehensible and memorable, and to this end we have resorted to a variety of pedagogical devices. We have endeavoured to use a clear, honest-to-God style from beginning to end, giving you the gist of the theory rather than the maze of opinions and counteropinions. Because we are fully aware that even the clearest of explanations is not sufficient to ensure rapid understanding and memorability, we make use of a panoply of mnemonics, as follows:

- each chapter opens up with a list of key points to be covered, hopefully in a style that you will understand at once
- throughout the chapter, we purposely interact with you by means of grey boxes, which should ensure that you connect with the text
- margin notes summarize the main points in the text as we go along: you should definitely endeavour to remember them
- the contents of each chapter are summarized in a dark box at the end
- each chapter is followed by a set of key questions for you to answer, and by a set of exercises for further practice
- each of the three parts of the book is preceded by a concise summary of its substance
- chapter 20 further sums up what we say throughout the book

In addition, we give all technical terms in full capitals in the place in the text where they are defined or become central. Many of these terms, and a number of others, are brought together in a glossary at the end of the book, to facilitate matters further. We also include a copy of the latest official version of the IPA alphabet, and a key to the special symbols we use throughout the book. A list of references follows chapter 20 to enable you to take your reading as far afield as your need or your yearning may drive you. Last, but not least, there is a subject index, a language index, and an author index.

Our advice to the reader is to make use of all these facilities in the manner that best fits personal needs. For instance, if you are a complete beginner, you will probably gain much benefit from reading the matter in the grey boxes, more or less systematically. If you already know some phonology, however, you may find some of these boxes distracting, particularly in the preliminary chapters, and therefore you will be best advised simply to skip them. Similarly, you may wish to ignore the grey boxes, or at least some of them, in subsequent readings of the text. In a nutshell, we provide you with a range of materials, grey boxes included, for your benefit, not for your punishment: it is you who must decide how many of these materials you use and when. The whole idea is that the text should not be approached as inert matter, but, rather, as a flexible interactive partner. We obviously wish you success. We also hope that you will genuinely enjoy the task.

KEY TO SYMBOLS

The following list includes most of the special symbols used in the book. You must pay attention to the fact that many of them are used for several purposes, often unrelated or even contradictory.

< > ANGLED BRACKETS:
indicates a two-way implication between the strings thus enclosed; marks extrametricality (or, more generally, extraprosodicity) of the material thus enclosed

→ ARROW:
signals that the material on its left 'rewrites as' the material on its right

» ARROW HEAD (DOUBLE):
used in OT to mean 'ranked higher than'

> ARROW HEAD (SINGLE):
signals that the material on its left 'precedes' the material on its right

* ASTERISK:
marks the ungrammaticality of the material it is prefixed to; signals metrical prominence, thus making up metrical grids; in OT tableaux, it signals constraint violation; as a superscript, it indicates optional recursion; signals "accent" in both stress and tones

{ } BRACES:
enclose several subrules to signal their joint participation in a single rule, as in the English Vowel Shift; indicate disjunctivity of features, as in the environment "[+sonorant] or [−continuant]" in the English rule of Spirantization

, COMMA:
in OT, it signals lack of ranking

~ DASH (SWUNG):
negates the material it is prefixed to; separates alternants

! EXCLAMATION MARK:
in OT, it indicates a fatal constraint violation;

in tonal phonology, it is frequently used to signal downstep (the IPA symbol is ↓, with ! standing for a (post) alveolar click)

⊃　IMPLICATION SYMBOL:

indicates that the material on its left 'implies' the material on its right

μ　MU [mju]:

a shorthand for "mora"

( )　PARENTHESES:

enclose feet;

enclose optional material

☞　POINTING FINGER:

in OT tableaux, it singles out the winning candidate

Σ　SIGMA (CAPITAL):

a shorthand for "foot"

σ　SIGMA (LOWER CASE):

a shorthand for "syllable"

/　SLASH:

separates focus from environment in rules

//　SLASHES:

enclose underlying representations;

enclose phonemic material

[ ]　SQUARE BRACKETS:

enclose distinctive features;

delimit distinctive feature matrices;

enclose constituents (phonological, morphological or syntactic);

enclose surface representations;

enclose phonetic material

[ ]$_x$　SUBSCRIPT NOTATION:

an alternative to the class node formalism

⌢　TIE BAR:

links two phonetic symbols to indicate the unitary nature of the sound

PART ONE

PHONETICS AND PHONOLOGY

This book is about sound in language. The first distinction we must draw is between sound as sound ("phonetics") and sound structure ("phonology"). By sound as sound we mean the sound we make with our vocal organs when we speak, an activity equivalent to the playing of the instruments by an orchestra: it is as if we were all carrying an orchestra in us! These sounds have their own physical characteristics, which can be described: here we focus on the description of the movements we make with our organs in order to produce such sounds ("articulatory phonetics"). The sounds made by an orchestra are not random, however, but, rather, the materialization of a symphony. Similarly, the sounds we make when we speak any particular language implement the particular symphony that constitutes the phonic structure of that language ("phonology"). Here we differentiate two levels, which we can illustrate with the two *p*s of the English word *paper*: they are the same "sound", but still sound different. They are the same sound in as much as they are not *b*s, or *t*s, or *k*s, etc. They sound different in as much as you could conceivably blow out a candle with the first *p* of *paper*, but not with the second one. Therefore, the message is that each language possesses an inventory of distinctive sounds ("phonemes" or "lexical segments", depending on the theoretical framework), but that each of these sounds can have a number of different realizations ("allophones" or "surface sounds"), contingent on environmental conditions, a bit like the way we dress up warmly when we climb up a frozen mountain, but undress when we lie in the sun on a beach: one important source of sound alternation thus concerns "contamination" by neighbouring sounds, a process globally known as "assimilation". In order best to understand assimilation, and other sound alternations, we decompose sounds into atomic units, or "features", to which we grant a certain degree of mutual autonomy: a *p*, therefore, is not a *p*, but a web of interconnected features, just as the hand with which we write is basically a constellation of molecules. The distinctive features of sounds are grounded in the gestures involved in their articulation, and thus in phonetics. Formally, features connect to each other by means of "autosegmental" lines. Sound processes mapping lexical sounds onto surface sounds (equivalently, but not identically, phonemes onto allophones) involve readjustments of such lines, a bit like a game of musical chairs. The linearization of speech is expressed in a line, or "tier", of abstract timing units, also known as the "skeleton": long sounds, like the *o* in *vote* or the *ee* in *feet*, are associated with two such units, and short sounds like the *o* in *cot* with one. The introduction of the skeleton allows us naturally to differentiate processes involving length changes from processes involving changes in the substance of the segments.

CHAPTER ONE

HOW ARE SOUNDS MADE?

THE PRODUCTION OF OBSTRUENTS

Chapter Objectives

In this chapter you will learn about:
- What is characteristic of speech sounds.
- The organs involved in making speech sounds.
- How we create an airflow from the lungs and then interrupt it to produce a variety of sounds.
- The specific ways in which such an interruption is implemented.
- The parts of the mouth active in the production of speech sounds.
- The role of humming in increasing the number of speech sounds.
- How to write speech sounds down in an unambiguous way.

The primary aim of this book is to present the principles and practice of current phonology in a manner which is both accessible and stimulating to the uninitiated reader. Phonology is the study of linguistically significant sound patterns, that is, of the organization of the sounds of speech. This definition will become clearer as we proceed. In order to study the organization of speech sounds, we must first be able to identify the sounds themselves, and we make a start on this task in the present chapter.

Phonology is the study of linguistically significant sound patterns

1 Speech Sounds

We can compare the act of speaking with the act of playing a recorder, with which many of us are familiar from childhood. You may of course substitute any similar instrument: the analogy will still hold. To start with, when you want the recorder to produce a noise, you have to blow air from your lungs through the mouthpiece. The sounds that we produce when we speak also need to be powered by air from the lungs. In fact, the physical act of speaking can be likened to "playing" our mouths and larynxes with the air coming out of the lungs through the windpipe linking the lungs to the mouth, technically known as the "trachea". The LARYNX is of course the voice box

The act of speaking can usefully be compared with the act of playing a recorder

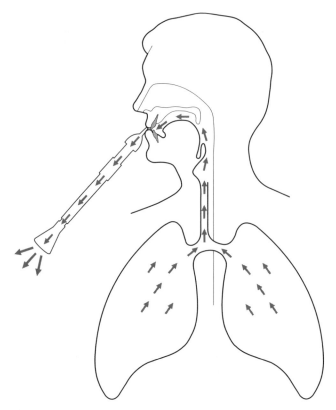

Figure 1.1   Playing a recorder

at the top of the trachea, which in the throat of males protrudes as the Adam's apple. A picture is worth a thousand words, and therefore we will adopt the practice of illustrating many of our statements with drawings (figures 1.1 and 1.2, above and on the next page, respectively).

At this point, a question arises. We take air into our lungs and let it out again every time we breathe. How come then that we are not continuously producing speech sounds? An easy experiment will give the answer. Quite simply, if you pick up a recorder and place the mouthpiece to your lips while breathing normally, you will find that the recorder only makes a faint wheezy sound, and that in order to play the recorder you need to discharge an extra amount of air. In the same way, if you wish to make a speech sound, you must breathe out more air than usual, and, of course, in order to breathe out more air, you must have taken in more air in the first place.

Compare for yourself the difference in the intake of air when you prepare to speak and when you are breathing normally.

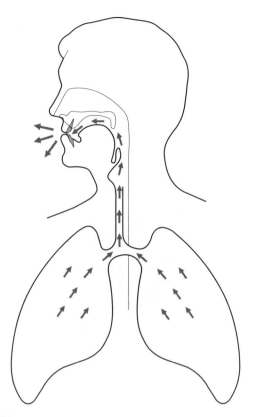

Figure 1.2 Speaking

You have now got the recorder making a noise. In order to play a tune, however, you need to do more than blow extra air through the recorder. Specifically, you need to move your fingers over the different holes on the body of the instrument. Why? Suppose you leave all the holes uncovered. Air will then come out through all the holes simultaneously, and the recorder will play a single note. Covering different holes at successive times will, however, enable you to produce different sounds. By covering (some of) the holes you are effectively putting up obstacles to the exit of the air through those holes. Similarly, in order to make the various speech noises, we have to interfere in various ways with the flow of the air on its way out through the larynx and, especially, the mouth. We will now look at some of the ways in which we "play" our vocal organs, starting off with the mouth.

Think for a minute or two about the analogy between playing the recorder (or any other such instrument) and making speech sounds.

2 Fricatives: Place and Manner of Articulation

Suppose that you place your lower lip loosely on the lower edge of your upper teeth and force air out of the mouth, after having filled your lungs aplenty. The situation is depicted in figure 1.3 (any new technical terminology in the drawings will be explained directly).

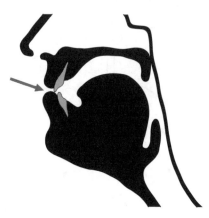

Figure 1.3   Labiodental fricative

What will happen? The obstacle you have created by the loose contact of the lower lip with the upper teeth does not totally block off the air, and therefore air will continue to flow out.

> Test the accuracy of this statement, with the help of a mirror if necessary: notice that the mirror gets misted up if you hold it close enough to your mouth.

Because the teeth and the lip are touching each other, the air rushing past will cause friction, and therefore a noise will be produced.

> Feel this friction and hear the air escape as you repeat the previous experiment.

The noise made by the air escaping between the lower lip and the upper teeth will sound exactly like the *f* at the beginning of *fat*, simply because this is how *f* is made, or "articulated". The ARTICULATORS of *f* are thus the lower lip and the upper teeth, hence the label LABIODENTAL given to this type of sound: *labial* is a Latin-based adjective meaning 'of the lips', and *dental*, related to *dentist*, means 'of the teeth'. Because the noise made by the air escaping through the obstacle being described is caused by friction, we refer to this type of sound as a FRICATIVE. Accordingly, the sound *f* at the beginning of *fat* can be (partially) described as a "labiodental fricative".

> Explain to yourself the meaning of this (composite) label without looking at the text.

"Labiodental" defines the place where the sound is made, its PLACE OF ARTICULATION, and "fricative" defines the manner in which the sound is made, its MANNER OF ARTICULATION.

Where a sound is made is its PLACE OF ARTICULATION. How a sound is made is its MANNER OF ARTICULATION

3 Phonetic Transcription

The labiodental fricative we have just discussed is the first of a range of fricative sounds which we are going to explore. Before we do this, however, it will be useful to introduce a method to write sounds down. An analogy with numbers will make the issue clearer. We call a certain number, say, "one thousand five hundred and sixty-five", but we do not usually write out this lengthy expression; indeed, calculations would be very difficult if we did. Instead, we use a shorthand version with the four digits one-five-six-five: 1565. In a similar way, we can and shall use a single symbol as a shorthand for the phrase "labiodental fricative".

How are we going to write down speech sounds? At first sight, this looks like a rather silly question – surely we already have a method of writing down speech sounds: we call it a "spelling system", the very one we are using right now to put our thoughts on paper. So, you may think, of course we are going to write the first sound of *fat* as *f*, the second sound as *a*, and the third sound as *t* – what else is the spelling there for? Well, there is actually something rather unsound about this line of reasoning. One example will bring out the problem. If indeed we are going to write the first sound of *fat* as *f* because that's the way it's spelled, are we also going to write the last sound of *laugh* as *gh* because that's the way it is spelled, and the first and the penultimate sounds of *philosophy* as *ph*? The point is that the first sound of *fat* and the last sound of *laugh* are identical, but their spellings are not. This is a bit like writing the number one sometimes as "1", and other times as "4", "23", etc.: clearly confusing! In fact, of course, there is no reason not to write "one" with the same symbol every time, say, as "1". The reasoning carries over to sounds. The best system of representation is thus one where the same symbol is always and only used for the same sound. This way there will be a one-to-one correspondence between each sound and each symbol, and we will be able to work out what sound we are referring to just by looking at the symbol – always assuming familiarity with the table of sound-symbol correspondences, which we will be supplying as we go along.

Clearly, ordinary English spelling is very far from being an adequate system for transcribing sound. In fact, no conventional spelling of any living language is, but English orthography is notoriously further removed from the ideal than average, as highlighted by Bernard Shaw's famous witticism that the word *fish* could equally well have been written *ghoti*: *gh* as in *laugh*, *o* as in *women*, and *ti* as in *nation*.

> Ordinary English spelling is very far from being an adequate system for transcribing sound

> Provide a few other alternative (perhaps facetious) spellings for a handful of English words. Explain their rationale.

English spelling is based on the late medieval pronunciation of English, and is indeed grossly inadequate for representing the way the modern language sounds. Awareness of spelling shortcomings spurred on the birth of systems of phonetic transcription in Britain and other European countries from at least the sixteenth century. At the end of the nineteenth century, a group of language teachers and phoneticians led by the Frenchman Paul Passy set up the International Phonetic Association and devised one such transcription system – soon to join was the British phonetician Henry Sweet, traditionally thought to have inspired the character of Professor Higgins in *Pygmalion/My Fair Lady*. The transcription system of the International Phonetic Association was gradually enriched to make it applicable to all languages, and it has by now been adopted by most practising phoneticians the world over. The system is known as the "alphabet of the International Phonetic Association", "IPA alphabet" for short. It is called an alphabet because it is based on letters – in fact, as we will see, essentially the letters English is spelled with, the Roman alphabet. The chief remit of the International Phonetic Association is to ensure the well-being of the international phonetic alphabet, which it regularly updates and publicizes.

> The goal of the IPA alphabet is to have each symbol always stand for the same sound, and only for that sound, and, conversely, to have each sound always represented by the same symbol

From now on, when we describe a sound, we will also give its IPA symbol. Remember that the goal of the IPA alphabet is to have each symbol always stand for the same sound, and only for that sound, and, conversely, to have each sound always represented by the same symbol. You will be pleased to learn that the IPA symbol for the first sound in *fat* that we have been describing is [f]: conventionally, phonetic symbols are enclosed in square brackets.

You should equally not be surprised to hear that [f] also represents the last sound in *laugh*, and the first and penultimate sounds in *philosophy*.

Square brackets are conventionally used to enclose phonetic symbols

> Why are we saying that you should not be surprised at the identity of phonetic symbol for *f*, *gh* and *ph* in the given words?

4 A Hissing Fricative

We now proceed to the description of other fricative sounds. How does the articulation of the sound at the beginning of *sip* differ from the articulation of [f]?

> Explore ffff and ssss for yourself before reading on (it is good practice to read out phonetic symbols as the sound they represent, rather than in the way letters are usually read out in English).

When we pronounce *s*, as in *sip*, we place either the "blade" or the "tip" of the tongue close to the ridge out of which the top teeth grow. The BLADE is easily recognizable as the most mobile and versatile part of the tongue, located behind the front point, itself known as the TIP (many non-specialist people actually call the whole blade of the tongue the "tip"). The blade is in fact the part of the tongue that sticks out most easily (figures 1.4 and 1.5).

The BLADE is easily recognizable as the most mobile and versatile part of the tongue, located behind the TIP

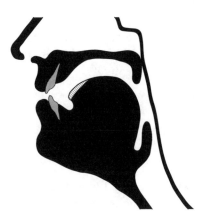

Figure 1.4   The tip and blade of the tongue

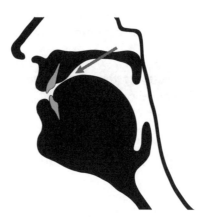

Figure 1.5   Alveolar fricative

If you blow air through the narrow gap between the blade of the tongue and the upper tooth ridge, in the manner you did through the gap between the lower lip and the upper teeth for [f], a hissing noise will be produced, which we transcribe as [s].

> Pronounce the two sounds [f] and [s] in succession, paying close attention to the different positions of the vocal organs. A useful technique to help awareness of precisely what bits of the vocal anatomy are involved in making a particular fricative sound consists in pronouncing that sound and then, without changing the position of the articulators, inverting the direction of the airflow, that is, breathing in, instead of breathing out: you will feel distinctly cold at the site of the friction.

Now some terminology in connection with [s]. Because [s] is articulated on the (upper) tooth ridge, it is given the label ALVEOLAR: *alveolus* is the Latin word for 'socket', and the teeth obviously grow out of "sockets", hence the expression "alveolar ridge". We can therefore describe [s] more fully (but still partially) as an "alveolar fricative".

> Say which of the two words making up the expression "alveolar fricative" describes the manner of articulation, and which the place of articulation.

Note that, strictly speaking, we ought to use the label "linguoalveolar": both the alveoli and the tongue, *lingua* in Latin, contribute to the articulation of [s]. The prefix *linguo-* is omitted on the grounds that the tongue is the organ most commonly involved in sound articulation, its intervention therefore being taken for granted in the absence of information to the contrary.

5 A Fricative in the Back of the Mouth

We have now described the articulation of two fricative sounds pronounced in the front region of the mouth: [f] (labiodental) and [s] (alveolar). The mouth is quite a big cavity, and other parts of it can also be used in sound production. In fact, there are so many locations available that typically languages do not make use of all of them.

The tongue is the most important articulator, and is almost exclusively composed of muscles, eight in all, some of them quite long – surprisingly so when you consider we can comfortably tuck the whole lot into the mouth. In addition, the wealth of innervations and the complex arrangements of the fibres of its muscles give the tongue a remarkable degree of versatility, which makes it particularly apt for the articulation of speech sounds. Consequently, there are many sections of the tongue available for contact with the structures that lie above it from the teeth to the pharynx. Note that, contrary to popular belief, the PHARYNX is the backmost part of the mouth, above the larynx, rather than the uppermost part of the throat (pharyngitis is therefore an inflamed back mouth, rather than a sore throat). See figure 1.6.

> There are many sections of the tongue available for contact with the structures that lie above it from the teeth to the pharynx

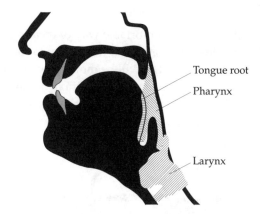

Tongue root

Pharynx

Larynx

Figure 1.6 The pharynx, larynx and tongue root

We have explained that [s] is made by positioning the blade of the tongue in the vicinity of the alveolar ridge. Suppose, instead, that you make the constriction at the back of the palate, that is, in the soft palate region. The PALATE is commonly referred to as the "roof of the mouth", and the SOFT PALATE is the soft area of the palate at the back. The technical term for the sounds made at the soft palate is VELAR, from VELUM, the anatomical word for the soft palate, derived from the Latin word *velum* 'veil' (figure 1.7).

Identify the soft palate by curling back your tongue tip and feeling the palate as you move the tongue backwards: you will notice that the front and middle areas of the palate are hard, but the back area is soft, since it is not supported by bone, hence the label "*soft* palate".

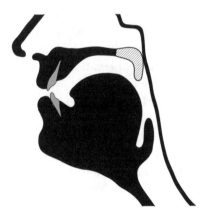

Figure 1.7   The soft palate

Clearly, the quickest and most comfortable way of creating a velar stricture will not be with the blade of the tongue, as the feeling exercise just suggested is likely to have revealed. Instead, it will be more convenient to use the part of the tongue which normally lies under the soft palate: the back part of the body of the tongue. The BODY is the section of the tongue behind the blade, more massive and less mobile than the blade (figure 1.8).

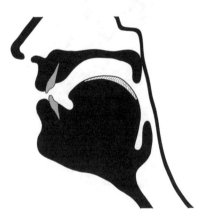

Figure 1.8   The body of the tongue

Indeed, the ACTIVE and PASSIVE ARTICULATORS involved in the production of a sound, that is, the articulator that moves and the inert articulator, more often than not lie directly opposite each other. Suppose now that you move the back of the body of the tongue up towards the soft palate, to create the same sort of narrow gap as for [f] and [s] (figure 1.9).

ACTIVE and PASSIVE ARTICULATORS more often than not lie directly opposite each other

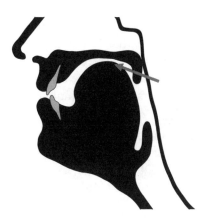

Figure 1.9   Velar fricative

The air rushing through will produce the sound that occurs at the end of *loch* as this word is pronounced in Scotland, and also the sound in such German words as *acht* ('eight') or *Bach* (the composer).

> Try this sound making sure that the airflow is not completely blocked, or else you will produce a sound more like the sound that corresponds to *k*, which we shall discuss below.

The phonetic symbol for this sound is [x]. You must of course not confuse this symbol with the letter *x*, which in English corresponds to two successive sounds.

> Work out what the two sequential sounds spelled as *x* are by pronouncing such words as *exam* and *box* (we will provide the answer in due course).

On the other hand, [x] is spelled *ch* in both Scots and German, therefore with two letters, despite being a simple sound. The spelling of [x] in other languages confirms the arbitrariness of spelling conventions: as either *g* or *j* in Spanish (depending on the vowel that follows), and as *h*, as well as *ch*, in

Polish. In the face of this diversity, the usefulness of a truly international standard for the representation of language sounds should be becoming obvious.

6 A Laryngeal Fricative

We shall now present another fricative sound which is pronounced even further back than [x]. In fact, it is articulated so far back that it is not articulated in the mouth at all, but rather in the larynx – as we said above, the larynx, or voice box, is the part of the throat that can stick out as the Adam's apple: we give cross-sections of the larynx in figure 1.10 below. The sound we are now introducing occurs at the beginning of the word *high*.

The larynx is the part of the throat that can stick out as the Adam's apple

> Pronounce this sound by itself: you should get something like a strong exaggerated puff, the noise you make when you blow condensation onto a pane of glass.

Clearly, there is no obstacle to the airflow in the mouth here, and yet one can distinctly hear friction. What is happening, then?

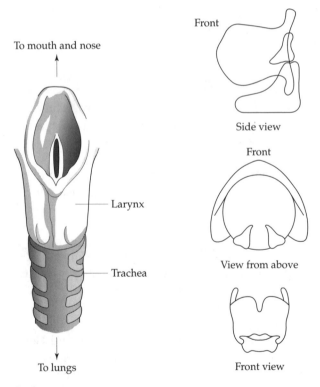

Figure 1.10 The larynx

When the air comes up the windpipe, it obviously has to pass through the larynx before reaching the mouth. Anatomically, the larynx is a cylindrical frame made up of cartilage, across which stretch two folds of muscle, called the VOCAL FOLDS – also, and perhaps more commonly in a non-linguistic context, VOCAL CORDS, a somewhat misleading term anatomically. The vocal folds are shaped like a pair of small lips and are highly mobile – they are responsible for the sudden reflex movement that prevents us from choking when a foreign body threatens to make its way into the windpipe (figure 1.11).

> The larynx is a cylindrical frame made up of cartilage, across which stretch two folds of muscle, called the VOCAL FOLDS

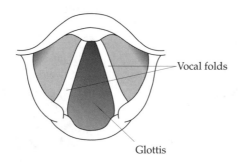

Figure 1.11 The vocal folds

In order to create the necessary friction for [h], the sound under observation, we position the vocal folds near each other to create turbulence in the airflow, but not so close together that they vibrate, as they do when we hum (figure 1.12).

> Try making a longish [h]. Now hum. Alternate between [h] and humming, trying to get a feel for the respective states of the vocal folds.

Figure 1.12 Glottal friction

The space surrounded by the vocal folds is known as the GLOTTIS, and therefore [h] is said to be a GLOTTAL fricative.

7 Voice

We have just mentioned humming, and a sort of humming plays a very important role in the production of many of the sounds of speech.

If you bring the vocal folds together closer than for the fricative sound [h], and tighten them somewhat, although not so much as simply to stop the airflow, the air passing through will cause them to vibrate, giving a humming effect (figure 1.13).

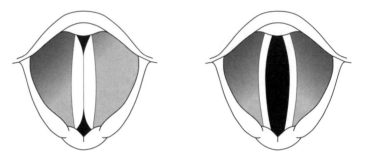

Figure 1.13   Positions of the vocal folds during voicing (initial and widest aperture)

You will feel the vibration of the vocal folds for yourself if you put your index finger and thumb on either side of the larynx and hum. Also, if you hum with covered ears, you will hear the hum as a buzz.

When the vocal cords are brought close together and tightened somewhat, the air passing through causes them to vibrate, giving a humming effect known technically as VOICE

This humming effect is known technically as VOICE. Voice can be superimposed on any of the sounds that we have already practised, just as we could get the combined sounds of a trumpet and a clarinet by playing the two instruments plugged into one another, with the same airstream powering both instruments: the mouth "instrument", which gives us the majority of the fricative sounds we have examined, is in effect permanently plugged into the larynx "instrument", with which we obtain voice. Clearly, this new set of sounds, composed of oral friction (that is, friction at some place in the mouth) and voice (that is, vibration of the vocal folds) will sound different from the simple set of voiceless sounds we have been reviewing so far: in this way, we will effectively double the inventory of speech sounds.

If you repeat the action by which you produced [f] in *fat* and super-impose voicing, the result will be a different sound: instead of *fat*, you will get *vat*. The two articulators, the teeth and the lower lip, are in the same position for both sounds (see figure 1.3 above), which are only differentiated with regard to voicing. The phonetic symbol for this new sound is, unexcitingly, [v].

> Place your finger tips on either side of the larynx, and pronounce [fffvvv]: as before, you will be able to feel the voicing as tickling. Now alternate the sounds [fvfvfvf] to gain further control over voice production.

The two other oral fricative sounds we described above also have voiced analogues. If you add vocal fold vibration to the [s] in *sip*, you will hear *zip*. Therefore, the only difference between [s] (as in *sip*) and [z] (as in *zip*) is again voicing: [s] is voiceless, and [z] voiced.

> Repeat the experiment you just carried out substituting [sz . . .].

Adding voicing to the sound at the end of *loch* does not give us a common sound of English. This is not terribly surprising, since [x] itself is not a sound of modern English either – *loch* is originally a Gaelic word, and most non-Scottish speakers of English pronounce it like *lock*. The voiced velar fricative [ɣ] (a phonetic symbol resembling the Greek letter gamma) is found in Greek and Arabic, among other languages.

> Assuming you are not familiar with either language, try to pronounce [ɣ] by composing it out of the more familiar [x] and (crucially, simultaneous) voicing.

We have now presented four voiceless fricatives ([f], [s], [x] and [h]), and three voiced ones ([v], [z] and [ɣ]). Voicing of [h] may appear impossible, since the organ responsible for the friction of [h], the vocal folds, is also the organ responsible for voice: it would seem out of the question to have one and the same instrument execute two apparently incompatible actions simultaneously. Surprising though it may seem, we can indeed perform this feat, given a bit of vocal fold gymnastics: the vocal folds must be placed close together at one end whilst held a little further apart at the other end. The closed end vibrates, while at the more open end there is air friction (figure 1.14).

Figure 1.14   The position of the vocal folds for voiced *h*

In order to identify the new sound, you can compare the *h* of *head* with the *h* of *ahead*. In *head*, there is no vocal fold vibration on the *h*, whereas in *ahead* voice runs through the entire word.

> Pronounce both tokens in succession, paying attention to the noted voice difference in the *h*. You can also try a phrase like "He arrived *ahead* of me because he had *a head* start".

We must of course differentiate graphically between the two types of *h*, and accordingly we use the phonetic symbol [ɦ] for the voiced *h*. This sound completes our initial survey of fricative sounds, which we now tabulate (table 1.1). Notice that the two relevant criteria for the classification are place of articulation and voicing.

Table 1.1   Fricatives (first inventory)

	Place of articulation			
	Labiodental	*Alveolar*	*Velar*	*Glottal*
Voiceless	f	s	x	h
Voiced	v	z	ɣ	ɦ

8 The Stop Gesture

We now know that the common denominator for fricatives is the gesture with which these sounds are produced: the two articulators are held close together, but not so close that the air is prevented from getting through and causing friction. Obviously, if the contact is tightened up, the airflow will be interrupted. Surprising though it may seem, momentarily stopping the airflow is another common method of producing speech sounds: another "manner of articulation". We shall now examine exactly how this is done.

Clearly, if you simply block the air, no sound will be made.

> Demonstrate this to yourself by trying to blow air out with closed lips. As long as the lips remain closed (and no air comes out through the nose) there will be no sound: all that will happen is that your cheeks will quickly fill with air.

However, if after blocking the airflow for a fraction of a second, you abruptly release the closure to allow the air to rush out, a sound will be produced. For instance, if you close both lips tightly and then open them suddenly, you will hear the sound [p], corresponding to the spelling *p* in the word *spy* – do bear in mind, however, that you need to have built up sufficient air pressure in the lungs for the "vocal instrument" to "sound" at all. The type of sound we are now introducing is obviously not a fricative, because the main phase of its realization does not involve the slow friction that characterizes fricatives. Instead, the articulation of [p] involves air stoppage, hence the generic name STOPS given to these sounds (figure 1.15).

If, after blocking the airflow for a fraction of a second, you abruptly release the closure and allow the air to rush out, a STOP sound will be produced

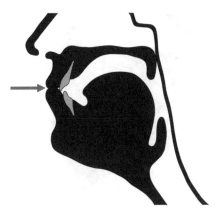

Figure 1.15   Bilabial stop

> Practise the bilabial stop [p] comparing it with the labiodental fricative [f]. You will notice that during the production of the fricative there is sound all the way through, even though the vocal folds are not vibrating. When you switch to the stop, however, there is no sound until the air is released.

If you vibrate the vocal folds during the closure phase of the lips, you will hear the sound [b] of the word *obey*.

> Repeat the previous exercise with the words *sober* and *over*. Notice how both [b] and [v] involve vocal fold vibration.

The sounds [p] and [b] share both manner of articulation and place: they are stops and BILABIAL, since they are articulated with both lips. Therefore, [p] and [b] only differ with regard to voice.

9 More Stops

We shall now describe the stop correlates of the rest of our by now familiar fricatives. If you place the blade of the tongue roughly in the same position as for [s], but this time interrupt the airflow by tightening up the contact, you will get the [t] of the word *sty* (figure 1.16).

Figure 1.16   Alveolar stop

If you increment [t] with voicing, the result will be the [d] of *adorn*. What will happen if you stop the air by placing the back of the tongue against the soft palate, in approximately the same position as for the fricatives [x] and [ɣ]? The respective stop sounds will now be [k], without voicing, as in *sky*, and [g], with voicing, as in *again* (figure 1.17).

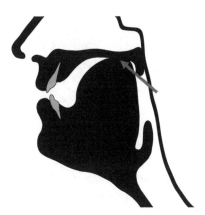

Figure 1.17 Velar stop

> Compare *loch* with *lock* and notice that in the latter word the last sound involves a complete blockage of the air-passage by the tongue, whereas in the Scottish pronunciation of the former no such stoppage occurs.

We now have all the information we need in order to give the promised phonetic interpretation to the English letter *x*: the *x* of *box* corresponds to the sound sequence [ks] (notice that *box* rhymes with *socks*), and the *x* of *exam* to [gz] (compare *eggs*).

The remaining fricatives in the inventory in table 1.1 are [h] and its voiced counterpart [ɦ]. They are both glottal, as their production involves air friction in the glottis – remember: the space surrounded by the vocal folds. Does either of these fricatives have a stop counterpart? If you say *ah* (as when asked to do so by the doctor), then close the vocal folds, and then open them again with another *ah*, the result will be the sound that is thought of as a "dropped *t*", heard in words like *butter* or *bottle* in many British accents (in *bottle* also in some American accents).

> Pronounce a few such dropped *t*s to become aware of the mechanics of this sound.

The technical name for this "dropped *t*" is, unsurprisingly, GLOTTAL STOP (figure 1.18).

Figure 1.18   Glottal stop

In order to pronounce a glottal stop, the vocal folds come together to close the glottis, causing a momentary break in the airstream. This closure is then released suddenly, exactly as with the remainder of the stops. The gesture involved in making the glottal stop is in fact similar to the gesture involved in coughing. Glottal stops do have to be voiceless, since it is not possible for the vocal folds to vibrate if no air is passing through, just as it is impossible for a flag to flap in the absence of wind. The phonetic symbol for the glottal stop looks like a question mark without the dot: [ʔ].

The addition of [p], [b], [t], [d], [k], [g] and [ʔ] notably enlarges our inventory of speech sounds, as we now encapsulate in table 1.2, which obviously supersedes table 1.1 above.

Table 1.2   Stops and fricatives (second inventory)

| | | | *Place of articulation* | | | | |
| | | | *Mouth* | | | | *Larynx* |
			Bilabial	*Labiodental*	*Alveolar*	*Velar*	*Glottal*
M	Stops	Voiceless	p		t	k	ʔ
a		Voiced	b		d	g	
n		Voiceless		f	s	x	h
n	Fricatives						
e		Voiced		v	z	ɣ	ɦ
r							

Try out the articulation of each of the sounds represented by each of the symbols in this table.

10 Still More Fricatives

Fricative and stop sounds with the obstruction to the airstream in the mouth are known as OBSTRUENTS: the glottal sounds [h], [ɦ] and [ʔ] are therefore not considered obstruents. In stops, the obstruction takes the form of a total blocking of the air, while in fricatives the air forces its way through the obstruction. You may well think that the list in table 1.2 exhausts the inventory of obstruents. In fact, there are quite a few more in store, even if we don't look beyond English.

Fricatives and stops made in the mouth are known as OBSTRUENTS

The sounds we will now examine also come in voiced–voiceless pairs. If you place the blade of the tongue on either the inside or the edge of the upper teeth, allowing the appropriate narrow gap for friction, you will get the sound at the beginning of *thigh* if you don't voice, and the sound at the beginning of *thy* if you superimpose vocal fold vibration (figure 1.19).

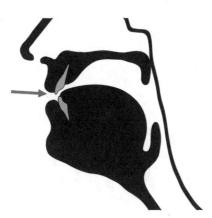

Figure 1.19 Dental fricative

Notice that our spelling system cannot distinguish between these two sounds, but the phonetic alphabet of course must. The respective IPA symbols are [θ] (the Greek letter "theta"), for the voiceless sound in *thigh*, and [ð] (the Old English letter "eth"), for the voiced sound in *thy*.

Place your fingers on either side of the larynx or cover your ears and feel the difference between these two sounds, [θθθð ðð], as you did in the earlier experiment with [f] and [v].

Note that it is also possible to make stop sounds on the inside of the upper teeth. Indeed, this is the place where speakers of Spanish pronounce their *t*s and *d*s (as also do some speakers of English). This is also the usual rendering by Southern Irish speakers of the common English sounds [θ] and [ð], which thus still remain distinct from the alveolar stops [t] and [d].

Compare the difference in both sound and feel between the *t* and the *d* made by placing the tongue blade against the tooth ridge (as in most accents of English), and the *t* and the *d* made by placing the blade against the back of the upper teeth.

Another fricative we have not yet discussed is the first sound in *ship*, also used extralinguistically to call for silence (*shhh!*). The phonetic symbol for this sound is [ʃ]. English spelling has some difficulty in representing [ʃ] – normally *sh*; but also, if followed by a vowel, *ti*, as in *ration*, or *si*, as in *mansion*; and even, if followed by *u*, as a simple *s*, as in *sure*. The articulation of the sound [ʃ] involves drawing the blade of the tongue to the area where the tooth ridge joins the hard palate – the part of the roof of the mouth which feels hard, as we mentioned above.

Practise pronouncing [ʃ] to see exactly how you make it. Pay successive attention to the action of the tongue and to the position of the lips: the gap for [ʃ] is in fact slightly wider than the gap for [s], and there is also a simultaneous slight rounding of the lips.

Because their place of articulation straddles the palate and the alveoli, sounds like [ʃ] are known as PALATOALVEOLARS (figure 1.20 below).

Notice that the composite label "palatoalveolar" defines the passive articulator. Which is the active articulator for these sounds? Why is it not usually included in the descriptive label?

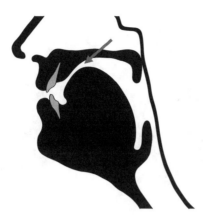

Figure 1.20   Palatoalveolar fricative

If you add vocal cord vibration to [ʃ], you get a sound which, although also used in English, has no specific representation in the English spelling system. This sound is found in the ordinary word *measure* and in the loanword *rouge*, and its phonetic symbol is [ʒ]. This is also the sound which appears in French at the beginning of *genre* 'class, kind' or *Jean*, the French equivalent of *John*.

> Practise the voiceless–voiced pair of sounds [ʃʃʃ**ʒʒʒ**]. Now compare [ʒ] with [z] as you did earlier with [ʃ] and [s].

Some authors, particularly in North America, use the symbol [š] for IPA [ʃ], and [ž] for IPA [ʒ].

11 Affricates

There is a third and final type of obstruent which is a composite of a stop and a fricative made in rapid succession, without changing the position of the articulators. These sounds are known as AFFRICATES – the phonetic similarity to *Africa* may be a useful mnemonic for this rather unusual word. The affricates familiar to speakers of English are the sounds found at the beginning and the end of *church* and *judge*.

In order to produce these sounds, we raise the tongue to the same position as for [ʃ] and [ʒ]. Instead of leaving a gap between the tongue and the roof of the mouth, however, as we do for [ʃ] and [ʒ], we create a total blockage of the air, as for a stop (figure 1.21).

A third type of obstruent sound is a composite of a stop and a fricative, and is known as an AFFRICATE

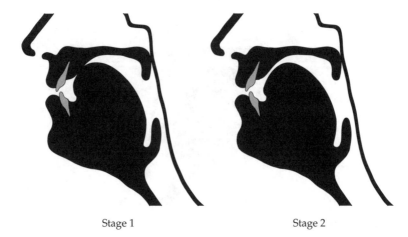

Stage 1   Stage 2

Figure 1.21 Palatoalveolar affricate

Crucially, at the moment of release the articulators do not come apart cleanly, as they do for stops, and therefore the outgoing air causes strong friction.

> Observe how this happens as you pronounce *church* or *judge*.

The phonetic symbols for these affricate sounds reflect their compositional nature. The symbols [t] and [ʃ] are combined into [ʧ] to represent the voiceless obstruent in *church* – equivalently, [t͡ʃ], with a TIE BAR linking both symbols to indicate the unitary nature of the affricate. In turn, [d] and [ʒ] are combined into [ʤ] (or [d͡ʒ]) to represent the voiced obstruent in *judge*. Note that the transcription [t] and [d] is strictly speaking inaccurate in this context, since the stop element of these affricates is palatoalveolar, as are [ʃ] and [ʒ], rather than alveolar, like [t] and [d]. An alternative, non-IPA symbol for [ʧ], particularly popular in North America, is [č]. Its equivalent for [ʤ] is [ǰ].

12 Summing Up

We will now bring the chapter to a close. You need, of course, to familiarize yourself with all the aspects of the sounds we are describing until you feel totally comfortable in handling them. Before ending the chapter, we recapitulate our findings in table 1.3.

Table 1.3 Stops, fricatives and affricates (third inventory)

		Place of articulation						Larynx
		Mouth						
		Bilabial	Labiodental	Dental	Alveolar	Palatoalveolar	Velar	Glottal
Stops	Voiceless	p		t̪	t		k	ʔ
	Voiced	b		d̪	d		g	
Fricatives	Voiceless		f	θ	s	ʃ	x	h
	Voiced		v	ð	z	ʒ	ɣ	ɦ
Affricates	Voiceless					tʃ		
	Voiced					dʒ		

M
a
n
n
e
r

Two final brief notes about this table. First, as we have hinted, [θ] and [ð] can be pronounced interdentally (that is, between the teeth) instead of dentally – the choice of place of articulation seems to be a matter of individual preference here (figure 1.22).

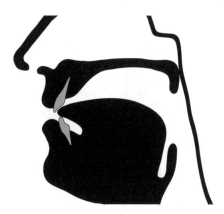

Figure 1.22 Interdental fricative

Second, the dental and alveolar symbols for *t* and *d* in the table are identical except for the extra mark, or DIACRITIC, "ˌ" under the dentals. Diacritics serve the purpose of increasing the descriptive power of the phonetic alphabet without unduly cluttering up the system with new symbols. Following on from this, we should transcribe the interdental fricatives with a special interdental diacritic. However, no such diacritic is available in the regular IPA alphabet, and therefore we resort to the general diacritic "₊", which simply signals an articulation slightly forward of the point represented by the symbol: [θ̟], [ð̟].

> Diacritics serve the purpose of increasing the descriptive power of the phonetic alphabet without unduly cluttering up the system with new symbols

C h a p t e r   S u m m a r y

This chapter has focused on the physical properties of speech sounds, with particular emphasis on obstruents, those sounds produced by setting up an obstruction in the path of the air from the lungs. Such an obstruction is made by bringing together two articulators, which either totally stop the airflow, then releasing it (a stop), or create a partial closure leading to turbulence of the air particles (a fricative). The third type of obstruent, the affricate, combines these two types of closure. The number and variety of obstruents result directly from the fact that these manners of articulation can be used at various points in the vocal tract. These points, referred to as places of articulation, are generally described in terms of where in the vocal tract contact is made (the alveolar ridge, the teeth, etc.), rather than in terms of the identity of the active articulator involved. Each of the combinations of manner and place of articulation may also be accompanied by vocal cord vibration or voicing. We showed that the set of (mainly English) obstruents discussed come in voiced and voiceless pairs. The IPA symbols supplied are laid out in table 1.3. Learning the description-to-symbol relationship is an essential part of learning phonology.

Key Questions

1 What is the larynx and what is its role in the production of speech?
2 How is speaking similar to or different from playing the recorder?
3 Discuss the manner of the release of air in the production of the three different types of obstruent.
4 When we talk about "place of articulation", what are we referring to? Enumerate the distinctive places of articulation we have discussed in the text.
5 What does a phonetic symbol represent? What are the advantages of the IPA alphabet?
6 What is the difference between a phonetic symbol and a letter? Why

should we never talk about letters when we are doing phonetics (or phonology)?
7 What do the terms "active" and "passive" articulator mean?
8 The set of obstruent sounds available to a language can be doubled by the addition of "voice". What is voice?
9 What is the purpose of a diacritic in phonetic transcription? Illustrate your answer.
10 Define the term "articulation".
11 Enumerate the sounds for which the soft palate is an articulator. Which other articulator would you expect to be involved?

Further Practice

Sound to Spelling

We have pointed out that, as phonologists, we are interested in speech sounds and not in spelling. We also pointed out that there is often, in English as indeed in other languages, more than one way to represent a single sound in the spelling system. We list below the phonetic symbols for a number of obstruent sounds. List as many different words as you can think of containing each sound with a different spelling (under each symbol is a number indicating the number of different spellings we have been able to think of):

[f] [k] [s] [z] [ʃ] [ʒ] [ʧ] [ʤ]
5   9   5   5   11   5   5   5

Articulation and Phonetic Symbols

a   Write down the IPA symbols representing the following descriptions, and illustrate each of the sounds with two English words:

A voiced labiodental fricative
A voiceless alveolar fricative
A voiced palatoalveolar affricate
A voiced glottal fricative
A voiceless bilabial stop
A voiceless dental fricative
A voiced velar stop

b   Provide full descriptions of the sounds represented by the following phonetic symbols (you will need to have recourse to the full IPA chart for some of the symbols):

[ɣ] [ç] [d̪] [ts] [ʒ] [β] [ð̪]

c   Arrange the sounds below into groups according to the following criteria:

(i)   Voicing
(ii)   Place of articulation
(iii)   Manner of articulation

[x] [k] [b] [ʃ] [ʒ] [z] [d] [p] [f] [g]

Spelling to Sound

Give the phonetic symbols for the sounds represented orthographically by the emboldened letters in the words below:

rough Thomas think pen phail fact stuff seed cede rise gnome
agnostic Stephen sheep cage jaw gold fission station chocolate
chaos dough kilt knowledge acknowledge question freeze bus
there castle muscle spaghetti fussy busy fuzzy casual causal
sugar Russia rushes cutlass table sign flight bomb vanity
bombard duke of off ascension escape succeed division

CHAPTER TWO

INTRODUCING PHONOLOGY

ASSIMILATION

Chapter Objectives

In this chapter you will learn about:
- How the pronunciation of obstruent sounds we presented in chapter 1 can be influenced by the context.
- How language is organized.
- How what we think we say and hear is not necessarily what we actually say and hear.
- How these two levels of reality can be formally related.
- In particular, how the actual pronunciation of strings of sounds constituting words and phrases can be "derived" from the idealized pronunciation stored in our mental dictionary.
- What the difference is between phonology and phonetics.

In the previous chapter we surveyed the production, or ARTICULATORY PHONETICS, of a number of consonants, obstruents and glottals in particular – we naturally assume some pretheoretical familiarity with the dichotomy consonant–vowel, from your learning of the alphabet if nothing else. We will now put the tools we have acquired to good use and make a start on the study of phonological structure, the primary object of this book. We will introduce some additional phonetic observations as we go along, as a necessary background to some of the discussion of phonology. As a preliminary to the delimitation of phonology from phonetics, we shall present several cases of sound "alternation" in English, and we shall provide a sketch of the way language in general is organized.

There are three basic parameters responsible for the phonetic differentiation of obstruent consonants: place of articulation, manner of articulation, and voice or its absence

1 On How Bilabial Stops Become Labiodental

In chapter 1 we saw that there are three basic parameters responsible for the phonetic differentiation of obstruents: place of articulation, manner of articulation, and voice or its absence. Pending the introduction of several additional such parameters for the description of other sounds, we shall focus the discussion on the three distinct series of oral stops that result from place of articulation differences in English.

> Enumerate the different places of articulation that we encountered in the previous chapter.

You will recall that English has a voiceless–voiced pair of stops for each of the bilabial, alveolar and velar places of articulation.

> Pronounce sounds that correspond to each of these places of articulation in English. Then write them down using the appropriate phonetic symbol.

Thus, for instance, we explained at the time that both [p] and [b] are bilabial sounds, involving the closure of both lips. In our presentation of these sounds we made use of such words as *spy*, *obey*, etc. But now consider other forms where the sounds corresponding to the *p* or *b* spellings immediately precede the labiodentals [f] or [v], as in the single words *cupful* and *subvert* or in the compounds *cup-final* or *cab-fare*. The question is, are *p* and *b* still bilabial in this context?

> Pronounce the words in question and try and find out whether the sounds represented as *p*, *b* in the spelling are bilabial or something else.

Chances are that you don't pronounce the sounds corresponding to the spellings *p*, *b* in *cup-final* or *cab-fare* as bilabial, as you do when you say the words *cup*, *cab*, etc. in isolation. Instead, in *cup-final* or *cab-fare* *p* and *b* are pronounced labiodentally. In the absence of an official IPA candidate, we will adopt the ad hoc symbols [ℙ], for the labiodental voiceless stop, and [ℬ], for its voiced counterpart.

> Explain what exactly is meant by the labels "labiodental voiceless stop" and "labiodental voiced stop". List the labiodental sounds we gave in chapter 1.

The discovery that *p* is [ℙ] in *cup-final*, and *b* [ℬ] in *cab-fare*, may have come as a mild surprise. Taking our search one step further, we shall ask why the situation should be precisely the way it is. Crucially, *cup* is the same word whether we say it by itself (*cup*), as an integral part of the longer word *cupful*, or as a component of the compound *cup-final*. In particular, the meaning of *cup* is the same in all three cases, and the difference in articulation we are now focusing our attention on is beyond the threshold of untrained consciousness. Words which clearly have the same meaning but sound different, like *friend, mate, pal, chum* and *buddy*, are technically known as SYNONYMS: most obviously, though, the *cup* of *cup* and the *cup* of *cupful* or *cup-final* are not synonyms, but simply the same word. Indeed, in *cupful, cup-final*, etc. we do not set out deliberately to change the way we pronunce the *p*: if we did, we would have been aware of the phenomenon all along. So, why are we making our lives complicated by pronouncing the word *cup* (and, even worse, any other word ending in the same consonant!) in two different ways, rather than sticking to the single pronunciation [p]?

> Do you have any idea why this may be so? Would it indeed be simpler always to pronounce *cup* in the same way?

One possible reason for the two pronunciations could be that bilabial stops do not sit comfortably in the middle of (simple or complex) words. If this were indeed so, the *p* and *b* in *lip-service, laptop, lapdog, sob-story, adoptive*, etc. ought also to be pronounced labiodentally.

> Check whether they are, by saying each of these forms out loud several times and gradually becoming aware of the way you pronounce the sounds in question. Do not slow down your speech unduly, or else you will distort your normal pronunciation.

In *lip-service*, etc., *p, b* are, however, not pronounced labiodentally, but bilabially, in exactly the same way as when they are word-final in *lip*, etc. This result inevitably leads to the abandonment of our current hypothesis and the search for an alternative. The slightly grand term HYPOTHESIS is used to refer to an idea that explains some body of data. We will gain familiarity with this important concept as we go along.

The term HYPOTHESIS is used to refer to an idea that explains some body of data

> Think of an alternative hypothesis to account for the present behaviour of *p, b*. Explain the real substance of the new hypothesis to yourself, in a fully explicit and rigorous manner.

In the present case it is not too difficult to come up with an alternative hypothesis. We shall follow our usual strategy and arrive at this alternative experimentally. If you try to pronounce *cupful* with a sound sequence bilabial–labiodental (for the *p* and *f* spellings, respectively) you will make at least two findings.

> Try and pronounce *cupful* really as *cu*[pf]*ul*. What do you find? In particular is this pronunciation easy, and does it feel natural?

First, you will probably feel rather awkward, as if the articulatory movements you are making were somewhat unusual, and unduly complex. Second, if you listen to yourself you will notice a stilted and unnatural diction. The reason for these two related results is, obviously, that the conscious pronunciation you have adopted for the sake of the experiment is not the pronunciation you use in ordinary speech. So, why should it be more difficult here to maintain the usual bilabial pronunciation of *p*, *b* than to shift it to labiodental? The answer is obvious: the simplest pronunciation involves only *one* articulatory gesture for both consonants. However, if you don't make the preceding stop labiodental, you will need *two* sequential gestures, first the closure of both lips, and then the motion of the lower lip towards the upper teeth. This is thus the answer to our question: in order to simplify the articulation, we allow the usually bilabial articulation of *p*, *b* to be "contaminated" by the labiodentality of its neighbour. Such "contamination" by (usually adjacent) sounds is a common occurrence in language, and is technically known as ASSIMILATION. As we shall see directly, assimilation abounds, in English and in other languages. Note, however, that assimilation clearly cannot have a free rein, or else we would end up with just one sound in every utterance!

"Contamination" of a sound by other (usually adjacent) sounds is commonplace in language, and is technically known as ASSIMILATION

> Explain why unbridled assimilation would lead to one-sound utterances.

2 Total Place Assimilation in Stops

The last sounds in the words *that* and *red* are alveolar stops, voiceless and voiced, respectively.

> Check that this is so. Take special care to refer to the standard pronunciation of such words in isolation, not to the colloquial variant with a glottal stop [ʔ] in lieu of [t] or [d], common in some accents.

Consider now the following simple phrases:

(1) that pen
     that box
     red pen
     red box

Let us pay close attention to the pronunciation of the sounds spelled *t* and *d* in these phrases. In particular, let us find out whether they can still rightly be transcribed [t] and [d], respectively.

> Provide an answer to this question after the appropriate experimentation: say each of the phrases in (1) aloud several times, paying special attention to your pronunciation of the sounds spelled *t*, *d* in *that*, *red*, respectively. You must ensure that your pronunciation is relaxed and natural (for instance, do not pronounce the phrases too slowly), or else the experiment will be worthless.

The answer is that the *t*s and the *d*s are indeed [t] and [d] if you pronounce the phrases in (1) rather slowly, paying special attention to what you are saying. However, when you utter them casually, as you do in the course of normal conversation, you are liable to pronounce them as bilabial: *tha*[p] *pen*, *tha*[p] *box*, *re*[b] *pen*, *re*[b] *box*.

> Try out the experiment once more if you didn't get this result in the previous trial.

Consider next the set of phrases in (2):

(2) that can
     that gate
     red can
     red gate

What is now the place of articulation of the sounds behind the spellings *t*, *d*?

> Conduct the appropriate experiment along the usual lines.

A small amount of attention will reveal that the sounds are now pronounced as velar (*tha*[k] *can*, *tha*[k] *gate*, *re*[g] *can*, *re*[g] *gate*), rather than bilabial, as they were in the set in (1) (*tha*[p] *pen*), or alveolar (*tha*[t], *re*[d]), as they are pronounced otherwise.

Let us add the final set in (3) to our pool of data:

(3)   that table
       that door
       red table
       red door

What is now the pronunciation of the sounds under scrutiny?

> Carry out the appropriate experiment. By now you should be sufficiently familiar with this type of experimentation, and with the precautions that need taking.

You will observe that *t*, *d* have now reverted to their original alveolar articulation: *tha*[t] *table*, *tha*[t] *door*, *re*[d] *table*, *re*[d] *door*.

Facts like the ones we have gleaned stimulate the researcher to act. The next step is of course to look for an explanation for why things are precisely the way they are. And the first stage in this process of explanation is the formation of a hypothesis, in much the same way as a detective comes up with a hypothesis about the identity of the criminal. Clearly, in order to get to a hypothesis, we must pay very close attention to the facts. For the detective this involves examining all kinds of material evidence, and for the phonologist it involves examining the exact shape of sounds. Indeed, we may have to look at the facts several times over before we reach a conclusion. At some point along the way, however, we will hopefully come up with "an idea". This idea, which often seems to spring up suddenly, is what we are calling a "hypothesis".

What is the most reasonable hypothesis to handle the data we are discussing?

> Propose one such hypothesis, ensuring that you remember all the facts at once and understand their significance.

If you look at the data closely you will realize that the place of articulation of the stop ending the words *that* and *red* is consistently the same as the place of articulation of the stop which begins the following word. Now, why should this be so?

> Try to answer this question. Notice that your answer, whatever it may be, also constitutes a hypothesis.

The answer should be obvious after the discussion in the previous section. Simply, what under normal circumstances is an alveolar stop (indeed as reflected in the spelling) systematically assimilates to the place of articulation of the stop that immediately follows it. This is another instance of REGRESSIVE ASSIMILATION, that is, assimilation to the following segment – in the opposite type of assimilation, PROGRESSIVE ASSIMILATION, there is assimilation to the preceding segment, as happens in *cubs* and *cups*.

> Say in what way *cubs* and *cups* illustrate progressive assimilation. Hint: pay particular attention to the pronunciation of the *s* in both words.

The reason there is no change in the set in (3) is that there the second stop is also alveolar, and therefore the assimilatory process is vacuous – it has no material consequences. In front of a bilabial or a velar consonant, however, the alveolar articulation is replaced by a bilabial or velar articulation. We summarize the processes in (4):

(4) *tha*[p] *pen*   *tha*[k] *can*   *tha*[t] *table*
     tha[p] *box*   *tha*[k] *gate*   *tha*[t] *door*

     re[b] *pen*   *re*[g] *can*   *re*[d] *table*
     re[b] *box*   *re*[g] *gate*   *re*[d] *door*

Notice that, in all the cases of assimilation we have discussed, we are assuming that one of the alternative articulations is more "basic" than the others. Thus, we have proposed that the labiodental realization of *p* in *cupful* is just a "deflection" of a basic [p], caused by "contamination" from the adjacent labiodental [f]. Similarly, the basic articulation of the last sounds in *that* and *red* is alveolar, and their alternative bilabial and velar realizations are brought about by assimilation.

> In all the cases of assimilation we are assuming that one of the alternative articulations is more "basic"

> State the position we are taking and defend it explicitly.

After all, if [t] and [d] were not basic, why should these sounds turn up when no consonant follows, namely, when the words are pronounced in isolation or when the next word starts with a vowel, as in *that apple*?

> Pronounce the phrase *that apple* in a standard accent and satisfy yourself that the *t* in the spelling indeed corresponds to an alveolar sound.

Sounds can be replaced by other sounds, under the appropriate contextual circumstances

What we are finding, thus, is that sounds can be replaced by other sounds, under the appropriate contextual circumstances: the changes in question are not random, but occur in particular, well-defined phonetic contexts. Notice that you also change clothes, makeup or hairstyle according to circumstances – crucially, you remain the same person, although sometimes it may be hard to tell just by looking at you.

> Explain in your own words the role of the context in the occurrence of any particular variant, both in language sound and in the analogy just given.

3 Voice Assimilation

We shall briefly consider one more case of assimilation before we propose a formalization for the phenomenon.

In chapter 1 we presented the following voiceless–voiced consonant pairs, among others:

(5) [f] [v]
     [s] [z]
     [ʧ] [ʤ]

> Pronounce these sounds, both in isolation and in a few words, to ensure continuing familiarity with the phonetic symbols and their phonetic realizations.

The sounds in the top two pairs in (5) are fricatives, and those in the bottom pair affricates. The words in (6) illustrate the voiceless–voiced contrasts in word-final position:

(6) a. Fife   b.   five
         loose   lose
         etch   edge

> Pronounce these and any other similar pairs that may spring
> to mind, making sure that you perceive the voice contrast.

Now consider the following phrases:

(7) five tons
     lose ten-nil
     edge trimmer

The first word in each of these phrases comes from the set in (6b), where
we saw that it ends in a voiced fricative or affricate. From a seriously experimental perspective, however, the assumption that in (7) these sounds are
also voiced needs to be tested.

> Conduct an experiment to check out the voiced status of the
> sounds in question in your casual speech, along the lines of
> the experiments previously suggested.

In fact, a minimal amount of observation should reveal that in (7) none of
these sounds is voiced.

A possible hypothesis to account for this fact, HYPOTHESIS A, would
be that the sounds in question are only voiced when the word is said in
isolation. You are becoming familiar with the need to put scientific hypotheses to the test before accepting them: an argument such as "because I say
so" does not cut much ice in science. Let us, accordingly, test out HYPO-
THESIS A with an additional list of phrases that include the words under
scrutiny:

(8) five or six
     lose eight-nil
     edge of the world

Here the words also appear in a phrasal context, and, therefore, HYPO-
THESIS A predicts that the sounds we are investigating ought also to be
voiceless. The empirical question of course is, are they?

> Pronounce the phrases in (8) and provide an answer to the question. You may want to have several trials before you consider your answer definitive.

Again, a small amount of observation will reveal that the sounds in question are voiced in (8), and therefore HYPOTHESIS A fails. Suppose next that we modify HYPOTHESIS A minimally into HYPOTHESIS B, by attributing the voicelessness of *v*, *s* and *dg* in (7) above to the presence of a following consonant – the mind is reluctant to abandon existing hypotheses, and therefore it is only human to modify hypotheses as little as possible.

> Explain how the small change we are proposing in the hypothesis would account for the data in (8), while still being compatible with the preceding data.

Whether the modification is minimal or drastic, HYPOTHESIS B must also be tested. Consider the following list:

(9)   five days
      lose data
      fridge door

In (9), the sounds we are discussing are followed by a consonant and therefore, according to HYPOTHESIS B, they also ought to be voiceless there. The question is, are they really?

> Answer the question after the appropriate experimentation.

The answer is that in (9) the sounds we are investigating are in fact voiced. This means that HYPOTHESIS B also fails.

Having reached this point, you may be tempted to ask yourself whether there is any way of accounting for the voicelessness of the sounds in the original set in (7): there is of course no a priori reason why natural phenomena, whether in the physical world or in the world of language, should be amenable to explanation. The assumption of the linguist and of fellow researchers in other branches of science is that there usually is an explanation, for otherwise there would be no more to say, and hence no linguistics or science in general. Fortunately, in the present case an explanation is readily available.

Can you now think of a better hypothesis – call it HYPO-THESIS C – as to why the set of sounds under consideration is only voiceless in the set in (7)?

The answer is that in the set in (7), but crucially not in those in (8) and (9), the sounds under observation are followed by a voiceless obstruent. Why should the voicelessness of the following obstruent matter? Because, as in the cases of assimilation we examined in the previous sections, the voicelessness of this obstruent can (and does) "contaminate" the (usual) voicefulness of the preceding fricative or affricate. Therefore, the devoicing of such sounds in (7) is simply a consequence of assimilation. Note that the parameter involved in the present assimilation process is not place of articulation, as was the case in the preceding sections, but, rather, voice. Indeed, assimilation can involve any of our familiar phonetic parameters, although assimilation of manner of articulation is considerably rarer.

Assimilation can involve any of our familiar phonetic parameters

We will wind up this section with an additional set of data which bring out minimally and strikingly the devoicing process we have examined:

(10)   five to five
       nose to nose
       edge to edge

In what way do these data minimally and strikingly bring out the process of devoicing?

4 The Organization of Language

Having prepared the ground by investigating a number of assimilation phenomena, it is time to turn our attention to the main subject matter of this chapter: presenting phonology and segregating its concerns from those of phonetics. As a preliminary, it will be useful to reflect briefly on the way language is organized.

We can start with the obvious: all languages have words. In fact, it is likely that for the layman the words of a language *are* the language. In reality, however, things are a little more complicated, although, fortunately, still not hard to understand.

We can indeed usefully view words as the building blocks of (any) language. What we do when we speak is put words together into phrases and sentences. The way words come together varies (at least partially) from language to language. Its study constitutes the subject matter of SYNTAX, one of the branches of LINGUISTICS, itself the analytic study of language. In this book we are of course concerned not with syntax, but, rather, with sound.

Besides syntax and sound, language (its words as well as its sentences) has meaning, studied by another branch of linguistics, known as SEMAN-TICS. How do we get sentences to have a meaning? For instance, how do we get the sentence *children love sweets* to mean precisely what it does? Well, it is not so difficult once we have the individual meanings of the words *child* (of which *children* is the plural), *love* and *sweet* (singular of *sweets*): in essence, all we do in order to understand the sentence is combine the meanings of its component words. But why does *child* mean 'child', *love* 'love' and *sweet* 'sweet'? Note that if we were speaking French then we would use *enfant* to mean 'child', *aimer* to mean 'to love' and *bonbon* to mean 'sweet'. Why?

> Try to answer this question. If you succeed, you will have proved your understanding of one of the most fundamental properties of human language, which we discuss in the text below.

The answer to the question of why words mean what they mean is tautological: words mean what they mean because they do. There is no other reason. In particular, the sound shape associated with the meaning of each word is arbitrary, and simply has to be taken on board and memorized. So, the first thing we need to carry in our minds in order to have a language is a pretty gigantic list of words, each word essentially consisting of a certain sound shape and a meaning glued together.

The sound shape associated with the meaning of each word is arbitrary

The famous Swiss linguist Ferdinand de Saussure (1857–1913), usually considered the founder of modern linguistics (linguistics has existed for millennia in a variety of guises), called the basic elements of language LINGUISTIC SIGNS. Each linguistic sign is thus made up of two integral and complementary parts, rather as the two sides of a coin make up the coin: a characteristic meaning, which Saussure called the sign's SIGNIFIED, and a characteristic sound, which he called the sign's SIGNIFIER. Following Saussure, the linguistic sign for *cup* can be represented graphically as in figure 2.1, where, in line with tradition, we represent the signified by means of a drawing, and the signifier with the italicized conventional spelling.

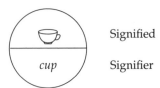

Figure 2.1   Linguistic sign

Saussure went on to point out that the association between the signifier and the signified that make up any one linguistic sign is arbitrary: he referred to this fact as "l'arbitraire du signe", 'the sign's arbitrariness'. From this arbitrariness follows the need for the brute-force memorization we alluded to above.

It is reasonable to assume that each sign only has one signifier and one signified. In fact, there is a strong logic to this assumption, namely, that it is precisely the conjunction of one signifier (that is, a certain sound shape) and one signified (that is, a certain meaning) that makes up a linguistic sign (a word, for our present purposes). If two meanings occur with a single form, as with the English *bank*, either a financial institution or the side of a river, we will assume two linguistic signs, rather than one sign with a double signified. We now display these two alternative construals in figure 2.2. Cups are of course easier to draw than sides of rivers or financial institutions, and therefore, following convention, we represent complex signifieds by means of ordinary language expressions enclosed in single quotation marks.

> Each sign has only one signifier and one signified

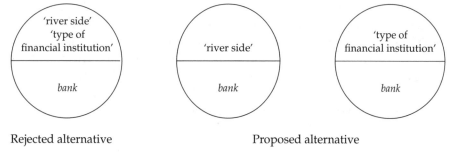

Rejected alternative   Proposed alternative

Figure 2.2 Two ways of representing intersecting signifiers

Following the same logic, the signifier of each linguistic sign will also be unique. For instance, we will assume two linguistic signs for the synonyms *pal* and *mate*, rather than just one sign with a double signifier. We display these two alternatives in figure 2.3, where we arbitrarily adopt 'friend' as a representation of the meaning shared by the two words:

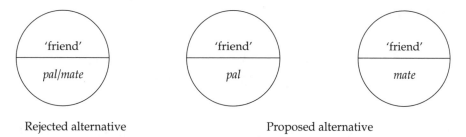

Rejected alternative   Proposed alternative

Figure 2.3 Two ways of representing intersecting signifiers

Signifier uniqueness appears difficult to reconcile with the dual pronunciation of the *p* of *cup* as [p] or [𝒫], with the multiple pronunciation of the *t* of *that* as [t], [p] or [k], or with the dual pronunciation of each of *v*, *s* and *dg* as [v], [z], [dʒ] or [f], [s], [ʧ]. In particular, aren't all these alternative pronunciations defining independent signifiers, and thus independent signs, by the logic adopted?

> Would this necessarily be a bad outcome? Think about the matter carefully and provide a reasoned answer.

We want to prevent the proliferation of linguistic signs

There are at least two reasons why we want to prevent the proliferation of linguistic signs. First, there is a general principle of economy acting as a backdrop to the whole enterprise of linguistics, a manifestation of an old philosophical dictum known as "Occam's razor", after its fourteenth-century formulator William of Occam: "entities must not be multiplied beyond necessity". This of course just means that we must keep things simple unless there are good reasons not to do so. The second reason to avoid the proliferation of linguistic signs is more psychological: as speakers of the language we have a feeling or intuition that *cup* is the same word in all its contexts, and similarly for the other forms discussed. Such feelings must be taken seriously in linguistics (even if not necessarily accepted at face value), since the very nature of language is psychological, not for example geological or artistic.

> What exactly do we mean when we say that language is psychological?

We select one of the competing candidates as the "official" signifier of the sign

If we accept that *cup*, *that*, *five*, etc., correspond to a single sign each, whatever varied realizations the last consonant of each such form may have, we must inevitably select one of the competing candidates as the "official" signifier of the sign.

> Why must we select between competing candidates, and which are these competing candidates, anyway?

The question is, will there be any criterion for the selection of one candidate as the "official" form, or will it be random?

> Make an educated guess, making use of all your common (and linguistic) sense, and of the knowledge of the data you have accumulated.

The answer is in fact implicit in our previous discussion, and should be pretty obvious by now. As you will recall, we have systematically construed one of the alternatives as basic, because this alternative is more frequent and general (for instance, it turns up when the word is said in isolation), because it is the alternative we constantly think we are pronouncing or hearing (even when objectively we are not!), because it corresponds to the conventional spelling of the sound (this is of course a secondary criterion, given the problems associated with spelling, but still worth bearing in mind as a possible reflection of the way we "think" about the sound), and so on.

> What are the problems associated with spelling we are referring to?

Clearly, this basic alternative will be the one included in the linguistic sign. All the other variants will be "derived" from their basic counterpart in the appropriate contexts, in the way we shall explain next.

> List the basic and non-basic variants of all the forms included in the total data set we have been examining. Rehearse the arguments for declaring a form basic in preference to its counterparts.

5 Basic and Derived Forms

Let us introduce some simple standard terminology. The set of all linguistic signs making up the vocabulary of a language is known as the LEXICON of that language. In fact, the label "linguistic sign" is not much used in current linguistics – it is usually associated with the type of linguistics propounded by Saussure, many details of which have been superseded by subsequent developments. The expression "linguistic sign" therefore tends to be replaced by the expression LEXICAL ITEM or LEXICAL ENTRY, which simply suggests a unit in the lexicon. Like linguistic signs, lexical items contain all the information relevant to sound and meaning that must be memorized as part and parcel of the process of mastering a language, whether a second language, the words of which we may memorize consciously, or

The set of all linguistic signs making up the vocabulary of a language is known as the LEXICON

The expression
LEXICAL ITEM or
LEXICAL ENTRY
simply suggests a
unit in the lexicon

a first language, where memorization happens automatically at an early age. The lexical entry for *cup* will therefore include the information that its final sound is [p], the lexical entry for *that* that its final sound is [t], and the lexical entry for *five* that its final sound is [v]. We refer to the information thus contained in a lexical item as its LEXICAL REPRESENTATION.

> Summarize the basic account of the structure of language we have just offered.

We refer to the
information con-
tained in a lexical
item as its LEXICAL
REPRESENTATION

It should be quite clear by now that the lexical representation of a word is not always identical to its PHONETIC REPRESENTATION, that is, to the way the word is heard or said. Thus, for *cup* in *cupful*, you will not hear (or pronounce) the [p] that we have just suggested is present in its lexical representation. Similarly, in the phrases *that pen* or *that can*, you will usually not be hearing (or pronouncing) the [t] we assume for *that* in its lexical representation. Likewise, in *five tons* the lexical [v] of *five* will not occur in the normal pronunciation of this phrase. You know by now what the motivation for these divergences is. What we obviously need next is a formalism that accommodates unity in the face of diversity, or, equivalently, diversity in spite of essential unity.

> Remind yourself what the unity and diversity we are taking about refer to: you must really be very clear about this if you are to understand the points we are making.

Fortunately, the way forward is pretty straight. At the moment, we already have lexical representations for *cup*, *that* and *five*. In particular, we have proposed that the last lexical sounds in these words are /p/, /t/ and /v/, respectively: lexical sounds are enclosed in slashes, to make them visually distinct from phonetic sounds, an important convention you must scrupulously adhere to.

Lexical sounds
are customarily
enclosed in
slashes, to make
them visually dis-
tinct from pho-
netic sounds

> Explain the import of the word "propose" when we say that we have proposed /p/, /t/ and /v/ as the last lexical segment of *cup*, *that* and *five*.

Now, we must assume that, under normal circumstances, phonetic sounds are identical to lexical sounds. Therefore, circumstances allowing, the last phonetic sounds of *cup*, *that* and *five* will also be [p], [t] and [v], respectively:

this is indeed the reason we postulate /p/, /t/ and /v/ as the respective lexical sounds in the first place. Under some restricted set of circumstances, however, we know that the phonetic sounds of the forms in question are different from their lexical sounds. What are these circumstances?

> Jog your memory about what the lexical–phonetic correspondences are, for each of the cases.

The circumstances under which the /p/ of *cup* becomes [𝒫] can be stated as follows:

(11)   /p/ is realized as [𝒫] when it immediately precedes /f/

Likewise, the observed changes in the realization of /t/ can be summarized thus:

(12)   /t/ is realized in the same place of articulation as the stop that immediately follows it, namely, as [p], [t] or [k]

Similarly, the change from /v/ to [f] in *five tons* can be accounted for by the statement in (13):

(13)   /v/ is realized as [f] when it is immediately followed by a voiceless obstruent

> Go through the relevant data and verify the appositeness of the statements in (11), (12) and (13).

Clearly, the three statements we have just given are sufficient to generate all and only the correct phonetic forms of these and other similar words. Thus, suppose we intend to say the word *cup* by itself. In this case, we retrieve the lexical representation, with /p/ in final position, and simply pronounce it: [p].

> Why are we writing [p] now, even though we wrote /p/ just a few words before?

Suppose, instead, that we intend to say *cup* in *cupful*. As before, we retrieve the lexical representation with a final /p/. In this case, however, we will not realize this /p/ as [p], because the statement in (11) above will "deflect" /p/ into [𝒫].

Before you go on, apply the same method to one or two of the other cases we have discussed.

At one level, statements such as those in (11) to (13) are simple observations of reality. In particular, it is indeed the case that /p/ is realized as [𝒫] when it immediately precedes /f/, and this is what the statement in (11) says. At another level, however, such statements can be construed as regulators of our phonetic behaviour, which they appear to monitor and guide. From this perspective, such statements are therefore RULES, and we will henceforth refer to them as such: rather as a road diversion sign directs traffic onto a certain route, phonological rules divert the realization of lexical sounds in certain directions. The state of affairs we are describing can be represented schematically as in (14):

Phonological rules divert the realization of lexical sounds in certain directions

(14)   Lexical representations

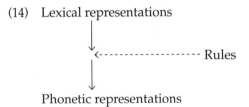

Phonetic representations

As (14) displays, lexical representations can be interfered with on their way to phonetic realization by rules, which "divert" or "deflect" them accordingly – the break in the vertical arrow is intended to convey a visual impression of this deflection. In psychological terms, you can think of this process as one of modification of the lexical sound stored in memory before articulatory implementation: the phonetic realization that will come out of the mouth will accordingly correspond to the form modified by the rule, rather than to its lexical base.

It should be clear at this point that rules are as much part of the machinery of the sound component of language as are lexical representations. In particular, we must learn the rules of a language if we are ever going to get its pronunciation right, since the differences in pronunciation between different languages, or between different accents within the same language, are (at least in part) the result of the presence of different rules in those languages. When we are taught a second language, sometimes such rules are pointed out to us, and we purposely learn them and try to apply them as well as we can. In the case of our first language, however, we have simply extracted these rules from the speech around us, in some rather mysterious way. Such are the wonders of first language learning, which have led linguists, notably Noam Chomsky (the man who has most influenced our ideas about language since Saussure), to suggest that the human brain is innately in possession of a LANGUAGE ACQUISITION DEVICE that allows it to acquire language spontaneously in childhood.

6 The Formalization of Rules

We shall now propose a formalism to encapsulate the concepts we have introduced. Formalism can be thought of as a shorthand notation that allows the eye to see the whole picture at a glance, and consequently it must be cherished rather than feared. It also forces us to be more rigorous and precise than we usually are when we write in ordinary prose.

> Formalism can be thought of as a shorthand notation that allows the eye to see the whole picture at a glance

> Explain in a few words the basic mechanics of some formal system outside linguistics you are familiar with (for instance, simple arithmetic).

We are already in possession of a set of phonetic symbols (the IPA symbols), and of the convention of enclosing them in slashes to refer to lexical forms, and in square brackets to refer to phonetic forms. Indeed, the proposed split between the lexical and the phonetic levels of representation is also part of the formal theory we are constructing to introduce order into the apparent real-world chaos. A word often used to refer to such scientific idealizations of reality is MODEL. We are accordingly engaged in the building of a model which hopefully will give us a better understanding of the mechanics of sound in language.

> Clarify to yourself the idea of a "model". Sketch out (mentally or graphically) the model of language we are proposing.

In the preceding section we stated several rules in prose, and we shall now trim them down to a leaner format. A number of ways of formalizing rules suggest themselves. By way of illustration, let us examine the rule changing /p/ to [𝒫]. Here is one reasonably obvious possibility:

(15)   / ... pf ... /
       [... 𝒫f ...]

The first line is flanked by slashes, to indicate lexical status, and the second line by square brackets, to indicate phonetic status. All we have done is write the sequence "pf" in the first line, preceded and followed by dots to indicate the irrelevance of additional material on either side, and the sequence "𝒫f", also with dots, in the second line. The obvious implication of this formalism is, therefore, that a lexical /p/ becomes a phonetic [𝒫] in the given environment: immediately before /f/.

One reasonable way of bringing out the idea of change graphically is by means of an arrow between the lines, as follows:

(16) /...pf.../
              ↓
      [...𝒫f...]

The arrow suggests the idea "goes to" or "becomes", and therefore we will consider this representation an improvement over its predecessor in (15).

Suppose now that we want to save space – we did say earlier, after all, that formalization amounted to a shorthand notation. One simple way of achieving this is to merge the lines:

(17) /...pf.../ → [...𝒫f...]

Let us take our trimming exercise one step further. Assuming a single format for all rules, we can dispense with the slashes and the brackets: given the linear arrangement we are adopting, the material to the left of the arrow will automatically be interpreted as the input (here the lexical input), and the material to the right of the arrow as the output (here the phonetic output):

(18) ...pf... → ...𝒫f...

Next, we can quite safely omit the dots, since they signal material which is by definition irrelevant:

(19) pf → 𝒫f

We have almost reached the end of our trimming exercise. Indeed, you may well feel that we can go no further, since all the material that is now included in the rule would seem to be substantial. Notice, however, that "f" appears on both the left- and the right-hand side of the arrow, to the right of "p" and "𝒫", respectively. Moreover, there is a significant difference between the role of "f" and the role of "p" or "𝒫" in the rule – and, correspondingly, in the real-world process. Specifically, "p" represents the segment to be altered and "𝒫" the result of the alteration. By contrast, "f" represents the constant environment or context in which the alteration takes place: in the absence of /f/, /p/ remains unaffected and will indeed be realized as [p]. When we take these facts into account, it becomes obvious that it is useful to separate the rule's ENVIRONMENT ("f") from the rule's FOCUS ("p" → "𝒫"), as follows:

(20) p → 𝒫 /___f

This is the final format of the rule. Formalized phonological rules thus contain two main parts, conventionally separated by a slash, not to be confused with the slash pairs that lend lexical status to phonetic symbols. These two parts are: (i) the focus, formalizing the change, and (ii) the environment, formalizing the contextual trigger for the change. We spell this out in (21) for the case we are discussing:

(21) Focus: p → 𝒫
      Environment: __f

In fact, in this formalism the focus is represented twice: once explicitly, with the actual input and output separated by the arrow (p → 𝒫), and once implicitly as a horizontal line adjacent to the environment (__f). Probably a more perspicuous formalization of the rule being scrutinized would therefore be as follows:

(22)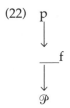

Indeed, this format can be nicely integrated into our graphic model of the organization of linguistic sound in (14) above, as follows:

(23)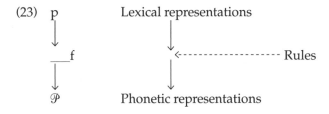

It is obvious, however, that the gain in perspicuity is more than offset by the spatial loss, and consequently we will adhere to the slightly more abstract format in (20), indeed the standard one.

> Formalize the change of /t/ in *that* in *that pen*, and the change of /v/ in *five* in *five tons*, making use of the standard rule formalism we have just proposed.

7 Derivations

Rules only represent one aspect of the organization of sound in language. The other two aspects are the lexical representation and the phonetic representation

Rules of course only represent one aspect of the organization of sound in language. The other two aspects we have considered are the lexical representation, which corresponds to the way language sound is inertly stored, and the phonetic representation, which corresponds to the way this sound is dynamically realized.

> We have just used the expressions "inertly stored" and "dynamically realized". Do you get a feel for the contrast we want to express? Try and put it into words.

We shall now examine how these three aspects of sound structure – lexical representation, phonetic realization and rules – are formally related.

In fact, we have already given the nub of this relationship: quite simply, the rules change lexical representations into phonetic representations. Equivalently, the rules can be thought of as a formal device bridging the gap between lexical and phonetic representations. This relationship can be visualized with the help of the diagram in (14) above, which we now repeat:

(24)   Lexical representations

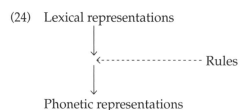

Phonetic representations

Let us see how this schema is implemented in the case of the [p] ~ [ℙ] alternation in *cup*. Crucially, whichever sound is chosen it does not affect the identity of the word, contrary to what happens if we replace [p] with [b] or

[f], as in *cub* and *cuff*, respectively. The reason for the difference in outcome is that in English [p], [b] and [f] are minimal units of sound contrast, or "phonemes", but [𝒫] is not. The word PHONEME therefore refers to a unit of explicit sound contrast: the existence of a MINIMAL PAIR, like the ones made up by *cu*[p] and *cu*[b], or *cu*[p] and *cu*[f], automatically grants phonemic status to the sounds /p/, /b/, /f/ responsible for the contrasts: notice that the symbols of phonemes are enclosed in slashes, just like the symbols for lexical sounds, an ambiguous use that should not cause confusion, given the quite different theoretical contexts associated with the two constructs. Each contextual variant of a phoneme is an ALLOPHONE of that phoneme: in the case we are discussing, /p/ can be realized as either [p] or [𝒫], which are correspondingly allophones of /p/. The words "allophone" and "allophony", derived from the Greek words *allos* "other" and *phonos* "sound", are, however, connotative of an approach to phonology closely associated with Saussure's style of linguistics, now superseded. From a more contemporary perspective, we refer to the phenomenon as ALTERNATION, and to the elements partaking in it, such as *cu*[p] and *cu*[𝒫] in the case at hand, as ALTERNANTS.

> Each contextual variant of a phoneme is an ALLOPHONE of that phoneme

We know what the lexical representation and the phonetic representations of *cup* (or rather, of the part of this form we are focusing on: we ignore the remainder for the sake of simplicity) are supposed to be: *cu*/p/, and *cu*[p] or *cu*[𝒫], respectively. These representations thus make up the LEXICAL or UNDERLYING LEVEL and the PHONETIC or SURFACE LEVEL, also respectively, as we illustrate in (25). Notice that the use of slashes and brackets is unnecessary in these representations, since we are defining the two levels explicitly:

> Variant realizations of a lexical form are ALTERNANTS

(25)   Lexical level: *cu* p

   Phonetic level: *cu* p   *cu* 𝒫

At the lexical level we have entered the hypothesized /p/, and at the phonetic level the actual phonetic alternants [p] ~ [𝒫].

Why are we saying that the /p/ is hypothesized?

While this layout conveniently displays the level-bound difference between the lexical and the phonetic forms, it obviously fails to account for the DISTRIBUTION of the alternants, that is, for the fact that [𝒫] only occurs before [f]. It is precisely the role of rules to express this.

Suppose then that we include the appropriate rules in the representation. In the present case, only one rule is relevant, to be referred to by the transparent label "Labiodentalization". The result is as follows ("NA" = not applicable):

(26)   Underlying level: *cu* p   *cu* p f *ul*

       Rules:

          "Labiodentalization"   NA   𝒫

       Phonetic level: *cu* p   *cu* 𝒫 f *ul*

> Why doesn't "Labiodentalization" apply to *cup*? Go back to (20) above to check the formalism of the rule.

What we are now doing is feeding lexical forms (in context, where necessary) through a given set of rules (here only "Labiodentalization"), writing in each line the accumulated results of the application of the rules. Finally, in the last line we enter the result of the operation of all the rules (again, only one rule is relevant in the present case). Such an output obviously corresponds to the phonetic realization, and will consequently constitute the phonetic transcription of the form in question. Constructs like the one in (26) are known as DERIVATIONS, because they embody the derivation of the phonetic sounds from the lexical sounds through the mediation of the rules.

DERIVATIONS embody the derivation of the phonetic sounds from the lexical sounds through the mediation of the rules

8 Phonetics and Phonology

We are now in a position where we can begin to understand the substance of phonology, and how it differs from phonetics.

As you now know, phonetics describes sounds: articulatorily (positions and movements of the speech organs), acoustically (patterns in the air, detectable with the appropriate technology) and perceptually (impact of the sound on the ear and subsequent transmission of the signal to the brain). For instance, in the cases we examined above, phonetic analysis will yield a description of the bilabial stop in *cup* as labiodental before [f], of the alveolar *t* in *that* as bilabial before bilabials and as velar before velars, and of the last fricative in *five* as voiceless before voiceless obstruents. Moreover, phonetics will help us to understand the articulatory motivation of these phenomena in terms of "coarticulation", the term by which phoneticians express essentially what phonologists refer to as "assimilation".

In terms of the display in (26) above, the concern of phonetics is, therefore, what we have been calling the phonetic (or surface) level: the level reflecting the real world of articulatory, acoustic and perceptual events. This limitation in the scope of phonetics obviously leaves both the lexical (or underlying) level and the rules uncatered for. Consequently we need another discipline to look after these aspects of the model. This discipline is, of course, PHONOLOGY.

Now, simplicity is not a bad companion, in science as in other aspects of life (once again, Occam's razor can be called forth in this connection), and we can legitimately ask ourselves what the point is of complicating things by introducing "phonology" alongside "phonetics". The answer is that in science, again as in life, division of labour often yields rich rewards. Thus, by splitting the remit of sound investigation between phonetics and phonology, we can allow the former to focus on the description of physical speech sound, while the latter will be aimed at its more abstract aspects. Specifically, the object of inquiry of phonetics (physical sound) is amenable to experimental investigation, while the object of study of phonology is by its very nature of a more hypothetical kind.

> The concern of PHONETICS is what we have been calling the phonetic (or surface) level. PHONOLOGY is concerned with the lexical (or underlying) level and with the rules

> Explain what is meant by this contrast, and provide some justification for proposing it.

Thus, it is not difficult to verify that the *p* of *cup* in *cupful* is [ℙ], rather than [p] – an experiment to this effect was indeed suggested above. By contrast, our postulation of /p/ as the underlying (or lexical) form of [ℙ] is purely idealistic – it is contingent on our hypothetical interpretation of the system, rather than on directly material data, which would indeed be very hard to come by in this connection: even if we could peep directly into somebody's grey matter, it is most unlikely that we would see anything of relevance to the issue. A similar remark is apposite with regard to our analysis of the [ℙ] alternant as the product of a rule, clearly only one of many possible ways of formalizing the situation, if a particularly apt one in the context of the overall model we are presenting: an alternative to rules and derivations will be discussed in chapter 19. All in all, therefore, both the type of work and the tools needed for the investigation of what we are calling phonetic events differ considerably from the type of work and the tools needed for the investigation of what we are dubbing phonological phenomena. This difference will undoubtedly have practical repercussions, and, more likely than not, different individuals will be drawn to focus their work on either area, further cementing the conventional separation of the two fields.

Chapter Summary

This chapter has presented the foundations of phonological investigation. By examining such cases as *cupful* or *red pen*, or the devoicing of fricatives before adjacent voiceless segments, we have shown that the signifier of any one linguistic sign may have more than one single physical manifestation. We have considered a number of hypotheses to account for such contextual variations. Hypotheses must be testable, and the preferred solution will be the one which fits the most facts: the nature of the adjacent following segment in the cases examined. Speakers assume that there is only one signifier for the sign CUP and are clearly unaware of the observed changes. Consequently, speakers do not make a conscious choice of *cu[𝒫]* when articulating *cup* as part of *cupful*. The principle of Occam's razor has been invoked in defence of lexical economy in the face of phonetic diversity. In line with our purpose of relating phonetics to phonology, we have introduced the concept of the phoneme, an abstract contrastive unit of sound, roughly (although not exactly) equivalent to the lexical level. Lexical forms and phonetic forms are formally related by means of rules, by their very nature capturing the generality of the patterns, which transcend any specific word. The display of the staged changes brought about by rules on any one form constitutes a derivation. The discipline of phonology is concerned with the study of such formal structures, thus contrasting with phonetics, which deals with the physical aspects of sound.

Key Questions

1 In what way can the articulation of one sound influence that of an adjacent sound?

2 Assimilation processes are either "progressive" or "regressive". What is the difference?

3 What are the two complementary parts of a linguistic sign?

4 What are the terms of "Occam's razor"? How does it constrain phonological analysis?

5 What is a phonological rule?

6 What is the connection between lexical items and their phonological representations?

7 What sort of information is contained in the lexicon?

8 What are the "focus" and the "environment" of phonological rules?

9 Explain the terms "phoneme" and "allophone".

10 What is a "minimal pair"? What does it help us to recognize?

11 Define "alternants".

12 What is a derivation?

13 Distinguish the concerns of phonology from those of phonetics.

F u r t h e r   P r a c t i c e

Catalan Obstruents

Consider the obstruent alternations (shown in broad phonetic transcription) in the following masculine/feminine pairs from Catalan, a language spoken mainly on the eastern side of Spain:

Masc.	Fem.	
llo[p]	llo[b]a	'wolf'
mu[t]	mu[d]a	'dumb'
ce[k]	ce[g]a	'blind'
francè[s]	france[z]a	'French'
ti[p]	ti[p]a	'satiated'
peti[t]	peti[t]a	'small'
se[k]	se[k]a	'dry'
gro[s]	gro[s]a	'fat'

(i)   Describe the differences between the alternants in each pair.
(ii)   Describe the environment for each alternant.
(iii)   Hypothesize a lexical form for each pair.
(iv)   Is there a pattern to the alternations? What is it?

English Past Tense

The following words are all regular past tense forms of English verbs:

jumped, talked, played, toyed, begged, rubbed, washed, dredged, fetched, keyed, showed, passed, caused, writhed, frothed

(i)   How is the past tense formed in English spelling?
(ii)   Does this correspond to a uniform sound?
(iii)   If not, how many sounds are there?
(iv)   Is it possible to postulate one lexical form for the past tense morpheme? If so what is it?
(v)   What is the reason for the surface variation?
(vi)   Show by means of a rule how the lexical and phonetic representations are connected.

CHAPTER THREE

SONORANT CONSONANTS

Chapter Objectives

In this chapter you will learn about:

- A type of consonant sound known as "sonorant", that does not involve constriction of the airflow.
- The secondary channels involved in the articulation of these sounds.
- The existence of two major types of sonorant: air escapes either through the nose, or out of the mouth over the top of the tongue or down the sides.
- The articulation of some sonorant sounds which may be less familiar to the English speaker.
- The phonetic symbols used for sonorants.

In the previous chapter we offered a succint sketch of phonology, backed up by an analysis of some assimilation phenomena involving obstruents. The phonetic properties of obstruents and glottals were examined in detail in chapter 1. Clearly, though, there are many speech sounds besides obstruents and glottals.

List a few speech sounds that you are aware of and have not been dealt with in chapter 1.

In line with our policy of alternating the presentation of phonetics and phonology in these preliminary chapters, we now turn our attention to the phonetics of sonorant consonants. We will make some further remarks pertinent to phonology as we go along, but will of course reserve the bulk of the phonological discussion on sonorants for chapter 4.

1 General Properties of Sonorants

The common denominator in obstruents is the presence of an obstruction to the airflow in the mouth; hence the label "obstruent". The contrasts between the various obstruents follow from differences in place of articulation (the anatomical point where the obstruction is made), manner of articulation (the degree of obstruction, according to which we classified obstruents into stops, affricates and fricatives), or vocal fold activity, by which obstruents are divided into voiced (pronounced with vocal fold vibration) and voiceless (without vocal fold vibration).

> Jog your memory by providing at least one sound exemplifying each of the categories just mentioned.

At this point you may be tempted to think that the production of speech sound necessarily involves some such obstruction – how else could sound be made?, you may wonder. As we shall see in this and successive chapters, however, this is in fact far from being the case. Indeed, in all the sounds to be introduced from now on, the air comes out through a channel wide enough to avoid friction. Such unobstructed sounds are known as SONORANTS, because, as follows from the greater openness of the channel, they carry a greater amount of sound than their obstruent counterparts – cf. Latin *sonus* 'sound', *sonor* 'resonance', *sonorus* 'sonorous'.

Unobstructed sounds are known as SONORANTS

Actually, sonorancy can be construed as a specific setting for manner of articulation. It should be obvious by now that the articulatory channel exhibits increasing openness progressively along the scale stops–affricates–fricatives–sonorants. This means that sonorants are the most open of consonants. In table 3.1 we summarize the settings we have now available for manner of articulation. You will see that the degree of channel opening is relative for all categories but stops – "f > a", for instance, indicates that the channel for fricatives is more open than the channel for affricates, without specifying the precise size of the opening:

Sonorants are the most open of consonants

The degree of channel opening is relative for all categories but stops

Table 3.1   Manner of articulation settings

Category	Degree of channel opening
Stops	Ø
Affricates	a (a > Ø)
Fricatives	f (f > a)
Sonorants	s (s > f)

Rank the following segments with regard to their sonority load: [ʤ], [s], [f], [p], [ʒ], [k].

A further property of sonorants is that they are voiced, under normal circumstances, in most languages. This means that, of the three criteria we introduced in chapter 1 for the classification of consonants, namely, voice, manner of articulation, and place of articulation, usually only place of articulation implements contrasts between sonorants. However, the articulation of sonorants involves additional channels or gestures that play no part in the articulation of obstruents, and divide the class of sonorants into several subclasses.

2 Nasality

The blockage or constriction of the air characteristic of obstruents is located at some point in the mouth. This point, therefore, defines the place of articulation of the obstruent.

However, in all the sounds we have examined so far, the airflow is also systematically blocked at a second location, which we left unstated in our descriptions. In particular, we have taken it for granted all along that, as we attempted to pronounce each of the sounds we presented, the soft palate would be raised to prevent the exit of air through the nose – you will recall that the soft palate, or "velum", is the softish area at the back of the roof of the mouth (figure 3.1).

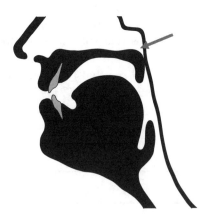

Figure 3.1   Raised soft palate

Now, what will happen if the soft palate is not raised during the production of speech? See figure 3.2.

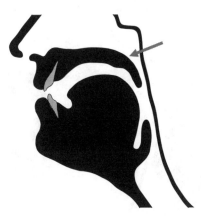

Figure 3.2   Lowered soft palate

Let us experiment by deliberately lowering the soft palate as we pronounce [b].

> Pronounce *stabber* several times (the sound represented as *bb* in the spelling here is of course a single [b]), and then lower the velum while continuing to articulate [b] with the lips. What sound comes out?

The resulting sound will obviously be different from [b]: if you utter *stabber* while lowering the velum for the sound represented as *bb*, you will hear *stammer*. This can only mean that [m] (the phonetic symbol for the sound spelled *mm* in *stammer*) is identical to [b] in all respects but one: the position of the soft palate.

> Write down a full phonetic description of both [b] and [m] and underline the difference(s).

The difference between the two sounds, therefore, involves nasality. On the one hand, [b] is an ORAL SOUND, since during its production no air comes out through the nose due to the raised soft palate. By contrast, [m] is a NASAL SOUND, since the lowered velum allows air to come out through the nose.

> Try and figure out what happens to your speech when your nose is blocked by a cold.

Nasality aside, [b] and [m] are identical: bilabial stops (figure 3.3).

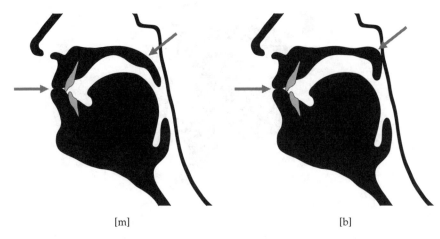

[m]   [b]

Figure 3.3   Articulation of [m] and [b]

They are bilabial because they are articulated with the two lips. They are stops because they involve total blockage of air in the mouth, even though in the case of [m] air keeps coming out through the nose.

> Try to lengthen the [m] as you pronounce *stammer*. Now try the same with [b] in *stabber*. Do you notice any differences? What is their cause?

At first sight, the continuous stream of nasal air makes the classification of [m] as a stop appear contradictory: in chapter 1 we said that sounds with no air blockage, such as fricatives, are not stops by definition.

> Try and guess why [m] and other nasals, to be examined directly, are classified as stops.

The answer is that, of the two articulatory actions you now know partake in the production of [m] and other nasals (the stricture in the mouth and the lowering of the velum), the stricture in the mouth is more important. Because sounds are characterized by their PRIMARY ARTICULATOR, [m] will be defined as a (bilabial) stop.

Sounds are characterized by their PRIMARY ARTICULATOR

Turning now to vocal fold activity, you know that both [b] and [m] are voiced, and that [b] without voice is in fact [p]. What will a voiceless [m] amount to?

Think about this question for a few seconds.

In fact, no voiceless [m] exists in English at the level at which the basic sound contrasts between the words of the language are catalogued, the lexical level. Thus, while English could have a word *stapper* forming a minimal pair with *stabber*, it could not have a word *sta*[m̥]*er* minimally contrasting with *stammer* – the IPA underscripted diacritic "ᵒ" indicates voicelessness, and consequently [m̥] is the symbol for a voiceless [m].

Does the availability of the diacritic "ᵒ" for voicelessness render such a symbol as [p] otiose? You ought to understand the logic of the question, even if you cannot give it a full answer at this stage.

Indeed, we have already mentioned that sonorants (of which nasals, and therefore [m], are instantiations) are typically voiced in all languages, for reasons of physics which need not concern us here. The upshot of this is that English lacks a phoneme /m̥/, and voiceless sonorant phonemes in general.

Some languages of South East Asia do have voiceless nasal phonemes, however: for example, the words [ma] and [m̥a] form a minimal pair in Burmese, the former signifying 'hard' and the latter 'notice'.

3 The Universal Nasal

The sound [m] does not exhaust the inventory of nasal sounds.

Mention at least one more nasal sound of English.

One obvious additional nasal sound in English, and probably in all of the world's languages, is present in such words as *knit* or *tin*, initially and finally, respectively (notice the purely orthographic value of *k* in *knit*). Having established the close correspondence of [m] with [b], you will not be surprised to hear that the sound symbolized as [n] also has an oral counterpart.

Try to work out the oral congener of [n] before you continue reading.

In order to discover which this is, you have to work out the place of articulation of [n], and then identify the English voiced oral stop articulated at the same place.

> You can now have a second go at finding the oral correlate of [n], after ascertaining the place of articulation of [n] through the appropriate exploration: go back to chapter 1 to refresh your memory, if necessary.

The articulation of [n] takes place on the alveolar ridge, and consequently [n] is an alveolar stop. It is also voiced, as we know all nasals (and other sonorants) are in English and most other languages. On the basis of these settings, the identification of the oral partner of [n] will offer no special difficulty: it must be a voiced alveolar oral stop. Familiarity with the information presented in the preceding two chapters will enable you to identify this sound as [d] (figure 3.4).

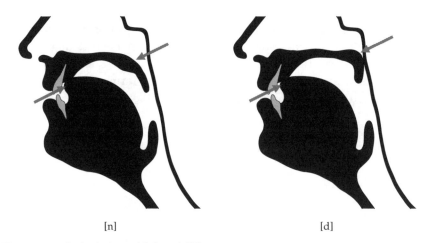

[n]   [d]

Figure 3.4   Articulation of [n] and [d]

Nasal consonants are characterized by the presence of a second resonating chamber: the nasal cavity

---

It should be clear by now, both conceptually and experientially, that nasal consonants are characterized by the presence of a second resonating chamber, the nasal cavity, in addition to the oral chamber that also characterizes obstruents – the precise meaning of the term "resonating chamber" bears on the physics of sound, or "acoustics", and need not concern us here: we can be satisfied with the idea of a space filled with air in which sound is produced. The fact that there are two resonating chambers in nasals confirms our statement at the outset that the articulation of sonorants involves channels that are not present in the articulation of obstruents.

The articulation of obstruents can, however, also involve two sources.

> Can you say which these are?

In particular, you will recall that, in addition to the oral source, the articulation of obstruents can involve a glottal source contributing voice. It follows that the pronunciation of nasals involves three (rather than just two) sound sources: the oral source (also present in obstruents), the nasal source (defining nasals), and the glottal source – remember that nasals are usually voiced. We can construe these various sound sources as sound-defining parameters, alongside manner of articulation. A PARAMETER is therefore a criterion for classification, akin to one type of building block. Within the musical universe we have been drawing analogies from, a parameter can be likened to an instrument in the orchestra: the tune played by this instrument is obviously one of the components that make up the symphony.

A PARAMETER is a criterion for classification

4 Other Nasal Consonants

A third nasal consonant is quite common in English.

> Can you think which this nasal is? Give at least one word that includes it.

The nasal in question never occurs at the start of a word. In fact, we will see that there are reasons to believe that this nasal is not a lexical segment of English, that is, that it is not present in the lexical level, from which alternation is excluded, as you know.

> Explain briefly to yourself the notion of alternation and the difference between the lexical and surface levels, as presented in chapter 2.

This third English nasal does, however, occur at the phonetic level in non-word-initial position. It is exemplified in such words as *wing, sung* or *gong,* which contrast minimally with *win, sun* and *gone* in most accents. *Wing* and *win,* for instance, make up a minimal pair in these accents. Even if the the final orthographic *g* is pronounced, as is typical, for instance, of Birmingham or Liverpool, in England, the *n* of *wing* will be phonetically different from the *n* of *win*, in spite of their orthographic identity.

> Explore the pronunciation of the *n* of *wing*, trying to elucidate its place of articulation.

The place of articulation of the *n* in *wing* is identical to the place of articulation of [g]. Accordingly, such *n* is the nasal counterpart of [g] (figure 3.5).

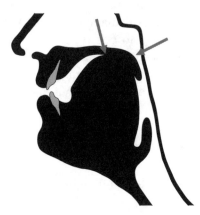

Figure 3.5   Articulation of [ŋ]

> Write down the defining traits of both [g] and its nasal counterpart in terms of our familiar parameters.

The phonetic symbol for the velar nasal is [ŋ].

If [ŋ] is absent from the lexical inventory of English, the question arises of why it occurs at the phonetic level. The answer is that English [ŋ] comes about as the result of assimilation of the place of articulation of a lexical /n/ to that of a following /g/, which is subsequently deleted in many accents. As we are seeing repeatedly, assimilation is one of the major factors responsible for the differences between the lexical and the phonetic levels postulated in chapter 2.

> Explain how assimilation accounts for many of the differences between the lexical and the phonetic levels.

In some languages, [ŋ] is a legitimate lexical segment. In those languages we would not expect the same limited distribution of [ŋ] we find in English, where it can never occur word-initially. For example, in Malay [ŋ] can occur in all positions, including word-initially: [ŋ]*eri* 'terrified' forms a minimal pair with [n]*eri*, a type of plant.

> Pronounce the word *singer* a few times. Do you pronounce the g? If you don't, try to slow down the delivery and split *singer* into two words, making each of them consonant-initial: *si-nger*. The initial sound of the second word ought to be [ŋ] (but do not worry unduly if you can't get it: the experiment is somewhat artificial for an English speaker, and therefore you may not get the desired results).

Looked at from a more traditional perspective, [ŋ] is therefore phonemic in languages like Malay, hence formally /ŋ/. Phonemic status has also been claimed for English [ŋ], on the basis of minimal pairs like those given above: *wing* vs. *win*, etc. You can now see that phonemic status does not necessarily imply lexical status: phonemic status follows from the existence of systematic contrastiveness in the surface, whereas lexical status requires constrastiveness at the lexical level.

> Remind yourself why [ŋ] does not appear to be contrastive at the lexical level in English.

A fourth nasal, reasonably common across languages, is very marginal in English. This nasal can turn up in such words as *onion* or *canyon* when said casually.

> Pronounce these words and see if the nasal you pronounce is different from [m], [n] or [ŋ]. If it is, try and figure out where in the mouth you are articulating the nasal. (This exercise is not as easy as it sounds, because as soon as you pay attention to your delivery you will tend to slow down and lose spontaneity.)

The place of articulation of this new sound, [ɲ], standard in French, Spanish or Italian, among others, is similar, although not identical, to the place of articulation of the [dʒ] of *judge* (figure 3.6 below). In particular, as we explained in chapter 1, [dʒ] is a palatoalveolar sound, pronounced in the area between the palate and the alveolar ridge. By contrast, [ɲ] is purely palatal: the blockage takes place entirely on the hard palate. Notice that the term PALATAL is reserved for sounds articulated on the hard palate: you already know that sounds articulated on the soft palate are referred to as "velar", the adjective of "velum", which we said in chapter 1 is the Latin word for the soft palate.

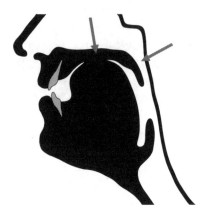

Figure 3.6   Articulation of [ɲ]

Define [ɲ] in terms of all the familiar phonetic parameters.

Although many languages have a contrastive palatal nasal, conventional orthographies do not have a letter for it. Thus, in French and Italian, [ɲ] is spelled by means of the digraph *gn* (French *agneau* 'lamb'; Italian *ogni* 'every'), in Spanish as *n* with a tilde (*ñ*, as in *año* 'year'), in Dutch as the digraph *nj* (*Spanje* 'Spain'), in Portuguese as the digraph *nh* (*anho* 'lamb'), and so on. The historical reason for this spelling diversity is that this sound did not exist in Latin, and therefore there was no letter for it in the Roman alphabet, from which the alphabets of these and other Western European languages were taken.

In Spanish, French and many other languages, there are many minimal pairs involving [ɲ] and the other nasals: Spanish *ca*[ɲ]*a* 'rod' vs. *ca*[n]*a* 'grey hair' and *ca*[m]*a* 'bed', for instance. In the absence of contrary evidence, /ɲ/ must therefore be analysed as a phoneme in these languages. From the updated perspective on phonology we are adopting here, it is reasonable to assume that /ɲ/ also has lexical status in these languages, but obviously not in English.

Explain the difference between being a phoneme and having lexical status. Why doesn't /ɲ/ have lexical status in English?

5 Liquids

So far in this chapter we have been seeing that nasal consonants are characterized by a second resonating chamber, the nasal cavity. Nasalization thus functions in a similar way to voice: it provides an additional source of sound which supplements the oral source to give rise to a complex sound. An important difference between nasalization and voicing is the manner in which the two sound sources are connected, sequentially for voice, but in parallel for nasality, as we represent in the following diagrams:

Air ⟶ Voice ⟶ Oral articulation ⟶ Sound
Sequential coupling of voice

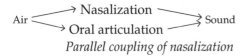

Parallel coupling of nasalization

Resorting once more to a musical analogy, we suggested in chapter 1 that the addition of voice to an oral articulation is reminiscent of the plugging of a recorder into a trumpet: the wind will first power one instrument and then the other. In the case of nasality, however, a more apposite analogy would be the bagpipes, where the chanter pipe, responsible for the main melody, and the drone pipe(s), providing the typical background buzz, are activated *simultaneously* by the air coming out of the bag.

Sketch out the progression of the air in the bagpipes and in the trumpet-cum-recorder contraption.

You also know from the preceding discussion that the primary articulation of nasals, located in the mouth, is of a stop kind, whereas their secondary articulation, responsible for their nasality, is of a continuant kind: the sound continues for as long as air is available in the lungs. In nasals, therefore, a CONTINUANT and a NON-CONTINUANT mode of articulation are effectively superimposed onto one another.

> Nasalization functions in a similar way to voice: it provides an additional source of sound which supplements the oral source to give rise to a complex sound

> Sonorants have a simultaneous continuant and non-continuant articulation

Sonorants can also be articulated exclusively in the mouth, with no nasal component. These non-nasal sonorants still have a simultaneous continuant and non-continuant articulation: during their production one part of the oral channel is blocked, while another part remains unobstructed and allows the air to escape freely. Such sounds are commonly referred to as LIQUIDS (perhaps because they sound fluid), and we now turn our attention to them.

6 Laterals

Let us compare the middle consonant in *mellow* (the doubling of the letter in the spelling is of course immaterial) with its counterpart in *meadow*.

> Spend a few seconds exploring the respective articulations and making a comparison between them.

The articulation of both these sounds is alveolar, that is, it involves placing the blade of the tongue on the upper alveolar ridge. Both sounds are also voiced. Last, they both involve a complete closure at the upper front alveolar area. Given these striking similarities, what is it that makes these two sounds different?

> Think about this question and advance an answer.

If you pay close attention to the articulation of the two sounds in question, you will notice that, in the case of [d], the tongue presses firmly against the upper teeth all around, not just at the front, but also on the sides, to prevent any air from escaping.

By contrast, for the sound found in the middle of *mellow*, represented by the phonetic symbol [l], the sides of the tongue (only one side in some speakers) do not touch the complete set of upper teeth, and air comes out continuously through the resulting gap. Because the air flows over sides of the tongue, these sounds are known as LATERALS: Latin *lateralis* means 'of the side(s)', from *latus* 'side' (compare such English expressions as *lateral thinking, collateral,* etc.).

As regards place of articulation, [l] is defined as an alveolar sound, exactly like [d] (figure 3.7).

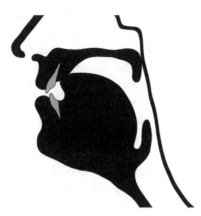

Figure 3.7   Articulation of [l] and [d]

The definition of [l] and [d] as alveolar obviously suggests that the gesture made by the blade of the tongue is regarded as primary, and the gesture made by the sides of the tongue (closing for [d] and opening for [l]) as subsidiary. Indeed, primary articulation is commonly related to the median line of the tube through which the air flows out: to the mouth's median plane, in more technical parlance. In addition, [l] is voiced, also like [d], unsurprisingly so, since we stated above that sonorants (of which class liquids, and thus [l], are members) are characteristically voiced across languages. Finally, [l] is also oral, since the velum remains raised during the whole of its production, just as it does with [d]. The difference between [l] and [d], therefore, lies exclusively in the respective status of these two sounds with regard to LATERALITY, the term referring to the lowering of the sides of the tongue during articulation: [l] is lateral, while [d] is not.

Primary articulation is commonly related to the central area of the mouth

> Make a list of all the defining phonetic traits of [t], [d], [l] and [n], highlighting the differences between them.

In the opening paragraph of the section we said that [l], like [d], involves air stoppage at the front. We now know that during the articulation of [l] air continues to flow out of the mouth through the gap formed by the sides of the tongue and the upper teeth on the sides of the mouth. We came across a similar situation earlier for nasals, characterized by air stoppage in the mouth but continuous airflow through the nose, and we attributed their conventional description as stops to the fact that the articulation in the mouth is regarded as primary.

Phonologically, nasals always function as stops, and therefore their classification as such is uncontroversial. The tendency for [l] is also to function as a stop, but in a few languages it appears to pattern with the continuants. Consequently, we must leave the classification of this sound somewhat flexible. Articulatorily, however, [l] is always considered alveolar: this confirms the privileged status of the central region of the mouth in the identification of the primary articulatory gesture.

An additional lateral sound, a patalal lateral, bears a similar relationship to [l] to that which [ɲ] bears to [n]. The phonetic symbol for the palatal lateral is [ʎ], an inverted "y". The articulation of this sound, spelled *gli* in Italian (*zabaglione*) and *ll* in Spanish (*paella*), is a bit exotic for the English speaker, and we will accordingly put some extra care into its description. Pronunciation guides tend to suggest the lateral sound in *million* as a close English equivalent, but this correspondence is subject to a number of caveats. To produce [ʎ], the body of the tongue (that is, the area behind the blade) must be raised to the roof of the mouth to block the exit of air, as was the case for the nasal [ɲ]. However, for [ʎ] the sides of the tongue must be allowed to hang free, to let the air flow out through the resulting gap, in the familiar lateral gesture.

> Experiment with the articulation of [ʎ], which you may find a trifle difficult. Try to listen to the pronunciation of native speakers of this sound if you have the opportunity.

In the British context it is perhaps advisable to caution the reader about the Welsh sound spelled *ll*, as in such place names as *Llandaf, Llandudno, Llangollen, Llanelli, Llanfairpwllgwyngyllgogerychwyrndrobwillllantysiliogogogoch*, etc. (*llan* simply means 'church, village' in Welsh). Although also an alveolar lateral, this sound involves frication, caused by a considerable narrowing of the lateral gap(s). Therefore, it is not a sonorant, since the defining criterion for sonorants is unobstructed exit of air. Indeed, the Welsh sound in question is an obstruent, which is moreover voiceless. The phonetic symbol for this sound is [ɬ].

> Give yourself a little practice of [ɬ]. As usual, try to listen to native speakers if you can.

The correspondences in place of articulation between nasals and laterals are completed with the velar laterals that exist in a handful of languages.

In the Mid-Waghi language of New Guinea, for instance, the word [aʟaʟe] 'dizzy', with the velar lateral [ʟ], contrasts (although not minimally) with the word [alala] 'speak incorrectly', with the ordinary alveolar [l]. The sound [ʟ] is also reported to occur in some English accents in some contexts (for instance, before labial or velar consonants), but it is otherwise rare. The velar lateral [ʟ] must not be confused with the *velarized* alveolar lateral [ɫ]. The sound [ɫ] occurs allophonically in English in word-final position, and syllable-finally generally (syllables are dealt with in chapters 9 and 10), as in *pill*, *mole* or *cool*, although some accents only have plain, or "clear", *l*s (general Irish), or velarized, or "dark", *l*s (general Scottish).

> Pronounce *pill*, *mole* and *cool* trying to notice the difference in the sound of the *l* with their close phonetic correlates *pillar*, *molar*, *cooler*. Now pronounce each pair paying particular attention to the different positioning of the back of the tongue for each type of *l*.

In languages like Russian, [ɫ] functions phonemically: *moɫ* 'pier' and *poɫka* 'polka', with [ɫ], contrast with *mol* 'moth' and *polka* 'shelf', without. The articulatory difference between the velarized *l*, [ɫ], and its plain counterpart [l] lies in the additional bunching of the body of the tongue at the back that characterizes [ɫ] (figure 3.8).

> Repeat the last exercise if you had difficulties in finding this out.

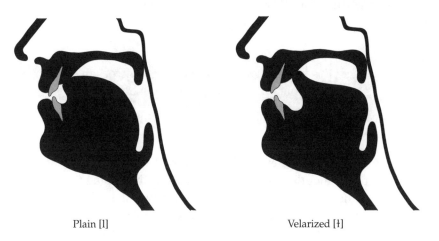

Plain [l]   Velarized [ɫ]

Figure 3.8   Plain and velarized *l*

In some accents (London Cockney, for instance) the velar lateral [ɫ] loses its alveolar contact and takes on lip rounding, effectively becoming the sound represented by *w* in *bow*.

We have seen that both laterals and nasals can be realized at a range of articulatory places. However, all laterals must by our definition involve the tongue in their articulation; labial nasals, by contrast, are realized exclusively with the lips.

All laterals involve the tongue in their articulation

7 Rhotics

The label RHOTICS refers to a class of sounds that are "r-like". The members of this class do not necessarily have much in common with each other phonetically

"Rho" is the Greek name for the letter *r*, and the label RHOTICS therefore refers to a class of sounds that are "r-like". It will soon become apparent, however, that the members of this class do not necessarily have much in common with each other phonetically: their common grouping as "rhotics" is grounded on similarity of phonological behaviour, rather than on shared phonetic substance.

> Explain carefully the difference between these two criteria.

The sound represented by the letter *r* in most accents of English is very different from its counterpart in many other languages. In turn, the *r* sound typical of Scottish English is different from its common English equivalent, as we will see below. The phonetic symbol for the common English *r* is [ɹ], an inverted *r*. The articulatory gesture for [ɹ] is almost the opposite of the articulatory gesture for [l], hence the tongue twister "red lorry, yellow lorry".

> Say this tongue twister out loud a couple of times, to experience for yourself the articulatory connection between [l] and [ɹ].

In the previous section we explained that for [l] we blocked the air in the central part of the mouth by pressing the blade of the tongue firmly against the alveolar ridge, while letting it flow freely down the sides. By contrast, for [ɹ] the sides of the tongue touch the back teeth, while a fairly wide gap is created in the centre of the mouth for the air to pass through without causing friction (figure 3.9).

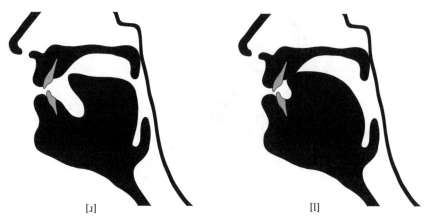

[ɹ]   [l]

Figure 3.9 Articulation of [ɹ] and [l]

> Try comparing the action of the tongue during [ɹ] and during
> [l]. Then focus your attention on where exactly you place the
> tip of your tongue.

There are two ways in which the blade of the tongue may be positioned for [ɹ]. The chances are that speakers from Britain will keep the blade flat, leaving a channel open at the front for the air to escape (figure 3.10).

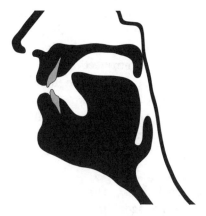

Figure 3.10 Plain (British) [ɹ]

American speakers, on the other hand, are more likely to curl back the blade towards the roof of the mouth (without of course touching it or drawing the tongue too close to it). See figure 3.11.

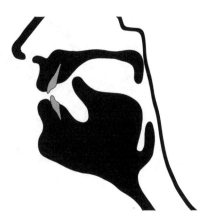

Figure 3.11   Retroflex (American) [ɹ]

Fortunately, the effect of this articulatory difference on the resulting sound is not great. The action of curling back the tongue is known as RETRO-FLECTION, and the sounds thus produced are referred to as RETROFLEXES.

> Try pronouncing *rip* and *rye* and see if you can decide how you form your *r*.

Not only *r*s can be retroflected, but also all other sounds that involve the tip of the tongue in their articulation. For instance, the *d* at the end of the Swedish word *smörgåsbord* is retroflex. In IPA phonetic transcription, retroflection is indicated by the addition of a tail to the symbol of the corresponding non-retroflex, hence [ɹ] for the English retroflex *r*, [ɖ] for the Swedish retroflex *d*, and so on. In an alternative notation, in common use for typographical convenience, retroflection is represented diacritically by means of an underscripted dot: [ṛ], [ḍ], etc. Retroflex sounds are particularly frequent in languages of the Indian subcontinent. For instance, in Malayalam, the main language of the state of Karala, in Southern India, *ku*[ʈ]*i* 'child', with a retroflex [ʈ], makes up minimal pairs with *ku*[t̪]*i* 'stabbed', with a dental [t̪], and *ku*[t]*i* 'peg', with an alveolar [t].

> Retroflection tends to carry over to English in the speech of speakers originating in the Indian subcontinent. Experiment with a range of sounds that are alveolar in ordinary English to see how much you can retroflect them.

A minimal amount of self-observation will make it obvious that the mechanics of tongue positioning for [ɹ] are rather subtle, if not downright fiddly.

Not surprisingly, therefore, children often have difficulty in pronouncing [ɹ] and substitute *w*, so *rock* becomes *wok*. Some adult speakers (including some well-known personalities) also have a so-called "defective" *r*, similar, but not identical, to *w*: the typical "defective" *r* is produced by drawing the upper teeth onto the inside of the lower lip further back than for [f] or [v], and not quite close enough to cause friction.

You may want to have a go at this sound, which is noticeable as a feature of popular speech both in London and in New York.

The "defective" *r* is perceptually similar to the more common English *r*, in spite of the striking articulatory difference between the two. The "defective" *r* is defined phonetically as a (voiced oral) labiodental approximant. Its IPA symbol is [ʋ]. The term APPROXIMANT, related lexically to *approximate* and *approximation*, in turn connected to *approach*, is applied to sounds that are continuant and frictionless.

A very common rhotic, found in Spanish, Russian, Greek and many other languages, as well as in Scottish English, at least historically, involves vibrating the tip of the tongue against the upper tooth ridge, hence the label "alveolar TRILL" (also, informally, "rolled *r*"): Spanish *rosa*, Russian *roza*, Greek (arch.) *roðo*, all 'rose'. Mechanically, and aerodynamically, the production of this sound parallels the production of voice, although, obviously, the articulators are different. You will recall that voice is caused by the vibration of the vocal folds. Most importantly, such vibration is not created by actively moving the vocal folds against one another, in the way we actively move our hands against one another to clap. Rather, it is brought about by positioning the vocal folds appropriately (not too close, not too far apart; not too tight, not too loose) and letting the high-pressure air passing through induce the vibration, like the flapping of a flag in the wind.

Vocal fold vibration is undoubtedly part and parcel of the sound inventory of all languages, and consequently it is unlikely that readers of this book will face difficulties with voicing (naturally, pathologies aside). This is not the case with the alveolar trill, which at least some speakers of English emphatically claim they are unable to produce, even though this sound is used extensively by young boys to mimic the firing of machine guns! Obviously, this inability cannot be physiological (again, true pathologies aside), and must simply be attributed to a failure to take the articulatory steps needed for the production of this sound, which we will now make explicit.

In fact, whether or not you think you can pronounce the alveolar trill, it is most likely that you already have another trill in your non-linguistic repertoire, namely, the trill we use more or less unconsciously to indicate cold, and which involves bilabial vibration.

> Produce this sound and observe what exactly you do to make it: not just in the lips, but also elsewhere, particularly in the lungs.

As was the case with the production of voice (humming), the production of a bilabial trill requires the lungs to be well filled with air, in order to increase the air pressure inside, and concomitantly the force with which the air comes out. The lips must also be positioned next to each other, without undue tightening up or slackening. When pressurized air is let out, the lips vibrate automatically.

Suppose now that, instead of bringing the lips together, you place the tip of the tongue just above the upper tooth ridge, again neither too tightly nor too loosely, taking care that the sides of the tongue press against the set of lateral upper teeth tightly enough to prevent air from escaping through the sides. If you now let through a substantial amount of high-pressure air, this air will automatically set the tip of the tongue vibrating, exactly as it sets the two lips vibrating in the cold gesture. An apposite musical analogy is the reed of a wind instrument, which obviously the player does not manipulate directly, but rather through the intermediary of the current of air.

> Have a good go at articulating the alveolar trill. If you can't do it, keep on trying until you succeed. Remember that the goal will inevitably be achieved if you take all the necessary measures to produce the trill: follow the instructions in the text, adapting them to your own idiosyncrasies as you go along.

The phonetic symbol for the alveolar trill is [r]. This symbol is obviously identical to the letter *r*, and it is sometimes used loosely (for typographical convenience, particularly when there is no likelihood of misinterpretation) for other phonetic varieties of *r* also. This includes the English *r*, which we saw above is a very different sound, and must strictly speaking be transcribed as [ɹ]. Such liberal use of phonetic symbols is for better or worse a fact of transcription life, and must be accepted by the budding phonologist philosophically, if perhaps not always joyfully.

The reader familiar with Spanish will be aware that there is another *r* in this language besides the alveolar trill just described, as demonstrated by the phonetic contrast between such words as *pero* 'but' and *perro* 'dog', with the digraph *rr* representing the alveolar trill. This softer *r* is also found in other languages, whether or not in contrast with [r]. Indeed, it is nowadays more typical of Scottish English than the alveolar trill, contrary to popular stereotype.

We will ease our way into describing the soft *r* by thinking of the typical American pronunciation of *t* in such words as *waiting* (similarly in many Irish varieties). Such a *t* does not of course sound anything like the [t] we described in chapter 1: it is indeed a different sound, which substitutes for [t] in various contexts in American English (see chapter 11 for details).

> Think of a context where even Americans would use [t] under any circumstances. Then think of another context (or contexts) where you know (or suspect) they may not use it.

How exactly is the sound we are referring to produced?

> Have a go at it, whatever your national origin: the chances are you will have come across American speech (on television, in songs, in films, etc.) more than once during your lifetime.

It clearly involves a single flap or tap of the tongue tip, which is essentially thrown against the alveolar ridge. This means that we are dealing with yet another alveolar sound.

> You will have noticed that there is no shortage of these, in English, as in other languages. List a few such sounds you have already come across.

The sound in question is also oral, since the velum is raised during its production, and, being a sonorant, it is voiced.

> Make the sound again and observe carefully its characteristics.

You may find the classification of this sound as a sonorant somewhat puzzling, given the fact that its production involves oral closure, and it is neither a nasal nor a lateral. The reason it is thought of as a sonorant is that the contact between the tongue tip and the alveoli is fleeting in the extreme, and therefore the airflow remains essentially unaltered. The argument carries over to the interruptions that make up the trill, also commonly considered a sonorant.

The American *t* in *waiting* we have just described is usually referred to as a FLAP. The Spanish *r* in *pero* 'but', or the typical Scottish *r*, is similar, but perhaps not absolutely identical, and is usually dubbed a TAP. The difference between a tap and a flap is subtle, but has been argued in the specialized literature. It is not in our interest to go into this level of detail here, and we will accordingly leave the matter as it stands. The phonetic symbol for the tap (as in Spanish *pero* 'but') is [ɾ]. This symbol is also proposed for the flap of the American *waiting* in the latest version of the IPA symbol chart. American authors, however, have tended to use a capital *d* to represent the flap, hence [D].

We shall now wind up our survey of rhotics – there are still more across languages, but the present inventory is quite sufficient for our purposes. As we pointed out at the outset, while they are spelled *r* in most languages, rhotics can differ considerably from each other in their articulation. To add to the confusion, the letter *r* is also used to represent sounds that are not even sonorants. For instance, the standard French and German *r*s are uvular fricatives, rather than rhotics as such: [ʁ] (voiced) or [χ] (voiceless). The UVULA is the appendix found at the end of the soft palate, and therefore the place of articulation of these sounds lies between the place of articulation of such velars as [x] or [ɣ] and the place of articulation of the glottal [h] (figure 3.12).

> Rhotics can differ considerably from each other in their articulation

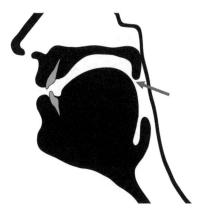

Figure 3.12   Uvular fricative

> *r*s tend to function as sonorants, even when they are not so phonetically

What is interesting, indeed puzzling, is that all the phonetically quite different *r*s function similarly in the respective phonological systems. In particular, they tend to function as sonorants, even when they are not so phonetically, undoubtedly the reason they are generally construed as rhotics.

Explain what we mean when we say that rhotics tend to have a similar phonological function.

Indeed, in languages like German, Dutch, Swedish and others, *r* is pronounced as the alveolar sonorant trill [r] in some dialects, or even individually, and as the voiced uvular fricative [ʁ], a phonetic obstruent, in other dialects or idiolects.

8 Summing Up

In this chapter we have examined the articulation of sonorant consonants: nasals, laterals and rhotics, the last two grouped together as liquids. Following our practice in chapter 1, we now tabulate all of these sounds under their respective IPA symbols (table 3.2).

Table 3.2 Sonorant consonants

	Bilabial	Labiodental	Alveolar	Postalveolar	Palatal	Velar
Nasals	m		n		ɲ	ŋ
Laterals			l		ʎ	
Rhotics		ʋ	ɾ	ɹ		
		(in "defective" English)	(flap or tap)	(in standard English)		
			r (trill)			

Study table 3.2 carefully, until you are satisfied that you understand it.

We have also described the lateral fricative alveolar [ɬ] (as in the Welsh place name *Llandaf*). While not a sonorant, this sound is of course closely related to the lateral sonorant [l]. Also obstruents, rather than sonorants, are the uvular fricatives [ʁ] and [χ], which we have just mentioned are used for *r* in several languages. On the other hand, there exists a uvular trill [ʀ], which, as a trill, must be considered a phonetic sonorant. This uvular trill is somewhat reminiscent of gargling to the ear of the English speaker. It occurs in some older dialects of French, and can be heard in recordings of the singer

Edith Piaf (cf. her classic "Je ne regrette rien"). It is also found in Lisbon Portuguese, while the usual sound for *r* in Brazilian varieties of this language is [x] or [h]. We gather all these heterogeneous sounds in table 3.3, to facilitate comparison.

Table 3.3 Additional consonant sounds discussed in the text

	Alveolar	*Palatal*	*Velar*	*Uvular*	*Glottal*
				ʁ	
Plain			x	χ	h
Laterals	ɬ				
Trills				ʀ	

Chapter Summary

In this chapter we have further extended our repertoire of consonant sounds by introducing sonorants. These sounds are so called because they are louder than the obstruents introduced in chapter 1, by virtue of the fact that they involve a greater volume of air. As in the case of obstruents, a constriction is set up in the primary channel, but in addition air is deflected through a secondary channel. Because sonorants are usually voiced, of the three parameters encountered in chapter 1 effectively only place of articulation is relevant to their description. Sonorants fall into two major categories in terms of the place of the primary constriction and the identity of the secondary source. The first is nasals, in which the air is diverted from the blocked oral cavity (hence their construal as stops) into the nasal cavity through the outlet created by the lowering of the soft palate. The other category of sonorant is known as liquids. In this case both the primary constriction and the secondary source are located in the mouth: in the articulation of lateral sounds air is deflected from an obstruction made at the centre of the tongue to pass laterally (down the sides of the tongue), whilst in the case of rhotics it is deflected from a lateral obstruction to pass centrally over the tongue. We have also offered some help with the articulation of sounds which may prove difficult for some readers. As in the case of chapter 1, the IPA symbols of these newly introduced sounds are tabulated to ease recognition. The discussion of the various phonetic parameters we have introduced anticipates the core matter of the next chapter.

Key Questions

1   How does a sonorant sound differ from an obstruent?
2   What role does the soft palate play in the articulation of speech sounds beyond those listed in chapter 1?
3   Define "nasality".
4   What do we mean by a "primary articulator"? Suggest what a secondary articulator is.
5   List the parameters relevant to the description of consonant sounds.
6   How does the relationship of nasality with oral articulation differ from that of voice with oral articulation?

7   What does a "continuant" mode of articulation refer to?
8   Define "laterality". What is lateral airflow?
9   Why do lateral sounds always involve the tongue?
10   Enumerate the variety of "rhotic" sounds. Why are they generally grouped together?

Further Practice

Sound to Spelling

We have represented the consonant sounds in the words below by phonetic symbols according to our pronunciation. Work out what the spelling is.

[n]e[v]er	[n]eu[m]o[n]ia	[n]ow[l]e[dʒ]e	au[t]u[m]
[n]e[m]o[n]i[k]	[θ]i[ŋ]	[θ]i[ŋk]	fi[ŋ]ger
[b]o[m]	[k]u[ɹ]y	[ɹ]i[t]	[t̪]y
[l]i[t]	[f]u[ɫ]	[f]u[l]y	[k̥]ear
[m]e[nʃn]	[t]a[l]ia[t]e[l]i	[n]a[t]	ca[ɲ]on

Odd One Out

Find the odd one out in the following sets and state reasons.

a.   [v x k p ʃ s]
b.   [m v β p b]
c.   [l k ɹ ɾ]
d.   [z d ð ʃ χ v]
e.   [k d b ʧ t g]
f.   [ɣ k ŋ g ɲ x]
g.   [q χ ɴ n ɢ]
h.   [l r ʎ ɭ ʟ]
i.   [θ ʃ t p s ʧ]

Articulation and Phonetic Symbols

a. Give the IPA symbol which corresponds to the descriptions below:

A labiodental approximant
A retroflex nasal stop
A voiceless uvular fricative
A velar nasal stop
An alveolar lateral stop
A voiced lateral fricative

b. Provide full phonetic descriptions for the sounds represented by the symbols below:

[ʟ]   [ɻ]   [ɾ]   [ɱ]   [ʙ]   [ɴ]   [ʎ]   [ŋ]

CHAPTER FOUR

NATURAL CLASSES OF SOUNDS

DISTINCTIVE FEATURES

Chapter Objectives

In this chapter you will learn about:
- Interpreting phonetic parameters as phonological dimensions we call "distinctive features".
- Minimizing the number of distinctive features to ensure maximum clarity and economy of lexical representation.
- The active articulator being criterial in the identification of the place of articulation.
- A linguistically more revealing formalism for writing rules.
- The grouping of sounds into natural classes.
- How different distinctive features may have a similar function.
- How the presence of certain features is contingent on the presence of others.

In the previous chapters we have described the phonetic characteristics of both obstruent and sonorant consonants. In addition, in chapter 2 we presented phonology and disentangled its concerns from those of phonetics, against the backdrop of the general structure of language. In the present chapter we introduce a number of formal devices central to the model of phonology we are concerned with. We first introduce the phonological correlate of the phonetic parameter: the "distinctive feature". We will see that most distinctive features are naturally binary, with two complementary values, but some features are intrinsically unary, and that distinctive features define natural classes of segments. Most importantly, we will see that the elements that make up phonological structure, the features in particular, are in principle structurally independent of each other, a state of affairs commonly referred to by the label "autosegmental phonology".

1 Descriptive Phonetic Parameters

In chapters 1 and 3 we reviewed in some detail the articulatory phonetics of several groups of consonants relatively familiar to the English speaker. Each consonant was described on the basis of a range of dimensions, or parameters, each representing a relevant aspect of its articulation.

> Try to remember what the parameters in question are.

Thus, for instance, [p] was described as a voiceless bilabial stop obstruent, [z] as a voiced alveolar fricative obstruent, [ŋ] as a voiced velar nasal stop sonorant, and so on.

> Jot down the parameters we used to define [ʧ] and [l] in English.

Distinct segments must by definition differ in the setting of at least one such parameter. Segments kept separate by only one parameter are minimally contrastive. For instance, the pair *sip ~ zip*, mentioned in chapter 1, is kept separate by the fricative obstruents [s] and [z], which differ only in their value for voice: [z] has voice, since it is pronounced with vocal fold vibration, but [s] does not, since it is pronounced with the vocal folds inactive.

Distinct segments must by definition differ in the setting of at least one parameter.

> Provide a couple more sound pairs contrasting minimally in one parameter. Explain how the parameter implements the contrast in each case.

In most cases, however, the contrast between two segments involves more than one parameter. For instance, in our present terms, [n] is defined as a voiced alveolar nasal stop sonorant, while [f] is defined as a voiceless labiodental oral fricative obstruent: [n] and [f] therefore differ in the setting of all the parameters mentioned, although of course they still overlap in being non-lateral consonants.

> Mention one lateral sound. Compare it with one or two additional pairs of sounds with which it exhibits substantial differences in the settings of the parameters.

The advantages of a system based on parameters are obvious. First, such a system enables us to describe each of the sounds of any language in a reasonably economic and uniform manner: [p], for instance, will be a voiceless bilabial obstruent stop in any language; indeed, [p] = voiceless bilabial obstruent stop. A second, related advantage of the parameter system is that it allows us to see at a glance what the significant differences between any two sounds are. For example, if we write [p] and [b], in standard IPA symbols, the differences between the sounds thus represented are not obvious to the eye: "p" is graphically no closer to "b" than it is to "q", for instance, and "b" is at least as similar to "d" as to "p". By contrast, if we write "voice**less** bilabial obstruent stop" (= [p]) and "voice**d** bilabial obstruent stop" (= [b]), respectively, we can immediately see that the difference between the two sounds hinges on the voice parameter. A third advantage of our parameter-based system is, of course, its phonetic motivation: we are not defining the sounds in question with arbitrary labels, but with labels that are directly grounded on their phonetic realization.

> Summarize for yourself the three advantages of the parameter system we have just mentioned.

2 Distinctive Features

One disadvantage of this phonetic grounding concerns the need to proliferate labels to keep pace with the phonetic facts. Indeed, we have come across quite a number of these labels already, but we are likely to need many more if we are going to add a label for each phonetic detail. This result runs against the grain of Occam's razor, which we mentioned in chapter 2 as favouring simplicity in scientific modelling. To counter this it could be argued that complex facts impose richness of both concepts and terminology. This is of course true if we remain close to the phonetic ground. However, the focus of this book is not on phonetics, but on phonology. Phonology is concerned with structural patterns rather than with phonetic minutiae, and therefore a simplification of the repertoire of parameters is in order here.

> Explain in your own words the rationale for the simplification we are advocating.

Phonology is concerned with structural patterns rather than with phonetic minutiae, and therefore a simplification of the repertoire of parameters is in order

One of the possible strategies we can follow to achieve this simplification highlights another disadvantage of the system we have been using: many of the labels we have supplied are complementary, in as much as the state of affairs one label refers to is the opposite of the state of affairs designated by the other label. For instance, "oral" is the precise opposite of "nasal" ("oral" = "non-nasal", and "nasal" = "non-oral"), "sonorant" is the opposite of "obstruent", and so on.

> Supply the opposite labels for "consonant", "voiceless", "oral", "fricative", "glottal", "voiced", "vowel", "stop".

Duplication of labels is potentially misleading

Besides being uneconomical, duplication of labels is potentially misleading, or at least confusing. In particular, it is easy to lose track of the fact that "obstruent" means exactly the same as "non-sonorant" (and "sonorant" the same as "non-obstruent"), and similarly for a number of other label pairs.

> Find a similar duplication with a number of other labels you are already familiar with.

The obvious solution to this problem involves the adoption of one of the two complementary labels as the only "official" label, its counterpart being entirely disposed of, or at least relegated to informal prose. The terminological gap left behind will of course be filled with the negated term of the surviving label: the dichotomy "sonorant" vs. "obstruent" now becomes "sonorant" vs. "non-sonorant", and so on. You must, however, be aware of the fact that the selection of labels has sadly not been carried out uniformly by all practitioners. For instance, the opposition "sonorant" vs. "non-sonorant" is expressed as "non-obstruent" vs. "obstruent" by some, and likewise for other oppositions, a minor inconvenience we will have no choice but to tolerate. This is one reason you still need to gain familiarity with the less common labels. Another reason is that many such labels are in current use in the phonetic literature, to which the phonologist must of course have ready access.

As a further small, but still important, step in the process of formal rationalization we are engaged in, we shall express the negation "non-" by the negative algebraic symbol "−", so that, for instance, we will write "non-sonorant" as [−sonorant]. For reasons of symmetry, we will write "sonorant" with the opposite algebraic symbol, "+": [+sonorant].

> Do this with the labels you got from the previous exercise.

We now have the kernel of the formalization we will be adopting henceforth: a restricted set of DISTINCTIVE FEATURES ("distinctive" because they keep sounds distinct; "features" because they express properties of the sounds: "parameters" would of course have been just as good a label), which are endowed with an alternative binary value, positive if the property named by the label is present in the sound being defined, and negative if it is not. Some such distinctive features simply translate the phonetic parameters you are already familiar with in a self-explanatory manner: [±sonorant], [±voice], [±nasal], [±lateral] and [±continuant] ([±continuant] was mentioned in chapter 3, and refers to continuous airflow through the central area of the mouth).

DISTINCTIVE FEATURES are endowed with an alternative binary value

Fill in the + or − values for each of the sounds in the following table:

	[f]	[v]	[m]	[t]	[d]	[n]	[l]	[ɹ]	[k]	[g]	[ŋ]
[sonorant]											
[voice]											
[lateral]											
[nasal]											
[continuant]											

Note that, by convention, distinctive feature labels are always enclosed in square brackets. Such labels are preceded by the operators + or − expressing the precise value of the feature: [±sonorant] stands for either [+sonorant] or [−sonorant], and so on.

The list of distinctive features is provided once and for all for all languages: it is assumed to be part of UNIVERSAL GRAMMAR, the set of principles for language all humans are endowed with innately. We will be presenting this list gradually, then providing a unified picture in chapter 17. Note that, while the list of features is assumed to be universal by pretty well all phonologists, its actual contents vary slightly from proposal to proposal: you must not lose sight of the fact that, like any other aspect of phonology, this list is hypothetical, given the conjectural, rather than mechanistic, nature of the enterprise.

The list of distinctive features is provided once and for all for all languages: it is assumed to be part of UNIVERSAL GRAMMAR

What exactly do we mean when we say that phonology is conjectural, rather than mechanistic? Hint: refer back to the notion of hypothesis we presented in chapter 2.

The system we are proposing – with a fixed list of distinctive features, each assigned one of two values (+ or –) – is ideal to implement classification, which is after all what we have been doing so far with the sounds of speech, the set of consonants, to be more precise. It is rather like classifying people into [+female] or [–female] (equivalently, [–male] or [+male]), bicycles into [+racing] or [–racing], or animals into [+pet] or [–pet]: the obvious advantage of such a system is that it immediately brings out both the criteria for classification and the exact position of any given element in the system. Notice that the system is maximally simple (it should only contain the features necessary to implement classification), clear (each value is immediately transparent: [–sonorant], for instance, refers to non-sonorants, that is, obstruents), and unambiguous: there is no chance of missing the complementarity between [+sonorant] and [–sonorant], as there would be if we used the labels "sonorant" and "obstruent". A further, even more important advantage will be discussed in the following sections.

3 Naturalness and Formal Economy

Phonetic symbols are very useful when we want a written record of language sounds. However, such symbols are not at all helpful when we want to find or explain sound patterns

In the preceding chapters we saw that phonetic symbols are very useful when we want a written record of language sounds. In this chapter, however, we are seeing that such symbols are not at all helpful when we want to find or explain sound patterns.

Consider for instance the assimilation of /p/ to [℘] examined in chapter 2 ([p] is of course bilabial, while [℘] is our ad hoc symbol for a voiceless labiodental stop). We saw then that the context for such assimilation is the presence of a labiodental sound, such as [f], in the following position.

Refresh your memory about this process: do the expressions *cupful* and *cup-final* ring a bell? Go back to page 32 in chapter 2 if you feel the need.

The rule we proposed for the description of the change from /p/ to [℘] reads as follows:

Explain why we are enclosing /p/ in slashes and [℘] in square brackets.

(1) $p \rightarrow \wp \; / \_\_ \; f$

> Examine this rule carefully and expain to yourself all the details
> of its formalism.

Now, you already know that /b/ changes to [ℬ] (remember, our ad hoc symbol for a labiodental voiced stop, in the absence of an official IPA proposal) in the same context, which also triggers a change of /m/ into [ɱ] (the IPA symbol for the labiodental nasal), as in the phrase *come for tea*.

> Pronounce this phrase and check that the *m* in the spelling comes
> out as labiodental. Remember to utter it naturally, at more or
> less normal speed: otherwise you will probably disengage *come*
> from the following [f].

The addition of [ℬ] and [ɱ] to [𝒫] means that we need two new rules in our rule repertoire: /b/ → [ℬ] and /m/ → [ɱ].

> Formulate these two rules in writing.

In actual fact, we will need to double our present set of three rules, since the assimilation process also occurs in front of /v/, not only before /f/, as in rule (1) above: *home video, top value, subvert,* etc. So, we will need six individual rules in total, not a very economical outcome. Moreover, both common sense and linguistic intuition are telling us that underlying the six rules is one single phonological process, by which lexically bilabial sounds are pronounced as labiodental before a labiodental sound.

> Explain what we mean by "lexical". You can go back to chap-
> ter 2 if your memory needs refreshing.

If we used phonetic symbols, we would miss an important linguistic generalization. At first blush, our reinterpretation of phonetic symbols as distinctive features does not take us any further: if anything, the string of phonological labels that replaces the string of phonetic symbols in each of the six rules seems an even more complex formula.

The problem extends to all instances of assimilation, of which we examined a few in chapter 2. We will be looking at a handful more in the remainder of this chapter, with a view to finding a solution to the problem.

4 Place Assimilation in Nasals: Natural Classes

Consider the following data:

(2) a. intolerant   b. indefinite
         interminable   indistinct
         intractable   indiscreet

All these forms start with the negative prefix *in-* – a PREFIX is an ante-posed affix; an AFFIX is a morpheme that needs to be attached to a base; a MORPHEME is a minimal unit of grammatical function.
   Compare now the forms in (2) with the ones in (3):

(3) a. impossible   b. imbalance
         imperfect
         impure

The examples in (3) contain the prefix *im-*, also negative. Is *im-* simply a different prefix from *in-*? If we are really confronted with two negative pre-fixes, what are the principles governing their distribution? Why don't we get *imtolerant* and *inpossible*, for instance? Linguistic intuition tells us that *in-* and *im-* are in fact one and the same prefix. In particular, both forms convey the same meaning, and are remarkably similar in phonetic composition, even in the diverging segments [n] and [m], only differentiated by their place of articulation: they are both [+sonorant], [−continuant], [+voice] and [+nasal].

> Specify in what way [n] and [m] are different in their place of articulation. Advance a hypothesis to explain the alternation *in-* ~ *im-*.

It does not require a great deal of observation and thinking to realize that the alternation between [m] and [n] in the prefix in question can also be attributed to assimilation: the labial [m] shows up before a labial ([p] in *impossible*), and the alveolar [n] shows up before an alveolar ([t] in *intolerant*). In order to formulate the rule responsible for this alternation, we will have to decide between /m/ and /n/ as the lexical consonant.

> Make sure you understand exactly what we mean by this. What is a lexical consonant? Why does the identity of such a con-sonant have to be decided on?

How are we going to select the lexical consonant? The general idea is that the sound that has the wider distribution (that is, turns up in most contexts) is lexical, whereas the sound or sounds with a more limited distribution is or are created by contextually restricted rule(s). Particularly important is the form that occurs in as neutral a context as we can find, where by "neutral" we mean unable or unlikely to induce assimilation. One such neutral context in the present case would be the word end: when a word is said in isolation there is no following consonant to trigger assimilation. Unfortunately, prefixes by definition cannot be word-final, and so this particular test is not available for the set of data we are discussing.

At this point we have two choices: we can look for the next best environment in the same set of forms, or we can extend the data set. We will now see that in the present case both strategies lead to the adoption of /n/ as the lexical segment.

> The sound that has the wider distribution is basic, that is, lexical, whereas the sound or sounds with the more limited distribution is or are created by contextually restricted rule(s)

> What would a reasonably neutral context be for the data we are discussing?

Let us first look for the next best environment to the word's end. Clearly, the context we are seeking involves a vowel-initial base, because there is little reason to believe that the prefix-final nasal will assimilate to a following vowel:

(4)   inability
      inevitable
      inoperable
      inimitable

We have purposely supplied forms with an assortment of initial vowels, to allay any suspicions that the identity of the vowel may after all affect the place of articulation of the nasal. You can see that the nasal in the prefix turns up as [n] in all cases. Crucially, no parallel forms starting with *im-* can be found.

> Verify this by trying to find examples with *im-* before a vowel. What can you say about *immature*, for example?

The facts instantiated in (4) therefore point to /n/ as the lexical form of the prefix.

This conclusion is confirmed when the data set is expanded in other directions, the second strategy for selecting the lexical form. Consider the pronunciation of word-final nasals:

(5)   ten pens
      ten boxes
      ten tables
      ten doors

> Pronounce these phrases trying to take notice of the pronuncia-
> tion of the *n* of *ten*. Is it uniform? If so, what is it? If not, what
> sounds correspond to this letter, and is there any special reason
> for their distribution?

The normal pronunciation of these sequences is, in fact, *te*[m] *pens*, *te*[m] *boxes*, *te*[n] *tables* and *te*[n] *doors*. These data therefore parallel the data with the prefix *im-* ~ *in-* in (3) and (2) above. Crucially, however, we can extricate *ten* from any possible assimilation context by pronouncing it in isolation. When we do so, we of course get *te*[n], confirming /n/, rather than /m/, as the lexical representation. Indeed, forms that must be assumed to have lexical /m/, like *some*, manifestly fail to undergo assimilation under the circumstances:

(6)   some tables
      some doors
      some pens
      some boxes

> Pronounce these phrases in succession to satisfy yourself that
> the final sound in *some* is also [m] before /t/ and /d/. Why
> then does /m/ undergo assimilation to /ɱ/ in front of [f]
> and [v]?

The data in (6) suggest that a putative lexical prefix *im-* would never become *in-*, as it would need to have done in *intolerable*, etc., at least other things being equal.

By contrast, we have encountered abundant evidence supporting the assimilation of /n/ into [m]. Therefore, we postulate /ɪn/ as the lexical form of the prefix we have been discussing, although of course this is a hypothesis, not a factual conclusion.

> Say in what way a hypothesis differs from a factual conclusion.

At this point in the exposition, we can propose the following (streamlined) rule of labial assimilation for nasals:

(7)   Labial assimilation in nasals:
$$[\text{coronal}] \rightarrow [\text{labial}] \;/ \left[\underline{\hspace{2cm}} \atop +\text{nasal} \right] [\text{labial}]$$

Notice that we are now replacing phonetic symbols with distinctive features. The feature [+nasal] is self-explanatory, while [labial] implies involvement of the lips in the articulation, as in labials and labiodentals. As for [coronal], all we need to say for now is that it formalizes alveolar articulation: in the next section we discuss this feature and give the rationale for the particular terminology.

> Explain the formulation of the rule in (7) and spell out the process(es) it expresses.

As formulated, rule (7) simply states that a coronal nasal immediately preceding a labial itself becomes labial. Notice that we are writing the features [labial] and [coronal] without the "+" sign: we give the reason for this practice in section 6 below.

> Why might we expect [labial] and [coronal] to be written as [+labial] and [+coronal] instead?

The superiority of distinctive features over phonetic symbols in the formulation of rules should now be apparent. Even for the limited data set we have been considering, the use of phonetic symbols would entail four distinct nasal assimilation rules, triggered by __ p, __ b, __ f and __ v, respectively: coronal nasals also become labial in front of [f] and [v].

> Formulate the four rules in question fully, for practice, making sure you understand what you are doing.

Once more, this four-rule outcome would come up against Occam's razor. Moreover, postulating four rules misses the generalization that their four contexts constitute one single natural class: the class of [labial] consonants.

Notice that we have not included [±sonorant] and several other feature specifications in rule (7). Indeed, features are omitted from rules when they are irrelevant to the process described in the rule (for instance, [–voice] is irrelevant to the operation of (7)) or when they are predictable from the features that are present (for example, we know from chapter 3 that [+sonorant] is predictable from [+nasal]). We will return to this important matter in chapter 17, simply bearing in mind for the moment that rules should be formulated in as economical a manner as possible.

Rules should be formulated in as economical a manner as possible

5 The Feature "Coronal". Active and Passive Articulators

We must now explain and justify the feature [coronal] that we included in the nasal assimilation rule in (7).

We said at the time that [coronal] encodes alveolar place of articulation. This is true, but not the whole truth: it is more accurate to say that [coronal] refers to a movement of the blade of the tongue. You will recall that the blade is the flexible portion at the front of the tongue that can be curled back or stuck out unproblematically. The blade enjoys considerable mobility, and therefore it can articulate in an area larger than just the tooth ridge.

The feature [coronal] refers to activity of the blade of tongue

> Mention a couple of non-alveolar sounds articulated with the blade. Specify where exactly in the mouth they are articulated.

Thus, for instance, the blade can go forward beyond the alveoli to produce such a dental or interdental sound as [θ] in *thigh* or *thistle*. It can also position itself further back than the alveoli, as it does for the sounds [ʃ] or [ʧ] of *sherry* and *cherry*, respectively. Now, as will become apparent later in the chapter, all these sounds, while different, behave in a similar way with respect to a number of phenomena. The assumption behind the distinctive feature model is, of course, that similarity of behaviour follows directly from membership of a common class: each feature defines a class. The feature relevant in the present case is "coronal". The sounds [t], [d], [s], [z], [θ], [ð], [ʃ], [ʒ], [ʧ] and [ʤ], among others, are defined as [coronal], since they all involve a gesture of the tongue blade.

Turning briefly to the terminology, the expression "coronal" is defined as 'pertaining to the blade of the tongue'. A more transparent label would obviously have been "bladal", except that this word does not exist in

English. An alternative strategy to preserve terminological transparency would have involved the reconstruction of the noun "crown" from the adjective "coronal", therefore talking about the "crown of the tongue", rather than the "blade of the tongue". As it happens, however, phonologists have settled for "blade" for the area of the tongue in question, and for "coronal" as its related adjective.

A more substantial point in connection with the feature [coronal] concerns the reference it makes to the active, rather than the passive, articulator: notice that there are no features [alveolar], [dental], etc.

> Remind yourself of the difference between active and passive articulators.

The grounding of distinctive features in the active articulator is not arbitrary. In particular, while both articulators are equally important phonetically (obviously, no sound would be possible without the passive articulator), only the active articulator is believed to be endowed with cognitive, or, more strongly, neural, substance. Using a computer analogy, phonetics is concerned with the hardware, while phonology is concerned with the software: the passive articulator obviously falls outside the scope of the software, since it is motionless.

Only the active articulator is believed to be endowed with cognitive substance

6 Single-Value Features

We pointed out above that the features [labial] and [coronal] appear without an algebraic operator: they are not given as [+labial], [+coronal], respectively. What is the reason for this?

There is a crucial difference between features like [labial] or [coronal], on the one hand, and [±voice] or [±nasal], on the other. Thus, as we said above, a binary formalization +, − is ideal to capture a situation of complementarity: when one value is present, the other value must of necessity be absent. From this perspective, [voice] or [nasal] indeed are binary features, since any particular sound will be voiced (= [+voice]) or voiceless (= [−voice]), but not both or neither. The same remarks apply to [±nasal] and many other features.

A binary formalisation +, − is ideal to capture a situation of complementarity

The obvious consequence of binarism is, of course, that the negation of one value implies its opposite.

> Give one or two examples of this.

For instance, if we know that a segment is not [+nasal], we will automatically know that it is [−nasal] (= oral), and therefore that we must articulate it with a raised velum. Consider now a feature such as [labial]. Knowing that a given sound is not labial still does not tell us what it is: there are more than two places of articulation, of which the feature [labial] only defines one. Another such place of articulation is, of course, [coronal], the other feature included in rule (7). A third place of articulation, [dorsal], defines sounds articulated with the body of the tongue against the velum, or soft palate. The rationale for the label "dorsal", rather than "velar", parallels the rationale for the label "coronal": "velar" refers to the passive articulator, while "dorsal" (from the Latin *dorsum* 'back', here referring to the body of the tongue) denotes the active articulator, that is, the articulator that moves. As we have already said, only the active articulator is thought to have cognitive (and neural) reality, hence its selection to underpin the distinctive features.

An important difference between one-valued features like [labial], [coronal] or [dorsal] and such obviously binary features as [±voice] is that unary place of articulation features can co-occur, since the gesture each such feature represents is not incompatible with the gesture represented by the others – by contrast, the two values of a binary feature are by definition mutually exclusive. For instance, the English sound spelled *w* in *wet* or *war* is articulated with narrowing both at the lips and at the velum, thus containing the features [labial] and [dorsal].

The unary place of articulation features [labial], [coronal] and [dorsal] can co-occur

---

> Try out *w* for yourself to prove that two articulators are simultaneously operative.

More spectacularly perhaps for most of us, many West African languages have stops that are not simply labial or simply dorsal, but rather a combination of the two, that is, labiodorsal: [k͡p] and [g͡b], where the tie bar indicates this unity. In Yoruba, a language of Nigeria, for instance, [ak͡pa] 'bridge' contrasts with both [aka] 'wheel' and [apa] 'lizard', and [ag͡ba] 'jaw' contrasts with both [aga] 'axe' and [aba] 'palm nut'

> Have a go at the "exotic" [k͡p] and [g͡b] by trying to say [k͡p]*ah*, [g͡b]*ah*, etc. (do not get excessively worried if you find it difficult).

All the facts we have considered confirm that at least [labial], [coronal] and [dorsal] are unary, that is, features with only one value, in this way differing from their binary counterparts like [±voice]. Note that the unary approach to place of articulation features is relatively recent: in the older formalism, associated with the monumental work *The Sound Pattern of English*, authored by Noam Chomsky and Morris Halle, all distinctive features were binary. In fact, some recent trends attempt to extend the unary approach beyond the set of place of articulation features (you can refer to chapters 8 and 17 for more information).

7 Constraining Rules: Autosegmental Formalism

The assimilation rule in (7) above obviously yields the desired result: it replaces the nasal coronal with a nasal labial before a labial consonant. There is a very serious shortcoming in this formalism, however. In order to understand this shortcoming, you must bear in mind that a rule like (7) is found not only in English, but also in many of the world's languages: there is clearly something very natural about this type of process, which speakers are extremely reluctant to suppress. Consider now the following formally possible rules:

(8)   [coronal] → [labial] $/\left[\begin{array}{c} \underline{\hspace{1cm}} \\ +\text{nasal} \end{array}\right]$ [coronal]

(9)   [coronal] → [labial] $/\left[\begin{array}{c} \underline{\hspace{1cm}} \\ +\text{nasal} \end{array}\right]$ [dorsal]

> Can you tell what is odd about these rules?

The difference between these rules and the rule in (7) lies in the relationship between the output and the context: in rule (7) the output feature is identical to the contextual feature, but in (8) and (9) it is not. In (8) the nasal becomes labial immediately before a coronal, and in (9) immediately before a dorsal, and the sequences [mt], [md], and [mk], [mg], respectively, are thereby created. The fact that rules of this kind do not exist, in English or (almost for certain) in any other language, clearly cannot be coincidental. Rather, the process expressed by the attested rule in (7) must be more natural than its logically possible but unattested counterparts in (8) and (9), which are so unnatural as to fail to occur.

> Can you offer a reason why rule (7) is more natural than rules (8) and (9)?

The reason is, of course, that the rule in (7) is a genuine assimilation rule, but the rules in (8) and (9) are not. In particular, the rule in (7) brings the substance of the input segment (the coronal nasal) closer to the substance of the contextual segment (the labial); indeed it makes it identical to it in place of articulation. Clearly, nothing of the kind happens in rules (8) and (9).

The bottom line is that the natural relationship between the output of assimilation rules and their context is not easily expressible in the rule formalism we have been using up to now. This formalism is essentially that of the early generative phonology literature, as compiled in *The Sound Pattern of English*, "*SPE*", to which we have already referred. Accordingly, we will now introduce a more restricted and up-to-date formalism.

We shall proceed in small steps, to ensure that we leave no room for uncertainty. First, you know that the segment that is input to the rule must contain the features [coronal] and [+nasal], since only coronal nasals are affected by this assimilation. In the type of theory propounded in *SPE*, this information would be represented in a unified feature matrix, as in (10):

(10) $\begin{bmatrix} \text{coronal} \\ \text{+nasal} \end{bmatrix}$

 e.g. [n]

We obviously need other features for a complete description or definition of [n], the incumbent segment, but we have already said that features that are not relevant to rules or are predictable from the features present in the rule are customarily left out, for the sake of simplicity.

The second ingredient in our assimilation rule is obviously the contextual feature [labial], since the change only takes place when the nasal is immediately followed by a labial. Accordingly, we need to add the context [labial] to our representation:

(11) $\begin{bmatrix} \text{coronal} \\ \text{+nasal} \end{bmatrix}$ [labial]

 e.g. [n   p]

We now have a string of two feature matrices, which define the sound sequences [np] and [nb], among others.

Flesh out a few of these sequences into features.

Upon application of the rule, [labial] replaces [coronal] in the first matrix, as follows:

(12) $\begin{bmatrix} \text{labial} \\ +\text{nasal} \end{bmatrix}$ [labial]

  e.g. [m   p]

In the formalization in (7) above, the input and output feature matrices are related by means of an arrow, indicating the transition. The equivalent formalization for (11) and (12) is as in (13) (rule (7) was of course further streamlined by factoring out the environment):

> Explain exactly what we mean by "factoring out the environment".

(13) $\begin{bmatrix} \text{coronal} \\ +\text{nasal} \end{bmatrix}$ [labial] $\rightarrow$ $\begin{bmatrix} \text{labial} \\ +\text{nasal} \end{bmatrix}$ [labial]

  e.g. [n   p] $\rightarrow$ [m   p]

What we are now seeing is that this type of formalism is also consistent with other, non-occurring processes, illustrated in rules (8) and (9) above.

> Can you think up one or two more such processes?

Suppose therefore that we reformulate rule (7) as in (14):

(14)   Labial assimilation in nasals:

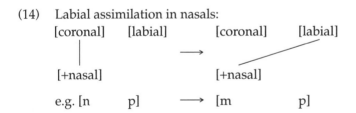

  e.g. [n   p] $\longrightarrow$ [m   p]

All we have done, in effect, is break up the unified multifeature matrix and grant functional (and, correspondingly, graphic) autonomy to each of its component features, [coronal] and [+nasal] here. The association line linking these two features indicates that they occur simultaneously in the input. In the output, the association line has been transferred from [coronal] to [labial], to encapsulate the assimilation process.

> Check carefully the mechanics of the rule in (14).

The simple innova-
tion of breaking
up multifeature
matrices into as
many single-
feature matrices
as features they
contain captures
the essence of
the AUTO-
SEGMENTAL
approach to
phonology

The simple innovation of breaking up multifeature matrices into as many single-feature matrices as features they contain captures the essence of the AUTOSEGMENTAL approach to phonology, which grants autonomy of action to each feature.

> Explain how the features have "autonomy of action" in (14).

The label "autosegmental" is a perhaps not quite felicitous blend of "autonomous" and "segmental", where "segmental" should really be paraphrased as "featural", since segments have been autonomous all along.

The advantage of writing the assimilation process in this novel way should be clear. In particular, the autosegmental rule in (14) includes the following information:

1   there is a sequence of two segments, the first containing the auto-segmental features [coronal] and [+nasal], and the second containing [labial];
2   the link between [coronal] and [+nasal] in the first segment gets severed: notice the absence of an association line between these two features in the rule's output;
3   the [+nasal] feature associates instead to the adjacent [labial] autosegment.

The assimilation
process is
autosegmentally
interpreted as a
simple change in
the association of
one feature

The crucial difference between this autosegmental formalism and its predecessor is that in the autosegmental formalism the assimilation process is interpreted as a simple change in the association of one feature: [+nasal] is connected to [+coronal] in the input, and to the adjacent autosegment [labial] in the output. The result we were seeking is thus achieved in a way which expresses the assimilation process directly. By contrast, the two pseudoassimilation rules in (8) and (9) above simply cannot be formulated autosegmentally – or, if they could be formulated in such a way, their unnaturalness would immediately be evident.

> Try formulating these rules and see why this is so.

8 Functional Groupings of Features

In its present formulation, the assimilation rule in (14) is confined to labials. We shall now show that this restriction is unwarranted.

Consider the data in (15):

(15) a. inconceivable   b. ingratitude
          incorrect   inglorious
          incapable

These words contain our familiar *in-* prefix, spelled precisely in this way. Spelling is of course no sure guide to pronunciation, and therefore you should not be unduly surprised to hear that in these forms the final nasal in the prefix is not [n].

> Pronounce some of the forms in (15) to find out what the exact pronunciation of the nasal is (make sure your pronunciation is natural).

Indeed, it would be rather strange for a nasal to assimilate to a following labial (/p/ in *impossible* and /b/ in *imbalance*), but not to a following velar. Now, in *inconceivable* and *ingratitude* the segments following the nasal are indeed velar (/k/ and /g/, respectively), and therefore we expect the nasal to come out as [ŋ].

> Did you not get this result in the previous test? If you didn't, repeat the experiment trying to feel how you articulate the nasal with the body of your tongue, rather than with the blade.

Assimilation to a velar is, however, not predicted by the rule in (14), which is specifically contextualized to labials. Therefore, in order to account for the data in (15), we need an additional assimilation rule. We formulate this new rule autosegmentally in (16), where we have collapsed the input and the output into one single schema – specifically, the crossing out of the relevant association line indicates dis(as)sociation, and the dotted line association:

(16) Dorsal assimilation in nasals:

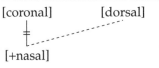

> Explain the formalism of rule (16) in your own words.

Rule (16) says that a coronal nasal immediately followed by a dorsal consonant loses its coronality and becomes dorsal (the feature [dorsal], as you know, expresses velarity).

While the rule of nasal labialization and the rule of nasal dorsalization are not identical, they are functionally similar, as they both implement assimilation of nasals. Therefore, economy as well as intuition call for the reduction of the two rules to one.

The reason that the assimilation process affects the unary features [labial] and [dorsal] in the same way is, of course, that both these features express place of articulation, the object of the assimilation in question. One simple way of formalizing this type of functional unity involves adding a common mark to all the features thus related, say, a subscript "ₚ", for "place of articulation", in the case we are discussing: [labial]ₚ, [dorsal]ₚ. This formalism allows us to refer to all places of articulation simultaneously simply by replacing the specific feature labels with a variable ranging over them: $[X]_P$, or, perhaps more perspicuously, $[\ldots]_P$. A more complex, but essentially equivalent, formalism will be presented in chapter 17.

The common process of place assimilation in nasals can now be expressed straightforwardly, as in (17):

(17)   Place assimilation in nasals:

The interpretation of this rule is as follows:

1   a [coronal, +nasal] consonant is followed by another consonant, of irrelevant place of articulation, as indicated by the emptiness of the second P-subscripted matrix;
2   the autosegmental feature [+nasal] of the first consonant loses its association to the P-subscripted coronal;
3   [+nasal] reassociates to the place autosegment of the consonant following [coronal]ₚ, whatever the specification of such a place autosegment may happen to be.

Explain how (17) accounts for the data in (3) and (15) above.

A question that arises at this point is whether, in its present more general formalization, rule (17) is not too unrestricted.

A subscript "ₚ", for "place of articulation", allows us to refer to all places of articulation simultaneously by the simple strategy of replacing the specific feature labels by a variable ranging over them, thus $[X]_P$, or, perhaps more perspicuously, $[\ldots]_P$

> Can you see what we are driving at?

In particular, it is possible to interpret the variable "…" of (17) as [coronal]$_P$, and thus to predict that coronal nasals become coronal, an apparent tautology:

(18)   Coronalization of nasals:

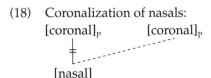

Even if it isn't outright wrong, such an extension of the rule's scope may seem otiose and wasteful. Note importantly, however, that the application of the rule in this context will at worst be vacuous: while it will have no positive effects, it will do no harm either, since we saw in (2) above that lexical coronal nasals are indeed pronounced as coronal in front of coronals. This means that we can leave things as they are at no cost: the rule in (17) is in any event needed in its present general formulation.

> Vacuous application of a rule has no positive effects, but does no harm either

> Why exactly is (17) needed?

Indeed, it would be more costly to attempt to exclude coronals from the context of rule (17), in the same way as it takes a greater effort to prevent the alarm clock from going off at the daily preset time on the occasion the sun or a noise happen to awaken us earlier.

> Show how any attempt to exclude [coronal] from the context of rule (17) would make the rule more complex.

Actually, we will see in the next section that, contrary to initial appearances, the rule in (18) has specific empirical consequences.

9 Feature Dependencies

Consider the forms in (19):

(19)   a.   tent   b.   tenth   c.   trench
             hint   plinth   finch
             punt   month   bunch

The nasal in the a. forms is alveolar, as would be expected from the fact that the following segment is alveolar: /t/. The question is, are the *n*s in the forms in the other two columns also alveolar?

> Pronounce these forms to ascertain whether their *n*s are indeed alveolar.

It should be obvious that they are not alveolar. In the b. forms (*tenth*, etc.) the passive articulator is the inside of the upper teeth, or the tooth edges, depending on whether [θ] is pronounced as a dental or as an interdental. In turn, for the forms in c. (*trench*, etc.) the blade of the tongue is retracted relative to the tooth edge, onto the palatoalveolar area where [ʃ] and [tʃ] are pronounced. All the consonants in question are, however, still [coronal], because they all have the blade of the tongue as their active articulator. Therefore, the differences between these various segments must hinge on features other than [coronal].

The feature
[±distributed]
refers to the
"distribution"
of the tongue
over the passive
articulator

One such feature is [±DISTRIBUTED], which refers to the "distribution" of the tongue over the passive articulator. "Distribution" is perhaps not the most transparent of terms to refer to the length of tongue area involved in the articulation, but once more we will have to make do with standard usage. The substantive point is that the noted versatility of the tongue blade makes it possible for a substantial portion of it to be engaged in the articulation: [+distributed]. Alternatively, the portion of the blade carrying out the constriction may be minimal, essentially the tip: [−distributed]. With regard to the precise part of the tongue involved, the contrast corresponds to a LAMINAL vs. an APICAL gesture, that is, a gesture with the full blade of the tongue vs. a gesture with just the tip. The binary contrast [+distributed] vs. [−distributed] thus captures the difference in place of articulation between dental [θ] or [t̪], on the one hand, and alveolar [t], on the other.

> List some other sounds made with the full blade of the tongue, and some other sounds made with just the tip of the tongue.

[±distributed]
comes by
definition autoseg-
mentally attached
to [coronal], of
which it consti-
tutes a subdivision

The crucial point in the present context is that the feature [±distributed] comes by definition autosegmentally attached to [coronal]: only coronal sounds can be [+distributed], and therefore the feature is only relevant to coronals, at least on our current conception of distinctive features – in older models, *SPE* for instance, the scope of [±distributed] included other places of articulation.

> Do you think that the broader scope of [±distributed] in SPE would be better able to account for the contrast between [p] and [𝒫] we discussed in chapter 2 and again earlier in this chapter?

The geometric consequence of the dependency of [±distributed] on [coronal] is that of the structures in (20) below; only a. is well formed. To make the dependency relation visually clear, we will systematically misalign dependents from their superordinates, and reduce the font size of their labels:

(20)   Yes   No   No

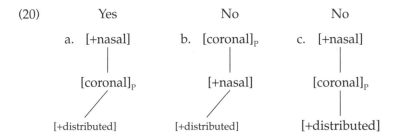

If [±distributed] must by definition be a dependent of [coronal], the fact that in b. and c. it is not makes these configurations illegitimate.

> What features are dependent and of what in each of the structures in (20)?

The graphic misalignment of the dependent feature is also aimed at suggesting that it occupies a different plane from that of its superordinate. Indeed, phonological representations are multiplanar, not just multitiered. In (20a), the nasal and coronal tiers share the same plane, but [+distributed] occupies a different plane, which branches off the [coronal] tier, in a manner reminiscent of the leaf of a drop-leaf table.

Phonological representations are multiplanar

> State what the difference is between a tier and plane in this context.

The multiplanar mode of representation has far-reaching repercussions for the theory of phonology, as we will have plenty of occasion to observe.

Let us now explore the consequences for coronals of our rule of place assimilation in nasals in (17) above. We have suggested that the application of this rule to coronals is not vacuous, contrary to first appearances. Consider, for instance, the effects of the rule on the relevant string in *te*/nθ/ (we are of course assuming at this point that [±nasal] and [coronal]$_P$ occupy the same plane, since neither is a dependent of the other):

(21)   Distributed assimilation in nasals:

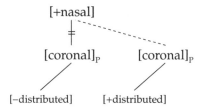

Although the rule has no visible effect at the [coronal]$_P$ level (NB both the input and the output segments are coronal), it does have consequences at the level of the dependent [±distributed], which is automatically dragged along by [coronal]$_P$. This result matches the facts in (19b) above, thus providing strong backup for our approach, which includes the general assimilation rule (17) and the built-in dependency of [±distributed] on [coronal]$_P$.

The argument carries over to the set of data in (19c) above (*trench*, etc.). Here the relevant feature is [±anterior]. This feature divides the hard palate into two regions, the forward or anterior region, with the alveolar and dental areas, and the posterior region, which includes the palatoalveolar and palatal areas (figure 4.1).

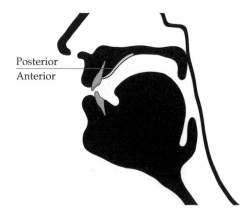

Figure 4.1   The anterior and posterior areas

Mention a couple of [+anterior] segments and a a couple of [−anterior] segments.

The feature [±anterior] is the only distinctive feature that refers to the passive articulator – indirectly, however, it still refers to the active articulator, which must retract or otherwise to meet the passive articulator.

> In the light of our discussion in section 5 above, say why relating to the passive articulator may matter.

The feature [±anterior] was first proposed in *SPE*. Like [±distributed], its scope used to extend over all places of articulation, but it is now also generally restricted to coronal sounds. Formally, therefore, [±anterior] is a further dependent of [coronal]ₚ:

[±anterior] is restricted to coronal sounds: formally, [±anterior] is a further dependent of [coronal]

(22)

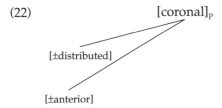

The assimilation observed in *tre*/nʧ/ will consequently be expressed as in (23):

(23)   Anterior assimilation in nasals:

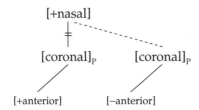

As is the case with [±distributed] in (21) above, linking to the second [coronal]ₚ has a side effect on the dependent, here the replacement of [+anterior] with [−anterior]. Therefore, the process is not vacuous.

We finish the chapter with the tabulation of all the distinctive features we have introduced, specifying their values in the segments we are familiar with (we have simply ticked unary features where present). We have arranged the segments by place of articulation from labial to velar, indenting dependent features under their superordinate (table 4.1).

Table 4.1 Distinctive features

	p	b	t	d	k	g	f	v	θ	ð	s	z	ʃ	ʒ	x	ɣ
Sonorant	−	−	−	−	−	−	−	−	−	−	−	−	−	−	−	−
Continuant	−	−	−	−	−	−	+	+	+	+	+	+	+	+	+	+
Voice	−	+	−	+	−	+	−	+	−	+	−	+	−	+	−	+
Nasal	−	−	−	−	−	−	−	−	−	−	−	−	−	−	−	−
Lateral	−	−	−	−	−	−	−	−	−	−	−	−	−	−	−	−
Labial_p	✓	✓					✓	✓								
Coronal_p			✓	✓					✓	✓	✓	✓	✓	✓		
Anterior			+	+					+	+	+	+	−	−		
Distributed			−	−					+	+	−	−	+	+		
Dorsal_p					✓	✓									✓	✓

	tʃ	dʒ	m	n	ɲ	ŋ	l	ʎ	ɬ	ʋ	ɹ	r	ɾ	ʁ	ʔ	h
Sonorant	−	−	+	+	+	+	+	+	−	+	+	+	+	−	+	+
Continuant			−	−	−	−	−	−	+	+	+	+	+	+	−	+
Voice	−	+	+	+	+	+	+	+	−	+	+	+	+	+	−	−
Nasal	−	−	+	+	+	+	−	−	−	−	−	−	−	−	−	−
Lateral	−	−	−	−	−	−	+	+	+	−	−	−	−	−	−	−
Labial_p			✓							✓						
Coronal_p	✓	✓		✓			✓		✓		✓	✓	✓			
Anterior	−	−		+			+		+		−	+	+			
Distributed	+	+		−			−		−		−	−	−			
Dorsal_p					✓	✓		✓						✓		

> Say why we have not provided a value for [±continuant] for affricates. Also, discuss whether labials and glottals could in principle be assigned the value [+lateral].

Palatals and velars are undifferentiated in this table: compare the values of [ɲ] and [ŋ]. The features which distinguish palatal from velar sounds will be introduced in chapter 6, with additional discussion in chapter 17. Notice also that we have purposely left the glottal stop [ʔ] and the glottal fricatives [h] and [ɦ] out of the place of articulation count: in phonology, "place of articulation" specifically refers to place of articulation *in the oral cavity*.

Chapter Summary

The three themes of this chapter have been: first, the introduction of the concept of the phonological distinctive feature as a part of universal grammar; second, autosegmental theory; and finally, feature dependencies. Sounds are made up of a combination of distinctive features which are construed as cognitive units referring to the active articulator rather than the passive. We showed that the phonetic parameters used so far in the description of sounds, whilst informing their phonological counterparts, involve a considerable degree of redundancy, and that many of the labels applied in these descriptions stand in a complementary relationship to one another. Thus, by opting for one of a complementary pair of labels (such as "sonorant") and the use of the algebraic operators + and −, we can introduce further formal economy into the system, since we know that the absence of one specification in the label necessarily implies the presence of the other. Rules gain more generality by referring to distinctive features, as we were able to demonstrate in the case of the bilabial sounds /p/, /b/ and /m/, all of which assimilate to the place of articulation of the following labiodental /f/ or /v/. If we had been unable to describe these sounds in terms of their common features, we would have been obliged to postulate six rules instead of one. Thus, the breaking down of segments into their component features allows us to show that speech sounds fall into natural classes by virtue of a shared feature or features, and that all segments in the same class undergo the same processes. Whilst perhaps the majority of features have binary + or − values indicating complementary sets of sounds according to which value is attached, the multivalued place of articulation features cannot be so marked. These are formalized as unary-value features, because the lack of one place feature gives no indication as to the identity of the appropriate feature. The second important theme of the chapter has been autosegmental theory, which holds that features can act independently of one another. This observation is amply demonstrated in the assimilation cases, where we showed a single feature spreading from the position to which it is attached onto the adjacent position. The use of autosegmental formalism in the writing of phonological rules allows the naturalness of those rules to be represented in an obvious way not available with the formalism used in chapter 2. Further generality and clarity of exposition are achieved by grouping certain features, such as place of articulation, into classes. Finally we showed that, notwithstanding the observation about the autonomy of features, some of the features are postulated as dependent on another.

K e y   Q u e s t i o n s

1 What is the relationship between distinctive features and the phonetic parameters discussed in earlier chapters?

2 Explain "binarity" with respect to distinctive features.

3 In what way is it more revealing to break sounds down into thei component features than to represent them in terms of their phonetic symbol?

4 The place of articulation of a sound is the point at which the active and passive articulator come into contact. Why do we refer only to the active articulator when defining place of articulation in phonology?

5 Why do some distinctive features only have a single value, as opposed to a binary value?

6 Define the term "coronal".

7 What do we mean by "autosegmental formalism"? Describe the advantage of this type of formalism over that involving feature matrices. Why is it more revealing?

8 What is the advantage of the subscript system in the grouping of features?

9 In what respect are some features dependent on others? What does a setting for the feature [±anterior] necessarily imply?

F u r t h e r   P r a c t i c e

Natural Classes

a.   In each of the groups (i–vi) below there is one odd member, the rest belonging to a natural class which can be identified by means of one or more common feature(s). Identify the odd one out and say which feature(s) is or are common to the remainder. (There may be more than one possible answer in some cases.)

i.   [v, n, m, ʋ, β]
ii.   [θ, ʃ, t, s, ç]
iii. [ɣ, x, ð, v, β]
iv.   [n, l, ʎ, d, ŋ]
v.   [d, ʒ, z̪, f, ð]
vi.   [x, ɣ, ŋ, k, p]

b.   Consider the following putative processes:

i.   /m, b, p/   →   [n, d, t]
ii.   /n, d, t/   →   [ŋ, g, k]
iii. /s, z/   →   [ʃ, ʒ]

iv. /b, d, g/   →   [β, ð, ɣ]
v.   /ɸ, θ, f, s, ʃ/ →   [β, ð, v, z, ʒ]
vi. /l, n/   →   [l̪, n̪]
vii. /b, d, ɖ, ɟ, g/ →   [m, n, ɳ, ɲ, ŋ]
viii. /g, x, k, ɣ/   →   [b, ɸ, p, β]

(i)   State the common features of the groups involved.
(ii)   Which feature changes are represented by the arrows?
(iii) Write the rules out using distinctive features and autosegmental representations.

Selayarese Reduplication

Reduplication is a process in which all or part of the phonological material of the base is repeated. In the case of Selayarese, an Austronesian language spoken in Indonesia, a reduplicated form conveys the meaning of what might roughly be translated as 'sort of':

Basic form		Reduplicated form	
[pekaŋ]	'hook'	[pekampekaŋ]	'hook-like object'
[tunruŋ]	'hit'	[tunruntunruŋ]	'hit lightly'
[keloŋ]	'sing'	[keloŋkeloŋ]	'sort of sing'
[jaŋaŋ]	'chicken'	[jaŋaɲjaŋaŋ]	'bird'
[hukkuŋ]	'punish'	[hukkuŋhukkuŋ]	'punish lightly'
[maŋŋaŋ]	'tired'	[maŋŋammaŋŋaŋ]	'sort of tired'
[gintaŋ]	'chili'	[gintaŋgintaŋ]	'chili-like object'
[roŋaŋ]	'loose'	[roŋanroŋaŋ]	'rather loose'

(i)   Is the reduplicated form identical to the base form in all these data?
(ii)   Why?
(ii)   Write a rule accounting for the facts.
(iii) Give the reduplicated forms for the following:

[dodoŋ]   'sick'
[nungaŋ] 'hit'
[bambaŋ] 'hot'
[soroŋ]   'push'

CHAPTER FIVE

VOWEL SOUNDS

CARDINAL VOWELS

C h a p t e r   O b j e c t i v e s

In this chapter you will learn about:
- Sounds known as vowels, which involve no constriction to the airflow whatsoever.
- The way the identity of vowels can be varied by altering the shape and size of the chamber in which the air particles resonate.
- A set of reference points against which to describe the vowels of the world's languages.
- Basic vowel systems.
- A set of parameters by which to measure vowels, using tongue height and backness, and lip rounding.

In chapters 1 and 3 we deliberately relied on English for the presentation of the articulation of consonants, introducing them where possible with the help of one or more English words containing the sound in question. The rationale behind this strategy is twofold. First, it is our belief that real understanding of each sound can only be achieved by relating abstract description to intuition and experience, hence our selection of English as the main exemplificatory language. Second, the basic mechanics of consonant articulation are readily accessible through guided self-exploration. We trust that our goal has been met, and that by now you feel reasonably in command of the panoply of consonants we have been discussing. Unfortunately, the presentation of vowels cannot follow the same pattern, for the simple reason that the mechanics of vowel articulation are far less accessible to observation. In order to see why this is so, we must first gain some understanding of the differences between vowel and consonant sounds.

Can you hazard a guess as to the main difference between consonants and vowels?

1 On What Vowels Are and How They Are Made

The key articulatory difference between vowels and consonants resides in the fate of the airflow coming out of the lungs as it passes through the mouth. In consonantal sounds the airstream finds a radical constriction or even total blockage at some point along the central passage in the oral cavity. By contrast, when a vowel sound is pronounced, no such obstacle is present.

Not surprisingly, a musical analogy will help us understand the nature of vowels. At the beginning of chapter 1 we commented on the fact that if you blow air through a recorder without covering up some of the holes in turn, there will be no melody: just one single, invariant note. We now want to focus on a different aspect of the music. In particular, whatever note we play, the sound quality of a recorder is readily distinguishable from the sound quality of a trumpet or a clarinet. You may think that the reason for this is simply that the recorder is a different instrument. This is tautologically true, of course. Consider, however, the fact that recorders come in different sizes: recorder fans will be able to name the sopranino, descant, treble, tenor, etc. These different types of recorder are all the "same" instrument, and yet they also produce different sound qualities, according to recorder size. This clearly suggests that the instrument's size (that is, not just its shape, material, etc.) plays a crucial role in the determination of the instrument's sound quality. The sound quality of the instrument is of course crucially different from the notes we play on it: all notes can be played on all instruments, although they still sound different.

From now on, we shall simply assume the veracity of our finding that sound quality is a function of the size of the instrument – this is indeed a fact of physical life, the technical reasons for which do not concern us here. Now, in a recorder concert recorders of different sizes will play at different time intervals, giving the effect of a symphony of recorder sound qualities. Suppose, however, that we only have one recorder to play the symphony with: how can we produce the same variety of sound quality? The answer is, obviously, that we cannot if our recorder is made of rigid wood or plastic, as recorders conventionally are. Imagine, though, that new technologies allow our single recorder to be flexible, so that we can vary its size by stretching or compressing it as we play along, as effectively happens with electronic gadgets. In this case, we will indeed be able to play the symphony with just the one recorder – at least if only one of the different-sized recorders is required to play at a time: in real-life symphonies, several different-sized recorders can of course find themselves playing *simultaneously*.

How does all this relate to vowels? Each vowel sound is like the sound made by one of the different-sized recorders of the analogy. Specifically, vowels differ from each other only in sound quality, in the same way as

When a vowel sound is pronounced, no obstacle is present

Sound quality is a function of the size of the instrument

Vowels differ from each other only in sound quality

the sounds given out by the different-sized recorders. In the case of vowels, however, we clearly have only one instrument to make them with: the mouth. The question therefore is: how can we vary the size of the mouth to produce the different vowels present in language? After all, the mouth is made of rigid materials, namely, the different bones that give it its basic shape and structure, and therefore you are likely to wonder how the variation in the size of the mouth that we need to produce different vowels can be attained.

> In what ways do you think we can vary the size of our mouth "instrument"?

If you think carefully about the anatomy of the mouth, you will realize that not all of it is rigid. For instance, the mouth can be opened and closed. More to the point here, we can and do form a tube inside the mouth, with the roof of the mouth, the position of which, of course, we cannot alter, and the tongue, which we *can* move. By drawing the tongue closer or less close to the roof of the mouth, we can vary the size of this tube. As you just learnt from our discussion on recorders, each such tube size will produce a different sound quality, hence a different vowel.

By drawing the tongue closer or less close to the roof of the mouth, we can vary the size of the tube. Each such tube size will produce a different sound quality, hence a different vowel

You can verify this prediction on yourself. Suppose you utter the sound *ah*, as when asked to do so by the doctor.

> Implement the proverbial doctor's instruction on yourself, observing carefully the position adopted by the articulators.

Clearly, *ah* is a real sound of language, similar in fact to the sound spelled *a* in such English words as *spa* or *father* in most accents (see the caveat on p. 119). How is it made? You can guess the answer from the function of the doctor's request. Obviously, the doctor wants to look down your throat, and consequently needs your mouth to be as open as possible, with the tongue at its lowest. What is interesting is that, instead of instructing you to carry out these actions, the doctor asks you to say *ah*, a sound with which you are familiar since an early age and which you can therefore reproduce automatically. It follows logically that the pronunciation of this sound must involve an open mouth and a tongue away from the roof, so as not to interfere with the doctor's field of vision down the throat.

We now have one vowel in our repertoire, just like one recorder in the range of recorders. Remember that there is no constriction of any kind in the mouth when we say *ah*. Let us contrast this sound with another one which is, in many ways, its polar opposite. In particular, push the body of your tongue as high and forward as you possibly can without making contact or creating a constriction with the roof of the mouth – if you do block the passage or create a constriction, the sound will of course not be a vowel, but a consonant.

> Why will the sound be a consonant if you create a constriction?

When you feel that you have got the tongue to the desired position, let out the air: the sound that will come out of your mouth will be similar to the vowel in the English words *bee* or *sea*. This sound thus constitutes a second vowel, which we can add to our list. Again, it is important to notice that the air flows out of the mouth unimpeded, precisely as is characteristic of vowels. The reason this second vowel sounds different from the first one is, of course, that the size of the tube in which it is produced is different. In fact, it is considerably different: the doctor would have quite a job examining your throat while you pronounce the vowel *ee*.

> Do you think a skilful doctor could still examine your throat if you say *ee*? Observe yourself in a mirror before answering.

2 The Two Basic Cardinal Vowels

The number of vowels in the world's languages can vary dramatically, from one or two to ten or twenty. We said above that our awareness of exactly how each vowel is pronounced is less than with consonants. You now know why this is so. In consonants we can find out easily where we are making the constriction or blockage. The pronunciation of vowels, however, involves creating a makeshift tube with the tongue and the roof of the mouth, and our awareness of such a tube and its properties is usually very poor, unfortunately for the student of phonetics. In addition, the tube is well inside the mouth, and therefore we cannot observe it directly, even if we enlist the aid of a mirror. We could of course take still X-rays, or even motion pictures, as we articulate the vowels, and indeed these and other such techniques have led to important advances in our understanding of how vowels are produced. Clearly, though, this technology is well beyond the reach of the average reader – and must anyway, for medical reasons, be used with great care, under proper supervision only.

> The pronunciation of vowels involves creating a makeshift tube with the tongue and the roof of the mouth

Naturally, phoneticians have been aware of the problem for a long time. In the early 1900s, the English phonetician Daniel Jones developed a chart on which to plot vowels in a way reminiscent of the cardinal points in nature. For the cardinal points we look for the point in the horizon where the sun rises, and we define such a point as the east. If we now face east (which we have just established), we automatically define west, south and north, as the points behind our back, to our right and to our left, respectively. Once we have these four cardinal points, we can define any intermediate points (south-west, north-east, etc.) simply by dividing the space accordingly.

We will now do something similar with vowels. We already have two CARDINAL VOWELS: *ah* and *ee*. As we have explained, *ee*, roughly as in *bee* or *sea*, is articulated with the body of the tongue as high and forward as is compatible with a vowel sound – in particular, there must be no blockage or constriction of the airstream. If you observe yourself in a mirror as you do this, you will notice that your lips spread automatically. The articulatory instructions for the *ah* of *father* or *spa*, or at the doctor's surgery, are the opposite: the tongue is pulled back and lowered, with the concomitant lowering of the jaw (unless the speaker happens to be chewing a pipe!).

> Try comparing your articulation of these two vowels with the aid of a mirror.

If you observe yourself in a mirror as you articulate *ah*, you will notice that the lips are in a neutral position: neither spread nor rounded. At the moment, such lip movements are quite automatic: our articulatory instructions concern exclusively the tongue. However, it will become clear later that lip position also plays an important role in the articulation of vowels.

The interest of the two vowels we have just considered is that they can be produced simply by following the given articulatory instructions, in a manner similar to what we saw in previous chapters is the case with consonants. In this respect, these two vowels are exceptional, as we will see. Their usefulness lies in the fact that they provide us with the two basic cardinal points to use as a reference to define the rest of the vowels.

The IPA symbols for our two current cardinal vowels are [ɑ], for *ah*, and [i], for *ee*. We have been saying all along that these vowels are similar to the vowels in the English words *father* or *spa*, and *bee* or *sea*, respectively. However, although they are similar, they are not identical, for two reasons. First, the cardinal vowels are by definition artificial, made by following a set of articulatory instructions, and there is no guarantee that the resulting articulatory gesture will be picked up literally by any natural language. Second, we will see below and in successive chapters that vowels have a tendency to

Cardinal vowels are by definition artificial, made by following a set of articulatory instructions

move about in the articulatory space much more than consonants. There-fore, vowels are likely to acquire their own nuances and idiosyncrasies in each language, or even in each dialect or idiolect (the word IDIOLECT refers to the specific manner of speaking of one speaker). By contrast, the cardinal vowels are idealized reference points, analogous to the metre standard kept in the Pavillon de Breteuil in Paris: the metre standard is stored under ideal conditions of temperature, humidity, etc., quite unlike the circumstances found in the outside world, and therefore no other metre stick will have exactly the same length as the standard, although it will of course be equivalent to it for all practical purposes. So, when we talk about the cardinal vowels [ɑ] and [i] henceforth, you must bear in mind that, although they are similar to the vowels in *father* and *bee*, they are bound not to be absolutely identical, and likewise for the other cardinal vowels we will introduce.

> When we talk about specific cardinal vowels, you must bear in mind that they are bound not to be absolutely identical to the vowels of any language

Try an experiment with the two vowels [ɑ] and [i]. Start articu-lating them at the cardinal points mentioned in the text above, and see how far you can stray from these points whilst still pro-ducing sounds recognizable as these two vowels.

3 The Four Corner Primary Cardinal Vowels: Two Axial Parameters

Before we proceed, we must issue an important caveat. The vowel system of English is remarkably complex in two ways. First, English has a much larger number of vowels than is usually the norm: something in the region of twenty. Second, as English speakers will be well aware, there is striking variation in the way these vowels are pronounced throughout the English-speaking world, and these pronunciations are still changing. The difficult-ies in illustrating the pronunciation of the cardinal vowels with English are therefore considerable, and, like other writers, we are bound to rely on the best-known or "standard" accents, namely, RP for British English and GA for North American English. The term RP ("Received Pronunciation") refers to a socially, rather than geographically, determined accent, traditionally associated with the English upper middle classes and their "preparatory" and "public" schools. This accent has, also traditionally, been favoured by the national media, hence the alternative expression "BBC English". The expression "General American" (GA) refers to a pronunciation of English common in North America, characterized by lacking any obvious regional traits – "Network English" is an alternative label. Hopefully, the wide-spread access to these standard accents in the respective communities will

> The vowel system of English is re-markably complex

help most readers grasp without much trouble the points we are end-eavouring to make. We will also appeal to more localized accents when required by the facts being discussed – we will indeed find Scottish English particularly useful to identify some of the primary cardinal vowels. In the final analysis, however, readers need to refer our descriptions to their own specific accents if true understanding is to emerge.

We saw above that, once we have the four cardinal points, we can define an infinite number of intermediate points in the intervening space. We will now show that something similar happens with cardinal vowels.

The cardinal points are of course plotted in an open space. The space available to vowels is, however, confined to the volume delimited by the roof of the mouth and the (moving) tongue. Geometrically, the vertical section of this space can be construed as a trapezoid, as we represent schematic-ally in figure 5.1. Note that, by convention, the vowel space systematically faces left.

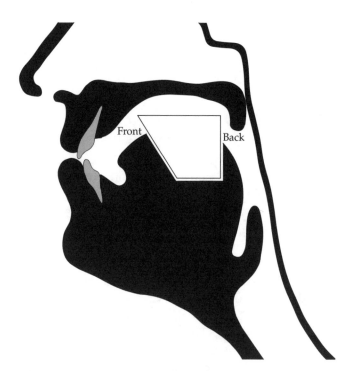

Figure 5.1 The vowel space

The space thus shaped is imposed by the anatomical structures of the mouth and the tongue. Such space limits the scope of the tongue's move-ments inside the mouth, and therefore it defines the maximum size of the tube responsible for the vowel sounds. Smaller tube sizes will be formed by the appropriate tongue movements inside the space, as we now represent in figure 5.2, again schematically (the strings of arrows are intended to suggest the airflow).

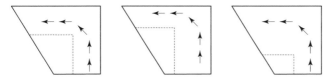

Figure 5.2   Tongue positions and tube sizes

In figure 5.2 it is visually apparent that different positionings of the tongue result in tubes of different sizes and shapes. Each such size and shape will of course produce a different vowel sound, as we know from our earlier discussion – you can usefully refer back to the analogy of the range of recorders in this connection.

> Vowel quality is a function of the size of the tube through which the airstream exits the mouth

In the same way as the set of cardinal points conventionally contains four primary points, the set of PRIMARY CARDINAL VOWELS is conventionally made up of eight vowels. We already have two primary cardinal vowels in our repertoire, which we will now plot in the vowel space (figure 5.3).

> The set of PRIMARY CARDINAL VOWELS is conventionally made up of eight vowels

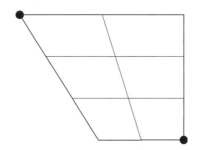

Figure 5.3   Points of the two basic cardinal vowels

The two blobs in figure 5.3 stand for the two points where our first two cardinal vowels are plotted. Clearly, given the convention that the vowel space faces left, the blob in the top left-hand corner identifies the position where [i] is articulated, and the blob in the low corner on the right of the figure the position for [ɑ] (figure 5.4).

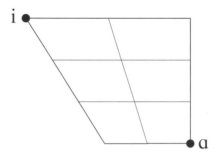

Figure 5.4   The two basic cardinal vowels

Having plotted these two vowels in the top left and the bottom right angles, respectively, two other vowels naturally suggest themselves in the two remaining corners. The IPA symbols for these vowels are [a] and [u] (we will, however, propose another symbol for [a] in section 6 below). See figure 5.5.

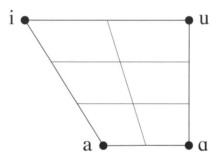

Figure 5.5   The four corner cardinal vowels

You can obtain these two vowels articulatorily from the two more basic vowels by sliding the tongue forwards, for [a], or backwards, for [u], while maintaining its height constant in each case.

The vowel [u] is instantiated (again, approximately) in the words *shoe* and *clue*. Its articulation thus involves simultaneous retraction and raising of the tongue. Additionally, the lips purse out rather heavily: the technical term for this lip gesture is "rounding".

> Experiment with this sound, pushing the back part of the tongue as far up to the velum as you can without making contact, not forgetting the lip rounding, which should come naturally. Now see how far away from this point you can go whilst still producing a sound recognizable as [u].

For [a], by contrast, the tongue needs to go down (as it does for [ɑ]) and come forward (in contrast to [ɑ]). A sound similar to cardinal vowel [a] is found in such words as *heart* in eastern New England, and also in *hat* and *tap* in some accents of Northern England, in Yorkshire for instance. For [a], as for [i] and [ɑ], there is no lip rounding.

> You can practise [a] by starting with [ɑ] and pushing the tongue forward whilst still keeping it very low in the mouth. Listen to yourself carefully a few times.

A glance at figure 5.5 above will reveal that the two basic parameters for vowels are height, on the vertical axis, and backness–frontness, on the horizontal axis. According to these parameters, [i] and [u] are both high vowels, whereas [a] and [ɑ] are low vowels. Simultaneously, [i] and [a] are front vowels, and [u] and [ɑ] back vowels. We summarize this distribution in the table in (1):

The two basic parameters defining vowels are height, on the vertical axis, and backness–frontness, on the horizontal axis

(1)

	High	Back
[i]	+	−
[a]	−	−
[ɑ]	−	+
[u]	+	+

▮4▮ Four Perceptually Intermediate Primary Cardinal Vowels: The Roundness Parameter

We said above that there are eight cardinal vowels, and we must now describe the remaining four. Importantly, no particular articulatory instructions can be issued for these four vowels, which instead fill in the perceptual space at regular intervals at the front and back. The idea is that, once we have [i] and [a] at the front, we can pronounce a vowel which sounds one-third of the way closer to [i] than to [a], and another vowel which sounds one-third closer to [a] than to [i]. These two vowels are represented in the IPA alphabet as [e] and [ɛ], respectively (figure 5.6).

Once we have [i] and [a] at the front, we can pronounce a vowel which sounds one-third of the way closer to [i] than to [a], and another vowel which sounds one-third closer to [a] than to [i]

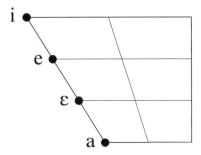

Figure 5.6　The front cardinal vowels

In order to pronounce both [e] and [ɛ], we must position our tongue some-where in between [i] and [a]. The size of the tube must therefore increase along the scale [i], [e], [ɛ], [a] – exactly how this is achieved is too complex a matter to go into here: what is relevant to us is that [e] sounds half-way between [i] and [ɛ], and [ɛ] sounds half-way between [e] and [a].

The cardinal vowels [e] and [ɛ] approximate to the Scottish English vowels in words like *late* or *raid*, and *let* or *red*, respectively. In more common English, the vowel in *late* is diphthongal, as we shall explain in chapter 7, while the vowel in *let* is higher than [ɛ]. The cardinal vowels [e] and [ɛ] also occur in more or less their pure form in French (*bébé* [bebe] 'baby'; *bête* [bɛt] 'beast') and in German (*See* [ze] 'lake'; *Bett* [bɛt] 'bed').

> Practise the four front cardinal vowels and notice how the tongue gradually moves to a lower position in the mouth. What other part of the anatomy is also moving?

The perceptual space between the back vowels [u], [a] can be filled in at equal intervals with the vowels [o], one-third close to [u], and [ɔ], one-third close to [a]

The situation we have described carries over to the back vowels [u], [a]. In particular, the perceptual space between these vowels can be filled in at equal intervals with the vowels [o], one-third close to [u], and [ɔ], one-third close to [a] (figure 5.7).

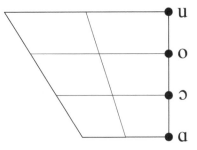

Figure 5.7　The back cardinal vowels

Lip rounding is restricted to the primary cardinal vowels of the back set, and increases with height. We already know that [ɑ] is unround, whereas [u] is round. The intermediate vowels [o] and [ɔ] are also round, [o] more heavily so than [ɔ], and less so than the high vowel [u]. Lip rounding makes up for the shallowness of the back area of the mouth, as compared with the area at the front. Thus, you know by now that vowel quality is a function of the size of the tube through which the airstream exits the mouth. The lips are pursed to varying degrees to compensate for the reduced volume at the back of the mouth, so as to achieve differences in tube size equivalent to those in the front vowels.

Our two new vowels [o] and [ɔ] again occur in Scottish English, respectively in *coat* or *road*, and *cot* or *rod*. They also occur in French (*beau* [bo] 'beautiful'; *botte* [bɔt] 'boot') and in German (*Sohn* [zon] 'son'; *sonst* [zɔnst] 'otherwise').

> Now practise the four back vowels we have presented, [a, ɔ, o, u], observing the gradual increase in degree of lip rounding.

We now summarize the complete set of primary cardinal vowels, plotted on the vowel space. To highlight their a priori nature and make reference easier, each cardinal vowel is standardly provided with a number, which we include in figure 5.8.

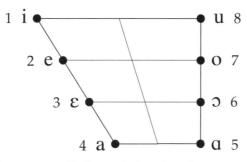

Figure 5.8   Set of primary cardinal vowels (numbered)

As we have already explained, the two main vowel parameters are height and frontness–backness. The vowels [i], [e], [ɛ] and [a] are front, while [u], [o], [ɔ] and [ɑ] are back. With regard to height, [i] and [u] are high, while [a] and [ɑ] are low. The intermediate vowels [e], [o], [ɛ] and [ɔ] are considered mid: [e] and [o] mid-high, and [ɛ] and [ɔ] mid-low. An additional ROUNDNESS parameter has been implicit in the discussion. With regard to this third parameter, [u], [o] and [ɔ] are round, and all the other vowels unround.

A ROUNDNESS parameter has been implicit in the discussion

> Pronounce i/u, e/o and ɛ/ɔ and observe carefully the position of the tongue and the activity of the lips.

5 Cardinal Vowels and Real-World Vowels: Diacritic Symbols

The cardinal vowels are idealized vowels

We have been pointing out that the cardinal vowels are idealized vowel sounds evenly distributed around the vowel space. The cardinal vowels do not therefore necessarily correspond to the real vowels of any natural language. We have, of course, offered some approximate illustrations to help readers understand the sound quality of each such vowel, but none of these strictly corresponds to the pristine cardinal vowels – recordings of these vowels by Daniel Jones, and others after him, are available commercially.

This said, some vowels in some languages approximate more to the cardinal vowels than some vowels in other languages. Unfortunately for most of us, the common English vowels are far from being good representatives of the cardinal vowels, even in cases where there is a reasonable correspondence: we shall see this in detail when we carry out a survey of English vowels in chapter 7. For instance, we have provided words like *sea* and *shoe* to illustrate the high cardinal vowels [i] and [u], respectively. Two similar-sounding words exist in French, although their meanings are quite different: *si* 'yes' and *chou* 'cabbage'. In IPA symbols, both English *sea* and French *si* will be transcribed [si], and both English *shoe* and French *chou* will be transcribed [ʃu]. In spite of this, there is a perceptible shade of difference between the pronunciation of the two English words and the pronunciation of their French correlates, which a speaker of one language will readily attribute to the presence of a "foreign" accent in the speaker of the other language. One of the reasons the two high vowels sound slightly different in the two languages is precisely that the French vowels are closer to the corresponding cardinal vowels than are the English vowels, which deviate from the cardinal specimens in several ways we will examine in chapter 7. Of course, similar considerations apply to the differences between English accents the world over. These differences are in fact far from trivial, in particular with respect to vowels, again as we will see in some detail in chapter 7.

The cardinal vowels are therefore equivalent to the straight lines we draw in real life, which can never be absolutely straight – the gap between conceptual objects and real-world objects is well known to philosophers, and is quite beyond dispute. Naturally, this caveat also applies to the other sounds represented in the IPA alphabet, except that for consonants no claim has ever been made of absolute uniformity across languages: [s], for instance, is defined as a voiceless alveolar fricative, and so any voiceless alveolar fricative can and must be transcribed as [s], whatever additional nuances it may possess. In the case of the cardinal vowels, however, each vowel is defined to a level of precision that leaves no room for latitude, and therefore most, if not all, real-world vowels will technically be at variance with the cardinal vowels.

The IPA alphabet does provide a set of diacritic symbols to express at least some of these deviations. Such diacritics are added to the basic vowel symbol to indicate the nature of the divergence. For instance, greater tongue lowering is indicated by underscripting "ˎ" to the vowel symbol, and a small degree of increased tongue height by underscripting "ˏ". Similarly, a slightly greater backing is represented by underscripting "ˍ", and a slightly greater fronting by underscripting "₊". We illustrate these symbols in (2):

> The IPA alphabet provides a set of diacritic symbols to express subtle deviations

(2)   ẹ, e̞, e̠, o̟

> Interpret the exact realization of each of the vowels in (2), in accordance with the instructions given in the text.

While use of diacritics enhances the precision of the IPA alphabet, it also quite clearly encumbers the transcription. Consequently, phoneticians tend to be sparing in the use of such symbols, reserving them for cases where confusion may arise between two otherwise similar sounds: in all other cases the IPA symbol is used with no accessories. For instance, the English vowels in *sea* and *shoe* will normally appear transcribed as [i], [u], exactly as the vowels in the French words *si* and *chou*, despite the fact that there is a perceptible difference between them – as we said, the French vowels are reasonably close to the cardinal specimens 1 and 8; the common English vowels are, among other things, slightly lower.

> Compare the vowel sounds in the French and English words [si] and [ʃu], if possible with the assistance of a native French speaker.

6 Some Vowel Typology: The Basic Vowel Triangle

We have seen that the set of primary cardinal vowels is made up of eight vowels. Four of these are basic, two of which are fundamental to the procedure, as they can be defined on an articulatory basis quite precisely.

Which are which?

Not surprisingly, not all eight primary cardinal vowels show up in all the world's languages, whether in their pure form or even approximately. A vowel system with one or two members is obviously not very functional. Some North Caucasian languages are claimed to have only two vowels, although these possess numerous allophones (we have talked about allophones and phonemes in chapter 2). The vowel system commonly considered basic to language in fact contains three vowels, the two high vowels [i], [u] and a central low vowel articulated between [a] and [ɑ], that is, between cardinal vowels nos. 4 and 5, in fact the common Scottish pronunciation of the vowel in *hat*. Quite unexpectedly and most inconveniently, there is no special IPA symbol for this vowel, which is usually transcribed with the same symbol as cardinal vowel no. 4, that is, [a]. This practice can only induce confusion in the reader, who will need extensive textual support to be sure whether the vowel referred to at any particular point is the front vowel or the central vowel. This vagueness runs against the very heart of the philosophy of the IPA. In order to keep to the standard of formal precision we are purposely adopting for this book, we shall reluctantly take the bold step of departing from IPA doctrine and substitute [æ] (a symbol known as "the ash") for [a] to designate cardinal vowel no. 4, the vowel of Yorkshire *hat* or eastern New England *heart*. This obviously frees the symbol [a] for the central low vowel, the vowel of Scottish *hat*. We wish to emphasize that we are not making this move light-heartedly, but on balance it seems to us that grasping this particular nettle will in the long run be more beneficial than trying to bury our heads in the sand. We return to this matter in chapter 7 in connection with the pronunciation of the English vowels.

> We shall reluctantly take the bold step of departing from IPA doctrine and substitute [æ] for [a] to designate cardinal vowel no. 4

The three basic vowels [i], [u], [a] pattern in the manner displayed in (3):

(3)   i   u

      a

> The most common vowel system world-wide is the five-member vowel triangle i, e, a, o, u

Notice that these three vowels are as far apart in the space as any vowels can be. With regard to the vowel parameters, [i] and [u] are high, and [a] low; [i] is front, [u] back and [a] central; and [i] has spread lips, [u] rounded lips and [a] neutral lips.

Systems with more than three vowels simply tend to add other vowels to this basic three-vowel system. Indeed, the most common vowel system world-wide is the five-member vowel triangle schematized in (4):

(4)   i   u
    e   o
      a

This system obviously results from the enrichment of the basic vowel triangle with the intermediate vowels [e] and [o]. Note that in these systems [e] and [o] are genuinely half-way between [i]–[a] and [u]–[a], respectively, and therefore the symbols [e] and [o] are strictly speaking misleading.

> Why exactly are the symbols [e] and [o] misleading here?

The reason for this lax use of phonetic symbols has to do with typographical economy, always an important consideration in transcription practice, sometimes perhaps excessively so. The practical motivation that inspired the IPA alphabet historically also often lends transcription practice a phonemic orientation that is not always consistent with the goal of phonetic faithfulness. Phonetically oriented transcription is known as NARROW TRANSCRIPTION, and phonemically oriented transcription as BROAD TRANSCRIPTION.

> Phonetically oriented transcription is known as NARROW TRANSCRIPTION, and phonemically oriented transcription as BROAD TRANSCRIPTION

> Think of at least one case of English transcription where phonemic orientation can be claimed to distort phonetic reality.

Note that the adoption of [e] and [o], rather than [ɛ] and [ɔ], as representatives of the intermediate sounds is also down to typographical considerations: the characters "e" and "o", but not their counterparts, are part of the Roman alphabet, and thus included in all standard typing and printing sets.

7 Quantum Vowels

An interesting question arises at this point concerning the basic three- and five-member vowel sets given in the previous section. In particular, it is perhaps not obvious why precisely the vowels [a], [i] and [u] are included in those sets, rather than, for instance, [ɑ], [o] and [ɔ].

> Can you suggest any reason?

One plausible reason for the prevalence of the three basic vowels [a], [i], [u] could be that they are easier to articulate. If we interpret ease of articulation as minimal movement, however, [a], [i], [u] don't seem easier to articulate, since they require extreme positions of the tongue and lips, with concomitant greater articulatory effort. On the other hand, minimizing articulatory effort cannot be the only consideration for the selection of sounds in language, since, if it was, only one sound (the sound easiest to pronounce) would be in existence universally.

The vowels [a], [i], [u] are called QUANTUM VOWELS because each of them can be articulated over a reasonably broad space with minimal effect on perception

What is special about the vowels [a], [i] and [u] is that each can be articulated over a reasonably broad space with minimal effect on perception. For instance, while we said that cardinal vowel no. 1 [i] corresponds to an extreme forward and upward movement of the tongue, the essential sound quality of the vowel will still be obtained with a more relaxed movement: the difference in articulation may of course be perceptible, as we saw above in connection with English *sea* and French *si*, but the vowels in question will still be identified as, broadly, [i]. For this reason, [a], [i] and [u] are given the label QUANTUM VOWELS, suggesting a perceptual quantum leap between them. By contrast, variation within each such vowel will at best be perceived as a matter of nuance, or "accent". This state of affairs arises from the fact that the relationship between the size of the tubes and the sound they produce is not a direct one – this matter falls within the domain of acoustic physics, and therefore its details do not concern us here.

8 Secondary Cardinal Vowels: Front Round Vowels

We have seen that the eight primary cardinal vowels [i], [e], [ɛ], [æ], [ɑ], [ɔ], [o], [u] are basically definable by means of the parameters of height and frontness–backness. In particular, the first four such vowels ([i] down to [æ]) are front, while the second four ([ɑ] up to [u]) are back. Concomitantly, [i] and [u] are high, [æ] and [ɑ] low, and [e] and [o] mid. All these descriptive expressions refer of course to the positioning of the tongue in the mouth cavity, which creates differences of size and shape in the tube it forms with the roof of the mouth.

We have also seen that the space is somewhat more limited at the back of the mouth, the lips accordingly undergoing rounding in all back vowels but [ɑ], to compensate. Rounding of the lips for the primary cardinal vowels nos. 6, 7 and 8 comes therefore quite naturally.

Suppose now that we reverse the normal setting and round the lips for all the primary cardinal vowels but precisely these three. What will happen? Clearly the sizes and shapes of the resulting eight new tubes (one tube for each cardinal vowel) will be different from the sizes and shapes of the tubes that correspond to the original eight primary cardinal vowels. If the tubes are different (considerably different, in fact, since the contribution of the lips is not negligible), the sound they will produce will obviously be different. So, in effect, we will have doubled our vowel inventory, from eight to sixteen members.

The vowels produced by deliberately reversing the normal action of the lips are known as SECONDARY CARDINAL VOWELS. We will now review these vowels, bearing in mind that they are not well represented in the most common accents of English, and therefore we will be forced to refer to other languages for description and exemplification more often than we would have wished.

Fortunately, most of the front secondary cardinal vowels exist in languages with which readers are likely to be reasonably familiar, French or German, for instance. The round vowel in the front high position corresponding to [i] is transcribed as [y] ([ü] in an alternative transcription not uncommon in America), and is present in the French word *rue* [ʁy] 'street' and in the German word *früh* [fʁy] 'early'.

> If you are unfamiliar with this sound or find it difficult to produce it correctly, as many native speakers of English do, you may wish to experiment by pronouncing [i] and then gradually rounding the lips (crucially, without altering anything else in the articulation) until you are satisfied that the sound you hear is clearly distinct from [i].

Interestingly, it is not uncommon among English learners of French and German to replace [y] with the vowel sound in the English word *cue*. While this is obviously wrong, the rationale for the process is both clear and logical, since the word *cue* contains precisely the vowel sounds [i] and [u] in succession: [kiu]. These learners are therefore "aware" that the target vowel [y] overlaps with [i] in frontness and with [u] in rounding, but find it difficult to combine frontness and roundness *in the same* vowel. Consequently, they resort to the strategy of articulating frontness and roundness *in succession*, precisely as in the English sound represented in *cue*: [y] is in fact one of the historical sources of the modern English sound [i͡u]. In chapter 8 we briefly discuss some formal machinery that makes direct sense of this behaviour.

We now incorporate [y] (a front high round vowel) into our familiar vowel chart, retaining its primary cardinal vowel counterpart to facilitate comparison. The two vowels are articulated in exactly the same point (figure 5.9).

The vowels produced by deliberately inverting the normal action of the lips are known as SECONDARY CARDINAL VOWELS

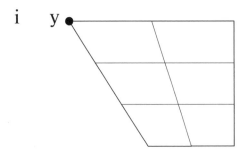

Figure 5.9   The secondary cardinal vowel [y]

The next secondary cardinal vowel down the chart is [ø] ([ö] sometimes in America), the round counterpart of [e]. Again, this vowel does not occur in English, but it does in French and in German: *feu* [fø] 'fire' and *schön* [ʃøn] 'beautiful', respectively. Monolingual English speakers are likely to have difficulties with this sound, and simply replace it with an unround central vowel which we shall discuss in chapter 7. In particular, there is no sequence [eo] or [oe] in English to fall back on, the way that there is [iu] for [y].

> Practise [ø] by gradually introducing lip rounding in [e] (unfortunately a vowel not present in most accents of English either, as you know), of course making sure that the position of the tongue remains constant.

The updated vowel chart looks as shown in figure 5.10.

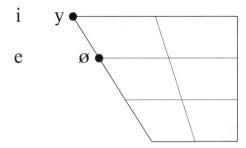

Figure 5.10   The secondary cardinal vowel [ø]

The next round front vowel is [œ] (also [ɔ] in America), corresponding to the primary vowel [ɛ]. As with the other front round vowels, this vowel does not exist in English, although again it does in French and German: *coeur* [kœʁ] 'heart' and *zwölf* [t͡svœlf] 'twelve', respectively.

> Practise [œ] in the same way as you did for the previous two rounded sounds, except that now you should start from [ɛ].

We now incorporate [œ] in the vowel chart (figure 5.11).

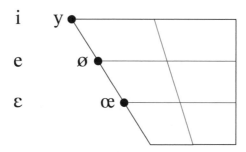

Figure 5.11 The secondary cardinal vowel [œ] added

The last front round vowel is the low vowel [Œ], corresponding to the primary cardinal vowel [æ]. This sound is truly rare among the world's languages. It is, however, reported to exist in a Bavarian dialect of Austria. The extreme rarity of this sound is evidence of its unnaturalness, easily traced back to the physiological difficulties in lip rounding inherent to low vowels, and to the weak perceptual salience of the sound that follows from the tenuousness of the rounding. All this makes the practice of [Œ] unnecessary, although we will still add it to our chart for completeness, as an additional reference point (figure 5.12).

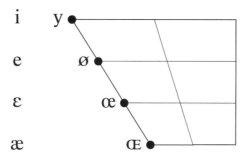

Figure 5.12 The front cardinal vowels (primary and secondary)

9 Back Secondary Cardinal Vowels

You are well aware by now of the tendency of back vowels to be spontaneously round, and of the fact that this tendency does not extend to the low back primary cardinal vowel [ɑ].

> Do you remember why this is so?

If [ɑ] is unround, its corresponding secondary cardinal vowel will have to be round, if only slightly so on account of the difficulty in rounding low vowels referred to at the end of the previous section. The IPA symbol for the back low round vowel is [ɒ], and for once this vowel exists in most accents of England, Wales and the southern hemisphere, in such words as *hot* or *loss*. A remarkably precise version of [ɒ] is found in Yorkshire. In North America and Southern Ireland, these and similar words tend to exhibit the vowel [ɑ], despite the identity of the spelling. However, in some of these accents the sound [ɒ] can still be found to some degree of approximation in words like *cloth, caught, claw, watch, horrid*, etc.

> Compare the sounds [ɑ] and [ɒ], as represented in RP *heart* and *hot*.

The vowel [ɒ] completes the inventory of round secondary cardinal vowels, which we now display in the familiar vowel chart (figure 5.13).

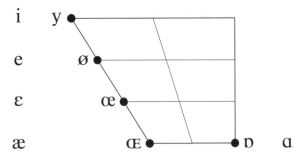

Figure 5.13   The set of round secondary cardinal vowels

The remainder of the back secondary cardinal vowels are unround, a reversal of their primary condition. The unround counterpart of the primary cardinal vowel no. 6, [ɔ], is [ʌ]. This vowel (or something quite similar to this vowel) existed in pre-Second World War RP English in such words as *up* or *cuff*, but its position has now shifted forward. In spite of this change, this vowel sound is still usually transcribed with the IPA symbol [ʌ], confusingly for RP English and similar accents: in some North American and southern Irish accents the vowel of *up* or *cuff* does approximate to the cardinal vowel [ʌ] (the accents of northern England typically have a much higher vowel in these words).

In order to practise [ʌ] and other back unround vowels you will naturally have to reverse the process of the rounding of front vowels. For [ʌ], pronounce the vowel [ɔ] (as in French *mode* 'style' or German *Sonne* 'sun') and attempt to spread the lips gradually, taking care to keep the position of the tongue constant (this exercise presupposes some familiarity with [ɔ] itself, which may not be forthcoming in at least some English-speaking readers).

We now incorporate [ʌ] into our vowel chart (figure 5.14).

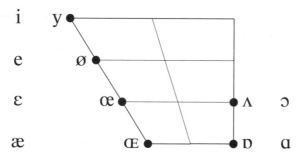

Figure 5.14   The back secondary cardinal vowel [ʌ] added

The next secondary cardinal back vowel on our way up the chart is [ɤ], the unround version of [o]. This vowel also does not exist in common varieties of English. It can, however, be heard in words like *up* and *cuff* in the speech of (normally south-dwelling) speakers of northern English origin in their attempt to approximate RP – as mentioned above, the vowel of these words in genuine northern English accents is higher, and also round: we will describe this vowel in detail in chapter 7. We now add [ɤ] to the vowel chart (figure 5.15) – if you wish to practise this vowel you simply have to unround your pronunciation of [o], as expected.

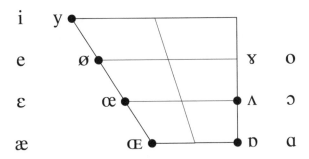

Figure 5.15 The back secondary cardinal vowel [ɤ]

The last secondary cardinal vowel is [ɯ]. This is a high back unround vowel, the unround counterpart of [u]. This vowel occurs in Vietnamese, where [kɯ] 'continue' contrasts with [ku] 'owl' and with [ki] 'note'. A bit closer to home, it also turns up in Turkish: [dɯʃ] 'exterior'.

> As the vowel [ɯ] is perhaps more common across languages than its back unround counterparts [ɤ] and [ʌ], some practice in its production may well repay the effort. You can follow the usual method of unrounding, but not fronting, the corresponding ordinary back vowel, here [u].

We give the complete set of cardinal vowels in figure 5.16.

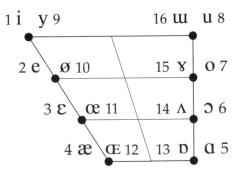

Figure 5.16 Complete set of cardinal vowels

As you can see, there are sixteen cardinal vowels in all, of which eight (nos. 1 to 8) are primary, and the rest secondary (from 9 to 16). As one would expect, secondary cardinal vowels, being less natural than their primary counterparts, are less widespread, but they are all still found in some languages – some of them in quite a few languages. We have mentioned an alternative, but less common, transcription system for the front rounded vowels: placing a dieresis on the symbol of the corresponding round back primary vowels ([ü], [ö], [ɔ̈]). This system, particularly associated with North America, is potentially confusing, since the dieresis indicates centralization (*not* fronting) in the more widely used IPA system.

There are in all sixteen cardinal vowels, of which eight (nos. 1 to 8) are primary, and the rest secondary (from 9 to 16)

10 Central Vowels

We have already observed that vowels can be advanced or retracted – as noted earlier, the corresponding IPA underscripted diacritics are "₊" and "_", respectively. Suppose now that we simultaneously retract a front vowel and advance a back vowel of the same height until the two vowels meet in the middle. When we get to this position, it will obviously be difficult to say whether we are dealing with a retracted front vowel or with an advanced back vowel, since the intermediate sound is both and neither. As a consequence, it will be useful to set up a third set of vowels which are neither front nor back. This set of CENTRAL VOWELS is not part of the official inventory of cardinal vowels, for historical reasons, but is in common use: for instance, central vowels are included in the IPA chart.

A third set of vowels are neither front nor back, but "central". Central vowels are not part of the official inventory of cardinal vowels, but they are still important

We have already noted that the low vowel of three- or five-member vowel systems, [a], is central: [i], [a], [u], and [i], [e], [a], [o], [u], respectively. A slightly higher variety of this vowel, represented in IPA transcription by means of an inverted "a", [ɐ], occurs in European Portuguese: [ˈɐnɐ] *Ana* 'Ann'. It is also the most common pronunciation of the vowel in words like *up* or *cuff* in current RP English and similar accents, despite its usual mistranscription as [ʌ], which we have seen is a legacy of history.

If you have a southern English-type accent or a North American one, you could attempt to locate the vowel in the word *cuff* in your own speech by reference to the cardinal vowel [ʌ] described above.

Moving up the central vowel space we come across the most neutral of all vowels: the vowel that, so to speak, comes out of the mouth without any tongue or lip movement. In English, many stressless vowels are realized thus. The IPA symbol for this central mid vowel is an inverted "e": [ə]. This vowel is endowed with its own label, in recognition of its importance: schwa (pronounced [ʃwa]), the old Hebrew term for a diacritic indicating a missing vowel (Hebrew writing usually only includes consonants). Schwa is a very common sound in the world's languages, although it is important to realize that not all the sounds thus labelled (or indeed transcribed) are in fact phonetic schwas. For instance, schwa is supposed to occur abundantly in French (in correspondence with non-silent orthographic *e*s), but it has been argued that such alleged schwas are phonetically [œ], rather than [ə]. Similar situations obtain in other languages, mutatis mutandis.

We shall now examine briefly the two central high vowels [ɨ] and [ʉ], unround and round, respectively. The vowel [ɨ] occurs in northern Welsh: *un* 'one'. A similar vowel can be heard in words like *bit* or *wish* in some accents of English, notably Scottish and Northern Irish, as well as in New Zealand. Scottish and Northern Irish English (but not New Zealand English) often have [ʉ] in words like *choose* or *foot*. This sound occurs more generally in other languages, such as Norwegian or Swedish: Swedish [hʉs] 'house', [fʉl] 'ugly', [nʉ] 'now'.

Practice [ɨ] and [ʉ]. First retract the tongue from [i] until the vowel quality is noticeably changed: [ɨ]. Now round the lips: [ʉ].

We now enter in the chart the position of the central vowels we have discussed (figure 5.17).

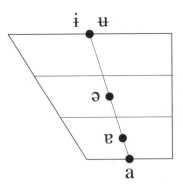

Figure 5.17   Central vowels

We wind up the chapter with a chart of all the vowels we have presented, and with a tabulation of these vowels in terms of the basic parameters "front"/"back", "high"/"low", and "round" (figure 5.18 and table 5.1).

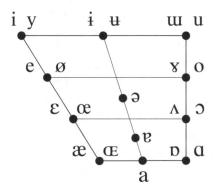

Figure 5.18   Complete vowel chart

Table 5.1   Parametric vowel table

	Front		Central		Back	
	Unround	Round	Unround	Round	Unround	Round
High	i	y	ɨ	ʉ	ɯ	u
Mid High	e	ø	ə		ɤ	o
Mid Low	ɛ	œ			ʌ	ɔ
			ɐ			
Low	æ	Œ	a		ɑ	ɒ

C h a p t e r   S u m m a r y

This chapter has been concerned with the description of vowel sounds through the medium of a set of reference points known as cardinal vowels. The speech sounds known as vowels are fundamentally different from the consonants we have been discussing in the preceding chapters in that they are articulated with no constriction to the airflow. This ensures that an even greater volume of air will escape than does with sonorant consonants, making vowels the loudest and most salient of sounds. The fact that no constriction exists raises the question of how we vary vowel quality. Variation is achieved by the tongue changing the size and shape of the cavity in which the air particles resonate. In this chapter we have concentrated on the cardinal vowels, analogous to cardinal points in geography. The cardinal vowels divide the vowel space in the mouth into equal parts by marking off eight equidistant points round the schematic trapezoid, between the highest and most forward position, the vowel [i], and the lowest and furthest back position, the vowel [ɑ]. The basic reference points for cardinal vowels are tongue height and backness. Lip rounding occurs with non-low back vowels, and increases with the height of the vowels. The cardinal vowels are numbered for ease of reference. The relationship of the cardinals to real-world vowels is, in the majority of cases, only approximate, greater precision being achievable with the use of diacritics. Not all of the eight cardinal vowels, or even approximations of them, occur in all of the world's languages, but the minimal three-vowel system, consisting of the quantum vowels [i], [a] and [u], which represent the maximal contrast, does tend to occur in some form or other in all languages. The more common vowel system consists of five vowels, with [e] and [o] added. Given the impossibility of symmetrically plotting a five-point figure onto an eight-point one, only the two high vowels in such vowel systems approximate to actual cardinal points. In the languages of the world it is natural for non-low back vowels to be accompanied by lip rounding, and for the other vowels to be articulated with spread lips. Nevertheless, the inventory of vowels can be increased by reversing this rounding relationship, thereby changing vowel quality. Such a move adds eight more vowels to the list: the secondary cardinal vowels. We have also discussed some central vowels, which do not form part of the cardinal sets, but nevertheless warrant their own IPA symbols. Finally, we have alerted readers to the not infrequent lax use of phonetic symbols in transcriptions and in phonological texts.

K e y　Q u e s t i o n s

1　What distinguishes a vowel from a consonant?

2　How do we modulate vowel quality?

3　What are "cardinal vowels"? How are they identified? List the primary set.

4　What do the initials RP and GA stand for?

5　How do cardinal vowels differ from real-world vowels? What is their use for descriptive purposes?

6　Define the terms "broad" and "narrow" phonetic transcription.

7　What are the minimal and the most common vowel systems in the languages of the world?

8　Define the term "quantum vowels". What are the particular attributes of these vowels?

9　Which of the settings for primary cardinal vowels is reversed in the secondary set?

10　List the parameters used for the characterization of vowels.

F u r t h e r   P r a c t i c e

Vowel Sets

What properties do the following sets of vowels share?

a. [y œ ø Œ]   d. [a æ ɑ ɒ]
b. [i ɨ ʉ y u ɯ]   e. [ɒ ɔ o ʊ u]
c. [ɯ ɤ ʌ ɑ]   f. [æ i ɜ e]

Vowel Systems

Study the following vowel systems. Explain how each of the sets can be described as either symmetrical or asymmetrical. What would be required to make the asymmetrical sets symmetrical?

Italian			*Albanian*			*Sundanese*			*Papago*		
i	u		i	y	u	i	ɨ	u	i	ɨ	u
e	o										o
ɛ	ɔ		ɛ	ə	ɔ	ɛ	ə	o		a	
	a				ɑ		a				

Itonama			*Persian*			*Hungarian*					
i	ɨ	u	i	u		i	y	ʊ	iː	yː	uː
e	o		e	o		ɛ	œ	ɔ	eː	øː	oː
	a		æ	ɑ				ɒ		aː	

Azerbaijani				*Chuckchi*			*Chuvash*			
i	y	ɯ	ʊ	i		u	i	y	ɯ	u
	ø		o	ɛ	ə	ɔ	ɛ			
ɛ					a					
æ			ɑ					ɑ		

Vowel Descriptions and Phonetic Symbols

a. Provide phonetic symbols for the following descriptions:

A high-mid unrounded front vowel
A high-mid unrounded back vowel
A high rounded central vowel
A low rounded front vowel

A low-mid rounded back vowel
A mid unrounded central vowel
A low unrounded back vowel
A high rounded back vowel

b.   Provide descriptions to match the following phonetic symbols:

[ɐ]   [ʌ]   [ø]   [ɨ]   [ɤ]   [ɛ]   [ɯ]   [y]

CHAPTER SIX

PHONOLOGICAL PROCESSES INVOLVING VOWEL FEATURES

Chapter Objectives

In this chapter you will learn about:
- The distinctive features used in the description of vowels.
- More feature dependencies.
- Features that are not specified in the lexicon, as illustrated, in particular, by some facts of Turkish.
- A mechanism for filling in those features in the phonetic form, through the spreading of lexical features.
- A similar historical interpretation of German umlaut and irregular singular–plural alternations in English.
- A synchronic interpretation of these phenomena by means of a "floating" feature.

In chapter 4 we saw that the primitive units of phonological sound are the distinctive features, and we presented and discussed a substantial number of them. In this chapter we will augment the universal list with a handful of additional features specifically relevant to vowels.

> Study table 5.1 at the end of chapter 5 and suggest which distinctive features might be relevant to the description of vowels.

We will put these features to work in Turkish "vowel harmony" and in German and English vowel "umlaut". The Turkish phenomenon will show the need for feature "underspecification", that is, for assuming that certain distinctive features are altogether absent in some lexical forms. Turkish vowel harmony will also demonstrate the prohibition against crossing association lines, one of the pillars of autosegmental phonology.

1 Distinctive Features for Vowels

Table 5.1 at the end of chapter 5, classifying vowels phonetically by the parameters height, frontness–backness and roundness, can be reinterpreted almost verbatim in terms of distinctive features.

We must first formally differentiate between consonants and vowels, by means of the feature [±consonantal], which we define as follows:

[+consonantal] sounds involve a drastic constriction in the central area of the mouth

[+consonantal] sounds involve a drastic constriction in the central oral passage

By "drastic constriction" we mean a constriction that results in total blockage of the airflow, as for stops, or in restricted air exit causing friction, as in fricatives. The condition that the constriction must involve the central oral passage implies that obstruents, nasals, laterals and most rhotics will be [+consonantal], whereas all vowels (possibly with some constriction *on the sides* of the mouth) will be [−consonantal].

We can now turn to the features that distinguish the various vowels. If we first consider the height parameter, you will remember that some vowels are high, in that they involve the raising of the body of the tongue ([i], [u]), some are low, involving the lowering of the body of the tongue ([æ], [ɑ]), and some are neither ([e], [o]).

> What do you think may be the most straightforward manner of formalizing the height distinctions between vowels in terms of distinctive features?

A tripartite classification of vowels *vis-à-vis* height can be implemented by means of the binary features [±high] and [±low]

This tripartite classification of vowels with respect to height can be implemented by means of the binary features [±high] and [±low]. We illustrate this in (1) for the familiar, and highly natural, five-member system:

(1) | | [i] | [e] | [a] | [o] | [u] |
     |--------|-----|-----|-----|-----|-----|
     | [high] | + | − | − | − | + |
     | [low] | − | − | + | − | − |

Mathematically, there is of course another possible combination, namely, [+high, +low], but this is ruled out on the reasoning that the body of the tongue cannot be simultaneously raised and lowered.

> Two pairs of the five-vowel system are shown in (1) with the same feature values. The two vowels in the pairs in question do not sound the same, though, so how do you think they will be distinguished in terms of distinctive features?

The major difference between [i], [e], on the one hand, and [u], [o], on the other, is one of backness. We captured this difference by means of a feature [±back] bearing on body of the tongue retraction, as we now illustrate for a six-vowel system:

The difference in backness is captured by means of the feature [±back]

(2)

	[i]	[e]	[æ]	[a]	[o]	[u]
[high]	+	–	–	–	–	+
[low]	–	–	+	+	–	–
[back]	–	–	–	+	+	+

In systems with an odd number of vowels the unpaired central low vowel [a] is usually considered [+back] phonologically.

> Of the vowels discussed in the chapter so far, all but one come from the primary set of cardinal vowels. What is the major difference separating this set from the set of secondary cardinal vowels? Can this difference be expressed by means of the distinctive features we have identified so far in this chapter?

Secondary cardinal vowels are differentiated from the primary cardinal vowels exclusively on the basis of inverted roundness. The phonological interpretation of this parameter is the distinctive feature [±round], as we now illustrate, first for the primary cardinal vowels, and then for their secondary counterparts:

The roundness parameter involves the distinctive feature [±round]

(3)

	[i]	[e]	[ɛ]	[æ]	[a]	[ɔ]	[o]	[u]
[high]	+	–	–	–	–	–	–	+
[low]	–	–	–	+	+	–	–	–
[back]	–	–	–	–	+	+	+	+
[round]	–	–	–	–	–	+	+	+

(4)

	[y]	[ø]	[œ]	[Œ]	[ɒ]	[ʌ]	[ɤ]	[ɯ]
[high]	+	–	–	–	–	–	–	+
[low]	–	–	–	+	+	–	–	–
[back]	–	–	–	–	+	+	+	+
[round]	+	+	+	+	+	–	–	–

The four features proposed distinguish all the segments reviewed but the two mid vowels in each of the front and back sets. We obviously need a further feature to differentiate the vowels in these pairs. Before we go into this matter, it will be useful to notice the existence of dependencies between the features we have just presented and some of the features we introduced in chapter 4.

There are dependencies between features

> We explained in chapter 4 that phonological distinctive features are typically grounded in the active articulator. The vowel features we have mentioned so far refer to the articulatory gesture. Which articulators are involved in the formation of each of the cardinal vowels?

2 Feature Dependencies

Consider first [±round]. Clearly, the rounding captured by this feature is implemented by the lips. In chapter 4 we introduced a unary feature [labial] to capture involvement of the lips in articulation, all labial sounds being phonologically classified as [labial]. We are now seeing that [+round] sounds are necessarily [labial], suggesting that [+round] is a dependent of [labial]. If [+round] is a dependent of [labial], [−round] will also have to be, for the simple reason that [−round] is not a different feature from [+round], but the same feature with the opposite value:

[+round] is a dependent of [labial]

(5)

Notice that the only reason to specify a sound as [−round] is that it could conceivably have been [+round]. If so, the sound in question must of necessity be [labial]. For instance, the consonants [p], [f], [b], etc., are all [labial] and [−round]. By contrast, consonants like [t], [d], etc., are articulated with the blade of the tongue, as we know, and therefore [±round] is simply irrelevant to them.

> Go back to the vowel tables in (3) and (4) and say which vowels will have to be specified as [labial].

Let us now examine [±high], [±low] and [±back]. We already know that these features capture movements of the body of the tongue upwards, downwards and backwards – notice that the blade can simultaneously be tucked in behind the lower teeth.

> Experiment on yourself by pronouncing the front vowels [i] and [e] with the blade first raised, then lowered and finally curled back. What does this tell you about the relevance of the place of articulation feature [coronal] to vowels?

It follows from this that [±high], [±low] and [±back] are dependents of [dorsal] (see, however, chapter 17 for a different opinion):

[±high], [±low] and [±back] are dependents of [dorsal]

(6)

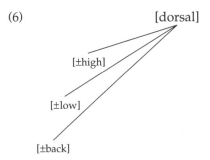

Notice that each of the dependent features is placed on a different plane, in line with the multiplanar geometry we introduced in chapter 4. Once more, if a segment is not [dorsal], the dependents of this feature will simply be irrelevant to it.

In the feature tables in (3) and (4) above, the mid vowel pairs [e]/[ɛ], [o]/[ɔ], etc., are not differentiated by the four features discussed so far. We will now explain how these vowels are distinguished.

3 Two More Distinctive Features

As follows from our remarks in chapter 1, the tongue is an organ of considerable length. Consequently, you will not be surprised to hear that a further section hides behind the body of the tongue, the tongue ROOT, which we now illustrate (figure 6.1).

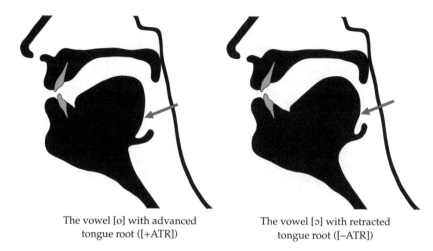

The vowel [o] with advanced
tongue root ([+ATR])

The vowel [ɔ] with retracted
tongue root ([–ATR])

Figure 6.1   Advanced and retracted tongue root

The tongue root has both phonetic and phonological relevance. In particular, if the tongue root is brought forward during the articulation of vowels, the pharyngeal cavity gets enlarged. Concomitantly, the size of our familiar tube responsible for vowel quality is modified: vowels with such a pharyngeal enlargement will automatically sound somewhat different from vowels which are identical apart from the enlargement. The forward movement of the root of the tongue is captured by the distinctive feature [±ATR] (ADVANCED TONGUE ROOT), a dependent of the unary feature [radical], a word meaning 'of the root':

(7)   [radical]

        [±ATR]

[±ATR] accounts
for the difference
between the two
shades of mid
vowels

The incorporation of the feature [±ATR] into our feature inventory allows us to specify mid-high vowels positively as [+ATR], and mid-low vowels as [–ATR]:

(8)   [e]   [o]   [ɛ]   [ɔ]
      [ATR]   +   +   –   –

> Do you notice the advancement of the tongue root when you articulate [e] and [ɛ]? Are there any attendant effects?

We have now defined the sixteen cardinal vowels (eight primary cardinal vowels and eight secondary cardinal vowels) in terms of a set of only five phonological distinctive features.

Remind yourself of what these features are.

The features we have available cannot differentiate the central vowels we added to the vowel repertoire at the end of the previous chapter. This deficiency could be overcome by enriching the distinctive feature inventory with a feature [±front] to supplement [±back], paralleling the contrast between [±high] and [±low]. A [±front] feature, however, does not form part of most current theories of distinctive features: central vowels are analysed phonologically as unround back vowels. There are two reasons for the absence of [±front]. The first is that central vowels are thought never to contrast phonologically with unround back vowels. The second is that the articulatory gesture that would justify a feature [±front], a deliberate forward movement of the body of the tongue, is claimed not to be viable.

Central vowels are analysed phonologically as unround back vowels

Before finishing the section, we will draw your attention to the existence of implicational relationships between features over and above the relationships implicit in the dependency relations we have been examining. Thus, for instance, if a sound is specified as [−consonantal], it is automatically also [+sonorant] and [+continuant]: these two values are therefore redundant and can be left out of the representation, then said to be "underspecified" for these features.

Why does the specification of a sound as [−consonantal] make the values [+sonorant] and [+continuant] redundant?

"Underspecification" will be found to be particularly useful in the next section. In-depth discussion of this construct can be found in chapter 17.

4 Back Harmony in Turkish

There are languages where the class of vowels which occur in a given domain, typically the word, is restricted in some way. This phenomenon is commonly known as "harmony", on the grounds that the vowels harmonize for some feature or features in the domain in question. The vowel harmony of Turkish has been thoroughly investigated in the literature, and provides a convenient point of entry into this area.

There are languages where the class of vowels which occur in a given domain is restricted in some way

Consider the following data:

(9)

	Nom.sg.	Gen.sg.	Nom.pl.	Gen.pl.
'rope'	ip	ipin	ipler	iplerin
'hand'	el	elin	eller	ellerin
'girl'	kɯz	kɯzɯn	kɯzlar	kɯzlarɯn
'stalk'	sap	sapɯn	saplar	saplarɯn

> How many manifestations of the genitive and plural markers can you isolate in (9)?

At a purely descriptive level, we can say that the Turkish genitive singular is formed by the addition of either [in] or [ɯn] to the nominative singular, the nominative plural by the addition of either [ler] or [lar] to the nominative singular, and the genitive plural by the addition of either [in] or [ɯn] to the nominative plural. We could streamline these statements by construing the nominative singular as the common base (or ROOT), to which the suffix [ler]/[lar] is added to signify plural, and the suffix [in]/[ɯn] added on to signify genitive. A SUFFIX is, of course, a morpheme concatenated to the right of some base; we assume that the concept of PLURAL needs no explanation; GENITIVE refers to the form of the word, or CASE, used to indicate possession, a function expressed in English by the preposition *of* or the possessive *'s*, as in *John's*.

The description we have just offered is quite satisfactory from the perspective of MORPHOLOGY, the branch of linguistics that studies the structure of words.

> Recall the definition of "morpheme" we gave in chapter 4, page 92.

In particular, the Turkish words in (9) have a structure ROOT (+ PLURAL SUFFIX) (+ GENITIVE SUFFIX), where the parentheses indicate optionality (not all words are plural or genitive), and the order of concatenation is as given. If we look at the data from the perspective of phonology, however, we will inevitably notice the vowel alternations in the plural and the genitive suffixes. In chapter 2 we set ourselves the task of reducing surface alternations to a common lexical representation, accounting for the mismatch between lexical and surface representations by means of phonological rules. We will now attempt to do this for the Turkish data we are considering.

> Before we proceed, can you suggest a reason for the distribution of the suffixes in question?

In order to elucidate what is actually going on in Turkish we first need to decompose the alternating segments into their relevant distinctive features: you are well aware by now that IPA phonetic symbols are only a shorthand for the feature substance of the corresponding sounds. You can see in (9) that the alternating vowels are [i] and [ɯ] in the genitive suffix (cf. [in] vs. [ɯn]) and [e] and [a] in the plural suffix (cf. [ler] vs. [lar]). In (10) we display the composition of these segments in terms of the features [±high] and [±back]:

(10)   i   ɯ   e   a
      [high]   +   +   −   −
      [back]   −   +   −   +

The two features [±high] and [±back] are sufficient to differentiate the four Turkish vowels, and the remaining features are therefore redundant – the system only has two degrees of height, for instance, and [±low] plays no role.

> Explain why we cannot replace [±high] with [±low] in Turkish.

If you examine the table in (10), you will notice that the difference between the two vowels that alternate in each suffix concerns the feature [±back]. The obvious question is why in these suffixes the feature [±back] takes on the value "+" in some words, and the value "−" in others.

> Go back to (9) and see if you notice anything special about the context in which each of the genitive and plural allomorphs occurs.

Pursuing our assumption that the reason for the alternation is phonological, not morphological, we shall look at the feature composition of the vowel in the root. Notice that the suffix consonants are identical in both alternants, and therefore cannot be responsible for the alternation.

> Spell out the details of the two alternative analyses we have just mentioned: the morphological analysis and the analysis that involves suffix consonants.

We could try to attribute responsibility for the alternation to some other factor, for instance to the consonants of the root, but we will not consider this obviously incorrect hypothesis, to save ourselves time and effort.

Instead, we will consider the relationship, if any, between the vowels in the root and the vowels in the suffix. Sometimes this relationship is one of absolute identity ([ipin], [sɑplɑr], etc.), but sometimes it is not ([elin], [kɯzlɑr], etc.). Does this mean that the reason for the suffix alternation does not lie in the root vowel after all? Not necessarily. Notice in particular that, while the relationship between the two vowels in question is not always one of total identity, it is systematically one of partial identity, as we illustrate in (11):

(11)　　　i p i n　　s ɑ pl ɑ r　　　e l i n　　k ɯ zl ɑ r
　　　[+high] [+high]　[–high] [–high]　[–high] [+high]　[+high] [–high]
　　　[–back] [–back]　[+back] [+back]　[–back] [–back]　[+back] [+back]

> Which feature or features has or have identically paired values throughout?

You will notice that the values of the feature [±high] need not be uniform across the root and the suffix. The values of the feature [±back], however, always are: [±back] harmonizes throughout the Turkish word, and consequently we say that Turkish has [±back] harmony for vowels. We should of course check some more data before making such a general statement, but we will once more save ourselves the time and the energy.

[±back] harmonizes throughout the Turkish word

5 Lexical Underspecification

Having discovered the essence of the Turkish alternation, we will now propose a formalization for it. The vowels in [ipin] and [sɑpɯn] will be represented as in (12) – to facilitate identification, we provide full IPA transcriptions at the top:

(12)

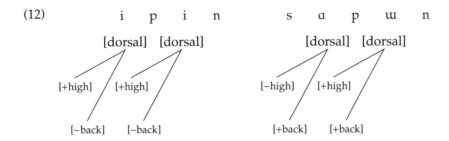

You will notice that in the genitive the suffix vowel is consistently [+high], but its value for [±back] varies according to the value of this feature in the root vowel: this is of course simply a restatement of the [±back] vowel harmony of Turkish. The most straightforward formalization of this situation involves leaving the feature [±back] lexically unspecified in the genitive and plural suffixes: the lexical representations of these suffixes will therefore be left blank for [±back], but the genitive suffix will of course be lexically [+high], and the plural suffix [–high].

> Summarize the proposal we are making and its motivation.

The lexical representations of [ipin] and [sɑpɯn] will consequently be as follows:

(13)

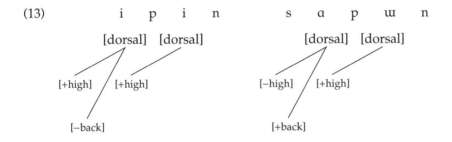

Notice that, while the root vowels contain the appropriate specifications for [±back] (compare *[ɯp], *[sep], respectively: by convention, incorrect forms are starred), this feature is missing from the suffix vowels. We know, however, that in the phonetic representation of these words the suffix vowels are [–back] and [+back], respectively, through agreement with the root vowel, as represented in (12) above. How can this target be attained?

> Can you guess the answer to the question?

Surface representations borrow the specification for [±back] from the neighbouring vowel

The answer is straightforward in the context of an autosegmental approach. In particular, the most direct strategy involves borrowing the specification for [±back] from the neighbouring vowel, along the lines of the assimilation processes we examined in chapter 4:

(14)

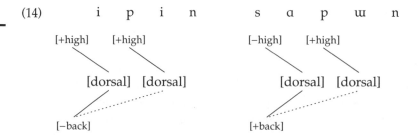

This analysis thus provides a principled explanation for the fact that the suffix vowel always shows up with the same value for [±back] as the root vowel. Clearly, the process also takes place in forms with a chain of suffixes, as we now illustrate for the pair [iplerin], [kuɯzlɑruɯn]:

(15)

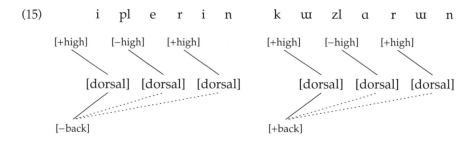

The prediction of the approach is that the number of vowels following the root will be irrelevant to the operation of the process of back harmony. This prediction is obviously correct for the data examined. It is also correct for comparable data not discussed, but that once more we could and ought to test: you know from chapter 2 that the accounts phonologists come up with only have the status of hypotheses.

6 Vowel Disharmony

The analysis as it now stands predicts that vowels will always have the same value for [±back] in the suffix(es) and in the stem. Consider, however, forms like the following:

(16) a. iki   'two'   b. ikigen   'two-dimensional'
          altɯ   'six'   altɯgen   'hexagonal'
          yedi   'seven'   yedigen   'heptagonal'
          sekiz   'eight'   sekizgen   'octagonal'

> Can you see anything unusual in any of these forms? What, and in which?

The forms in (16b) are obviously made up by suffixation of the stems in (16a) with the suffix *-gen*. The form *gen* of this suffix is predicted when the stem contains front vowels: quite simply, the [–back] specification of these vowels will trigger the [–back] specification of the vowel [e] in *gen*. When the base contains back vowels, as it does in *altɯ*, we would of course expect a back vowel in the suffix also: **altɯgan*. This is, however, not the case, since this suffix invariably turns up with the front vowel [e], regardless of the specification of the vowel(s) of the stem for [±back]: *altɯgen*. The form *altɯgen* therefore exhibits vowel disharmony, since the value of [±back] is not identical in all its vowels:

(17)

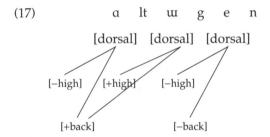

Even more striking instantiations of vowel disharmony are provided by such bisyllabic suffixes as *-vari* '-like', *-lejin* 'during', *-istan* '-land'. Consider the following forms:

(18) a. eʃ   'partner'   b. eʃvari   'partner-like'
          balɯk   'fish'   balɯkvari   'fish-like'
          fil   'elephant'   filvari   'elephant-like'
          kedi   'cat'   kedivari   'cat-like'

          sabah   'morning'   sabahlejin   'during the morning'
          gedʒe   'night'   gedʒelejin   'during the night'
          akʃam   'evening'   akʃamlejin   'during the evening'

          ermeni   'Armenian'   ermenistan   'Armenia'
          arap   'Arab'   arabistan   'Arabia'

kazak	'Kazak'	kazakistan	'Kazakistan'
hint	'Indian'	hindistan	'India'
afgan	'Afghan'	afganistan	'Afghanistan'
madʒar	'Hungarian'	madʒaristan	'Hungary'

Say in what way these suffixes exemplify disharmony.

In *ermenistan*, the first vowel of the suffix, [i], harmonizes with the vowels of the stem: all the vowels are [−back]. However, in *arabistan* this same vowel shows up disharmonic: [i], instead of the expected [ɯ]. Worse still, the second suffix vowel, [a], clearly does not harmonize with its predecessor [i] in the same morpheme. If it did harmonize, the morpheme would systematically be *-isten*, but it obviously is not.

Vowel disharmony is also observable in stems. So far, we have provided stems which are either monosyllabic, and therefore vacuous for harmony, or polysyllabic with harmony. Indeed, polysyllabic harmonic stems are the norm, as we further exemplify in (19):

(19)	baɫɯk	'fish'	bilezik	'bracelet'
	jatak	'bed'	dilek	'wish'
	jɯlan	'snake'	bilet	'ticket'
	altɯm	'gold'	endiʃe	'worry, anxiety'
	iʃkembe	'tribe'	salak	'stupid'
	salatalɯk	'cucumber'	hɯjar	'cucumber'

You can easily verify that in the forms in (19) all the vowels have the same specification for [±back]: they are all either [+back] or [−back]. However, disharmonic roots also exist – indeed, their number is not inconsiderable. We offer a small sample in (20):

(20)	anne	'mother'	fijat	'price'
	hamsi	'anchovies'	adet	'item'
	mezat	'auction'	takvim	'calendar'
	haber	'news'	vazijet	'position'
	elma	'apple'	battanije	'blanket'
	fakirlik	'poverty'	jemekhane	'dining hall'
	basit	'simple'	ikametgah	'residence'
	sefalet	'poverty'	serinkanlɯ	'cool-headed'

In what way are these roots disharmonic?

The stems in (20) exhibit a mixture of back and front vowels, and therefore contradict vowel harmony.

> Make a proposal to account for disharmony formally.

We will account for disharmony through the idiosyncratic lexical specification of [±back]. We exemplify with -istan, for suffixes, and with *adet* 'item', for stems:

(21)

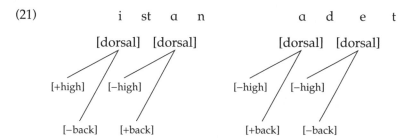

The presence of the appropriate specification of [±back] in the lexicon blocks any further association, since Turkish [±back] harmony, like other harmony systems, only operates on underspecified representations.

> Provide the full autosegmental representation for the vowels in *arabistan*.

7 The No-Crossing Constraint

Forms like *altugenler* 'hexagonals', with the familiar plural suffix -ler added to the base *altugen* 'hexagonal', raise an interesting question. In particular, we know from our discussion in section 4 above that the Turkish plural suffix has two alternants, -ler and -lar, as a result of vowel harmony. This being so, we might expect vowel harmony to be triggered from the root, the strongest morpheme both morphosyntactically and semantically. Therefore, we might expect the form **altugenlar*, erroneously.

> Why should we expect **altugenlar*?

The fact that we get *altugenler* instead shows that the harmony cannot have been induced by the root. This situation is indeed systematic for all harmonic suffixes:

(22) altɯgenler   'hexagonal' (pl.)   ermenistanlar   'Armenia' (pl.)
      adetler   'items'   elmalar   'apples'
      takvimler   'calendars'   fijatlar   'prices'
      vazijetler   'positions'   jemekhaneler   'dining halls'

If you examine the forms in (22) carefully, you will notice that in all cases each prespecified vowel (an OPAQUE VOWEL) starts off a new harmony domain. To make your task easier, we make this explicit in (23):

Each prespecified vowel (an OPAQUE VOWEL) starts off a new harmony domain

(23) **a**ltɯgenler   ermenistanlar
      adetler   elmalar
      t**a**kvimler   fij**a**tlar
      v**a**zijetler   jeme**x**haneler

> Attempt an autosegmental account of the distribution of the vowels in the forms in (23).

In (23) the vowels emboldened are prespecified in the lexicon as [+back] or [–back]. On the reasonable assumption that the unemboldened vowels are unspecified for [±back], they manifestly take the value for this feature from the immediately preceding vowel. The question we are asking is why they do not take it from the root vowel(s) instead.

Let us investigate what such an outcome would formally entail. We shall use the form *altɯgenler* as a test case. In (24) we provide the autosegmental configuration of the alternative, but non-existent, *altɯgenlar, which would indeed be derived if the harmony trigger were located in the root:

(24)   a   lt   ɯ   g   e   nl   a   r

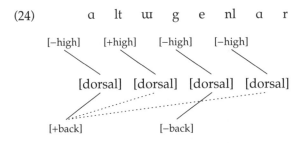

> Explain the mechanics of this representation.

In (24), the [+back] of the first vowel of the root has spread to the second vowel, as predicted. Its spread to the third vowel has been blocked by the prespecified value [−back] associated with this vowel in the lexicon, in line with our previous discussion. The question now is why [+back] cannot in fact associate to the last vowel, in -*lar*: we might expect that it could, given the fact that this vowel does not carry any [±back] prespecification. If it did, we would of course get the illegitimate form **altugenlar*.

> Can you advance a reason why [+back] does not associate to the vowel in -*lar*?

The reason the structure in (24) is not possible is that it contains a crossing of lines on the [±back] plane. In particular, the line linking [+back] to the suffix vowel crosses the line linking this vowel to the prespecified value [−back]. This configuration infringes a general, inviolable principle of autosegmental theory, the NO-CROSSING CONSTRAINT:

(25)   No-crossing constraint:
       Association lines may not cross

The rationale for the No-Crossing Constraint is straightforward.

Association lines may not cross (= "No-Crossing Constraint")

> Can you guess what the rationale for the No-Crossing Constraint is? Hint: look at the linearization of the associated elements.

Consider (24) again. This representation in fact contains the implicit claim that the specified feature [+back] both precedes and follows the specified feature [−back]. The reason for this may not be obvious, since it would appear that in this representation [+back] only precedes [−back]. In its line indeed it does. However, once the multidimensional nature of autosegmental representations is taken into account, the contradictory claim we referred to comes through. In particular, [+back] is associated both with a vowel that precedes the vowel associated with [−back] (precisely as it should) and with a vowel that follows the vowel associated with [−back]. This contradiction accounts for the illegitimacy of this type of representation, encapsulated in the No-Crossing Constraint.

Because the No-Crossing Constraint rules out the representation in (24), the correct derivation will be as in (26):

(26)

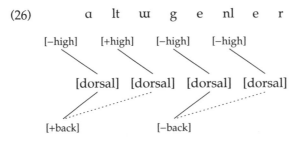

In (26) there is no crossing of lines. Instead, the prespecified feature [−back] spreads from *-gen* to the vowel of the plural suffix, correctly yielding the allomorph *-ler*.

> Construct similar rules for some of the other examples in (23) to make sure you understand.

8 German Umlaut

Turkish is likely to be rather an exotic language for most of the readers of this book, who may be tempted to think of vowel harmony as something equally out of the ordinary. As it happens, however, languages closer to home, such as German and English itself, exhibit essentially the same phenomenon.

Consider the following German forms:

(27)

	Singular		*Plural*	
Bruder	Br[u]der	'brother'	Br[y]der	Brüder
Sohn	S[o]hn	'son'	S[ø]hne	Söhne
Tochter	T[ɔ]chter	'daughter'	T[œ]chter	Töchter

> State what changes occur in the stem vowels of the words in (27).

These singular–plural alternations illustrate the well-known German phenomenon of vowel mutation, or UMLAUT, which involves the fronting of the vowel in the plural (as you can see in (27), vowel fronting is indicated by a dieresis in the German spelling):

(28)   *Plain vowel   Umlauted vowel*

[u]	[y]
[o]	[ø]
[ɔ]	[œ]

Not all German plurals are umlauted, however:

(29) Blume   Bl[u]me   'flower'   Bl[u]men   Blumen
      Rose   R[o]se   'rose'   R[o]sen   Rosen
      Roß   R[ɔ]ß   'horse'   R[ɔ]sse   Rosse

Indeed, plural umlaut appears as an idiosyncrasy in contemporary German.

Historically, German plural umlaut is reducible to an account similar to the analysis of Turkish. In particular, the class of nouns that underwent umlaut had a plural suffix -[i] in Old High German, some thousand or so years ago. In (30) we trace the development of the umlauted plural of *Sohn* 'son', slightly idealized for ease of exposition:

(30)

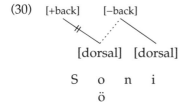

You can see that all we have to assume is that the feature [–back] of the plural suffix -[i] spread leftward, and dislodged the adjacent [+back] value associated lexically to the root vowel. There are two obvious differences between the German vowel umlaut and the vowel harmony of Turkish. First, the direction of association in German umlaut is the reverse of the direction of association in Turkish harmony: right-to-left in German vs. left-to-right in Turkish. Second, the German umlaut involves the substitution of a lexical feature: Turkish disharmony is of course incompatible with this procedure.

> Show in what way Turkish disharmony is incompatible with the substitution of a lexical feature.

The German plural marker -[i] eventually evolved into schwa, completing the change to the modern form [zønə], where the motivation for the umlaut has obviously been obscured.

A similar situation arose with such derivational suffixes as the adjective-forming suffix *-lich* or the adverbial *-ig*:

(31) T[o]d   'death'   t[ø]d+lich   'deadly'
      Br[u]der 'brother' br[y]der+lich 'brotherly'
      v[ɔ]ll   'full'   v[œ]ll+ig   'fully'

Here the trigger of the umlaut survives into contemporary German: /i/. However, the umlaut process is no longer automatic, since other suffixes similar on the surface fail to trigger it:

(32) M[o]de   'fashion'   m[o]d+isch   'fashionable'
      R[u]he   'silence'   r[u]h+ig   'quiet'
      d[ɔ]rt   'there'   d[ɔ]rt+ig   'of that place'

Notice that German has two phonetically identical suffixes -ig, reminiscent of English -ly: the umlaut-triggering adverbial in (31) (*völlig*), and the adjectival formative in (32), which does not trigger umlaut (*dortig*). We can encode this difference in the contemporary grammar by including an additional [−back] feature in the lexical representation of umlauting suffixes, as follows:

(33)

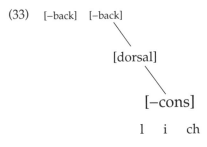

You can see in (33) that this [−back] autosegment is not linked to any of the sounds that make up the suffix -lich. Instead, it is an extra feature that FLOATS in the lexical representation of the suffix, to the left of the [−back] associated to the vowel. Consider in this light the derivation of *tödlich*:

(34)

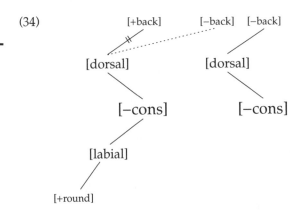

> Explain how the introduction of a floating autosegment allows us to derive the forms in (31) and (32) (also those in (27)).

The crucial aspect of the derivation in (34) is that the feature [–back] responsible for the umlaut in the root is unassociated in lexical representation. Therefore, in modern German only lexically floating features undergo association in the course of the derivation, in contrast to Old High German, where we saw in (30) that lexically associated features were liable to further association derivationally. Suffixes that do not trigger umlaut despite containing a high front vowel simply do not include such a floating feature in their lexical representation:

(35)

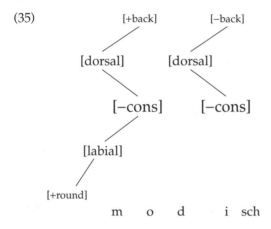

m   o   d   i   sch

In the purely umlauting plural forms in (27) above, we assume that the floating autosegment [–back] constitutes a lexical entry by itself. This makes perfect sense, in as much as the umlaut effected by this autosegment constitutes *the only* mark of the plural in nouns like *Bruder* (pl. *Brüder*) or *Tochter* (pl. *Töchter*) (NB the *e* preceding the final *r* in the spelling corresponds to phonetic schwa, which can be considered a phonetic artifact, and therefore we omit it from the representation):

(36)

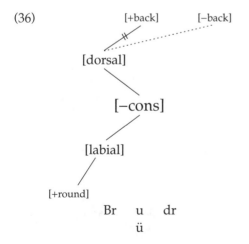

Br   u   dr
     ü

9 English Plurals

The regular rule of English plural formation is simple enough: essentially, add -s, -[z], to the singular: see chapter 19 for specific discussion.

> Why are we saying that the English rule of plural formation is "essentially" add -s?

However, English has a number of idiosyncratic plurals, which have to be memorized – unsurprisingly, children make mistakes on these for quite some time.

One set of irregular English plurals involves a process of vowel fronting similar to German umlaut, as we illustrate in (37):

One English irregular plural involves a process of vowel fronting similar to German umlaut

(37)   goose   [gus]   geese   [gis]
       tooth   [tuθ]   teeth   [tiθ]

> How would these alternations be described in terms of distinctive features?

As in German, the process is entirely opaque in the contemporary language. In Old English, however, there was a plural suffix -[i], again similar to German. In addition, but irrelevantly for our present concerns, the root vowels in these words were [o] in the singular and [e] in the plural, as still reflected in the spelling (more on this in chapter 8):

(38)   *Singular*   *Plural*
       gos   gosi
       toθ   toθi

> Can you guess how the eventual plural forms were arrived at?

What happened next is easy to guess. Specifically, the [–back] feature of the suffix spread to the root vowel, thus fronting it:

> Why must [–back] spread in this direction and not in the opposite one?

(39)

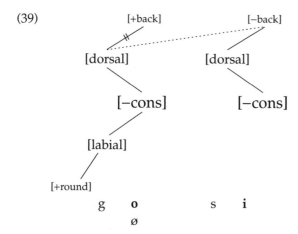

Subsequent developments involved the unrounding of all front round vowels and the loss of the inflectional suffix -[i]: [ges]. At a later stage, the mid vowels [e] and [o] underwent raising to [i] and [u], respectively, to yield the contemporary [gis] and [gus]: we examine this raising process in detail in chapter 8.

In the modern language, it is possible to analyse the phenomenon along the same lines as its German counterpart in (36) above, that is, by means of a floating [−back] plural marker:

(40)

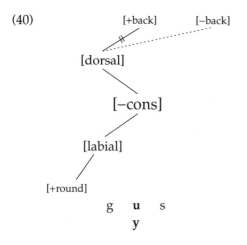

In the modern language, the phenomenon can be analysed by means of a floating [−back] plural marker

We must of course assume that the front round vowel of the output [gys] is subject to an unrounding procedure, a synchronic reflex of the historical event, to yield the surface [gis].

The processes of umlaut and vowel fronting in modern German and English, respectively, are undoubtedly less well behaved than vowel harmony in Turkish: their lexical incidence is basically unpredictable, and therefore the synchronic analysis demands a considerable amount of abstractness. The three phenomena are, however, essentially identical in kind, and thus reducible to basically the same analysis.

C h a p t e r   S u m m a r y

In this chapter we have translated the phonetic parameters high, low, back and round, used to categorize vowels, into phonological features, on a direct one-to-one basis. These features further extend the set of feature dependencies. Thus, [round] refers to a gesture of the lips, and must of necessity imply the place feature [labial]. Likewise, [high], [low] and [back] refer specifically to the position of the body of the tongue, and are, therefore, [dorsal] dependents. Combinations of the binary settings of these four subordinate features are sufficient to distinguish six out of the eight cardinal vowels in each the primary and the secondary sets. In order to obtain the four degrees of height encoded in the cardinal vowels, a further feature was introduced to distinguish between such pairs of mid vowels as [e] and [ɛ], [o] and [ɔ], etc. This binary feature, [±ATR], permits the distinction between vowels pronounced with the root of the tongue advanced, which leads to an increase in height and tenseness (cf. [e, o]), and [−ATR] vowels where no such effect occurs (cf. [ɛ, ɔ]). Just as we discovered that not all languages have even approximations of the entire cardinal vowel set in their inventories, so it is clear that languages may choose not to employ the entire range of available features, some of which will then be redundant. Values for other features may be entirely predictable and therefore do not need to be lexically specified. The notions of redundancy and underspecification of lexical forms for certain features were illustrated through vowel harmony in Turkish. Harmony is a phenomenon which leads all vowels (or more rarely consonants) in a given domain to bear the same value for some feature or features. For example, it may be that all the vowels in a word are round or high. We examined a subset of four Turkish vowels, distinguished by the two features [±high] and [±back]. We saw that the suffix vowels are normally unspecified for [±back], the eventual value of which is supplied by the adjacent stem vowel through spreading. In some special cases, suffix vowels or additional stem vowels do bear a lexical specification for [±back]. Discussion of these phenomena allowed us to continue our presentation of autosegmental theory and to introduce the very important No-Crossing Constraint, which prohibits the crossing of lines of association. The harmony at work in Turkish is transparent, but in modern German and English only the residual effects of harmony from earlier forms of the language remain. The case of German umlaut (vowel fronting) was used to introduce floating segments (not associated in lexical representation), here the residue of Old High German lexically associated features. A similar explanation was suggested for English alternations of the type goose/geese.

Key Questions

1 How do the phonetic parameters relevant to vowels convert into phonological distinctive features?
2 Which of the distinctive features defining vowels relate to the general place of articulation features and how?
3 What is meant by [±ATR]? How does this feature distinguish pairs of vowels?
4 What is meant by "lexical underspecification"? How does it help to explain harmony phenomena?
5 Explain the No-Crossing Constraint. How does this constraint account for disharmony in harmonic systems?
6 What is meant by "umlaut"?
7 How do processes operative in German and English resemble those of Turkish?
8 What is the historical explanation for umlaut in German?
9 Explain how a floating autosegment can be called upon to explain umlaut in modern German and English.

Further Practice

More Turkish

In section 4 we discussed backness harmony in Turkish vowels and displayed a feature matrix for four vowels. Turkish, in fact, has eight vowels:

i ɯ y u
e ɑ ø o

(i) Which further feature(s) will allow for the additional four sounds?
(ii) Show the complete feature matrix of Turkish vowels.

Now consider the following forms:

	Nom.sg.	Gen.sg.
'face'	jyz	jyzyn
'stamp'	pul	pulun
'village'	køj	køjyn
'end'	son	sonun

(iii) List the genitive suffixes.
(iv) Following from what you learned in this chapter, can you postulate one single underlying representation for the genitive suffix?
(v) Show how each surface form is obtained.

Now consider the data below:

	Nom.pl.	*Gen.pl.*
'face'	jyzler	jyzlerin
'stamp'	pullɑr	pullɑrɯn
'village'	køjler	køjlerin
'end'	sonlɑr	sonlɑrɯn

(vi)   Explain these cases.

Finnish Vowel Harmony

The Finnish vowel system is as follows:

i   y   u
e   ø   o
æ   ɑ

(i)   List the distinctive features of the vowel sounds.

Many Finnish suffixes occur in two different forms according to features of
the stem vowels. Consider the examples listed below (notice that some of
the vowels are "transparent" to harmony):

talo-ssɑ	'in the house'	kylæ-ssæ	'in the village'
turu-ssɑ	'in Turku'	kæde-ssæ	'in the hand'
pori-ssɑ	'in Pori'	venee-ssæ	'in the boat'
porvoo-ssɑ	'in Porvoo'	helsiŋŋi-ssæ	'in Helsinki'
tuo-ko	'that?'	tæmæ-kø	'this?'
tuo-ssɑ-ko	'in that?'	tæ-ssæ-kø	'in this?'
nɑise-ltɑ	'from the woman'	tytø-ltæ	'from the girl'
sisɑre-ltɑ	'from the sister'	velje-ltæ	'from the brother'

(ii)   What are the alternating forms of the suffixes meaning (a) 'in', (b)
         interrogative and (c) 'from'?
(iii)   Which feature undergoes harmony?
(iv)   What causes the harmony?
(v)   Which vowels are transparent to the process?
(vi)   The data can best be explained if we assume one of the values of the
         harmonizing feature to be filled in by a default rule. Which is the
         default value?
(vii)   Write the default rule.
(viii)   Write a rule to provide the non-default value.
(ix)   In what order must these two rules apply?

CHAPTER SEVEN

THE VOWELS OF ENGLISH

Chapter Objectives

In this chapter you will learn about:
■ The relationship between the set of English vowels and the cardinal vowels.
■ The identity of the simple (steady state) vowels of English.
■ How the English vowel inventory is further increased by a set of complex vowels called "diphthongs".
■ Diphthongs where the tongue rises during the articulation.
■ Diphthongs which end up at the centre of the vowel space.

In chapter 5 we provided the inventory of the cardinal vowels developed by Daniel Jones as a set of reference points to aid with the description of the vowels of the world's languages: sixteen cardinal vowels in all, eight primary and eight secondary. We saw that these vowels can be produced mechanically by any healthy human by following a set of simple articulatory instructions, or by targeting certain perceptual points defined by reference to the articulatorily established vowels. We pointed out that the idealized nature of the cardinal vowels makes absolute sameness with the vowels of any natural language unlikely. Nevertheless, the vowels of natural languages are whenever possible identified with a neighbouring cardinal vowel, for obvious ease of reference, while of course making explicit in the description what the differences are between the cardinal vowel and the vowel in question. In the present chapter, we adopt this strategy to survey the complete inventory of English vowels.

1 Variation in English

We have already cautioned in chapter 5 that the vowels of English are subject to remarkable variation world-wide. This means that there is no single English vowel system or inventory, but, rather, very many. This situation

The vowels of English are subject to remarkable variation world-wide

obviously does not make easy the presentation of the English vowels in a unified chapter.

The strategy we shall adopt is as follows. We will build our discussion on the set of cardinal vowels we presented in chapter 5 – indeed, we shall follow a similar order of presentation. For each IPA vowel relevant to English we shall list a number of English specimens, ranked from closest to most distant, each with the appropriate geographical or social identification. Our goal is, of course, not to survey the wealth of pronunciations of English vowels, but to enable readers to home in on those they are most familiar with, in particular their own, and in this way identify the vowels experientially – vowels, a bit like wines, can only be properly understood when they are tasted.

Some accents of English are of course more "standard" than others, and accordingly they are better known. Two of these accents actually stand out as being widely recognizable: North American GA and British RP.

Some accents of English are of course more "standard" than others

> Remind yourself of what is meant by the labels RP and GA, which we introduced in chapter 5.

These two accents will therefore play a central role in our discussion, but we will make incursions into other varieties when useful. It goes without saying that these other varieties are in all as worthy as their better-known counterparts: in language, as in biology, what we each have is by definition best, prestige and social recognition aside.

As a preliminary to our descriptions, we will give an overview of the main accents of English across the world, and of the principal characteristics of each. English, of course, originated in Britain, and consequently it is here that we find the most fragmentation in accent and in dialect. The main accents in the British Isles, with their respective chief distinctive traits at present, are as follows:

- **Scotland:** rhoticity, no distinctive vowel length, tendency for pure vowels, [j] in *new*, aspiration in *when*, only dark *l*s, no distinct vowel in *foot* relative to *food*.
- **Northern England:** mostly non-rhoticity, occasional linking and intrusive *r*, distinctive vowel length, tendency for pure vowels, [j] in *new*, dropping of *h*, no aspiration in *when*, no distinct vowel in *cup* relative to *put*.
- **South West England:** rhoticity (even hyper-rhoticity), distinctive vowel length, diphthongization, [j] in *new*, dropping of *h*, no aspiration in *when*.
- **London Cockney:** non-rhoticity, linking and intrusive *r*, distinctive vowel length, dropping of *h*, glottal stop for *t*, other plosives, and even fricatives;

extensive vowel shifts, no aspiration in *when*, vocalization of final *l*, vowel nasalization before nasal consonants, dental fricatives replaced by labio-dentals (*three* → *free*).

- **RP:** non-rhoticity, linking and intrusive *r*, distinctive vowel length, diphthongization, [j] in *new*, no aspiration in *when*, [ɑ] in *bath* set, pre-glottalization of stops, simplifications of diphthongs in some environments.
- **Estuary English:** a variable accent intermediate between RP and Cockney, widespread over south-eastern England and spreading to other parts of the south.
- **Southern Ireland:** rhoticity, full range of vowels before *r*, no dental fricatives [θ, ð] (dental stops [t̪, d̪] instead), intervocalic *t* weakening (t̪ > [t̪] > [r]), aspiration in *when*, [ə] as only reduced vowel, clear *l* in all positions, "dark" *r* ([ɻ]), [e] and [o] monophthongs.
- **Northern Ireland:** rhoticity, no distinctive vowel length, no [ʊ], intervocalic *t* tapping ([r]), tendency for pure vowels or centring diphthongs (see section 8 below), clear *l* in all positions (except in Belfast), retroflex rhotic *r* ([ɻ]), aspiration in *when*.

RHOTICITY refers to the occurrence of the sound represented by *r* in all positions, whereas in non-rhotic accents *r* only occurs before vowels (we talk about HYPER-RHOTICITY when *r*s turn up where they shouldn't, as in the pronunciation of *china* as *china*[ɹ]). DISTINCTIVE VOWEL LENGTH means that at least some vowels are kept apart by their length, only or principally: one member of the pair will be short, and the other long. DIPHTHONG-IZATION refers to the tendency of many vowels in many accents of English not to be uniform from beginning to end, the way pure vowels are. LINK-ING *r* and INTRUSIVE *r* refer to pronouncing an *r* between a non-high vowel and a following vowel, whether or not that *r* is pronounced when the word is said in isolation, and whether or not it appears in the spelling: cf. *hair and nails* ("linking"), *law-r-and order* ("intrusive"), and the like.

The expression "non-rhotic" refers to the absence of [ɹ] in all positions but before a vowel

Check the features of your own accent against this description.

Of the accents just listed, the Scottish vowel system clearly stands apart: in fact, it lies closest to the cardinal vowels. Consequently, we will make special use of it in our description, even though numerically it is a minority accent. The accent of northern England (itself varied, like most others, but we cannot go into many details here) is in some respects half-way between Scottish and southern English, and we will also find it of use at times, with special reference to the accent of (West) Yorkshire. The main accent of Britain is, of course, RP, the prestige of which indeed spreads beyond the

The Scottish vowel system lies closest to the cardinal vowels

white cliffs of Dover. RP is probably the most studied and best described of all English accents, and therefore we will make ample reference to it throughout the chapter. While related to RP, the London accent diverges in a number of important traits, most particularly its traditional Cockney variey. Finally, the English south-west converges with North American English in many of its features, not least in its rhoticity and its dislike of low rounded vowels. These traits are shared with Irish English, itself divided into the accents of Northern Ireland and the Irish Republic, the former related to Scottish.

North American English of course has the largest number of speakers of any variety of English. Its accent is far less diversified than that of the old metropolis, for obvious reasons of more recent history. Indeed, it is only in the east, where the colonists first settled, that anything resembling the heterogeneity of England can be observed, and only to a limited extent at that. While some regional and individual variation is inevitable in a country of the size and demographic weight of the USA, only four of its accents are worth differentiating for our present purposes:

> English is far less diversified in North America than in the British Isles

- **Eastern New England:** non-rhoticity, linking and intrusive *r*, centralization of the vowel of *father*, rounded vowel in *cot* (and *caught*) distinct from *cart* (and, of course, *cat*), occasionally [j] in *new*.
- **New York City:** non-rhoticity, linking and intrusive *r*, pretty back vowel in *father* and often in *nice*, same vowel in *cot* as in *cart*, no aspiration in *when*.
- **The South:** non-rhoticity, no linking or intrusive *r*, monophthongs diphthongize and some diphthongs monophthongize, [j] in *new*, southern drawl.
- **General American:** rhoticity, no [j] on *new*, *cot* (and possibly *caught*) with the (unround) vowel of *cart*, flapping of intervocalic *ts*, aspiration in *when*, dark *l* after vowels.

Check your accent for the features described.

> The *r* of the spelling corresponded to an *r*-sound in all positions in all varieties of English until the eighteenth century

There are of course other accents in the area, but they are not very distinct, and we will ignore them to keep things simple. The most notable difference between GA and its three counterparts concerns its rhoticity. This is a by-product of history. In particular, the *r* of the spelling corresponded to an *r*-sound in *all* varieties of English until the eighteenth century, when non-rhoticity began to hold sway in the London area, from where it gradually spread to other neighbouring zones (the process is still ongoing), and across the Atlantic. There, it took hold on the eastern seaboard: New York

City, Boston and eastern New England in general, and also the southern states, through such main centres of population as Richmond or Charleston. However, since the Second World War a process of uniformization in the direction of GA has been under way, and some of the old local accentual traits are on the retreat, to different degrees in different areas and social classes, although they are still by no means extinct. Further north in North America, the accent of Canada can be safely subsumed under the label GA, at least for our present purposes, with the notable exception of one specifically Canadian phenomenon to which we will refer in due course.

Elsewhere in the world, English is spoken as a first language in three large countries of the southern hemisphere, each of them endowed with its own variety:

- **Australian English:** non-rhoticity, linking and intrusive *r*, raised front lax vowels (*bad*, *bed*, *bid*), heavy diphthongization in *see* and *Sue*, [j] in *new*.
- **New Zealand English:** non-rhoticity, linking and intrusive *r*, heavy centralization of the vowel in *bid*, other front lax vowels raised (*bad*, *bed*), heavy diphthongization in *see* and *Sue*, [j] in *new*.
- **South African English:** non-rhoticity, no linking and intrusive *r*, strengthening of *r* usually into a tap, contextual centralization of the vowel in *bid*, other front lax vowels raised (*bad*, *bed*), far back vowel in *father*, [j] in *new*.

Although the three countries are reasonably far apart geographically, their accents share important traits, to the extent that it is often possible to refer to them together under the label "southern hemisphere English".

There are of course many other parts of the world where English is spoken, many Caribbean islands among them. However, we obviously have to draw the line somewhere, and we will ignore these further varieties in order to keep the chapter within manageable limits.

2 The Four Corner Vowels

As we have already said, in our exploration of the vowels of English we will adopt the same order of presentation as for the cardinal vowels in chapter 5, for similar reasons. We shall therefore start with the four corner vowels [i], [æ], [ɑ] and [u]. Remember, crucially, that these vowels are relatively easy to define articulatorily.

Let us remind ourselves of the position of these vowels in our familiar chart (figure 7.1).

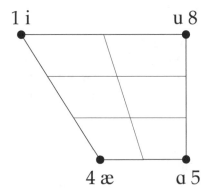

Figure 7.1   The four corner vowels

> Jog your memory about the pronunciation of these vowels by
> referring to the descriptions in chapter 5.

We will now review each English vowel in detail, starting with the correspondents of cardinal vowel no. 1, [i], as in *heat*, *seed* or *key*. The correspondents of this vowel in English are as follows:

- [i] in Scottish English and the English of other Celtic areas
- [ɪ] both in conservative or careful RP and in the GA short variant (*heat*)
- otherwise slightly diphthongized in RP and GA (*seed*, *key*) and in accents of southern England (see section 6 below), particularly in the longer variants
- clearly diphthongized in Australian English and in Cockney (see section 6 below).

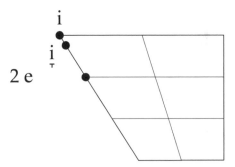

Figure 7.2   The vowel of *heat*

> Try your own pronunciation of this vowel. Do you reckon you pronounce a pure [i] all through?

We have just made reference to short and long variants. Indeed, in GA, in RP and in many other accents of English (but not in all), vowels automatically vary in length according to the nature of the following consonant: they are longest if there is no such consonant (*key*), and shortest if the following consonant is a voiceless obstruent (*heat*), with intermediate degrees of length otherwise (*seem, seed*). This length variation takes place irrespective of the identity of the vowel. The IPA transcription system includes a special length diacritic "ː" for long vowels, hence *k*[iː]. In turn, half-long vowels are assigned the diacritic "ˑ": *s*[iˑ]*m*. To keep the representations simple, however, we will only make use of these diacritics where length is directly relevant to the discussion.

In many accents of English, vowels automatically vary in length according to the nature of the following consonant

Going now over to cardinal vowel no. 4, [æ], we already know that is low and front. The most common accents of English, among them traditional RP, southern English and GA, do not have this precise vowel. In accents that do, or almost, the spelling can be disconcerting:

The IPA transcription system includes the special length diacritic "ː" for phonologically long vowels, and a half-length diacritic for vowels of intermediate length

* the vowel of *hat* in typical Yorkshire and Southern Irish accents: [hæt]
* the vowel of *heart* in Yorkshire, Australia, New Zealand and the traditional (non-rhotic) Boston accent: [hæt]
* the vowel of *hot* in the North Central area of the US: [hæt].

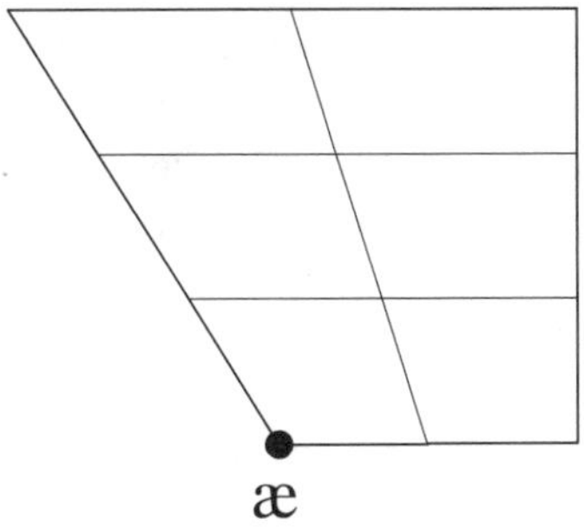

æ

Figure 7.3   The vowel of *hat* in Yorkshire and Southern Ireland

You can see that the spelling needs to be interpreted in the context of each particular accent. For instance, the vowel in both Yorkshire and Boston *heart* can sound like the vowel in Yorkshire *hat*, although the RP and GA pronunciation of these two words would be quite distinct. The point of the present exercise is, of course, not so much to untangle the relationship between spelling and sound as to provide reasonable illustrations of the basic sounds of English, and of their relationship with the cardinal vowels.

The spelling needs to be interpreted in the context of each particular accent

The more standard vowel sounds in *heart* and *scotch* will be presented below. In some accents of English, among them traditional RP and varieties of GA, the vowel in *hat*, while close to cardinal vowel 4, is a raised [æ], in effect a half-way vowel between cardinals 4 and 3: [æ̞].

> Compare the articulation of [æ̞] and [æ]. Say the vowel in *hat* as a non-regional TV newscaster might (you might usefully avail yourself of a recording here). Now notice how the tongue perceptibly lowers in order to produce the [æ] of a northern English accent.

The occurrence of this vowel in RP at the time of the formation of the IPA alphabet led its promoters to assign the special "ash" symbol [æ] to it, quite exceptionally, since variants of cardinal vowels are usually indicated by diacritics. As you know from chapter 5, though, we have decided to adopt the ash [æ] for cardinal vowel 4, and the plain "a" [a] for the central low vowel, to avoid ambiguity. In addition to the arguments we offered in chapter 5, we must point out that the intermediate pronunciation that originally warranted [æ] is now probably a minority pronunciation throughout English. In particular, over the past few decades, the traditional RP [æ̞] of *hat* has been lowering back to [æ], and in the pronunciation of many RP speakers this vowel is now probably as good a representative of cardinal vowel no. 4 as is the Yorkshire [æ]. Moreover, the vowel of *hat* is raised to cardinal vowel [ɛ] in much of the southern hemisphere and, possibly diphthongized, in Cockney. The raising can go further in North America, also usually accompanied by diphthongization. Indeed, in New York City, for instance, the vowel in *bad* can overlap with the vowel in *beard*, discussed in section 8 below. We now list the English correspondents of cardinal vowel 4:

- [æ̞] or [ɛ̞] in traditional RP and GA
- [æ] more and more in RP
- [ɛ] in the southern hemisphere and in Cockney (here possibly diphthongized)
- [ɛ], [e] or even a lax [i] (see section 4 below), all with diphthongization, in North America.

(See Figure 7.4 on the next page.)

> Compare your pronunciation with those listed.

Obviously, of the instantiations listed above only the second corresponds to the cardinal vowel [æ] per se, the others falling outside its range. Indeed,

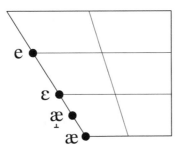

Figure 7.4 The vowel of *hat* across accents

as we have already cautioned and will be seeing all along, lack of identity between English vowels and cardinal vowels is the common situation.

Turning now to the back vowels, in chapter 5 we used the words *father* [fɑðə] and *hoot* [hut] to exemplify cardinal vowels nos. 5 and 8, respectively. As usual, the English vowels tend not to coincide exactly with their cardinal counterparts, which have a somewhat more extreme articulation. In particular, English [ɑ] tends to be slightly advanced with respect to cardinal vowel no. 5, and English [u] slightly lowered relative to cardinal vowel no. 8. Moreover, English [u] is advancing towards the centre in a number of accents.

The range of correspondents of cardinal vowel no. 5 in English words like *father* is as follows:

- a literally back articulation [ɑ] in New York City and, in particular, in South African English
- a slightly advanced variety [ɑ̟] in RP and in GA
- a central variety [a] in Scotland and in some accents in the US
- front varieties [æ] in many parts of northern England (Yorkshire, for instance), in Australia and New Zealand, and in eastern New England.

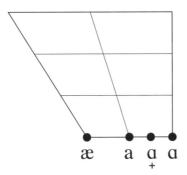

Figure 7.5 The vowel of *father*

> Again, test your own vowel in *father* to compare it with those listed.

In turn, the English correspondents of cardinal vowel no. 8 are as follows:

- back and slightly lowered [ʊ̝] in conservative RP (possibly slightly centralized), in GA short variants (*hoot*), and in southern Irish English
- centralized towards [ʉ] in Scotland, in the southern hemisphere, in the US south, and in popular speech in England, advanced into the front area in some accents
- also centralized towards [ʉ] along the US Atlantic coast as far north as New York City, and in much of the central midland
- diphthongized to some degree in long variants in GA (*mood, whom*) and across the board in most other accents
- clearly diphthongized in Cockney and Australian English (see section 6 below).

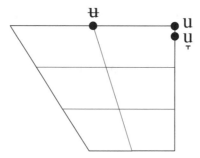

Figure 7.6   The vowel of *hoot*

> Compare your own vowel with those listed, again. Is your vowel diphthongized?

This completes the presentation of the English correspondents of the four corner cardinal vowels.

3 Intermediate Primary Vowels

We shall now turn our attention to the correspondents of the intermediate primary cardinal vowels: [e] and [ɛ] at the front, and [o] and [ɔ] at the back.

Cardinal vowel no. 2, [e], is represented to various degrees of approximation by the vowel in *late*, as follows:

- literally [e] in Scottish English: *late* [let], *lay* [le]
- perhaps a little lower in Yorkshire accents, and in GA in words like *v[e̞]cation*
- diphthongized otherwise in GA, and generally in RP (see section 6 below), where it is also a little lower ([e̞])
- lowered further (in addition to diphthongizing) in Cockney and in the southern hemisphere.

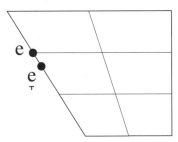

Figure 7.7   The vowel of *late* in some accents

> Try the vowel in the words *late* and *lay*. Does your vowel resemble any of those listed? Is it diphthongized?

Cardinal vowel no. 3, [ɛ], is fairly closely related to the vowel in *let* or *red* in many accents, but not in all:

- usually [ɛ] in Scottish English and Yorkshire English
- slightly higher in GA: [ɛ̝]
- even higher in RP, but not as high as [e]: [e̞]
- diphthongized to various degrees in the American south.

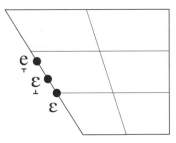

Figure 7.8   The vowel of *let*

> Refer to your own pronunciation of the *e* of *let* or *bed* to locate the cardinal vowel [ɛ].

For the back primary cardinal vowels, cardinal vowel no. 4, [o], partly parallels its front counterpart [e]:

- literally [o] in Scottish English (*coat* [kot], *low* [lo])
- slightly lowered and possibly advanced in Yorkshire accents
- tending to diphthongize in GA (see section 6 below)
- consistently diphthongized in RP (see section 6 below)
- the first part of the diphthong can be centralized ([ɵ]) and unrounded ([ɜ]) – we return to this matter in section 6 below.

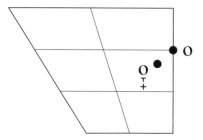

Figure 7.9   The vowel of *coat* in some accents

Do you have a monophthong or a diphthong here? See if you can locate it on the chart.

The correspondences of cardinal vowel no. 6, [ɔ], are as follows:

- [ɔ] in words like *caught* in Scottish and Yorkshire English: [kɔt]
- a lower [ɔ̞] or [ɒ] in GA: [kɔ̞t]/[kɒt]
- can be lowered further to [ɒ] in North America, from where it can unround into [ɑ]: [kɒt], [kɑt]
- in RP, raised and pretty heavily rounded: [kɔ̜t] (the underscripted diacritic "ₒ" signals extra roundness)
- can be diphthongized towards schwa from [ɒ]/[ɔ̞] in New York City, in the American south and (when not prevocalic) in Cockney.

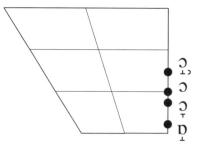

Figure 7.10   The vowel of *caught*

What differences, if any, can you perceive in your pronunciation of *caught* and *cot*?

It may be worth pointing out that the RP vowel of *caught* is similar in
quality to the Spanish vowel [o] in *loco* [loko] "mad" – it is half-way
between cardinal vowels nos. 6 and 7: Spanish [o] obviously does not correspond to cardinal vowel no. 7 either. The RP vowel of *caught* is, however,
considerably longer and tenser than the Spanish vowel of *loco*, and has more
lip rounding.

We round off the section with a chart of the primary cardinal vowels, and
the charts of the related vowels of Scottish, GA and RP English alongside,
to facilitate cross-comparison (figure 7.11).

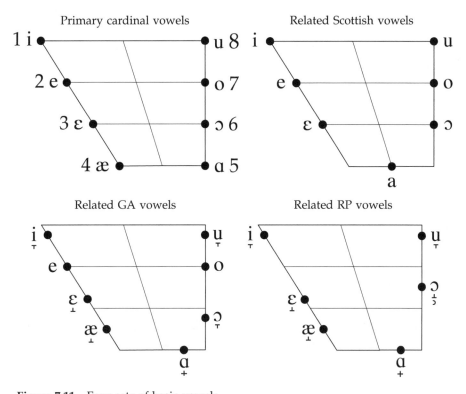

Figure 7.11   Four sets of basic vowels

4 More Lax Vowels

We shall now examine four additional non-central lax vowels of English.
The first such vowel is the one in words like *cot* or *rock*. We have already
mentioned that Scottish English has a vowel equivalent to cardinal vowel

no. 6 here, similar to the French vowel of *cotte* 'overalls'. In Yorkshire accents this vowel is remarkably like secondary cardinal vowel no. 13, [ɒ]. You will recall that secondary cardinal vowels are produced by reversing the lip position of their primary counterparts. This means that secondary cardinal vowel no. 13 will be identical to primary cardinal vowel no. 5 in all but lip rounding – secondary [ɒ] is rounded, whereas primary [ɑ] is not. The set of correspondents of this vowel across English accents is as follows:

Secondary cardinal vowels are produced by reversing the lip position of their primary counterparts

- literally [ɒ] in Yorkshire English: [kɒt]
- also usually [ɒ] in GA before *r* in such words as *horrid, orange, forest,* and after *w* (*w*[ɒ]*ter, w*[ɒ]*sp, w*[ɒ]*tch*): the latter also in midwestern and western areas
- [ɒ] generally in eastern New England and parts of the coastal US south
- slightly raised in RP and similar accents: [ɒ̝] to [ɔ̞]
- unrounded to [ɑ] in the English south-west and in southern Irish English
- also unrounded to [ɑ], and then often advanced to [ɑ̟] or even [ɐ], in most words in GA and in most of the US south
- further centralized to [a] in New York City (and possibly diphthongized) and in the north central area of the USA.

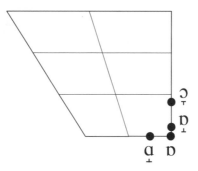

Figure 7.12   The vowel of *cot*

> Attempt the pronunciation of *cot* with each of the vowels [ɒ], [ɑ] and [ɔ], to get a flavour of the various English accents.

English has two vowels that can be construed as particularly lax pronunciations of [i] and [u]

The next two vowels we will consider are not cardinal vowels, primary or secondary. Instead, they can be construed as particularly lax pronunciations of [i] and [u], as we shall explain.

The front lax vowel occurs in such words as *hit* or *lick*. If you compare these words with their close phonetic correlates *heat* and *leek*, you will notice that the vowel in *heat* involves considerable tensing of the vocal apparatus, in a way that the vowel in *hit* or *lick* obviously does not. This tensing is often thought to go hand in hand with an advancement of the root of the tongue, captured by a positive specification of the distinctive feature [±ATR] introduced in the preceding chapter. According to this interpretation, the forward movement of the root of the tongue would be present in the [i] of *heat* and *leek*, and absent from [ɪ], its lax counterpart in *hit* or *lick*. Laxing and lack of tongue root advancement result in a certain degree of lowering relative to [i], and also in a certain amount of centralization (figure 7.13).

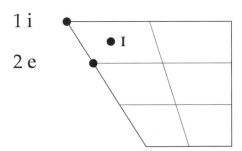

Figure 7.13   The vowel of *hit* in GA and RP

Pronounce the two vowels [i] (as in *heat*) and [ɪ] (as in *hit*) to experience the relaxation and lowering of the tongue concomitant with the retraction of the tongue root.

On simple visual inspection of figure 7.13, we could be tempted to interpret the new vowel [ɪ] as a raised, retracted version of [e], namely [ë]. This interpretation would, however, be at odds with the disparity in tensing between the two vowels, since in English [e] is tense, and [ɪ] is lax. Note also that tensing tends to push vowels towards the edges of the vowel chart, and [ɪ] is characteristically centralized. Moreover, as we show below, and again in the next chapter in more detail, [ɪ] pairs up phonologically with [i], not with [e] or [ɛ]. We conclude from all this that [ɪ] is the lax counterpart of [i]. Because [ɪ] plays a distinctive role in the vowel system of English, it is endowed with its own individual phonetic symbol, in fact two, since an alternative to [ɪ], also accepted by the IPA, is [ɪ].

The correspondences of [ɪ] across English accents are as follows:

- [ɪ] in GA and RP
- raised in Australian English: [ɪ̝]
- considerably lower and/or more retracted in popular Scottish accents
- centralized to [ɨ] in New Zealand

- centralized to [ɨ] in some contexts in South Africa, and raised to almost [i] in others
- diphthongized generally, and centralized to [ɨ], except before a velar, in the US south.

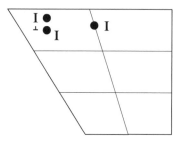

Figure 7.14 The vowel of *hit* across accents

The back counterpart of [ɪ] occurs in such words as *hood*, *put* or *look*. We will analyse it as a lax, [–ATR] version of [u], matching the relationship between [ɪ] and [i]. The vowel in *hood* and its companions is usually transcribed as [ʊ], although the symbol [ɷ] is also countenanced by the IPA. As in the contrast between [ɪ] and [i], [ʊ] is lower and more central than its tense counterpart [u].

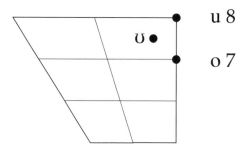

Figure 7.15 The vowel of *hood* in GA and RP

> Compare [u] as in *food* and [ʊ] as in *hood* focusing on the difference in tongue tension.

The proximity of [ʊ] to [o] in figure 7.15 is reminiscent of the proximity of [ɪ] to [e]. As in the case of the [ɪ]–[e] pair, however, this spatial closeness does not correspond to a phonetic or phonological relationship, for precisely the same reasons.

The vowel [ʊ] is missing from Scottish and Northern Irish English. Scottish English substitutes [u]/[ʉ]. In many other accents, [ʊ] is undergoing centralization, and unrounding, a pronunciation [ʊ̈] being far from uncommon nowadays (the underscripted diacritic "." stands for loss of rounding). For completeness, we now list the correspondences of [ʊ]:

- traditionally [ʊ] in RP, GA and most other accents (but not in Scottish and Northern Irish English)
- progressive tendency to centralize and unround in many accents
- some tendency to diphthongize in North America.

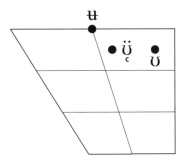

Figure 7.16   The vowel of *hood* across accents

Try pronouncing *good*. Is your vowel back and rounded or is it centralized and unrounded? If you have neither of these vowels, plot the one you do pronounce on figure 7.16.

The last vowel we shall examine in this section occurs in words like *hut*, *up* or *cuff* in GA and in Scottish English. It resembles [ʌ], the secondary vowel that corresponds to the primary vowel [ɔ]: [ʌ] is [ɔ] without the rounding. The English vowel is, however, slightly advanced *vis-à-vis* its cardinal counterpart, hence [ʌ̟]:

- advanced [ʌ] in GA and Scottish English: [ʌ̟].

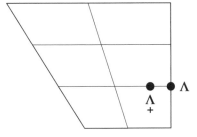

Figure 7.17   The vowel of *hut* in GA and Scottish English

As we said in chapter 5, the same pronunciation ([ʌ] or [ʌ̟]) existed in RP before the Second World War, but its position has now shifted. We examine the new RP vowel in the next section. In northern England this vowel simply does not exist, words like *hut*, *up* or *cuff* having the same vowel as *foot*: [ʊ].

5 Central Vowels

In present-day RP, and in RP-like accents, the vowel in *hut*, *up* or *cuff* corresponds to a raised central low vowel, for which we said in chapter 5 that the IPA official table provides the symbol [ɐ] (= an inverted "a").

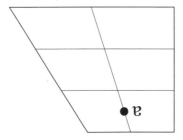

Figure 7.18   The vowel of *hut* in RP

Confusingly from a phonetic perspective, this RP sound [ɐ] is still usually transcribed with the symbol [ʌ], like its backer and higher GA and Scottish counterpart.

We now list this and other correspondents, to be added to the Scottish and GA [ʌ] or [ʌ̟] we introduced at the end of the previous section:

- a central raised low vowel [ɐ] in RP and RP-like accents
- raised to schwa [ə] in Wales
- further raised to [ɘ] in much of the American south.

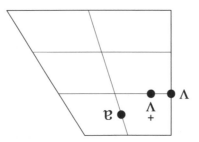

Figure 7.19   The vowel of *hut* across accents

Which vowel do you produce in *hut*?

Moving up within the central region, we enter the area of schwa, [ə]. We mentioned in chapter 5 that schwa is extremely frequent in English, representing as it does the stressless, "reduced" pronunciation of most vowels, although some stressless vowels reduce to [ɪ] or [ʊ], rather than to schwa.

Schwa is extremely frequent in English

Mention a few cases of vowel reduction to [ɪ] and [ʊ], rather than to [ə].

We now offer a small sample of English words containing schwas, with the letters that represent the phonetic schwa underlined:

<u>a</u>go   c<u>o</u>llect   t<u>e</u>leph<u>o</u>ny   at<u>o</u>m   <u>a</u>tomic   col<u>u</u>mn   hipp<u>o</u>pot<u>amus</u>

Next, we incorporate schwa into our chart of English central vowels, deliberately keeping its spatial range somewhat fuzzy.

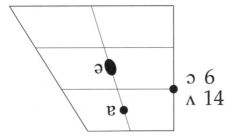

Figure 7.20   Schwa added

The realization of schwa is remarkably uniform across accents, perhaps precisely because of its loose range. However, some Scottish accents substitute [ʌ] for schwa. In rhotic accents, schwa can be "*r*-coloured": [ɚ]. The expression R-COLOURED refers to the [ɹ]-type quality superimposed on a vowel, usually achieved by curling the tip of the tongue up, in a gesture of retroflection.

The last central vowel we will present constitutes a strong version of schwa, and occurs in words like *bird* or *lurk*. This is in fact the vowel that we referred to in chapter 5 as likely to be used by English speakers for the rounded vowels [ø] and [œ] of other languages. This vowel is usually transcribed as [ɜ] when non-rhotic, and as [ɝ] when rhotic. The symbol [ɜ] used to share the centre of the vowel space with [ə] in the IPA chart. However, in the latest version of the chart the symbol [ɜ] is allocated a well-defined position, as a mid-low unround central vowel, with the mid-high central vowel space assigned to [ə].

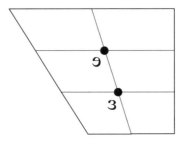

Figure 7.21 Central mid-vowels

> Practise the sound in (non-rhotic) *bird* in comparison with [ə] in e.g. *about*.

The implication that [ɜ] is a mid-low vowel seems appropriate for RP, but not necessarily for other accents. The range of correspondents of [ɜ] is in fact as follows:

- [ɜ] in RP, most RP-like accents, and eastern New England
- *r*-coloured [ɝ] in GA and other rhotic accents, Scottish excepted; also (curiously) in some non-rhotic accents
- raised to [ə] or even [ɨ] in Birmingham and Liverpool (England) and much of the southern hemisphere
- centralized and rounded in New Zealand, and possibly raised: [œ̈] to [ö]
- a diphthongized [ɜ] in traditional New York City and some US southern states (see section 8 below).

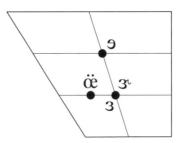

Figure 7.22 The vowel of *bird*

> Try out all these variations in *bird* to get a flavour of the range of possibilities.

It is worth noting that the lexical incidence of this vowel is severely restricted in Scottish English, many varieties of which allow practically all lax vowels to precede a final *r*, in striking contrast with most other accents of English.

We have now completed the inventory of the simple vowels of English. We have seen that many of these vowels have a tendency to diphthongize – we examine diphthongs in the next section. Despite this diphthongizing tendency, it is useful to consider some of the vowels as primarily pure, and others, still to be reviewed, as primarily diphthongal. Paradoxically, we will see that some diphthongs actually tend to be pronounced monophthongally in some accents, and some pure vowels tend to diphthongize.

At this point it will be helpful to chart all the basically pure vowels, of which there are twelve in RP and eleven in GA (also twelve if we count in the *r*-coloured schwa). We will display these systems in parallel with the cardinal vowels to make cross-comparison easier (remember that RP [ɐ] is usually (mis)transcribed as [ʌ], the IPA symbol for the unround mid-low back vowel).

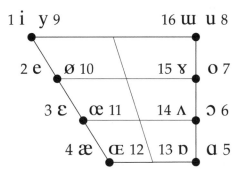

Figure 7.23A   Cardinal vowels

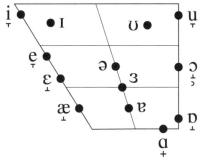

Figure 7.23B   RP pure vowels

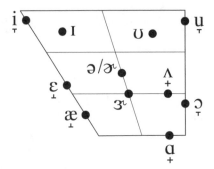

Figure 7.23C GA pure vowels

Finally in the section, we tabulate all the RP and GA vowels we have examined, against the classificatory criteria we have used (table 7.1).

Table 7.1 Parametric classification of RP and GA pure vowels

	Front		Central		Back			
					Round		Unround	
	Tense	Lax	Tense	Lax	Tense	Lax	Tense	Lax
High	i̧	ɪ			ṷ	ʊ		
Mid		e̞, ɛ̞	ɜ, ɝ	ə, ɚ	o̝, ɔ̞			ʌ̞
Low		æ̞		ɐ		ɒ̞	ɑ̞	

6 Homogeneous Diphthongs

In our discussion of "pure" vowels above we have frequently commented that some particular vowel has a tendency to diphthongize in some accent. In the remainder of the chapter we turn our attention to this type of phenomenon.

We said above that words like *late* and *coat* have the mid-high primary cardinal vowels [e] and [o] in in Scottish and Yokshire English, and to a limited extent in GA. Elsewhere, words like these have diphthongs.

> Before we describe these sounds, try to discover experimentally how the vowels in *late* and *coat* differ from the cardinal vowels nos. 2 and 7 in the standard accents.

Thus, in the majority accents the vowel in *lay* or *raid* is not a pure vowel, with a constant quality throughout, but rather a diphthongal vowel, with the sound quality changing half-way through. The phonetic tools we have at our disposal allow us to transcribe this vowel as [eɪ]. This is a vowel of non-steady realization: its first phase corresponds more or less to cardinal vowel no. 2, [e] (usually a little more open: [ẹ]), and its second phase to the now familiar vowel [ɪ]. The articulation of this complex vowel, or DIPH-THONG, in fact glides from [e] to [ɪ]. The standard transcription [eɪ] obviously suggests two independent vowels and, to this extent, it is misleading. One way around this problem involves the addition of a tie bar, thus [e͡ɪ]. However, we already know that phoneticians favour simple representations and often ignore phonemically irrelevant phonetic detail. Indeed, in the specific case of English diphthongs, the inclusion of the tie bar is the exception rather than the rule in the literature.

> The transcription [eɪ] obviously suggests two vowels and, therefore, it is slightly misleading

One obvious characteristic of the vowel [e͡ɪ], besides the non-steady nature of its sound quality, is its relative length, as you will find out if you compare the pronunciation of the vowels in such pairs as *late ~ let, raid ~ red, sale ~ sell, tames ~ Thames*, etc.

> Pronounce carefully each of these pairs, paying close attention to the differences between the two vowels in articulation and in length.

You may be inclined to think that the difference in length between [e͡ɪ] and [ɛ] inevitably follows from their difference in complexity: according to this construal, a composite vowel would inherently take longer to pronounce than a simple one. As it happens, however, English has simple vowels that are as long as complex vowels like [e͡ɪ]. One such long vowel is the low back vowel [ɑ] of *father*, which is pronounced long with a pure, steady sound in most accents: *f*[ɑː]*ther*.

> RP English has simple vowels that are as long as complex vowels

> Compare the length of [e͡ɪ] and [ɑ] by pronouncing some words containing these vowels (notice the contrast in the pronunciation of *tomato* between the US and the UK).

Paradoxically, though, [e͡ɪ] is never transcribed [e͡ɪ], presumably on the grounds that the two symbols "e", "ɪ" already take up two spaces in the line.

The range of correspondences of [e͡ɪ] is as follows:

- [e͡ɪ] in RP, in Southern England in general, and generally in GA
- [ɐɪ] in Cockney and in the southern hemisphere
- monophthongal [e] in Scottish and northern English
- monophthongal [e] ([ɛ] in a few words like *great*) in parts of the US south, rediphthongized as a centring diphthong before a consonant in some areas (see section 8 below).

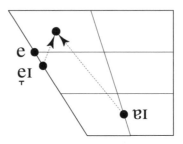

Figure 7.24   The vowel of *late*

> Is your vowel a monophthong or a diphthong? Where does your diphthong in *lay* start? Try to locate it in figure 7.24.

The diphthong corresponding to [eɪ] at the back is [oʊ]. This diphthong turns up in many accents of English in such words as *coat* or *foam* ([koʊt], [foʊm]), but GA is reported to exhibit a certain tendency to a monophthongal realization, in particular when the vowel is short ([kot]). This monophthong, identifiable with cardinal vowel no. 7, is general in Scottish English, and also in much of northern England. When diphthongal, the first phase of the diphthong is actually central in many accents. The specific range of diphthongal correspondents of this sound is as follows:

- [oʊ] or [oᵘ] in GA, particularly in long variants: *dome*, *low* (shorter variants as in *coat* can be monophthongal)
- lowered to [ɒʊ] before a final *l* in London and the southern hemisphere: *dole* [dɒʊł] (or even [dɒːł] in South Africa)
- central start in the middle Atlantic and western Pennsylvania areas of the US: [əʊ]
- unround central start in RP: [ɜʊ]
- further lowered start in London and the southern hemisphere, [ɐʊ], undergoing fronting in younger speakers.

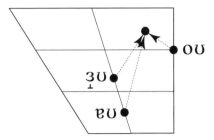

Figure 7.25 The vowel of *coat*

> What is the starting point of your vowel in *dome*? Does it dif-
> fer from that in *dole* or that in *coat*?

The high front vowel in *heat*, *seem* or *see* is also intrinsically long in most accents – in Scottish English vowels do not carry any intrinsic length differences, however.

> Pronounce *heat* and *hit* to compare the length of the vowels.
> If you have any experience of a Scottish accent, try the same
> in Scottish to see that the two vowels have identical length.

We have already said that the quality of this vowel varies from pure [iː] through [ĩi] to [ɜɪ]. The geographical distribution of the diphthongal realizations is as follows:

- tendency to diphthongize to [ĩi], particularly in longer variants (*seem*, *see*) in GA and in accents of southern England
- definitely diphthongized and lowered as far as [ɜɪ] in Australian and Cockney English.

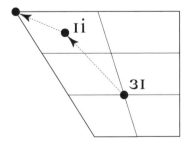

Figure 7.26 The diphthongized vowel of *heat*

Compare the pronunciation of *hate* in RP with that of *heat* in Cockney, if you have had any exposure to this accent.

The long high back vowel [uː] undergoes diphthongization under the same circumstances as its front counterpart [iː]: [ʊu], [əu] or [ɜu], hence [fʊud], [fəud] or [fɜud] for *food*. The distribution of the diphthongal realizations of this sound is as follows:

- tendency to diphthongize to [ʊu], particularly in longer variants (*mood*, *who*), in GA and in accents of southern England
- centralized, diphthongized and lowered as far as [ɜʉ] in Australian and Cockney English.

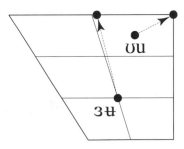

Figure 7.27   The diphthongized vowel of *food*

Compare the pronunciation of *food* with a constant tongue position ([uː]) with the diphthongal versions [ou͡], [ɜu͡], etc.

| Diphthongization, or "breaking", of long vowels is not unusual across languages |

The "breaking" of long vowels into diphthongs is not unusual across languages, as if the articulators got tired or bored of maintaining the same sound throughout and opted for change. Indeed, this is the origin of [eɪ] and other English diphthongs – English [e͡ɪ] was a monophthong [eː] at some previous stage.

Of the diphthongs we have discussed in this section, we are considering both [i͡i] and its variants, and [u͡u] and its variants, as realizations of the pure vowels [iː], [uː]. By contrast, we are considering [e͡ɪ] and [o͡u] as primarily diphthongal. The reason for this different treatment lies in the respective fate of these vowels in the more prestigious accents, contemporarily and historically: we have in fact seen that the four vowels can be realized as diphthongs or monophthongs, depending on the accent.

The diphthongs [eɪ] and [oʊ] are homogeneous in as much as both phases of the diphthong are close in articulatory position and share the lip gesture. In the next section we examine three other primary diphthongs of English, which are heterogeneous. In section 8 we will examine a final set of English diphthongs, which mainly arise as a result of contact with [ɹ].

7 Heterogeneous Diphthongs

The set of heterogeneous English diphthongs has three members, instantiated in the words *buy*, *bough* and *boy*.

A common realization of the diphthong in *buy* has a central low vowel [a], in its first phase, and a high front lax vowel [ɪ], in its closing phase, hence [aɪ]. Forms with this diphthong include *buy*, *eye*, *sigh* and *ice*. The heterogeneous nature of [aɪ] hinges on the fact that it combines a low central vowel articulation ([a]) with a high front vowel articulation ([ɪ]). The obvious question that arises is how such a divergent combination could ever have arisen. The answer has already been hinted at: vowel sounds, including vowel sounds that make up diphthongs, can and do move around the vowel space as time goes by. Thus, unlikely as it may seem, the historical source of the diphthong [aɪ] is a long vowel [iː] similar to the [iː] of *heat* in contemporary English. This vowel is attested to have lowered to [eɪ] (perhaps after a stage as [iɪ]), eventually yielding [aɪ] after centring and further lowering: all this is discussed in more detail in chapter 8 below. To make these matters clear, we now represent the evolution of [iː] into [aɪ] in the vowel chart (the numbers correspond to the stages).

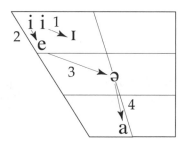

Figure 7.28   Historical evolution of [aɪ]

Test the diphthong [aɪ] for yourself.

In Canada, the vowel [a] of [aɪ] undergoes raising before a voiceless consonant: *bite* [bɜɪt]. This phenomenon is also reported for Virginia and coastal

South Carolina. A similar realization [ɜɪ] (or a lower [ɐɪ]) in all positions is typical of rural accents in southern England and in eastern New England. Curiously, the diphthong [ɜɪ] (or something very much like it) substitutes in traditional New York City speech for the more commonly pure vowel [ɜ:] of *bird* before a consonant.

We now list the correspondents of [aɪ] throughout the English-speaking world:

- [aɪ] in RP and GA
- [ɑɪ] in Cockney and much southern English urban speech, in the southern hemisphere, and in New York City
- [æɪ], sometimes monophthongized to [æ] (or even [ɛ̝]) in the north of England
- [a] generally in the American south
- [ɐɪ] before a voiceless consonant in coastal South Carolina
- [ɜɪ] in rural southern England and eastern New England, and before a voiceless consonant in Canada and Virginia
- [ɜɪ] before a voiceless consonant or a voiced stop in Scotland.

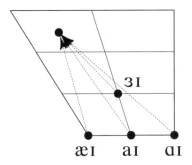

Figure 7.29 The vowel of *bite*

Is the sound you produce in *bite* a diphthong? Which of the diphthongs listed above does your diphthong most resemble?

The second heterogeneous English diphthong is [aʊ], as in *how* or *gout*, with the same first phase as [aɪ], [a], but with a high back rounded lax vowel [ʊ] as a second phase. The disparity of lip gesture between the two phases makes this diphthong more heterogeneous than [aɪ]. The source of [aʊ] mirrors the source of [aɪ], that is to say, a long high back vowel [u:] evolved into [aʊ] through the stages [ʊʊ], [oʊ] and [əʊ] (we respect the common transcription of the first phase of this diphthong as a schwa in the historical literature).

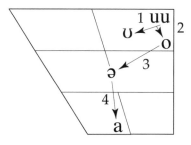

Figure 7.30 Historical evolution of [aʊ]

Try [aʊ] to feel the movement of the articulators.

The diphthong [aʊ] exhibits variation reminiscent of that of [aɪ]:

- [aʊ] in RP and GA
- [æʊ] in the US south and in popular speech in southern England, particularly in Cockney, where it can monophthongize to [æ:]
- [ɑʊ] in South African English
- [ɐʊ] in Scotland, in coastal South Carolina before a voiceless consonant, and in rural speech in general
- [ɜʊ] before a voiceless consonant in Canada and Virginia: *doubt* [dɜʊt].

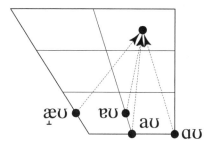

Figure 7.31 The vowel of *gout*

Where does your diphthong start? Do you experience any difference between the sounds in *lout* and *loud*?

The last of the three heterogeneous diphthongs general in English is [ɔɪ], represented in such words as *boy* or *voice*. The closing phase of this diphthong is identical to the closing phase of [aɪ]: [ɪ]. The opening phase is standardly represented as [ɔ], hence [ɔɪ]. Notice that the [ɔ] in [ɔɪ] differs considerably from the [ɔ] of RP *caught*, which we saw is significantly tenser and longer. Indeed, the [ɔ] vowel in [ɔɪ] approximates to cardinal vowel no. 6, [ɔ], to a degree substantially greater than the vowel in *caught* in many accents. While unusually uniform throughout the English-speaking world, the diphthong [ɔɪ] still exhibits some variation:

- [ɔɪ] in most accents, including GA and RP
- [ɒɪ] in parts of the south of England
- [æɪ] or [ɒɪ] in parts of Ireland and the US
- possibly [ɜɪ] in New York City, in which case it merges with the traditional [ɜɪ] of *bird* (*bird* also has [ɜɪ] in the US deep south).

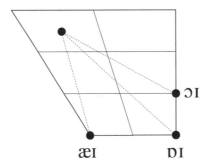

Figure 7.32   The vowel of *voice*

Find out which if any of these positions your diphthong in *boy* starts in. If it is none of these, try to plot the starting position for your own diphthong.

You can see that most variants of the diphthong [ɔɪ] straddle the vowel space from back to front, uniquely so among the five standard English diphthongs – all the other diphthongs are localized exclusively in either the front or the back area ([eɪ] vs. [oʊ], respectively) or involve a rising movement from the centre ([aɪ], [aʊ], [ɜʊ]/[ɵʊ]), at least in the standard accents.

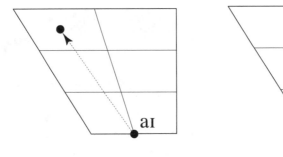

Figure 7.33   Diphthongs from the centre

The diphthong [ɔɪ] is also the only diphthong of contemporary English whose historical origin is exclusively diphthongal: *boy*, for instance, was already [bɔɪ] in Middle English, in contrast with the diphthongs in *time*, *town*, *hate* and *boat*, which at some point were all simple vowels: [iː], [uː], [aː] and [ɔː], respectively.

8 Centring Diphthongs

We shall now examine a final set of English diphthongs, in which the movement is towards the centre of the vowel space.

Consider the following words:

pier   poor
dare   door

The final *r* in the spelling of these words is purely orthographic in non-rhotic accents such as RP, which are defined by precisely this trait. The question now is: how exactly are these words pronounced in these varieties, granted that the final *r* is only orthographic?

The typical non-rhotic pronunciation of the forms in the first column above is [pɪə] and [dɛə], respectively. Two aspects of this transcription are noteworthy. First, the final sound is a schwa, [ə]. Second, the preceding vowel is lax: [ɪ], [ɛ], respectively. These two properties give a clue to the historical evolution of these sounds. In particular, before its disappearance in the eighteenth century, *r* (a trill at the time) caused diphthongization of the preceding vowel, and then laxing, so that [pir] *pier*, for instance, came to be pronounced [pɪər], and correspondingly for the other forms in question. Clearly, after the *r* went, the schwa remained the sole trace of its former presence.

The net effect of this process in RP and the other non-rhotic accents is an additional set of "centring" diphthongs, that is to say, diphthongs with an initial phase somewhat towards the edges of the vowel space and with the central vowel [ə] (often lowered as far as [ɐ] in word-final position) as a closing phase.

> Before its disappearance in the eighteenth century, *r* caused diphthongization of the preceding vowel, and then laxing

> Examine your own pronunciation of the relevant words and decide whether your accent has undergone breaking and loss of [ɹ], just breaking, or neither.

We now exhibit the four centring diphthongs exemplified at the start of the section.

> In RP there is a maximum of four centring diphthongs

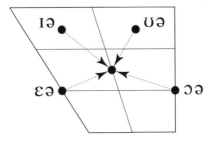

Figure 7.34   Centring diphthongs

We have already commented on the [ɪə] of *pier*. The back counterpart of [ɪə] is [ʊə], as in *poor*. In RP, forms like *door* also had a centring diphthong [ɔə] until the post-Second World War period, but are now more commonly pronounced with the long tense steady vowel of *caught*, hence [dɔ̧]. However, in other non-rhotic accents (eastern New England, New York City, US south) [ɔə] persists. In RP, the vowel of *poor*, traditionally [ʊə], as we just said, is also merging with [ɔ̧] in many speakers, hence [pɔ̧ː]. The RP tendency to monophthongize centring diphthongs extends to the front mid vowel: *dare* is more and more pronounced monophthongally as [dɛ̧ː]. By contrast, some other non-rhotic accents exhibit a greater number of centring diphthongs. For instance, in the traditional accent of New York City the vowel in *star* is [ɑə], and in that of eastern New England the vowel in *square* is [æə]. In US southern states, the front lax vowels [ɪ], [ɛ], [æ] break into [ɪə], [ɛə], [æə] in such entirely *r*-less words as *bid, bed* or *bad*, with the result that *bid* and *beard* may become homophonous. On the other hand, the RP tendency to monophthongize centring diphthongs is also present to varying degrees in other accents: for example, in New York City all centring diphthongs can become long monophthongs: [ɪː], [ɛː], [ɑː], [ɔː] and [ʊː].

> Do you produce diphthongs or monophthongs in the words *poor, door* and *square*?

Breaking and laxing before [ɹ] also took place after the set of non-centring diphthongs [aɪ], [aʊ], [eɪ], [oʊ] and [ɔɪ]. This resulted in the development of the centring TRIPHTHONGS [aɪə], [aʊə], [eɪə], [oʊə] and [ɔɪə], as in *fire, hour, layer, lower* and *coyer*, respectively. Of these, the first two ([aɪə] and [aʊə]) are considered triphthongal more often than the rest, perhaps more for reasons of morphological makeup than of phonetic realization as such. This said, it is not unusual for triphthongs to simplify in many accents, either by breaking up into a diphthong followed by a simple vowel ([aɪ-ə], etc.)

or by smoothing up the initial diphthong into a monophthong, as happens more and more in RP: *fire* [faə], *tower* [taə] or [tɑə], and so on, and similarly in the American south. A further step in this development involves the monophthongization of the resulting centring diphthong: [faː], [tɑː], etc.

Compare *higher* with *hire* and *hour* with *our*. Are these pairs homophonous? If not, what is the difference?

C h a p t e r   S u m m a r y

In this chapter we surveyed vowels in a range of major accents of English relative to the cardinal set discussed in chapter 5. Throughout the survey we indicated the divergence of pronunciations of each of the vowels that can be encountered in these accents. English boasts up to twelve steady state vowels and five systemic diphthongs, but does not overall exhibit the range of contrasts implied in the primary and secondary cardinal vowel sets. Of the simple vowels, perhaps only three can be claimed to be anywhere near their cardinal equivalents in the two main accents, RP and GA, although in no case is the English version so extreme as the cardinal. These three are [i], [u] and [ɑ]. Of the others some are raised or centralized in relation to cardinal positions, and these divergences can be made explicit with the use of diacritics. Lip rounding is only marginally contrastive in English, but an equivalent to cardinal no. 13 occurs in some accents (including RP). Some vowel pairs are distinguished in terms of relative tenseness and laxness, the phonetic manifestations of the values + and − for the phonological feature ATR, introduced in chapter 6. Laxing of a vowel leads to a certain degree of lowering and centring: [ɪ], the lax congener of [i], is in fact somewhere between cardinal no. 1 [i] and cardinal no. 2 [e]. There are, however, phonological as well as phonetic reasons for claiming [ɪ] and [ʊ] (the lax congener of [u]) to be related to [i] and [u], rather than [e] and [o]. We introduced the tense mid central vowel [ɜ], found in words like *bird* in non-rhotic accents. Many of the monophthongal vowels discussed are short, and the set of historically long vowels of the language is completed by a number of diphthongs, the result of breaking. Of the five diphthongs in which the tongue glides up to a close position two are homogeneous, that is, articulated throughout in either the front or the back area. In addition there are three heterogeneous diphthongs in which the tongue position moves across areas. Two of these originated as steady state vowels, whilst the third originated as a diphthong. We introduced the length diacritic "ː", usually added only to monophthongs.

The present maximal list of seventeen vowels (twelve steady state and five diphthongs) is augmented by the so-called centring diphthongs, the origins of which we explored. Breaking and laxing after non-centring diphthongs gave rise to centring triphthongs.

Key Questions

1 List the basic differences between RP, GA and standard Scottish English.
2 What is rhoticity?
3 What is meant by "distinctive vowel length"?
4 What are "linking" and "intrusive" /r/? Why are there two terms?
5 How do most English vowels differ from the cardinal vowels? Which variety is the exception to this?
6 What is meant by "tense" and "lax" vowels? What is their phonological feature correlate?

7 In which positions in a word do we find schwa in English? Is schwa a distinctive vowel in English?
8 What is a diphthong? Describe the articulation of a diphthong.
9 How accurate is the IPA alphabet for the transcription of English vowels?
10 What is the origin of the four centring diphthongs of English?

Further Practice

Homophones

The following data contain a number of homophones. They also contain a number of homographs (same spelling, different pronunciation). Some of the words pair both ways.

(i)   Identify and transcribe the homophones.
(ii)   Give the alternative pronunciations of the homographs, also in phonetic transcription.

pier	dear	read	bead	fair	red	reed	pear	peer	bread	breed
pair	rite	lead	fare	led	choir	right	bough	quire	rough	row
bow	dough	grown	pare	sore	doe	saw	sow	so	groan	blew
aught	blow	blue	court	ought	caught	gone	lone	done	loan	dun
soar	write	ruff	seize	fleas	fleece	seas	kernel	dew	berry	key
colonel	boy	quay	bury	due	cow	cough	shower	flower	beer	bear

Phonetic Transcription

Transcribe the following sentences into normal orthography:

ɒn ə klɪə deɪ jʊ kn si fə maɪlz
fɜst ɪmpreʃnz kaʊnt fəɹ ə lɒt
jə ðə lɑst pɜsn aɪ ɛkspɛktɪd tə si hɪə tədeɪ

ðɪ aɪdɪə ðət ðɪ ɜθ ɪs flæt ɪs toʊtli ɹɪdɪkjələs
hɪ ʤɑgz ɛvɹi mɔɹnɪŋ hwʌɹɛvɚ ðə wɛðɚ
aɪl hæf tə get sʌmwʌn ɪn tə fɪks ðə ɹuf

Put the sentences below into IPA transcription:

(i)   for your own accent
(ii)   for a standard accent you are familiar with.

That man is far more important than the prime minister
How many professors does it take to change a light bulb?
All work and no play makes Jack a dull boy
They arranged all the Christmas presents around the tree
It is a truth universally acknowledged that a single man in possession of a
    good fortune must be in want of a wife
Mr Salteena was an elderly man of 42 and was fond of asking people to stay
    with him

Sound to Spelling

Below are a number of vowel sounds. How many spellings in English
words can you find to correspond to the sounds listed?

[aɪ]   [eɪ]   [ɑː]   [ɛ]   [iː]   [aʊ]   [oʊ]   [ju]   [ɔː]   [ə]

CHAPTER EIGHT

THE TIMING TIER AND THE GREAT VOWEL SHIFT

Chapter Objectives

In this chapter you will learn about:

■ An extension of the autosegmental model.
■ Alternations which appear to be inexplicable and yet are widespread in English.
■ A way of differentiating between long and short vowels which share the same features.
■ The introduction of separate tiers to represent time and features.
■ How processes may apply at either of these levels.
■ The use of the two-tier model to offer a better analysis of affricates.
■ The story of the English Vowel Shift to offer an explanation of the seemingly inexplicable.
■ How the two-tier model helps to analyse these facts.

In previous chapters we have introduced and substantiated the autosegmental nature of phonology. In particular, we saw that the very common phenomenon of partial assimilation between segments can readily be understood if we assume that each distinctive feature is free to act independently of the other features it may be associated with: this freedom of action allows each feature to influence a neighbouring segment irrespective of whether other associated features do so. In chapter 7 we saw that vowels (English vowels in particular) can be long or short, and the question arises of how this contrast should be formalized. In the present chapter we introduce an additional, and most important, tier into our autosegmental model. This tier is made up of abstract "timing units", which associate with bundles of features to indicate their length. In particular, a short segment will be associated with one timing unit, and a long segment with two. Conversely, a single timing unit can be doubly associated with two values of a feature, as is the case with affricates. The introduction of the timing tier makes possible a reasonably transparent analysis of the English Vowel Shift, one of the most important processes affecting vowels in English. At the end of the chapter we will suggest that the timing tier constitutes the baseline which supports the remainder of the autosegmental structure.

1 A Puzzle with Affricates

In chapter 1 we introduced the affricate consonants [ʧ] and [ʤ], instantiated in the English words *church* and *judge*, respectively. We explained then that an affricate is articulated as a stop with a partial release equivalent to a fricative.

> Identify the two phases as you pronounce the affricates [ʧ] and [ʤ].

Phonologically, the question arises of whether affricates (and other complex sounds) constitute in fact one or two segments. Notice that the IPA symbols [ʧ] and [ʤ] could be interpreted either way: they correspond at the same time to one segment ([ʧ] and [ʤ], respectively) and to two segments ([t] + [ʃ] and [d] + [ʒ], respectively). The phonological evidence is also equivocal: some facts suggest that affricates are monosegmental, whereas other facts suggest that they are bisegmental.

Let us examine the evidence for monosegmentality first. English words may not start with two obstruents, setting aside the sequence **s + obstruent**, which we discuss in chapters 10 and 16. Indeed, when native speakers of English encounter such words as *tsar*, *psychology* or *pterodactyl*, with an initial cluster in the spelling, they normally simplify the cluster: [s]*ar* or [z]*ar*, [s]*ychology*, [t]*erodactyl*. The clusters [ts], [dz], [ps], [pt], etc., are, however, perfectly acceptable in many other languages: in French, for instance, there is [ps]*ychologie* 'psychology', [ps]*eudonyme* 'pseudonym', [ps]*aume* 'psalm', [pt]*érodactyle* 'pterodactyl', [pt]*olémaïque* 'ptolemaic', [dz]*ar* 'tsar', [dz]*igane* 'gypsy', [ts]*é-*[ts]*é* 'tse-tse', etc.

The simplification of these clusters in English leads us to expect that the pronunciation of word-initial [ʧ] and [ʤ] would also be problematic for English speakers.

> Can you identify the reason?

The fact that it is not problematic provides obvious support for a monosegmental analysis of these sounds. Indeed, in *The Sound Pattern of English* Chomsky and Halle analysed affricates as [−continuant] (= stop) sounds with the added feature [+delayed release]. The specification [+delayed release]

Phonologically, the question arises of whether affricates (and other complex sounds) constitute in fact one or two segments

defines the second, fricative, phase of [ʧ], [ʤ], thereby keeping these sounds distinct from the corresponding plain stops [t], [d].

> Would you say that the devoicing of [ʤ] to [ʧ] in *edge trimmer* we discussed in chapter 2 also supports the analysis of [ʤ] as a single segment?

There are other facts that suggest that [ʧ] and [ʤ] are bisegmental, however. We just mentioned that word-initial *sC-* clusters *are* allowed in English. However, *s* + **affricate** clusters are not: *[sʧ], *[sʤ]. Similarly, English words can begin with a single obstruent followed by the liquids [l] and [r], with certain restrictions which we will discuss in chapter 10: think, for instance, of *pride, plate, trip, crate, clear*, with stops, and *fry, fly, thrive, slit, shrink*, with fricatives. **Affricate + liquid** clusters are, however, never found: **chroke*, for instance, is not possible. These two gaps in the distribution of segments would obviously follow from an analysis of affricates as two segments.

> Explain in what way the two distributional gaps in question would follow from a bisegmental analysis of affricates

Additional evidence for a bisegmental analysis of affricates comes from the choice of plural and past tense allomorphs. An ALLOMORPH is a contextual variant of a morpheme – the term is coined in the mould of "allophone", which, as we explained in chapter 2, designates the variants of a phoneme. A noun like *match* forms its plural with the same allomorph as forms ending in plain [ʃ] (*match*[ɪz], *bush*[ɪz]). Similarly, verbs ending in [ʧ] and in [ʃ] select the same past tense allomorph (*match*[t], *mash*[t]), different from the allomorph selected by forms ending in a non-continuant coronal like *pat* and *pad* (*patt*[ɪd], *padd*[ɪd]). *Pat* and *pad* also select the short allomorph in the third person singular (*pat*[s], *pad*[z]). All this again falls into place under the analysis of the affricates as [t] + [ʃ] and [d] + [ʒ], respectively.

> Explain how the bisegmental analysis of affricates accounts for the data we have just discussed.

In order to break the stalemate between the monosegmental and the bisegmental interpretations of [ʧ] and [ʤ], we need to enrich our formal apparatus, in the manner that we shall explain in the next section.

2 The Timing Tier

The machinery in question involves the autosegmentalization of segment length. We shall develop this formalism in connection with vowels first, before returning to the issue of affricates.

We have been marking long vowels with the diacritic ":", which suggests a doubling of the length of the segment it modifies. In the pair [æ], [æː], therefore, [æ] stands for the shorter vowel and [æː] for the longer vowel.

As we explained in chapter 5, the addition of diacritics to phonetic symbols denotes a difference in the sound represented equivalent to the use of an independent symbol: [i̦], for instance, can in principle be construed as being as different from [i] as [i] is from [ɪ].

> Explain the exact differences between the segments in these two pairs.

Following this logic, the members of the pair [æ], [æː] would not stand in any closer relationship than the members of pairs like [æ] and [ɒ], or [æ] and [y]. This conclusion is, however, patently wrong, because [æ], [ɒ] and [y] are vowel sounds of different quality, whereas the pair [æ], [æː] contains one and the same vowel sound, albeit with two different lengths.

> Demonstrate the accuracy of this statement using the relevant distinctive features introduced in chapter 6.

In order to achieve the correct result, we shall enlist the help of the autosegmental formalism. You will recall that this formalism allows us to separate out (conceptually, functionally and graphically) the various elements that make up a sound we perceive as a unit: our description of English nasal assimilation in chapter 4, and of Turkish vowel harmony and English and German vowel fronting in chapter 6, showed how individual features can (and do) change association loyalties without affecting other features with which they are also associated at some level. We shall now extend the autosegmental approach to the formal expression of segmental length.

Segmental length is a matter of timing: when we say that [æː] is twice as long as [æ], we are simply saying that [æː] takes twice the time to say as [æ]. Suppose then that we create a special autosegmental unit of timing, which we shall write as "X", in line with standard practice. The difference between [æː] and [æ] will now be represented as in (1):

We create a special autosegmental unit of timing, which we write as "X"

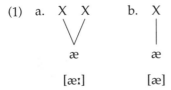

(1) a. X X   b. X

æ   æ

[æː]   [æ]

The interpretation of these diagrams is straightforward. Formally, in (1a) the vowel is associated with two timing units, whereas in (1b) precisely the same segment is only associated with one timing unit. The suggestion is, of course, that the delivery of the segment in (1a) should take twice as long as the delivery of the segment in (1b). This statement is correct, provided we replace "delivery" with "abstract" or "intended" timing, since in real life the actual delivery of sounds can be (and often is) affected by non-linguistic factors.

> Can you think of one or two such factors? How come these factors do not affect abstract timing?

Chomsky draws a distinction between "performance" and "competence"

This mismatch motivates the distinction forcefully drawn by Chomsky between "performance", that is, language in the real world, and "competence", that is, the language system that underlies performance, and which must be assumed to be permanently present in the brain, in some form. In line with this, the Xs that make up the "timing tier" need to be construed as units of phonological (and thus abstract) timing, and are not intended to correspond to actual phonetic measurements. The expression TIMING TIER we have just used refers of course to the tier made up of such Xs.

The Xs in the TIMING TIER are units of phonological (and thus abstract) timing

Applying this formalism to some real data, consider the English contrasts between long and short vowels in such pairs as *beat* ~ *bit*, or *boot* ~ *put*. These contrasts can be formalized straightforwardly by means of the timing tier, as follows:

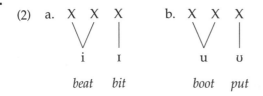

(2) a. X X X   b. X X X

i   ɪ   u   ʊ

beat *bit*   *boot* *put*

Notice that these configurations provide an unambiguous representation of the two component parts of these or any other vowels: their quantity and their quality. In particular, the first member of each pair is shown to be both long, as expressed by the two Xs in the timing tier, and tense, as expressed by the symbols "i", "u" in the melody tier – MELODY is a generic label referring to quality, that is, phonetic substance, as against quantity, that is, length. The second member of (2a) and (2b), on the other hand, is short (it only carries one X) and lax (cf. "ɪ", "ʊ"). The independence of these two aspects of a single sound is confirmed when we consider the pronunciation of pairs of words like *cart* and *cat* in Yorkshire accents where there is no [æ] ~ [ɑ] contrast:

> The label MELODY refers to quality, that is, phonetic substance, as against quantity, that is, length

(3)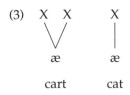

cart   cat

How might the vowels of *cart* and *cat* be represented in RP and other accents of English?

We can now return to affricates. The introduction of the timing tier predicts the possibility of the mirror-image relationship between timing elements and melody elements, as represented in (4):

(4)

The schema in (4) implies a timing of a single segment, but an internal composition of two melodies – precisely the configuration we will give to the affricates [ʧ] and [ʤ]:

(5)   X   X
     /\   /\
    t ʃ   d ʒ

The configurations in (5) capture the fact that affricates are simultaneously monosegmental, with a single X slot, and bisegmental, since they involve a dual sequential articulation. Each of the two melodies of this sequence will of course obey its own "phonotactic constraints": PHONOTACTIC CONSTRAINTS are the restrictions on the distribution of sound sequences in the words of any given language (we return to this matter in chapters 9 and 10 below).

> PHONOTACTIC CONSTRAINTS are the restrictions on the distribution of sound sequences in the words of any given language

3 A Strange Set of Vowel Alternations in English

In chapter 6 we examined the fronting processes involved in some German and English plurals (Br[uː]der 'brother' vs. Br[yː]der 'brothers', and g[uː]se vs. g[iː]se, respectively), and attributed them to the presence of a floating autosegment [–back] in the lexical representation of the plural suffix. In the same chapter, we showed that the vowels of each Turkish word normally exhibit a uniform specification for the feature [±back].

These processes are very natural: they simply involve the spreading of a certain feature value to neighbouring segments, as admirably captured by the autosegmental formalism. Consider now the following pairs of English words:

(6)   divine   divinity
      serene   serenity
      sane   sanity

Think carefully about the relationship between these pairs of words. Jot down the vowels which alternate in each of the pairs.

Each of the pairs in (6) consists of an adjective and a noun derived from the adjective by the addition of the suffix -ity. Both members of each pair have stress on the same orthographic vowel, emboldened in (6) (stress will be discussed in chapters 11 to 13). Despite the constant spelling, these vowels alternate phonetically according to the following patterns:

(7)   [aɪ]   ∼   [ɪ]
      [iː]   ∼   [ɛ]
      [eɪ]   ∼   [æ]

Two things are noteworthy here. First, the length of the vowels in each column is uniform: in the first column the vowels are long, and in the second column short (English diphthongal vowels are, of course, intrinsically long; the extra length of [iː] is represented by the appropriate diacritic). An alternation based purely on length is very natural:

An alternation based purely on length is very natural

(8)   [iː]   ∼   [i]
      [eː]   ∼   [e]
      [æː]   ∼   [æ]

Clearly, though, the English alternations in (7) do not only involve length. Another example of a natural melodic alternation is the above-mentioned vowel fronting of German, repeated in (9), where the symbol [ʏ] represents the [−ATR] counterpart of [y]:

(9) [u] ~ [y]
     [ʊ] ~ [ʏ]
     [o] ~ [ø]
     [ɔ] ~ [œ]

> Say in what way the alternation in (9) is natural.

By contrast, the English alternations in (7) are bizarre in the extreme. This bizarreness may lead us to expect such alternations to be relegated to a marginal and restricted set of words, along the lines of the *goose ~ geese* set. However, the pairs in question, further illustrated in (10), run well into their hundreds:

Alternations like *div*[aɪ]*n ~ div*[ɪ]*nity* are bizarre in the extreme

(10) severe   severity   inspire   inspiration
      fertile   fertility   profane   profanity
      deprave   depravity   impede   impediment
      vain   vanity   incline   inclination
      wise   wisdom   brief   brevity
      invite   invitation   recite   recitation

> Can you think of a few more such pairs?

The situation we are describing obviously poses a considerable challenge to the phonologist, whose working assumption of necessity is that the sound patterns of natural languages are principled, rather than random. We will meet this challenge in the remainder of the chapter, providing additional evidence for the timing tier along the way.

> Comment on the import of the expression "of necessity" we have just used with reference to the phonologist's working assumption.

4 Short ~ Long Vowel Alternations

One puzzling aspect of the *divine ~ divinity, serene ~ serenity* and *sane ~ sanity* pairs in (6) is the constant spelling of the phonetically alternating vowels: *i, e* and *a*, respectively.

We know from previous chapters that the relationship between sound and spelling in English is often fairly remote, for historical reasons. In particular, English spelling was reasonably close to the pronunciation until the fifteenth century, but many English sounds have undergone considerable evolution since. However, the spelling has typically remained unchanged, especially after the invention of printing towards the end of that century, for the obvious complementary reasons of printers' inertia and readers' habit. This means that some current spellings reflect more the pronunciation of English before that time than in our time. We will now see that this historical dimension sheds crucial light on why the phonetically alternating vowels in (6) have the invariant spellings *i, e* and *a*.

At the time we are talking about, the alternations in question exclusively involved length, as we illustrate in (11). The sound originally corresponding to the final *e* in the spelling had already been lost then, and so we parenthesize it to avoid confusion:

> **English spelling was reasonably close to the pronunciation until the fifteenth century**

> **In the fifteenth century the alternation between *divine* and *divinity* exclusively involved vowel length**

(11)   *div*[iː]*n(e)*   *div*[i]*nity*
       ser[eː]*n(e)*   *ser*[e]*nity*
       s[æː]*n(e)*   *s*[æ]*nity*

All the relevant vowels in (11) have the structural representation in (12), where [–cons] abbreviates [–consonantal], which of course formalizes vowelhood. Notice, importantly, that the contrast between the two columns is carried by the timing tier, since the melody is constant:

(12)

Can you suggest in what ways one of the structures in (12) might be derived from the other?

Now, the natural assumption is that *divine* and *divinity* share the morpheme *divin*, *serene* and *serenity* share the morpheme *seren*, *sane* and *sanity* share the morpheme *san*, and so on. Therefore, we must decide which of the two configurations in (12) is included in the lexical entry of the respective forms:

the non-basic configuration will be derived from the basic one by rule. The two alternatives we have available are as follows:

(13)   a. $X \quad \rightarrow \quad X \quad X$ b. $X \quad X \quad \rightarrow \quad X$

       [−cons]   [−cons]   [−cons]   [−cons]

In a., a short vowel becomes long, while in b. the opposite process takes place.

The scope of the rule in (13a) will need to be restricted to word-final position: we want the rule to lengthen the /i/ in *divin(e)*, but not in *divinity*, where it is followed by the suffix *-ity*. This approach produces the desired results in the alternating vowels:

(14)   a.   *div*/i/*n(e)* → *div*[iː]*n(e)*   by rule (13a)
     b.   *div*/i/*nity* = *div*[i]*nity*   rule (13a) not applicable

Once this procedure is in place, however, the last vowel in forms like *trim*, *pin*, *acid* (cf. *acidity*) and very many others will also lengthen, in defiance of the facts:

(15)   *tr*/i/*m* → **tr*[iː]*m*
     p/i/*n* → **p*[iː]*n*
     ac/i/*d* → **ac*[iː]*d*

> Say exactly why this lengthening takes place.

We could of course mark these forms as exceptions to rule (13a): indeed, phonological rules often do have exceptions, a fact of life we must simply accept. Countenancing exceptions by the thousand, however, clearly borders on the perverse.

> Think of other examples that would be wrongly captured by rule (13a).

Countenancing exceptions by the thousand borders on the perverse

This problematic result is avoided if we adopt (13b) as the rule responsible for the alternations. On this analysis, the lexical form will contain the long vowel, /iː/ in the current example. The short alternant [i] will now be derived by (13b) in forms where /iː/ is followed by at least two other vowels, as indeed is the case in (10) above (we return to the issue of vowel shortening in chapters 15 and 18):

(16) div/iː/$nity \rightarrow div$[i]$nity$ by rule (13b)
div/iː/$n(e) = div$[iː]$n(e)$ rule (13b) not applicable

This new procedure works as well as the procedure in (13a) in cases where there is an alternation. In addition, it circumvents the undesirable effects of (13a) on *trim, pin* and similar non-alternating forms, which simply fail to meet the environment of (13b), and therefore will remain unchanged. It is of course possible in principle that this positive result may be offset by some negative development elsewhere, but this does not seem to be the case here.

5 The Great Vowel Shift

Our account of the alternation between long and short vowels affecting a sizeable set of English forms crucially relies on the availability of the timing tier. We illustrate the alternation again in (17):

(17)

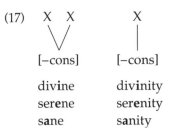

divine	divinity
serene	serenity
sane	sanity

The qualities of the related vowels in Modern English are of course significantly different from their counterparts in Middle English, that is, in the English that resulted from the mixture of the purely germanic Old English with the Norman French of the conquerors, and which towards the end of the fifteenth century became Modern English. Indeed, we deliberately chose to go back to a time when the alternation only involved length in order to shed some light on the apparently capricious state of affairs found in Modern English, repeated in (18) as a reminder:

(18) Modern English vowel alternations:
div[aɪ]ne div[ɪ]$nity$
ser[iː]ne ser[ɛ]$nity$
s[eɪ]ne s[æ]$nity$

The problem with the modern English situation is that the long vowels [aɪ], [iː], [eɪ] do not correlate phonetically with their predecessors [iː], [eː], [æː], respectively, in any obvious way – by contrast, the short vowels have only undergone laxing, a minimal and highly natural change: [ɪ], [ɛ], [æ], respectively. The solution to the puzzle posed by the quality of the long vowels can again be found in the history of the language. In particular, the Middle English long vowels [iː], [eː], [ɛː] and [æː] (and correspondingly for the back vowels, although the situation is more complex with the back set) underwent a series of changes which ultimately led to their modern incarnations [aɪ], [iː], [eɪ]. If such processes are followed step by step, the motivation for each individual change becomes apparent.

The reconstruction that we are about to present is based on history, but we have divided up historical stages where we deemed it necessary for maintaining the clarity of the exposition. We shall start the discussion with a display of the relevant set of the long vowels in Middle English:

> If the change from the Middle English long vowels [iː], [eː], [ɛː] and [aː] to their modern incarnations [aɪ], [iː], [eɪ] is examined step by step, the motivation for each individual change becomes apparent

(19) [iː] *divine*
     [eː] *serene*
     [ɛː] *meat*
     [æː] *sane*

The series of changes which eventually yielded [aɪ], [iː] and [eɪ] are known collectively as the GREAT VOWEL SHIFT. The first stage of the Great Vowel Shift involved the diphthongization of [iː] into [eɪ]. This process took place in two steps. In the first step, the second timing slot of [iː] dissimilated in tenseness from the the the first element [i]:

(20) iː → iɪ   *div*[iː]*n(e)* → *div*[iɪ]*n(e)*

The autosegmental formalization in (21) brings out the exclusively segmental nature of the process. Notice in particular that the number of timing slots is not altered:

(21)

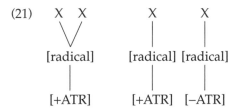

This formalization makes it obvious that the process involves melodic breaking, or diphthongization, a tendency which is still active in various contexts in Modern English, as we saw in chapter 7.

Jog your memory on some of the ongoing processes of diphthongization.

The second step in the process of diphthongization of [iː] into [eɪ] involved the lowering by one degree of the melody associated with the first timing slot of [ɪɪ]:

(22) ɪɪ → eɪ   *div*[ɪɪ]*n(e)* → *div*[eɪ]*n(e)*   *divine*

The result of this process in the set of English vowels at the time is as follows:

(23) [eɪ]   *divine*
       [eː]   *serene*
       [ɛː]   *meat*
       [æː]   *sane*

Notice that the system no longer has a high vowel [iː]. On the other hand, there is considerable phonetic proximity between the relevant vowels of *divine* and *serene*, [eɪ] and [eː], respectively. The distance between these two vowels was increased as [eː] raised to [iː]:

(24) eː → iː   *ser*[eː]*n(e)* → *ser*[iː]*n(e)*   *serene*

We now have the system in (25):

(25) [eɪ]   *divine*
       [iː]   *serene*
       [ɛː]   *meat*
       [æː]   *sane*

There is of course no [eː] in this system. This gap was filled as [ɛː] raised to [eː]:

(26) ɛ → eː   *m*[ɛː]*t* → *m*[eː]*t*   *meat*

The system is now as in (27):

(27) [eɪ]   *divine*
       [iː]   *serene*
       [eː]   *meat*
       [æː]   *sane*

In this system there is no [ɛː], a gap filled as [æː] raised:

(28) æː → ɛː   *s*[æː]*n(e)* → *s*[ɛː]*n(e)*   *sane*

The sum total of the changes we have considered led to the system in (29):

(29) [eɪ]   *divine*
      [iː]   *serene*
      [eː]   *meat*
      [ɛː]   *sane*

We offer a summary of the various changes so far in (30):

(30) Input   iɪ   *div*[iɪ]*n(e)*,
               eː ɛː æː   *ser*[eː]*n(e)*, *m*[ɛː]*t*, *s*[æː]*n(e)*
       Output eɪ   *div*[eɪ]*n(e)*,
               iː eː ɛː   *ser*[iː]*n(e)*, *m*[eː]*t*, *s*[ɛː]*n(e)*

Notice that the process involves a one-degree raising of all the vowels that remained long. In turn, the first member of the diphthong [iɪ], not being able to rise any higher, lowered instead, also by one degree. The chain of raisings iː ← eː ← æː was apparently triggered by the lowering of [i(ɪ)] to [e(ɪ)] – it is as if the vacuum thus left in the [i] slot had had a suction effect, dragging up all the remaining vowels by one degree. Appropriately, this type of chain reaction is referred to as a "drag chain" (also "pull chain").

The system in (29) is still not quite that of Modern English, and we must now examine the remaining changes.

The diphthong [eɪ] (remember, originally from Middle English [iː]) first centralized to [əɪ] (thus transcribed with a schwa in the historical literature), and eventually lowered to its Modern English position [aɪ]:

(31) eɪ → əɪ → aɪ   *div*[eɪ]*n(e)* → *div*[əɪ]*ne* → *div*[aɪ]*n(e)*

In turn, [eː] raised to [iː], with the concomitant merging of the *meat* and *serene* vowels:

(32) eː → iː   *m*[eː]*t* → *m*[iː]*t*   *meat*

The slot left vacant by [eː] was occupied by [ɛː] (from Middle English [æː]) through raising:

(33) ɛː → eː   *s*[ɛː]*n(e)* → *s*[eː]*n(e)*   *sane*

Finally, this long [eː] diphthongized to [eɪ]:

(34) eː → eɪ   *s*[eː]*n(e)* → *s*[eɪ]*n(e)*   *sane*

In (35) we display all the stages of the Great Vowel Shift, with the changes at each stage emboldened and boxed in:

(35)   *divine   serene   meat   sane*

iː	eː	ɛː	æː	Stage 0
iɪ	eː	ɛː	æː	Stage 1a
eɪ	eː	ɛː	æː	Stage 1b
eɪ	iː	eː	ɛː	Stage 2
əɪ	iː	eː	ɛː	Stage 3
əɪ	iː	iː	eː	Stage 4
aɪ	iː	iː	eː	Stage 5
aɪ	iː	iː	eɪ	Stage 6

As would be expected from a historical sequence of events, not all these changes have taken place in all English-speaking areas. This failure is of course an important source of difference between accents. We hope that our exposition has brought out the considerable degree of phonetic naturalness of each of the steps in the Great Vowel Shift. This naturalness is obviously obscured in the final output, which effectively compresses the chain, hence the puzzling nature of the vowel alternations in Modern English. Importantly for us here, the processes we have examined provide strong confirmation of the autonomy of the timing tier in relation to the melodies: the alternation in length is quite independent of the changes in the melodies.

6   The Synchronic Reflex of the GVS. Vowel Primes and Vowel Processes

The slightly idealized historical account of the Great Vowel Shift we presented in the previous section attempts to make sense of the outcome of the shift, which permeates the contemporary phonology of English: cf. the samples in (6) and (10) above. We must now come up with a formalism to capture these contemporary alternations. We will operate on the crucial assumption that the lexical representations have not changed from Middle to Modern English. This assumption is argued for in *SPE* and is accepted by many.

The three rules in (36) account for the three changes in height that underlie the three alternations, provided that the rules apply simultaneously:

(36)   a.   [−high]   →   [+high]/$\left[\underline{\hspace{1cm}} \atop -\text{low} \right]$ e → i   *serene*

b.   [+low]   →   [−low]/$\left[\underline{\hspace{1cm}} \atop -\text{high} \right]$ a → e   *sane*

c.   [+high]   →   [+low]   i → a   *divine*

The problem with these rules is that they state the changes in a piecemeal fashion, despite their obvious structural unity. An autosegmental version of these rules will not improve matters.

Verify this assertion by writing an autosegmental version of the rules in (36).

This failure could be interpreted as an indictment of the standard binary approach to features. One proposal of some interest designed to overcome problems of this kind formalizes the whole range of vowels as the product of the three basic vowel sounds [a], [u], [i], the most natural set of vowels: [a], [u], [i] are the quantum vowels, as we explained in chapter 5.

One proposal of some interest formalizes the whole range of vowels as the product of the three basic vowel sounds [a], [u], [i]

Why do we say that [a], [u], [i] are the "most natural" vowels?

The alternative approach in question replaces the features of the standard theory with the three basic vowels as undecomposable phonological units. Let us represent these three vowel primitives with the symbols <a>, <i> and <u> – we are maintaining the convention that symbols in square brackets represent sound, and introducing the ad hoc, but crucially different, notation of angled brackets for the three vowel primitives. In isolation, these three vowel primitives yield the vowels [a], [i] and [u] directly. So far, therefore, nothing very spectacular has been achieved.

Let us now turn to the mid vowels, and to secondary vowels like the rounded front vowels and the back unrounded vowels. Under the vowel-primitive approach, these objects will have the representations in (37):

(37)   [e]   [ɛ]   [o]   [ɔ]   [y]   [ɯ]   [ø]   [ɤ]   etc.
       <i>   <a>   <u>   <a>   <i>   <u>   <i>   <u>
        | | | | | | | |
       <a>   <i>   <a>   <u>   <u>   <i>   <a>   <a>
                                                 | |
                                                <u>   <i>

The representations in (37) bring out the two essential components of the approach: (i) all vowels are built out of the three quantum vowels, whether by themselves or in combination with each other; (ii) such combinations crucially involve a hierarchization of the primitives, such that [e] results from the dominance of <i> over <a>, [ɛ] from the dominance of <a> over <i>, and so on – the notational expression of dominance is, obviously, vertical precedence. The not infrequent interpretation of cardinal vowel [y] as [ĩu] by untrained English speakers to which we referred in chapter 5 above could of course be taken as evidence for the vowel-prime analysis we are presenting.

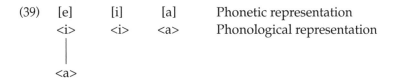

Explain how the interpretation of [y] as [ĩu] supports the vowel-prime analysis.

Let us now analyse the vowel changes which make up the Great Vowel Shift in this framework. The structure of the vowel melodies that are input to the Great Vowel Shift will be as in (38):

(38)   [a]   [e]   [i]   Phonetic representation
        <a>   <i>   <i>   Phonological representation
                    |
                   <a>

After the shift, the respective composition of these vowels will be as in (39):

(39)   [e]   [i]   [a]   Phonetic representation
        <i>   <i>   <a>   Phonological representation
         |
        <a>

This alternative formalism does not in fact make the process any clearer. Consider first the raising of the mid vowel [e] to [i]. The formalization of this process as the loss of <a> from the representation of [e] is appealing, and arguably does shed light on the event. It will therefore not be unreasonable to expect an equivalent operation in the raising of [a] to [e]. Here, however, the formalism forces us to insert the element <i> into the bare input representation <a>, at the same time demoting this original <a> in the dominance ranking to prevent the formation of the mid-low vowel [ɛ]. Finally, the mutation of [i] to [a] requires the brute force substitution of <a> for <i>. In the end, thus, no unified pattern emerges, and the approach is not particularly well supported by these data. We will consider a related proposal for the analysis of vowels in chapter 17.

7 The *SPE* Account

We now offer a summary of the ingenious pre-autosegmental formalization of the Great Vowel Shift advanced by Chomsky and Halle in *The Sound Pattern of English*. To keep the exposition simple, we shall adapt Chomsky and Halle's rule to the set of front vowels we have been discussing.

Chomsky and Halle split the process of vowel shift into two parts. In the first part, the value of the feature [±high] is inverted in non-low vowels:

Chomsky and Halle split the process of vowel shift into two parts

$$(40) \quad [\alpha high] \quad \rightarrow \quad [-\alpha high] / \begin{bmatrix} \underline{\qquad} \\ -cons \\ -low \end{bmatrix}$$

> Have a go at interpreting this rule before you read the explanation we provide in the text.

Let us dissect rule (40) to ensure full understanding. The restriction of the scope of the rule to non-low vowels is appropriately formalized by the inclusion in the environment of the specifications [−consonantal] (= vowels) and [−low] ([−consonantal, −low] = non-low vowels, namely, [i] and [e]). The process these vowels undergo involves the inversion of the value for [±high]: an input [αhigh] becomes [−αhigh] in the output. By convention, the value of each GREEK LETTER VARIABLE (α, β, γ, etc.) is arbitrarily set as + or −, independently for each variable. Accordingly, if we interpret the α in the input of rule (40) as + (thus defining the vowel [i] in our present context), we must also interpret α as + in the output. Consequently, the rule will express the change from [+high] [i] to [−high] [e]: $-\alpha = -$, if $\alpha = +$. On the other hand, if we interpret α as −, rule (40) will change [−high] [e] to [+high] [i]: $-\alpha = +$, if $\alpha = -$. All this is of course in accordance with the ordinary rules of algebra and logic.

The value of each GREEK LETTER VARIABLE (α, β, γ, etc.) is arbitrarily set as + or −, independently for each variable

> Explain in what way these results accord with the principles of algebra and logic.

The overall effect of rule (40) will be an interchanging of /i/ and /e/, precisely as desired:

$$(41) \quad \begin{array}{llll} /i/ & \rightarrow & e & div/\textbf{i:}/ne \rightarrow div[\textbf{e:}]ne \\ /e/ & \rightarrow & i & ser/\textbf{e:}/ne \rightarrow ser[\textbf{i:}]ne \end{array}$$

> Work through the unified rule in (40) again, interpreting α first as + and then as −, to make sure you follow the procedure.

The second part of Chomsky and Halle's Vowel Shift rule inverts the value for [±low] in non-high vowels:

(42) $[\beta low]$ → $[-\beta low]/$ $\begin{bmatrix} \underline{\hspace{2em}} \\ -cons \\ -high \end{bmatrix}$

> Now work through rule (42), interpreting β as we did α in rule (40).

The mechanics of rule (42) parallel those of rule (40), with the appropriate substitutions of the affected and contextual features. Notice the crucial use of a different Greek letter variable, [αhigh] in rule (40) and [βlow] in rule (42), to encode the independence of the respective values. The effect of rule (42) will be the exchange of /e/ and /æ/:

(43) /e/ → æ   *div*[eː]*ne* → *div*[æː]*ne*
      /æ/ → e   *s*/**æː**/*ne* → *s*[eː]*ne*

At the moment, we have two rules formalizing the vowel shift process: (40) and (42). However, these two rules can be reduced to a single rule by factoring out [−consonantal] as the common input, as in (44):

(44)

$[-cons]$ → $\begin{Bmatrix} [-\alpha high] \ / \begin{bmatrix} \underline{\hspace{2em}} \\ \alpha high \\ -low \end{bmatrix} \\ [-\beta low] \ / \begin{bmatrix} \underline{\hspace{2em}} \\ \beta low \\ -high \end{bmatrix} \end{Bmatrix}$ Branch a. = (40)

Branch b. = (42)

BRACES signal participation in a single rule

The BRACES enclosing the two branches signal participation in a single rule. Crucially, the motivation for the unification goes beyond notational expediency: it relates to the fact that the two processes in question take place in strict succession in the order given, with no other rule intervening between them, as could happen, in principle, if each process were formalized independently.

> Explain carefully, either in prose or by means of some formal apparatus, why we don't want any rule to intervene.

We wind up the section with a summary of the effects of the two branches of rule (44), ordered in strict succession:

(45)   i

$$\downarrow\ \uparrow \qquad \text{Branch a. (cf. rule (40))}$$

e

e

$$\downarrow\ \uparrow \qquad \text{Branch b. (cf. rule (42))}$$

æ

Notice that the relative success of Chomsky and Halle's formalization hinges on the breaking down of the lowering of [i] to [a] into two steps, corresponding to branches a. and b. of rule (44), respectively. The output of the first branch feeds the second branch. In this way, each step corresponds to a natural change in height: [i] → [e], and [e] → [æ], and conversely.

> Check how the rules in (44) relate to the historical stages outlined in section 5. Notice that some parts of the historical description are factored out in the rules.

The Vowel Shift rule in (44) is of course to be understood to apply only to long vowels. The availability of the timing tier allows us to formalize such length as two timing slots, without interfering with the melody.

The availability of the timing tier allows us to formalize length as two timing slots, without interfering with the melody

8 Further Repercussions of the Vowel Shift

The Great Vowel Shift has interesting repercussions in unexpected areas of the English vocabulary, and we shall now mention some of these briefly.

In chapter 6 we discussed the vowel fronting that occurs in a small handful of English plurals: *goose* → *geese*, *tooth* → *teeth* (also *foot* → *feet*, with additional laxing of [u] to [ʊ] in the singular). Now consider the following additional plural alternations:

The Great Vowel Shift has interesting repercussions in unexpected areas of the English vocabulary

(46) mouse [maʊs]   mice [maɪs]
      louse [laʊs]   lice [laɪs]

The alternations in (46) involve the weak element of the diphthong, and are therefore strange from a phonetic perspective. When the historical evolution of the alternations is investigated, however, they are seen to be essentially reducible to the same analysis as *goose* ~ *geese*, etc.

> In the light of what you know about the vowel shift, explain why these alternations are essentially part of the same process as goose ~ geese.

The historical antecedent of [aɪ] was [iː], and the historical antecedent of [aʊ], [uː]. This means that in Old English the first stage of the plural process in (46) must have involved the fronting of the singular vowels by the plural suffix *-i*, the very process that we saw in chapter 6 affecting *goose* ~ *geese*, etc.:

(47)   muːs+i   →   myːsi

Rounded front vowels obviously underwent unrounding, the plural suffix *-i* disappearing also at some point:

(48)   myːsi   →   miːs

We now have the contrasting forms *m*[uː]*s* (singular) and *m*[iː]*s* (plural). These forms then underwent vowel shift, hence their respective modern counterparts *m*[aʊ]*s* and *m*[aɪ]*s*, all in the expected manner.

> Why are goose and geese not pronounced g[aʊ]se and g[aɪ]se, respectively? Hint: look at the spelling (you can check section 5 in chapter 6 if the answer still does not come easily). Why do we bother to ask the question in the first place?

A further set of alternations involving Vowel Shift concerns a set of so-called STRONG VERBS, where the expression "strong" refers to a vowel alternation in the stem which contrasts with the more common inflectional realization of past tenses (cf. *fine* → *fined*, *found* → *founded*):

(49)   find   [faɪnd]   found   [faʊnd]
       bind   [baɪnd]   bound   [baʊnd]
       wind   [waɪnd]   wound   [waʊnd]
       grind   [graɪnd]   ground   [graʊnd]

The interest of this group lies in the apparent reversal of the direction of the backness shift: compare *mouse* → *mice* with *find* → *found*.

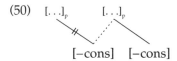

Historically, the alternation in (49) also arose from the spreading of vowel features from the suffix to the stem. The past tense suffix was *-on* at the time. The specified features [+back] and [+round] spread from the suffix *-on* to the stem, via association of the [. . .]$_p$ nodes of the suffix vowel to the [−consonantal] node of the stem vowel. The process is formalized in (50):

(50)   [. . .]$_p$ [. . .]$_p$

           [−cons]   [−cons]

The effect of this rule on *findon* is as in (51):

(51)

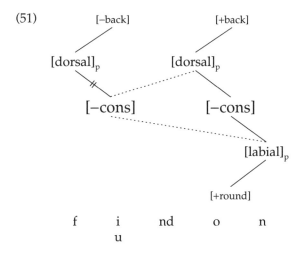

The vowels [i] (in the present) and [u] (in the past) subsequently underwent vowel shift. By then, the suffix *-on* had disappeared, and the backing of the root vowel remained as the only mark of past tense.

Synchronically, we may consider relating the process to the familiar one of plural formation: *mouse → mice = found → find*.

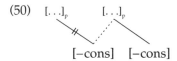

This solution obviously involves the derivation of the present from the past. From Saussure's perspective that the signifier is independent of the signified, there is, of course, no reason to assume that the form of the present is basic. However, work by another great linguist, Roman Jakobson, suggests that morphological and semantic "markedness" usually go hand in hand – MARKEDNESS is the nominalization of MARKED, a label which suggests 'less expected', 'more complex', 'less natural', and the like (see chapters 17 and 19 for further discussion). If morphological and semantic markedness go hand in hand, we would expect the semantic unmarkedness of the present, revealed in its more general scope, to correspond to a morphologically underived form. This naturally leads to an analysis of the strong preterites with a floating feature [+back] as a past marker.

> The label MARKED suggests 'less expected', 'more complex', 'less natural', and the like

Spell out the formal details of the analysis we are proposing.

The formalization of Modern English umlaut by means of floating features was introduced in chapter 6, and you can refer back to it if your memory needs jogging.

9 Multidimensional Phonology: The Skeleton

In this chapter we have encapsulated the temporal dimension of phonological structure in the timing tier. In particular, we have shown that melodies can exhibit different lengths, irrespective of the identity of the melody: vowel melodies, for instance, can be short or long, and consonant melodies can enjoy full independence or be part of an affricate. In the current formal model, these situations are represented as mismatches between the timing tier and the melody tier: a melodic element can be associated with one or two timing slots, and a timing slot can be associated with one or two melodic elements. We represent these various configurations in (52):

> Our present model allows for mismatches between the timing tier and the melody tier

(52) a. One timing slot:

       (i) One melody   (ii) Two melodies

  b. Two timing slots:

       (i) One melody   (ii) Two melodies

In both (52ai) and (52bii) there is a one-to-one correspondence between timing slots and melodies. In (52aii) and (52bi), however, there is a mismatch between the two tiers, as corresponds to affricates and long vowels, respectively.

We have seen the timing tier to be made up of a succession of Xs, the abstract unit of timing. The timing tier and the melody tier make up a plane: geometrically, two lines necessarily make up a plane. The association lines relating the melodies to the timing elements run on this plane. As we know from this and previous chapters, however, melodies do not constitute indivisible lumps, but are in fact constellations of distinctive features. In turn, distinctive features enter certain universally determined dependency relations. This means that the structures in (52) are only shorthand abbreviations for their full versions in (53). Note in (53aii) that the proper representation of affricates contains not only one timing unit, but also one feature [+consonantal], from which the two successive phases [+continuant] and [−continuant] branch off in the [±continuant] tier:

(53)   a.   i.

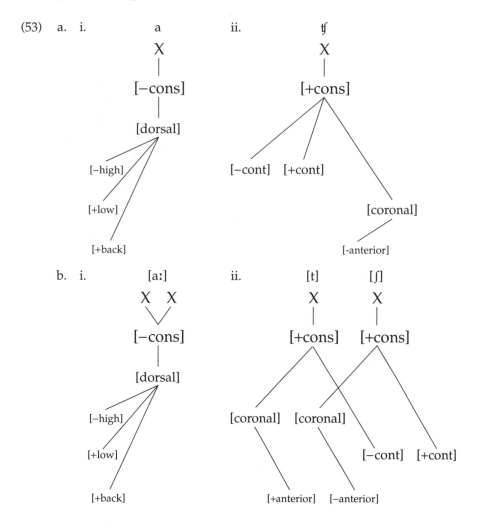

You can see that phonological structures resemble the mobiles that hang down from the ceiling over the cots of babies, or, perhaps more accurately, the pull-outs that come out of some pages in some books. These figures are easier to see and comprehend in the real three-dimensional space than on the two-dimensional drawings of the pages of a book, and we must ask you to make a special effort with your imagination really to understand their structure. Notice that the timing tier makes up the baseline of the structure. Concomitantly, the timing tier is often given the label SKELETON, suggestive of its basic function in sound structure: the rest would simply be the flesh. Correspondingly, the timing units can be referred to as SKELETAL SLOTS.

Phonological structures resemble the mobiles that hang down from the ceiling over babies' cots

The timing tier, or SKELETON, constitutes the baseline of the edifice of sound in language

Chapter Summary

This chapter has seen the extension of the autosegmental model of phonology to the representation of length, in a new tier independent of segment substance. Vowel length can be the only distinguishing factor between two words, yet length is not a defining feature of vowels: [iː] and [i] have the same articulatory properties. The autosegmental solution to the problem is to represent length on a tier (the timing tier) separate from the substance of the sound (the melody tiers). In the case of short vowels there is a one-to-one correspondence between a slot (marked 'X') on the timing tier and the segment on the melody, whereas long vowels would occupy two time slots. The recognition of this independent tier leads to a neat analysis of affricates, shown to occupy only one slot on the timing tier but two ([–continuant] [+continuant]) in the melody. This account solves the conundrum brought about by conflicting evidence as to whether affricates are monosegmental or bisegmental: the two-level solution allows them to be both. The main body of data in the chapter concerned the English Vowel Shift, most strikingly illustrated by the seemingly inexplicable but very widespread alternations in the stem vowel of such pairs as *div*[aɪ]*ne*/*div*[ɪ]*nity*. The lexical form of this stem (here *div*/iː/*n*) undergoes processes on the two tiers. Affixation triggers a shortening process on the timing tier by which one slot is deleted, whilst in the unsuffixed stem the vowel remains attached to two slots but undergoes diphthongization in the melody tier. The autosegmental formalism allowed us to demonstrate both these processes. However, the change in the quality of the first phase of the diphthong is awkward to represent, and we offered two solutions. The first account introduced the phonological primitives <a>, <i> and <u> in place of the distinctive features conventionally accepted, but the solution did not prove very revealing. An *SPE*-based alternative account offered a justification for the use of Greek letter variables in unified rules in a two-part process. The consequences of the Vowel Shift are far-reaching in English phonology, both historically and synchronically, and we showed how the Vowel Shift also interacts with the fronting alternations discussed in chapter 6, and with a backness shift apparent in a number of English strong verbs, such as *find/found*. Throughout the chapter, the segregation of the timing and melody tiers has been instrumental to the various analyses. In the final section we spelled out the multidimensional form of phonological structure, with the skeleton as the central line and the various features cascading off, in a manner reminiscent of a mobile (made up of sheets, rather than wires).

Key Questions

1 Rehearse the arguments for a mono-segmental and a bisegmental analysis of the affricate.
2 How can an autosegmental analysis solve the affricate problem?
3 What are the "timing tier" and the "melody"?
4 Define the term "phonotactic constraints".
5 What is odd about the pervasive vowel alternations of English as exemplified in such pairs as *divine~divinity*, etc.?
6 How and why does English spelling disguise the oddity of these alternations?

7 Which two types of process are involved in the alternations of the Great Vowel Shift?
8 On which tier does vowel shortening take place?
9 How are these alternations good evidence for the two-tier approach?
10 What is the basis of the analysis of vowels involving vowel primitives?
11 What is the purpose of Greek letter variables? What is the purpose of braces?
12 What do you understand by the term "marked"?

Further Practice

Turkish

The following alternations are found in Turkish between formal speech and casual speech:

Formal	Casual	
kahja	kaːja	'steward'
fihrist	fiːrist	'index'
tahsil	taːsil	'education'
kahve	kaːve	'coffee'
mahsus	maːsus	'special to'

(i)   What is the nature of the alternation?
(ii)   Does the alternation affect the timing tier or a feature tier?
(iii)   Give an autosegmental account of the process.

Vowel Shifts

Albanian

The diagrams below represent the shift of a number of Proto-Indo-European (PIE) vowels to their Modern Albanian descendants. The overall effect is that PIE /ɑ/, /o/ and /u/ have become [ɔ], [ɛ] and [i] respectively in Albanian, and the diphthong /au/ has become [ɑ].

$$
\begin{array}{ccccc}
[i] & \leftarrow & /y/ & \leftarrow & /u/ \\
[\varepsilon] & \leftarrow & /\varnothing/ & \leftarrow & /o/\text{/}[\mathrm{ɔ}] \\
& & & & \uparrow \\
& & & & /\mathrm{ɑ}/ \\
& & [\mathrm{ɑ}] & \leftarrow & /au/
\end{array}
$$

Give an account of the feature changes which occurred in the course of these shifts.

New Zealand English

Compare the New Zealand English pronunciation of the vowels in the following words with those in standard northern hemisphere varieties.

bit   [bɨt]
bet   [bɪt]
bat   [bɛt]

(i)   Which vowels are affected?
(ii)   How does this vowel shift compare with the Great English Vowel Shift?
(iii)   Provide a diagram to represent the shift.

London English

The relationship between various RP English diphthongs and their Estuary (= popular London) English and Cockney equivalents is represented in the diagrams below:

RP	iː	eɪ	aɪ	ɔɪ
	↓	↓	↓	↓
Estuary	ɪ̯i	ɐɪ	ɑɪ	ɒ̯ɪ
	↓	↓	↓	↓
Cockney	əɪ	aɪ	ɒɪ	oɪ

Describe the relationship between the three accents as involving a vowel shift.

PART TWO

SUPRASEGMENTAL STRUCTURE

In part I we formalized speech as an array of timing slots, each supporting a cluster of distinctive features. We saw that this mode of representation allows a remarkably natural and constrained account of many of the phonological processes present in languages, assimilation in particular. In part II we show that this structure needs to be augmented in two ways. First, there is a whole dimension to speech that involves a type of singing ("intonation" and "tones"), and this requires the enrichment of the model with a tone plane independent of the segmental planes, or cluster of planes. The tone plane thus connects to the skeleton from a different angle to the segmental planes, and contributes to the configuration of phonological structure in a manner reminiscent of a book, with one spine and several pages fanning out from it. The reason for the postulation of a separate tone plane is, of course, that tones (by themselves or in intonational phrases, or "tunes") engage in their own processes, quite independently of the segments. In addition to the tonal plane, we need to augment phonological structure in a second way. In particular, the slots linearized in the skeleton enter specific, family-like relations with each other: more technically, they group themselves into constituents. We know they do because otherwise a vast number of phenomena in natural languages would be entirely arbitrary, indeed incomprehensible, but they become quite simple and natural as soon as such suprasegmental, or "prosodic", structure is brought into the picture. We will come across two levels of prosodic structure. The first level is made up of "syllables", each syllable with its own internal constituency. We shall see that the linear distribution of segments is constrained in ways relatable to syllable constituency, and that syllable constituency also plays a crucial part in delimiting the scope of phonological processes. The second level of prosodic structure gathers syllables into "metrical feet", and hierarchizes the metrical feet included in such grammatical constituents as the simple word, the compound word or the phrase. The main, but by no means exclusive, manifestation of metrical feet is "stress", which materializes as prominence or, perhaps more perspicuously, as the main anchor for intonational association. While at first sight more abstract than segments, tones have played a major role in the shaping of the autosegmental approach to phonology, and of the principles that regulate such an approach, and therefore they well deserve the attention of the phonologist.

CHAPTER NINE

THE SYLLABLE

Chapter Objectives

In this chapter you will learn about:

- A curious bias in the phonology of children's early utterances.
- The need for grouping sounds together into units we call "syllables".
- The terminology used in the analysis of syllable structures.
- The constituents that make up the syllable.
- The types of syllable that occur in the languages of the world.
- The interaction between syllable structure and the timing tier.
- How the relative loudness of different types of sound controls positions in syllable structure.
- What combinations of sounds make up possible syllables.

In previous chapters we have illustrated the distinction between lexical and phonetic representations with processes like assimilation of voice and of place of articulation, vowel harmony, or umlaut. In essence, all these processes involve the action of one segment on another – or, more precisely and more technically, of one feature on another.

> Explain briefly why it is important to draw a difference between segments and features in the present context.

Some of these processes provide direct evidence for an autosegmental representation made up of various interconnected levels, or "tiers", significantly different from traditional unilinear transcription, and from standard writing.

> Say in what way our multitiered, indeed multiplanar, structure differs from the traditional unilinear representation.

In this and subsequent chapters we will see that many phenomena relevant to the phonology of languages cannot be properly understood unless we enrich the representation with certain structures which are abstract to the extent that they are not, and by definition cannot be, pronounced directly in the way that segments are. These structures express relations between (concrete) elements. We assume that these structures are real because they can reasonably be thought to be behind many of the phonological phenomena observable in languages.

1 The Shape of Children's Early Utterances

At a certain point in a child's early development we dignify its utterances as "words". In the very early stages of life an infant goes through a crying and wheezing stage, to which "cooing" (contented vocalizations) is then added. At around four or six months comes the period of "vocal play", during which the child experiments with a multitude of possibilities of what might be construed as consonant articulations. Then, at around six or nine months of age, the child starts "babbling", that is, combining consonants and vowels into recognizable words: [baba], [mama], [dada], [nana], and so on.

> Based on what you have read in this book so far, what comments can you make about the form of these early utterances?

The following utterances by "Timmy" are representative of the early speech of many children (the corresponding adult forms are given on the right):

(1) [pʰə]   ball   [11 months]
     [pæ]   book   [11 months]
     [gaː]   duck   [11 months]
     [ʔa]   hi   [11 months]
     [həkːʰa]   key   [11 months]
     [kə]   kitty   [11 months]

     [bæː]   bird   [15 months]
     [gɛː]   cow   [15 months]
     [ka]   cup   [15 months]
     [gæː]   dog   [15 months]
     [kʌː]   girl   [15 months]
     [ʔəmːa]   moon   [15 months]

[pæ]	baby	[16 months]
[pæ]	block	[16 months]
[pæ]	boat	[16 months]
[k'akʰi]	cookie	[16 months]
[ʔʌɸæ]	flower	[16 months]
[nʌmæ]	Simon	[16 months]

These words obviously consist of a consonant followed by a vowel (for instance, [pæ], [gɛː]), or of a string of such **consonant + vowel** pairs ([nʌmæ], [k'akʰi]). Note that they could just as well have consisted of a string of just consonants or just vowels (say, [bmk] or [aəɛ], respectively), or of a **vowel + consonant** sequence ([æp], [ɛːg], and so on). You may think that the reason these possibilities do not materialize is that the adult forms the child hears do not have this structure. However, if you pay close attention to the data, you will notice that the adult forms are systematically more complex than those of the child, who only retains the **consonant + vowel** pairs.

> Check out in (1) that this is indeed the case.

For instance, adult *ball* is reproduced as [pʰə] by the child, not as [əpʰ], adult *duck* is reproduced as [gaː], not as [aːg], and so on. It is as if all the child is bothered about is the sequence **consonant + vowel**.

At this point we could conclude that the speech of this child is simply peculiar. Indeed, there are some children (not many) with speech problems which require the services of the speech therapist. However, a child's speech is only deemed problematic when the "defect" persists beyond a certain, reasonably mature, age – were this not to be the case, we would all have needed the therapist in our early years: the distortion of adult speech by children is common and typical. What is relevant for us here is that such distortion obeys certain unwritten and unconscious laws, of which the sample in (1) above is a fairly representative output.

Children's distortion of adult speech obeys certain unwritten and unconscious laws

> If you know some real children of this age, you may want to take the opportunity to listen to them and compare their speech with your own.

Before we start investigating these laws, we shall look briefly at a curious phenomenon involving the pronunciation of English words by Japanese adults. Japanese has been importing and is still importing many words from English. However, when the Japanese pronounce these words, they do not pronounce them in quite the way English speakers do, as we illustrate in (2):

(2) *English*   *Japanese*
     Christmas   kurisumasu
     text   tekisuto
     club   kurabu
     dress   doresu
     glass (for drinking)   gurasu
     disc   disuku
     slum   suramu
     plus   purasu
     bolt   boruto
     grotesque   gurotesuku

> What is the common denominator behind the Japanese versions of the English words?

Essentially, Japanese adults seem to be doing what we saw English children do: aiming at pronouncing **consonant + vowel** strings, rather than strings of consonants or strings of vowels. However, the way they go about achieving this result is different – while we saw that English children drop the consonants they hear in English adult speech to make words more pronounceable, we are now observing that Japanese adults prefer inserting vowels into the English consonant clusters. It thus seems that Japanese adults are guided by the same unwritten and unconscious laws as English children, but implement them differently.

The laws we have been alluding to govern the way segments are abstractly connected in clusters known as SYLLABLES. Segments that are not consistent with these laws fall overboard, so to speak, and are not pronounced: segments need to be members of a syllable if they are to be pronounced. It is the purpose of this and the next chapter to present and discuss the conditions for such membership, that is, to spell out the conditions under which segments can be incorporated into a syllable.

Segments need to be members of a SYLLABLE if they are to be pronounced

2 Structure of the Core Syllable

We have seen that young children's syllables tend to be made up of a consonant and a vowel. This obviously means that the syllabic structure available to the child is rather rudimentary compared with the syllabic structure that is available to adults, at least in English. We formalize the structure of the child's typical syllable in (3) with the help of a tree. A TREE is just a visual representation of a network of hierarchical relations. The informal symbol "C" stands for a consonant, that is, a segment defined as [+consonantal], and the symbol "V" for a vowel, that is, a [−consonantal] segment. You can see in (3) that such C and V are gathered under the umbrella of σ, the Greek letter "sigma" equivalent to the Roman s, here a shorthand for the word "syllable":

A TREE is a visual representation of a network of hierarchical relations

(3)

What is the structure in (3) telling us?

The structure in (3) is simply telling us that a syllable is made up of a consonant followed by a vowel. This structure is, of course, abstract, but none the less real. For instance, the structure in (3) explains the rendering of adult *book* as [pæ] by the child in (1) above – quite simply, the syllable template in (3) acts as a filter to the more complex input [buk]:

(4)

Look back at the data in (1) and list some of the complexities of adult speech the child is leaving out.

The Japanese adaptations of English words we illustrated in (2) above suggest that something similar is happening in the Japanese adult language.

Explain exactly in what way.

The component parts of the syllable are given special names, to make it easier to identify them and to refer to them. Let us assume at this point that syllables always contain a vowel, the centre or NUCLEUS of the syllable – reality is a little more complex, but this assumption will do for the time being. In the forms in (1) and (2) above, this vowel is preceded by a consonant, which acts as the ONSET of the syllable. The core syllable, conveniently illustrated by the child's utterances in (1) and the Japanese renderings of

Syllables contain a vowel, the core or NUCLEUS of the syllable, preceded by a consonant, which acts as the ONSET

English words in (2), is thus made up of a nucleus preceded by an onset. We represent this more detailed structure in (5):

(5)
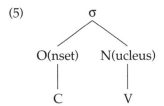

We now apply this schema to our database in (1) and (2) above:

(6)   a.

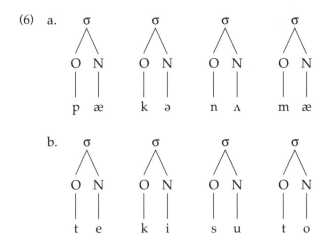

b.

The label "O" on [p], [k], [n] and [m] in a. and on [t], [k], [s] and [t] in b. simply indicates that these consonants fill the role of onset in their syllable. In turn, the label "N" indicates that the vowels it dominates fill the role of nucleus.

The CV syllable is legitimately considered the CORE SYLLABLE. Some languages only have CV syllables. More commonly, languages allow for syllables of greater complexity: this is obviously the case in adult English, and Japanese also allows for other types of syllables besides the ones we have mentioned, as illustrated by *abusutorakuto* 'abstract', *sutoraiki* '(labour) strike', *aisukuriimu* 'ice cream', *burakku* 'black' and *doragon* 'dragon'.

> In what way are these syllables more complex than the core ones?

The core syllable is, however, found in every language, whether or not the language also allows more complex syllables.

The CV syllable is the CORE SYLLABLE

Write down up to ten longish English words. Underline the core syllables that you find in these words.

The cross-linguistic omnipresence of the core syllable offers an interesting parallel with its also invariable occurrence in early child language. The correlation between the frequency of a sound in the sound systems of the world's languages and the order in which sounds and sound structures are acquired by children was insightfully drawn over fifty years ago by Roman Jakobson, one of the giants of modern phonology and linguistics in general, to whom we have already referred in chapter 8.

3 Sonority and the Syllable

So far we have encountered the universal core syllable, made up of an onset, usually a consonant, and a nucleus, usually a vowel. We must now motivate this particular configuration.

In chapter 3 we mentioned the fact that some sounds are more sonorous than others. We explained at the time that being more sonorous means having more sound (*sonus* means 'sound' in Latin). The obvious implication is that some sounds have more sound than others. There is no paradox here: it is just that the word "sound" is being used in two different senses, to signify 'segment' and to signify 'quantity of sound'. Another way of putting it is to say that not all segments (bundles of features, as you know) carry the same amount of sound.

Being more sonorous means having more sound

It is not hard to see that vowels have more sonority than consonants. After all, when we want to attract someone's attention we typically shout "oy!", "eh!", etc., with a fairly open vowel carrying the call. The point is that we would not dream of shouting [p], or even the fricative [f], or the liquid [l].

We do use [ʃʃʃʃ] to call for silence, though: why?

Notice also that if we shout out for help it is the vowel we will lengthen for emphasis: *heeeelp*, not *hhhhelp*, *hellllp* or *helpppp*. The reason for all this is that vowel sounds carry at a greater distance than consonants, precisely because vowels are more sonorous than consonants.

We know by now that the segmental structure of the core syllable is CV, rather than, say, CC, VV or VC. The arrangement of segments within the syllable is therefore such that sonority goes up from the onset to the nucleus, and then down to the next onset, like the ground in hilly terrain. We represent this situation in (7):

Segments are arranged within the syllable in such a way that sonority goes first up and then down

(7) Sonority profile of speech:

        N   N   N   More sonorous

    O   O   O   Less sonorous

Given the greater intrinsic sonority of vowels, it is not surprising that vowels, rather than consonants, should occupy the syllable nucleus, and consonants, rather than vowels, the onset.

> Explain in your own words why exactly we expect vowels in the nucleus and consonants in the onset.

Human speech consists in essence of a succession of vowels punctuated by consonants

The sonority profile outlined in (7) replicates the reality of human speech, essentially a succession of vowels punctuated by consonants, or, from a more reductionist perspective, a long modulated vowel sound regularly interrupted by consonants, rather as the meat is regularly constricted by knots in a string of sausages. The alternation of opening and closing that constitutes speech thus underpins the core status of the ON (or CV) syllable.

4 The Coda

We will now see that syllable structure can be considerably richer than we have been allowing.

Consider the following words of adult English:

(8) captain   active   septic

     rustic   kaftan   rectum

It should be intuitively obvious that each of these words is made up of two syllables (more on this in chapter 10). Clearly also, the segmental strings that make up the words in (8) do not fit into the syllable template in (4) above, as we now illustrate for *captain*:

(9)

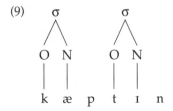

You can see that [p] and [n] remain outside our current syllable structure. We have already said that segments that are not affiliated to a syllable fail to be pronounced. However, the prediction that [p] and [n] are not pronounced in *captain* is obviously false for adult English (child English may well realize *captain* as [katɪ], precisely because in such child language only the core CV structure is available). In technical parlance, syllables act as "licensers" of phonetic material. We can draw a useful analogy with the "licensing" of humans by the issue of a birth certificate. Without a birth certificate, a person does not officially exist, and in the case of the segments the unlicensed segment will simply not be pronounced. The fact that *captain* is [kæptɪn] in English therefore means that the /p/ and the /n/ are both licensed, and consequently they must be part of a syllable.

> Syllables act as "licensers" of phonetic material

> On the basis of what you know so far, do you think that English and Japanese syllables have the same structure?

The inclusion of the /p/ and /n/ of *captain* in a syllable implies that English syllable structure admits more segmental material than the core syllable in (4). In particular, English syllable structure allows for a consonant after the nucleus. This new constituent is known as the CODA, a label we will abbreviate to "Cd" (reserving "C" for "consonant", as we have been doing so far):

> A consonant after the nucleus constitutes the syllable CODA

(10)

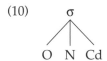

The addition of the coda to syllable structure allows for the representation of *captain* as in (11):

(11)

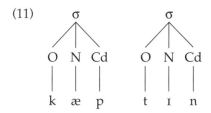

You can see that the orphan consonants of (9) are now affiliated to the syllable coda. This correctly predicts that these consonants will have a phonetic realization.

> Draw trees similar to (11) for some of the other words in (8).

5 The Rime

In (10) and (11) above we connected the subsyllabic constituents O, N and Cd directly to the syllable node σ. We shall now see that there are reasons to make the structure of the syllable slightly more complex.

Consider the words in (12):

(12) pat   bat   cat   fat
      [pæt] [bæt] [kæt] [fæt]

> Can you find any relation in sound between these words?

These words clearly rhyme with each other (we assume you are familiar with the device of rhyming in English verse). Compare these forms with those in (13):

(13) a. pat   pan   pad   pack
          [pæt] [pæn] [pæd] [pæk]
      b. pat   pit   pot   put
          [pæt] [pɪt] [pɒt] [pʊt]

> Do these words also rhyme? Why do they (or not, as the case may be)?

The words in the two sets in (13) do not rhyme with each other, even though they exhibit the same amount of phonetic overlap as those in (12): [æt] in (12), [pæ] in (13a), and [p . . . t] in (13b). Clearly, thus, rhyming is not just a matter of amount of overlap. Rather, the overlap must affect a certain position within the syllable, namely, the sequence **N + Cd**: the onset simply does not enter into the computation of rhyme.

The joint participation of the nucleus and the coda in poetic rhyming is not coincidental: the same pairing plays a crucial role in many phonological processes, as we shall see in due course. This leads to the replacement of the flat structure of the syllable in (10) with a structure where the nucleus and the coda group together in a constituent RIME, with the spelling difference conveniently highlighting the phonological relevance of the construct. The enriched structure of the syllable is displayed in (14):

The nucleus and the coda group together in a constituent called RIME

(14)   σ

     O R(ime)

        N Cd

In (15) we match this new syllabic template to the segmental sequence [pæt] of *pat*:

(15)   σ

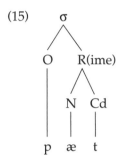

The structure in (15) includes all the standard syllabic subconstituents: O, R, N and Cd, organized as shown. As we know from our brief discussion of child phonology, simpler syllables also exist. In the next section, we review the four most basic structures of syllables found in the world's languages.

6 Basic Syllable Typology

We now have two types of syllable in our repertoire, namely, ON and ONCd, which we are still assuming correspond to CV and CVC segmentally. The nucleus is, of course, essential to the syllable, in the way that the heart or the brain is essential to the human body: without a nucleus there is simply no syllable. By contrast, syllables without an onset do exist, whether or not with a coda. The four most basic types of syllable are, therefore, as follows:

(16)   a. ON   b. ONCd   c. NCd   d. N

> Provide a handful of English words illustrating these structures.

Of the structures in (16), we have seen (16a) to be the core syllable. The non-core syllables are in effect minimal deviations from this core syllable. In particular, the core syllable template ON can undergo two minimal changes. First, it can shed its onset:

The core syllable template can undergo two minimal changes: first, it can shed its onset; second, it can take on a coda

(17)   ON → N   (equivalently at the segmental level, CV → V)

Second, it can take on a coda:

(18)   ON → ONCd   (equivalently at the segmental level, CV → CVC)

The representation of these two alternatives in terms of Cs and Vs is as in (19):

> Try out this alternative formalism, for practice.

(19)   a.   C → Ø /___V
          b.   Ø → C /V___

The effect of these two rules on the core syllable CV is shown in (20):

(20)   CV ⇒ V   by (19a)
          CV ⇒ CVC   by (19b)
          CV ⇒ VC   by (19a) and (19b)

> Which of these syllable types do you think will be least likely to occur in languages generally? Why?

The degree of complexity of each of the four basic syllable types can be read directly from this formalism. In particular, the core syllable CV is simplest, because it is not subject to any particular operation. The VC syllable is the most complex because it requires the application of both rules. Finally, the two other syllables (V and CVC) have intermediate complexity, each being derived by means of one rule.

We now provide RP English examples of each of the four syllable types we have described:

The core syllable CV is simplest, the VC syllable is the most complex, the two other syllables (V and CVC) have intermediate complexity

(21)

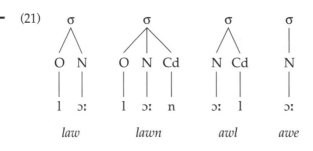

law   lawn   awl   awe

> Can you suggest other examples for each of these syllable types?

English syllable structure can of course accommodate more complexity than is present in these four types. We start addressing this matter in section 9 below, and take it further in chapter 10.

The differences in complexity between the four basic syllable types rendered explicit by our formalization in (17) to (19) above are made explicit in the implicational hierarchy in (22) ("⊃" = 'implies'):

(22) $\text{VC} \supset \begin{Bmatrix} \text{V} \\ \text{CVC} \end{Bmatrix} \supset \text{CV}$

> Restate in plain English prose the relations expressed in (22).

The hierarchy in (22) is backed up by fact over a wide spectrum of superficially unrelated areas: children acquire the different syllable types in precisely the order predicted by the hierarchy; the presence of a more complex type in any one language presupposes the presence of its simpler counterpart(s); syllable-related historical change tends to go in the direction of greater syllable simplicity; in languages with a rich range of syllable patterns, simpler syllables are more frequent, both statically, in the inventory, and dynamically, in actual language use; and so on.

> Mull this over.

We complete this part of the discussion listing a few languages that instantiate each of the four basic syllable types. Notice that the sample confirms the implicational hierarchy in (22):

(23) CV only   Senufo   Hua
                         (W. Africa)   (Papua New Guinea)
      CV, V   Maori   Cayuvava
                         (New Zealand)   (Bolivia)
      CV, CVC   Klamath   Arabic
                         (N. America)   (Middle East, N. Africa)
      CV, V, CVC, VC   French   Finnish   Spanish   English

7　The Nature of the Syllable

In section 3 above we referred to the role of sonority in the syllable. In particular, we said that the essence of speech is a sequence of elements of high sonority, so far embodied in vowels, interrupted by elements of lower sonority, embodied in consonants. Correspondingly, syllables are made up of a segment of high sonority flanked by segments of lower sonority. A syllable is therefore a cluster of sonority, defined by a sonority peak acting as a structural magnet to the surrounding lower sonority elements – the analogy of crystals in geology or of pearls in biology may be helpful in this connection.

A syllable is a cluster of sonority defined by a sonority peak

---

> Explain one or both of these analogies.

In turn, speech is a sequence of such sonority clusters, as we represent in (24):

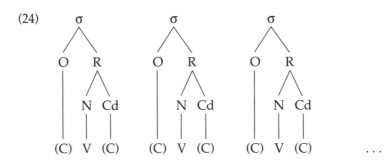

(24)

The pivotal role of the sonority peak in the syllable becomes more obvious if we formalize the whole syllable as a projection of its nucleus, as in (25a), otherwise equivalent to (25b):

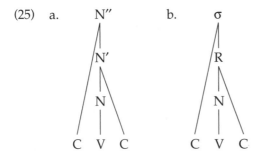

(25)　a.　　b.

> In what way does (25a) make more obvious the role of the nucleus as the hub of the syllable?

If you are familiar with Chomskyan syntax, you will recognize in (25a) the so-called "X-bar" template, adapted to syllables. If you are not, you simply need to notice that in (25a) the syllable margins (that is, onsets and codas) are in effect formal excrescences of the nucleus N. In particular, the "trunk" of the tree in (25a) is made up of layered copies, or PROJECTIONS, of the nucleus node N. The highest projection, N″, constitutes the syllable node, which branches off to its left as the onset. The intermediate projection, N′, constitutes the rime node, branching off to its right as the coda. As we said, these higher nodes are supported by the nucleus node, N, which is in turn projected from the vowel, the head of the syllable – the HEAD of a constituent is the core element of the constituent, that is, the element without which there would simply be no constituent.

For our immediate purposes, it will not really matter whether we formalize syllables with the schema in (25a) or with the perhaps more familiar one in (25b), since we have introduced the "X-bar" formalism only to help you grasp the nature of the syllable.

> The HEAD of a constituent is the core element of the constituent

> Explain carefully in your own words what the nature of the syllable consists of.

What does matter is that you should have reached a reasonable level of understanding of both the nature and the basic structure of the syllable, in preparation for the further intricacies we will be examining in the remainder of this chapter and in chapter 10.

8 Complex Nuclei

In chapter 8 we saw that vowel length is contrastive in English.

> Explain briefly what "being contrastive" means.

We provide further examples of vowel length oppositions in (26):

(26) a. peak   [piːk]   b. pick   [pɪk]
          pool   [puːl]   pull   [pʊl]
          caught   [kɔːt]   cot   [kɒt]

The vowels in the words in (26a) are long, and the vowels in the words in (26b) short. The remainder of the sounds are identical in each pair, and therefore each contrast is minimal. Of course, the long vowels are also tense, and the short vowels lax, but this additional difference is not contrastive by itself, since contrasts like [pik] vs. [pɪːk], etc., are not possible in English.

> Make sure you see that length, rather than tenseness, is contrastive in English.

We are now faced with the challenge of fitting long vowels into rime structure.

> Can you think why fitting vowels into rimes might present a problem for the rime structure we have available?

Long vowels are by definition associated to two timing slots. Strictly speaking, syllable structure is built on the timing tier, not on the segments themselves as we have been doing so far, to keep the representations simple: as we said at the end of the previous chapter, the skeleton constitutes the baseline of the edifice of sound in language. Now, long vowels cause a mismatch between our present syllable structure and the timing tier. In (27) we display two alternative interpretations of this mismatch:

(27)

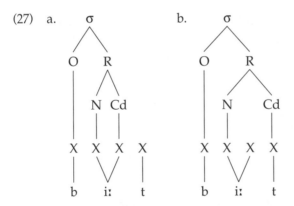

> What is the difference between these two structures?

In (27a), the timing slots associate to the syllable terminals one to one from left to right, irrespective of the feature content of the segments. The consequence is that the second part of the long vowel links to the coda, and no syllable terminal remains for the slot of the final /t/ to link to. In (27b), the feature content is taken account of, strictly keeping vowels for the nucleus. The consequence is that only one of the two slots of /iː/ can be incorporated into the structure. Given the function of syllable structure as a segmental licenser, (27a) predicts that the /t/ will not be pronounced, while according to (27b) the vowel will be pronounced short.

> Explain what we mean when we say that syllable structure acts as a segmental licenser.

Neither prediction is, of course, correct: if /t/ were not realized phonetically, *beat* would sound like *bee*, and if the vowel were short it would sound like *bit*, after the concomitant laxing, or as impossible b[i]t, if there was no laxing.

The obvious course of action to achieve an exact match with the timing units involves augmenting the number of syllable terminals. The question is whether such an increase ought to affect the coda or the nucleus. If we assign one part of the /i/ to the coda (as we did in (27a)), we will conflict with the typical pattern of association of [−consonantal] segments with the nucleus. While we will see in the next chapter that this pattern does sometimes break down, it is all the same quite robust. Accordingly, we fit the long vowel into the syllable by augmenting the nucleus to two units:

We fit long vowels into the syllable by augmenting the nucleus to two timing units

(28)

```
              σ
           /     \
          O       R
          |      / \
          |     N   Cd
          |    / \   |
          X   X   X  X
          |    \ /   |
          b    iː    t
```

> Can you assign syllable structure to *bite* on the strength of what you have learned so far?

The representation in (28) nicely captures the sameness of *beat* and *bit* with regard to both syllable structure and melody identity (abstracting away vowel tenseness, which in English we assume follows from vowel length, in line with our findings in chapter 8): the two words only contrast with regard to the number of skeletal slots in their respective nuclei. On the other hand, *bee* and *bit* also differ with regard to syllable structure, since *bit* has a coda, but *bee* does not.

> Write out and compare the syllable structures of *bee* and *bit*.

A nucleus with two slots also accommodates diphthongs, since we assume that a diphthong is equivalent to a pair of vowels, both in the melody and in the skeleton:

A diphthong is equivalent to a pair of vowels, both in the melody and in the skeleton

> How then will two consecutive vowels and a diphthong be distinguished formally?

(29)

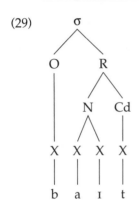

We hope that the need in English for nuclei with two timing slots, alongside nuclei with only one slot, is by now quite clear.

9 Complex Onsets

The syllable template we have available at the moment (maximally CVVC) cannot account for the English forms in (30):

(30) plot   blot   flag
     press   brick   frock

     clock   glad
     crack   grill

     trap   dress   thrill
                    slum
                    shrill

> How would the forms in (30) relate to the syllable templates we have available?

In particular, the first two segments in the forms in (30) are consonants, and our current syllable template only accommodates one consonant in the onset.

> Show in a diagram that this is so.

The obvious solution to the problem posed by the consonant clusters in (30) involves allowing for onsets with two timing slots, in the way that we have allowed nuclei with two timing slots. Augmentations of this kind manifestly involve more structural complexity, but the ultimate goal of phonology, and of linguistics in general, obviously has to be the modelling of reality, not the attainment of economy of representation at all costs.

We allow for onsets with two timing slots

> Reflect briefly on this statement and then explain it to yourself or, even better, to a friend. Is the statement compatible with Occam's razor?

We formalize the proposed augmented onset in (31), in each of the two alternative modes of representation we have at our disposal:

(31) a.   σ   b.   N″

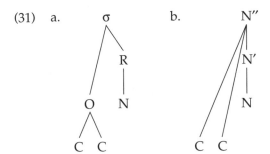

We have now enriched the structure of the syllable with two-member nuclei and two-member onsets. In the next chapter we will encounter an apparent need for two-member codas also.

10 The Sonority Hierarchy

The inventory of English branching onsets in (30) above contains a number of gaps. In particular, only the consonant clusters in (32) actually occur:

(32) [pl] [bl] [fl]   [sl]   [kl] [gl]
        [pɹ] [bɹ] [fɹ] [θɹ] [tɹ] [dɹ]   [ʃɹ] [kɹ] [gɹ]

> The list in (32) omits a number of apparent complex onsets of English (to be discussed in the next chapter), all of which have one aspect in common. Can you think what these apparent onsets might be?

Why do consonant combinations other than those in (32) not turn up in the onset, including, for instance, combinations which simply reverse the order of the two actually co-occurring consonants, such as [lp], [ɹp], etc.?

If you examine the clusters in (32), you will notice that the second timing slot is always filled with a liquid, namely, [l] or [ɹ]. In turn, the first slot accommodates all the obstruents of English but the affricates ([ʧ], [ʤ]) and the voiced fricatives ([v], [ð], [z], [ʒ]).

> Can you advance an explanation for each such exception? If you can (there is of course no guarantee that a solution will be available for all problems!), check whether the explanation is specific to one set or generalizes across sets.

The pairing of obstruents and liquids in the onset is obviously subject to some further restrictions (there is no [θl] or [sɹ], for instance), but we will postpone discussion of these in order to maintain the continuity of the exposition.

We could of course formalize the confinement of English onsets to **obstruent + liquid** clusters simply by writing the appropriate requirements directly into our syllable templates, as we do in (33), with "Ob" and "Lq" as informal abbreviations for obstruent and liquid, respectively:

(33) a.

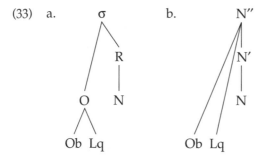

The problem with these syllable templates is that, while they do indeed do their job, they only do it by brute force.

Are you clear about what we mean by "brute force" in this context? Explain what is undesirable about it.

Thus, why should the two slots of complex onsets need to associate precisely with an obstruent and a liquid, and in this order? The answer to this and many other questions concerning the constraints on the distribution of segments within the syllable is found by reference to the SONORITY SCALE, also known as the "Sonority Hierarchy", a universal ranking of segment classes on the basis of sonority. We will build up the sonority scale in stages, to ensure that each step is motivated by explicit argument. At this point in the exposition, we shall propose the embryonic scale in (34):

(34) Sonority scale (first version):
    Most sonorous 4 Vowels
                  3 Liquids
                  2 Nasals
    Least sonorous 1 Obstruents

The sonority scale is relevant to our present problem because, as you already know, syllables constitute in effect sonority mountains: the sonority profile of a syllable rises, reaches a peak, and then falls. We illustrate this profile in (35) for a syllable with a complex onset and a coda:

(35) a.

b.

Syllable structure

Sonority profile

The sonority profile of the syllable is regulated by a universal principle known as SONORITY SEQUENCING:

(36) SONORITY SEQUENCING:
    The sonority profile of the syllable must rise until it peaks, and then fall.

The sonority profile of the syllable must rise until it peaks, and then fall

Explain how sonority sequencing rules out the type of onset we are finding to be non-existent.

As we show in (37), an onset such as *lp*, the converse of existing *pl*, would violate sonority sequencing:

(37)   a.   b.   Syllable structure

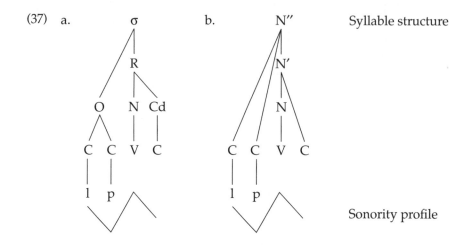

Sonority profile

The sonority trough in the onset in (37) obviously contravenes sonority sequencing in (36). This is the reason for the absence of this sequence from the inventory of onsets in English and other languages.

11 Sonority Distance

In (32) above you may notice that [ps] (**stop + fricative**), [pn] (**stop + nasal**) and suchlike do not occur in English onsets, even though these sequences are consistent with sonority sequencing.

Justify the claim that the clusters in question comply with sonority sequencing.

Similar sequences do turn up in other languages, however. For instance, in Greek they are part of words like [ps]*ychologia* 'psychology', [pn]*efmonia* 'pneumonia', [ks]*enos* 'stranger', *sym*[pn]*oia* 'accord', *kom*[ps]*os* 'elegant', *ed*[ks]*e* 'attraction', etc. Is their absence from English therefore purely arbitrary?

If you work out the distance between [p] and [l] on the sonority scale in (34) above, you will find out that it involves two points: liquids = 3, obstruents = 1, therefore 3 − 1 = 2. On the other hand, [ps] scores a difference of 0 on this scale, and [pn] a difference of 1.

> Work it out for yourself why [ps] scores 0 in sonority distance.

In many languages, the segments of complex subsyllabic constituents need to satisfy a minimum of sonority distance. We shall formalize this requirement through a MINIMAL SONORITY DISTANCE parameter. The setting of this parameter for English complex onsets will be as in (38), with reference to the sonority scale in (34) above:

> We refer to the requirement of a certain minimum of sonority difference between the segments of complex subsyllabic constituents as MINIMAL SONORITY DISTANCE

(38)   Minimal sonority distance in English onsets:
       The minimal sonority distance between the two elements of an English complex onset is 2

In the next chapter we will provide the reason for setting this sonority distance as minimal, rather than as a constant.

> Try out a fixed value of 2 on the data in (32) above. Does it work?

We will not go further into specifics here, for the issue is truly complex across languages. However, we will emphasize that, while the sonority hierarchy is essentially uniform across languages, the requirements of minimal sonority distance between "sibling" elements in a given constituent need to be specified language by language, and constituent by constituent (we are using the term SIBLING to refer to nodes that are immediately dependent on the same PARENT node; the terms "sister" and "mother" are also in use in this connection). In our present context, it will suffice to know that the architecture of the syllable in any given language is the joint product of invariable universal principles, such as sonority sequencing in (36), and parameters with a fixed range of values, one selected by each language, as Minimal Sonority Distance in (38) has exemplified in our discussion.

C h a p t e r   S u m m a r y

In this chapter we have introduced abstract structures which cannot themselves be pronounced ("syllables"). We saw that infants' early utterances consist principally of CV syllables, also basic in the languages of the world:

there are languages where syllables are organized solely in this way, and none where such syllables do not occur. The technical terms used to describe the consonant and vowel positions in these basic syllables are "onset" and "nucleus", respectively. Obviously, this basic structure can only accommodate segment strings which consist of alternating consonants and vowels, but syllable structure is richer than this in most languages, and we need to add a further position after the nucleus: the "coda". We demonstrated that the nucleus and the coda form a unit (the "rime") – words that differ only in their onsets rhyme (in verse), whereas those differing in other positions do not. We presented an inventory of basic syllable types in terms of onset/nucleus/coda combinations, with illustrations from English demonstrating the optionality of the positions "onset" and "coda" and the essential presence of the "nucleus", which is the defining part of the syllable. Syllable complexity can be gauged on the basis of the optimal CV syllable, a hierarchy of syllable types being definable in terms of their degree of deviation from it. In turn, this leads directly to an implicational chain of syllable types: VC ⊃ CVC/ V ⊃ CV. We then referred to the relationship between syllable structure and the timing tier, and showed that a long vowel occupies two timing slots, associated with the (now branching) nucleus. We saw that the distribution of vowels and consonants within a syllable (in the nucleus and the margins, respectively) is a consequence of sonority differences between these two classes of segments, where "sonority" simply refers to the amount of sound carried by the segment. In this context, speech is nothing but a string of elements with high sonority (= vowels) interrupted by elements of lower sonority (= consonants). The constraints on possible branching onsets in English and other languages are also partly explained by the principle of sonority sequencing (enforcing a rising sonority profile up to the peak, and a falling one thereafter), and partly by the Minimal Sonority Distance parameter (imposing a minimal distance in sonority between siblings of syllabic constituents).

Key Questions

1 How does the syllable structure of children's early utterances and English loanwords in Japanese differ from that of adult English?

2 What is the structure of the core syllable?

3 Which other constituent combines with the onset and the nucleus to make up a more complex syllable? What is the larger constituent formed by this other constituent and the nucleus?

4 Provide evidence for the rime as a constituent.

5 What is sonority? What is its role in syllable structure?

6 How does the second timing slot of a long vowel or diphthong fit into syllable structure?

7 How does sonority determine the structure of the complex onset?

8 What is the "sonority scale"? List it.

9 What is the role of sonority sequencing in the determination of syllable structure?

10 How does minimal sonority distance constrain onset formation?

F u r t h e r   P r a c t i c e

Sonority

Arrange the following sounds according to their relative sonority:

[a] [p] [l] [ɹ] [ʃ] [e] [z] [m] [ŋ] [i] [d] [ʌ]

Draw the sonority profiles of the following words. Identify the nuclei and the syllable boundaries:

compass   cocoa   trigger   asparagus   acumen   hippopotamus

Which of the following hypothetical words are syllabifiable in English? Explain the reasons for the failures to syllabify.

[pnɛkil]   [kɛpnil]   [bɹældɪn]   [ldæbɹɪn]   [nɪndɪp]   [ɪdɹikɹæl]

Spanish

In many varieties of Spanish [s] and [h] are in complementary distribution. Consider the following examples:

ca[s]a	'house'	ca[s]a[h]	'houses'
ca[h]co	'helmet'	cen[s]o	'census'
[s]e[s]o	'brain'	[s]e[s]o[h]	'brains'
[s]e[h]go	'slant'	e[h]to[h]	'these'
to[h]	'cough'	to[s]e[h]	'coughs'

Describe the distribution of the two segments taking into consideration all the possible factors, including adjacent segments, word position and syllable position.

Yawelmani Vowels

Consider the following forms of Yawelmani verbs:

Future passive	Passive aorist	Precative gerundial	Dubitative	
xilnit	xilit	xilʔas	xilal	'to tangle'
maxnit	maxit	maxʔas	maxal	'to procure'
meknit	meːkit	mekʔas	meːkal	'to swallow'
sapnit	saːpit	sapʔas	saːpal	'to burn'
tannit	taːnit	tanʔas	taːnal	'to go'

(i)   Describe the alternations between the long and short vowels in the data.

(ii) Formalize the alternation on the basis of syllable structure.

SYLLABLE COMPLEXITY

ENGLISH PHONOTACTICS

Chapter Objectives

In this chapter you will learn about:
- Falling sonority in apparently complex codas.
- Further restrictions on codas.
- The existence of non-vocalic nuclei in English.
- Vowels in the onset.
- Refining the sonority hierarchy.
- An explanation for missing obstruent–sonorant combinations in branching onsets.
- The integration of the diphthong [i͡u] into syllable structure.
- How onsets take precedence over codas.
- How medial consonant clusters are syllabified to reflect this precedence.
- Maximizing the possible onsets for the same reason.
- Residual problems and suggestions for a solution.

In the previous chapter we introduced the syllable, a structure with largely universal characteristics that imposes a certain organization on the string of segments. We saw that syllables are minimally made up of a nucleus, and maximally of an onset, a nucleus and a coda, the latter two constituents being conventionally gathered into a rime. We have been assuming throughout that nuclei are filled with vowels, and margins with consonants. While this correlation is essentially sound, it will have to be slightly relaxed in order to take account of certain facts in many languages, English included. In this chapter we also continue the survey of English phonotactics. English syllables are useful because of their complexity, which will force us to enrich our theoretical machinery: understanding the nooks and crannies of English syllables will stand us in excellent stead to understand syllables universally.

1 Complex Codas

In chapter 9 we motivated the existence of onsets and nuclei with two elements, respectively in sections 9 and 8. The data we will now present suggest that we may need to extend this (minimal) constituent complexity to codas.

Consider the following set of nonsense words in phonetic transcription:

(1) [kɪnp] [pɪmt] [pɪŋt] [pɪŋp] [kɪtp]
     [kɪtk] [kɪpk] [pɪkn] [pɪpn] [pɪpl]

> Try pronouncing these "words" (make sure you pronounce each of them as *one* syllable). Are they possible words of English?

We hope you will agree that none of these forms is possible in English. Clearly, the reason is not simply that the forms are (deliberately) nonsense: another nonsense word, *blick*, has repeatedly been proposed in the literature as a possible word of English – *blick* could, for instance, be the brand name of a newly launched product, say, a new washing powder or a new soft drink. Indeed, we must draw a tripartite distinction in all languages between existing words, non-existent but possible words, and non-existent and impossible words.

> Are we right in not including a fourth category of existing impossible words?

The dimensions of possibility and existence need to be kept carefully apart

Thus, the dimensions of possibility and existence need to be kept carefully apart. Possibility has to do with phonological well-formedness, a matter directly related to the grammar of the language, while existence has to do with lexical inclusion, an essentially haphazard affair.

> Explain in your own words the distinction between phonological well-formedness and lexicalization.

You may think that a more plausible explanation for the impossibility of the forms in (1) in English concerns the fact that they all have the structure CVCC, since our present maximal syllable template only allows one C after the nucleus, in the coda. Consider, however, the following set of also nonsense forms:

(2) [kɪmp] [pɪnt] [sɪnd] [sɪld] [tɪŋk]
    [kɪpt] [kækt] [pɪlk] [pɪlp] [hɪlb]
    [pæln] [wɪlm] [hɛlf] [hɛlv] [hɛlʃ]
    [hɛlz] [hɛls] [bɛnz] [bɛns] [hɪsp]
    [hɪsk] [dɛst] [laɹt] [kaɹm] [hɔɹθ]

> **Can you pronounce these forms?**

These forms can be pronounced by English speakers without any problem.
Therefore, we must conclude that, like *blick*, they qualify as possible words
of English. Crucially for our purposes here, they also have two consonants
after the nucleus. Indeed, parallels for the forms in (2) can easily be found
in the set of real words, as we show in (3):

(3) camp   punt   fond   build   pink
    kept   fact   silk   pulp   bulb
    kiln   film   shelf   twelve   Welsh
    fells   pulse   lens   fence   clasp
    risk   west   part   farm   forth

These facts are similar to those we came across in the previous chapter with
regard to the onset and the nucleus. Therefore, if we take these facts at face
value, we will need to accommodate a complex coda in our syllable template, along the lines of (4):

> We provisionally
> accommodate a
> complex coda
> in our syllable
> template

(4)

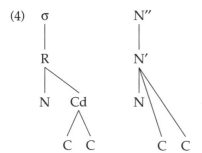

For the moment we will indeed adopt such complex codas, although at the
end of the chapter we shall see that there are reasons to favour a different
approach.

    Incorporating complex codas into the English syllable still does not account
for the contrast in grammatical status between the nonsense sets in (1) and
(2) above, instantiating impossible and possible English forms, respectively.

Now, if you compare the two sets in question, the following facts about the putative complex coda will come to your attention:

1   the liquid [l] only occurs as a left sibling, and similarly for [ɹ] in rhotic accents: [pɪlk], [hɛlf], [kɑɹm];
2   when nasals occur as left siblings they assimilate in place of articulation to their right sibling: [kɪmp], [pɪnt], [tɪŋk];
3   when both siblings are non-sonorant stops, the right one is coronal: [kɪpt], [kækt].

The restriction in 3 will be discussed in section 8 below. The restriction in 2 follows from the rule of place assimilation in nasals we examined in chapter 4. The restriction in 1 appears to mirror the restriction on onsets we examined in the last section of chapter 9.

> The coda conditions just given fail to account for one type of coda shown in (2)/(3). Which is this? (We shall discuss the cases in question later in the chapter.)

The requirement of a sonority gap of at least two degrees between the two elements of onsets is, obviously, relaxed in codas. In *camp, pink, kiln* or *film*, for instance, the two coda consonants differ by only one degree in the sonority scale in (34) of chapter 9, which we now repeat as (5):

(5)   Most sonorous   4   Vowels
                      3   Liquids
                      2   Nasals
      Least sonorous 1   Obstruents

> Why do the two coda consonants differ in sonority by only one degree?

In turn, in actually occurring *kept* or *fact* there is simply no sonority difference. This raises a question about the interpretation of sonority sequencing: we would expect sonority sequencing to require sonority to *fall* in codas, indeed as we stated in (36) in chapter 9. The fact that sonority does not fall in *kept* or *fact* hints that either this requirement is too strong or that *pt, kt,* etc., do not constitute complex codas after all. We will be addressing this dilemma in the remainder of the chapter.

2 Non-Vocalic Nuclei

At this point you may feel tempted to take a leap and interpret the laxer sonority distance requirement in codas as a hint that there are in fact no sonority restrictions on English complex codas. Notice, however, that sonority does not *rise* in such putative complex codas in any of the forms we have provided. Consider now the forms in (6), crucially bearing in mind that in these words only the first vowel in the spelling has phonetic reality:

> What exactly do we mean when we say that only the first spelled vowel in the forms in (6) has phonetic reality?

(6) prism
  button
  thicken
  sickle
  funnel
  brother (in rhotic accents)
  colour (in rhotic accents)

A word like *prism* does not strike the eye of the English speaker as odd in any way. Indeed, *prism* appears to comply with all the requirements built into our syllable: the structure C(C)VCC of this and the other words in (6) is at first sight syllabifiable as **onset** (simple or complex) **+ simple nucleus + complex coda**, thus apparently replicating the words in (3) above. However, closer inspection reveals that, while the forms in (3) are monosyllabic, those in (6) are bisyllabic. We make this difference explicit in (7) (the underscripted diacritic "ˌ" indicates nucleus status, and "." a syllable boundary, in IPA notation):

(7) [pɹɪ.zm̩]
  [bʌ.tn̩]
  [θɪ.kn̩]
  [sɪ.kl̩]
  [fʌ.nl̩]
  [bɹʌ.ðɹ̩] (in rhotic accents)
  [kʌ.lɹ̩] (in rhotic accents)

We do trust that your intuition agrees with ours on this matter.

  Two questions arise at this point. The first question is why we are assigning the final two consonants to the coda in the words in (3) but not in those in (6) – compare *silk* with *sickle*, or *think* with *thicken*, for instance:

(8) a.   b.

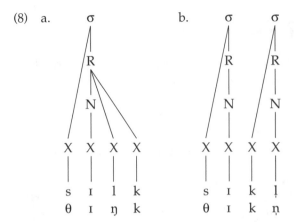

The second question is why (and how) we are assigning the word-final sonorant consonant in (6) to the nucleus, in contradiction to the prerequisite we
have been operating with so far that nuclei are vowels.

> Compare the monosyllabic *kiln* with the bisyllabic *kennel*,
> or, more perspicuously to the eye, *schism* with *skims* (the fact
> that *kennel* includes an *e* before the *l* in the spelling is, of
> course, immaterial). What is responsible for the differences in
> syllabification?

The reason for the divergent syllabification of the forms in (3) and (6) is
that in the coda cluster [lk] of *silk* the first element, [l], is more sonorous
than the second element, [k] (3 vs. 1), whereas in the last two consonants of
sickle this relationship is reversed (1 vs. 3). This is relevant with respect to
the sonority profile of the syllable, which you know rises on its way to the
peak (= the most sonorous element in the nucleus), and then falls. We display this profile once more in (9):

(9)   N   More sonority
      O   Cd   Less sonority

The principle responsible for this state of affairs is, of course, SONORITY
SEQUENCING, which we stated in (36) of chapter 9, and repeat here as (10):

(10) Sonority Sequencing:
      The sonority profile of the syllable must rise until it peaks, and then
      fall.

Clearly, a monosyllabic *silk* does comply with this principle:

(11) O N Cd

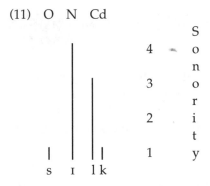

A putative coda [kl] in the word *sickle* would, however, contravene Sonority Sequencing, since the second element, [l], has more sonority than the first one, [k]:

(12) O N Cd

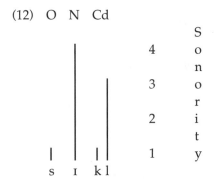

Say what is wrong with the "syllable" in (12).

The sonority trough on [k] prevents [kl] from being a valid coda. Faced with this situation, English (and other languages, but not all) relaxes the requirement that nuclei must be vowels, and allows sonorant consonants in the nucleus under the circumstances, as already represented in (8b):

(13) O N O N

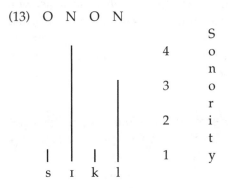

Explain how the problem of (12) has been solved in (13).

English nuclei can accept a sonorant consonant under pressure from the sonority profile of the segmental sequence

So, while it is true that English nuclei normally aim for a sonority minimum of 4 and therefore normally contain vowels, they can lower this minimum to 2 and accept a sonorant consonant under pressure from the sonority profile of the segmental sequence, precisely as happens in the cases we have just examined.

Show the sonority profiles of *schism* and *skims*.

In section 4 we will present the opposite phenomenon, and argue that English onsets can accommodate vowels.

3 Vowels in Disguise

Consider the syllabic structure of the words in (14):

(14) a. well   wish   wag
      b. yes   yob   yum

You will most probably recognize a CVC syllable here, analysing the first segment of these words (spelled *w* and *y*, respectively) as a consonant.

Check whether this is indeed your construal of the data.

At this point we need to pause and ask ourselves what kind of consonant these might be. Remember that consonants are divided into obstruents, with a radical constriction to the airflow in the central passage in the mouth, and sonorants, with the airflow also constricted in the central passage, but still flowing out unimpeded through some other channel: the nose for nasals, or the sides of the tongue for laterals, for instance.

Jog your memory on these important differences between consonants, going back to the appropriate chapters if necessary.

Now, if the sounds spelled *w* and *y* in (14) were consonants, they would most certainly not be obstruents.

> Explain why *w* and *y* cannot be obstruents.

They are obviously also not nasals or laterals.

> Explain why *w* and *y* cannot be nasals or laterals.

What can they be, then? There is, of course, a further class of sonorants, rhotics, but in these sounds the air is interrupted (albeit most fleetingly) at the front of the mouth, and this is clearly not the case with *w* and *y*.

> Reassure yourself that *w* and *y* are not rhotics.

So, what kind of consonant can *w* and *y* be? If you turn to the literature, you will find a variety of labellings: "glides", "semivowels" and "semiconsonants", as well as "yod" for *y* in a diachronic context. Sometimes, *w* and *y* are also included in the more general class of "approximants", indeed a feature in a system we will examine in chapter 17. Now, what exactly lies behind these labels?

If you (artificially, and most unnaturally) lengthen the initial segment of *well*, you will come up with the form [uːɛl], and if you do likewise with *yes* you will find yourself pronouncing [iːɛs].

> Do precisely what we have just suggested. Does the result agree with our prediction?

This simple experiment therefore reveals that *w* and *y* are really vowels, even if particularly short ones – the diacritic "˘" is actually available to indicate extra shortness, hence [ŭ], [ĭ]. They are also pronounced with a higher tongue than in the words *hoot* and *heat*, in fact more or less literally as IPA [i] and [u]. If *w* and *y* are phonetic vowels (despite the ambivalence of much of the literature on this matter), you may think that the forms in (14) above have, after all, no onset – only a complex nucleus made up of a high vowel ([u], [i], regardless of the spelling) followed by a second vowel, as represented in (15):

Articulatorily, w and y are vowels

(15)   a.   b.

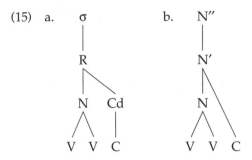

Consider now the forms in (16):

(16)   a.   womb   weep   wade
       b.   yeast   yawn   you

> Can you see what problem the words in (16) may pose?

In these forms the initial high vowel is followed by a long vowel, and there-fore, following the logic of the argument, we would have to assume a three-member nucleus:

(17)   a.   b.

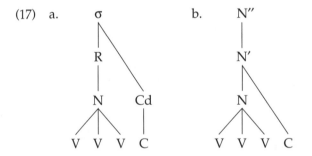

If the facts stopped here, we would have no alternative but to recognize the existence of three-member nuclei, despite our overt disinclination to increase the size of syllabic subconstituents.

> What is the rationale for this disinclination?

As it happens, however, other facts take us away from the structures in (17), and, concomitantly, from those in (15). These facts concern poetic rhyme and the ban on [w] after labial consonants.

4 Onset Vowels. The "OCP"

Let us compare the forms in (18) with their counterparts in (19), which replicates (30) of chapter 9 minus *slum* and *shrill*, since these are best analysed separately, as we will see in section 7 below:

(18) a.   twin   dwell   queen   Gwyn
                                              thwart
                                              swell

     b. pew   beauty   cute   argue
         few   view
         mute

     c. (in RP and most British-type accents)
                                              tune   dune
                                              Thew
                                              suit   Zeus
                                              news

(19)   plot   blot
            press   brick
            flock
            frock
                    trap   dress
                    thrill
                            clock   glad
                            crack   grill

We know from the previous chapter that the forms in (19) have a complex onset. Those in (18), by contrast, would have a complex nucleus according to the analysis sketched in the previous section (cf. (17) above). If so, the nucleus of forms like *twine* or *queen* would have three members.

> Explain why the nucleus of these forms would have three members.

This additional complexity in the nucleus cannot be welcome, but we will have to accept it if life is indeed like that.

Life, however, is not quite like that. First, *twin* rhymes with *tin, bin, sin,* etc., in the same way as *play* or *pray* rhymes with *pay*. The relevance of this is that, as we know from the previous chapter, the criterion for rhyming in English verse is that the segments in the syllable rime be identical. Therefore, if the left-most high vowel in the words in (18) were part of the rime, *twin* would simply not rhyme with *tin*, and so on. The fact that *twin* does rhyme with *tin* therefore suggests that the high vowel represented by *w* in the spelling is assigned to the onset.

The possibility of assigning high vowels to the onset receives specifically phonological support from the absence from the English native vocabulary of forms with the structure **labial consonant + labial high vowel + another vowel**. This sequence does occur in words of Spanish or French origin: *pueblo*, *bueno*, *poids*, *foie*, etc., with a labial consonant followed by [we] or [wa] respectively, as in the expressions "Pueblo Indians", "Buenos Aires", "avoirdupois", "foie gras". In native English words, however, sequences **consonant + labial high vowel + another vowel** are limited to the environments we listed in (18a). We transcribe these phonetically in (20), where we are representing onset /u/ as [w] to highlight its non-nuclear status (a less common alternative transcription is [u̯], with the non-nucleus status signalled by the underscripted diacritic "˯"):

> High vowels can be included in the onset

(20) a. [θw] [tw] [dw] [sw]   b. [kw] [gw]

Notorious absentees from this list are, of course, the clusters [pw], [bw], [mw], [fw] and [vw].

> Can you advance some reason to explain why these clusters should not be in the list in (19)?

In order to understand the bearing these gaps have on the role of [w] in the syllable, we need to take note of the fact that [tl], [dl], [θl] and [ðl] are also absent from English onsets. There are simply no words beginning with such clusters in English ([ð] and the other voiced fricatives do not occur in branching onsets of any kind). Moreover, in a word like *atlas*, where one of the clusters occurs word-medially, the [t] and the [l] do not join as a complex onset. Instead, the [t] makes up the coda of the first syllable: *at.las* (remember that "." represents a syllable boundary). We return to this matter in section 7 below, simply trusting for the moment that the syllabification *at.las* does not conflict with your intuition.

> Test out your intuition with regard to the syllabification of *tl* in *atlas* and similar words. Can you think of any reason why the clusters in question should be disfavoured as onsets?

The reason [tl], [dl], [θl], [ðl] are banned from the onset, while [pl], [bl], [fl], [kl] and [gl] are not, has to do with the fact that [l] shares the specification [coronal] with [t], [d] and [θ]: all these sounds are alveolar or dental, that is, [coronal] in distinctive feature theory. Like many other languages, English dislikes segments with an identical place of articulation in the same subsyllabic constituent, a situation akin to phonological incest! The reason for the non-occurrence of the onset clusters [pw], [bw], [mw], [fw] and [vw] is of course similar, since both the sounds in these clusters have the feature [labial].

> Check your understanding of the argument by explaining it to yourself or to a friend.

The tendency of constituent siblings not to have similar places of articulation is stated formally in the picturesquely named OBLIGATORY CONTOUR PRINCIPLE (OCP). The principle, and its label, originated in the context of tonal phonology (tone will be discussed in chapter 14). While all-pervasive in various ways in all components of phonology, with the principled exception of the timing tier for obvious reasons, the OCP is subject to a considerable number of exceptions, and its precise status therefore remains uncertain.

The tendency for constituent siblings not to have similar places of articulation is formalized as the OBLIGATORY CONTOUR PRINCIPLE

> Why should it be obvious that the OCP cannot apply to the timing tier?

The OCP is in fact more a tendency than a principle as such. We offer a provisional and deliberately somewhat loose definition in (21):

(21)   OCP (Obligatory Contour "principle"):
       Similar melodies are disfavoured as constituent siblings.

If high vowels can, after all, occur in the English onset, we need to weaken our current conception of the distribution of segment categories among the constituents of the syllable. In particular, we will now have to say that syllable margins are mainly (NB crucially, not only) occupied by consonants. In order to provide a formal basis for this situation, we need to introduce an additional level in our sonority scale, as we do in (22). This version obviously supersedes its predecessor in (5) above:

Syllable margins are mainly (NB crucially, not only) occupied by consonants

(22)   Sonority scale (second version):

Most sonorous   5   Non-high vowels
                4   High vowels
                3   Liquids
                2   Nasals
Least sonorous   1   Obstruents

We can now answer the question from the previous chapter as to why we formulate the sonority distance restriction on English onset siblings as a minimum of 2, rather than giving it a fixed value. The answer is that such legitimate onsets as [tw] or [kw] have a sonority distance of 3 (NB not 2) on the scale in (22): [t] and [k] are obstruents, and [w] (= [u]) a high vowel, thus $4 - 1 = 3$.

> Make a list of the extended set of possible English onsets, having regard to the OCP.

The conclusion that high vowels may be included in the English onset leads to a new statement of English onset phonotactics, as in (23), where reference to the new sonority scale in (22) replaces the brute-force onset template of (33) in chapter 9:

(23)   a.    b.

Sonority conditions: (i) $y \leq 4$
                       (ii) $x = 1$
                       (iii) $y - x \geq 2$

> Paraphrase these sonority conditions in your own words, to satisfy yourself that you understand them.

Notice that (23) is more accurate than its predecessor, but this accuracy is achieved at the cost of greater formal complexity, in the form of conditions.

Indeed, as is becoming increasingly evident and will be confirmed as we go along, the formal description of English syllable phonotactics is a matter of considerable intricacy.

> Are forms like *womb* and *yeast* consistent with the OCP? Explain carefully what the problem could be and propose a solution. Hint: the answer is effectively contained in our formulation of the OCP in (21).

5 Syllabification of [ĭu]

In the previous section we split the sequence **[w] + vowel** in words like *twin* or *quack* between the onset and the nucleus. This analysis is compatible with a formalization of the [w] and the following vowel as independent lexical segments: in the same way that we assume that the [ɹ] and the [æ] in *crack* are lexically independent, the [w] and the [æ] in *quack* can be /u/ and /æ/, respectively, in the lexicon. At first blush, the situation with the sequence [ĭu] in *fume* is analogous.

The sound [ĭu] occurs in the words in (18b, c) above, repeated now as (24) (remember that in some accents, General American for instance, the forms in (24b) do not have [ĭuː], but simply [uː]):

(24) a.   pew   beauty   cute   argue
           few   view
           mute

      b.   tune   dune
                          Thew
                          suit   Zeus
                          news

The vowel cluster [ĭu] is idiosyncratic in several respects. For instance, articulating [ĭu] involves no raising of the tongue in moving from the first to the second phase, contrary to what happens in the English primary diphthongs. Also, [ĭu] is the only instantiation of the sequence **[ĭ] + vowel** after a consonant: in a simple onset, [ĭ] can be followed by pretty well any nucleus vowel (see (14) and (16) above), but as part of a complex onset it only combines with the nucleus [uː] (or its reduced versions [ə] and [ʊ], where appropriate), as the examples in (24) above illustrate.

Thus, English speakers avoid the sequence **[ĭ] + vowel** (in one syllable) unless the vowel is [u] and/or no tautosyllabic consonant precedes the [ĭ] (the prefix TAUTO-, which also occurs in "tautology", signifies 'same').

Explain the meaning of "tautosyllabic".

One set of exceptions to this generalization, irrelevant for our immediate purposes, will be accounted for in chapter 18.

The dislike of English for [ĭ] in sequence with vowels other than [u] is forcefully brought out by the English pronunciation of such Spanish words as *fiesta*, *siesta*, *(San) Diego*, *Santiago*, etc. In Spanish, the vowel sequence is diphthongal: [i̯e], [i̯a], etc. (we mentioned above that the underscripted diacritic "ˎ" signals lack of syllabic independence). In English, however, such vowel sequences are systematically pronounced with a hiatus ([i.e], [i.a], etc.), except possibly in fast speech, where many of the restrictions we are discussing (although by no means all) appear to be flouted.

The following place names are not Spanish: *Kiev*, *Vienna*, *Lyon*, *Siena*, *Kyoto*. Do you (normally) pronounce the vowels of the spelling in two separate syllables or as a diphthong (we anticipate that the former will be the case)? Can you think of other similar cases? Are there any counterexamples?

The apportioning of all post-consonantal [i]V sequences but [ĭu] to two different nuclei shows that English generally rejects the integration of the /i/ of /iV/ into a complex onset. The question that obviously arises is why such integration is not rejected in [ĭu]. One reasonable answer would be that [ĭu] is a diphthong, since it seems sensible to assume that the very nature of diphthongs prevents them from being split between two syllables: all uncontroversial diphthongs of English ([aɪ], [ɔɪ], [oʊ], etc.) are indeed tautosyllabic.

Now, if [ĭu] is a diphthong, we might expect it to be allotted whole to the nucleus.

> English generally rejects the integration of the /i/ of /iV/ into a complex onset. Such integration is not rejected in [ĭu]

Explain why.

There is, however, specific evidence that the [i] of [ĭu] is assigned to the onset.

In the early seventeenth century, there was a diphthong [ɪu̯], with the syllable peak on [ɪ], and the second element [u̯] as an offglide, in much the same way as in the current primary diphthongs [aʊ], [oʊ], etc.: indeed, there seems to be a requirement for the first nucleus element to be the syllable peak. By the end of the seventeenth century, however, the peak of [ɪu̯] had been transferred to the second element, [u], and [ɪ] raised to [i]: [ĭu]. All these facts make it reasonable to construe present-day [ĭu] as a diphthong with a lexicalized peak on [u]. Given this analysis, the assignment of the [i] to the onset follows automatically as a matter of formal necessity: from this perspective, [ĭu] will be [ju], where the symbol [j] indicates onset status, parallelling the use of [w] for onset [u] ([y] is often used for [j] in North America, rather confusingly from an IPA perspective).

> Explain how the assignment of the [i] of [ĭu] to the onset follows as a matter of formal necessity.

This outcome is backed up by empirical evidence. Thus, English systematically lacks [ju] after onsets with two consonants, even in accents that admit the sequence **coronal + [ju]** in the onset: compare *bl*[u] (NB not **bl*[ju]) with the possible *l*[ju]*d* (*lewd*), *l*[ju]*rid* (*lurid*), and even *l*[ju]*te* (*lute*), *l*[ju]*dicrous* (*ludicrous*), etc.

> Can you guess the relevance of this to the issue of the syllabification of the [i] of [ĭu]?

Assuming that onsets cannot have more than two elements, in English and perhaps in other languages, an already binary onset such as [bl] will simply leave no room for [j] – thus failing to be licensed, [j] will not surface. This analysis crucially presupposes that the /i/ of /ĭu/ is assigned to the onset: if it were assigned to the nucleus, it would have been licensed there, in some way, and it would have been pronounced in all cases.

Further evidence for the assignment of [i] of [ĭu] to the onset comes from the selection of the "weak" article allomorphs *th*[ə] and *a* before [j] (*a ewe*, *th*[ə] *ewe*), as they always are before an onset (*a/th*[ə] *bow*, *a/th*[ə] *blow*), but not otherwise (*an/th*[i] *owl*).

Finally, and most revealingly, a handful of receding accents do have [blɪ̯ʊ], and [ɪ̯ʊ] in general for [ĭu], with the *first* element of the sequence as the peak.

> Say exactly how [blɪ̯ʊ] can be possible.

The behaviour of the [i] of /iu/ confirms that high vowels can partake in the English onset. In section 4 we showed that sonorant consonants can be assigned to the nucleus. These two complementary facts obviously force the relaxation of our early identification of ONCd with CVC.

High vowels can partake in the English onset

6 Onset Fulfilment

Our "parsing" of segments into syllables and into syllabic subconstituents has been guided by the sonority profile of the sequence of segments – the word PARSING denotes allotment of elements to constituents, and is well worth becoming familiar with. In a nutshell, English peaks normally require a sonority level of at least 4 on the scale in (22) above, that is, they need to be vowels. We illustrate in (25) with the words *traffic*, *napkin* and *pumpkin*:

(25)

Segments to the left of the nucleus are parsed in the onset, to a maximum of two, and segments to the right of the nucleus in the coda, at the moment also to a maximum of two:

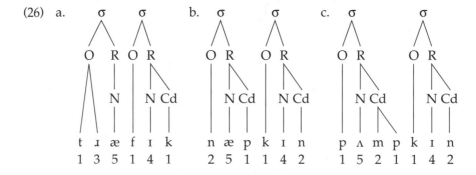

(26) a.   b.   c.

This parsing is, of course, conditional on compatibility with Sonority Sequencing and the other general principles of syllabification. The lowering of the sonority requirement on nuclei to level 2 on scale (22) that we discussed in section 2 is but a strategy to circumvent one specific problem for Sonority Sequencing without paying the price of deleting segments, which would be the obvious alternative.

Languages show a strong tendency to assign an inter-vocalic consonant to the onset, as encapsulated in the principle of MINIMAL ONSET SATISFACTION

> What problem are we referring to? How would segment dele-tion be an alternative solution?

An intervocalic consonant such as /f/ in *traffic* qualifies in principle as an onset or as a coda. As it happens, languages show an overwhelming tendency to assign an intervocalic consonant to the onset, as in (26a) above. We express this situation in the principle of MINIMAL ONSET SATIS-FACTION in (27):

(27)   Minimal Onset Satisfaction:
        Minimal satisfaction of onsets takes priority over satisfaction of codas

Following from Minimal Onset Satisfaction, a sequence ... VCVCV ... will be syllabified ... V.CV.CV ... , and not ... VC.VC.V ...

> On the basis of what you read in chapter 9, hazard a guess as to why Minimal Onset Satisfaction exists in language.

The syllabification ... V.CV.CV ... of course tallies in with our finding in chapter 9 that CV is the universal core syllable: a parsing ... V.CV.CV ... creates two such core syllables, whereas a parsing ... VC.VC.V ... creates none.

Specific evidence for the principle of Minimal Onset Satisfaction is also available. Consider such words as *carriage*, *car* and *cart*. In non-rhotic accents, there is no phonetic [ɹ] in *car* and *cart*, since these accents by definition do not admit [ɹ] in codas. In words like these there is of course no other possible parsing for the *r*. In *carriage*, however, the /ɹ/ can also be parsed as an onset, since it is followed by a vowel – the question is, will it indeed be parsed as the onset of [ɪ], or will it still be parsed as the coda of [æ]? The fact that non-rhotic speakers pronounce such an /ɹ/ answers our question: the /ɹ/ is parsed in the onset, for otherwise it would have no phonetic realization in these accents. This result obviously supports the principle of Minimal Onset Satisfaction in (27).

> Say exactly why the pronunciation of the *r* of *carriage* endorses the principle of Minimal Onset Satisfaction.

7 Onset Maximization. English Stop Allophony

Consider the forms in (28), with two or three intervocalic consonants:

(28)   recline   entreat   comply   surprise   contrive
        redress   congress   comfry   pam[f]let   conflate
        recruit   encroach   actress   undress   poultry
        include   en[θ]ral   impress   culprit   portrait

> Before we continue our discussion, decide where the syllable boundaries come in the words in (28). What are the reasons for your choice?

The question that arises in connection with the intervocalic consonants in (28) is whether they will all be parsed in the onset of the second syllable or whether they will be split between the two syllables, and if so how.

> Explain why they could not all be parsed as the coda of the first syllable.

Intuitively, the relevant syllable divisions in the words in (28) are as in (29):

(29)   re.cline   en.treat   com.ply   sur.prise   con.trive
       re.dress   con.gress   com.fry   pam.[f]let   con.flate
       re.cruit   en.croach   ac.tress   un.dress   poul.try
       in.clude   en.[θ]ral   im.press   cul.prit   por.trait

The formal procedures we have in place also allow for the parsings in (30), still assuming complex codas:

(30)   rec.line   ent.reat   comp.ly   surp.rise   cont.rive
       red.ress   cong.ress   comf.ry   pam[f].let   conf.late
       rec.ruit   enc.roach   act.ress   und.ress   poult.ry
       inc.lude   en[θ].ral   imp.ress   culp.rit   port.rait

Notice that the parsings in (30) do not incur any violation of Sonority Sequencing, since the resulting syllables do not contain sonority troughs.

> Show how this is so.

The parsings in (30) are obviously also compatible with the principle of Minimal Onset Satisfaction in (27) above.

> Say how they are compatible.

Intuitions are to be taken seriously in phonological (and other linguistic) research, for they are often, if not invariably, the tip of the iceberg of phonological (or linguistic) cognitive structure. The phonologist, however, wants to find empirical confirmation of such intuitions, which may conceivably be coloured, or even caused, by extralinguistic factors.

> Any idea what one such extralinguistic factor could be?

Empirical evidence for the parsings in (29) does indeed exist. This evidence concerns some stop allophony, and it confirms the principle of Minimal Onset Satisfaction (27).

In chapter 1 we illustrated the difference between English voiced and voiceless stops with word-medial, rather than word-initial, instantiations. The reason is that in word-initial position the contrast is not implemented by means of simultaneous vocal fold vibration or its absence, respectively. Rather, it is a function of the length of the time lag between the release of the closure and the start of vocal fold vibration for the following vowel: in "voiceless" stops the time lag is considerable, and in "voiced" stops very short, or possibly null. Word-initially, therefore, English "voiced" stops are actually voiceless!

Word-initially, English "voiced" stops are actually voiceless

> Explain the apparent paradox that English word-initial "voiced" stops are voiceless.

Consider, for instance, the pairs of words in (31):

(31)   a.   pie   b.   buy
           tie   die
           cow   guy

> Place your forefinger close to your lips and pronounce each of these words in turn. In the first word of each pair you should be able to detect a puff of air immediately before the voiced vowel, whereas, in the second word of the pair, there should be no such puff of air.

The period between the release of the closure and the start of vocal fold activity for the vowel is clearly longer in (31a), where it can be felt physically as

Aspiration charac-
terizes voiceless
stops in English

a puff of air known as ASPIRATION. Aspiration characterizes voiceless stops in English, not only word-initially, but also word-internally in the onset of a stressed syllable (we trust that you can identify the "stressed syllable" intuitively; we examine stress in detail in the next three chapters): *paper, repeat, terminal, deter, cover, recall,* etc.

> Compare the [p] in *repeat* with that in *rapid*. Although you may experience very slight aspiration in the second of these, you should again be able to feel a clear difference between the two *p*s.

Now, the parsings in (29) above are confirmed by the aspiration test.

> The aspiration test is only relevant to some of the words in (28). Which are these?

Thus, in words like *surprise* or *recline* the obstruent stop is aspirated, to the extent of rendering the following sonorant voiceless (recall that there are no lexical voiceless sonorants in English and in most other languages).

> Why isn't the sonorant voiceless in *congress* or *redress*?

The narrow phonetic transcription of the relevant sounds is therefore as in (32), where the underscripted circle of course represents voicelessness:

(32)   sur[pɹ̥]ise   re[kl̥]ine

It could be thought that devoicing is simply caused by the adjacency of the two relevant segments, irrespective of their syllabic constituency: according to this construal, syllable structure would be irrelevant to the spread of voicelessness. Consider, however, forms like those in (33), already referred to in section 4 above:

(33)   atlas   athlete

On the surface, the consonantal clusters [tl] and [θl] are similar to their counterparts in (32). However, if you observe your own pronunciation of [tl] and [θl] you will notice that [l] is now fully voiced, even though it also follows a voiceless obstruent. This situation follows from the syllabifications in (34):

(34)   at.las   ath.lete

There is in fact a good reason for the contrast in syllabification between the forms in (32) and the forms in (33): as we mentioned in section 4 above, the OCP in (21) prevents the occurrence in the same constituent of clusters with a similar place of articulation, such as [pw], [bw], [tl], [dl], [θl], [ðl].

> Restate the OCP in your own words and explain its function.

The facts of aspiration therefore show that the consonant clusters in (28) above (*recline, comply,* etc.), in all respects similar to those in (33), are parsed as complex onsets.

> Try out the same test on *atlas*. Does the outcome tell you anything about the internal syllable boundary in this and similar words?

Likewise, most speakers may pronounce *t* glottally in *atlas*, but not in *petrol*, for instance: the reason is, again, that in *petrol* /t/ would be parsed, not in the coda, but in the onset.

   The conclusion to draw is that intervocalic consonant clusters are allotted to the onset unless prevented by the familiar conditions on syllabification. We formulate this bias towards the onset as the principle of ONSET MAXIMIZATION:

(35)   Onset Maximization:
       Maximal formation of onsets takes priority over formation of codas

> In English, two intervocalic consonants are parsed in the onset unless prevented by the syllabification conditions

It would seem at this point that Onset Maximization subsumes our previous Minimal Onset Satisfaction principle in (27) above. This is, however, not so, since the two principles can show a different strength of application. For instance, in French the voiceless alveolar stop *t* is usually not pronounced at the end of words (*pet*[i] 'small'), although it can be pronounced when the following word beings with a vowel (*pet*[it] *enfant* 'small child'). One simple way of formalizing this contrast involves a prohibition against parsing /t/ in the coda, similar to the prohibition against parsing /ɹ/ in the coda in English non-rhotic accents. Now, the fact that the final /t/ of *petit* is pronounced in the phrase *petit enfant* indicates that Minimal Onset Satisfaction has impelled the parsing of this /t/ as the onset of the next vowel: *pe.ti.ten.fant*. What is interesting, and directly relevant to our present concerns, is that such parsing does not take place in a phrase like *petit roi* 'little king', which is invariably *pet*[iʁ]*oi* (not **pet*[itʁ]*oi*), even though the sequence [tʁ] is otherwise quite legitimate in French onsets: [tʁ]*ois* 'three' (cf. *pet*[i] [tʁ]*ois* 'little three'!). The reason for the opposing behaviour of the word-final /t/ in *petit enfant* and *petit roi* is that, in French, Minimal Onset Satisfaction is operative across words, hence *pe.ti.ten.fant*, but Onset Maximization is not, hence *pe.tit.roi* (= *.pe.tit.* + *roi*.): Minimal Onset Satisfaction is therefore stronger than Onset Maximization.

> Why doesn't Minimal Onset Satisfaction also force *pe.ti.trois* 'little king'?

It may be helpful to construe Onset Maximization and Minimal Onset Satisfaction as the maximal and minimal implementation, respectively, of a more general ONSET FIRST PRINCIPLE favouring onsets over codas. This result may be derivable from a still more fundamental principle favouring a maximal jump in sonority at the start of the syllable, and a minimal drop in sonority at the end.

A general ONSET FIRST PRINCIPLE favours onsets over codas

> Explain how not having a coda is better than having some coda under the principle favouring a maximal jump in sonority at the start of the syllable and a minimal drop at the end.

8   No Complex Codas in English

The structure of the syllable as we have it at the moment is fairly symmetrical, and thus quite pleasing. Summing up, syllables are made up of two constituents, the onset (optional) and the rime (obligatory), the latter made up of the nucleus (obligatory) and the coda (optional). The melodic contents of each subconstituent are restricted on the basis of sonority: nuclei prefer vowels, although they accept sonorant consonants under duress, and margins prefer consonants, although the onset can also accommodate high vowels. Each subconstituent is maximally binary, at least in English. Further principles governing syllabic parsing are Sonority Sequencing, Minimal Sonority Distance (both related to sonority), Minimal Onset Satisfaction, Onset Maximization, and the OCP.

Some word-final consonant clusters are problematic for our present approach. Consider first the forms in (36):

(36) clamp tent   link
             tend

      help   bolt   milk
      bulb   gild
      film   kiln

> The pronunciation fil[ə]m is common in Ireland. Give an analysis of this pronunciation after reading this section.

These words seemingly contain a complex coda made up of a sonorant followed by another consonant. The sequences in question clearly obey Sonority Sequencing, since the first sonorant invariably has more sonority – if it had less, an additional syllable would be formed, as we explained in section 2 (cf. *sickle* vs. *silk*). In fact, the clusters in (36) almost mirror their counterparts in onsets, as we mentioned in section 1: complex onsets allow for a cluster **C + liquid**, and the complex codas in (36) for a sequence **sonorant + C**. The difference between the two cases therefore hinges on minimal sonority distance: 2 in onsets (liquids = 3, obstruents = 1), but apparently nil in codas, given forms like *kept*, *fact*, etc. This poses an obvious problem for Sonority Sequencing.

A further difference between complex onsets and the putative complex codas is that complex onsets occur freely word-medially, as well as word-initially: indeed, the formation of word-medial complex onsets is favoured by Onset Maximization (35).

> Give some examples of complex onsets in both positions.

By contrast, the distribution of complex codas is heavily skewed towards word-final position, at least in English. This statement may appear to be wildly inaccurate, in the face of forms like *parenthood*, *thankless*, *boldness* and a great many others. However, we will argue in chapter 16 below that the clusters in question are effectively also word-final in these cases: *parent*, *thank(s)*, *bold*, etc., are words in their own right. Another group of apparent counter-examples has a stop between a homorganic nasal and an obstruent – the stop can be analysed as a purely phonetic transition, that is, as non-lexical: *pumpkin* and one or two other forms ending in *kin* (*pumpkin* is actually *pu*[m]*kin* for many speakers), *resumptive*, *redemption*, *assumption*, and so on. Among the few truly genuine examples of word-medial complex codas is *arctic* in rhotic accents, but a pronunciation *a*[ɹt]*ic* or [aːt]*ic*, with no [k] is far more common.

English complex codas are essentially limited to word-final position

The effective restriction of complex codas to the right edge of the word is obviously puzzling. One way out of the conundrum involves abandoning the complex coda analysis for the consonant clusters in question. This move receives support from forms like those in (37):

(37)   claim   leak
      hail   like
      bowl
      file

> Say why these forms support the move against the complex coda.

The forms in (37) end in a consonant preceded by a long vowel or a diphthong. Again, this configuration is not found word-internally – the only genuine counterexamples are the rather technical *deictic*, *deixis* and *seismic*: in words like *chamber*, *dainty*, *council*, *ancient*, *angel*, *poultry*, *shoulder* and a handful of others the "coda" sonorant shares its place of articulation with the onset, which can therefore be argued to license it, in a way we will explain in chapter 16.

The common denominator of (36) and (37) is, of course, the presence of an extra consonant after an ordinary rime word-finally: this is the analysis we will adopt. In particular, we will assume that the word-final consonant of English words affiliates directly to the σ node, not indirectly via the R node, as we would expect:

We will assume that the word-final consonant of English words affiliates directly to the σ node

(38)   a.

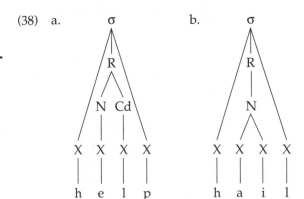

This analysis has the advantage of allowing us to preserve the statement that English codas are simple throughout the word: the coda is the consonant licensed by R, and so the word-final consonant in (38) does not partake in the coda. At the same time, such a final consonant remains inside the syllable, and therefore the compliance of such clusters with Sonority Sequencing is correctly predicted (cf. (8a) vs. (8b) above): the exception inevitably involves final coronals (*act*, *apt*, and so on), and will be seen to directly (remember that we said in section 1 that when both siblings in an apparent coda are non-sonorant stops, the right one needs to be coronal).

As we have just hinted, coronal obstruents can follow any type of segment word-finally, irrespective of sonority, to complicate the English syllable still further. We show this in (39):

(39) a. left   raft   lift
      b. act   apt   concept   erect
      c. buzzed
      d. lapse   si[ks]
      e. bread[θ]   wid[θ]

> What happens to such coronals when they are not in word-final position, as in *rafter* and *aptitude*?

Indeed, coronal obstruents appear to occur unrestrictedly on the right edge of the English word. A rather spectacular instantiation of extra word-final coronal obstruents is offered by the forms *sixths* and *contexts*, with no fewer than three coronal obstruents after /k/, at least in careful diction: [sɪksθs], [kontɛksts].

Coronals appear to occur unrestrictedly on the right edge of the English word

> Which constraints are being violated here?

Situations of this kind pose a serious challenge to the constrained framework we have been endeavouring to develop for the syllable.

> Say exactly in what way these situations are a challenge to the constrained syllable. Now give the analysis of *fil[ə]m* asked for in the grey box below (36) above

We return to these issues and advance a solution in chapter 16.

9 The Antics of /s/

The limitation of the English coda to one consonant that we have just proposed appears to be contradicted by /s/, which can follow any coda consonant word-internally: *institute, transfer, abstain, instruct, conscript, obstacle,* etc.

> Summarize the differences between onsets and codas with regard to the distribution of consonants.

Faced with these facts, we could think of accepting complex codas with /s/ as their second element. However, this solution would be problematic for Sonority Sequencing as it stands at the moment, as we illustrate in (40) – remember that stops and fricatives are level in sonority in the scale in (22) above:

(40) clasp crisp tusk risk

You can see that, as a possible first element of the new complex coda, /s/ patterns with sonorants, even though /s/ is level with stops in the sonority scale in (5). One answer would be to split fricatives and plosives in the sonority ranking, in a more precise sonority scale – objectively, fricatives are indeed more sonorous than stops:

(41)   Potential sonority scale:
       Most sonorous   6   Non-high vowels
                       5   High vowels
                       4   Liquids
                       3   Nasals
                       2   Fricatives
       Least sonorous 1   Stops

The /s/ + stop coda now obviously complies with Sonority Sequencing. However, /s/ is the only fricative licensed in the English coda before non-coronals, as attested by the impossibility of forms like *lefp*, *lefk*, etc. (in contrast to *left*, which ends in a coronal). Therefore, the scale in (41) still falls short of solving the problem, and therefore we shall not adopt it.

> Why doesn't the scale in (41) solve the problem posed by the extra *s*?

The idiosyncrasies of /s/ extend to the onset. Consider the words in (42):

(42) a. slum
      b. small   snow
      c. spy   sty   sky
          sphere

These forms apparently have a complex onset. However, the parsing of the
initial *s*C cluster in the onset would put some of our current generalizations
in jeopardy.

> If the initial *s*C
> cluster were
> analysed as an
> onset, some of
> the standing gen-
> eralizations would
> be put in jeopardy

> List a few of the current generalizations, without thinking too
> hard.

First, an onset *s*C would be incompatible with the setting 2 we have given
to the Minimal Sonority Distance parameter: in the forms in (42b) the distance between *s* and C is only 1 (obstruents = 1; nasals = 2), while in (42c)
the score is even (1, since voiceless stops and /s/ are both obstruents), all
according to the hierarchy in (5) above. Next, an onset *sl*, as in *slum*, would
violate the OCP, which we know bans *[tl], *[dl], *[θl] from the onset. Likewise for an onset *shr* [ʃɹ], as in *shrill*, best analysed as derived from /sɹ/ by
assimilation, since [sɹ] never occurs word-initially in English, even when
prompted by the spelling: *Sri Lanka*.

> Explain exactly what we mean by [ʃɹ] being derived from /sɹ/.
> Provide some empirical evidence to back up this claim.

The problems for an onset parsing of *s*C clusters get compounded in forms
like those in (43):

(43) **spr**ay   **str**ay   **scr**ap
      splay   **scl**erosis
      spew   **st**ew   **sk**ew
                            squash

> What is different about the onsets in the words in (43)?

These consonant clusters can only be parsed in the onset if we admit three-
member onsets:

(44)   [spɹ]   [stɹ]   [skɹ]
       [spl]   [skl]
       [spj]   [stj]   [skj]
                       [skw]

> Do you notice anything else special about these onset clusters?

You are well aware that an increase in the size of syllabic subconstituents is undesirable, on grounds of grammatical stringency. Moreover, the fact that the first segment in such putative three-member onsets is always [s] would be a coincidence.

The changes in onset sonority distance that took place in the historical development of English also militate against the inclusion of /s/ in the onset. In Old and Middle English, forms like *knave* and *gnat* were pronounced as spelled, on a par with the contemporary German *knabe* [knabə] 'boy' or *gnädig* [gnɛdiç] 'gracious'. In Early Modern English, the initial stop was lost (although it survived in the spelling). By contrast, initial [s] was retained, not only prenasally but, more generally, preconsonantally.

> Explain in what way the preservation of preconsonantal initial [s] militates against its inclusion in the onset.

The behaviour of /s/ is idiosyncratic across the board, in English and in many other languages

All the facts we have considered provide strong motivation for granting word-initial [s] special status, in English and in other languages. We formulate a specific proposal along these lines in chapter 16.

C h a p t e r   S u m m a r y

In this chapter we have investigated further principles which govern syllabi-fication, concentrating specifically on the phonotactic constraints of English branching onsets and on codas. Branching onsets typically consist of an obstruent followed by a sonorant consonant. We came to the conclusion that English does not countenance branching codas, although an extra word-final consonant can be licensed directly from the syllable node. As expected, Sonority Sequencing is operative throughout the syllable: word-final sequences of consonantal elements with rising sonority are dealt with by the creation of a syllable with a non-vocalic nucleus (e.g. *sickle* [sɪkl̩]).

We have also shown that, while vowels will generally form syllable nuclei and consonants syllable margins, in a significant minority of cases Sonority Sequencing drives sonorant consonants into nuclei. We also showed that high vowels (/i/ and /u/ in English) can be parsed in the onset when they immediately precede another vowel (onset /i/ and /u/ are traditionally transcribed /j/ and /w/, respectively). Phonotactic discrepancies between C/w/ and C/l/ onsets are accounted for by the Obligatory Contour Principle (OCP), which disfavours similar melodies in constituent siblings. Thus, /w/ involves labial activity, and may not co-occur with labial consonants (/p, b, f, v, m/), while coronal /l/ may not co-occur with coronals (/θ, ð, t, d/). The parsing of word-medial consonants is governed by two principles. The first, Minimal Onset Satisfaction, imposes the formation of a (minimal) onset in preference to a coda in the preceding syllable, to conform to the universally basic CV syllable. The second, independent principle, Onset Maximization, favours the parsing of word-medial clusters as onsets. The pronunciation of intervocalic r in non-rhotic accents shows support for Minimal Onset Satisfaction, and the syllable-initial aspiration of voiceless stops for Onset Maximization. The intervention of /s/ creates problems for some of the generalizations made, but the solution will not be tried out until chapter 16 below.

Key Questions

1 What are the basic constraints on apparent complex codas in English?

2 Under what conditions may consonants form nuclei in English?

3 Under what conditions may vowels occur in an onset? Which vowels?

4 What evidence is there for high vowels being analysed as part of an onset, when followed by another vowel, rather than forming part of a complex nucleus?

5 What is the Obligatory Contour Principle (OCP)? What influence does it have on onset formation in English?

6 What is unusual about the sequence /iu/ in English? How is it syllabified?

7 Which two principles can be combined to make up the Onset First Principle? What is the difference in the provisions of these two principles?

8 How does the possible word-internal coda differ from its apparent word-final counterpart?

9 Some words end in clusters of three or four consonants. What is special about these consonants? Can the extra consonants be considered part of a complex coda?

10 List the problems inherent in a claim that sC clusters may form complex onsets.

F u r t h e r   P r a c t i c e

French

French high vowels can be syllabified in two different ways ([ɥ] is the symbol used for [y] in non-nuclear position, in parallel with [w] for [u] and [j] for [i]):

a. il joue   [ilʒu]   'he plays'
    jouer   [ʒwe]   'to play'
    jouable   [ʒwabl]   'playable'

    il tue   [ilty]   'he kills'
    tuer   [tɥe]   'to kill'
    contribution   [kɔ̃tribysjɔ̃]   'tax'
    contribuable   [kɔ̃tribɥabl]   'taxpayer'

    il lie   [illi]   'he ties'
    lier   [lje]   'to tie'
    colonie   [kɔlɔni]   'colony'
    colonial   [kɔlɔnjal]   'colonial'

(i)   Can you see any reason for the different syllabifications?

Compare the data in a. with those in b.:

b. plier   [plie]   *[plje]   'to fold'
    prier   [prie]   *[prje]   'to pray'
    clouer   [klue]   *[klwe]   'to nail'
    trouer   [true]   *[trwe]   'to make a hole in'
    cruauté   [kryote]   *[krɥote]   'cruelty'
    influence   [ɛ̃flyɑ̃s]   *[ɛ̃flɥɑ̃s]   'influence'

(ii) What do these new facts suggest about the structure of syllabic subconstituents in French?

Southern Welsh Rime Phonotactics

Monophthongal Southern Welsh vowels, except for schwa, fall into groups, long and short. The list is as follows:

/iː ɪ eː ɛ aː a oː ɔ uː ʊ ɜ i ə/

In some circumstances the long and short vowels can be shown to be contrastive but in other situations only one or other group may occur. Consider the following representative examples of monosyllabic words:

a. /diːn/   'man'   /gwɪn/   'white'
    /heːn/   'old'   /prɛn/   'tree'
    /taːn/   'fire'   /man/   'place'
    /soːn/   'speak'   /brɔn/   'breast'
    /suːn/   'noise'   /grʊn/   'ridge of ploughland'
b. /biːd/   'world'   /jɛt/   'gate'
    /ɬeːd/   'width'   /at/   'to'
    /boːd/   'to be'   /ɬɔk/   'sheepfold'
    /taːd/   'father'   /krʊt/   'boy'
    /knuːd/   'crop'
c. /priːð/   'earth'   /r̥iːχ/   'furrow'
    /beːð/   'grave'   /hwɛːχ/   'six'
    /ɬaːð/   'to kill'   /moːχ/   'pigs'
    /moːð/   'way'   /huːχ/   'sow'
    /kiːɬ/   'hazel'   /gweːɬ/   'better'
    /ɬaːɬ/   'other'   /hoːɬ/   'hole'
d. /kiː/   'dog'   /ɬeː/   'place'
    /daː/   'good'   /toː/   'roof'
    /ɬuː/   'oath'
e. /pɪnt/   'pound'   /gwɛrθ/   'value'
    /plant/   'children' /gɔlχ/   'children'
    /kʊsk/   'sleep'

(i)   Is vowel length contrastive in all environments?
(ii)   What conditions are there on the distribution of long and short vowels?
(iii) Make a suggestion about the shape of the rime in southern Welsh.
(iv)   Compare the possible rime in southern Welsh with that of English outlined in section 8.

CHAPTER ELEVEN

THE PHENOMENON OF STRESS

RHYTHM

Chapter Objectives

In this chapter you will learn about:

- Unequal prominence among syllables both in words and in word sequences.
- Syllable prominence interpreted as "stress".
- The difference in stress location between phrases, where stress falls on the final element, and compounds, where it falls on the first.
- How these differences can be represented formally as a "metrical grid", where all syllable nuclei are marked with an asterisk, and an additional, higher, asterisk singles out the most prominent syllable.
- The rhythm of English compared with the rhythm of French.
- A method of maintaining rhythm and preventing adjacent prominent elements, through the retraction of stress where a clash occurs.
- Segmental evidence for stress from the weakening of intervocalic /t/ and the reduction of unstressed vowels to schwa.

In the previous two chapters, we argued for the enrichment of phonological representation with abstract PROSODIC structure, over and above the structure that corresponds to the linear arrangement of segments and to the relations between the features inside the segments – the word *prosody* ultimately derives from the Greek *pros* 'to' + *ōidē* 'song', with the meaning 'song sung to music', or, more to the point here, 'tone of a syllable'. So far we have identified such prosodic structure with the syllable, and we have gone to some lengths to present and justify the internal architecture of this construct. In this and the next two chapters we will examine a level of prosodic organization larger than the syllable. The principal manifestation of this higher prosodic level is what is commonly known as "stress", and in this chapter we provide ample illustration of the phenomenon, conveniently tapping the intuitions of the English speaker. The specific prosodic nature of stress will become clear as the exposition proceeds, in this and subsequent chapters.

1 Syllable Prominence

In line with the hands-on methodology we are adopting, let us try to gain first-hand experience of the phenomenon of stress by pronouncing the words in (1):

(1) increase imprint relay   torment   upset
     contest   contract escort decrease protest
     contrast implant survey convict   digest

> Pronounce these words. Do you encounter any problems? Explain what they are.

The task of pronouncing the words in (1) ought to be child's play for any fluent speaker of English, but it turns out to be tricky, for the simple reason that each of the words in question can be pronounced in one of two ways, which we represent impressionistically in (2):

(2) INcrease   inCREASe
     CONtest   conTEST
     CONtrast   conTRAST
     ....

Each of these pairs of words is basically made up of the same string of segments – indeed, the spelling is constant. The words in the first column of (2) have, however, more prominence on the first syllable, while in those in the second column the second syllable is more prominent. We hope that this contrast will be obvious to any fluent English speaker, but we contextualize it in (3) to remove any possible doubts:

(3) a. another tax increase   b. taxes continue to increase
         when is the beauty contest?   when will the beauties contest?
         an unexpected contrast   they unexpectedly contrast

> Do you see any difference in the function of the words in the two columns?

The words we are examining are of course being used as nouns in column a. and as verbs in column b. We are now seeing that this grammatical difference goes hand in hand with a difference in the location of the word's highest prominence: the first syllable in (3a) and the last syllable in (3b). The prominence in question is what we call STRESS. The data we have considered thus show that one of the syllables of each English word is singled out as the word's stress carrier.

Each English word has one of its syllables singled out as the word's stress carrier

2 Word Prominence

Let us take our awareness of stress one step further by considering the two-word string in (4):

(4)   time flies

We just saw that in each word one syllable has more prominence, that is to say, carries more stress. The question now is whether one of the two words in the sequence in (4) is also more prominent than the other, and, if so, which.

In a sequence of words one of the words carries more stress than the others

Have a guess.

The answer will again come readily to any fluent speaker of English: the second word, *flies*, is more prominent:

(5)   time FLIES

We are, of course, assuming a "neutral" context, that is, a context that does not involve a contrast with another word, as would be the case, for instance, in *space doesn't fly: TIME flies*, with the emphasis on *time* for contrast.

Experiment with a few other similar phrases until you feel comfortable locating their stress.

The string in (6) looks very much like its predecessor in (4):

(6)   time-flies

The meaning of *time-flies* is intended to parallel the meaning of the forms in (7):

(7)   mayflies
       horseflies
       greenflies
       white flies
       black flies

Time-flies is, therefore, the plural of *time-fly*, the potential name of a fly species. Of course, no such object exists, but it could have existed and may well exist in the future. This again shows that a language is much more than the words in the dictionary, since *time-fly*, albeit a well-formed word in English, is not likely to be found in any English dictionary.

> How can a well-formed word of English not be found in any English dictionary?

The relevant question here is whether an utterance of *time-flies* will be confused with an utterance of *time flies*. The two strings are in fact indistinguishable with regard to both word identity and word order. They do not, of course, look the same when we write them down, since in *time-flies* we are separating the two words with a hyphen. However, it ought to be obvious from our repeated comments that spelling conventions are simply that, and cannot automatically be assumed to have a phonetic correlate. The broad transcription in (8) confirms that the segments of the strings in (4) and (6) are indeed identical:

> We mentioned the difference between "narrow" and "broad" transcription in chapter 5, section 6. Would a narrow transcription make any difference in the present case?

(8)   [taɪm flaɪz]   "time flies" or "time-flies"

Puzzlingly, although the segments of the two phrases are identical, there will be no confusion between *time-flies* and *time flies* when we say them.

> Conduct a test on a friend or even on yourself, involving saying or recording, respectively, a random sequence of tokens of the items in question, to prove that there is indeed no perceptual confusion.

At first sight, the statement that *time-flies* and *time flies* are pronounced differently conflicts with their identical phonetic representation in (8). The conflict, however, is resolved when we look for a difference beyond the makeup of the segments.

> What indeed is the difference?

While, as you now know explicitly, *time flies* has the main prominence on *flies* (*time FLIES*), in *time-flies* *time* is more salient, assuming again a neutral context:

(9)　TIME-flies

As we have just hinted, *flies* in *time-flies* will be contrastively emphasized if we are comparing such a fly species with another time-connected species: *I'm not talking about time-ants; it's time-FLIES I'm interested in*. Contrastive stress, however, falls outside our present remit and, therefore, we will ignore it in the rest of the discussion: essentially, any English word or syllable can be stressed for emphasis.

> Explain to yourself the difference between "normal" and "contrastive" stress.

We superimpose a hierarchical structure on syllables and on words, functionally analogous to the prosodic structure that gathers segments into syllables

Emphasis or no emphasis, the data in (4) and (6) reveal that in a sequence of words one of the words has greater prominence than the others. We already know that in each word one of the syllables is more prominent than the rest. We shall give a common formal expression to these two facts by superimposing a specific hierarchical prosodic structure on syllables and on words. This prosodic structure is functionally analogous to the prosodic structure that gathers segments into syllables and that we discussed in chapters 9 and 10, in as much as it also gathers elements into prosodic constituents.

> Remind yourself of how a syllable is but a hierarchy of segments based on sonority.

The configurations of the two structures are, however, significantly different, as we shall see. We present the prosodic structure associated with stress in the next section.

3 Metrical Grids

We will now introduce a formal notation for the representation of the prosodic structure we are proposing, and consequently for stress itself. Consider once more the now familiar contrasts between (*to*) *implant* and (*an*) *implant*, or *time flies* and *time-flies*. A straightforward representation of these contrasts is given in (10) and (11), respectively:

(10) a.   *   b.   *   Stress line
              *   *   *   *   Baseline
         (to) implant   (an) implant

(11) a.   *   b.   *   Stress line
              *   *   *   *   Baseline
            time flies   time-flies

These graphics can be interpreted at a glance: stressed elements are more heavily starred than their stressless counterparts, a bit like higher-ranking army officers being more heavily starred than officers of lower rank. Thus, consider (10). In the baseline we mark with an asterisk all and only the segments that qualify to bear stress, normally the syllable heads – we said in chapter 9 that the head of a constituent is the element defining the constituent: the head of a syllable is, normally, a vowel. The reason that only syllable heads can be stress bearers should be obvious in the context of the theory of the syllable we presented in the previous two chapters.

> Spell out what the reason is for stress-bearer status being limited to syllable heads.

Quite simply, we know that the syllable head constitutes the true core of the syllable: it is its sonority peak. As a consequence, only syllable heads qualify to bear stress, and it is this potential for stress that the baseline is meant to formalize. In contrast to the stress potential formalized by the baseline, the stress line signals the actual presence of stress on the element it singles out: *a* in (10a) and *i* in (10b), for instance. From this perspective, we can construe stress as the projection of certain syllable heads onto a higher structural level (we came across the notion of "projection" in the context of syllable nuclei in chapter 9): formally, the baseline asterisk dominating the privileged syllable head is projected onto the stress line.

Stress can be construed as the projection of a certain syllable head onto a higher structural level

> What sort of "projection" did we encounter in chapter 9? Explain the meaning of the term in your own words.

Diagrams (10) and (11) are made out of a series of rows intersecting with a series of columns, in the style of a grid (more obviously so when the number of rows and columns of asterisks is increased), hence the official label METRICAL GRID. The exact import of the key word "metrical" will be clarified as we go along. From now on, we will use metrical grids to formalize the stress patterns of words and word collocations.

We will use metrical grids to formalize the stress patterns of words and word collocations

4 Motivating Stress Constrasts

Having availed ourselves of a reasonable formal notation for the representation of stress, we will now try to find the factor behind the differences between the two stress patterns in (2) (*INcrease* vs. *inCREASe*) and between the two stress patterns in (4) and (6) (*time FLIES* vs. *TIME-flies*).

We have already pointed out that the different location of stress in the words in the two columns in (2) can be attributed to the categorial opposition noun vs. verb: *INcrease* is a noun and *inCREASE* a verb. You may be inclined to think that the contrast between *time FLIES* and *TIME-flies* hinges on meaning: the stress shifts implementing contrastive emphasis in *TIME flies* and *time-FLIES* are indeed related to meaning.

> Say in what way the contrasts *time FLIES* vs. *TIME flies* and *TIME-flies* vs. *time-FLIES* are dependent on meaning.

Note, however, that *time flies* has at least two different readings. The meaning most likely to spring to mind is that time moves at great speed. The collocation has, however, a second possible meaning, just as real and legitimate, if perhaps a little less obvious.

> Try and figure out this second possible meaning.

This alternative meaning involves a command by the speaker to the hearer to engage in the timing of flies (A: "What shall I do for fun?"; B: "Time flies!"). In this sense, *time flies* contrasts with *time fleas* or *time ants*, or, more realistically, with *time horses* or *greyhounds*. Of course, it also contrasts with *kill flies*, *collect flies*, *admire flies* or even *race flies*.

> Pronounce this second batch of phrases, making sure you don't give them contrastive stress.

What is directly relevant to the discussion is that this additional meaning of *time flies* is not marked prosodically. The hearer must, therefore, interpret *time flies* simply on the basis of the background and contextual information available. This shows that there is no necessary connection between stress and meaning.

> Introspect for a few seconds to check whether you are convinced that there is no necessary connection between stress and meaning.

There is no necessary connection between stress and meaning

A more productive line of inquiry into the stress difference between *time flies* and *time-flies* involves grammatical structure. In particular, you will notice that *time flies* (in either of its senses) is a sentence, with a subject, *time*, and a predicate, *flies*, or alternatively a predicate, *time*, and a direct object, *flies*, depending on the sense (do not worry excessively if you are not fully conversant with this syntactic terminology). By contrast, *time-flies* is a (compound) noun – we could, for instance, order someone to *time time-flies*. We provide further illustration of the stress contrast between phrasal and compound constructions in (12):

The stress difference between time flies and time-flies concerns grammatical structure

(12)   green HOUSE   GREENhouse
       (the house is painted green)   (where tomatoes grow)
       black BIRD   BLACKbird
       (could be a rook)   (the female of the species is brown)
       playing CARDS   PLAYing cards
       (to pass the time)   (in a pack)

Compounds, of course, abound in English, as we now (modestly) illustrate:

(13)   child minder   phone book   dolls house
       oak apple   clothes horse   horse box
       house plant   tie rack   trouser press
       alarm clock   baby alarm   coffee pot

In fact, English compound formation resembles sentence formation in having no apparent limit. As Chomsky observed in his book *Syntactic Structures*, which set the programme of generative grammar in motion in the late 1950s, the number of sentences in English, or any natural language, is by its very nature infinite. For a similar reason, most compounds we use in real life are not in the dictionary.

> Do you see why most compounds are not in the dictionary? Make up a few more compounds to satisfy yourself of how productive the procedure is.

Summarizing the discussion so far, we have seen that in words with more than one syllable one of the syllables has more stress than the others, and that in phrases or compounds one of the words also exhibits more prominence. Moreover, we have seen that, in the data we have considered, the location of prominence is not dependent on meaning, but, rather, on the category of the word (noun vs. verb) or the word collocation (phrase vs. compound).

5 The Distribution of Stress in Personal Names

In this section we will examine a class of apparent counterexamples to the stress patterns we have been observing in phrases, and we will suggest a reason for the situation. Conveniently, this will involve the manipulation of additional stress data.

Consider the English double names in (14), either attested or sufficiently realistic:

(14)   Sue Ann
       Sarah Jane
       Donna Jo
       Peggy Sue
       Maggie May
       Mary Lou
       Billy Jean
       Peter John
       Christopher Robin

> Test these out for stress. Experiment with a few other such names you can think of.

In all the collocations in (14) the second name is more prominent (*Sue ANN*, etc.), indicating that these constructions are stressed like phrases, rather than like compounds. It is indeed a fact of English that some compounds receive stress in the manner of phrases (and it is actually not clear how complex names should be analysed syntactically).

First names can, of course, be followed by surnames:

(15)   Sue Ann Cook
       Sarah Jane Brown
       Mary Lou Jones

> Which of the three words carries the main stress in the collocations in (15)?

In these constructions, the main stress still falls on the right-most item, that is, on the surname (*Sue Ann COOK*, etc.). Two further, related facts are directly of interest here. First, the remaining two words (making up the double first name) are not pronounced with equal prominence but, instead, one of them bears more prominence than the other. We would expect this greater prominence to be carried by the second word (*Ann, Jane*, etc.), on the basis of the data in (14) above (*Sue ANN*, etc.). As it happens, however, it is the first word (*Sue*, etc.) that bears this subsidiary prominence. This second fact is intriguing in the light of the present discussion.

> Why should the subsidiary prominence of the first word be intriguing?

In order to solve the puzzle, we need to examine the grid representation of the stress pattern in question:

(16)   *   Stress line 2
            *   *   Stress line 1
          *   *   *   Baseline
        Sue Ann Cook

Notice that we have now increased the number of stress lines in the grid, to take account of the intermediate degree of stress carried by *Sue*. Indeed, we will see as we proceed that the number of lines in the grids of word collocations is in principle open-ended – it is simply a function of the number of words in the construction: the more words, the more grid lines.

Formally, the problem is why in the grid in (16) the line 1 stress should be located on *Sue*, since this stress is located on *Ann* when the double name *Sue Ann* is said in isolation:

The number of grid lines for word collocations is a function of the number of words in the construction

(17)   *   Stress line 1
        *   *   Baseline
      Sue Ann

We offer a solution in the next section.

6 Stress Retraction under Clash

You will now see that our grid formalism provides an elegant resolution to our paradox. Consider what the structure of the grid corresponding to the string *Sue Ann Cook* would look like if *Ann*, rather than *Sue*, had a line 1 mark:

(18)   *   Stress line 2
             *   *   Stress line 1
        *   *   *   Baseline
      Sue Ann Cook

The grid in (18) contains a "stress clash". There is a STRESS CLASH between two asterisks in any grid line when they are adjacent and there is no asterisk in between the corresponding pair of asterisks in the line immediately below. In (19) we show with the aid of a box that this is precisely the case in the grid in (18):

There is a stress clash between two asterisks adjacent in any grid line when there is no asterisk in between the corresponding asterisks in the line immediately below

(19)
Sue Ann Cook

The structure boxed in includes two adjacent asterisks in line 1, without any asterisk separating the corresponding asterisks in the line immediately below, the baseline.

> Go back to the diagram in (19) and point at the clash with your finger.

English and languages with similar metrical systems strongly resist stress clash

English and similar languages strongly resist stress clash. The stress clash in (18) has of course resulted from the concatenation of the double first name *Sue Ann*, which we saw in (17) has the main stress on *Ann*, and the surname *Cook*, which bears the main stress of the entire construction *Sue Ann Cook*.

The clash between *Ann* and *Cook* is resolved by movement of the subordinate stress from *Ann* to *Sue*. From now on, we informally signal the original location of the moved asterisk with an arrow. We also embolden clashing asterisks, to make them more salient to the eye:

(20)
```
            *                  *      Stress line 2
     *      *           *  ←   *      Stress line 1
  *  *      *           *  *   *      Baseline
  Sue Ann Cook   →   Sue Ann Cook
```

Stress movement of this kind is very frequent in English, and is generally seen as the result of the RHYTHM RULE in (21) – the motivation for the label "Rhythm Rule" will be given in section 9:

Stress movement is very frequent in English, and is generally analysed as the result of the Rhythm Rule

(21) Rhythm Rule:
```
     *  *      *      *
  *  *  *  →   *  *  *
```

You will notice that the left-most of the two clashing asterisks moves back by one position: as a result of this movement, the output is free of clash.

The Rhythm Rule gives English much of its characteristic metrical flavour, as even a modest survey of the phenomenon reveals.

> Illustrate the action of the Rhythm Rule in a handful more cases.

Thus, the situation we just investigated with personal names is general in the language. Compare, for example, the strings in the two columns of (22):

(22) a. South American   b. South American music
          Sydney Harbour   Sydney Harbour Bridge
          apple pie   apple pie bed

> Check these for stress contour.

In the shorter construction *South American*, the main stress falls on the second word, *American*. As before, we would have expected this pattern to survive when the word *music* is added to form the longer phrase. Specifically, the metrical structure of *South American music* ought to be a composite of the metrical structure of *South American* and *music*. As we show in (23), however, this is not the case:

(23)

a. South American   b.   South American music

How do the grids in (23) differ from those in (20)? How is this difference justified? Hint: some of the words in (23) are polysyllabic.

In *South American music* the second highest stress column rests, not on *American*, but on *South*. This structure parallels that of *Sue Ann Cook* in (15). Indeed, the reasons are the same, namely, avoidance of stress clash, in compliance with the Rhythm Rule in (21) above:

(24)

a. South American   b.   South American music

By contrast, in *South American modern music*, *American* does retain its subsidiary stress, simply because in this collocation *American* does not incur a stress clash:

(25)

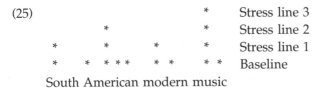

South American modern music

Explain why there is retraction in (24), but not in (25).

In the construction in (25), made up of the shorter phrases *South American* and *modern music*, the line 2 asterisks on *American* and *music* are separated by a line 1 asterisk on *modern*. Consequently, no clash arises, and stress does not have to move.

In this section, we have seen that stress clashes in English word collocations are resolved through movement of the first clashing asterisk to a word further to the left. In the next section we show that leftward stress movement can also happen inside words.

7 Word-Internal Stress Retraction

In all the cases we have examined, stress has ended up in a word to the left of the word that originally bore it. Now consider the words in (26a) and the collocations in (26b), made up of each of the words in (26a) followed by another word:

(26) a. Suzanne   b. Suzanne Morris
          Michelle   Michelle Pfeiffer
          Heathrow   Heathrow Airport
          Berlin   Berlin Wall
          Dundee   Dundee marmalade
          Cornell   Cornell hockey
          Aberdeen   Aberdeen Angus

> How do you stress the words in (26a)?

All the simple words in (26a) have main stress on the final syllable (some of the words admit idiolectal variation, but the patterns we are citing are widespread):

(27)   *   Stress line 1
          *   *   Baseline
        Suzanne

When the words in (26a) appear in the larger collocations in (26b), however, the subsidiary stress of the phrase invariably falls on their initial syllable:

(28)   *   Stress line 2
          *   *   Stress line 1
        *   *   *   *   Baseline
        Suzanne Morris

The high frequency of this stress retraction in real life can lead to permanent stress shift. For instance, the pronunciation *HEATHrow*, with unetymological stress on the first syllable, may nowadays be heard even when the word is said in isolation or in non-clash contexts.

Clash-triggered retraction is, of course, not restricted to proper nouns. For instance, the words in (29a) have a different stress contour in isolation and in the collocations in (29b):

The high frequency of stress retraction in real life can lead to permanent stress shift

(29) a. antique   b. antique chair
          fifteen   fifteen children
          bamboo   bamboo table

Here also, stress retraction in the collocation is impelled by stress clash:

(30)   *   *   Stress line 2
              *   *   *   *   ←   *   Stress line 1
        * *   *   *   *   * *   *   Baseline
        antique antique chair → antique chair

Formally, the process falls within the scope of the Rhythm Rule in (21), clearly a fundamental principle for the organization of English stress.

Interestingly, stress movement can cause the merger of the verb and noun patterns we mentioned in section 1:

> Remind yourself quickly of what the noun and verb stress patterns are.

(31) a. INcrease TAxes   b. TAX INcrease
          IMplant SYlicone   SYlicone IMplant
          DISpute BOUNdaries   BOUNdary DISpute

The collocations in a. are phrasal (Chancellor of the Exchequer: "What can I do to avoid bankruptcy?"; Advisor to the Treasury: "Increase taxes!"), while those in b. are compounds (TV newscaster: "The government is planning a tax increase"). We know from section 1 that the verbs in (31a) normally exhibit final stress:

(32) inCREASe taXAtion
      imPLANT susPIcions
      disPUTe inTENtions

> Why doesn't the Rhythm Rule operate on examples of the type in (32)?

In the phrases in (31a), however, the verb pattern merges with the noun pattern in avoidance of stress clash, as we display in (33):

(33)

```
                   *                    *        Stress line 2
            *      *              *  ←   *        Stress line 1
      *     *     *  *         *     *     *  *   Baseline
   a.  increase taxes   →    increase taxes
```

The stress clash in *tax increase* in (31b) obviously cannot be corrected by leftward movement. It could be corrected by rightward movement of the asterisk on *in*, but the English Rhythm Rule in (21) above does not provide for rightward movement.

> Show how the English Rhythm Rule does not provide for rightward movement.

We return to this matter in the next section.

In all the data we have considered, the retracted stress has ended up in the word's first syllable, and therefore it would be possible for this to be the decisive criterion in the choice of landing site for the moving asterisk. However, the data in (34) reveal that the landing site is actually chosen on grounds of asterisk adjacency in the line immediately below the clash:

> The criterion responsible for the choice of landing site is asterisk adjacency in the line below the clash

(34) a. MonongaHEla   b. MoNONgahela RIver
          tyrannoSAUrus   tyRAnnosaurus REX

You can see that stress does not retract onto the word-initial syllable here. The reason becomes transparent when we examine the grid:

(35)

```
                              *              Stress line 3
            *            *   ←  *             Stress line 2
      *     *         *     *     *           Stress line 1
   *   *   *   *  *    *   *   *   *  *   *  *  Baseline
   Monongahela    Monongahela River
```

> Satisfy youself that you understand what is happening.

The line 2 clash created by the concatenation of *MonongaHEla* and *RIver* in (35) is again resolved by asterisk movement. The retracted asterisk lands on the closest syllable with a line 1 asterisk. As it happens, this syllable is no longer the word's first syllable, but the non-initial syllable *non*.

8 Retraction Failures: The Continuous Column Constraint

Phrases like *antique chair*, with stress retraction, strikingly contrast with compounds like *antique dealer*, with no retraction in spite of the clash.

> Check that you perceive this difference.

Consider the metrical structure of *antique dealer*:

(36)   *   Stress line 2
         *   *   Stress line 1
     *   *   *   *   Baseline
     antique dealer

This structure contains a stress clash. However, the grid of *antique dealer* differs crucially from the grid of *antique chair* in (30) above with regard to the position of the main stress.

> What would happen if we tried to resolve the stress clash in (36)?

Notice now what would happen if *antique* underwent stress retraction in *antique dealer*:

(37)   *   *   Stress line 2
         *   *   * ←   *   Stress line 1
     *   *   *   *   *   *   *   *   Baseline
     antique dealer   →   antique dealer

> Can you see anything anomalous with the structure in (37)?

The asterisk column on *ti* has now been broken. This situation is formally unacceptable, since columns obviously need to be continuous if they are to have any real substance. We formulate this common-sense requirement in the universal CONTINUOUS COLUMN CONSTRAINT of (38):

Metrical grid columns must be continuous, that is, they cannot have gaps

---

(38)   Continuous Column Constraint:
       Metrical grid columns must be continuous, without skipping lines

> Try and motivate the Continuous Column Constraint in your own words. Why exactly should we want to bar a process such as that in (37)?

If you re-examine the *antique chair* grid in (30) above you will notice that the metrical configuration of this construction after retraction does comply with the constraint in (38), in contrast to the *antique dealer* grid in (37). Consequently, *antique chair* will indeed undergo stress movement, but *antique dealer* will not.

> What is the stress pattern of the expression *antique dealer* when it refers to a dealer who is old? Why?

Stress clash also persists in constructions like *sports contest*, *cash register* or *house hunting*:

```
(39)    *                Stress line 2
        *    *           Stress line 1
        *    *    *      Baseline
    sports contest
```

Stress movement could be carried out in *contest* without contravening the Continuous Column Constraint of (38) above:

> Any idea how this result can be achieved?

```
(40)    *                Stress line 2
        *    →  *        Stress line 1
        *    *    *      Baseline
    sports contest
```

The output of this operation is, however, illegitimate in English: *SPORTS conTEST* would imply that sports, not something else, are the contestants! In German, by contrast, an analogous outcome is obligatory:

```
(41)  a.              b.   *                 *                    Stress line 2
          *                *    *            *    →   *           Stress line 1
          *    *           *    *    *       *    *    *          Baseline
       Marschall        Feld Marschall  →  Feld Marschall
       'marshal'                           'field marshal'
```

The reason for the difference between the two languages lies in their respective formulations of the Rhythm Rule. In English, the Rhythm Rule only implements leftward movement, as we made explicit in (21) above. In German, however, no such limitation exists, as we illustrate further in (42) with word-internal contrasts:

In English the Rhythm Rule only implements leftward movement

(42) a. SICHTbar   'visible'   b. UNsichtBAR   'invisible'
          ANziehen   'to put on'   den ROCK anZIEhen 'to put the
                                                              skirt on'

The fact that the English Rhythm Rule only sanctions retraction explains the asymmetry of our familiar noun–verb pairs with regard to stress merger – the shift to word-initial position caused by clash in verbs is not matched by a mirror-image shift in nouns:

(43)   TAX INcrease

The clash in (43) could only be resolved by moving stress to the right: TAX *inCREASe. However, the English Rhythm Rule does not provide for this result, which we have just seen would be fine in German.

So far in the chapter we have been examining the mechanics of stress movement. In the next section we offer a motivation for the phenomenon.

9 Rhythm

The label "Rhythm Rule" we have given to the rule responsible for stress movement in (21) appropriately suggests a connection with rhythm.

Music, of course, has rhythm, and so usually does poetry. Consider the following children's poem by Spike Milligan, where we have marked the strong beats with capitals:

(44)   MAry PUGH was NEARly TWO
       when SHE went OUT of DOORS.
       She WENT out STANding UP, she DID,
       and CAME back ON all FOURS.

> Notice that *she* and *went* occur both stressed and stressless: why? This aside, do you notice any pattern regarding which words have stress, and which don't?

A reading of this poem reveals an alternation of stressed and stressless syllables, precisely the favourite rhythm of English.

The favourite rhythm of English involves an alternation between stressed and stressless syllables

> Poetry is, of course, a stylized activity, and accepts other rhythms also:
>
> WHAT is the MAtter with MAry JAne?
> She's PERfectly WELL and she HAsn't a PAIN,
> And it's LOvely rice PUdding for DInner aGAIN! –
> What IS the MAtter with MAry JAne?
>
> What type of alternation does this verse by A.A. Milne illustrate?

The strong liking English has for binary rhythm has interesting (and perhaps unexpected) consequences for more mundane activities than the writing or reciting of poems. For instance, English speakers usually count objects emphasizing the odd numbers and de-emphasizing the even numbers, as follows:

(45)   ONE two THREE four FIVE six SEVEN eight NINE ten

You may think that this is the only possible way of counting (or at least the only natural way), but a comparison with French reveals that this is not the case:

(46)   UN DEUX TROIS QUATRE CINQ SIX SEPT HUIT NEUF DIX

You will notice that French speakers emphasize all the numbers. The difference between the two patterns is nicely captured by our metrical grid formalism:

(47)   a.   *   *   *   *   *
            *   *   *   *   *   *   *   *   *   *
            ONE two THREE four FIVE six SEVEN eight NINE ten

       b.   *   *   *   *   *   *   *   *   *   *
            UN DEUX TROIS QUATRE CINQ SIX SEPT HUIT NEUF DIX

You can see that each numeral carries a stress of its own in both languages. Moreover, a higher metrical layer is erected in English to provide the first word of each pair with greater emphasis. This additional metrical layer is missing from French altogether.

The respective behaviour is deeply engrained in the speakers of the two languages. Given a string of nonsense syllables *la*, English speakers will also assign alternating stresses, whereas French speakers will pronounce it flat:

(48)   a.   English: LA la LA la LA la LA la
      b.   French: LA LA LA LA LA LA

This difference can again be accounted for on the assumption that English speakers build an additional level of metrical structure.

> Try out these rhythms. When you are satisfied you've got the hang of it, write down the respective grids.

10   Segmental Evidence for Stress: Vowel Reduction

So far, we have been trying to gain familiarity with the reality of stress by accessing what are sometimes subtle intuitions about the different degrees of prominence exhibited by different syllables in words, or by different words in word constructions. In this section, we complement this evidence with some more easily accessible segmental data.

Consider the forms in (49):

(49)   a.   Pat   b.   Patricia
         Sam   Samantha
         prop   propeller
         prep   preparatory

The forms in column a. are monosyllabic truncations of the words in column b., and therefore we would expect their segmental makeup also to be a section of the fuller string – their spellings certainly are. However, the pronunciation of the vowel is clearly different in the two contexts.

> Say what the respective pronunciations of the first vowel are in the words in (49).

In particular, the identity of the vowel in the monosyllables in (49a) is unpredictable ([æ], [ɒ], [ɛ], . . .), but its correspondent in the polysyllables in (49b) is invariably the reduced vowel schwa ([ə]):

(50) a. P[æ]t   b.   P[ə]tricia
          S[æ]m   S[ə]mantha
          pr[ɒ]p   pr[ə]peller
          pr[ɛ]p   pr[ə]paratory

Crucially for our purposes here, the two sets of forms also differ in their stress patterns. In particular, the lone syllable of the forms in (49a) is stressed. This is to be expected, since under normal conditions fully meaningful words include a stressed syllable, in English and in most other languages. This particular syllable is, however, stressless in the polysyllabic forms in (49b), which are stressed elsewhere (*PaTRIcia*, etc.).

The reduction of stressless vowels to schwa (or to [ɪ] or [ʊ] in specific contexts) is one of the most characteristic traits of English.

The reduction of stressless vowels is one of the most characteristic traits of English

> **Can you think of a few cases of reduction to [ɪ] or [ʊ]?**

In chapter 7 we saw that the articulation of schwa is less precise than the articulation of other vowels. Schwa is also intrinsically weak, at least in English, in as much as it is less salient than other vowels and can even delete under the appropriate circumstances: *p[ə]tato*, for instance, can become *p'tato*, and so on. The use of schwa in stressless positions is therefore not surprising, given the intrinsic association of stress with prominence, and conversely.

11 Stop Allophony

The position of stress can also influence the pronunciation of consonants. For instance, the weakening of /t/ (to a glottal stop in some British dialects or to a flap in American English and a number of other accents world-wide) is directly contingent on stress. We saw in chapter 3 that the articulation of the flap involves the active articulator lightly hitting the passive articulator as a consequence of a rapid ballistic movement. We also know from chapter 1 that the glottal stop is a stop made with the vocal folds.

The position of stress can influence the pronunciation of consonants

Word-initial /t/s obviously never weaken:

(51) *t*en
      *t*aramasalata
      *t*abasco
      etc.

Word-internal /t/s do weaken, but not indiscriminately, as illustrated in (52):

(52)   a. cutting   b. mastery   c. attain
            waiting   after   retort

> Try out the words in (52), observing the different pronunci-
> ation of *t* in each group.

The forms in a. can exhibit glottalling (*cu[ʔ]ing*) or flapping (*cu[ɾ]ing*), but
not so those in b. or c. Comparison of (52a) with (51) suggests that intervocalic position is a precondition for /t/ weakening. This conclusion is
confirmed by the absence of weakening in the forms in (52b), where the /t/
is preceded by a fricative. The forms in (52c), however, do not undergo
weakening either, even though their /t/ is intervocalic. The difference
between (52a) and (52c) becomes clear when stress is brought into the picture: a further condition on weakening is that the vowel following the /t/
must be stressless. The full formalization of English /t/ weakening is thus
as in (53), where we have ignored some additional complexities to keep
matters simple:

(53)   English /t/ weakening:
        t → ɾ OR ? /[−consonantal] _____ [−consonantal]
        Condition: the second [−consonantal] does not support a grid column

The central role of stress in the weakening process is expressed by the condition on rule (53). As a consequence, the presence of a flap or a glottal stop
provides indirect evidence about the distribution of stress, and a fortiori about
its existence.

> Explain why and how exactly the rule of flapping would over-
> apply if vowels were all stressless.

We find more evidence for stress in the aspiration of voiceless stops. In
chapter 10 we made brief reference to the fact that English voiceless stops
are kept apart phonetically from their voiced counterparts by the puff of
air, or "aspiration", that follows the release of the closure. As it happens,
the degree of aspiration of voiceless stops is not uniform across contexts:

(54)   a. pend   b. append   c. happened   d. spend
            tale   entail   retail   stale

Test these forms in (54) for aspiration. Notice that two of the columns exhibit strong aspiration, one weak aspiration and one no aspiration at all: which is which?

It should not be difficult to verify that aspiration is weaker in (54c), and altogether missing in (54d), after /s/. Saying that aspiration only occurs word-initially will obviously not do, because (54b) has as much aspiration as (54a). The relevant criterion is again stress: there is strong aspiration when the vowel after the stop is stressed (and the preceding segment is not /s/). Once more, therefore, segmental allophony provides a strong clue about the position of stress, and consequently about its existence.

The overall message of this chapter has been that there is a hierarchy of prominence among syllables in words, and among words in compounds and phrases. This prominence hierarchy is grounded in rhythm, and we can appropriately represent it in a metrical grid. We have seen that the drive to preserve rhythm can induce stress movement. We have accounted for the differences in the location of stress between nouns and verbs, or between compounds and phrases, by appeal to differences in grammatical category. In the next chapter we shall investigate the actual mechanics of stress assignment in simple words, first in English, and then in other languages.

Chapter Summary

This chapter has introduced the phenomenon known as "stress". We showed that within words and in word collocations one element is more prominent than its neighbours. This prominent element will be a syllable in words, and a word (through its prominent syllable) in collocations. Pairs of word strings which are identical segmentally can, nevertheless, be distinguished by the location of stress, which falls on the final element in phrasal collocations and on the first element in two-word compounds. We introduced the metrical grid in order to represent these differences in a formal way. An asterisk is placed in the baseline of the grid over all the syllable nuclei, prominence being recorded by a second asterisk in a line above the baseline. As the number of elements to be metrified increases, so new lines need to be added to the grid. In order to maintain an alternating pattern of stressed and unstressed syllables it is necessary to prevent the emergence of adjacent stressed elements. Asterisk clash at any grid level above the baseline is resolved by the "Rhythm Rule", which moves the asterisk to the nearest landing site. Failures of the Rhythm Rule to apply are accounted for by the "Continuous Column Constraint", which bans gaps from the column of asterisks, and by a direction setting, which allows only leftward movement in English (but not in German, where clashing asterisks can also move to the right). We demonstrated the pervasiveness of the stressed/stressless rhythm of English words and phrases by reference to the verse and counting patterns used by native speakers. Finally, we offered segmental evidence for stress from the reduction of vowels to schwa, the weakening of /t/ when it does not precede a stressed vowel, and the distribution of aspiration in stops.

Key Questions

1 What is a metrical grid? What is its function?
2 How is the stress pattern instrumental in differentiating between nouns and verbs, and between compounds and phrases?
3 Is there any connection between word stress and meaning?
4 Does the stress pattern of double proper names comply with that of compounds or with that of phrases?
5 What is the cause of stress retraction?
6 What is a stress clash?
7 Show how the Rhythm Rule works.

8 Why does the Continuous Column Constraint prevent some cases of retraction even though an apparent clash occurs? State the terms of the Continuous Column Constraint.
9 What is the directional setting for the Rhythm Rule for English? How does the Rhythm Rule operate in German?
10 What is the basic rhythm of English? How does it differ from that of French?
11 What segmental evidence can be adduced for stress in English?

Further Practice

Catalan

The seven vowels in a. occur in stressed syllables in Central Catalan, but in unstressed position only the three in b. are found:

a. i   u   b. i   u
       e   o   ə
       ɛ   ɔ
            a

With this information in mind, work out where the stress falls in the following words (orthographic accents have been suppressed):

ull	[uʎ]	'eye'	ulleres	[uʎerəs]	'eye glasses'
camio	[kəmjo]	'truck'	camionet	[kəmjunɛt]	'truck' (dim.)
cosa	[kɔzə]	'thing'	coseta	[kuzɛtə]	'thing' (dim.)
roda	[rɔðə]	'wheel'	algu	[əlɣu]	'someone'
menja	[menʒə]	'he eats'	menjar	[mənʒa]	'to eat'
llibre	[ʎiβrə]	'book'	llibreta	[ʎiβrɛtə]	'notebook'
el dia	[əldiə]	'the day'	engany	[əŋgaɲ]	'deception'
pasta	[pastə]	'dough'	pasteta	[pəstɛtə]	'dough' (dim.)
pruna	[prunə]	'plum'	pruneta	[prunɛtə]	'plum' (dim.)

On the basis of these data, can you suggest which reduced form corresponds to each of the full vowels?

English Rhythm

Compare the words in column a. and the phrases in column b. below. Draw the relevant grids for each of the words and phrases showing where retraction has occurred and why:

a. Piccadilly
   piccalilli
   Mississippi
   Hallowe'en
   Mediterranean

b. Piccadilly Circus
   piccalilli chutney
   Mississippi Delta
   Hallowe'en party
   Mediterranean Sea

Poetic Rhythm

Consider the following snatches of English poetry. Work out their patterns and say how they relate to the rhythms of speech we have been demonstrating.

a.   The curfew tolls the knell of parting day,
      The lowing herd wind slowly o'er the lea,
      The ploughman homeward plods his weary way,
      And leaves the world to darkness and to me. (*Thomas Gray*)

b.   Old Meg she was a Gipsy,
      And liv'd upon the Moors:
      Her bed it was the brown heath turf,
      And her house was out of doors. (*John Keats*)

c.   Eye of newt, and toe of frog,
      Wool of bat, and tongue of dog,

Adder's fork, and blind-worm's sting,
Lizard's leg, and howlet's wing. (*William Shakespeare*)

d.   Tomorrow, and tomorrow, and tomorrow,
Creeps in this petty pace from day to day,
To the last syllable of recorded time;
And all our yesterdays have lighted fools
The way to dusty death. (*William Shakespeare*)

e.   'The time has come,' the Walrus said,
'To talk of many things:
Of shoes – and ships – and sealing wax –
Of cabbages – and kings –
And why the sea is boiling hot –
And whether pigs have wings.' (*Lewis Carroll*)

CHAPTER TWELVE

METRICAL PRINCIPLES AND PARAMETERS

Chapter Objectives

In this chapter you will learn about:

- The general principles of stress assignment.
- How one single parameter is responsible for stress in both phrases and compounds.
- Disregarding peripheral elements.
- The role of the "metrical foot" in word stress.
- How foot structure reflects language rhythm.
- Three parameters responsible for the assignment of main stress to nouns.
- The difference in the stress patterns of nouns and verbs.
- The stress profile of multiply stressed words.
- How variation in parameter settings accounts for the diverse stress patterns of the world's languages.

In the previous chapter we surveyed a variety of stress patterns in English, with the explicit aim of gaining familiarity with the phenomenon. We paid special attention to the procedure by which these patterns are modified to avoid clash. In the present chapter we turn to the procedures by which the original stress patterns are arrived at. In the first part of the chapter we examine the stress patterns of English phrases and compounds, and then extend the inquiry to simple words. In the second part of the chapter we show how the varied stress patterns of the languages of the world are accounted for simply by introducing slight variations in the procedure we originally set up for English.

1 English Phrasal and Compound Stress

In chapter 11 we saw that in English phrasal collocations main stress falls on the right, whereas in (binary) compounds the greatest prominence tends to be on the left (remember that personal names pattern like phrases with regard to stress).

Stress on the edge of some domain is a very frequent occurrence across languages. This situation is straightforwardly formalized in (1):

(1) END STRESS:
     Project the right-most/left-most asterisk

It should be quite obvious by now that the expression "project the right-most/left-most asterisk" simply means that the last/first asterisk in a metrical line is copied onto the line immediately above, created for the purpose if necessary.

Consider, for instance, the sentence *time flies* from the previous chapter. To keep the presentation simple, let us assume that there is only one baseline asterisk for each component word – this simplification is of course made more plausible because the words involved are both monosyllabic. Phrasal stress can now be assigned to the collocation simply by applying End Stress (1) in its "right-most" setting:

(2)   *   Stress line 1
          *   *   *   *   Baseline
        time flies   →   time flies
                 End Stress [Right]

You can see that the last baseline asterisk, directly above *flies*, has projected onto the newly created line 1. The resulting grid appropriately expresses the fact that *flies* has greater prominence than *time*.

Were we to apply the same procedure to the compound *time-flies*, we would of course obtain an identical output. This result would be incorrect, since we know that in this and many other compounds the first word is more prominent:

(3)   *   Stress line 1
      *   *   Baseline
     time-flies

The expression "project the right-most/left-most asterisk" simply means that the last/first asterisk in a metrical line is copied onto the line immediately above

We obviously need to introduce some change in the procedure to bring about this result.

2 Extrametricality

One possible way to get the correct stress in compounds would simply be to switch the setting of End Stress in (1), that is, to select "left" for compounds, rather than "right":

(4)   *   Stress line 1
            *   *   *   *   Baseline
        time-flies   →   time-flies
                End stress [left]

In (4), the left-most asterisk in the baseline (directly above *time*) is projected onto line 1, which the projection procedure in fact creates.

This procedure can, however, be objected to on the grounds that it requires multiple settings for the same parameter in a single language.

> Why should multiple settings for the same parameter in a single language be objectionable?

An alternative procedure, consistent with the "right-most" setting of End Stress for compounds too, involves concealing the right-most asterisk in the input of (4). You will probably find this strategy rather baffling at this point, but if you bear with us you will see that it receives considerable backing.

In real life, we could simply cover up the asterisk we want to render invisible with a finger, thus ensuring that we ignore it in the ensuing computations.

> Cover up the offending asterisk in the input of (2) and (4) above and see for yourself what the result is.

In the more stylized medium of scientific writing we need some symbol to achieve the same end, and a pair of angled brackets ("< >") is commonly used for the purpose. The device is given the name EXTRAMETRICALITY, because it excludes the element it acts upon from the computations in the metrical grid. We provide a general statement of extrametricality in (5):

The device known as EXTRAMETRICALITY involves excluding the element it acts upon from the computations in the metrical grid

(5) Extrametricality:
     Make the right-most/left-most asterisk extrametrical
     (notationally: *   →   <*>)

Of course, extrametricality needs to be assigned in a specific context in each particular case, since we clearly do not want the right-most/left-most asterisk of all lines in all grids to be extrametrical.

> Why don't we want all lines in all metrical grids to contain extrametrical material?

In the case we are currently discussing, extrametricality is only relevant to compound structures, since we know that phrases and sentences do not require it (indeed, do not allow it), at least in English.

Only elements that are peripheral in the appropriate domain are allowed to be extrametrical

The restriction that only elements that are peripheral in the appropriate domain are allowed to be extrametrical has solid empirical grounding: extrametrical behaviour has been found to be associated with peripheral elements in language after language. The restriction is also common sense, because, were unbridled extrametricality to be allowed, we could end up with any number of extrametrical elements anywhere in the string, in a quite ad hoc manner.

> Explain briefly what would happen if we did not have the proposed restriction.

The restriction in question is made explicit in (6), under the label PERIPHERALITY CONDITION:

(6) Peripherality Condition:
     Only peripheral elements can be extrametrical

Let us now observe the effect of (right-most) extrametricality on the stress of English compounds:

(7)   *   *   *   <*>   Baseline
      time-flies   →   time-flies
                       Extrametricality

Extrametricality makes the asterisk on *flies* invisible, and consequently the output of (7) now includes only one baseline asterisk. The action of End Stress [Right] (1) on this structure places the main stress of the collocation in the correct position:

(8)   *   Stress line 1
      *   <*>   *   <*>   Baseline
   time-flies   →   time-flies
         End Stress [Right]

> Explain carefully how we have arrived at the grid in (8).

The procedure we are adopting obviously yields the right results. Importantly, it also allows us to retain the setting "right" for End Stress throughout the language in domains above the simple word. In fact, we will see below that this setting also encompasses the domain of the simple word. This is clearly an advantageous outcome, both formally and from the point of view of learnability, as we will explain in section 9 below.

> Why are we bringing learnability into the argument?

3 The Elsewhere Condition

The last baseline asterisk in compounds is a potential target for both End Stress [Right] and Extrametricality [Right], but we just want Extrametricality to apply. Therefore, the interaction between the two procedures needs to be regulated.

Suppose we were to allow End Stress [Right] to apply before Extrametricality:

(9)   *   *   Stress line 1
      *   *   *   *   *   <*>   Baseline
   time-flies   →   time-flies   →   time-flies
         End Stress [Right]   Extrametricality

> Do you see anything wrong with this outcome? What is it?

The result is very dubious from a formal point of view. First, can a dominated asterisk be the target of extrametricality? Second, doesn't the resulting grid violate the Continuous Column Constraint in (38) of chapter 11? Third, how is the grid in (9) to be interpreted anyway? In particular, which of the two words is predicted to bear greater prominence, and why? All these difficulties are avoided if Extrametricality applies before End Stress, precisely

EXTRINSIC ORDERING is widely disfavoured, and only accepted as a last resort

as it does in (7) and (8) above. We could, of course, simply stipulate this ordering. However, EXTRINSIC ORDERING of this kind is widely disfavoured, and only accepted as a last resort when there is no viable alternative (we deal with ordering in detail in chapter 18). We will now see that in the case we are discussing a viable alternative does indeed exist.

The answer is contained in the formal relationship between End Stress [Right] in (1) and Extrametricality in (5) in English compounds. We spell out the two procedures in (10), to facilitate comparison:

(10)   a.   End Stress [Right]:
                  Project
                       the right-most asterisk
          b.   Compound Extrametricality [Right]:
                  Make extrametrical
                       the right-most asterisk
                                 in compounds

Two rules can only conflict when they share the input, as (10a) and (10b) do: the right-most asterisk. The two aspects relevant to the interaction between these or any competing rules are:

1   the effect of the rule – here: "project" for end stress in (10a), and "make extrametrical" for the Compound Rule in (10b);
2   the environment or context in which the rule applies – here: no context for End Stress in (10a), and "in compounds" for the Compound Rule in (10b).

Now, the effects of the two rules in (10) are obviously incompatible, since they involve, respectively, the projection of the right-most baseline asterisk and the assignment of extrametricality to this very same asterisk.

> Explain how exactly the effects of the two rules are contradictory.

As for their environments, the environment of Compound Extrametricality in (10b) is more restricted than the environment of End Stress in (10a): Compound Extrametricality only applies in compounds, whereas End Stress has no built-in limitations.

> Check that it is indeed the case that Compound Extrametricality is limited to compounds but End Stress has no restrictions.

Over two thousand years ago, the Indian linguist Pāṇini noticed a very special relation between two rules when they produce incompatible results and the environment of one rule is included in the environment of the other rule: in such cases, the more specific rule (with the more qualifications, and thus with the more detailed environment) applies first. In its modern incarnation, Pāṇini's principle is commonly referred to as the ELSEWHERE CONDITION, because the more general rule (with the fewer qualifications, and thus with the less detailed environment) applies in all the contexts where the more restricted rule cannot, that is, "elsewhere".

> When two rules produce incompatible results and the environment of one rule is included in the environment of the other rule, the more specific rule applies first

> Explain how exactly the Elsewhere Condition works, with the help of a pencil and paper.

The Elsewhere Condition is active throughout phonology, and indeed other areas of language. We formulate it explicitly in (11):

(11)   Elsewhere Condition:
       Given two rules such that:
       (i)   their inputs are identical
       (ii)   their outputs are incompatible
       (iii)   the environment of one rule is the same as the environment of the other rule plus something extra
       then, the rule with the richer environment is ordered first, and, if it does apply, the other rule is skipped.

You can now see that our rule of Compound Extrametricality in (10b) will apply before End Stress in (10a) simply as a consequence of the Elsewhere Condition – there is no need to stipulate this order.

> Compound Extrametricality applies before End Stress as a consequence of the ELSEWHERE CONDITION

> Do you see why there is no need to stipulate the order between Compound Extrametricality and End Stress? Also, how come the application of End Stress isn't blocked, given the skipping clause at the end of (11)? Hint: pay attention to the identity of the asterisk each of the two rules ends up applying to.

4 Stress Assignment in Words

The stress pattern of French words is remarkably simple and provides a useful entry into our discussion of word stress. The procedure responsible for the stress patterns of English compounds that we discussed in section 2 also applies to French individual words, with minor adaptations. We illustrate the stress pattern of French words in (12). You should bear in mind that French orthographic accents bear no relation to stress, and that the final *e* in words like *extrème* (bracketed in (12) for ease of identification) usually has no phonetic correlate, although exceptionally it can be sounded as a "schwa" (in effect, the round front vowel [œ] in French):

> Is the French "schwa" really a schwa?

(12)   exTRÈm(e)   allocaTION   exTRA   candiDAT   opiNION

> Try and work out the pattern of French stress.

You can see that stress invariably falls on the right-most syllable, unless this syllable contains a "schwa", which is ignored for stress purposes. French word stress can therefore be formalized as in (13):

> Before you read on, formalize the French stress pattern making use of the metrical machinery we have available.

(13)   French word stress:
   a.   extrametricality: "schwa" on the right edge (if there is one)
   b.   asterisk placement: End Stress [Right]

All French words obey these simple principles, and therefore no more needs saying about the matter in the present context.

English word stress is considerably more complex. You can get a taste of this complexity from the small sample in (14), which replicates the French one in (12) above:

(14)   exTREme   alloCAtion   EXtra   CANdidate   oPInion

> Can you see a pattern to English stress in these data?

In *extreme* stress falls on the final syllable, or, equivalently, on the second syllable; in *allocation* it falls on the third syllable, which is also penultimate;

in *extra* and *candidate* it falls on the initial syllable, but if we count from the end, stress will be penultimate in *extra* and antepenultimate in *candidate*; finally, in *opinion* stress is located on the second or the antepenultimate syllable – you can take your pick!

Faced with this situation, it is small wonder that until fairly recently each English word was thought to have its own idiosyncratic stress. For instance, Daniel Jones, the one-time influential English phonetician to whom we referred in chapter 5 in connection with the cardinal vowels, wrote that "generally speaking there are no rules determining which syllable or syllables of polysyllabic English words bear the main stress" (*An Outline of English Phonetics*, 1967: 248). In the context of this belief, and of the type of data that supported it (cf. (14) above), the position of Chomsky and Halle that "both the placement of main stress and the stress contours within the word and the phrase are largely predictable from the syntactic and the non-prosodic phonological structure of an utterance" (*The Sound Pattern of English*, 1968: 59–60) was obviously daring and provocative.

> Until fairly recently, each English word was thought to have its own idiosyncratic stress

Indeed, Chomsky and Halle initiated the trend for in-depth research into the regular stress patterns of languages. Such research has gone a long way since then, and in what follows, as in the preceding chapter, we will base our exposition on the metrical theory that developed subsequently. We are seeing that in metrical theory stress is conceived of as a network of prominence relations, formally represented as a metrical grid.

> Chomsky and Halle initiated the trend for in-depth research into the regular stress patterns of languages

> Do you find this statement a bit of a mouthful? Explain it in your own words.

Crucially, metrical relations are assumed not to be present in lexical representation, but to be filled in by the action of the metrical procedures.

> Is the absence of metrical information from the lexicon advantageous?

All this will of course become progressively clearer as we go along.

5 Basic Stress Pattern of English Nouns

We shall start our empirical investigation of English word stress with the set of nouns in (15). From now on, we shall mark stress by means of an acute accent on the vowel that carries it:

(15)   cínema   plátypus   ténement   ímpetus
        álgebra   ánimal   vénison   fílament
        élephant   chócolate   áccolade   cústomer

Can you find a pattern to the stress of these words?

All the words in (15) have three syllables, the first of which is stressed, as signalled by the mark on the corresponding vowel. This mark is, of course, not included in ordinary English spelling, but is provided in standard dictionaries, usually in the form of a preceding apostrophe, as part of the phonetic information of each lexical item. Must we conclude from (15) that English nouns are simply assigned stress word-initially? The data in (14) above already gave a hint that this cannot be the case. Consider further the forms in (16):

(16)   aspáragus
        alumínium (British)
        alúminum (American)
        hypochóndriac
        metamórphosis
        hippopótamus
        pantéchnicon
        parallélogram
        gloxínia

You can see that stress is not word-initial in these (longer) words.

Can you form a hypothesis about the location of the stress in these words? (Make the hypothesis as basic and as preliminary as you need to.)

English noun stress is ante-penultimate, that is, it is located on the third syllable from the right edge of the word

Comparison of the sets in (15) and (16) reveals that in both cases stress is in fact antepenultimate: it is located on the third syllable from the right edge of the word. Can we achieve this result from the metrical procedures we have available at present? The answer is a clear "no". In particular, the only metrical devices currently at our disposal are Extrametricality, which in English effectively nullifies the right-most grid element, and End Stress, which, also in English, enhances the right-most element in the metrical grid.

Show how the result of this procedure is incorrect in the words in (15) and (16).

Application of Extrametricality and End Stress yields the wrong result for the data we are considering. Let us first try the familiar "right-most" setting for both rules:

(17)

| | | * | Stress line 1 |

* * * * *   * * * * <*>   * * * * <*> Baseline

hippopotamus → hippopotamus → hippopotamus

Extrametricality [R]   End Stress [R]

The output, *hippopotámus, does not match the correct pattern hippopótamus. Let us experiment with a setting "left-most" also for both rules:

(18)

| | | * | Stress line 1 |

* * * * *   <*> * * * *   <*> * * * * Baseline

hippopotamus → hippopotamus → hippopotamus

Extrametricality [L]   End Stress [L]

Again, the result is incorrect (*hippópotamus). Assigning opposite settings to end stress and Extrametricality clearly does not help (*hippopotamús, *híppopotamus), and therefore we need to introduce some significant modification in the procedure.

Write out the derivation of the illegitimate patterns *hippopotamús, and *híppopotamus availing yourself of the usual metrical devices.

6 The Metrical Foot

In the previous chapter we referred to the fact that English favours stress in alternate syllables, as revealed in the typical pronunciation of a sequence of the nonsense syllable la by an English speaker:

(19) lá la lá la lá la . . .

Notice, however, that there is another way of achieving alternating rhythm in the same sequence:

(20)   la lá la lá la lá . . .

The alternation of stressed and stressless syllables (equivalently, of S[trong] and W[eak] metrical elements) is preserved in (20), but the pattern is reversed: S–W in (19) and W–S in (20). As we will see, languages with alternating stress employ one or other of these two opposite metrical patterns.

> We call a pairing of S–W or W–S syllables a FOOT

We shall now introduce some formalism and terminology. Let us call a pairing of S–W or W–S syllables a FOOT. The word "foot" is also used in versification, but the two constructs, albeit related, must be kept apart firmly: we certainly do not wish to imply that ordinary language is verse (unfortunately, there is no handy spelling contrast here as there was with "rhyme" vs. "rime").

> At this point, you may want to work out the poetic feet of the verses in (44) and the next but one grey box in the previous chapter.

The first property of metrical feet, binarity, is implicit in the configurations S–W, W–S, each made up of precisely two syllables:

(21)   (S W)   or   (W S)

> Have we already come across some other binary constituent?

We are keeping to common practice and enclosing metrical feet in parentheses. The strong element of a foot is the HEAD of the foot: feet, like syllables and other constituents, have a core, or "head". Accordingly, we shall refer to the two feet in (21) as LEFT-HEADED and RIGHT-HEADED, respectively. Alternative terms, taken from classical metrics, are "trochee" and "iamb", respectively, but we shall avoid using these for the time being in order to maximize the transparency of the terminology. Our metrical machinery has, therefore, now been augmented with the two constructs in (22):

> Feet can be LEFT-HEADED or RIGHT-HEADED

(22)   left-headed foot   = (S W)
         right-headed foot = (W S)

We next need to give a grid interpretation to the abbreviations S and W, since we know that the metrical grid is the formal device for representing metrical structures:

(23) a.   *   Stress line 1
        left-headed foot   = (* *)   Baseline
       b.   *   Stress line 1
        right-headed foot = (* *)   Baseline

You can see that the extension of the foot is indicated by means of ordinary parentheses in the baseline, and the location of the foot head by means of an asterisk in line 1.

> The extension of a foot is indicated by means of ordinary parentheses in the grid's baseline, and the location of the foot head by means of an asterisk in line 1

> Reflect briefly on the graphic geometry of feet to make sure you fully understand it.

In the next section we will make use of binary feet to account for the basic stress pattern of English words.

7 Main Word Stress in English

The procedure in (24) assigns the correct main stress to the English nouns listed in (15) and (16) above. We will be refining this procedure as we go along, and therefore we number each successive version to allow you to keep track; the word ALGORITHM is in common use to designate a self-contained procedure:

(24) English noun stress algorithm (no. 1):
       1. Make the last element extrametrical
       2. Build a left-headed foot at the right edge

> Explain why the ordering of these two rules cannot be left to the Elsewhere Condition.

In (25) we illustrate this procedure with the noun *asparagus*:

(25)   *   Stress line 1
        * * * *   * * *<*>   * (* *) <*> Baseline
        asparagus   →   asparagus   →   aspara gus
                 (24.1)   (24.2)

In the first step in (25), the final element of the baseline becomes extrametrical (cf. the angled brackets), paralleling *hippopotamus* in (17) above. In the second step, a left-headed foot is constructed at the right edge, with the extrametrical element naturally outside the computation altogether. As a result of these two steps, main stress is correctly assigned to the syllable *pa*. A similar outcome obtains for the remainder of the nouns we are investigating.

> Try out the procedure on a few of these nouns.

The algorithm in (24) does not include all the steps you already know are necessary to assign primary stress to English nouns. We list the complete procedure in (26), again with the form *asparagus* as an illustration:

(26)   English noun stress algorithm (no. 2):
   1.   Input a lexical form, with no metrical structure:
        asparagus

   2.   Construct the grid baseline by projecting syllable heads:
        *   * * *   Baseline
        asparagus

   3.   Make the last element in the baseline extrametrical:
        *   * * <*>   Baseline
        asparagus

   4.   Build a left-headed foot at the right edge:
             *   Stress line 1
        * (* *) <*>   Baseline
        aspara gus

> Work through the algorithm in (26) with *hippopotamus*.

The algorithm in (26) works well for the bulk of both nouns (*médicine*, *magnanímity*, etc.) and suffixed adjectives (*medícin-al*, *magnánim-ous*, etc.). It does not, however, yield the correct stress pattern for verbs and unsuffixed adjectives. We present a sample of these in (27):

> What exactly is the difference in stress pattern between suffixed and unsuffixed adjectives?

(27)   implícit   insípid   imágine   impéril
       devélop   endéavour   admónish   endémic
       astónish   delíver   detérmine   pellúcid

Let us try out the procedure in (26) on *implicit*:

(28)

```
                                    *              Stress line 1
      *    * *         *    *<*>     (*    *)<*>  Baseline
      implicit  →   impli cit  →   impli cit
           Extrametricality      Footing
```

The output is incorrect: **ímplicit*. This problematic result should not be surprising, given that in the previous chapter we learnt that there is a stress contrast between nouns and verbs (and, as we are now seeing, also between suffixed and unsuffixed adjectives).

> Can you see how we may achieve the right result? What options are available?

Fortunately, the correct result is not hard to get – quite simply, we suppress the extrametricality clause in verbs and unsuffixed adjectives:

(29)

```
                          *          Stress line 1
      *    * *        *    (* *)     Baseline
      implicit  →   implicit
              Footing
```

We suppress the extrametricality clause in English verbs and un-suffixed adjectives

In (29) you can also see a left-headed foot at the right edge. In contrast to what happens with nouns, however, the last syllable is not excluded from the computation. The difference between verb and noun stress in English, therefore, is the product of the restriction of extrametricality to nouns.

8 Multiple Stress

Our present procedure yields one (left-headed) foot at the right edge of the word. Now, in words like *aluminium* or *metamorphosis*, the vowels in the first syllables are unreduced: [æ] and [ɛ], respectively. We know from the previous chapter that stressless short vowels in English undergo reduction. The fact that /æ/ and /ɛ/ surface unreduced in *aluminium* and *metamorphosis* suggests, therefore, that these vowels are stressed. Yet, the most prominent syllables in these two words are *mi* and *mor*, respectively.

The situation is further illustrated in (30), where we have highlighted unreduced vowels by underlining. Some of the words are admittedly, but irrelevantly, rather uncommon.

> Why is the strangeness of the words in (30) irrelevant, perhaps even helpful?

(30)   hamamelidanthemum
       mesembryanthemum
       pelargonium
       sanatorium
       pimpinellifolia
       serendipity
       hippopotamus

The algorithm in (26) assigns stress to the antepenultimate vowel, and therefore the full quality of this vowel is expected. What is still unexplained is the presence of other unreduced vowels in each of the words.

> Any idea why there are more unreduced vowels? Hint: you may find a clue in the contrast in the first vowel of *aluminium* and *aluminum*.

You may have noticed that the unreduced vowels are located at equal intervals to the left of the vowel stressed by the algorithm. This pattern provides a clue as to what's going on. You will recall that the basic rhythm of English involves an alternation of strong and weak elements throughout the word, not just at the right edge. If this is so, foot construction must sweep across the whole word, contrary to what we have been doing so far:

The basic rhythm of English involves an alternation of strong and weak elements throughout the word: English foot construction thus takes place iteratively

(31)
```
                                                  *                 Stress line 1
 *   *  * * *    *  <*>        *  *  * *(*    *)<*>                  Baseline
 hamamelidanthemum   →   hamamelidanthemum   →
              Footing

        *    *                    *      *    *      Stress line 1
 *   * (* *) (*    *) <*>     (*  *) (* *)(*    *) <*>  Baseline
 → hamameli danthe mum → hama meli danthe mum
   Footing                    Footing
```

You can see that in (31) foot construction takes place iteratively from right to left, where ITERATIVE means 'repeated' or 'recurring'.

> Explain why iteration cannot be left-to-right on the basis of (30) and the other data we have so far presented.

As a result of the right-to-left iteration of foot construction, the syllables *ha, me* and *dan* of *hamamelidanthemum* end up supporting foot heads, and, therefore, their vowels do not reduce. These additional peaks of prominence are referred to as SECONDARY STRESSES.

The existence of secondary stresses leads us to modify clause 4 of the stress procedure in (26) above, along the lines of (32):

(32)   4′.   Build left-headed feet iteratively from right to left

Note that the direction of foot construction needs to be stipulated language by language. In particular, while we are constructing English feet from right to left, in other languages (some of them to be considered below) feet are constructed from left to right. In English, left-to-right iterative foot construction would yield a wrong contour in words with an even number of syllables: **rhínocéros*.

> Additional peaks of prominence are referred to as SECONDARY STRESSES

> The direction of foot construction needs to be stipulated language by language

> Show how this contour is arrived at.

At this point we have three (left-headed) feet on *hamamelidanthemum*, with their heads on *ha, me* and *dan* (cf. (31) above). We know intuitively that the stress on *dan* is stronger, but in (31) there is no structural difference between this syllable and the two other foot heads, *ha* and *me*. This must mean that the grid in (31) is incomplete, since grids need to provide a complete representation of metrical structure. To make up for this shortfall, we submit the structure in (31) to End Stress [Right]:

(33)
```
                                        *              Stress line 2
      *       *   *              *       *   *          Stress line 1
    (*  *) (* *) (*    *) <*>   (*  *) (* *) (*    *) <*>  Baseline
    hama meli danthe mum  →  hama meli danthe mum
                    End Stress [Right]
```

We shall have more to say about End Stress further on, but for now we can be satisfied with the result we have obtained: a grid for *hamamelidanthemum* that signals greatest prominence on *dan*, and subsidiary prominence on *ha* and *me*.

> Work through the procedure with some of the other words in (30).

9 Stress Typology: Metrical Parameters

We have now accounted for the difference between the antepenultimate stress of English nouns (and suffixed adjectives) and the penultimate stress of English verbs (and unsuffixed adjectives) through the simple strategy of including an extrametricality clause in the metrical algorithm of nouns, but not in the metrical algorithm of verbs. This reveals that significant differences in the output can be due to a small difference in the grammar, opening the way for a parametric account of the metrical structure of languages in general. We spell out the details of such an account in this and the following section.

In (34) we list the metrical possibilities we have available at present:

Significant differences in the output can be due to a small difference in the grammar

(34)   Foot head location: Left/right
        Construction direction: Right-to-left/left-to-right
        Extrametricality: Yes(right/left)/no

The emboldenings in (35) specify the English settings for these parameters:

(35)   Foot head location: **Left**/right
        Construction direction: **Right-to-left**/left-to-right
        Extrametricality: **Yes(right**/left)/no   (nouns)
                                               Yes(right/left)/**no**   (verbs)

The settings required for English nouns yield the regular stress pattern of all types of words in (literary) Macedonian, and the settings for English verbs the regular pattern of all types of words in Polish (Macedonian is spoken in the Former Yugoslav Republic of Macedonia, and Polish, of course, in Poland). In (36) we provide a sample of words for each of these two languages (NB Polish *y* = [ɨ]):

(36)   a.   *Macedonian*   b.   *Polish*
             (= *English nouns*)   (= *English verbs*)
             'miller'   'marmalade'
             vodéničar   Sg.   marmólad   Gen. pl.
             vodeníčari   Pl.   marmoláda   Nom. sg.
             vodeničárite   Pl. def.   marmoladówy   Adj.

We illustrate the workings of the respective metrical algorithms in (37). Note that we are assuming that all syllables need to belong to a foot, even if some feet finish up monosyllabic as a result, as is the case with (*vo*) and (*mar*) in (37) – we return to this matter below:

(37) a. *Macedonian*   b. *Polish*

(= English noun parameters)   (= English verb parameters)

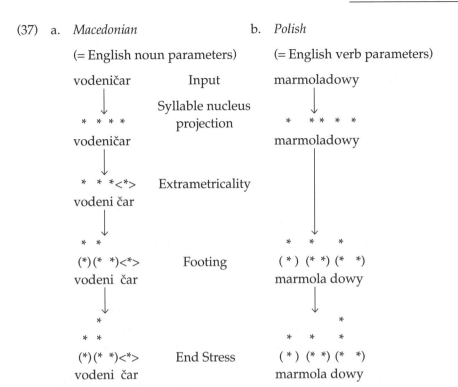

vodeničar	Input	marmoladowy
	Syllable nucleus projection	
* * * *		* * * * *
vodeničar		marmoladowy
	Extrametricality	
* * *<*>		
vodeni čar		
* *		* * *
(*)(* *)<*>	Footing	(*) (* *) (* *)
vodeni čar		marmola dowy
*		*
* *		* * *
(*)(* *)<*>	End Stress	(*) (* *) (* *)
vodeni čar		marmola dowy

You can see that the present procedures assign main stress in the correct place in both languages.

We can obtain other stress patterns by varying the settings of the parameters. Suppose first that we give the head location parameter the opposite setting from English, to produce right-headed feet:

We can obtain different stress patterns by varying the settings of the parameters

(38) Location of foot head: Left/**right**

If we keep the settings of all other parameters as in (35) above, with extrametricality as for English nouns, we will once more derive the pattern of Polish: word-penultimate main stress.

Show how this is the case.

However, if we do not select extrametricality (as we don't for English verbs), main stress will be assigned to the final syllable, and secondary stress to every other syllable to the left of the main stress. This turns out to be the pattern of Aklan, a language of the Philippines, which we illustrate in (39). Note that from now on some of the segmental transcriptions, taken directly from the literature, may not conform exactly to standard IPA practice, although, fortunately, this has no effect on the points we make:

(39) Aklan (right-headed, right-to-left, no extrametricality):
   bisá   'kiss'
   bísahí   'kiss' (Ref. imp.)
   suɣúguʔún   'servant'
   mátinámarún   'being lazy'

> Derive the stress of some of the words in (39).

Let us next reset the direction of foot construction to "left-to-right":

(40) Direction of foot construction: Right-to-left/**left-to-right**

We shall illustrate the consequences of this resetting with data from two Australian aboriginal languages, Maranungku, with left-headed feet, and Yidinʸ, with right-headed feet (n^y represents the palatal nasal [ɲ]; d^y = palatalized /d/). Notice that neither language has extrametricality, and that Yidinʸ does not allow monosyllabic feet, perhaps in avoidance of clash – the fate of monosyllabic feet is therefore best approached as parametric:

(41) Maranungku (left-headed, left-to-right, no extrametricality):
   pán   'friend'
   tíralk   'saliva'
   mérepét   'beard'
   yángarmáta   'the Pleiades'
   wóngowútanáwanʸ   'thunderhead'

(42) Yidinʸ (right-headed, left-to-right, no extrametricality):
   galbí   'catfish' (Abs.)
   gudága   'dog' (Abs.)
   wawádʸinú   'see' (Antipass. past)
   madʸímdaŋádʸiŋ   'walk up' (Trans. antipass. pers.)

> Work through a few of these examples. Where exactly would the absent monosyllabic feet be in Yidinʸ?

Extrametricality on the left edge is rather uncommon. It is, nevertheless, attested in the native American language Winnebago, which has a basic stress pattern otherwise analogous to Yidin^y (an alternative analysis of Winnebago stress without extrametricality is also available in the literature). We offer examples of Winnebago basic stress in (43) – notice that all vowels have been projected onto the baseline, and that there are also no clashing monosyllabic feet:

(43)   Winnebago (= Yidin^y with left extrametricality):
      waghighí   'ball'
      naaná?a   'your weight'
      hochichínik   'boy'
      haakítujík   'I pull it taut' (Plain)
      hakirújikshána 'he pulls taut'
      haakítujíkshaná 'I pull it taut' (Declined)

> Based on these data, carry out a metrical analysis of Winnebago stress, specifying the setting of the parameters and providing explicit derivations.

The data we have been reviewing back up our claim that small changes in the setting of the given parameters can have a considerable effect on the output. To the extent that this formal result matches the stress patterns of the world's languages, the parametric model of stress we are proposing receives empirical confirmation. The model is also superior from the point of view of learnability. In particular, it provides a very reasonable answer to the thorny question of how humans (specifically, children) manage to work out and learn the stress patterns of natural languages (some of them pretty diabolical on the surface!) simply from exposure to data, and to do so in a reasonably short space of time.

> Make explicit how this issue receives a satisfactory explanation in the context of the parametric model.

The approach based on Universal Grammar and parameter setting carries the implication that the child learner intuitively knows what to look for

Thus, the approach based on Universal Grammar and parameter setting carries the implication that the child learner intuitively knows what to look for: left vs. right foot-headedness, and so on. In this way, the child can home in on the data to achieve these modest goals without expending too much time and energy, and the learning task becomes manageable. The Universal Grammar cum parameter-setting model is of course also applicable to other branches of linguistics, syntax in particular, although, naturally, the identity of the parameters varies from branch to branch.

We end the section with a tabulation of the various parameter settings we have discussed and the names of the languages that instantiate each pattern:

(44)

Language	Foot head location		Construction direction		Extrametricality		
	l	*r*	*l-to-r*	*r-to-l*	yes *l*	yes *r*	*no*
English nouns	✓			✓		✓	
Macedonian	✓			✓		✓	
English verbs	✓			✓			✓
Polish	✓			✓			✓
≡ Polish		✓		✓		✓	
Aklan		✓		✓			✓
None?	✓			✓	✓		
Maranungku	✓		✓				✓
Winnebago		✓	✓		✓		
Yidinʸ		✓	✓				✓

10 Word-Level Stress: Line Conflation

The selection of the right-most foot as the carrier of the main word stress in English is achieved through a setting "right" for End Stress

In section 8 we saw that the selection of the right-most foot as the carrier of the main word stress in English is achieved through a setting "right" for End Stress: *hamamelidánthemum*, not *hámamelidanthemum*. An analogous situation obtains in Macedonian, Polish, Aklan and Yidinʸ, among the languages we have mentioned. We illustrate with Polish in (45):

(45)

```
                             *          Stress line 2
   *   *   *          *   *   *         Stress line 1
 (*) (* *) (*  *)    (*) (* *) (*  *)   Baseline
 marmola dowy    →   marmola dowy
           End Stress [Right]
```

In languages like Maranungku and Winnebago, by contrast, the initial foot is enhanced. We show this in (46) with the Maranungku word *wóngowù-tanàwan*ʸ 'thunderhead' (grave accents indicate secondary stresses, and the acute accent the primary stress):

(46)

```
                              *           Stress line 2
   *      *    *         *      *    *    Stress line 1
 (*   *) (* *) (*  *)   (*   *) (* *) (*  *)  Baseline
 wongo wuta nawan^y  →  wongo wuta nawan^y
             End Stress [Left]
```

Maranungku and many other languages are described in the literature as exhibiting the predicted pattern of secondary stress in the surface. However, in languages like Macedonian the secondary stresses are not realized phonetically. In other languages, like Polish or English, secondary stresses do appear in the surface, but not necessarily where we might expect from the iterative application of the primary stress metrical algorithm. In many cases, therefore, our metrical procedure is generating more structure than appears necessary.

> Explain in what way the metrical procedure generates more structure than necessary.

Two strategies are available to resolve this problem. One strategy involves enriching the model with an ITERATIVENESS parameter to control the repetition of footing: the setting for this parameter would be positive for Marunungku, so that feet be constructed over the whole domain, and negative for Macedonian, so that only one foot be constructed: *(yángar)(máta)* and *vodeni(čári)<te>*, respectively. The alternative strategy, LINE CONFLATION, allows iteration across the board in the first instance, and then deletes line 1 from the grid to dispose of all the feet but the one bearing the main stress. We illustrate this procedure in (47) with Macedonian:

```
(47)              *                                      Stress line 2
           *   *   *                           *         Stress line 1
          (*) (* *) (* *)<*>      *  *  * (* *)<*>   Baseline
          vo deni čari te    →   vodeni čari te
                    Conflation
```

> What exactly is the effect of conflation in (47)?

You can see that conflation does away with the line 1 of the input, and that line 2 of the input becomes line 1 in the output as a result. Notice also that, as feet are beheaded, the parentheses enclosing the relevant asterisks in the baseline are deleted: decapitated constituents automatically cease to exist. The reason for this lies in the indissoluble connection between a foot and its head: a constituent is nothing but the domain of a head, and therefore it cannot exist without its head. Conversely, of course, a head defines a constituent. This mutual implication between heads and constituents is formulated in the FAITHFULNESS CONDITION on grid structure in (48) – the word "faithfulness" naturally refers to the inseparability of the head and its domain:

Conflation does away with line 1 of the input

> Explain what we mean by "domain".

Each grid constituent must have a head, and each head must have a domain

(48)   Faithfulness Condition:
       Each grid constituent has a head (plotted in the line immediately above),
       and each head has a domain (delimited in the line immediately below)

When Line Conflation deletes line 1 in (47), the feet on *vo* and *deni* are deprived of their heads, and therefore they automatically cease to exist.

The Line Conflation analysis is reminiscent of the Duke of York's antics in the nursery rhyme, marching his men up to the top of the hill only to march them down again: we first create feet across the whole domain, only to end up destroying all but one of them. The Iterativeness parameter may therefore look like an obviously superior alternative: if nothing else, it is simpler, and it will be favoured by Occam's razor.

> Explain in what way Occam's razor is relevant here.

However, in the next chapter we will see that matters are a bit more complex than they may have appeared so far, and that Line Conflation is in fact supported by specific evidence.

At this point the question arises of whether the effect of End Stress is the simple provision of a line-2 asterisk, as we have been assuming, or whether it results in the creation of a full line-1 constituent.

> Explain what the formal difference between these two outcomes would be.

The construction of a line-1 constituent for the Maranungku word in (46) above would result in the grid in (49), with the line-1 asterisks enclosed by a pair of parentheses:

(49)   *   Stress line 2
       (*   *   *)   Stress line 1
       (* *) (* *) (* *)   Baseline
       wongo wuta nawan^y

The empirical evidence for this higher constituent is not overwhelming. None the less, its existence does follow from the logic of the Faithfulness

Condition, and therefore we will include it in our representations from now on. Some related discussion appears in chapter 16.

We have now completed our presentation of the prosodic structure pertinent to stress. In (49) above you can see that this structure consists of a foot layer and a word layer. The foot layer is formalized by means of asterisks marking foot heads in line 1, and of pairs of parentheses delimiting the foot's extension in the baseline. All the feet considered up to this point are maximally binary: they encompass a maximum of two syllables. The line-2 asterisk corresponds to the head of the metrical word, and the pair of parentheses enclosing the line-1 asterisks formalizes the inclusion of all the feet in the metrical word domain. The head of the metrical word shows up as the word's main stress, and the heads of the remaining feet as secondary stresses, unless such feet are suppressed by Line Conflation, as we have explained.

> The head of the metrical word shows up as the word's main stress, and the heads of the remaining feet as secondary stresses

C h a p t e r   S u m m a r y

In this chapter we have shown how a single set of principles and parameters can account for the apparently varied and unpredictable stress patterns of English, and how these same devices can be applied to the stress patterns of other languages seemingly quite unrelated. We showed that the simple strategy of rendering the right-most asterisk on a designated level extrametrical allows us to account for the contrasting English stress patterns of phrases and verbs/unsuffixed adjectives, on the one hand, and compounds and nouns/suffixed adjectives, on the other, while maintaining a single setting for End Stress ("right" for English): End Stress projects a baseline edge asterisk onto line 1 after extrametricality has effectively moved such an edge one position inward. Extrametricality is controlled by the Peripherality Condition, which ensures that only peripheral elements may be rendered extrametrical. The combination of End Stress and Extrametricality fails, however, to account for the antepenultimate stress in English nouns of more than two syllables. The problem is solved by the introduction of the metrical foot, which brackets together pairs of syllables, one of them projected onto the line immediately above as the head of the foot. English verbs and unsuffixed adjectives, with basic penultimate stress, are not subject to extrametricality. Metrical feet are further substantiated by the alternating pattern of stressed and unstressed syllables typical of longer words. The inventory of metrical parameters includes the location of the foot's head, the direction of foot construction, the presence and edge setting of extrameticality, and the edge setting of End Stress.

Key Questions

1 What is "End Stress"?
2 What is "extrametricality"? Why is the Peripherality Condition important in constraining extrametricality?
3 State the terms of the Elsewhere Condition.
4 How do the standard stress patterns of nouns differ from those of verbs? How does the stress algorithm deal with the discrepancies?
5 What is the structure of the metrical foot in English? What evidence do we have for it?

6 How can the direction of foot construction be determined by the sites of the stresses in words?
7 How can changes to the settings of the metrical parameters yield a wide variation of stress patterns in languages? List the parameters discussed. What are the settings for English?
8 What is the result of Line Conflation? Why is it necessary?
9 State the terms of the Faithfulness Condition. How does it relate to Line Conflation?

Further Practice

Araucanian

The stress pattern of the Penutian language Araucanian, spoken in Chile and Argentina, is illustrated below (assume orthographic *w* and *y* to represent non-nucleic [u] and [i], respectively):

wulé	'tomorrow'
ṭipánte	'year'
kimúbalùwulày	'he pretended not to know us'
elúmuyù	'give us'
elúaènew	'he will give us'

(i)   What are the parameter settings required to account for this pattern?
(ii) Show the processes through which stress is assigned, in the form of a grid.

Warao

Compare the stress pattern of Araucanian with that of Warao, spoken in Venezuela:

yiwàranáe	'he finished it'
nàhoròahàkutái	'the one who ate'

yàpurùkitàneháse   'verily to climb'
enàhoròahàkutái   'the one who caused him to eat'

(i)   What are the parameter settings for Warao?
(ii)   Show the processes in the form of a grid.

Weri

As in the cases of Araucanian and Warao, account for the stress pattern of
the New Guinean language Weri:

ŋintíp   'bee'   kùlipú   'hair or arm'
ulùamít   'mist'   àkunètepál   'times'

Hungarian

Now show the settings for Hungarian, in the same way as you have done
for the three languages above:

bóldog	'happy'
bóldogsàːg	'happiness'
bóldogtàlan	'unhappy'
bóldogtàlansàːg	'unhappiness'
légeslègmegèngesztèlhetètlenèbbeknèk	'to the very most irreconcilable ones'

Western Aranda

In the Australian language Western Aranda, primary stress falls on the first
or second syllable in trisyllabic or longer words and on the first syllable
if the word has fewer than three syllables. Examples of the patterns are shown
below:

a. *Consonant-initial words of three or more syllables*
    túkura   'ulcer'
    kútunùla   'ceremonial assistant'
    wóratàra   place name

b. *Vowel-initial words of three or more syllables*
    ergúma   'to seize'
    artjánama   'to run'
    utnádawàra   place name

c.   *Bisyllabic words*
    káma   'to cut'
    ílba   'ear'
    wúma   'to hear'

Allowing for an extrametricality clause in the algorithm, work out the settings for Western Aranda.

CHAPTER THIRTEEN

SYLLABLE WEIGHT

FURTHER METRICAL MACHINERY

Chapter Objectives

In this chapter you will learn about:
- The definition of "heavy" and "light" syllables.
- Word stress falling closer to the end of the word because of a heavy syllable.
- Marking heavy syllables as heads of feet in advance of the application of regular footing.
- The creation of monosyllabic feet to conform to the foot-head parameter setting.
- Final consonants outside the rime.
- Extrametricality blocking by long vowels.
- The "mora" as an alternative way of encoding syllable weight.
- Unbounded feet.
- Lexical marking of idiosyncratic accent.

The account of English stress in the previous chapter only works for a subset of nouns/suffixed adjectives and verbs/unsuffixed adjectives. This shortfall should not come as a surprise, in view of our earlier warning on the complexity of the English stress system. In this chapter we continue to investigate stress, adding to the theory as we need to along the way. The specific focus will be on the effect of syllable structure on stress assignment, and its implications for syllable theory. In the final sections we extend the metrical model to cases that fall outside the scope of the machinery as it stands at present.

1 An Additional Pattern of Stress in English

Consider the two samples in (1), nouns in a. and verbs and unsuffixed adjectives in b.:

(1) a. agénda   b. (to) incréase
         amálgam   (to) replý
         asbéstos   (to) recomménd
         incísor   oblíque
         meménto   (to) despíse
         debénture   inténse
         incéntive   (to) invént
         Octóber   (to) enthúse
         amanuénsis   (to) withdráw

Can you see anything new in the patterns in (1)?

In both sets stress falls one syllable further to the right than is predicted by the procedures we gave in chapter 12, now summarized in (2) as a reminder:

Briefly summarize these procedures before you read on.

(2) English stress algorithm (no. 3):
     a. Project syllable heads onto the baseline
     b. Make the right-most baseline asterisk extrametrical (in nouns and suffixed adjectives only)
     c. Construct line 1 by building left-headed feet iteratively from right to left
     d. Construct line 2 by applying End Stress [Right] on line 1

Work through the algorithm in (2) until you are comfortable with it. Go back to the data in (1) above and demonstrate what the problem with them is.

As we explained at the time, the steps in (2) follow from the settings of the relevant parameters, which we repeat in (3). Remember that we are crucially assuming that lexical forms are bare of metrical structure:

Lexical forms are bare of metrical structure

(3) English stress parameter settings:
     Extrametricality: Yes [right]   *Nouns*
                                          No   *Verbs*
     Location of foot head: Left
     Direction of foot construction: Right-to-left
     End stress: Right   *Onto line 1*

In (4) we illustrate these procedures at work in the forms *agenda* and *recommend*, from (1a) and (1b), respectively. The derivations incorporate line conflation, anticipating the evidence we present in chapter 15 to the effect that line conflation is also operative in English, contrary to our practice so far, which we based on the secondary stresses of forms like *hàmamèlidánthemum*:

Line conflation is also operative in English

> What exactly is the argument that emerges from forms like *hàmamèlidánthemum*?

(4)	agenda	Input	recommend	
	* * *		* * *	Baseline
	agenda	(2a)	recommend	
	* * <*>		* * *	Baseline
	agenda	(2b)	recommend	
	*		*	Stress line 1
	(* *) <*>		(*) (* *)	Baseline
	agenda	(2c)	re commend	
	*		*	Stress line 2
	*		*	Stress line 1
	(* *) <*>		(*) (* *)	Baseline
	agenda	(2d)	re commend	
	*		*	Stress line 1
	(* *) <*>		* (* *)	Baseline
	agenda	(Conflation)	recommend	

Obviously, the outputs **ágenda* and **recómmend* do not match up to the real data *agénda* and *recomménd*.

There are several things we can do next.

> Try and guess at least two ways of solving the problem posed by **ágenda* and **recómmend*.

We could, for instance, treat the noun *agenda* as an exception to the extra-metricality clause (2b). This move would not be too outrageous in principle, since phonological rules can be subject to idiosyncratic exceptions, as we will see in some detail in the last section of the chapter. However, the exception-based solution cannot solve the problem posed by the wrong contour **recómmend*.

> Explain why *recómmend* is not prevented by marking the word as an exception to extrametricality.

The reason *recommend* remains problematic is that verbs are not marked for extrametricality in the first place, and therefore making them exceptions to extrametricality will by definition be inconsequential.

An alternative explanation for the stress patterns of the forms in (1) could be that these forms are assigned right-headed feet, instead of the normal left-headed feet:

(5)   *   *   Stress line 1
       (* *) <*>   * (*   *)   Baseline
          agenda   recommend

This approach, however, goes against the reasonable assumption that metrical structure is uniform across the board in each language, so that, for example, in any given language all the feet are left-headed (or right-headed), End Stress invariably affects the left (or the right) edge, and so on. Under this alternative proposal, English feet would sometimes be left-headed (for instance, in *aspáragus* or *implícit*) and sometimes right-headed (in *agénda* and *recomménd*). Remember that the uniformity assumption has very positive implications for learnability, which would be lost, or at least considerably weakened, if we were to set the parameters word by word.

Metrical structure is uniform across the board in each language

> Spell out the implications of the parameter-based approach for learnability. Why would these implications be weakened by the analysis we are dismissing?

Before we go on to offer a solution, it is worth pointing out that the words in (1) are as regular as their predecessors in chapter 12 – forms in the mould of (1) are legion, and do not feel odd or exceptional in any way: on the contrary, it is *ágenda* and *recómmend* that feel un-English. The procedure by which stress is assigned to the words in (1) must therefore be as general as the stress procedure responsible for their predecessors.

2 Syllable Weight and Metrical Accent

Up until now, syllable structure has played no part in the construction of the metrical grid, beyond syllable peaks providing baseline elements. This

omission needs to be corrected. The syllable structure of the forms in (1) above
is as follows:

(6) a.gén.da   in.cr[íː]se
     a.mál.gam   re.pl[áɪ]
     as.bés.tos   re.co.mménd
     in.c[áɪ].sor   o.bl[íː]que
     me.mén.to   des.p[áɪ]se
     de.bén.ture   in.ténse
     in.cén.tive   in.vént
     Oc.t[óʊ].ber   en.th[júː]se
     a.man.u.én.sis   with.dr[ɔː]

Notice that in these words the stressed syllables are all HEAVY, in that their
rimes contain either a long nucleus ([iː] in *increase*, [aɪ] in *reply*, etc.) or a
coda ([n] in *agenda*, [n] in *recommend*, etc.).

> Why aren't we including the final *d* of *recommend* in the rime?
> Go back to chapter 10 if your memory needs jogging.

By contrast, in all the words we considered in the previous chapter, the stressed
syllable (antepenultimate for nouns and penultimate for verbs) was followed
by a LIGHT syllable, with neither a long nucleus nor a coda:

(7) cí.ne.ma   as.pá.ra.gus
     ál.ge.bra   a.lu.mí.ni.um
     é.le.phant   a.lú.mi.num
     plá.ty.pus   hy.po.chón.dri.ac
     lá.by.rinth   me.ta.mór.pho.sis
     ás.te.risk   hi.ppo.pó.ta.mus

> Check that the penultimate syllable is indeed light here.
> Reconsider other English data presented in chapter 12 to see
> if they fit the pattern we are now advancing.

For ease of reference, we now tabulate the correspondences between stress
and rime structure we are focusing on:

(8)   Rime structure and stress in English:

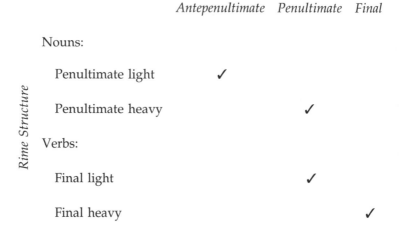

Stress

Antepenultimate   Penultimate   Final

The connection between the location of stress and the structure of the rime obviously needs to be encoded in the grid. In order to achieve this, we project the baseline asterisks of heavy rimes onto line 1. The word ACCENT is commonly used to refer to this projection, perhaps not very helpfully, given the other functions of the word, among them the designation of the graphic mark signalling stress.

> List and explain all the meanings of the word "accent" you can find.

We illustrate the accenting procedure in (9) with *agenda*:

(9)
```
                                        *          Stress line 1
                      *  *  <*>      *  *  <*>      Baseline
            a.gen.da  →  a.gen.da  →  a.gen.da
                 Baseline and         Accent
                 Extrametricality
```

> Say exactly what happens in (9).

In (9) all the syllable heads (including the /ɛ/ of *gen*) supply an asterisk to the baseline, as usual. In addition, the baseline asterisk dominating the /ɛ/ of *gen*, a heavy syllable, projects onto line 1 before footing (2c) is activated. This line-1 asterisk on *gen* defines the head of a foot. Now, we know from the previous chapter that heads imply constituents, and constituents heads,

The connection between the location of stress and the structure of the rime is encoded in the grid through the device ACCENT as encapsulated in the Faithfulness Condition in (48) of chapter 12, which we now repeat in (10):

(10) Faithfulness Condition:
Each grid constituent has a head (plotted in the line immediately above), and each head has a domain (delimited in the line immediately below)

It follows from the Faithfulness Condition that the output grid in (9) effectively contains one foot, with its head already explicit on *gen*:

(11)
```
     *                    *
 *   *   <*>      *  (*)  <*>
 a.gen.da    →    a.gen.da
         Faithfulness
```

Notice that, instead of making accent make the head explicit in line 1, we could make accent supply the corresponding parenthesis in the baseline, the line-1 asterisk then being automatically provided by the Faithfulness Condition in (10):

(12)
```
                          *           Stress line 1
 *  *  <*>     *  (*  <*>     *  (*)  <*>  Baseline
 a.gen.da  →   a.gen.da  →   a.gen.da
         Accent        Faithfulness
```

You will observe that the ultimate effect of the two procedures is identical. Consequently, we will have nothing further to say on the matter here.

> Show that the two alternative accenting procedures we mentioned indeed yield the same results for our data.

In order to remain notationally neutral, however, we shall enter in our grids both the asterisk and the parenthesis whenever we activate the accent procedure.

If footing were to disregard the pre-existing line-1 asterisk and its line-0 parenthesis, the effects of accenting would obviously be nullified, and the accent procedure would be futile:

(13)
```
     *            *           Stress line 1
 *  (*  <*>    (*  *)  <*>  Baseline
 a.gen.da  →   a.gen.da
         Footing
```

In order to avoid this result, we enrich the theory with a FREE ELEMENT
CONDITION limiting the action of metrical algorithms to the building of
structure:

(14)   Free Element Condition:
       Only metrically free elements may undergo metrical construction

If the pre-existing head mark on *gen* is to be respected by the footing procedure, in keeping with the Free Element Condition in (14), and if English
feet are necessarily left-headed, then the pre-existing head mark supplied
through accenting needs to be aligned with the left edge of the foot:

> Explain exactly why the accentual head mark needs to be left-
> aligned.

(15)   *   Stress line 1
       * (*) <*>   Baseline
       a.gen.da

Notice that the ensuing foot is DEGENERATE (it has its growth stunted!),
with only one syllable. This result shows that falling short of foot binarity
is preferable to contravening the Free Element Condition or the English setting of the headedness parameter.

> Remind yourself under what other circumstances degenerate
> feet are possible (go back to chapter 12 if you need to).

We have now successfully accounted for the penultimate stress of *agenda*
and similar nouns in (1a) through resort to SYLLABLE WEIGHT, that is, by
computing syllables with a complex nucleus or rime as heavy, and assigning them accent. The analysis also accounts for the final stress of the verbs
and unsuffixed adjectives in (1b), allowing for the general exclusion of these
categories from extrametricality marking:

(16)   *   *   *   Stress line 1
            *   *   *   * * (*   (* *)   (*)   Baseline
          re.co.mmend   →   re.co.mmend   →   re.co.mmend   →
                     Accent   Footing

```
                    *                       Stress line 2
        *           *               *       Stress line 1
      (* *)        (*)         * *  (*)      Baseline
   →   re.co.mmend   →   re.co.mmend
   End Stress            Conflation
```

Stress systems that require accenting of heavy syllables, as English does, are said to be QUANTITY-SENSITIVE, and stress systems that do not require accenting of heavy syllables are said to be QUANTITY-INSENSITIVE.

> Suggest why such a system as embodied in (16) is "quantity" sensitive.

We wind up the section with an update of the English stress algorithm, incorporating both the appropriate accent clause and conflation:

(17) English stress algorithm (no. 4):
    a. Project syllable heads onto the baseline
    b. Make the right-most baseline asterisk extrametrical (in nouns and suffixed adjectives only)
    c. Accent all (metrical) heavy syllables
    d. Construct line 1 by building left-headed feet iteratively from right to left
    e. Construct line 2 by applying End Stress [Right] on line 1
    f. Delete line 1

3 The Word-Final Consonant

The algorithm in (17) appears to run into difficulties when the data set of verbs and unsuffixed adjectives is extended.

Consider the forms in (27) of chapter 12, which we now repeat in (18) syllabified:

(18) im.plí.cit   in.sí.pid   i.má.gine   im.pé.ril
      de.vé.lop   en.déa.vour ad.mó.nish   en.dé.mic
      as.tó.nish   de.lí.ver   de.tér.mine pe.llú.cid

> Try and figure out what the problem is with the set in (18).

Side note: Stress systems that accent heavy syllables are QUANTITY-SENSITIVE, and stress systems that do not accent heavy syllables are QUANTITY-INSENSITIVE

The words in (18) end in a consonant ([n], [ʃ], etc.), and therefore their final syllable is heavy according to the definition of heavy syllable we gave in the previous section. Therefore, following our present reasoning, such a syllable ought to receive accent and carry stress, but it manifestly does not.

> What is the main point we are making?

This situation is obviously related to the observation we made in chapter 10 that the distribution of English consonants word-finally differs from their distribution word-medially.

> Jog your memory on this aspect of English syllable structure: what is the difference between the distribution of consonants word-finally and word-medially?

In particular, we saw then that the regular coda consonant can be followed by one extra consonant word-finally, in a manner only restricted by sonority sequencing (leaving aside some cases with two obstruents):

(19) camp   punt   fond   pink   fence
      build silk   pulp   bulb   belt
      shelf twelve pulse kiln   film
      farm   fort   ford   corn   harsh   (in rhotic accents)
      fork   harp   serve herb   surf   (in rhotic accents)

You will remember that we proposed affiliating this additional consonant directly to the syllable node.

> Recall the arguments for the direct affiliation of the word-final consonant to the syllable node.

We shall assume that the last consonant of English words lies outside the rime

Suppose now that the analysis is extended to all word-final consonants, whether or not they are preceded by another consonant. If this step is taken, the last consonant of English words will systematically lie outside rime structure, and the last syllables in the words in (18) will be light. We illustrate this situation with *imagine* and *recommend* in (20) and (21), respectively, with the non-rimal final consonant separated from the rime by a dash (we will propose an alternative in the next section):

(20)   *   Stress line 1
      *   *   *   * (* *)   Baseline
      i.ma.gi-ne   →   i.ma.gi–ne
                  Footing, etc.

(21)   *   *   Stress line 1
      *   *   *   *   *   *   * *   (*)   Baseline
      re.co.mmen-d   →   re.co.mmen-d   →   re.co.mmen–d
                    Accent   Footing, etc.

You can see in (21) that the final syllable of *recommend* remains heavy even after the exclusion of the word-final consonant from the rime. In *imagine* in (20), on the other hand, this exclusion makes the final syllable light: *gi*. As a consequence, this syllable is parsed as the weak element of a left-headed foot, just as we showed in (20).

4 Long Vowels in the Last Syllable

So far we have been assigning systematic right-most extrametricality to nouns and suffixed adjectives. The examples in (22) appear to confirm that this extrametricality is assigned irrespective of syllable weight, indeed of the number of word-final consonants:

(22) a. ínstrument   b. signíficant
          lábyrinth   revérberant
          détriment   éxcellent
          ínterdict   ígnorant
          ásterisk   irréverent
          cátapult   dóminant

Unexpectedly from this perspective, the nouns in (23) have final stress:

(23) chimpanzée   seventéen
      enginéer   macaróon
      brigadóon   margaríne
      brigadíer   magazíne
      smitheréens   referée
      millionáire   questionnáire

If the forms in (23) did not have final stress, do you think their stress would fall on the antepenultimate or on the penultimate syllable?

English extrametricality is blocked by a long vowel

Crucially, all the forms in (23) have a long vowel in their final syllable: English extrametricality is therefore blocked by a long vowel, although obviously not by a coda consonant.

> What do long vowels and coda consonants have in common in the present context?

An update of the English stress algorithm is desirable at this point:

(24) English stress algorithm (no. 5):
  a. Project syllable heads onto the baseline
  b. In nouns and suffixed adjectives, make extrametrical the right-most baseline asterisk **if it dominates a syllable with a simple nucleus**
  c. Accent all (metrical) heavy syllables
  d. Construct line 1 by building left-headed feet iteratively from right to left
  e. Construct line 2 by applying End Stress [Right] on line 1
  f. Delete line 1

There are nouns which end in a long open syllable and do not exhibit the expected final stress

Puzzlingly, there are nouns with a long open final syllable which do not exhibit the expected final stress:

> How is a long open syllable characterized structurally?

(25) búffal[ou]   Málib[uː]
      cálic[ou]   cárib[uː]
      mosquít[ou]   Méxic[ou]
      Kikúy[uː]   jujíts[uː]
      albín[ou]   commánd[ou]
      tomát[ou]   potát[ou]
      wínd[ou]   méad[ou]

A way of accounting for this situation involves treating these word-final vowels as short underlyingly (*buffal*/o/, etc.), to allow them to induce extrametricality. After stress has been assigned, these vowels will undergo lengthening:

> Why is the analysis of the word-final vowel of *buffalo* as short at all necessary? How would such forms be stressed otherwise?

(26)   buffal/o/

          <o>   Extrametricality

     *

    (* *)   Stress (NB left-headed footing)
         oː   Word-Final Lengthening
         oʊ   Diphthongization

> **What would happen if Word-Final Lengthening applied first in (26)?**

In (27) we formulate the rule of Word-Final Vowel Lengthening, somewhat informally. Notice that only high and mid vowels lengthen – the final low /æ/ of *algebra*, for instance, reduces to [ə] (compare *algebraic*, where that /æ/ is word-internal and becomes [eɪ], by Vowel Shift and Diphthongization):

(27)   Word-Final Vowel Lengthening:

$$V \rightarrow V\textrm{ː} \: / \left[\underline{\hspace{1.5em}} \atop -\text{low} \right] \#$$

The existence of rule (27) obviously makes the surface length of word-final vowels predictable, and therefore their underlying representation as short becomes plausible, indeed desirable on our familiar economy tenets.

> **What exactly are these economy tenets?**

Our repeated warning that English stress assignment is by no means a simple matter is certainly receiving ample confirmation.

5 Moras

Implicit in the discussion throughout has been the irrelevance of onsets to syllable weight. Consider in this connection the contrast between the two sets of words in (28):

(28)   a.   ággregate   b.   agénda
           réprimand   incísor
           ínstrument   vióla

In (28a) the penultimate syllables have a complex onset, but a light rime. In (28b), they have a heavy rime, but the onset is simple, or even null, as in *viola*.

Show how this is so by providing the syllabic parsings of some of the words in both columns of (28).

Now, while all the penultimate syllables in (28a) involve some form of internal complexity, only the forms in (28b), with a complex rime, bear penultimate stress. This confirms that it is only the rime that is relevant to the determination of syllable weight.

Only the rime is relevant to syllable weight

How does the conclusion that only rimes are relevant to weight follow?

The conclusion that only rimes determine syllable weight does not follow from our present formalism. Compare, for instance, the syllable structures of *gre* in *aggregate* and *gen* in *agenda*:

(29)

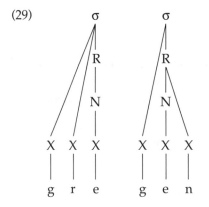

There are as many skeletal slots in *gre* as in *gen* (three), and yet only *gen* behaves as a heavy syllable.

Suppose then that we suppress the skeletal slots that correspond to the onset:

(30)   a.   b.

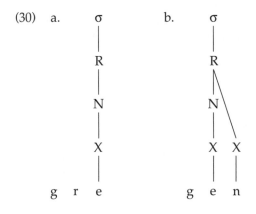

We can now compute syllable weight simply as a function of the number of skeletal slots in the rime: a syllable will be heavy if and only if its rime contains more than one skeletal slot. We spell this out in (31):

(31)

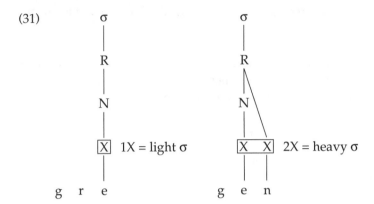

The syllable *gre* now contains only one skeletal slot, and therefore it is reckoned as light. By contrast, *gen* includes one additional slot, and therefore it is reckoned as heavy.

> Why exactly do we want to reckon *gre* as light and *gen* as heavy?

In the approach we are now developing, skeletal slots are referred to as MORAS. Traditionally, this term designates a basic unit of classic versification, and is also used in the phonological analysis of Japanese. Moras are conventionally represented by the Greek letter "μ" ("mu" [mju] in English):

Two moras define a heavy syllable, and one mora a light syllable

(32) a.   b.

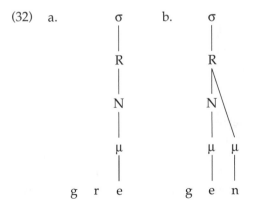

In the mora-based trees in (32) we have left the onset consonant unaffiliated, to make the presentation simpler. However, as we pointed out in chapters 9 and 10, all segments need to be part of prosodic structure in order to be licensed.

> Remind yourself of the rationale for this licensing requirement.

We can incorporate the onset consonant or consonants into syllabic structure in one of two ways – we can link them either to the first mora or to the syllable node directly, without any mora intervening:

(33)   a.   b.

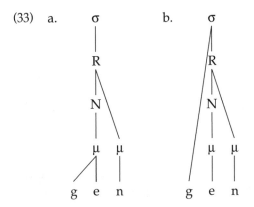

Either way, of course, the onset consonant will have no mora of its own, and therefore it will not contribute to syllable weight.

The replacement of skeletal slots with moras is generally assumed to make the intermediate R and N nodes superfluous:

(34)   a.   b.

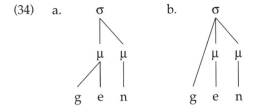

The structure in (34a) keeps moras (attached to σ) formally distinct from segments (all attached to μ). In the alternative structure in (34b), by contrast, onset segments are attached directly to σ, with no μ intervening.

One final question that needs addressing concerns the source of the moras themselves. One reasonable answer involves lexical projection from vowels, and structural projection from consonants that are preceded by a vowel and followed by a consonant, as is /n/ in *agenda* – this procedure is often referred to as WEIGHT BY POSITION:

Pause and reflect on weight by position.

(35)   a.   μ   μ   μ   μ

           | \ / |

           a   re na

     b.   μ   μ   μ   μ   μμ   μ

          | | | | |⋮| |

          a   gen da   →   a   gen   da
                          WBP

The final consonant in words like *imagine* will of course not project a mora, since it is not followed by another consonant:

(36)   μ   μ   μ

       | | |

       i ma gi n(e)

This structure obviously makes its predecessor in (20) redundant, since the final −*n* does not contribute weight.

6 Foot Structure and Universal Rhythm

The metrical parameters we have been using define the following symmetric inventory of feet:

Before you read on, enumerate the metrical parameters and the types of foot that are defined by their various settings.

(37)   Symmetric foot inventory (σ = syllable; L = light σ):

	left-headed	*Right-headed*	
Quantity-sensitive	(σ̇ L)	(L σ̇)	
	(σ̇)	(σ̇)	Regular
Quantity-insensitive	(σ̇σ)	(σσ̇)	Degenerate
	(σ̇)	(σ̇)	

Notice that in quantity-sensitive systems the head's sibling, if there is one, must be light.

Given the inventory in (37), we would expect each of the patterns it contains to have an even chance of being realized across languages. However, recent research has shown that reality does not live up to this expectation. In particular, only the patterns in (38) have been found strongly represented in the world's languages:

(38)   Asymmetric foot inventory (H = heavy σ):

	Left-headed	Right-headed
	*	*
Quantity-sensitive	(L L)	(L σ)
	*	*
	(H)	(H)
	*	
Quantity-insensitive	(σσ)	

> What logically possible feet are missing from this inventory?

L is of course equivalent to μ, and H to μμ. Therefore, from a mora perspective, the quantity-sensitive feet in (38) are constrained by the set of requirements in (39):

(39)   Constraints on quantity-sensitive feet:
   a.   Left-headed feet have precisely two moras
   b.   Right-headed feet have at least two moras
   c.   The head's sibling in a right-headed foot has precisely one mora

The point of these constraints is that syllable sequences that do not comply with them will fail to be footed. There is, however, some evidence that the degenerate (L) foot may be allowed parametrically: we saw in chapter 12 that such feet seemingly exist in Aklan and Maranungku, for instance (cf. *(má)(tiná)(marún)* 'being lazy' and *(mére)(pét)* 'beard', respectively).

In quantity-insensitive systems, the moraic makeup of the syllables plays no role in foot structure – indeed, it is reasonable to assume that in these systems all syllables are monomoraic by definition.

> Explain why it is reasonable to assume that in quantity-insensitive systems all syllables are monomoraic.

You can see in (38) above that, in the model we are discussing, foot type is severely restricted in quantity-insensitive systems. In particular, only left-headed binary feet are allowed for in these systems.

The lopsided foot system in (38) is grounded in limitations of rhythm perception by humans. Specifically, when humans hear a string of elements of even duration but uneven intensity, they perceive a succession of units made up of a strong element followed by a weak element, that is, a succession of left-headed feet. By contrast, when they hear a string of elements of even intensity but uneven duration, they perceive a succession of units made up of a short element followed by a long element, that is, a succession of right-headed feet.

The lopsided foot system in (38) is grounded in limitations of rhythm perception by humans

> Test this out with friends, by tapping alternative strong knocks (implemented as heavy and long in successive experimental conditions) and asking them whether the strong knock precedes or follows its light counterpart.

The formalization of this contrast in terms of moras is as in (40):

(40) a. Left-headed foot:

b. Right-headed foot:

These structures correspond to the maximal feet in the inventory in (38) above. The justification for their non-degenerate minimal versions ($((\overset{*}{\sigma})$ in both

types of feet, but $(\overset{*}{\sigma\sigma})$ in right-headed feet only) is less clear.

We formalize
the perceptual
foundation of
metrical rhythm
in the IAMBIC–
TROCHAIC LAW

We formalize the perceptual foundation of metrical rhythm in (41) as the IAMBIC–TROCHAIC LAW – remember that "iamb" and "trochee" are the names given in classical versification to right-headed and left-headed feet, respectively:

(41) Iambic–Trochaic Law:
a. Elements of uneven intensity (and even duration) pair up as left-headed feet (= trochees)
b. Elements of uneven duration (and even intensity) pair up as right-headed feet (= iambs)

The noted differences in frequency of foot types in the stress systems of the world obviously support the asymmetric foot inventory in (38) above. Note, however, that this is not the only possible interpretation for the rarity of some foot types. In particular, this rarity could also be attributed to performance factors related to the realities of human perception encapsulated in the Iambic–Trochaic Law. From this perspective, the Iambic–Trochaic Law would be irrelevant to the competence grammar that we must assume underpins metrical systems, and the parametric system in (37) above could be maintained as a model of metrical competence level in spite of the typological facts reported.

The rarity of some
foot types could
also be attributed
to performance
factors

> Remind yourself of the competence-performance opposition, set up by Chomsky and referred to in chapter 8.

7 Non-Rhythmic Stress

Binary feet are, of course, the formal incarnation of alternating rhythm, as we now remind ourselves of with the help of *hamamelidanthemum*:

(42)   *   *   *   Stress line 1
        (*   *) (* *)(*   *) <*>   Baseline
        hama meli danthe mum

Without left-headed binary feet, *dan* or *me* could not be stressed, since End Stress can only stress one syllable on the word edge, as you know.

Some languages do have a single surface stress located on the edge, with or without extrametricality. One such language is Bengali, spoken in Bengal (Bangladesh and Indian West Bengal):

(43) Bengali stress:
   ápon   'personal'
   dhópa   'Washerman'
   ápnar   'your own' (honorific)
   báʧorik   'annual'
   ónuʃɒron   'pursuit'
   páromanobik   'atomic, molecular'

> Propose an analysis for Bengali stress.

The pattern in (43) can obviously be derived by End Stress, without recourse to footing.

In yet other languages, the derivation of the single surface stress is less straightforward. Consider, for instance, the following data from (Khalkha) Mongolian, the official language of the Mongolian Republic:

(44) Mongolian stress:
   bosgúːl   'fugitive'
   bariáːd   'after holding'
   xoyərdugáːr   'second'
   garáːsaː   'from one's own hand'
   áli   'which'
   xŏtəbərə   'leadership'

Your first reaction to these data will probably be utter bewilderment.

> See if you can discern any pattern in (44).

Closer inspection reveals a rather simple pattern, however: Mongolian stress is carried by the first long vowel of the word or, in the absence of long vowels, by the first syllable.

> Work out in which of the words in (44) each of these two cases occurs.

This type of pattern poses an obvious challenge to our metrical model, and we now attend to it.

The distribution of stress in (44) suggests that in languages like Mongolian stress is not a direct consequence of rhythm. Therefore, it cannot be formalized through binary footing. Consider, for instance, *xốtəbərə*, where there are no fewer than three stressless syllables after the stressed syllable: rhythmic stress would of course favour **xótəbə́rə*. Similarly, *xoyər-dugáːr* ought to have been **xoyə̀rdugáːr*.

> Do any of the other words in (44) exhibit any kind of rhythm?

A quite convincing analysis of Mongolian stress runs as follows. We first subject all long vowels to accenting:

(45)

```
                        *   *             *   *    Stress line 1
       *   *   *        * (* (*      * (*) (*)     Baseline
     garaːsaː    →   ga raː saː   →   ga raː saː
            Accenting           Faithfulness
```

We then apply End Stress [Left] to enhance the first of these accents:

(46)

```
                        *           Stress line 2
          *   *         *   *       Stress line 1
       * (*) (*)      * (*)(*)       Baseline
     ga raːsaː    →   ga raːsaː
            End Stress [Left]
```

Finally, we apply line conflation to dispose of all secondary stresses:

(47)

```
       *                            Stress line 2
       *   *            *            Stress line 1
     * (*) (*)        * (*)  *       Baseline
     ga raːsaː    →   garaːsaː
            Conflation
```

The result is *garáːsaː*, exactly as required.

> Work through one of the other examples in the sample in (44) above.

The procedure is also successful in forms with no long vowels. In such forms the accenting clause will be inoperative. As a consequence, there will be no accent-induced marks on stress line 1 – indeed, no stress line 1 at all at this stage.

> Why won't there be a line 1 yet?

In the final stage, End Stress [Left] will simply enhance the word's initial syllable, as we show in (48):

(48)

| | * | | * | Stress line 1 |
| * * * * | | * * * * | (* * * *) | Baseline |

xötəbərə   →   xötəbərə   →   xötəbərə

       End Stress [Left]   Faithfulness

8   Unbounded Feet

The development we have just introduced also accounts for languages where stress falls on the first or the last heavy syllable (again independently of rhythm), but where the polar opposite syllable is stressed in the absence of heavy syllables.

> Ensure that you see conceptually the difference between this type of language and Mongolian.

This apparently more complex pattern can be illustrated with the Uralic language Selkup:

(49)   Selkup stress:

kə́	'winter'	sə́rɨ	'white'
ámɨrna	'eats'	qóːkɨtilʲ	'deaf'
qólʲtsimpatɨ	'found'	pynakɨsə́ː	'giant!'
kanaŋmíː	'our dog'	kárman	'pocket'
qumóːqi	'two human beings'	qúmɨt	'human beings'
úːtsɨqo	'to work'	úːtsɨkkak	'I am working'
uːtsɔ́ːmɨt	'we work'	uːtsɨkkóːqɪ	'they two are working'

The Selkup pattern is in one respect the mirror image of the Mongolian pattern: Selkup stress falls on the last (rather than the first) of a sequence of long vowels. However, in words with no long vowels, stress falls on the initial syllable, just as in Mongolian.

The Selkup pattern can be derived straighforwardly by constructing unbounded left-headed feet – notice that, crucially, we did not construct feet in Mongolian: more on this below. As is implied by the name, the number of baseline elements in an UNBOUNDED FOOT is undefined:

(50)   a.   *   *   b.   *   Stress line 1
            (*) (*   *)   (*   *   *) Baseline
            uːtsɔːmɨt   amɨrna

> Explain why these two words have been assigned different metrical configurations.

The left-headed unbounded feet in (50) are anchored on the heads supplied by the accenting procedure, or, in the absence of such heads, on the baseline. At word level, Selkup End Stress has the opposite setting to Mongolian – "right" in Selkup and "left" in Mongolian:

(51)   a.   *   Stress line 2
              (*   *)   *   Stress line 1
              (*) (*   *)   * (*   *)   Baseline
              uːtsɔːmɨt   →   uːtsɔːmɨt
                         Conflation

       b.   *   Stress line 2
            (*)   *   Stress line 1
            (*   *   *)   (*   *   *)   Baseline
            amɨrna   →   amɨrna
                     Conflation

Once more, we have achieved the desired result through the familiar parameters, simply enriched with unbounded feet.

We saw above that in Mongolian there is no foot construction.

> Show that Mongolian cannot accommodate foot construction.

In particular, Mongolian feet originate in the inevitable relationship between foot heads and foot boundaries encapsulated in the Faithfulness Condition. In (52) we offer the whole derivation of garaːsaː:

(52)

			*	Stress line 2
* *	* *	(* *)	*	Stress line 1
((*	* (*) (*)	* (*) (*)	* (*) *	Baseline

garaːsaː → ga raːsaː → ga raːsaː → ga raːsaː

    Faithfulness   End Stress [L]   Conflation

Crucially, the first syllable remains unfooted.

> Why is it crucial that the first syllable of *garáːsaː* should remain unfooted?

9 Idiosyncratic Accent

We have remarked in several places that exceptions to phonological rules are far from uncommon. Importantly, we shall now show that even exceptional forms are subject to the overall system of rules and principles.

   It would be most surprising to find an unsuffixed noun in English with the primary stress outside the customary THREE-SYLLABLE WINDOW on the right edge, allowances being made for some additional factors that we will examine in chapter 15. The three-syllable window is conveniently instantiated by the chain derivation *médicine, medícinal, medicinálity*, where stress can be seen to move rightwards to keep within the window (we observed a similar situation in the Macedonian data we presented in chapter 12). In the possible *médicinelessness*, the violation of the three-syllable window is only apparent, since suffixes like *-less* and *-ness* are systematically excluded from the domain of stress, as we will see in chapter 16. A potentially irreducible case of three-syllable window violation is provided by a word like *Kalevala*, the name of the Finnish national epic. The question is, how will English speakers (radio and TV presenters, for instance) stress this word? The answer is that they can assign it penultimate stress, *Kalevála*, by lengthening the penultimate vowel to [aː], or antepenultimate stress, *Kalévala*, by keeping the penultimate vowel short and ultimately reducing it to schwa. What would have been unexpected, indeed quite astonishing, would have been for the word to have received initial stress (*Kálevala*), in defiance of the three-syllable window. Crucially, though, this pattern is in itself neither absurd nor impossible: it is indeed the pattern the word has in Finnish, a language with systematic word-initial stress, like Bengali.

   We will now show that the device of lexical accent allows a natural interpretation of the ultimately lawful behaviour of exceptional stress. Consider the real English patterns in (53):

Even exceptional forms are subject to the overall system of rules and principles

The device of lexical accent allows a natural interpretation of the ultimately lawful behaviour of exceptional stress

(53)   a.   Kentúcky   b.   Berlín
             Mississíppi   violín

The forms in (53a) ought to have had antepenultimate stress (*Kéntucky*, *Missíssippi*), because their penultimate syllable is light (the *ck* and *pp* clusters are purely orthographic), and their last syllable extrametrical, as they are nouns.

> Show that *Kentucky* ought to have had antepenultimate stress.

The short vowel in the last syllable of the forms in (53b) ought also to have been extrametrical, and therefore stressless.

> Explain exactly why the last syllable in *Berlin* and *violin* ought to have been extrametrical.

The facts just mentioned reveal that the patterns in (53) contravene the rules of English stress. The question is whether this contravention is wild (as **Kálevala* would have been) or still constrained by the general principles.

Irregular stress can in fact be reconciled with the regular stress procedures, which remain in force in all cases. In particular, we shall assume that the vowels stressed in the forms in (53) idiosyncratically carry an accent in lexical representation:

(54)   (*   (*
        Kentucky   Berlin

Vowels with a lexical accent are effective foot heads before the derivation even starts. We illustrate in (55) for *Kentucky*. Notice that when nuclei are projected onto the baseline, the preassigned asterisk is raised to the next line up, to preserve differentials:

Vowels with a lexical accent are effective foot heads before the derivation even starts

(55)   *   *   *   * *   Stress line 1
            (*   * (*   *   * (*) *   * (*) <*>   (* (*) <*>   Baseline
        Kentucky → Kentucky → Kentucky → Kentucky → Kentucky →
              Baseline   Faithfulness   Extrametricality   Accent

```
                              *                      Stress line 2
        *   *                 (*   *)          *      Stress line 1
      (*) (*) <*>           (*) (*) <*>   *  (*) <*>  Baseline
   → Kentucky → Vacuous → Kentucky → Kentucky
   Faithfulness      Footing    End Stress [R]  Conflation
```

You can see that the desired result follows automatically. *Berlin* and *violin* in (53b) above obviously suggest that extrametricality is blocked by lexical accent.

> Why exactly do we have to assume that extrametricality is blocked by lexical accent?

Given this approach, a form like **Kálevala* is underivable. Let us see what happens if we hypothetically provide its first vowel with a lexical accent:

A form like **Kálevala* is underivable in English

(56)   *   *
     Kalev/æ/la or Kalev/ɑ:/la

The respective derivations will be as follows:

(57) a.   *   *   *   Stress line 1
         (*   (* *   *   *   (* *   * <*>   Baseline
        Kalev/æ/la → Kalev/æ/la → Kalev/æ/la →
                       Baseline   Extrametricality

```
                                    *                      Stress line 2
           *   *              (*   *)              *        Stress line 1
         (*)(*   *) <*>     (*)(*   *) <*>     *(*   *) <*>  Baseline
      →  Ka lev/æ/ la  →  Ka lev/æ/ la  →  Kalev/æ/ la
         Footing           End Stress         Conflation
```

b.   *   *   *   Stress line 1
   (*   (* *   *   *   (* *   * <*>   Baseline
  Kalev/ɑ:/la → Kalev/ɑ:/la → Kalev/ɑ:/la →
                  Baseline   Extrametricality

```
      *     *         *     *                  *          Stress line 1
    (* *  (* <*>    (* *) (*) <*>     *  *  (*) <*>       Baseline
  →  Ka lev/ɑ:/la  →  Kalev/ɑ:/la  →  Kalev/ɑ:/la
     Accent          Footing         End Stress, etc.
```

You can see that the lexical accent on *Ka* has no effect on the final output.

> Sum up in a few words why the first syllable of *Kalevala* will never carry stress in the surface in English.

If so, forms like **Kálevala* simply cannot exist in English. This outcome confirms the suitability of lexical accent for the formalization of stress exceptions. It also vindicates line conflation, which is obviously needed to dispose of stresses that are unwanted in the surface: *Kalevala*, for instance, can surface as *Kalévala*, but not as **Kàlévala*, with the lexical accent surfacing as a secondary stress.

Line conflation is needed to dispose of stresses that are unwanted in the surface

> Why is line conflation obviously needed to dispose of stresses?

The hypothetical English situation we have just discussed actually exists in Macedonian. In the previous chapter we saw that regular Macedonian stress is antepenultimate. There are, however, a few cases of penultimate or final stress in modern loanwords, exemplified in (58):

(58) a. literatúra   'literature'   b. citát   'quotation'
          romántik   'romantic'   autobús   'bus'
          konsumátor   'consumer'   restorán   'restaurant'

Upon suffixation, stress moves rightwards whenever it needs to in order to remain inside the three-syllable window, as is the case in the forms underlined in (59):

(59) literatúra   romántik   konsumátor
      literatúrata   romántikot   konsumátorot   Sg. def.
      literatúri   romántici   konsumátori   Pl.
      literatúrite   romantícite   konsumatórite   Pl. def.

This situation parallels the *Kalevala* case in (57) above, and can be approached in a similar manner.

> Try out the *Kalevala* analysis on the Macedonian forms.

The final case we shall discuss concerns Vedic Sanskrit, the language of the Veda, the ancient sacred texts of the Hindus. This case is related to the English and Macedonian cases we just described, but has an interest of its own.

The data in (60) illustrate the stress system of Vedic Sanskrit (hyphens signal morphological divisions, and *ś* represents a voiceless alveopalatal fricative):

(60) Sanskrit stress:
    a. áśv-a-nam   'horses'   b. áśv-a-vat-i-nam   'having horses'
       dev-á-nam   'gods'   pad-vat-i-nám   'having feet'

You may think that these patterns are truly beyond the powers of our familiar procedures. However, we have come up against similar situations before (the stress patterns of English are not famous for their simplicity), and have consistently been able to bring them to heel after a bit of hard thinking.

> Why do the forms in (60) appear to be beyond our procedures?

Let us suppose that some Sanskrit morphemes idiosyncratically carry an accented vowel lexically, as we indicate in (61):

(61)
```
   *   *  *      *   *          *          *  *                    *
  (*  (* (*     (*  (*         (*         (*  (*                  (*
  aśv-a-nam   aśv-a-vat-i-nam   dev-a-nam   pad-vat-i-nam
```

Of the morphemes in (60), the root *aśv* 'horse' and the suffixes *-a* and *-nam* are therefore accented, and the rest accentless. Once we take this simple step, we can account for the Sanskrit system by means of procedures we are already familiar with.

> Any idea which these familiar procedures are?

In particular, the Sanskrit system obeys the parameter settings we proposed for Mongolian earlier on: End Stress [Left], with no foot construction. We illustrate in (62) and (63) for *áśvanam* and *devánam*, respectively:

(62)
```
                                    *                        Stress line 2
  *  *  *      *  *  *         (*  *  *)      *               Stress line 1
 (* (* (*     (*) (*) (*)      (*) (*) (*)    (*)  *  *       Baseline
 aśvanam  →  aśva nam  →  aśva nam  →  aśvanam
    Faithfulness    End Stress [L]    Conflation
```

(63)

```
                                                              *          Stress line 2
        *  *              *  *           (*   *)             *           Line 1
     *  (*  (*         *  (*)  (*)      *  (*)  (*)        *  (*)  *      Baseline
     devanam   →   deva nam   →    deva nam   →   devanam
        Faithfulness        End Stress [L]       Conflation
```

> Work out the derivations of the forms in (60b) above.

We do not think it will be unreasonable to take this rather spectacular result as evidence that the metrical model we have been proposing is indeed on the right track.

Chapter Summary

In this chapter we have shown that in cases where English polysyllabic nouns bear penultimate rather than antepenultimate stress, and verbs and unsuffixed adjectives final rather than penultimate stress, the stressed syllables have branching rimes. Such syllables are defined as heavy, while those whose rime does not branch are light. In order to formalize the observation that heavy syllables are stressed regardless of their position in the word, the asterisk dominating the heavy syllable is projected onto line 1 (a process known as "accenting") in advance of the general construction of feet. Accented syllables will of necessity head a foot (degenerate if they have no syllable to pair with), since by the Faithfulness Condition each head corresponds to a constituent, and conversely. Verbs and unsuffixed adjectives with ostensibly final branching rimes do not, however, exhibit final stress. We can readily account for this fact if we exclude the word-final consonant from the final syllable, thus defining it as light. Such an "extrasyllabic" analysis of the word-final consonant is motivated by the strong tendency of apparent three-place rimes to be confined to the word-final position. Nouns with stress on a final long vowel suggest blocking of extrametricality by underlying vowel length. The observation that the onset plays no part in the calculation of syllable weight leads to an alternative model of syllables, with rime segments attached to "moras". This analysis provides a direct explanation for the behaviour of heavy syllables with complex nuclei, as well as those with a simple nucleus and a coda. Not all languages distinguish between heavy and light syllables in the calculation of stress: those which do are "quantity-sensitive", and those which do not "quantity-insensitive". Not all possible foot configurations are realized in the languages of the world: quantity-sensitive left-headed feet are precisely bimoraic, while quantity-sensitive right-headed feet contain two or three moras, and such asymmetries are captured in the Iambic–Trochaic Law. We also examined languages whose stress patterns are not reducible to binary feet. Finally, we considered cases which cannot be explained by any of the mechanisms hitherto introduced, and where it is necessary to mark the stressed syllable as accented in the lexicon. It is important to note, however, that the general principles of the language's stress system are still complied with in the presence of such lexical idiosyncratic accent.

K e y   Q u e s t i o n s

1 What is the explanation for the regular penultimate stress in some nouns and final stress in some verbs?
2 What is meant by "syllable weight"? Define a "heavy syllable".
3 What is a degenerate foot?
4 What do we mean by "accenting" in the context of stress assignment?
5 How does the Free Element Condition prevent normal foot construction overriding the effects of accenting?
6 What are quantity-sensitive and quantity-insensitive languages?
7 Why do final syllables with simple codas not count as heavy?

8 Under what conditions is noun extrametricality suppressed?
9 Define the "mora". Which syllable constituents are moraic?
10 What is "weight by position"?
11 What statement about stress systems is encapsulated by the Iambic–Trochaic Law?
12 How do unbounded feet differ from bounded ones?
13 What is the "three-syllable window"?
14 How can some apparently intractable stress assignments be explained by lexical accent?

F u r t h e r   P r a c t i c e

Latin Stress

Classical Latin word stress is either antepenultimate or penultimate. Consider the following data and say what parameter settings of the stress algorithm will produce the correct stress patterns (hint: conflation is operative in Latin):

amíːcus	'friend'	reféːcit	'set over' (3sg.perf)
agricoláːrum	'farmer' (gen.pl.)	agrícola	'farmer' (nom.sg.)
vólucres	'winged' (pl.)	pepérci	'spare' (1sg.perf)
símulaː	'snub nosed' (fem.)	magíster	'master'

Demonstrate the application of the stress algorithm to the data shown.

Cairene Arabic Stress

The dialect of Arabic spoken in Cairo has the following syllable types: light CV, heavy CVV and CVC, and superheavy CVCC and CVVC. Stress may fall on the final (as in a. below), penultimate (as in b.) or antepenultimate (as in c.) syllables (conflation is also operative here):

a. katábt   'I wrote'
    jadʒdʒáat   'pilgrimages'
    sakakíin   'knives'
b. ʕamálti   'you (fem.sg.) did'
    haðáani   'these (fem.du.)'
    katábta   'you (masc.sg.) wrote'
    mudárris   'teacher'
    martába   'mattress'
    katabítu   'they wrote'
    ʃadʒarátun   'tree'
    ʔadwijatúhu   'his drugs'
c. búxala   'misers'
    kátaba   'he wrote'
    ʃadʒarátuhu   'his tree'
    ʔadwijatúhumaa   'their drugs'

Making use of the machinery you have available, show the relevant parameter settings for the assignment of stress in Cairene. (Hint: all rime elements are stress bearers.)

Guajiro Stress

Consider the following sets of data from Guajiro, a language spoken in Venezuela and Colombia (adjacent vowels are tautosyllabic; all segmental symbols are IPA):

a. ipá   'stone'   b. tatʃéʔe   'my ear'
    eʔraháa   'to watch'   atýhaa   'to know'
    miʔirá   'party'   aʔjatáasy   'she works'
    iʃí   'a well'   oʔjotówaa   'to cut'
    aʔlanáa   'to fell'   iráma   'deer'
    iʃíi   'be sour'   oʔunýsy   'she goes'
    soʔú   'her eye'   aʔwanáahaa   'to change'
    saʔanýin   'she weaves'   aréepa   'corn bread'

c.	sapáatapy	'shoelace'	d.	áasajawaa	'to speak'
	akámaha	'to smoke'		éemerawaa	'to rest'
	óusahaa	'to kiss'		íipynaahee	'from above'
	átpanaa	'rabbit'		éirakawaa	'to turn one's eyes to something'
	óttahaa	'to distribute'		ʃíinaluʔu	'at the bottom'
	haʔjumúlery	'a fly'		ʃéemeraain	'she rests'

(i) Is there an extrametricality clause in the stress algorithm of Guajiro?

(ii) If yes, what are the criteria which determine extrametrical elements?

(iii) What is the foot structure of Guajiro?

(iv) Is Guajiro quantity-sensitive?

(v) What is the Guajiro setting for End Stress?

(vi) Does conflation apply?

(vii) Show how the settings of the Guajiro stress algorithm derive the stress of following words:

ʧeʔuháasy	'it is needed'	aʔjaláhaa	'to cry'
tóusahyin	'I kiss'	koʔói	'beehive'

CHAPTER FOURTEEN

TONAL PHONOLOGY

Chapter Objectives

In this chapter you will learn about:
- The variations in the vocal pitch referred to as "tones".
- How such variations are implemented.
- Different patterns of rising and falling tone sequences ("intonation") employed to express the speaker's intention.
- The extension of the autosegmental formalism to express the association between a tone and the syllable on which it is realized.
- Intonation providing direct evidence for stress.
- The lexical and morphological functions of tone in many of the world's languages.
- The principles of autosegmental association in operation in African languages.
- The all-pervasive nature of the OCP.

In the last three chapters we have reviewed stress, but still have not said specifically what stress is, having instead relied on general expressions like "prominence" or "salience" to identify the phenomenon. In chapter 11, we saw that vowels which do not support metrical structure in English tend to be pulled towards the centre of the vowel space, often becoming schwa: *Cánada* vs. *Canádian*. We also mentioned several phenomena affecting consonants equally related to stress, like the aspiration of voiceless stops and /t/ weakening. All these segmental facts provide evidence about the location of stress, and, by implication, about its existence. However, this evidence is indirect by its very nature. More to the point, it is only partial, since the correlations are by no means perfect: full vowels can be stressless (cf. *raccóon* in many accents), stressed vowels can have the quality of vowels plausibly analysed as reduced in other contexts (cf. [ɪ] in *distínguish*), aspirated voiceless stops occur in some stressless contexts (cf. *tenácious*), and so on. A more direct, and particularly salient, diagnostic for English stress is intonation, as we shall now explain. First, however, we must prepare the ground by describing succintly what intonation is. An understanding of the mechanics of intonation allows us to connect with other tonal phenomena that are absent from English, but are important in a world-wide context, and we will also discuss them in the chapter.

1 The Phenomenon of Intonation

Any English utterance, irrespective of length, can be delivered in a variety of tunes. Consider such simple monosyllables as *yes* or *no*. Suppose somebody says to us "Are you ready?". We answer "yes" or "no" to express agreement or disagreement, respectively, with the proposition "you are ready" contained in the question (the term PROPOSITION is used to refer to the logical content of utterances).

> Pause here and reflect briefly on the concept "proposition". How can we recognize the same proposition in "you are ready" as in "are you ready?", given the fact that the former expression is a statement, and the latter a question?

The way we will utter "yes", "no" or any other words will be very different from the flat, monotonous delivery typical of Daleks, robots or computers.

> Even gadgets like these are becoming less mechanical and more human-like in their speech: can you think why? (You may have to continue reading much of this chapter before you can approximate a principled answer, but nothing prevents you from advancing an educated guess at this point.)

Human delivery of language will almost certainly be "intonated", with the pitch rising and falling as we say the words, in a kind of simplified singing. In (1) we give three particularly common manifestations of such intonated delivery in English. We represent the modulation of the voice impressionistically, by means of falling or rising lines reminiscent of the lines an orchestra conductor draws in the air:

Human delivery of language will almost certainly be "intonated", with the pitch rising and falling as we say the words

(1) a. ＼ yes   b. ／ yes   c. \/ yes

         ＼ no   ／ no   \/ no

In (1a), the falling line represents the falling pitch of the tune characteristic of statements, a mode of delivery expressing agreement with the proposition ("yes, I'm coming") or disagreement ("no, I'm not coming").

> What exactly do we mean when we say that the contour in (1a) expresses simple propositional agreement or disagreement?

In (1b), by contrast, the line (and thus the tune it represents) rises, to signal incompleteness – (1b) can therefore be paraphrased as "yes/no, but I'm surprised you asked", or "yes/no, and so?". Finally, in (1c) the tune first falls and then rises, approximately conveying the meaning "yes/no, but . . .".

> Check whether you get the interpretations we are suggesting for the tunes in (1b) and (1c).

The simple set of data we have just examined appropriately demonstrates English intonation.

> Try out the various ways of saying "yes" represented in (1), to hear how these contours actually sound.

Our data also provide us with a first approximation to the physical substance of intonation, namely, singing-like movements with our voice which manifest as TUNES: melodies made up of a certain pitch pattern. Finally, we have seen that each of the tunes conveys a certain meaning, or meanings, which are often difficult to express in ordinary words: this difficulty provides an obvious functional motivation for intonation.

TUNES are melodies made up of a certain pitch pattern. Each tune conveys a certain meaning, or meanings, which are often difficult to express in ordinary words

> Explain how the difficulties involved in paraphrasing intonational tunes with words justify the existence of intonation.

2 The Mechanics of Intonation

In order to understand how intonation works, we first need to understand its physical mechanics. Fortunately, this is not a difficult task. We have already hinted at the involvement of voice in the process. You will recall from chapter 1 that "voice" is the technical term used in phonetics to refer to the vibration of the vocal folds. We said at the time that vocal fold vibration is induced indirectly, by the action of the air coming out of the lungs, much as a flag is caused to flap by the wind. Remember, in particular, that we cannot make the vocal folds vibrate directly: vibration happens by itself as a result of the physical dynamics caused by the air flowing through.

> Remind yourself of the precise mechanics of voice, referring back to chapter 1 if you need to.

In order for such aerodynamics to come about, we need to position the vocal folds in a particular way: not too far apart, not too close together, not too tense, not too lax, and we do have control over these gestures. We also have the capacity to regulate the thickness of the vocal folds, and through this thickness regulate the rising and falling of the intonational tunes: a thick set of vocal folds will produce a lower pitch than their thin equivalent, in the way that a guitar's thick strings give a lower note than its thin strings.

> Test out the correctness of this statement by humming a simple melody and noticing as much as possible the sensation caused by the varying thickness of the vocal folds.

We have already said that intonation is nothing but a hummed melody, albeit a radically simplified one. In a nutshell, then, INTONATION is modulated pitch. Different patterns of modulation correspond to different intonational contours, or "tunes", and we gave three of these in (1) above. We must warn at this point that, like stress, English intonation is a very complex area, and therefore our discussion in the following sections will have to be confined to the essentials.

INTONATION is modulated pitch

Different patterns of modulation correspond to different intonational contours, or TUNES

3 The Primitives of Intonation

In (1) above we represented the variations in pitch that make up intonational contours by means of falling or rising lines, which we compared with the lines drawn in the air by the conductor's baton. These lines are useful in that they can be interpreted immediately, and accordingly they have been made frequent use of in the literature on intonation, in a manner reminiscent of phonetic symbols for segments.

There is a crucial difference between the lines used for intonation and the symbols used for segments, though: what is this difference? Hint: bear in mind the contrast between "iconic" representations, which resemble some physical aspect of the object they represent, and "symbolic" ones, which do not.

You already know that phonetic symbols are merely a convenient shorthand, and that the real substance of segments is their distinctive features. In the case of intonation, we will assume that the pitch movements impressionistically evoked by the lines do not constitute its real phonological substance either. Instead, we will propose that the underlying components of the intonational melodies, equivalent to the distinctive features in segments, are pitch levels, essentially H and L, representing "high" and "low" pitch, respectively. This is a bit like a simplified musical scale: instead of the seven musical notes, from C to B, intonation would only have two, H and L. Also, the phonetic substance of H and L is less precisely defined than the substance of their musical correlates: the only general requirement is that H be realized at a higher pitch than L.

The underlying components of the intonational melodies are pitch levels, essentially H(igh) and L(ow)

There is of course much more than this to the way we use our pitch when we talk. For one thing, different languages (different varieties of languages even), as well as different individuals, have their own characteristic pitch ranges. In addition, pitch has an important "paralinguistic" function – PARALINGUISTIC means interacting with language without being part of it. For instance, when we are excited we expand our pitch range (and speed up our speech rate, etc.), whereas when we are bored or depressed we reduce the phonetic difference between our Hs and Ls; indeed, we bring down the pitch of the Hs noticeably. All this is undoubtedly important for human expression and interaction, but it falls outside language as such, and therefore it is beyond the scope of intonation: it is paralinguistic, rather than linguistic.

Think up a few speech phenomena that are paralinguistic. After you have isolated such phenomena, experiment a little to gain some familiarity with the distinction between linguistic and paralinguistic.

For strictly linguistic purposes, we will operate for the moment with the assumption that the component elements of intonation are H and L. Not surprisingly, matters are really a little more complex, but we will abstract away these complexities for the time being in order to keep the exposition clear.

4 Autosegmental Intonation

If the basic components of intonational melodies are not the slant lines, but the primitive elements H and L, then our original figures in (1) must be re-written as in (2), where the lines are meant as association lines, rather than as impressionistic representations of pitch movement:

> Before you go on, make explicit to yourself the difference between the two kinds of line.

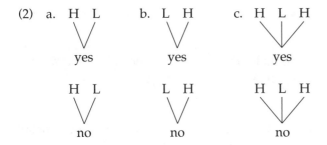

(2) a. H L   b. L H   c. H L H

         yes   yes   yes

         H L   L H   H L H

         no   no   no

The configurations in (2) closely resemble the autosegmental structures that we introduced and discussed in chapters 4 and 6 in connection with such phenomena as the assimilation of nasals in English or the vowel harmony of Turkish, and therefore they must be given a similar interpretation.

First, you will notice that the primitives H and L responsible for intonation are assigned to a specific autosegmental tier, distinct from the tier where we represent the segments (more rigorously, of course, a cluster of tiers, one for each feature).

> Jog your memory about some of the autosegmental tiers we have already introduced.

We will refer to the tier housing H and L as the TONE TIER, and to the elements H and L as TONES – the word "tone" is of course included in the word "intonation": in-**ton**-at-ion. You can see in (2) that the tone tier contains linear sequences of the tones H and L, in a manner that parallels the linearization of the segmental distinctive features in their corresponding tiers: [+back] [–back], [+round] [–round], etc., for features; HL in (2a), LH in (2b), and HLH in (2c), for tones. Also as is the case with features, H and L integrate into the structure by means of association lines. In particular, H and L associate to segments specifically licensed to carry this association, usually syllable

We refer to the tier housing H and L as the TONE TIER, and to the elements H and L as TONES

head segments. Strictly speaking, tones of course associate to the skeletal slot associated to the nuclear vowel. Thus, remember that in chapter 8 we identified the timing tier as the baseline of the whole autosegmental structure – the skeleton acts as a central distributor for all the autosegmental tiers (naturally, excluding those corresponding to dependent features), as the spine of a book acts as a central distributor for all the pages of that book:

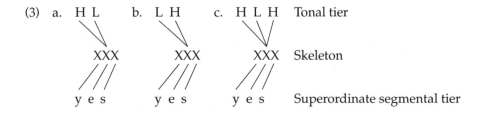

(3) a. H L   b. L H   c. H L H   Tonal tier

         XXX   XXX   XXX   Skeleton

         y e s   y e s   y e s   Superordinate segmental tier

> Why are we specifically referring to the superordinate segmental tier? Hint: what does *yes* really stand for?

To keep the representation simple, however, we will ignore this formal detail and continue using the abbreviated graphics of (2).

We are now ready to interpret the structures in (2) (or (3)). (2a), for instance, is telling us that the vowel [ɛ] of *yes* is pronounced with a high pitch followed by a low pitch, and similarly for the vowel [oʊ] of *no*. Naturally, the time interval between the start and the end of these or any other vowels is very short. Consequently, it would be impractical to raise the pitch for H, sustain it there for a while, stop vocal fold vibration, and then go through the same routine for L.

> Try to carry out these actions to convince yourself of their impracticability.

The structure in (2a) is instead implemented by a simple pitch movement, modulated from a high start to a low finish as we articulate [ɛ], precisely as the impressionistic lines in (1a) indicate. What we are now arguing is that such contours are a phonetic by-product of the simpler tonal primitives, which are the real targets for pitch.

Intonational contours are a phonetic by-product of the simpler tonal primitives, which are the real targets for pitch

> State the difference between contour and punctual targets with regard to intonation.

5 Stress and Intonation

In this section, we shall show that the autosegmental behaviour of intonation provides specific evidence for stress.

So far we have been analysing English intonation with the help of monosyllabic words. Obviously, though, English also has a great many polysyllabic words. In our monosyllabic words *yes, no,* all the tones of the tune were associated to the lone nucleus, and the question arises as to how such tones will associate to the several syllables of polysyllables. Will all the tones converge on the first syllable of the word? On the last syllable? Will they associate syllable by syllable in an orderly fashion? If so, will the association proceed from left to right, or from right to left? In any event, after each tone has been assigned to one syllable, will any excess syllables receive a tone and, if so, which?

The configurations in (4) offer a first approximation to phonetic reality and provide us with the key evidence we need to begin to answer these questions:

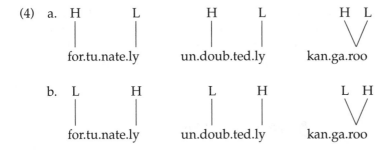

(4) a.   H   L   H   L   H L
           | | | | \\/
        for.tu.nate.ly   un.doub.ted.ly   kan.ga.roo

     b.   L   H   L   H   L H
           | | | | \\/
        for.tu.nate.ly   un.doub.ted.ly   kan.ga.roo

> Read out these intonated words.

The configurations in (4a) and (4b) (corresponding, respectively, to the statement and plain question tunes) puzzlingly reveal a diversity of patterns of tone association: in the third column the two tones converge on the final syllable; in the first column, they are as far apart as they can be, landing on the opposite edges; finally, the pattern in the middle column is similar, but with the first syllable skipped. At first sight, it doesn't seem possible to come up with a unified formal account of these patterns.

> Try to find a unified account before you read on.

If you scrutinize the patterns more closely, you will indeed find a common thread: in all cases, the second tone associates to the word's last syllable, while the first tone links to the syllable that carries the main stress. The privileged status of the main stressed syllable with regard to tone association is confirmed by the data in (5):

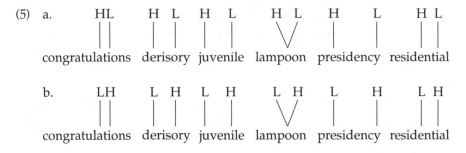

(5) a.

congratulations derisory juvenile lampoon presidency residential

b.

congratulations derisory juvenile lampoon presidency residential

> Say "congratulations" with the two intonational contours shown, and suggest an (approximate) meaning for each of them.

The systematic choice of the stressed syllable as the anchor for the association of the tonal melody provides particularly strong evidence for the reality of stress

The systematic choice of the stressed syllable as the anchor for the association of the tonal melody, irrespective of that syllable's linear position, provides particularly strong evidence for the reality of stress: if nothing else, pitch is measurable, and therefore we can now test syllables for stress instrumentally.

6 Non-Lexical Tones

One obvious question outstanding concerns the syllables we have been representing as toneless to the left of the stressed syllable.

> Why should this be a question at all?

The incorporation of M into the set of tones all but completes the inventory: in a minority of languages, the mid tone M is split into a high mid and a mid proper

The question arises because intonation is all-pervasive in the utterance: as we said, humans do not speak like robots or computers, and, therefore, all syllables will come out intonated. This means that syllables that do not receive a tone by the procedure as it stands need to receive a tone in some other way.

We shall assume at this point that initial syllables unmarked for tone are pronounced at a pitch intermediate between H and L, which we will transcribe as M, for "mid". The incorporation of M into the set of tones is widely supported cross-linguistically, and all but completes the tonal inventory: in a handful of languages, the mid tone M is split into a high mid and a mid proper.

Some of the structures in (4) and (5) above have toneless syllables sandwiched between two toned syllables, and we must now describe how these syllables are intonated. One logically possible answer would be that one of the available tones spreads to such syllables – we have already observed left-to-right spreading in the vowel harmony of Turkish, and right-to-left spreading in the plural umlaut of German and English. However, the mechanics of intonation are not quite like the mechanics of vowel assimilation. In particular, intonational tones do not appear to spread or, if they do, they do so to a very limited extent: we have just seen that initial toneless syllables have their tone assigned by default, rather than by spreading. In the case of medial syllables sandwiched between two toned syllables, no default tone is provided either. Instead, the pitch of the left tone changes gradually into the pitch of the right tone over the tonally empty space, a phenomenon technically known as INTERPOLATION, which we now illustrate in (6) (notice the affinity with the lines of our initial impressionistic notation):

> The gradual change of pitch over a tonally empty space between two toned syllables is known as INTERPOLATION

(6)

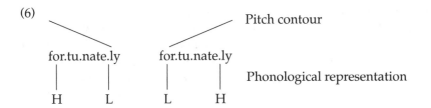

un.doub.ted.ly

7 Three Types of Intonational Tones

So far we have slightly simplified the tonal melody, for presentational convenience. As it happens, however, there are three types of tone included in each tune. We will refer to these three types of tone by the reasonably transparent labels "word tone", "phrase tone" and "boundary tone", corresponding to the "pitch accent", "phrase accent" and "boundary tone" of much of the literature. We illustrate the distribution of these three tone types in (7), again with the statement tune, previously simplified to H*L, but now given its full representation H*L⁻L%:

> Tones come in three categories: "word tone", "phrase tone" and "boundary tone"

(7) a.   H*   L⁻   L%
            | | |

     un.doub.ted.ly

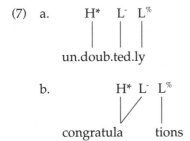

b.

The richer, and more rigorous, representation in (7) includes the three tone types we are now introducing: the word tone (H*), the phrase tone (L⁻), and the boundary tone (L%). The phrase tone bears the graphic mark "⁻" and the boundary tone "%", while the asterisk singles out the word tone, or, more rigorously, the dominant component of the word tone – English word tones can in fact be made up of two tones, graphically linked with a plus sign: all six of H*, L*, H*+L, H+L*, L*+H and L+H* can therefore be word tones in English, in different tunes, of course. In each complex tone one of the tones is the dominant tone (graphically, it bears the asterisk), and as such it will associate to the stressed syllable (dominant tones are commonly referred to as "accented" tones in the literature).

> Summarize the tone taxonomy we have just given, and its symbolization, to check your understanding.

The transparent terminology we are using provides a key to the function of the three tone types, and therefore to their linear pattern of distribution. The boundary tone associates to segmental material on the edge of the domain where intonational association takes place. The word tone associates to the word's stressed syllable. Finally, the phrase tone associates to material positioned shortly after the word tone, or, if no such material is available, to the same material as the word tone. The functions of the word tone and the boundary tone are obvious, as they signal the presence of words and boundaries, respectively. In turn, the postulation of the phrase tone is justified by the richness in pitch that gravitates to the last word tone in every utterance, as we will explain in the next section.

> Pause and reflect on the linear distribution of each type of tone.

8 Sentence Intonation

Up to this point we have illustrated intonation with isolated words. Clearly, though, most English utterances consist of more than just one word. So, suppose that, instead of uttering just "yes", "no" or "undoubtedly", we say "the dark clouds in the sky threaten imminent rain". The point about this or any long utterance is that it can be intonated in all the ways we have illustrated for single words (and, naturally, like the single words, also in many we have not illustrated).

How are tunes to be associated to the segmental material of longer utterances? The full intonational representation of the utterance we have just given is as in (8):

(8)

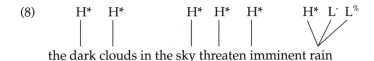

the dark clouds in the sky threaten imminent rain

Let us carefully dissect this structure. First, you will recognize our familiar statement tune H* L'L% on the right edge: its three tones are associated to the vowel of the right-most word *rain*, a monosyllable. If the right-most position were occupied by a polysyllable, the three tones would of course distribute themselves over the whole word:

(9)

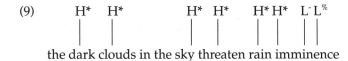

the dark clouds in the sky threaten rain imminence

Notice that the word tones associate to the main-stressed syllable of each word (the small stressless function words are known as CLITICS), and the boundary tone associates to the material on the edge of the domain. In turn, the phrase tone associates to material lying between the last word tone and the right boundary tone, here the syllable *mi* in *imminence*. The sequence **last word tone + phrase tone + boundary tone** obviously carries the main load of the tune, and is often given the label NUCLEAR TONE.

The privileged status of the tone complex at the end of the utterance warrants the special label NUCLEAR TONE often given to it

In (9) we have H*s as prenuclear word tones, but we could of course substitute another tone, to get a slightly different tune, naturally with a slightly different meaning. We exemplify in (10) with L*:

(10)

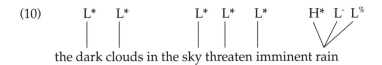

the dark clouds in the sky threaten imminent rain

Other variations are possible in the prenuclear tone sequence, to express various nuances of meaning. However, combinations of prenuclear tones are limited in comparison with the variety possible in the nuclear tone itself, or in the combinations of prenuclear and nuclear tones.

9 Tone Languages

We have now reached a point at which we can fully understand the precise nature and mechanics of stress, the question with which we opened the chapter. Quite simply, stress corresponds to rhythmic prominence, formally represented as greater column height in the grid. This metrical prominence

Stress corresponds to rhythmic prominence, formally represented as greater column height in the grid, and also manifested in a number of areas has manifestations in a number of areas, ranging from the distribution of intonational tones over the segmental string to the specific realization of some segments, for instance, vowels (cf. vowel reduction), *t*s (cf. *t* aspiration and weakening), etc. The close connection between intonation and stress is expressed by the association of word tones to stressed syllables.

There are other functions of tone, besides intonation, which are extremely common in the world's languages, even though they do not occur in English or most European languages. In particular, in "tone languages" tones serve to differentiate lexical items or to express morphological functions. In turn, in "pitch accent languages" tones mark each word with a fixed tune. We examine these other functions of tone in the remainder of the chapter.

Consider the words in (11), taken from a dictionary of Mandarin Chinese, the main Chinese language, nowadays referred to as Putonghua in the People's Republic. Notice that we temporarily revert to the impressionistic method of representing tones, in an effort to keep the presentation clear ("¯" indicates absence of pitch change, a situation referred to as "level tone"):

(11)   shū   'write'   shú   'sorghum'   shù   'technique'   shǔ   'category'
       mō   'feel'   mó   'plan'   mò   'end'   mǒ   'smear'
       xī   'sunset'   xí   'exercise   xì   'play'   xǐ   'wash'
       bāo   'wrap'   báo   'hail'   bào   'report'   bǎo   'treasure'
       rāng 'shout'   ráng 'avert'   ràng 'give way'   rǎng 'earth'

What is striking to the Western eye here is that the words in each line are kept apart not by their segments, which they all share, but by their tonal structure, which in turn is uniform in each column. It is rather as if the English *yes* or *no* (or *shoe*, which is segmentally reminiscent of the Chinese words in the first line of (11)) were different words when we pronounce them with the different tunes, not just different ways of pronouncing the same word.

> Can you now say how tones function in Chinese and similar languages?

In Mandarin Chinese and other TONE LAN-GUAGES tones encode lexical distinctions

In Mandarin Chinese and other TONE LANGUAGES, tones differentiate lexical entries. By contrast, in STRESS-AND-INTONATION LANGUAGES like English, tones provide the functional or emotional meaning of the utterance (NB not even of each individual word in the utterance).

Explain the differences in the use of tone between Chinese and English in your own words, to make sure you fully understand.

In most African languages and in a number of native American languages tone also has a morphological function, similar to the function of suffixes in European languages. For instance, in English we form the past tense (essentially) by adding the suffix -*(e)d* to the present, so that from *refuse* we get *refused*, and so on. In the Nigerian language Tiv, on the other hand, the difference between the general past and the recent past of *vende* 'refuse', for instance, is implemented through a change in the tonal makeup: *vèndè* vs. *vèndé*, respectively. Notice that tone is conventionally marked on the vowel that bears it with diacritics resembling the marks commonly used for orthographic "accent": an acute accent "´" indicates a high tone, and a grave accent "`" a low tone.

In most African languages and in a number of native American languages tone also has a morphological function

Do a count of the uses of "´" and "`" you have come across in the text.

10 Pitch Accent Languages

We will now see that Japanese is neither a "stress-and-intonation language", like English, nor a "tone language", like Mandarin Chinese, but, rather, a "pitch accent language". The slightly awkward expression PITCH ACCENT LANGUAGE refers to a situation where a single fixed tonal melody is associated to each word. In the Tokyo variety of Japanese, the melody in question surfaces as (L) H (L) in nouns, with the material enclosed by the parentheses only present when the circumstances are favourable, as we will see. You can get a first flavour of the system from the minimally contrastive pairs in (12):

The expression PITCH ACCENT LANGUAGE refers to a situation where each word has a single fixed tonal melody associated to it

(12) (Tokyo) Japanese surface pitch accent contrasts:

H L		L H	
hashi	'chopsticks'	hashi	'bridge'
mochi	'birdlime'	mochi	'durability'
ima	'now'	ima	'living room'

mushi	'disregard'	mushi	'insect'
shiro	'white'	shiro	'castle'
tsuyu	'dew'	tsuyu	'rainy season'
tabi	'socks'	tabi	'trip'
ame	'rain'	ame	'candy'

The point about these words is that they always turn up with the same tonal melodies. This makes the Japanese system distinct from a stress-and-intonation system like that of English: in a stress-and-intonation system *háshì* would simply be the statement realization of both 'chopsticks' and 'bridge', while *hàshí* would be its question counterpart.

> Explain why Japanese cannot be considered a stress-and-intonation system.

The three sets of words in (13) provide further evidence on the system (*-ga* is an enclitic particle marking the nominative: an ENCLITIC is a clitic that follows its "host", that is, the word that supports it):

(13) a. H L L
          hashi-ga   'chopsticks'
          mochi-ga   'birdlime'
      b. L H L
          hashi-ga   'bridge'
          mochi-ga   'durability'
      c. L H H
          hashi-ga   'edge'
          mochi-ga   'rice cake'

There are three surface melodies here: HLL, LHL, LHH; HLH does not occur, and cannot in fact occur. In order to account for these facts, we shall make the following assumptions about the Japanese pitch accent system:

(14) Assumptions about the Tokyo Japanese pitch accent system:
      (i)   The lexical tone melody is L%H*, where, as expected, H* is the tone associating to the word's accented syllable
      (ii) If the word has no accented syllable, H* associates to the word's last vowel
      (iii) H* spreads leftwards
      (iv) Tone bearers only support one tone

(v)   Syllables still toneless at this stage are assigned L by "default" (we expand on this notion in the next two sections)

(vi) An unassociated $L^\%$ deletes at the end of the derivation

> Read this list several times. Invent a derivation to try it out.

Following from the assumptions in (14), the derivations of the forms in (13) will be as in (15). Notice that the form for 'rice cake' has no accent. This is another key difference between pitch-accent languages, like Japanese, and stress-and-intonation languages, like English, where all non-clitic words need to carry stress:

(15)

	'birdlime'	'durability'	'rice cake'

Lexical accent / Tone association / Tone spread / L default / Stray $L^\%$ deletion derivations for 'birdlime' (móchìgà), 'durability' (mòchígà), and 'rice cake' (mòchígá).

You can now see that the Japanese system cannot be analysed as a tonal system along the lines of Chinese. In particular, given the two tones H and L and four syllables, a Chinese-type system allows for sixteen tonal contours: HHHH, HHHL, HHLL, HLLL, LLLL, LLLH, LLHH, LHHH, HHLH, HLHH, HLLH, HLHL, LLHL, LHLH, LHLL, LHHL.

> Explain the mathematics of tone combination. Hint: this will be easy if you are familiar with the concept "power".

Of the sixteen combinations just listed, only HLLL, LHLL, LHHL and LHHH show up in Japanese: *ínòtì-gà* 'life', *kòkórò-gà* 'heart', *àtámá-gà* 'head' and *nèzúmí-gá* 'mouse'. This limitation would be entirely arbitrary in a tone system, but is principled in the pitch accent system we are describing: a word made up of four syllables can have the accent on the first syllable (*ínòtì-gà*), on the second syllable (*kòkórò-gà*) or on the third syllable (*àtámá-gà*), or be accentless (*nèzúmí-gá*).

> Demonstrate how this situation is a consequence of the pitch accent account.

A handful of European languages commonly classified as "pitch accent" (Swedish/Norwegian, Lithuanian and Serbo-Croatian) are in fact quite different from Japanese. Among other things, these languages have a fully fledged intonational system along the lines of English. By contrast, intonation is considerably simplified in Japanese and in tone languages, for obvious reasons.

> Can you guess what these reasons may be?

In particular, because both tone and intonation are implemented through pitch, a full intonational melody would inevitably distort the tonal melody. Consequently, in tone and pitch accent languages intonation tends to be confined to relatively simple devices, for instance a contrast in the right boundary tone or an alteration of the pitch range, with a wider pitch range signalling a question.

The intonation system of tone languages and of pitch accent languages is relatively simple

One of the persistent themes of this book has been and is the autosegmental nature of phonology. As it happens, autosegmental theory was developed in the context of the tonal phonology of African languages. In the next two sections we review the mechanics of tone association in these languages, both for its own intrinsic interest and as a useful way of overviewing the general principles of autosegmental phonology.

11 Principles of Autosegmental Association

The repertoire of tone melodies of Mende, a language spoken in Sierra Leone, includes H, L, HL, LH and LHL. Revealingly, these melodies turn up irrespective of the number of syllables in the word, as the sample in (16) illustrates:

The tone melodies of Mende turn up irrespective of the number of syllables in the word

> What would the alternative be?

(16) H   L
    kɔ́   'war'   kpà   'debt'
    pélé   'house'   bèlè   'trousers'
    háwámá   'waistline'   kpàkàlì   'tripod chair'

    HL   LH
    mbû   'owl'   mbǎ   'rice'
    ngílà   'dog'   fàndé   'cotton'
    félàmà   'junction'   ndàvúlá   'sling'

    LHL
    mbā   'companion'
    nyàhâ   'woman'
    nìkílì   'groundnut'

> Can you see the patterns of tone association in these data?

Data such as those in (16) provide strong support for the autosegmental approach to tone. Notice, in particular, that all the tones of each tune are realized regardless of the number of syllables in the word: if syllables outnumber tones, then the last tone spreads onto the as yet tonally vacant syllables, and if tones outnumber syllables, then the excess tones are dumped onto the final syllable.

> Say where this happens in (15).

This mode of behaviour demonstrates the autonomy of the tonal and segmental tiers, and hints at the principles that govern their interaction. These principles were originally formulated as in (17):

The tonal and segmental tiers are mutually autonomous

(17) Original principles of autosegmental association:
1   Association Convention: associate tones and syllables one to one from left to right
2   Well-Formedness Condition: at each stage in the derivation, all syllables are associated with at least one tone, and all tones are associated with at least one syllable
3   No-Crossing of Lines: association lines may not cross

Not all these principles have endured subsequent testing. Principles 1 and 3 have proved to be quite resilient, apart from a few cases of right-to-left tone association. Principle 2, however, has subsequently been abandoned: the total association effects illustrated by data like those in (16) above are now interpreted as the result of language-specific rules, rather than of a universal Well-Formedness Condition inducing automatic spreading of tones onto vacant syllables (cf. Mende *háwámá* 'waistline') and automatic dumping of excess tones on already toned syllables (cf. Mende *mbã* 'companion').

Shona, a language of Zimbabwe, also shows the three association principles in action. In Shona, the suffixes *-es*, *-er* and *-a* show up either with a high tone, as in (18a), or with a low tone, as in (18b) (the dots on the left-hand side of the forms indicate that the stems concerned must be preceded by a prefix, a detail irrelevant to the present discussion):

> The Well-Formedness Condition induces automatic spreading of tones onto vacant syllables and automatic dumping of excess tones on already toned syllables

(18) a. . . . téng-és-á   'sell'
           . . . téng-és-ér-á   'sell to'
       b. . . . èrèng-ès-à   'make read'
           . . . èrèng-èr-à   'read to'

We could set up one lexical entry for each tonal variant of each suffix, but this duplication would obviously be uneconomical. Worse still, it would obscure the fact that the suffixes have no fixed tone.

> Do you see what we are saying and do you agree with the conclusion we draw?

A more satisfactory analysis draws on the parallel case of Turkish vowel harmony we discussed in chapter 6.

> Can you possibly advance the solution?

All we need to do in Shona is omit the tonal information from the single lexical entry of the suffixes:

(19)
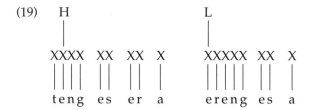

Notice that, while the stems -*teng*- and -*ereng*- carry their own tone (H and L, respectively), the suffixes are lexically toneless. Upon concatenation, the Well-Formedness Condition (17.2) will cause their association to the adjacent tone, here the only one available:

(20)
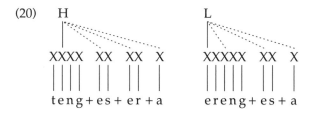

This outcome ostensibly confirms the appropriateness of the association conventions in (17) above.

Mysteriously, after the future prefix -*ngá* 'could' only low tones show up, even in stems with a lexical H, such as *tèng*- (cf. (19) above):

(21)

The solution to this puzzle lies in the Obligatory Contour Principle, formulated in (21) of chapter 10 in connection with syllabification as "Similar melodies are disfavoured as constituent siblings." As we hinted then, the impact of the OCP extends throughout the phonology. We offer a suitably general reformulation of the OCP in (22):

(22)   Obligatory Contour Principle:
       Similar adjacent elements are disfavoured

We said at the time that the OCP is not a principle as such, but rather a latent force motivating some of the rules and principles of languages, somewhat as the shifting of the earth's inner matter motivates volcanoes to erupt: the shifting is not the eruption. In the Shona case we are discussing, the OCP motivates "Meeussen's law" to dissimilate adjacent H tones, as in many other African languages.

The OCP is a latent force motivating some of the rules and principles of languages

> Say how the OCP will account for the situation in (19).

The autosegmental formalization of Meeussen's law is as in (23):

(23)   Meeussen's law:
        H → Ø /H___

> In what way is the formulation of (23) autosegmental?

Quite simply, Meeussen's law resolves the OCP violation through the deletion of the second H. The effect on the string *ngáténgésá* is as follows:

(24)

You can see that the deletion of just one H in the autosegmental tonal tier deprives no fewer than three syllables of tone. These syllables do not of course reassociate to the remaining H – if they did, Meeussen's law would be vacuous. Rather, these syllables are eventually supplied with L, the default tone in bitonal languages. The notion of default has already cropped up in previous chapters: it is an important concept, and we will return to it in earnest in chapter 17. Notice, importantly, that the observed effect of Meeussen's law on no fewer than three syllables would be very awkward to account for in a non-autosegmental model of phonology.

> Try to produce one such a non-autosegmental account.

12 Floating Tones

Some lexemes are purely tonal

We mentioned above that some lexemes are purely tonal. We will now introduce two such tonal lexemes and show that their behaviour can contravene the Well-Formedness Condition in (17.2) above. It follows from this that this condition cannot be upheld as a universal principle of tonal association.

Consider first the following forms from the recent past tense of Tiv, a language of Nigeria, as we have already indicated:

(25) a. óngó   'heard'   b. vèndé   'refused'
          yévésè   'fled'   ngòhórò   'accepted'

If you look closely at these forms, you will notice that the first tone differs across the two sets: it is H in a., but L in b. By contrast, the second tone is H throughout. Finally, if there is a third syllable, it invariably has L.

> Check that you see these patterns before you go on.

It will be helpful to compare the forms in (25) with their counterparts in the general past tense, which we display in (26) (the segmental allomorphy in the verb meaning 'heard' is irrelevant to the discussion):

(26) a. !úngwà   'heard'   b. vèndè   'refused'
          !yévèsè   'fled'   ngòhòrò   'accepted'

The tone in the second syllable is now L throughout, while the other tones are the same as in the recent past. In addition, the forms in (30a) exhibit an initial "!", which we will disregard for the time being.

> Again, ensure that you see these patterns before proceeding.

The tonal contrast between the two tenses in the second syllable suggests that H is the (purely tonal) marker of the recent past, as follows:

(27) Tiv recent past:

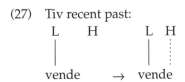

If there is a third syllable, it obviously does not receive its tone through spreading of this right-most H, as the Well-Formedness Condition in (17.2) above would predict, but rather by default assignment of L, similarly to what happens with the output of Meeussen's law in Shona (cf. (24) above):

(28) H   H   H H   H H L

          yevese   →   yevese   →   yevese

If the Well-Formedness Condition in (17.2) were indeed a universal principle governing the association of tones and segments, the output would have been *yévésé, with spreading of the recent past H onto the final syllable.

> Show how the Well-Formedness Condition in (17.2) imposes the output *yévésé.

The ungrammaticality of *yévésé thus provides evidence against the Well-Formedness Condition in (17.2), and shows the need for its replacement by language-specific rules in those cases where it was thought to be active.

> Say why the Well-Formedness Condition in (17.2) cannot be upheld.

At this point, we shall return to the general past forms in (26). The third tone in !yévèsè obviously also corresponds to the default L. The second tone, invariably L, could also be interpreted as default, or, alternatively, as the morpheme of the general past: after all, in (25) we identified second-position H with the recent past morpheme. However, the "!" at the beginning of the forms in (26a) prompts a different solution. The symbol "!" stands for a DOWNSTEP, a term that refers to the realization of a following H or sequence of Hs at a lower pitch than the previous Hs – this lowering is not so extreme as to turn Hs into Ls, however: tone differentials are maintained.

Downstepping is commonly thought to be triggered by a preceding FLOATING L, that is, an L which is not associated with any melody. Unlinked as it is, for reasons to do with the specific configuration and constraints of the language, this L still influences the tonal realization by downstepping the following H – the symbol "!" is just a diacritic commonly used to represent this situation (the IPA symbol is ↓).

The presence of downstep in (26a) provides the key to the analysis of the general past. All we need to do is to assume that the morpheme of the general past is a floating L prefix – not a suffix, which we saw the evidence in (26) above looks equally consistent with:

The term DOWNSTEP refers to a lowering in pitch of the following H tone(s). Downstepping is commonly thought to be triggered by a FLOATING L, that is, by an L which is not associated to any melody

(29)   L H   L L

    yevese   vende

This floating L prefix downsteps the lexical H of *yevese*, the Ls in the additional syllables being eventually supplied by default. In *vende* there can be no downstep, since the stem tone that follows the prefix L is also L. The L on the final syllable of the surface form *vèndè* is provided by default, in line with the general procedure.

> Go through the derivation of *!yévèsè* once more, explaining it in your own words.

The obvious question to ask at this point is why the initial L does not associate to the first syllable *ye*, in line with the association convention in (17.1) above, to create an LH contour. This association would of course pre-empt the downstep, since downstep is only induced by a floating L.

> Provide this spurious derivation, for practice.

In order to answer this question we need to acquaint ourselves with a device known as "the cycle", which constitutes the subject matter of the next chapter. In the meantime, you should notice that this failure of the floating L to associate provides further evidence against the Well-Formedness Condition in (17.2) above.

Chapter Summary

In this chapter we have discussed tonal phonology. "Tone" is the phonological correlate of vocal pitch. Pitch variation is induced by the control of the thickness of the vocal folds, employed to different effect in the languages of the world. We first considered the intonational patterns of English, where vocal pitch is used not to vary the propositional content of an utterance, but to express the speaker's intention in uttering it, as a statement, as a question, to express doubt or surprise, etc. We showed how the intonational patterns operate on a different autosegmental plane from the melody, each H(igh) or L(ow) associating with a syllable head (or tone-bearing unit). These associations provide direct and measurable evidence for stress, since the leading nuclear tones (H in the case of statement tunes and L for questions) associate to the syllable bearing the highest column in the metrical grid. We then went on to consider other ways in which vocal pitch is utilized in languages. In Chinese and other languages of South East Asia, tone patterns express lexical distinctions, whilst in many African and some native American languages they also have a morphological role, expressing such functions as tense and aspect, in much the same way as suffixes do in European languages. The third type of tonal system, which we illustrated from Japanese, is known as "pitch accent", where all words have a fixed tonal melody, here L%H*. The dominant H* tone is associated to the accented syllable and spreads leftwards, except for a first syllable already associated with the lexical L%. Syllables that are still toneless receive a default L, while the lexical L% ultimately deletes if unassociated. The principles of autosegmental association between the tone tier and the tone-bearing units of the melody were shown in operation in the Zimbabwean language Shona, in a manner reminiscent of Turkish vowel harmony discussed in chapter 6. Data from other languages (Tiv, for instance) militate, however, against an automatic spreading of tones. We saw evidence of the all-pervasive influence of the OCP. This "principle", which we reformulated to take account of its general application, motivates "Meeussen's law", which causes the dissimilation of adjacent H tones. Finally we introduced "floating" tones, shown to trigger the phenomenon known as "downstep", witnessed in many African languages.

Key Questions

1 What is meant by "intonation"? How is it manifested?

2 What is a "tune" in speech patterns?

3 What are the three basic components of the intonational melody?

4 In what way is intonation evidence for stress?

5 What is "interpolation"?

6 What are the three tone categories making up intonational patterns? What is a "nuclear tone"?

7 What are the four uses of tone in language? How does intonation differ from the other three uses?

8 What is "pitch accent"?

9 List the three original principles of autosegmental association. Which of these has been found not to be well supported?

10 What is Meeussen's law and how is it connected with the OCP?

11 Describe downstep. What triggers it?

Further Practice

Margi Tones

Consider the following forms from the Chadic language Margi, spoken in Nigeria:

sál	'man'	+árì (def.)	→	sálárì
kùm	'meat'	+árì	→	kùmárì

ʔímí	'water'	+árì	→	ʔímjárì
kú	'goat'	+árì	→	kwárì
tì	'mourning'	+árì	→	tjǎrì
hù	'grave'	+árì	→	hwǎrì
úʔù	'fire'	+árì	→	úʔwǎrì

(i) Explain how the tonal melody of the suffixed forms is obtained from the simple ones.

(ii) Formalize the process using autosegmental machinery.

Ci-Ruri

In some languages morphemes may be lexically marked as bearing a tone. In the Bantu language Ci-Ruri, verb stems are underlyingly either unmarked or marked on the first vowel of the stem. In the data presented below, the surface tone is located according to the following principles:

1. On the penultimate vowel if that syllable is lexically marked
2. Elsewhere on the syllable following the lexically marked syllable

Unmarked syllables receive default tone.

The following examples show the result of these principles:

a. *Unmarked*

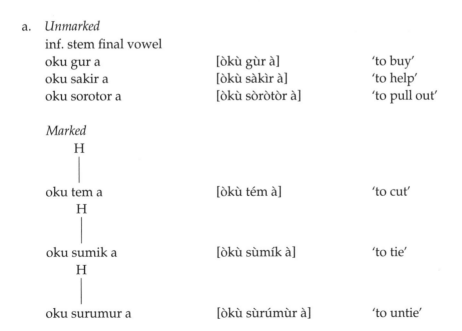

inf. stem final vowel

oku gur a	[òkù gùr à]	'to buy'
oku sakir a	[òkù sàkìr à]	'to help'
oku sorotor a	[òkù sòròtòr à]	'to pull out'

Marked

oku tem a   [òkù tém à]   'to cut'

oku sumik a   [òkù sùmík à]   'to tie'

oku surumur a   [òkù sùrúmùr à]   'to untie'

(i)   Show how tone is acquired by the forms in a.

Object prefixes are all marked:

b.

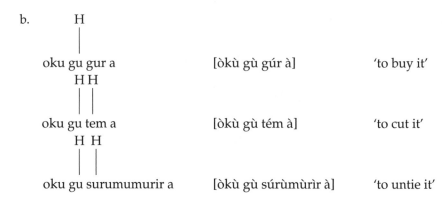

oku gu gur a	[òkù gù gúr à]	'to buy it'
oku gu tem a	[òkù gù tém à]	'to cut it'
oku gu surumumurir a	[òkù gù súrùmùrìr à]	'to untie it'

(ii) Bearing in mind the provisions of Meeussen's law in (23), show how
      the patterns in b. emerge.

PART THREE

ADVANCED THEORY

In the previous two parts we have laid the foundations of the edifice of phonology, essentially providing the autosegmental organization (together with the phonetic backup) in part I and the prosodic structure (stress and syllables) in part II, where we completed the autosegmental picture with the tonal tier. Now, in part III, we shall elaborate the model further, addressing three issues in particular. The first issue concerns the effect of grammatical structure on phonology. The specific question is whether grammatical structure (morphological structure in particular) provides domains for the application of phonological rules. One answer is that it does for some such rules (the "cyclic" rules), while other rules simply apply in the maximal domain (the word). It has also been argued in the literature that word construction can be sensitive to the previous action of phonology, and therefore that phonological rules need to be interleaved with word-formation rules: the model of "lexical phonology" provides a theoretical framework for the expression of this and other related aspects of word building. The model works less well in phrasal domains, where phonological domains were soon found to be at variance with syntactic structure. As a consequence, a theory of specific phonological domains, related, but not identical, to syntactic domains, was developed: it is commonly known as "prosodic phonology", somewhat confusingly. It is a moot point whether this theory must be extended to phonological domains below the word to resolve some mismatches with morphological structure, the so-called "bracketing paradoxes". A second issue we deal with in part III concerns the structure of the lexical forms, in particular their composition in terms of distinctive features. The combination of features is limited in two ways: intrinsically and extrinsically. Intrinsically, the features themselves are organized into a "feature geometry", by which they make up a web of dependencies, expressive of their autosegmental behaviour. Extrinsically, some combinations of features are disfavoured by the "markedness" conventions, designed to capture the degree of naturalness of phonological systems. While the markedness conventions (like the feature geometry) are universal, they interact with the systems of specific languages through the device of "underspecification", by which predictable feature values are left out of lexical representations. Unspecified features are of course predicted to be transparent to autosegmental spreading, and we shall see that in some cases such transparency is only achievable if we assume that certain (terminal) features are monovalent. The third issue we will address in this part is whether the best way of formalizing phonological relationships between forms is by means of rules and derivations (as has been typical of generative phonology) or by means of surface constraints, as proposed in Optimality Theory. Rules are crucially ordered, and OT constraints are like-wise ranked. The innovation brought in by OT is the claim that constraints are universal (the rankings, not the constraints themselves, are responsible for the language-specific grammars) and that they are violable, satisfaction of higher-ranked constraints taking precedence. Cyclic application and level ordering of rules is replicated in OT through "correspondence" constraints that relate surface forms to one another.

CHAPTER FIFTEEN

MODES OF APPLICATION

THE CYCLE

Chapter Objectives

In this chapter you will learn about:
- Some problems with the resolution of stress clash, and suggestions for their solution.
- Two modes of phonological rule application: "cyclic" and "non-cyclic".
- Cyclic application of the stress procedure, applying first in smaller domains and then in progressively larger ones.
- Word-internal cyclic rule application giving rise to downstep in Tiv.
- How English main word stress is derived in the cyclic mode, and secondary stress in the non-cyclic mode.
- Structure-changing phonological processes which apply only in derived contexts.
- The Principle of Strict Cyclicity formalizing this observation.

We ended the previous chapter with a question about the lack of association of the first L to the first syllable in the Tiv general past form *!yévèsè*. This form is derived by prefixing the general past tonal morpheme L to the stem *yevese*, lexically marked for H (the Ls in the last two syllables are both default). The question arises because of the general autosegmental principle that tones associate to vowels one-to-one from left to right, as formulated in the association convention in (17.1) of chapter 14. This convention leads us to expect that the prefixal L- tone will associate to the initial syllable of the stem, *ye*, and the lexical tone of the stem, H, with the second syllable, *ve*. However, the output **yèvésè* is incorrect. Instead, the prefixal L- remains unassociated (= floating) and downsteps the H associated to the initial syllable *ye*: *!yévèsè*. The question is how this result is achieved in the face of the said universal convention.

State exactly what the problem is.

We said at the time that the answer involves the cycle, or, more precisely, the cyclic mode of application of (some) phonological rules. In this chapter, we motivate this formal device and spell out its mechanics, with the appropriate exemplification. Following our usual strategy of building on the familiar and intuitively obvious, we shall first motivate the cycle with a set of the English data involving stress retraction which we discussed in chapter 11. After providing the analysis of Tiv downstep, we will show that the rules of English word stress also apply cyclically, as does a rule that accounts for the shortening of English vowels in certain contexts. Some loose ends of English stress will be tied up as we go along.

1 Staged Grid Construction

In chapter 11 we examined phrases like *Súzanne Mórris* or *Sárah Jane Brówn*, and pointed out that the left-most of the two stresses in these constructions originates in a syllable further to the right: *Suzánne* (not **Súzanne*), *Sarah Jáne* (not **Sárah Jane*), and so on.

What is the reason for the mismatch?

You will remember that the reason for the mismatch is that in the longer phrases the stress on the left undergoes leftward movement in order to avoid clash – *Suzánne Mórris* → *Súzanne Mórris*, etc.:

(1)

```
              *                    *      Line 3   phrase head
       *      *           * ←      *      Line 2   word heads
    *  *      *  *        *  *      *  *   Line 1   foot heads
    *  *      *  *        *  *      *  *   Line 0   baseline
    Suzanne Morris   →   Suzanne Morris
```

Now, in the case of *Sarah Jane Brown*, we did not concatenate the three words that make up the construction simultaneously. Indeed, had we done so, the stress clash would have been unresolvable:

We did not con-catenate the three words that make up *Sarah Jane Brown* simultaneously

(2)

```
              *        Line 3   phrase head
    *      *   *        Line 2   word heads
    *      *   *        Line 1   foot heads
    *  *   *   *        Line 0   baseline
    Sarah Jane Brown
```

Say exactly why the clash in (2) is unresolvable.

Notice that the line-2 clashing asterisk on *Jane* in (2) has no landing site in line 1 to go onto, and therefore it cannot move. However, if we first form the metrical grid of the double first name *Sarah Jane*, and then add the grid of the surname *Brown* to this grid, the desired result becomes attainable. This is precisely what we did in chapter 11, where we simplified grid structure slightly so as to not to complicate the presentation unnecessarily. We replicate the procedure in (3), where we are assuming a line-3 asterisk in *Brown* at the stage it is added to *Sarah Jane*, on the reasonable assumption that only phrases can concatenate to phrases:

(3) a.
```
            *        Line 3   phrase head
     *      *        Line 2   word heads
     *      *        Line 1   foot heads
     * *    *        Line 0   baseline
   Sarah Jane
```

   b.
```
                                            *       Line 4   long phrase
                                                              head (SJB)

           *     *               *     *    Line 3   short phrase
                                                              heads (SJ; B)
     *     *     *         *     *     *    Line 2   word heads
     *     *     *         *     *     *    Line 1   foot heads
     * *   *     *         * *   *     *    Line 0   baseline

   Sarah Jane Brown   →   Sarah Jane Brown
                    End Rule [R]
```

Explain the difference between this procedure and the one encapsulated in (2).

The clash between *Jane* and *Brown* in (3b) can now be resolved by leftward movement, in the familiar way:

(4)
```
            *       Line 4   long phrase head (SJB)
     *    ←  *       Line 3   short phrase heads (SJ; B)
     *    *  *       Line 2   word heads
     *    *  *       Line 1   foot heads
     * *  *  *       Line 0   baseline
   Sarah Jane Brown
```

As we explained at the time, the weaker of the two clashing asterisks moves leftwards onto the nearest asterisk in the line immediately below, here the line-2 asterisk in the column on *Sa*. Resolution of the remaining clashes is blocked by the Continuous Column Constraint in (38) of chapter 11, which we now repeat in (5):

(5)   Continuous Column Constraint (= (38) in chapter 11):
      Metrical columns must be continuous, without skipping lines

> Explain how the Continuous Column Constraint stands in the way of resolving the other clashes in (4).

We build the metrical grid in stages, as if the word sequence were organized in layers of Chinese boxes

The relevance of the stress movement in *Sarah Jane Brown* to the subject of this chapter is that we have built the metrical grid in stages, first on the shorter phrase *Sarah Jane* (naturally with prior grid construction on the individual words *Sarah* and *Jane*), and then on the longer construction *Sarah Jane Brown*. It is as if the word sequence were organized in layers of Chinese boxes (equivalent to Russian dolls, an object perhaps more familiar to many), with the grid being constructed box by box outwards from the core, rather than all at once across the board.

> Go back to (3) to see how this happens.

The structure in question is represented in (6):

(6)   [[[Sarah] [Jane]]   [Brown]]

The square brackets in (6) are the Chinese boxes of the analogy, and reflect the morphosyntactic makeup of the construction. In particular, the bracketing in (6) captures the following facts: (i) the basic elements in the longer phrase are *Sarah*, *Jane* and *Brown*; (ii) *Sarah* and *Jane* make up a unit, or CONSTITUENT; (iii) this constituent makes up a larger constituent together with *Brown*, namely, the longer phrase *Sarah Jane Brown*. Notice that the structure we are proposing appropriately matches our intuition that the surname *Brown* combines with the whole of the double first name *Sarah Jane*, rather than just with *Jane*.

> Pause and ensure you have got all this.

Once the multilayered structure in (6) is in place, the ground is clear for the application of phonological rules (in the case just discussed, grid construction) in the manner we described. This mode of rule application is referred to as CYCLIC, and the procedure that drives it as the CYCLE – words like "cyclic" and "cycle" appropriately carry an implication of repetition. English phrasal grid construction, therefore, takes place cyclically, first in the smallest, inner constituents, and then in successive layers of constituent structure, until the outer, largest constituent is reached: the thought of a Lilliputian Samson trapped in the innermost box and making his way out by pushing down the walls of the embedded boxes one by one after the appropriate phonological processes have taken place in that box may be helpful in this connection.

This mode of rule application is referred to as CYCLIC, and the procedure that drives it as the CYCLE

> Why are we suggesting that Samson pushes down the walls of the boxes?

2 Cyclic Tone Association

We shall now show that our Tiv *!yévèsè* problem has a ready solution in the context of rule cyclicity. You will recall that the problem is that, were tones to associate to vowels one-to-one from left to right, as the Association Convention (17.1) of chapter 14 says they must, the prefixal L- tone would finish up associated to the initial syllable *ye*, and the tone H of the root would finish up associated to the middle syllable *ve*:

(7)   L + H   L H

                 →   ⋮ ⋮   etc.

          yevese   yevese

> Complete the derivation in (7).

You know, however, that this is not what happens. Instead, the L- remains unassociated (= floating) and downsteps the H associated to the initial syllable: *!yévèsè* (you must recall that downstep involves relative pitch lowering of high tones). The correct configuration is therefore that in (8):

(8)   L H

          | etc.

       yevese

> Complete the derivation in (8).

In chapter 14 we attributed downstep to a floating L immediately before the downstepped H. Therefore, it is essential that the L which is left-most in (8) remain unassociated. The question is how this result can be achieved in the face of the said universal convention that free tones associate to free tone-bearing units one-to-one from left to right. A few languages associate tones from right to left instead, but clearly this is not the case here either.

> Show that right-to-left association does not work for Tiv.

As we anticipated at the time, the problem can be resolved by carrying out tone association cyclically. Let us first consider the makeup of *!yévèsè* prior to tone association:

(9) $\begin{bmatrix} L & \begin{bmatrix} H & \\ & \\ & yevese \end{bmatrix} \end{bmatrix}$

> Explain the structure in (9) before you go on.

In (9) there are two layers of structure, namely, the inner layer of the stem and the outer layer of the tonal prefix: we are therefore defining word-internal cyclic domains on a morphological basis, just as in the preceding section we defined word-external cyclic domains on a syntactic basis. We will introduce some important refinements on this in chapter 16, but for the time being this approach will do.

Let us next examine the mechanics of tone association in the two domains of *!yévèsè*, on the assumption that Tiv tone association is cyclic. Tone association will first take place in the stem *yevese*, the form's innermost constituent – we are emboldening the brackets enclosing the currently active domain to make the procedure clearer:

Tiv tone associa-
tion is cyclic

---

(10)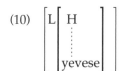

> Say exactly what happens here.

In (10) you can see H associating to *ye*, the left-most syllable of the stem, in compliance with the Association Convention in (17.1) of chapter 14. This completes the first cycle: you will recall that Tiv does not allow multiple association of tones, and therefore the remaining stem syllables, *ve* and *se*, must remain toneless for the time being. The second cycle is defined by the outer pair of brackets in (10) (the outer box, in our Chinese box analogy), housing the prefix L-. The structure input to this second cycle is as in (11):

(11) $\left[L \left[\begin{array}{c} H \\ | \\ | \\ \text{yevese} \end{array} \right] \right]$

> Say what will happen next.

The free tone L looks around for a vowel to associate with. However, this turns out to be a futile endeavour. First, L cannot associate to the first syllable *ye*, because this syllable is already associated to a tone, and we know that Tiv does not allow multiple tone association. Second, L cannot associate to the syllables *ve* or *se* either, because any such association would infringe the prohibition against the crossing of lines which governs the association of autosegmental elements universally:

(12)   No-Crossing of Lines ((17.3) in chapter 14):
       Association lines may not cross

> Show that crossing of lines would happen in (11).

If L- cannot associate to any syllable in (11), it has to remain floating. While floating status obviously prevents a direct phonetic realization, it is still compatible with an indirect manifestation as downstep, and this is precisely what happens in *!yévèsè*. What is relevant for us here is that this output is achieved through the cyclic association of the tone, providing further support for the cycle in phonology.

While floating status obviously prevents a direct phonetic realization, it is still compatible with an indirect manifestation as downstep

3 Non-Cyclic Refooting

In section 1 above we saw that the construction of metrical grids in English phrases takes place cyclically. In section 8 below we will see that some of the stress rules of English word stress also apply cyclically. However, it is not the case that all rules (whether for stress or otherwise) apply cyclically: some rules apply non-cyclically, that is, only once, in the largest domain. It is also possible for one and the same rule to apply both cyclically and non-cyclically.

> Explain to yourself the precise difference between cyclic and non-cyclic rule application, with the help of a pencil and paper.

The cyclic or non-cyclic status of any one rule is therefore idiosyncratic, and needs to be specified in the rule itself.

In this and the following sections we lay the foundations for the analysis of some of the rules of English word stress as cyclic. The first step involves the analysis of the patterns of secondary stress in English words. Consider the stress pattern of the forms in (13), which include some US place names:

> *The cyclic or non-cyclic status of any one rule is idiosyncratic*

(13)   Wìnnipesáukee
         àbracadábra
         Kàlamazóo
         hùllabalóo
         Tàtamagóuchi

> Remind yourself of the English stress algorithm we laid down in part II (there is a summary in (16) below). Do you notice anything special about the stress patterns of the words in (13)?

The forms in (13) are, crucially, monomorphemic, and therefore they cannot involve any word-internal cycle. The issue that interests us at present concerns the presence of *two* stressless syllables between the initial secondary stress and the primary stress. In particular, our present footing procedure predicts *Wìnnìpesáukee*, etc., with two secondary stresses (we assume that the final vowel *ee* is short underlyingly, and thus subject to extrametricality):

(14) a.

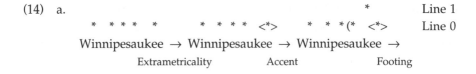

b.

```
                                                    *           Line 2
         *    *               *   *   *          (*   *   *)    Line 1
   * (* *)(*) <*>       (*) (* *) (*) <*>      (*) (* *) (*) <*> Line 0
   Winnipe saukee   →  Winnipe saukee   →  Winnipe saukee
           Footing              End Stress [Right]
```

The procedure in (14) matches the procedure we adopted for *hamamelidan-themum* in chapter 12, with footing sweeping leftwards across the word. The crucial difference between *hamamelidanthemum* and *Winnipesaukee* concerns the number of metrical syllables to the left of the main stress, even in the former (*ha.ma.me.li*) but odd in the latter (*Wi.nni.pe*). Because the number of such syllables in *Winnipesaukee* is odd, the standing procedure creates a degenerate foot in the left-most syllable, as we have shown in (14). This outcome does not match the evidence, since the second syllable of *Winnipesáukee* is in fact stressless. In chapter 12 we saw that some languages do not admit monosyllabic feet, but this constraint will not help here, since it will incorrectly predict **Winnìpesáukee*.

> Why will a ban or monosyllabic feet predict *Winnìpesáukee*?

We did anticipate in chapter 12 that, although English words have secondary stresses in the surface, the location of these stresses does not necessarily match the output of right-to-left footing, and accordingly we introduced a line conflation clause in the English stress algorithm, to get rid of all secondary stresses. The obvious paradox between this suppression and the presence of such stresses in the surface (albeit not necessarily in the same place) needs to be resolved now.

> Any idea how to solve the problem?

The solution we will provide involves an additional non-cyclic application of footing, that is, an additional once-only application in the domain of the whole word. Anticipating the discussion in section 8, we will assume that the procedure responsible for primary stress in English is cyclic, that is, applies constituent by constituent.

The derivation of English surface secondary stresses requires a non-cyclic application of footing

We resume the cyclic derivation of *Winnipesaukee* in (15), which starts with the last step of (14) above. To simplify matters graphically, we are adopting the informal practice of maintaining the word-level asterisk in line 2 after conflation – the graphic advantages of this informal practice will become apparent shortly:

(15)
```
                    *                          *          Line 2
         (*   *    *)                                     Line 1
         (*) (* *)(*) <*>        *  * * (*) <*>           Line 0
       Winnipesaukee   →   Winnipesaukee
                      Conflation
```

The application of conflation in (15) completes the cyclic procedures of English word stress, which we now list in (16) in the appropriate order, as a reminder:

(16)   English cyclic stress procedures:
       Extrametricality
       Accenting
       Foot construction
       End stress
       Line conflation

> Go through the whole cyclic derivation of *Winnipesaukee*, to make sure you understand it fully.

At this point we are in the outer box of our Chinese box analogy, in which all non-cyclic rules apply. The first non-cyclic rule we will propose is foot construction: remember that it is possible for one and the same rule to apply cyclically and non-cyclically. A literal non-cyclic application of footing to *Winnipesaukee* would obviously reverse the effects of conflation:

> Say why the effects of conflation would be reversed by a literal non-cyclic application of footing.

(17)
```
                    *                          *          Line 2
                                   *   *   *              Line 1
          *   * * (*) <*>        (*) (* *)(*) <*>         Line 0
       Winnipesaukee   →   Winnipesaukee
                      Footing
```

As before, we have generated one stress too many on the second syllable. Of course, this stress clashes with the stress on the first syllable, and therefore it will not be unreasonable for one of these two stresses to go. The obvious candidate for deletion is, however, the degenerate foot on the first syllable, inconveniently so.

> Why is the first foot a better candidate for deletion than its alternative?

We shall propose a solution in two steps, both of them to be justified independently as we go along. First, we shall postulate that the direction of non-cyclic footing (henceforth dubbed "refooting") is left to right. This change in directionality will naturally produce a different structure, and thus provide a concrete motive for the terminological split:

The direction of non-cyclic footing is left to right

(18)

$$
\begin{array}{llll}
 & * & & * & \text{Line 2} \\
 & & * & * \ * & \text{Line 1} \\
* \ * \ * \ (*) <*> & & (* \ \ *)(*)(*) <*> & \text{Line 0} \\
\text{Winni pe saukee} & \rightarrow & \text{Winni pe saukee} \\
 & \text{Refooting} &
\end{array}
$$

> In what way is this structure different from the one in (17)?

In (18) you can see that the degenerate foot is now on the third syllable, rather than on the first. You will also notice that refooting has not destroyed the word foot previously constructed on *sau*. This is in line with the Free Element Condition in (14) of chapter 13, which we now repeat in (19):

(19)   Free Element Condition:
       Only metrically free elements may undergo metrical construction

The second step in the derivation of *Winnipesáukee* involves the introduction of a non-cyclic rule of destressing, which we formulate in (20):

(20)   Destressing:
$$
\begin{array}{ll}
* \rightarrow \varnothing / \_\_ & * \quad \text{Line 1} \\
(*) (* & \quad \text{Line 0} \\
| & \\
\mu &
\end{array}
$$

> Examine this rule carefully and state its precise effects.

Destressing deletes a monomoraic degenerate foot when this foot immediately precedes the head of another foot

Destressing deletes a monomoraic degenerate foot, that is, a foot with only a light syllable, when this foot immediately precedes the head of another foot. The effect of Destressing in *Winnepesaukee* is as in (21):

(21)
```
                *                         *         Line 2
        (*    * *)              (*        *)        Line 1
        (*   *)(*)(*) <*>       (*   *)*(*) <*>     Line 0
      Winni pe saukee   →   Winnipesaukee
                   Destressing
```

The conjunction of left-to-right refooting and Destressing provides a simple account for many of the patterns of secondary stress in English:

(22) a. América   c. àbracadábra
          Dakóta   Kàlamazóo
      b. Àlabáma   d. Àpalàchicóla
          Càlifórnia   hàmamèlidánthemum

> Work through some of these words with the procedure we are proposing.

In the forms in b. and d., the binary feet created by left-to-right refooting exhaust the domain. In the forms in a. and c., by contrast, a degenerate foot is created next to the primary stress, and then disposed of by Destressing (20).

4 Final Stress Retraction

The procedure we have just adopted helps us to account for the surface violation of the three-syllable window in forms like *péregrinàte*, with the main stress four syllables from the end of the word. Like many other English words, verbs ending in the suffix *-ate* reject main stress in the final syllable and undergo asterisk retraction by a mechanism akin to our familiar Rhythm Rule.

Many English words reject main stress in the final syllable, and undergo asterisk retraction

> Think of a few *-ate*-final verbs and see if they all retract stress from the final syllable. Find a few other words that also do.

This retraction obviously cannot be triggered by asterisk clash in non-clash contexts, most particularly when the word is said in isolation. The pattern with retracted stress is, however, clearly more in sympathy with the over-all rhythmic structure of English. *Heathrow*, for instance, is currently under-going stress shift: *Héathrow Áirport* is motivated by clash, but *I'm leaving from*

Héathrow is not. *Maureen* has consolidated the shift in many accents: in England at least, most people don't say *Mauréen*, although quite a few still say *Heathrów*.

Whatever the reason for the noted dislike of word-final stress, the line-2 asterisk also undergoes leftward movement in words like *peregrinate*. To keep the presentation simple, at this point we shall derive the retracted pattern by means of the Rhythm Rule, which we formalized in (21) in chapter 11. The triggering environment of the rule must of course be extended accordingly, but we postpone the introduction of this technical detail until the next chapter:

(23)

*		*	←	Line 2
(* *)		(* *)		Line 1
(* *) *(*)		(* *) *(*)		Line 0
peregrinate	→	peregrinate		

Rhythm Rule

> See if you can find a way of construing the stress retraction in (23) as motivated by (abstract) clash in the input. Hint: one of the clashing elements will obviously not be an asterisk.

This word-bound application of the Rhythm Rule obviously needs to follow both refooting and Destressing, and consequently it must also be non-cyclic: if the Rhythm Rule did not follow refooting and Destressing the landing site would not be on *pe* at all.

> Explain why the Rhythm Rule cannot be applied cyclically before conflation.

The pattern of stress retraction in *péregrinàte* is actually not the most common one in *-ate* verbs, as we illustrate with the forms in (24), apparently more numerous than their initially stressed counterparts. Note that we have deliberately excluded obviously prefixed forms from the list, to take account of the possibility of such prefixes being systematically excluded from the domain of secondary stress, for reasons we will discuss in chapter 16:

(24)   capítulàte, hydrógenàte, pontíficàte, pacíficàte, matrículàte, ejáculàte, hypóthecàte, antícipàte, negótiàte, alléviàte, manípulàte, retáliàte, . . .

In these forms retraction stops on the second syllable to the left of the final syllable. Our present procedure is unable to yield this outcome:

(25)

	*		*		*	*		Line 2

```
                  *                *              *        *           Line 2
               *      * *        *      *       *       *          Line 1
    * * * (*)      (* *)(*)(*)     (* *) * (*)    (* *) * (*)     Line 0
    capitulate  →  capitulate  →  capitulate  →  capitulate
               Refooting        Destressing      Rhythm Rule
```

The output *cápitulàte* is obviously incorrect. In order to obtain the correct output, *capítulàte*, we shall declare the first grid element extrametrical in this and similar forms:

(26)

```
           *                *              *          Line 2
        *      *          *      *                   Line 1
    <*> * *(*)      <*>(* *)(*)    <*>(* *)(*)     Line 0
    ca pitulate  →  ca pitu late  →  ca pitu late
           Refooting        Rhythm Rule
```

Countenancing left-edge extrametricality in some forms is imposed on us by the facts

Countenancing lexical extrametricality of this kind is obviously not ideal, but it is imposed on us by the facts: we have already warned that the English stress system is oozing with complexity.

> Why is lexical extrametricality not ideal?

It may be possible to avoid total lexical idiosyncrasy in the assignment of such left-edge extrametricality, though: monomorphemic forms tend to eschew it, while polymorphemic forms appear to favour it.

5 Vowel Shortening

The deletion of monomoraic feet by Destressing as in (20) can be related to the universal predilection for binarity in feet. This predilection allows an elegant analysis of vowel shortening in the *divine ~ divinity* pairs we discussed in chapter 8 above. At the time, we examined the formal mechanics of these vowel alternations in some detail, both in Modern and in Middle English, but we did not give any reason for the shortening of the vowel in the longer form.

We further illustrate the surface alternations in (27):

(27) a. divine   b. divinity   [aɪ] ~ [ɪ]
          derive   derivative
          vile   vilify
          extreme   extremity   [iː] ~ [ɛ]
          brief   brevity
          compete   competitive
          profane   profanity   [eɪ] ~ [æ]
          chaste   chastity
          inflame   inflammatory

Note that in all cases the long vowel in the shorter form corresponds to a short vowel in the longer form. Suppose now that we add a moraic dimension to foot binarity, such that each foot is not allowed to contain more than two moras. The feet in both *(alge)bra* and *di(v/iː/ni)ty* obviously violate this constraint on foot structure, since they each contain three moras, which we have emboldened to make their recognition easier. The violation in *di(v/iː/ni)ty* is repaired by the rule of Vowel Shortening, to which we give a moraic formulation in (28) (Σ = foot):

> We add a moraic dimension to foot binarity, such that each foot is not allowed to contain more than two moras

(28) Vowel Shortening:

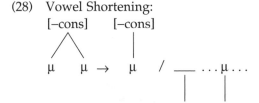

> **Explain this rule in common prose.**

The effect of the rule in (28) is the shortening of the vowel /iː/ in the stressed syllable *vi*, which subsequently laxes to yield *di(v[ɪ]ni)ty*, with a bimoraic foot. In words like *algebra*, by contrast, the violation of foot bimoraicity is maintained, as it must be if the input melodic material is to be preserved. Indeed, preservation of melodic material is apparently a powerful force in English phonology, as we will have the occasion to see again below.

> Preservation of melodic material is a powerful force in English phonology

> **Explain exactly how *algebra* violates the moraic binarity of feet.**

The framework we are proposing provides an explanation for the puzzling vocalic contrast in (29):

(29) a. t[ou]nal   b. t[ɒ]nic

> What is the contrast between *tonal* and *tonic*, and why is it puzzling?

Morphologically, both these forms derive from *tone*. The root vowel shortens in *tonic*, however, although not in *tonal*. This contrast falls in with certain independently motivated facts of extrametricality. In particular, in chapter 12 we saw that suffixes trigger extrametricality in English adjectives. However, *-ic* is clearly an exception to this generalization:

(30) a. pérsonal   b. masónic
          medícinal   atómic
          máximal   alcohólic
          signíficant   titánic
          vígilant   psychopáthic
          sónorous   Homéric
          magnánimous   telepáthic
          rígorous   morónic

> Say exactly what the difference is between the stress pattern of the words in (30a) and those in (30b), and where we can reasonably assume this difference comes from.

The forms in (30a) are all stressed in the same way as nouns, with the final syllable extrametrical, but those of (30b), with *-ic*, are stressed in the same way as verbs, with no extrametricality.

The extrametricality difference between *tonic* and *tonal* and the bimoraicity of feet conspire to explain the contrast in the root vowel of the two forms:

(31)

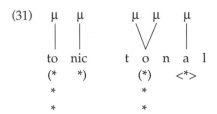

In both words the foot only contains two moras. If *tonic* kept the long vowel of *tone*, however, its foot would be trimoraic.

> Provide the derivation of *tonic*. Hint: you may find it useful to refer to rule (28) above.

On the other hand, there is no need to shorten /ɔː/ in *tonal*, where it instead undergoes vowel shift and diphthongization into [oʊ], exactly as in the base *tone*. This rather spectacular result provides obvious support for our approach.

6 Strict Cyclicity

There are well-known exceptions to Vowel Shortening:

(32)   a.   obesity, hibernate, isolate, probity, scenic, basic, phobic, anaemic, deictic, Vedic, rhotic, hyphenate, dangerous, vaporous, cyclic (in some accents)

   b.   rotary, notary, irony, decency, primary, primacy, papacy, vagary, vacancy, regency, potency, piracy, secrecy

   c.   nightingale, Abraham, stevedore, dynamo, protocol, dinosaur, boomerang, apricot, ivory, rosary, Averell, protege, Omaha, Clytemnestra, Polaroid, Oberon, Aubusson, bijouterie, dinothere, boutonniere, coterie, Obadiah, abelmosk, Novocain, rhododendron, Locofoco, ovolo, overture, rotifer, souvenir, troubador, edelweiss (in General American, also: wisenheimer, trilobite, dynasty, Bolshevik, bechamel, vitamin, ocarina, ocotillo, conquistador, nomenclature)

The forms in sets a. and b. are derived, and those in c. underived.

> This generalization is generally sound, but the morphological analysis of a few of the forms is perhaps questionable. Locate two or three of these and discuss the pros and cons of analysing them as simple or composite.

Some of the forms in (32b) also violate accenting: compare, for instance, *vácancy* with the expected *vacáncy*.

> Why should we expect *vacáncy* at all?

The suffix /-i/ spelled -y does not project a stress bearer

The forms in (32b) are systematically spelled with a final -y, apparently the orthographic encoding of a suffix /-i/ which, most idiosyncratically, does not project a stress bearer. If so, the whole string *cancy* in *vacancy* will correspond to one extrametrical line-0 element, and the *va* foot will only be bimoraic, with no need for shortening.

> Write down the analysis of *vacancy*, to make sure that you understand it fully.

Having thus regularized set b., only sets a. and c. remain as genuine exceptions to vowel shortening. Set c. is considerably more sizeable than set a. The property common to the forms in c. is that they are all underived. The fact that the majority of the exceptions to vowel shortening involve forms with no internal morphological structure clearly cannot be coincidental.

Indeed, it has been observed in case after case in language after language that some rules systematically apply in newly created environments, while failing to apply in pre-existing ones. A case in point is the rule of vowel shortening (28), which we are seeing applies in *divinity*, derived from *divine*, but not in *nightingale*, which is underived. An important hypothesis standardly made in this connection is that the rules that behave in this way are precisely the rules that change structure and apply in a cyclic mode.

> When does a rule change structure? What is the alternative?

Structure-changing cyclic rules can only apply in environments derived in that cycle, as encapsulated in the PRINCIPLE OF STRICT CYCLICITY

Structure-changing cyclic rules, therefore, only apply in environments derived in that cycle – "derived" in the sense of having been created by a morphological operation or, in some cases, by a structure-changing phonological process. This generalization is encapsulated in the so-called PRINCIPLE OF STRICT CYCLICITY, as follows:

(33)   Principle of Strict Cyclicity:
        Structure-changing cyclic rules only apply in environments derived in that cycle, where "derived" = resulting from a morphological process or, in some cases, from a phonological *change*

> Study this principle until you satisfy yourself that you understand it. How does the Principle of Strict Cyclicity account for the data in (32)?

The Principle of Strict Cyclicity is an important pillar in the edifice of phonological theory. It will directly account for the failure of the forms in (32c) to undergo shortening if the long vowel of these forms is already present in the lexicon.

> Explain exactly how lexical presence blocks shortening in (32c) but not in (32a).

On the other hand, the deviant behaviour of the forms in (32a) needs to be formalized by brute-force individual exception marking: we have already pointed out more than once that the existence of idiosyncratic exceptions is a fact of life in phonology.

7 Non-Cyclic Accenting

In section 3 above we used left-to-right refooting to account for the initial secondary stress in words like *Wìnnipesáukee, àbracadábra* or *Kàlamazóo*, with two stressless syllables before the main stress.

> Remind yourself of why exactly the secondary stress of *Wìnnipesáukee* and the like is word-initial.

Consider now the forms in (34):

(34)   Monòngahéla
        Valènciénnes
        Atàscadéro
        Manàntenína

In these forms the secondary stress falls not on the initial syllable, but on the second syllable, the initial syllable remaining stressless.

> Any proposal as to why stress is not initial in *Monòngahéla* and the other forms in (34)?

The obvious difference between these forms and those in (13) above concerns the weight of the second syllable, which is heavy in (34) (*Monongahela*) but light in (13) (*Winnipesaukee*). It will not be unreasonable to attribute the difference in secondary stress placement between the two sets to this difference in syllable weight.

The heavy syllables in second position in (34) will indeed receive stress as a consequence of the accent clause of the English stress procedure. However, this accent clause is at the moment cyclic, and therefore it will be followed by line conflation, which will dispose of the corresponding foot.

> Explain exactly how line conflation disposes of the feet derived by cyclic accenting.

The obvious way forward involves adopting the same strategy as for foot construction, and allow accenting to apply in a non-cyclic mode also. Following from this, the non-cyclic derivation of *Monongahela* will be as in (35):

(35)

```
              *                      *                    *          Line 2
                          *    *            (*  *      *)             Line 1
    * *   * (*) *        * (*  * (*)*      (*)(*   *) (*)*            Line 0
 Monongahel a    →     Monongahela    →    Mononga hela    →
        Accenting              Refooting
```

```
               *                                                     Line 2
          (*       *)                                                Line 1
       * (*   *) (*)*                                                Line 0
    →    Mononga hela
     Destressing
```

> Say exactly in what way the non-cyclic application of accenting is instrumental in accounting for the data.

Crucially, Destressing now affects the degenerate foot in the initial syllable. In *Winnepesaukee*, by contrast, the first syllable is the non-clashing head of a binary foot, as we saw.

At this point you may feel a little suspicious that our decision to reapply accenting non-cyclically, while convenient for the set we are examining, may be ad hoc and have adverse consequences elsewhere. There is, however, independent evidence for non-cyclic accenting. Consider in particular the also monomorphemic forms in (36):

There is independent evidence for non-cyclic accenting

(36) Hàlicàrnássus
      òstèntátion
      ìncàrnátion
      ìncàntátion

Say in what way the forms in (36) confirm non-cyclic accenting.

These words also have a secondary stress, and thus no vowel reduction, on vowels that need an input accent if they are to end up as foot heads.

Explain exactly what we mean.

Halicarnassus will indeed receive an accent on *car* in the cyclic phase. However, as usual, this accent will be disposed of by conflation at the end of this phase:

(37)   Line 2
            *   * *   *   *   *   Line 1
      * * * (* <*>   * *(* (* <*>   (* *)(*) (*)<*>   Line 0
      Halicarnassus →   Halicarnassus →   Hali carnassus →
                 Accent   Footing

                       *   *   Line 2
              (*   *   *)   Line 1
              (* *) (*) (*)<*>   * * * (*)<*>   Line 0
        → Hali carnassus   →   Halicarnassus
      End Stress [R]   Conflation

As a consequence of line conflation, the syllable *car* will come out of the derivation with no prominence at all unless we reapply accenting in the non-cyclic phase:

(38)   *   *   *   Line 2
                             *   *   (*   *   *)   Line 1
      * * * (*)<*>   * *(* (*)<*>   (* *)(*) (*)<*>   Line 0
      Halicarnassus →   Halicarnassus →   Hali carnassus
                 Accenting   Refooting

Why doesn't Destressing apply here?

The bimoraicity of *car* prevents the operation of Destressing, and the vowel will surface with a secondary stress.

The data we have considered provide reasonable evidence for the application of accenting in both a cyclic and a non-cyclic mode. Cyclically, accenting applies across the board without failure.

> What is the real import of this state of affairs? Hint: conflation destroys all feet but one.

Non-cyclically, however, accenting is subject to a not inconsiderable number of exceptions: *sèrendípity, èpistémic, Cònestóga, Trànsylvánia, Pènnsylvánia, ánecdòte,* and so on. By now you are well aware that many phonological rules do have exceptions.

We finish the section with an update of the English word stress procedures:

(39)   English word stress algorithm (update):
    Cyclic:
        Extrametricality
        Accenting
        Foot construction
        End Stress
        Line conflation
    Non-cyclic:
        Accenting
        Refooting
        Destressing
        Rhythm Rule

> Justify the ordering we have proposed for the four non-cyclic stress rules.

8   Word-Internal Stress Cycle

We now have all the ingredients we need in order to show that the rules of English word primary stress apply in a cyclic mode.

Consider the forms in (40):

(40) a. pèregrinátion   b. orìginálity
          clàssificátion   compàtibílity
          òxygenátion   precìpitátion
          tèrgiversátion   equìvocátion
          mèliorátion   capìtulátion
          vìtriolátion   syllàbicátion

> State what the difference in stress pattern is between the two columns.

The stress patterns of the two columns of (40) parallel those in (13) and (34) above, respectively: (40a) and (13) have initial secondary stress, while in (40b) and (34) secondary stress falls in the second syllable. We attributed the contrast between (13) (*Winnepesaukee*) and (34) (*Monongahela*) to the presence of a heavy syllable in second position in (34), but not in (13). In (40), however, the second syllable is light in both columns.

> Check out the weight of the second syllable in the two columns of (40).

The contrast in secondary stress between the two columns in (40) could of course have been accidental.

> Do you think it is? Can you find a criterion to differentiate between *pèregrinátion* and *orìginálity*, beyond the location of the secondary stress?

Close observation reveals that the bases of the forms in (40b) have their primary stress on the second syllable: *oríginal*, and so on. This is not the case for the forms in (40a). Therefore, it will be reasonable to attribute the difference between the two columns to the word-internal stress cycle.

The formal mechanics of the word-internal stress cycle differs in certain respects from the more general mechanics of the cycle, which we presented above in connection with phrasal grid construction and tone association. In particular, no word-internal stress metrical structure is carried over to subsequent cycles, as we demonstrate in (41) with *oríginal*, obviously derived from *órigin* (we simplify the derivations innocuously):

The formal mechanics of the word-internal stress cycle differs in certain respects from the more general mechanics of the cycle

(41)

```
                                        *
                *                      (*)                  *
    * *<*>          (* *)<*>        (* *)<*>        (* *)<*>
    ori gin    →   ori gin    →    ori gin    →   ori gin
           Footing         End Stress [R]      Conflation
```

```
                                                    *
      *                   *    *            *    *              *
    (* *) * <*>        (* *)(*)<*>       (* *)(*)<*>      * *(*)<*>
    ori gin al   →    ori gin al    →   ori gin al   →   origin al
           Footing            End Stress [R]         Conflation
```

Explain why we have ended up with the incorrect form *origínal*.

The preservation of the foot on *(ori)* in the second cycle incorrectly leads to a degenerate foot on *(gi)*: the resulting stress contour will be *origínal*, as in (41), or, even worse, *óriginal* if footing were to maintain stress differentials.

Explain how we can get *óriginal*.

In order to obtain the correct primary stress of *original*, we obviously need to start the second cycle anew:

(42)

```
                                        *
                *                      (*)                  *
    * *<*>          (* *)<*>        (* *)<*>        (* *)<*>
    ori gin    →   ori gin    →    ori gin    →   ori gin
           Footing         End Stress [R]      Conflation
```

```
                                          *                        *
               *    *                   *    *
    * * * <*>        (*)(* *) <*>       (*)(* *) <*>       *(* *) <*>
    origin al   →    o rigin al   →    o ri gin al   →    origin al
           Footing             End Stress [R]         Conflation
```

Non-cyclic binary refooting will next create a degenerate foot on the *o* of *original*, irrelevantly so because it will be disposed of by Destressing. In *originality*, however, left-to-right refooting would derive *òriginálity* on the output of cyclic conflation:

(43)

```
          *                      *                      *            Line 2
                       *    *  *                  *       *          Line 1
    * * *(* *) <*>      (* *)(*)(* *) <*>         (* *)* (* *) <*>    Line 0
    originali  ty   →   ori gi nali  ty   →   origi nali  ty
              Refooting              Destressing
```

The correct result *origínality* could of course be generated by adopting left extrametricality, along the lines of *capitulate* above. However, all forms in the mould of (40b) would require this setting, and these are precisely the forms where main stress falls in the same position in the source words: this correspondence would go uncaptured if we simply stipulated left extrametricality.

> Explain why this correspondence would go uncaptured if we were to stipulate left extrametricality.

Obviously, we need to go half-way between total preservation of prior metrical structure and total loss. In particular, we need to keep a trace of the primary stress of previous cycles. We will achieve this aim through a twofold strategy. First, we shall construct each cycle on a different plane:

(44)

```
        *                Line 2  ⎫
                         Line 1  ⎬  original plane
   * (* *)<*>            Line 0  ⎭

   ‾‾‾‾‾‾‾
   o rigi nal i  ty

   * * * (* *)<*>        Line 0  ⎫
                         Line 1  ⎬  originality plane
              *          Line 2  ⎭
```

Second, we will interpret all the syllables that support line-2 asterisks on any such planes as heavy, and will therefore subject them to non-cyclic accenting:

(45)

```
        *                Line 2  ⎫
                         Line 1  ⎬  original plane (only cyclic)
   * (* *)<*>            Line 0  ⎭

   ‾‾‾‾‾‾‾
   o ri gi nal i  ty

   * (* * (* *)<*>       Line 0  ⎫
        *      *         Line 1  ⎬  originality plane (cyclic
              *          Line 2  ⎭  and, here, non-cyclic)
```

In the case of word-internal stress we construct each cycle on a different plane and interpret all the syllables that support line-2 asterisks on any such planes as heavy

The remainder of the derivation on the non-cyclic plane of (45) is as follows:

(46)   Refooting   Destressing
o rigi nal i   ty   →   o ri gi na li   ty   →   o rigi nali   ty
* (* * (* *) <*>   (*) (* *) (* *) <*>   * (* *) (* *) <*>   Line 0
    *   *   * *   *   *   *   Line 1
       *   *   *   Line 2

You can see that we have now attained the same stress pattern in *originality* as in *Monongahela*, even though the relevant syllable of *originality* is not heavy. In *originality* the cyclic application of the stress rules is of course a necessary prerequisite.

9 The Structure of the Word-Final Syllable

In section 5 above we accounted for the length alternations in pairs like *divine* ~ *divinity* by means of the rule of Vowel Shortening in (28), which we repeat here as (47):

(47)   Vowel Shortening

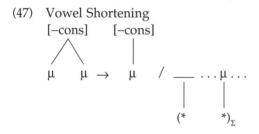

We will now show that this rule also accounts for the vowel length contrast in (48), where both alternants have the same number of syllables.

> If the number of syllables is constant, what is the difference between the two columns in (48)?

(48) a. deep   b. depth
          five   fifth
          dream   dreamt
          leave   left
          feel   felt
          sleep   slept
          heal   health

Syllable structure is responsible for the alternation in (48). In chapter 10 we suggested that English rimes include a maximum of two timing units, now interpreted as moras. However, in word-final position we observed the possibility of an extra consonant, as in *d*[iːp], *d*[ɛpθ], and the remainder of the forms in (48).

Also in chapter 10 we saw that word-final biconsonantal clusters need to comply with Sonority Sequencing (final coronal obstruents excepted, a matter we discuss in chapter 16). Given that the domain of Sonority Sequencing is obviously the syllable, we decided to affiliate the extra consonant directly to the syllable node. The moraic formalization of this configuration is as follows:

(49)

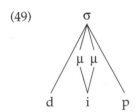

The incorporation of the structure in (49) into the syllabic repertoire of English raises the question of why it is not permitted word-internally.

> Is the structure in (49) really not permitted word-internally? Aren't there any exceptions?

The extra consonant affiliated to σ is only licensed at the right edge of the word

One crucial observation we made at the time is that the extra consonant affiliated to σ is only licensed at the right edge of the word. In particular, two or more such consonants cannot be licensed:

(50)

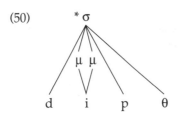

Does the requirement that the extra consonant must be on the edge ring a bell from some other domain?

The licensing of exactly one extra element in the periphery is reminiscent of extrametricality, a device we made ample use of in our discussion of stress: by the Peripherality Condition (6) of chapter 12, "only peripheral elements can be extrametrical". Were the one extra consonant at the end of words to be analysed as extrametrical, its peripheral nature would follow automatically, and indeed an analysis of this kind can be found in the literature. However, the analysis has clear disadvantages. At the conceptual level, it is not self-evident why extrametricality, a device responsible for skipping metrical elements in the metrical counting, should also be applicable to syllabic parsing, which is not metrical. Moreover, in the empirical arena, extrametricality of the extra consonant ought to make it impervious to Sonority Sequencing, but we know that this is not the case in English.

What actually seems to be happening is that the edges of words have special licensing powers, which materialize as metrical skipping (= "extrametricality") in the area of stress, as underparsing in the area of syllabification (= "extrasyllabicity"), and so on. By way of compromise, we shall refer to the special properties associated with word edges by the generic label "EXTRAPROSODICITY", and mark the elements subject to such special licensing with angled brackets, as we did earlier with extrametricality:

We shall refer to the special licensing powers of word edges by the generic label "EXTRA-PROSODICITY"

(51)

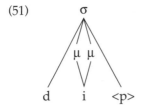

We wish to make it quite clear, however, that we are not proposing a uniform implementation of extraprosodicity across the various structural domains. In particular, we are not suggesting that the extraprosodic consonant should be ignored by Sonority Sequencing, at least in English.

Once this simple framework is in place, the account of the vowel length alternation in (48) becomes straightforward. In particular, the forms in (48b) have a (suffixal) extra obstruent. If the vowel did not shorten (d[i:p]th, etc.), these forms would, illegitimately, contain either three-mora rimes or a non-peripheral extraprosodic consonant, as we illustrate in (52):

(52)   a.   b.   c.

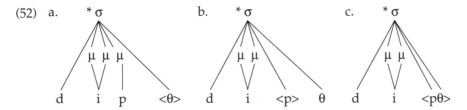

In a., the rime contains three moras. In b., the extraprosodic element is not peripheral. In c., extraprosodicity extends over two segments, the left-most of which is not peripheral. In the face of these licensing failures, Vowel Shortening (47) is called upon as a repair strategy. Shortening the vowel allows us to have our cake and eat it – all the segmental material of the input can now be parsed, at the small cost of dropping one of the moras originally associated with the vowel:

(53)

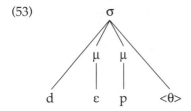

Shortening the vowel allows all the segmental material of the input to be parsed, at the small cost of dropping one of the moras

In the structure in (53) the *p* and its mora are licensed, despite the presence of the suffix -*th* in *depth*. Crucially, the addition of this suffix creates the environment for the application of Vowel Shortening (47), thus making the application of the rule compatible with the Principle of Strict Cyclicity.

The structure in (53) presents us with a new challenge.

In particular, the sequence [pθ] does not comply with Sonority Sequencing. We pointed out in chapter 9 that the sonority profile of the syllable must first rise, and then fall. In the cluster [pθ], however, there is obviously no fall in sonority – indeed, there will be a rise if fricatives are assigned a higher sonority ranking than stops, as we briefly explored in (41) in chapter 10 above. As a consequence of this infringement of Sonority Sequencing, the incorporation of [θ] (NB not [p]) into prosodic structure in *depth* becomes problematic.

> Do you see the problem now?

Importantly, /θ/ is a coronal obstruent, and we have already said that coronal obstruents are allowed on the right edge of English words, with no obvious restrictions. We shall give a formal analysis of this fact in the next chapter, in the context of which the problem of the licensing of /θ/ in *depth* will be resolved.

Chapter Summary

In this chapter we looked again at the cases of stress clash which we discussed in chapter 11. We showed that, whilst within words clashes may be resolved by simple retraction, the same is not obviously clear across words: bringing together the individual words *Sarah*, *Jane* and *Brown* results in an unworkable grid. This problem is resolved through the construction of grids first in smaller constituents, and then in progressively larger ones, a mode of application dubbed "cyclic". Cyclicity is also operative within words, where rule domains are created by the concatenation of successive morphemes. This procedure affords a solution to the problem pending from chapter 14 of justifying the floating low tone responsible for downstep in Tiv. We also saw that English main word stress applies in a cyclic manner, from the innermost to the outermost domain, while the secondary stress procedure applies only once (non-cyclically), in the largest domain, after all the passes of the cyclic rules. Main stresses from earlier cycles are effectively copied onto the grid, a procedure that provides an explanation for the differing secondary stress patterns of *pèregrinátion* and *orìginálity*. A large number of examples which are impossible to accommodate under this account led us to postulate non-cyclic, in addition to the cyclic, application of accenting, and left-to-right, rather than right-to-left, reapplication of footing. Combined with a rule that destresses the first of two clashing asterisks, these innovations allowed us to apply the intuitively appealing notion of cyclicity in the metrical procedures of English.

Phonological rules, then, apply in two different modes, either cyclically, domain by domain, or non-cyclically, across the board. The cyclic or non-cyclic status of a rule has to be specified with the rule, and some rules are specified as both. We showed that cyclic status is not exclusive to structure-building rules such as those involving stress and tone phenomena: we were able to show that the vowel-shortening rule responsible for the alternations between the vowels in such pairs as *divine ~ divinity* and *deep ~ depth* is confined to derivational contexts. This type of situation has been found to be true across languages: structure-changing cyclic rules may only apply in derived environments, as encapsulated in the Principle of Strict Cyclicity.

K e y   Q u e s t i o n s

1 What is meant by a "cyclic" mode of rule application?
2 How does cyclic rule application explain stress retraction in English phrases and tone association in Tiv?
3 Can the cyclic or non-cyclic status of rules be predicted from the way the rules are formulated? Name a non-cyclic rule.
4 How do we know that the word-bound application of the Rhythm Rule is non-cyclic?
5 What is the Principle of Strict Cyclicity?

6 How can Strict Cyclicity be called upon to show that Vowel Shortening is a cyclic rule?
7 List the cyclic and non-cyclic clauses of the English word stress algorithm.
8 How does word-internal stress assignment work?
9 How does Extraprosodicity, governed by the Peripherality Condition, prevent the application of Vowel Shortening in words such as *deep* (cf. *depth*)?

F u r t h e r   P r a c t i c e

Finnish

Finnish has a rule of "assibilation" which converts [t] into [s] before a suffixal [i], as we show in a.:

a. tilat-a 'to order'   tilas-i 'ordered'
   halut-a 'to want'   halus-i 'wanted'
   compared with:
   tila   'room'   æiti   'mother'

(i) What is the status of the assibilation rule with regard to cyclicity?

The language also has a rule raising [e] to [i] in word-final position:

b. joki   'river'   joke-na   'river' (essive sg.)
    æiti   'mother'   æiti-næ   'mother' (essive sg.)
    kuusi   'fir'   kuuse-na 'fir' (essive sg.)
    koti   'home'   koti-na   'home' (essive sg.)

Now consider the following forms:

c. vesi   'water'   vete-næ   'water' (essive sg.)
    kæsi   'hand'   kæte-næ   'hand' (essive sg.)

(ii)   Why does assibilation not apply in b.?
(iii)   Assuming both assibilation and *e*-raising to be cyclic, trace the derivation of the forms in a. and in c.

Slovak

Slovak contrasts long and short vowels at the lexical and phonetic levels, but in addition the language has morphologically conditioned vowel lengthening:

a. *Nom.sg.*   *Gen.pl.*
    blat+ɔ   blaːt   'mud'
    piv+ɔ   piːv   'beer'
    put+ɔ   puːt   'chain'
b. ʧɛl+ɔ   ʧiɛl   'forehead'
    kɔl+ɔ   kuɔl   'wheel'
    mæs+ɔ   miæs   'meat'

The evidence from b. suggests that there is a diphthongization rule in Slovak affecting the long versions of the vowels /ɛ/, /ɔ/ and /æ/:

ɛː → iɛ
ɔː → uɔ
æː → iæ

The process of diphthongization does not apply to certain etymological loan-words which otherwise behave exactly as native words:

c.   legeːnda   'legend'
     afɛːra   'affair'
     metɔːda   'method'
     betɔːn   'concrete'

This is not a matter of a native/loanword distinction, since other loanwords do undergo diphthongization.

Can the assumption of cyclic status for diphthongization explain its failure to apply to the examples in c.?

CHAPTER SIXTEEN

DOMAINS OF APPLICATION
LEXICAL AND PROSODIC PHONOLOGY

Chapter Objectives

In this chapter you will learn about:
- Suffixes ignored by the cyclic processes.
- Two classes of suffix, creating cyclic and non-cyclic domains respectively.
- Interleaving of phonology and morphology in lexical phonology.
- Problems for this model.
- Mismatches between phonological domains and morphological domains.
- Mapping between the two.
- Phonological domains larger than the word.

In the previous chapter we showed that some phonological rules apply cyclically, that is, in every domain defined by morphological structure, and other rules apply non-cyclically, that is, just once in the domain of the whole word. We pointed out that the selection of mode of application (namely, cyclic vs. non-cyclic) needs to be stipulated individually for each rule. For instance, of the rules assigning stress to English words, Destressing and the Rhythm Rule are specified as non-cyclic, and the remainder as cyclic, with the accenting and footing subprocedures as non-cyclic also. In this chapter we present and discuss some cases where morphological domains are ignored by cyclic rules, and develop the model further to meet this challenge.

1 Three-Mora Feet?

In the previous chapter we aimed at limiting the English foot, and a fortiori the rime, to two moras. As we showed then, this limitation accounts for the shortening of long nuclei, with the attendant vowel shift-related effects, in pairs like *d*[iː]*p* ~ *d*[ɛ]*pth*, *div*[aɪ]*ne* ~ *div*[ɪ]*nity*, and so on.

Remind yourself of the mechanics of these alternations.

The data in (1) and (2) plainly contradict the state of affairs we have been describing:

(1) deepness   divineness   lightly
     fivehood   chasteness   slothful
     dreamful   vileness   vagueness
     leaveless   extremeness   delightful
     creedless   briefness   painting
     sleepless   profaneness   attainment
     flightless   soundness   divinely

(2) breezily   wearisome   leaderless
     beautiful   likelihood   tidiness
     flavoursome   craziness   warily

> Make explicit in what way the data in (1) and (2) contradict shortening.

(1) deliberately includes some of the base words we used in chapter 15 to illustrate vowel shortening before a consonant cluster. In contrast to what we saw then, the relevant vowels remain long in (1), notwithstanding the apparent violation of the two-mora restriction on rimes they incur: *d*[iː**p**].*ness*, *div*[a**ɪn**].*ness*, etc. Similarly, in the forms in (2) the relevant vowels do not undergo shortening, even though the foot ostensibly contains more than the canonical two moras: (*br*[iː]*z*[i])*ly*, (*l*[aɪ]*kel*[i])*hood*, and so on.

> Go through sets (1) and (2) checking for the violations we are talking about.

There are many words where vowels remain long notwithstanding the apparent violation of the two-mora restriction on rimes they incur

One immediate reaction may be to attribute the anomalous behaviour of the forms in (1) to the word-internal position of the offending sequence, in contrast to its word-final position in *depth* and similar forms from the previous chapter. However, the licensing of the longer sequence word-internally, but not word-finally, would run against the observation we made in chapters 10 and 15 that it is precisely in word-final position (not word-internally) that extra elements turn up, in English and in many other languages. Indeed, nucleus shortening does take place word-internally in other forms under the expected conditions:

(3) a. convene   b. convention   [iː] vs. [ɛ]
         contravene   contravention
         intervene   intervention
         conceive   conception
         perceive   perception
         receive   reception
         redeem   redemption

         describe   description   [aɪ] vs. [ɪ]
         inscribe   inscription
         subscribe   subscription
         transcribe   transcription

         detain   detention   [eɪ] vs. [ɛ] (NB no vowel shift)
         retain   retention

The forms in (3a) have long vowels or diphthongs before the word-final consonant. In the forms in b., however, before a consonant-initial suffix, the corresponding vowels are short. Why, then, do long vowels persist under similar circumstances in the forms in (1) and (2)?

> Do you see the problem, and can you think of a solution?

2 Violations of the Three-Syllable Window

Before we address the problem posed by the long vowels in the forms in (1) and (2), we shall examine another puzzling, and, as it will turn out, related phenomenon. Observe the distribution of stress in the forms in (4):

(4) a. impétuous   b. impetuósity   c. impétuousness
         anónymous   anonýmity   anónymousness
         fínicky   fínickiness
         pernickety   pernícketiness
         úppity   úppitiness

> Is the position of stress in set c. compatible with our current account of English stress?

In the forms in (4a), which are embedded in those in (4b) and (4c), primary stress has been assigned by means of last-syllable extrametricality and right-to-left left-headed binary footing, the usual English procedure:

(5)

```
                        *                    *   *              Line 1
  *   * *<*>        (*   * *<*>        (*)  (* *)<*>            Line 0
  impetu ous   →   impetu ous   →   impetu ous   →
            Accent              Footing
```

```
            *                                    Line 2
        (*    *)                    *            Line 1
        (*)  (* *)<*>         *    (* *)<*>      Line 0
        →   impetu ous   →   impetu ous
  End Stress [R]          Conflation
```

You will notice that stress ends up three syllables (NB not, say, four) from the right edge of the word, as a fallout of the basic English stress algorithm as it stands at the moment. The restriction of the stress locus to one of the three peripheral syllables is in fact quite common cross-linguistically, and we have been referring to this state of affairs as "the three-syllable window". In chapter 15 we appealed to asterisk retraction to account for some surface violations of the three-syllable window in English, as in *péregrinàte*, for instance, where metrical structure does comply with the window prior to retraction.

> Refresh your memory on the derivation of *péregrinàte*.

The suffixation of -*ity* in the forms in (4b) gives rise to an additional cycle (on a new plane, as we know from chapter 15):

> Why do we need a new plane?

(6)   Second cycle

```
                      *                    *   *   *           Line 1
  *   * ** *<*>     (*   * ** *<*>      (*)  (* *)(* *)<*>     Line 0
  impetuosi ty   →   impetuosi ty   →   impetu osi ty
            Accent              Footing
```

```
            *                                        Line 2
        (*    *    *)                    *            Line 1
        (*)  (* *)(* *)<*>      *    * *(* *)<*>      Line 0
        →   impetu osi ty   →   impetu osi ty
  End Stress [R]          Conflation
```

The main stress lies further to the right in *impetuósity* than in *impétuous*, and thus complies with the three-syllable window – *impétuosity* would not comply with it.

> Check that you see how the three-syllable window fares differently in the two versions of *impetuosity*.

The forms in (4c) are also derived from their counterparts in (4a) by suffixation, and we would expect the stress contours in (7):

(7) a. *finíckiness   b. *impetuóusness
         *pernickétiness   *anonymóusness
         *uppítiness

> Explain how these forms would be derived.

In *impetuóusness* and *anonymóusness*, in b., stress is attracted to the heavy penult, while in *finíckiness*, *pernickétiness* and *uppítiness*, in a., the three-syllable window is utilised to its full extent. None of these forms is, however, correct. Moreover, their correct counterparts in (4c) (*impétuousness*, *anónymousness*, etc.) are all incompatible with the three-syllable window in a manner which does not appear to be reducible to a retraction analysis, in the way that *péregrinàte* is.

> Explain why retraction cannot have played any role in deriving the stress pattern of the forms in (4).

If you look carefully at the data, you will see that *impétuousness* and the other forms in (4c), with stress outside the three-syllable window, retain primary stress on the same syllable as their bases in (4a): *impétuous*, etc. What seems to be happening, then, is that the basic English stress algorithm simply does not reapply after the suffixation of *-ness*. This failure of the algorithm to reapply accounts both for the stresslessness of the heavy penults that precede *-ness* and for the violations of the three-syllable window.

The basic English stress algorithm does not reapply after the suffixation of -ness, and some other suffixes

> Check that this is the case in the data.

The obvious question now is: why does the basic English stress algorithm not reapply after the suffixation of *-ness*?

3 Cyclic and Non-Cyclic Affixes

Up until now, we have seen all the cyclic rules applying morphological layer by morphological layer, from smallest to largest. By contrast, the non-cyclic rules take no account of internal morphological structure and apply only once, to the fully formed word right at the end of the procedure. What we are now seeing is that this model oversimplifies reality, since cyclic rules (for instance, the English primary stress algorithm) can systematically fail to apply in some affixal domains (for instance, in the domain defined by -*ness*). This suggests that compatibility or non-compatibility between rules and domains with regard to cyclicity works in both directions: rules have to be specified as to whether they apply cyclically or non-cyclically, and domains (as defined by affixation) have to be specified as to whether or not they trigger cyclic rules.

> Cyclic rules systematically fail to apply in domains specified as non-cyclic

> All rules and all domains (as defined by affixes) are marked as to whether they are cyclic or non-cyclic

> Explain how the compatibility between rules and domains with regard to cyclicity works, and how it bears on the problem posed by *impétuousness* and similar forms in (4c).

The list of suffixes incompatible with cyclic rules in our present data includes -*ness*, -*ly*, -*ful*, -*some*, -*hood*, -*less*, -*ment*. We shall refer to these and similar affixes as NON-CYCLIC AFFIXES. You must of course realize that in the context of affixes the expression "non-cyclic" means 'only compatible with non-cyclic rules' – rules can "cycle" (= apply in cycles), but affixes obviously cannot: indeed, affixes cannot "apply" at all.

> Why cannot affixes "apply" at all, and in what way is the expression "cyclic affix" therefore a misnomer?

We shall represent the cyclic or non-cyclic status of any given rule or any given affix by means of the subscripts "c" (for "cyclic") and "nc" (for "non-cyclic"), as we illustrate in (8) for the cases related to stress we have been examining. You should bear in mind that cyclic status is, of course, confined to the domain defined by the cyclic affix – *all* forms eventually undergo the non-cyclic rules at word level:

(8) a. Rules: Extrametricality$_c$
             Accent$_{c, nc}$
             Footing$_{c, nc}$

End stress$_c$
Conflation$_c$
Destressing$_{nc}$
Rhythm rule$_{nc}$

b. Domains: Stem$_c$ (by general convention)
    -ity$_c$, -al$_c$, -ation$_c$, -ify$_c$, etc.
    -ness$_{nc}$, -ly$_{nc}$, -ful$_{nc}$, -some$_{nc}$, -hood$_{nc}$, -less$_{nc}$, -ment$_{nc}$, etc.

> Pause and ensure that you fully understand the mechanics of the algorithm in (8a).

With this background, let us look at the derivation of the forms *impetus* (cyclic, as a base), *impetuous* (with cyclic *-(u)ous*), *impetuosity* (with cyclic *-ity*) and *impetuousness* (with non-cyclic *-ness*):

(9)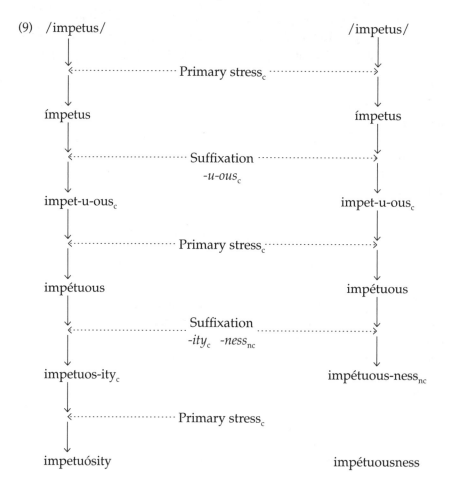

> Go through the derivation in (9) step by step, in its full richness of detail. Pick a couple of other words from (4) above and give their derivations in the mould of (9).

The crucial difference in the derivational history of the forms *impetuósity* and *impétuousness* is that only the former undergoes the primary stress procedure in the domain defined by its outermost suffix. The contrast follows from the fact that the rules of the English primary stress procedure are cyclic, and the domain defined by *-ity* is also cyclic, while the domain defined by *-ness* is non-cyclic: the mismatch between the cyclicity of the English primary stress procedure and the non-cyclicity of the domain defined by *-ness* prevents the application of this procedure in this domain.

> Introspect for a few seconds to see if you have any doubts. If you do, go over the argument again until it is clear.

4 The Interaction between Morphology and Phonology

We have just seen that our previous practice of strictly identifying cyclic domains with morphological layers was an oversimplification, since some morphological layers are non-cyclic, that is, do not define a domain of application for cyclic rules.

In (9) we presented the derivation of *impetuosity* and *impetuousness* as cumulative, in that we first entered *impetus*, then formed *impetuous*, and then *impetuosity* and *impetuousness* (in the first and the second column, respectively). The obvious advantage of this style of presentation is that the reader can follow step by step how the word is being built. In itself, however, the procedure is also compatible with a preformed word, inside which the cyclic rules simply work their way through the appropriate cyclic domains. Indeed, this is the practice we adopted for the cyclic derivation of *!yévèsè* when we presented the cycle in the previous chapter. There is an obvious, and crucial, difference between the two approaches. If we build the word in stages, the morphology and the phonology can apply in tandem, and each step in the construction of the word be immediately followed by the application of the relevant phonological rules.

> Can you see how morphology and phonology can interact if words are built in stages?

By contrast, if the word is fully formed first, the phonological rules cannot interact with word formation.

> Why can't morphology and phonology interact if the word is fully formed first?

How can we possibly adjudicate between the two alternatives just sketched? Consider the data in (10) and (11):

(10) a. arríve   appráise   b. arríval   appráisal
        construe   rehéarse   construal   rehéarsal
        revíve   procúre   revíval   procúral
        appróve   rént   appróval   réntal
        commít   trý   commíttal   tríal
        betráy   withdráw   betráyal   withdráwal

(11) a. delíver   b. *delíveral   cf. delívery
        abándon   *abándonal   abándonment
        édit   *édital   edítion
        endéavour   *endéavoural   endéavour
        devélop   *devélopal   devélopment
        consíder   *consíderal   consIderátion
        depósit   *depósital   depósit
        prómise   *prómisal   prómise

In (10b) we have listed a number of nouns formed from the verbs in (10a) by the addition of the suffix -al. Such a derivational relationship is impossible for the forms in (11).

> Is there any structural difference that may account for the different behaviour of the suffix -al in (10) and (11)?

The contrast between (10) and (11) with regard to the acceptance of the suffix -al can be attributed to one simple fact: all the base forms in (10) have final stress, but none of those in (11) does. If final stress is a precondition on -al suffixation (necessary but not sufficient, though: depárt → *depártal, etc.), then *arrive* needs to have stress assigned before -al suffixation takes place. This means that the morphology and the phonology are interleaved, not segregated. In particular, if they were segregated, with all the derivational processes preceding the phonology, phonological information would not

The morphology and the phonology are interleaved, not segregated be available to affixation. As a result, the derivations in *both* (10) and (11) would be blocked if *-al* suffixation were indeed stress-sensitive, since under the circumstances *-al* would simply not find the contextual stress it needs. Alternatively, if *-al* suffixation were not stress-sensitive, both groups of words would undergo *-al* suffixation, producing *arrival*, etc., and **deliveral*, etc., respectively. One or other outcome is of course incorrect for one of the sets.

> State explicitly what the problem is for a model that segregates morphology and phonology.

The derivation in (12) illustrates the interleaving of the phonology and the morphology we are talking about:

(12)

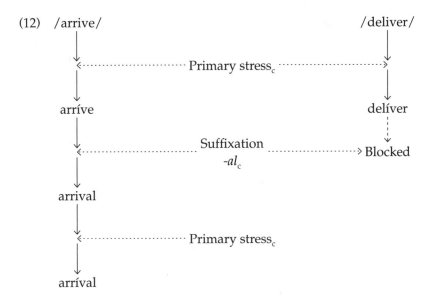

Derivational affixes of the *-al* type are of course heavily lexicalized, in that they cannot be added freely to stems to form new words.

> Can you see this? Have a few trials to prove the point.

Instead, affixes of this type belong in constructions that are, so to speak, fossilized, and thus most likely learnt as a block: notice that no English speaker will ever dream of saying **departal* or **arrivure*, even though the exchange of the two suffixes does not seem to be ruled out by any principle. This state of affairs is to be expected if words like *arrival* and *departure* are indeed learnt as one unit, rather than being composed by actively combining *arrive* and *-al*, and *depart* and *-ure*, respectively. This being so, the argument from *-al* we have just advanced for interleaving the phonology with the morphology could be objected to on the grounds that the distribution of *-al* has been fixed historically, and therefore falls outside the remit of the synchronic grammar.

> What exactly do we mean by "fixed historically"? Why should this have consequences for the synchronic grammar?

Similar cases of interleaving involving clearly productive affixes, however, do exist in many languages. One such case in English involves the colloquial (and unrefined) "infix" *-bloody-*, as in the expression *I have to go to uniBLOODYversity!* – an INFIX is an affix that neither precedes nor follows the stem, in the way that prefixes or suffixes, respectively, do: rather, it is inserted in the middle of the stem. The point about this extremely productive infix is that it cannot be inserted just anywhere, as the set in (13) clearly attests:

(13)   *uBLOODYniversity
       uniBLOODYversity
       *univerBLOODYsity
       *universiBLOODYty

You will notice that there are no fewer than four possible insertion sites, but only the second one listed (between *uni* and *versity*) is viable. At first sight, this restriction may appear totally mystifying.

> Study the data in (13) and see if you can predict where *-bloody-* needs to be inserted.

Our knowledge of metrical structure allows us to find the answer: the legitimate insertion site of *-bloody-* lies precisely between the two metrical feet of the word: $(uni)\downarrow(versi)<ty>$. Indeed, it immediately precedes the strongest foot *(versi)*. This is in fact the preferred location, as we illustrate in (14) with the longer form *Àpalàchicóla*, a place name in the USA:

(14)   *ABLOODYpalachicola
       ?ApaBLOODYlachicola
       *ApalaBLOODYchicola
       ApalachiBLOODYcola
       *ApalachicoBLOODYla

Apalachicola contains three feet: *(Apa)(lachi)(co)<la>*. What the set in (14) shows is that the best position for the infix *-bloody-* is immediately before the strongest foot, the rightmost one: *(co)*.

The best position for the infix *-bloody-* is immediately before the strongest foot

> Can you see the relevance of this to the discussion?

The relevance of all this to our present discussion is that *-bloody-* infixation, a morphological process, requires information about metrical structure, a phonological process. This means that metrical structure needs to be assigned to the base (*university* and *Apalachicola* in our examples) before infixation takes place. Consequently, a phonological operation (namely, footing) needs to precede a morphological operation (namely, *-bloody-* infixation), exactly as predicted by the interleaving model of morphology–phonology interaction we are presenting.

> Explain exactly what we mean by morphology–phonology interleaving.

5 The Scope of Peripherality

We have come some way in our understanding of the relationship between morphology and phonology, but we still have not accounted for such contrasts as *depth* vs. *deepness*, with which we opened the chapter. We shall now show that our present procedure cannot account for this type of data, and therefore it needs refining.

The reason our present procedure falls short of explaining these data is quite simple. You will recall that in the previous chapter we analysed the *p* of *deep* as extraprosodic ([di:<p>]), and construed this extraprosodicity as the source of its licensing.

> Explain in what way the *p* of *deep* is licensed by extraprosodicity.

When *th* is added to form *depth*, *p* ceases to be peripheral, and therefore it can no longer be extraprosodic. If the *p* of *depth* is not licensed by extraprosodicity, it will have to be licensed in the rime, but because of rime bimoraicity this can only happen if one of the two vowel moras is lost, hence the shortening of the vowel.

The problem now is that, if we extend the procedure to *deepness*, we will be predicting **d[ɛ]pness*. In fact, the correct outcome *d[iː]pness* suggests that *p* remains licensed by extraprosodicity in spite of its loss of peripherality. How can this be so?

> Can you see the problem? State it succinctly.

One logically possible answer would be that the Peripherality Condition on extraprosodicity is simply wrong. However, the evidence for this condition is so strong overall that it would be foolish to give it up.

> Jog your memory on some of the evidence we have given for the Peripherality Condition.

Indeed, if we did give up the Peripherality Condition, how would we explain that there is *d[ɛ]pth* rather than **d[iː]pth*?

> Can you see the paradox? State it.

Following on from the discussion in the previous sections, you may next think of relating the vowel contrast in *depth* and *deepness* to the by now familiar cyclic vs. non-cyclic dichotomy. Indeed, we have accounted for the stress contrast between *-ity* and *-ness* formations by declaring *-ity* cyclic and *-ness* non-cyclic. Could we use the same strategy now, assuming that *-th* is also cyclic (we have of course already established that *-ness* is non-cyclic)?

> Explain how this strategy would solve the problem.

Obviously, the implementation of this solution cannot be direct, since, as a condition, the Peripherality Condition is not subject to the cyclic vs. non-cyclic dichotomy: the cyclic vs. non-cyclic dichotomy is only relevant to rules, which can apply in the two different modes, and to affixes, which can define two different types of domain, compatible with cyclic and with non-cyclic rules, respectively. Evidently, therefore, an alternative implementation is called for if we are to call upon the Peripherality Condition to account for the *d[ɛ]pth* vs. *d[iː]pness* paradox.

The first step in this alternative implementation involves formalizing the Peripherality Condition on extraprosodicity as in (15):

(15)   *...<X>Y], for Y non-null

The key aspect of the formalization in (15), which otherwise simply restates the definition of the condition in chapter 12, is the "]" context. In particular, (15) makes it explicit that the extraprosodic element must immediately precede a morphological right bracket. With this in mind, let us consider the morphological representations of *depth* and *deepness*:

> An extraprosodic element must immediately precede a morphological right bracket

(16)   a.   [[dɛp]θ]   b.   [[diːp]nəs]

You will notice that [p] indeed immediately precedes a right bracket in *both* configurations. Consequently, according to (15), it should qualify for extraprosodicity in both cases, but it obviously does not in a.: some other factor must therefore be at work to prevent this result.

Why are we saying that *p* cannot qualify for extraprosodicity in (16a)?

We suggest that the factor in question is the degree of integration of the various morphemes in the word, as we shall now explain.

6 Word-Internal Cohesion: The Bracket Erasure Convention

In section 4 we mentioned the fact that such cyclic suffixes as *-al* in *arrival* occur with a fixed set of bases, rather than being productively attached to any base at the will of the speaker. This is also the case with *-th*. By contrast, suffixes like *-ness* are highly productive.

Test out the difference in productivity between both groups of affixes.

> The dichotomy productive vs. non-productive affix correlates well with the dichotomy non-cyclic vs. cyclic affix: cyclic suffixes LEXICALLY SELECT their bases

Importantly, the dichotomy productive vs. non-productive affix (corresponding to the opposition between non-lexicalized and lexicalized constructions, respectively) correlates well with the dichotomy non-cyclic vs. cyclic affix: the unproductive *-al* and *-th* define a cyclic domain, whereas the productive *-ness* defines a non-cyclic domain. Technically, we say that cyclic suffixes LEXICALLY SELECT their bases: the information as to what bases they attach to is an integral part of their lexical entry. Non-cyclic affixes are, however, not so restricted. We spell out the contrast between the two in (17) with a small sample of (simplified) lexical entries of the two kinds:

(17)   Types of lexical entry:
      a. Cyclic/Unproductive:
          -al /arrive _____, etc.
          -th /deep ____, etc.
      b. Non-cyclic/Productive:
          -ness
          -less
          -ful
          -hood

> Can you list (all?) the forms to which the nominalizing suffix *-th* can attach? Could you possibly do the same with *-ness*?

The obvious implication of the restrictedness of *-al, -th*, etc., *vis-à-vis -ness, -less*, etc., is that the degree of internal integration is greater in words with the former (cyclic) affixes than in words with the latter (non-cyclic) affixes.

Indeed, the internal unity that characterizes cyclic domains manifests itself in several spheres. For instance, semantically, non-cyclic suffixes tend to be compositional, with their meaning simply added to the meaning of the base: *neighbourhoodlessness* means exactly what *neighbour + hood + less + ness* mean. This is far less so the case with cyclic suffixes, which are often semantically integrated with the base. For example, a word like *transmission* (clearly derived from *transmit* morphologically) can refer to a specific part of an automobile, as well, of course, as to the act of transmitting. Expectedly, *transmissionful* or *transmissionless*, with the non-cyclic suffixes *-ful* or *-less* added to *transmission*, mean 'full of transmission' and 'without transmission', respectively, whatever the meaning of *transmission* may be: words with non-cyclic affixes are less prone to develop idiosyncratic meanings.

The internal unity that characterizes cyclic domains manifests itself in several spheres

> Can you think of another example of semantically non-compositional derivatives? Which of the groups in (17) are the suffixes of these derivatives in?

Another obvious manifestation of the close integration of cyclic affixes and the looser amalgamation of non-cyclic affixes has to do with phonological exceptionality: it is far more likely for words containing cyclic affixes to be exceptions to phonological rules than for words with non-cyclic affixes. For instance, we have already seen in chapter 15 that *obesity*, with the cyclic suffix *-ity*, fails to undergo vowel shortening: *ob*[i:]*sity*, not **ob*[ɛ]*sity*.

The particularly close unity characterizing cyclic domains in all areas is given formal interpretation in the following BRACKET ERASURE CONVENTION:

(18)   Bracket Erasure Convention:
        Internal morphological brackets are erased (= become invisible = become inaccessible) at the end of each level.

The implication of the Bracket Erasure Convention in (18) is that, after the cyclic derivation is completed, a word like *depth* will keep no trace of its original internal morphological structure:

(19)   [diː<p>]   →   [[diː<p>]θ]   →   [diː<p>θ]

Clearly, the representation [diː<p>θ], with *p* extraprosodic, violates the Peripherality Condition in (15), since the [p] does not immediately precede a morphological right bracket. This situation triggers the shortening of the vowel to allow the licensing of *p* by the rime, as we have explained. If *p* were not thus licensed, it would have fallen foul of the rule of STRAY ERASURE, which we must assume deletes material which is not prosodically licensed:

(20)   Stray Erasure:
        Delete material which is not prosodically licensed.

Let us now turn to *deepness*, with the non-cyclic suffix *-ness*, and no vowel shortening. At the point where Stray Erasure applies, the word *deepness* still has its internal morphological structure: [[dee<p>]ness]. Given this, *p* remains licensed by the morphological right bracket that immediately follows it, and consequently the conditions for Stray Erasure in (20) will not be met. This explains the difference between *depth* and *deepness*, and similarly for the parallel data we provided in section 1 above.

> Do you see the whole picture now? Summarize it.

7 Non-Cyclic Processes

The proposal we are advancing accounts for a rich array of data that go beyond vowel shortening, as we shall now briefly review.

In chapter 10 we came across the possibility of sonorant consonants occupying the syllable nucleus. We illustrate this again in (21):

(21) cycle
      centre   (in rhotic accents)
      rhythm

> Syllabify these three words after having drawn their sonority profiles.

As we pointed out at the time, this unexpected result is motivated by Sonority Sequencing, which would be violated if the sonorants were integrated in the previous syllable. Ostensibly, the situation in question can only arise word-finally, since word-internally the sonorants can readily be incorporated into the next onset:

(22) cyclic
      central
      rhythmic

> Compare your pronunciation of the words in (22) with that of their counterparts in (21), paying particular attention to the syllabic role of the sonorants we are discussing.

Paradoxically, however, in the forms in (23) the sonorant is not (necessarily) parsed in the onset:

(23) cycling
      centring   (in rhotic accents)
      rhythmish

> How do you pronounce the words in (23)? Do you only have one pronunciation, or a choice of two?

A considerable number of processes in English are contingent on the presence of a right morphological bracket

In (23), the sonorant may still be parsed in the nucleus, despite the fact that the **obstruent + sonorant** cluster is followed by a vowel, as in (22) above, and therefore the cluster is parsable in the onset. The paradox is resolved if we make the process of sonorant nucleus formation contingent on the presence of a right morphological bracket:

(24) Sonorant Nucleus Formation:

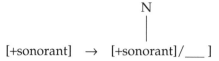

The rule of Sonorant Nucleus Formation is obviously non-cyclic: if it were cyclic we would indeed obtain *rhy.thm.ic*, and correspondingly.

> Explain how a cyclic Sonorant Nucleus Formation would yield forms like *rhy.thm.ic.*

On the other hand, if Sonorant Nucleus Formation is non-cyclic, it will not apply in *rhythmic*, since when this form reaches the non-cyclic block the relevant sonorant *m* is no longer followed by the required morphological right bracket, having been disposed of by the Bracket Erasure Convention in (18):

(25) Cyclic phase

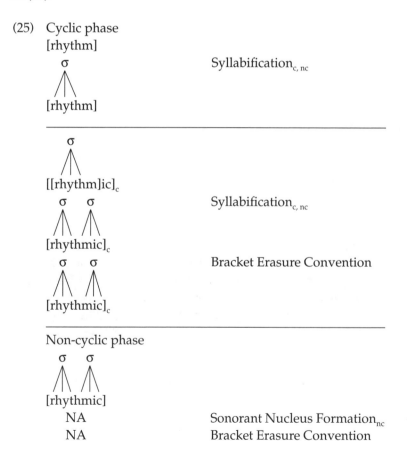

Sonorant Nucleus Formation as in (24) will, however, apply in both *rhythm*, where the *m* is word-final, and therefore necessarily adjacent to the required bracket, and *rhythmish*, where the suffix *-ish* is non-cyclic, and the word-internal bracket is therefore preserved:

(26) Cyclic phase

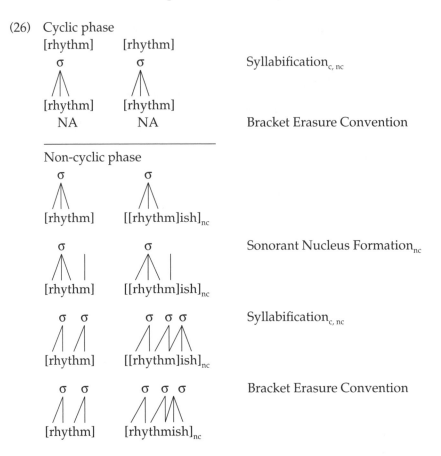

Study these derivations carefully, paying particular attention to the conditions for the nuclearization of *m*. Notice the final ambisyllabic parsing of *m* in *rhythmish*, with the *m* both in the nucleus and in the next onset: in similar words with a syllabic *l* (for instance, *tackling*), the first part of the *l* is velarized, and the second part clear.

Another phenomenon we have come across is the deletion of word-final *g* after a nasal in many accents of English (see chapter 3 above):

(27) lon**g̸**   stron**g̸**   . . .

> Think of a few more words in the mould of (27).

This process is matched by the deletion of *b* under similar conditions in all accents:

(28)   bomb̸   iamb̸   . . .

> Can you think of more words of the type exemplified in (28)?

The deletion of these stops word-finally after the nasal is probably motivated by a requirement of minimal sonority distance.

> Spell out this requirement for (28). Hint: compare forms like *pomp* or *lamp*.

The stop does surface word-internally in such derivatives as those in (29):

(29)   a.   bombard   b.   longest

> Why are *b* and *g* preserved here?

Unexpectedly at first sight, *b* and *g* are deleted word-internally in forms like those in (30):

(30)   a. bomb̸ing   b. long̸ing

Again, the matter is resolved if we include a right morphological bracket in the environment of the appropriate deletion rule:

(31)   Postnasal Voiced Stop Deletion:
       [−continuant] → Ø / [+nasal] ___]
       Condition: the input may not contain a path to [coronal]

> What do we mean by "path"? State the condition in (31) in plain words.

If Postnasal Voiced Stop Deletion as in (31) is non-cyclic it will apply, for instance, in [[*bomb*]*ing*], which keeps the word-internal bracket in the non-cyclic domain, but not, for instance, in [[*bomb*]*ard*], which loses it on exit from the cyclic domain: [*bombard*].

> Why exactly does [[*bomb*]*ard*] become [*bombard*]?

Also subject to word-final deletion is *n* following *m* (again, probably because of sonority restrictions):

> What types of sonority restriction could these be?

(32) a. hymn   b. hymnal
         condemn   condemnation
         autumn   autumnal

The lexical presence of the *n* is justified by the forms in b. In their base counterparts in a., however, this *n* disappears. Puzzlingly, *n* also disappears in the forms in (33), despite the fact that it is parsable as the onset of the next syllable, just as in (32b):

(33) hymning
        condemning
        autumny

> Can you guess what the solution is?

Once more, we shall assume that the relevant rule deleting the *n* is non-cyclic and includes a morphological right bracket in its environment (the deleting *n* must obviously be preceded by *m*: cf. *hen, kiln, barn* in rhotic accents, etc., with no deletion):

(34) Nasal Simplification:
        n → Ø /m ___]

As a final process affecting segments, consider the deletion of *g* before a word-final nasal:

(35) a. sign   b. signature
         paradigm   paradigmatic
         resign   resignation

In a., the sequence **g + nasal** is indeed word-final. In this context, the syllabification of *g* would violate Sonority Sequencing, and consequently the *g* deletes (NB there is no rule to parse the nasal as a nucleus here).

> Could English in principle have had a rule parsing *n* in the nucleus in *sign*? What would it have looked like?

In (35b), **g + nasal** is not word-final: therefore, the nasal can be onset to the following vowel, and the *g* does not delete. In this case also, there is an apparent paradox, illustrated by the data in (36):

(36) sig̸ner
      paradig̸my
      resig̸ning

> Say what the problem is, and suggest a solution.

In (36) *g* deletes despite the fact that in these forms the sequence *g* + **nasal** is not word-final, and the nasal could in principle be syllabified in the following onset. By this stage, the solution is completely obvious: the non-cyclic rule deleting *g* includes a right morphological bracket in its environment:

(37) Prenasal g Drop:

     g → Ø / ___ n]

The model we are proposing also provides an explanation for the retraction of stress in forms like *péregrinàting*, where the retracted stress is not word-final in the source structure, *peregrináting*. All we have to do, in fact, is make such non-cyclic retraction sensitive to the presence of a right bracket, rather than to the word end as such:

(38) Final Syllable Stress Retraction:

```
        *           *            Line 0
   *    *       *    *           Line 1
   * ... * ]  →  * ... * ]       Line 2
```

Clearly, this rule will enact retraction in both [*peregrinát*]*e* and [[*peregrinát*]*ing*], since the retractable asterisk is adjacent to a right bracket in both cases.

8 Ordered Affixes

The model of the interaction between morphology and phonology we have been presenting can be schematized as in (39):

(39) Interaction between morphology and phonology:

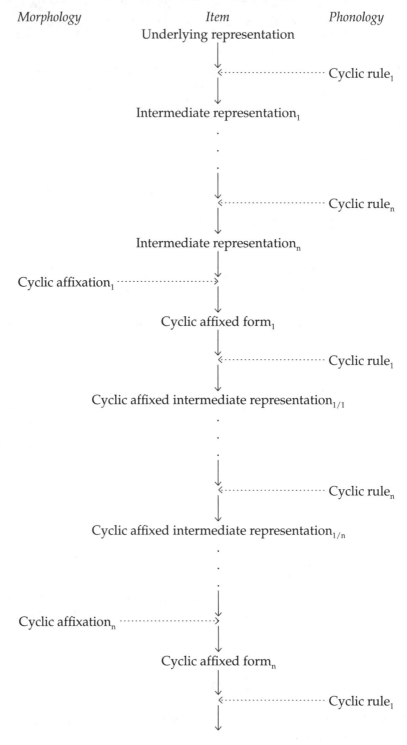

Morphology   *Item*   *Phonology*

Underlying representation

Cyclic rule$_1$

Intermediate representation$_1$

Cyclic rule$_n$

Intermediate representation$_n$

Cyclic affixation$_1$

Cyclic affixed form$_1$

Cyclic rule$_1$

Cyclic affixed intermediate representation$_{1/1}$

Cyclic rule$_n$

Cyclic affixed intermediate representation$_{1/n}$

Cyclic affixation$_n$

Cyclic affixed form$_n$

Cyclic rule$_1$

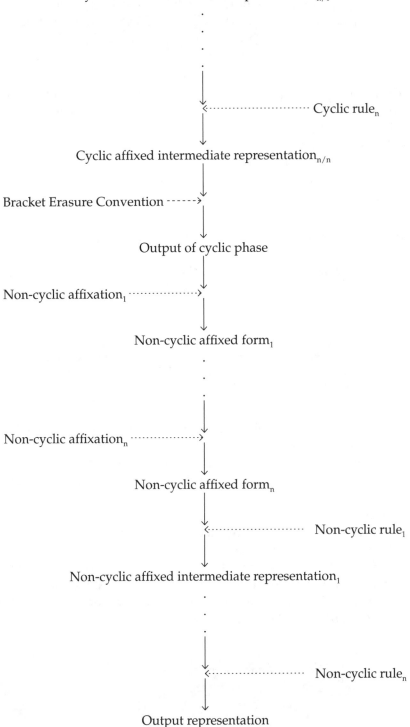

Cyclic affixed intermediate representation$_{n/1}$

Cyclic rule$_n$

Cyclic affixed intermediate representation$_{n/n}$

Bracket Erasure Convention

Output of cyclic phase

Non-cyclic affixation$_1$

Non-cyclic affixed form$_1$

Non-cyclic affixation$_n$

Non-cyclic affixed form$_n$

Non-cyclic rule$_1$

Non-cyclic affixed intermediate representation$_1$

Non-cyclic rule$_n$

Output representation

> Study diagram (39) carefully until you are satisfied that you understand it fully. You may want to test yourself before you go on.

Cyclic affixes are concatenated first, and non-cyclic affixes subsequently

The model in (39) implies that cyclic affixes are concatenated first, and non-cyclic affixes subsequently. The obvious implication is that no cyclic affix will ever occupy a more outward position than a non-cyclic affix: non-cyclic suffixes will occur to the right of cyclic suffixes, and non-cyclic prefixes to the left of cyclic prefixes.

There is a considerable amount of evidence for this hypothesis. We give a sample in (40):

(40)   a.   un-in-capable   b.   *in-un-capable
            nation-al-ist   *nation-ist-al
            Wilson-ian-ism   *Wilson-ism-ian
            creat-iv-ist   *creat-ist-ive
            immun-ity-ite   *immun-ite-ity

> Explain how the two classes of data in (40) substantiate the point we are making.

The forms in (40a), containing at least two affixes, are all legitimate. However, their counterparts in (40b) are not, even though they contain exactly the same affixes. The reason is, of course, that in (40b) the order of the affixes has been inverted, in violation of the strict order **cyclic affix > non-cyclic affix** we are referring to (the arrow head ">" indicates the obvious linear ordering).

The discovery that both affixes and phonological rules are allotted to classes which interact in the manner we have been describing, and that the order of affixes is fixed as between classes (the order of affixes in the same class is supposed in principle to be free, regulated only by syntactico-semantic considerations), is one of the most important contributions of the decade straddling the 1970s and the 1980s.

> Explain what we mean by "syntactico-semantic considerations". Hint: *white* can become *whiteness*, but *fight* cannot become *fightness*, or *night* *nightness*.

9 Lexical Phonology: Problematic Orderings

We have already seen that each class is defined both by order (stacking order for affixes, application order for rules) and by a set of contrastive properties (cyclic vs. non-cyclic application, early versus late internal bracket erasure, and other dichotomies listed in (52) below). This state of affairs was encapsulated in a model where both the morphology (that is, affixation) and the phonology are organized in autonomous interacting blocks, as schematized in (41):

(41)   Organization of the morphology and the phonology in blocks

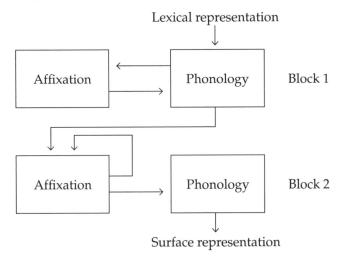

Lexical representation

Affixation   Phonology   Block 1

Affixation   Phonology   Block 2

Surface representation

> Stop and study the figure in (41), relating it to its antecedent in (39).

The blocks of our flow chart in (41) are often referred to as CLASSES, LEVELS or STRATA, and the model that incorporates them as LEXICAL PHONOLOGY or STRATAL PHONOLOGY. There have been several versions of Lexical Phonology through the years, varying in a number of technical details not sufficiently central to our present concerns to warrant discussion here. In essence, (41) merely compresses our more detailed diagram (39) above, and must be interpreted in a similar manner.

Blocks of rules and affixal domains are referred to as CLASSES, LEVELS or STRATA, and the model that incorporates them as LEXICAL PHONOLOGY

> Check the two figures again, to confirm their basic equivalence.

Both figures (39) and (41) are of course adapted to the requirements of English, and the exact mechanics of the blocks may differ in other languages. The number of blocks also differs from language to language, and even from proposal to proposal.

For completeness, we now summarize the properties characterizing the rules of each of the two blocks we have been proposing for English:

(42)   Rule properties:

Block 1	*Block 2*
Cyclic	Non-cyclic
Exceptions likely	Exceptions unlikely
May not refer to internal brackets	May refer to internal brackets
Non-productive	Productive
Common semantic opacity	Usual semantic transparency
Structure-preserving	Non-structure-preserving

STRUCTURE PRESERVATION refers to the fact that some phonological rules are strictly respectful of the basic structural properties of the language, such as the identity of lexical segments or the core syllable structure (in English CVX, or CVXC word-finally). Non-structure-preserving rules can, by contrast, violate these properties.

STRUCTURE PRESERVATION refers to the fact that some phonological rules are strictly respectful of the basic structural properties of the language

> Check that you understand the distinction between structure-preserving and non-structure-preserving rules by giving a couple of English rules in either category. Hint: Nasal Assimilation is not necessarily structure-preserving.

Lexical Phonology held considerable promise of reducing the interaction between morphology and phonology to a truly simple, compact formalism. As research went on, however, significant problems concerning the ordering of the affixes came to light: many (in fact most) legitimate affix combinations are missing, while a number of putatively illegitimate ones do occur.

As research went on, significant problems concerning the ordering of the affixes came to light

With respect to the non-occurrence of legitimate affix strings, it appears that, out of 1,849 logically possible combinations of the 43 most common English suffixes, only 40–50 exist. Many of the failures can perhaps be accounted for by syntactico-semantic factors: for instance, we cannot form **nightness* from *night* because the suffix *-ness* only attaches to adjectives (*whiteness* is fine, but *night* is a noun). After putting such cases aside, there is still a remnant of over 600 combinations that ought to be possible, but most of them fail to occur.

> Think of a few affix combinations that ought to be possible in English but do not seem to occur.

Obviously, therefore, Lexical Phonology is underpowered: it lets too much through.

> Explain why predicting too much reveals that a grammar is underpowered (at first sight this may look like a contradiction).

The other side of the coin is a subset of combinations which are predicted to be illegitimate but do occur. These have received considerable attention in the literature under the label ORDERING PARADOXES, and can appropriately be illustrated by the comparative formation *unhappier*. In Modern English, comparatives in *-er* are restricted to adjectives with at most two syllables, the second of which must moreover be light, as, for instance, in *ha.ppy*. Therefore, the morphological constituency of *unhappier* must be [*un*[*happier*]], since a base *unhappy* (*un.ha.ppy*) would simply not qualify for *-er* suffixation.

> Why exactly wouldn't it qualify?

The morphological bracketing [*un*[*happier*]], however, implies a meaning 'not happier', as against the real meaning 'more unhappy'. The true meaning of *unhappier* presupposes the bracketing [[*unhappy*]*er*], which is at odds with the derivational facts mentioned: hence the paradox.

> Explain the *unhappier* paradox in your own words.

This and other similar cases are bracketing paradoxes precisely because of the assumption we have been operating with that the domains available to phonological rules word-internally are provided by their morphological constituency. For the data we have been presenting, this assumption has indeed served us well, but we are now seeing that it runs aground when the data set is extended in certain directions. A proposal to circumvent this problem involves the abandonment of the assumption that morphological and phonological constituents are identical, and we will present it in section 16 below. First, however, we must turn our attention to domains bigger than the word, where by definition morphology is irrelevant.

Bracketing paradoxes are so because of the assumption that the domains available to phonological rules word-internally are provided by their morphological constituency

10 The Phonological Phrase

In chapter 11 above and at various points since we have referred to the very common English phenomenon of stress retraction under clash: *Sue Ánn* vs. *Sùe Ann Cóok, antíques* vs. *àntique cháir*, and so on.

The data in (43), however, do not exhibit retraction, in spite of the fact that they contain stress clashes:

(43)   Japanése ráilways and motorways
       Tennessée's pólitics and religion
       rabbits reprodúce quíckly enough
       Mary persevéres fírmly but gently

In particular, the asterisk clashes in the constructions in (43) are to all appearances identical to those that we have been saying all along are subject to retraction, as is the case in (44):

(44)   Jápanese ráilways
       Ténnessee's pólitics
       rabbits réproduce quíckly
       Mary pérseveres fírmly

We will now show that the answer to this problem involves assigning phonological rules to specifically phonological domains.

In principle, it might be reasonable to identify phrase-size domains of phonological rule application with syntactic constituents, in the same way as we have been identifying word-internal application domains with morphological constituents, quite successfully up to the end of the previous section. Indeed, this is what we assumed when we discussed stress retraction in previous chapters. The assumption that grammatical constituents (whether morphological or syntactic) double up as application domains for phonological rules was already made in *SPE*, and is of course maximally parsimonious and natural, providing as it does a ready-made interface between the phonology and the grammar.

> What do we mean when we say that designating grammatical constituents as domains for phonological rules provides a ready-made interface between the phonology and the grammar?

Although the identification of phonological phrasal domains with syntactic constituents is plausible in principle, it runs into considerable empirical difficulties. In the case we are discussing, it is clear that the phrases in (43) share their syntactic constituency with their counterparts in (44), and yet the two sets behave differently with regard to stress retraction: retraction takes place in (44), but in (43) the clash persists.

> Why is the syntactic constituency of the phrases in (43) and (44) identical?

Although the identification of phonological phrasal domains with syntactic constituents is plausible in principle, it runs into considerable empirical difficulties

In order to resolve this apparent paradox we have to accept that the extension of the syntactic phrase is not the same as the extension of the phonological phrase, and that the domain of application of the Rhythm Rule is the phonological phrase, rather than the syntactic phrase. The syntactic phrase and the phonological phrase are related, but they are still distinct, in ways that we shall now explain.

The construction of the phonological phrase is parasitic on the structure of the syntactic phrase. A typical syntactic phrase (a noun phrase, a verb phrase, an adjective phrase) has a head (a noun, a verb or an adjective, respectively) and (optionally) additional material on either side of the head:

The extension of the syntactic phrase is not the same as the extension of the phonological phrase

(45)

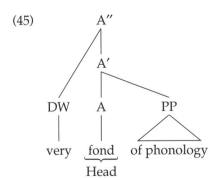

A″ = major adjective phrase

A′ = minor adjective phrase

DW = degree word

A   = adjective

PP = prepositional phrase

For any one language, one of the two sides of the phrase is "recursive" – in principle it admits of an unlimited number of "complements":

(46)   very fond of phonetics, phonology, morphology, syntax, semantics, pragmatics, . . .

> Try and add more phrases in the position of the dots in (46). When (if ever) do you have to stop?

The other side of the phrase, by contrast, is non-recursive, in that the elements it can take ("specifiers") are limited:

(47)   fond of phonology → very fond of phonology → not very fond of phonology → ??

> Can you modify the phrase in (47) further by preposing more elements?

The construction of the PHONO-LOGICAL PHRASE is parasitic on the structure of the syntactic phrase: it includes (obligatorily) the syntactic head and the elements in the non-recursive side which are not themselves syntactic heads

The syntactic configuration exemplified in (45) provides the criteria for the construction of the PHONOLOGICAL PHRASE, which includes (obligatorily) the syntactic head and the elements in the non-recursive side which are not themselves syntactic heads – if they are syntactic heads, they will constitute nuclei of independent phonological phrases.

> What will the phonological phrases be in (47)?

Optionally, phonological phrases include a single word on the complement side of the head, as we show in (48) (PP = phonological phrase; NB do not confuse it with PP = prepositional phrase above!):

(48)   [rabbits]$_{PP}$ [reproduce]$_{PP}$ [quickly]$_{PP}$
       or
       [rabbits]$_{PP}$ [reproduce quickly]$_{PP}$

> Explain why [*quickly*]$_{PP}$ can be integrated into [*reproduce*]$_{PP}$.

Crucially, if the complement side contains more than one word, it cannot be incorporated into the PP, as we illustrate in (49):

(49)   [rabbits]$_{PP}$ [reproduce]$_{PP}$ [quickly enough]$_{PP}$
        not
        [rabbits]$_{PP}$ *[reproduce quickly enough]$_{PP}$

> Can you see why [*reproduce*]$_{PP}$ cannot be augmented here?

We formalize the criteria for the formation of the phonological phrase in (50):

(50)   Phonological phrase formation:
        A phonological phrase is made up of:
        (i)   a syntactic head +
        (ii)   all the words on the non-recursive side of the head's phrasal
                domain +
        (iii)   optionally, a single-word constituent on the complement side of
                the head

> Go back to the exercises that follow (48) and (49) and relate
> the definition in (50) to them.

Given the definition in (50), we can account for the occurrence of retraction
in (44), but not in (43), simply by declaring the phonological phrase the domain
of the English Rhythm Rule:

(51)   a.   [Japanése ráilways]$_{PP}$ → [Jápanese ráilways]$_{PP}$
        b.   [Japanése]$_{PP}$ [ráilways and motorways]$_{PP}$

> How can phrases like *Sue Ann Cook* that we examined above
> be parsed into only one phonological phrase? Hint: think of
> the spellings of such composite first names as *Marianne*,
> *Joanne*, *Rosemary*, etc.

You can see that there is no formal stress clash in (51b) (and correspondingly in the other phrases in (43)): the clash occurs across the boundaries of
the phonological phrase and, therefore, formally it is only apparent.

> Explain exactly why (51b) does not contain a clash, despite the
> proximity of the stress of *railways* to the stress of *Japanese*.

11 The Intonational Phrase

The phonological phrase is the smallest of our phrasal phonological domains. The next phonological domain larger than the phonological phrase is the INTONATIONAL PHRASE, which is traditionally identified with the domain where the intonational melodies we studied in chapter 14 associate to the segmental material.

> What exactly do we mean by association of intonational melodies to segmental material?

As you will recall, just as intonational melodies associate to individual words uttered in isolation, they also spread over whole (and fairly lengthy) phrases, like *the dark clouds in the sky threaten imminent rain*. Clearly, domains such as these are potentially larger than phonological phrases, and therefore they need to be given independent formal status.

The criteria for delimiting the intonational phrase are less clear-cut than the criteria for delimiting the phonological phrase. In particular, while the phonological phrase appears to be definable on purely syntactic terms, as our formalization in (50) displays, the delimitation of the intonational phrase can also involve semantic and phonological factors, and even be influenced by performance. We list these heterogeneous criteria in (52), with the appropriate exemplification:

The delimitation of the intonational phrase involves syntactic, semantic and phonological factors, and is even influenced by performance

(52) Criteria for the delimitation of the intonational phrase (IP):
Syntactic criteria:
(i)   The PPs making up an IP must be *sequential*:

$[[Picasso]_{PP} \ [was \ a \ truly]_{PP} \ [great]_{PP} \ [painter]_{PP}]_{IP}$

therefore:
(ii) "Parenthetic" PPs (technically, PPs unattached to the highest sentence node) make up independent IPs:

Picasso $[[as \ you \ know]_{PP}]_{IP}$ *was a great painter*
Picasso was $[[as \ you \ know]_{PP}]_{IP}$ *a great painter*

> In what way is the phrase *as you know* in these two examples "parenthetical"?

and:

(iii)   Each of the remaining PP sequences attached to the highest sentence node makes up an IP:

[[*Picasso*]_{PP}]_{IP}
  [[*as you know*]_{PP}]_{IP}
    [[*was a great*]_{PP} [*painter*]_{PP}]_{IP}

[[*Picasso*]_{PP}[*was*]_{PP}]_{IP}
  [[*as you know*]_{PP}]_{IP}
    [[*a great*]_{PP} [*painter*]_{PP}]_{IP}

> Why should the two phrases flanking *as you know* above be attached to the highest sentence node?

or, optionally:

(iv)   IPs can be split up into smaller IPs
       usually after a noun phrase:

[[*Picasso*]_{PP} [*was a painter*]_{PP}]_{IP},
  [[*a lover*]_{PP}]_{IP},
    [[*and a bon viveur*]_{PP}]_{IP}

[[*My brother*]_{PP}]_{IP}
  [[*found*]_{PP} [*several two-pound*]_{PP} [*coins*]_{PP}]_{IP}
    [[*on the church floor*]_{PP}]_{IP}

or before a subordinate sentence:

[[*my brother*]_{PP} [*found*]_{PP}]_{IP}
  [[*that phonology*]_{PP} [*is a most interesting*]_{PP} [*subject*]_{PP}]_{IP}

> Why is the sentence starting with *that* subordinate?

Semantic criteria:

(v)   Contrastive prominence induces the breakup of an IP:

[[*Siegfried*]_{PP} [*loved*]_{PP} [*Brünnhilde*]_{PP}]_{IP}
  [[*before SHE*]_{PP}]IP
    [[*loved*]_{PP} [*HIM*]_{PP}]_{IP}

(vi)   IPs are not usually broken up between the verb and its follow-ing obligatory argument (an "obligatory argument" is a type of word the meaning of which is integrated in the meaning of the verb in a particularly close manner):

[[*I always*]$_{PP}$[*give*]$_{PP}$[*money*]$_{PP}$[*to the buskers*]$_{PP}$[*that cheer me up*]$_{PP}$]$_{IP}$

cf. [[*I always*]$_{PP}$ [*give*]$_{PP}$ [*money*]$_{PP}$]$_{IP}$
   [[*for the buskers*]$_{PP}$ [*that cheer me up*]$_{PP}$]$_{IP}$

Phonological criteria:
(vii)   The greater the length, the more likely the break-up of the IP:

[[*my brother*]$_{PP}$]$_{IP}$
   [[*only recently*]$_{PP}$ [*realized*]$_{PP}$]$_{IP}$
     [[*that his girlfriend*]$_{PP}$ [*of twenty years*]$_{PP}$]$_{IP}$
       [[*had been relentlessly pursued*]$_{PP}$]$_{IP}$
         [[*by a crowd*]$_{PP}$ [*of wealthy*]$_{PP}$[*suitors*]$_{PP}$]$_{IP}$
           [[*for the past*]$_{PP}$ [*ten years*]$_{PP}$ [*or more!*]$_{PP}$]$_{IP}$

Performance-based criteria:
(viii)   Rate and style of speech affect IP breakup: the slower and the more formal the style, the more IPs.

You can see that the criteria for the delimitation of intonational phrases are quite flexible, although some strict guidelines, included in (52), do exist.

There are also general conditions on the structure of all phonological domains, in particular a requirement of proper domain inclusiveness: for example, an IP cannot begin or end in the middle of a PP. The requirement that a phonological domain must properly include the immediately smaller domain, with no leftover, is encapsulated in the so-called "Strict Layer Hypothesis", which we formalize in (58), further below.

> Explain what "proper inclusion" means, and how the relationship between phonological domains is controlled by it.

Like other phonological domains, the intonational phrase can in principle serve as the domain of any type of phonological rule, not just of intonational association. In fact, there is some evidence that the intonational phrase may not after all necessarily constitute the domain of intonational mapping, paradoxically so if the label is taken seriously. Consider the two phrases in (53):

(53) a. But we are *not* telling John
      b. But we are *not* going John

> Compare the intonation of these two phrases, making sure you emphasize the *not* in both cases.

(53b) (conventionally written with a comma between *going* and *John*) must contain two IPs (one on each side of the comma) according to criterion (52ii). Yet its pattern of association of the intonational melody is identical to the pattern in (53a).

> Why must (53b) include two IPs?

Among the non-intonational processes that occur in the domain of the intonational phrase is optional nasal assimilation, a rule of English we introduced and discussed in chapter 4:

(54) The trai[m] passed us as we were going up the hill
      The trai[ŋ] came in late
      cf.
      They came by trai[n], Peter and Jane
      They came by trai[n], contrary to advice

There is some evidence that the intonational phrase may not necessarily constitute the domain of intonational mapping

> Analyse each of the utterances in (54) into their component intonational phrases, to verify that the domain of English nasal assimilation is indeed the IP.

The extension of the intonational phrase need not coincide with the extension of any type of syntactic phrase

It is clear from our discussion that the extension of the intonational phrase need not coincide with the extension of any type of syntactic phrase. A dramatic example of this, made classic by *SPE*, is provided by the rhyme *this is the cat that killed the rat that ate the malt that . . .* , with the syntactic constituency in (55a) but the intonational phrasing in (55b) (NP = noun phrase, VP = verb phrase, S = sentence, all syntactic constituents):

(55) a. [this [is [the cat that killed [the rat that ate [the malt]$_{NP}$]$_{NP}$]$_{NP}$]$_{VP}$]$_S$
      b. [this is the cat]$_{IP}$ [that killed the rat]$_{IP}$ [that ate the malt]$_{IP}$

12 The Phonological Utterance

One phonological domain even larger than the intonational phrase is the Phonological Utterance (PU). The phonological utterance constitutes the domain of application of such phonological rules as *r*-insertion (in RP, eastern New England and many other accents of English) and flapping (in General American, and also in some non-rhotic accents). A useful pair illustrating the role of this domain in *r*-insertion is given in (56):

(56) a. Don't sit on that sofa!: it's broken.
      b. Don't sit on that sofa! It's Mary.

> Assuming that you are a speaker of an *r*-inserting dialect, pronounce these two phrases and see if you insert an [ɹ], and where. If your accent is not *r*-inserting, but has flapping, you can substitute *mat* for *sofa* and apply this and successive tests to flapping.

In the phrase in (56a), pronounced with an intrusive [ɹ] (. . . *sofa*[ɹ]*it* . . .), we give the reason for not sitting on the sofa: it is broken. By contrast, in (56b) the two phrases are semantically unrelated: *it's Mary* refers, for example, to the knock on the door we hear as I say *don't sit on that sofa*. Most curiously, there is no [ɹ] intrusion here, even if the two phrases are said in absolute succession, with no break between *fa* and *it*.

> Pronounce the two phrases in (56) again to verify our predictions.

Indeed, each of the phrases in (56) can be pronounced with or without *r*-insertion, depending again on whether or not there is a semantic link between their two component phrases: compare *Don't sit on that sofa! It's broken*, with *it's broken* referring to an object other than the sofa, and *Don't sit on that sofa:* [ɹ] *it's Mary*, with *Mary* identified with the sofa (Mary had, for instance, disguised herself as the sofa!).

> Change your mental setting along the lines just suggested and pronounce the phrases again. Does your new pronunciation confirm our predictions on *r*-insertion?

It appears that the construction of the Phonological Utterance involves criteria from practically every component of the grammar, phonological or non-phonological, as we specify in (57), where the superscript * indicates optional recursion:

> The construction of the PHONO-LOGICAL UTTER-ANCE involves criteria from practically every component of the grammar, phonological or non-phonological

(57)   Conditions on the formation of the Phonological Utterance:
$[_X[\ldots]^*_{IP}$ X = a syntactic label
Condition: no deliberate internal pause

Conditions on (optional) merger of Phonological Utterances:
Pragmatic: utterer and addressee identity
Phonological: shortness and no pause
Syntactic: "ellipsis" or "anaphora" relation
   e.g. [*You didn't **invite Martha**.* [ɹ] *I did*]$_{PU}$
                                   (**invite Martha**)
or Semantic: "and", "therefore" or "because" relation
   e.g. [*Dont' sit on that sofa* [ɹ].   *It's broken*]$_{PU}$
                     (**because**)

13 Properties of Phonological Domains

The three phrase-level phonological domains we have been presenting (the phonological phrase, the intonational phrase and the phonological utterance) are commonly labelled PROSODIC DOMAINS, and the branch of phonology concerned with them PROSODIC PHONOLOGY. You must bear in mind, however, that the term "prosodic" has through the years been applied to a variety of phenomena, and is therefore potentially ambiguous. Remember, for instance, that in part II we referred to such suprasegmental constituents as the syllable and the foot as prosodic. Here as elsewhere in this book, we are endeavouring to select terminology which is transparent and cannot lead to misunderstanding, hence our use of the expression PHONOLOGICAL DOMAINS in preference to "prosodic domains".

The three phonological domains in question stand in a relationship of inclusiveness, such that the Intonational Phrase is made up of (one or more) Phonological Phrases, with no material left over, and the Phonological Utterance is made up of one or more Intonational Phrases, again, with no material left over. As we mentioned above, this requirement of proper inclusiveness is known as the STRICT LAYER HYPOTHESIS, which we now formulate in (58):

The requirement that a phonological domain must properly include the immediately smaller domain, with no leftover, is encapsulated in the STRICT LAYER HYPOTHESIS

(58)   Strict Layer Hypothesis:
        Each phonological domain contains precisely one or more phonological domains of the rank immediately below

> Mull over (58) until you understand it fully. Give the full list of phrasal phonological domains, from smallest to largest.

The Strict Layer Hypothesis fares reasonably well across domains and across languages, although some problematic cases are known to exist. We will be proposing a general solution to the problem of exceptional behaviour in phonology in chapter 19.

In the Lexical Phonology model of morphology–phonology interaction we introduced in section 8 above, phrasal phonological domains are directly identified with syntactic constituency, misguidedly, as we are now seeing. In Lexical Phonology, phonological rules that apply in phrasal domains are labelled POSTLEXICAL RULES, and are assumed to apply under conditions even more liberal than those on the rules in the lexical non-cyclic block.

Phonological rules that apply in phrasal domains are labelled POSTLEXICAL RULES

> Which are the conditions on rules of the non-cyclic block? (Go back to (42) if you need to.)

In (59) we provide a list of the properties originally thought to be associated with each type of rule:

(59) Lexical vs. postlexical rule properties:

	Lexical	Postlexical
Word-bounded	Yes	No
Access to word-internal structure	Yes	No
Cyclic	Yes	No
Only applies in derived environments	Yes	No
Structure-preserving	Yes	No
Only applies to lexical categories	Yes	No
May have exceptions	Yes	No

It is of course not surprising that the properties of lexical and postlexical rules should contrast, since the elements making up postlexical domains (= words) are even more self-sufficient than the non-cyclic affixes that make up the non-cyclic block. This notwithstanding, the divide between the two types of rule sketched in (59) is too sharp and neat, and was soon found to leak in both directions, as our earlier discussion of non-cyclic rules already hints (compare (59) with (42) above).

14 Subphrasal Phonological Domains

We shall now turn our attention to the phonological domains below the phrase, namely, the domains of word-size or shorter.

In the first part of this chapter we used words and (some of) their constituent morphemes as domains for phonological rules, in the general context of Lexical Phonology. In a parallel tradition, however, it is the foot, the syllable and, on occasions, the mora that are viewed as word-internal phonological domains, structured hierarchically in accordance with the Strict Layer Hypothesis.

> In what way are the phonological domains smaller than the word different from the phrasal domains (size apart, obviously)?

It is clearly desirable to bring these two traditions together, in a synthesis which would allow us to preserve the best of either camp. In order to attain this goal, several inconsistencies need to be overcome. Thus, if grammatical constituents do not have a direct role as phonological domains above the word, it appears reasonable to expect them not to have such a role below the word either, but they do in Lexical Phonology. In particular, there is an obvious inconsistency between delimiting phrasal phonological domains primarily through a mapping from syntactic structure, as we have shown we must, and identifying subphrasal domains directly with morphological constituency, without the mediation of a similar mapping.

> The word "mapping" is a little technical, but very useful. Make sure you understand it (compare it with the word "projection" we have been using on and off in the text).

On the other hand, if the word-internal phonological domains are to be identified with the foot, the syllable and the mora, as they are in the alternative tradition, the construction of these domains from scratch we adopted in chapters 9–13 above is inconsistent with the construction of their phrasal equivalents essentially through a mapping from the syntax.

> Why do we say "essentially"? What other factors can enter into the delimitation of phrasal phonological domains?

We draw a distinction between PHONOLOGICAL CONSTITUENTS, which make up phonological *structure*, and phonological domains, which supply the *spatial bounds* within which phonological rules apply

One possible response to the difficulties just mentioned is to draw a distinction between phonological constituents (the mora, the syllable, the foot) and phonological domains. From this perspective, PHONOLOGICAL CONSTITUENTS make up phonological *structure*, whereas PHONOLOGICAL DOMAINS simply supply the *spatial bounds* within which phonological rules apply.

> Do you understand the difference we are drawing between a phonological constituent and a phonological domain?

This division between phonological constituents and phonological domains allows us to formalize the word-internal phonological domains as mappings from morphological constituents, thus preserving the formal parallel with the mappings from syntactic constituents for phrasal domains.

> Do you see the formal parallel between phrasal and word-internal phonological domains in this proposal? Explain it in your own words.

Word-internal phonological domains contrast with their phrasal counterparts in that more often than not they are identical to morphological constituents, the stem and the word in particular.

Explain the difference between a morphological stem and a morphological word.

In the mapping approach, however, mismatches between the two domains (morphological and phonological) are possible.

Why are mismatches between the morphological and the phonological domains accommodated in the mapping approach only?

The largest subphrasal phonological domain, and thus the component element of the Phonological Phrase, is the PHONOLOGICAL WORD (PW). One of the characteristics of the Phonological Word in English we are already familiar with is the presence of a prominent foot, with the primary stressed syllable in the word. Such prominence is, of course, maintained when the word is included in larger domains:

> The largest subphrasal phonological domain, and thus the component element of the Phonological Phrase, is the PHONOLOGICAL WORD

Do you need reminding that phonological words include a prominent foot? Think of the function of the grid's line 2 in words.

(60)   uniVERsity
        the provision [of uniVERsity education]$_{PP}$
        [the provision of uniVERsity education]$_{IP}$ is one of the government's
            fundamental duties
        [the provision of uniVERsity education is one of the government's fundamental duties]$_{PU}$

You can see that the syllable *ver*, the head of the foot *versi*, is prominent in *university* irrespective of the size of the phonological domain: it is not the case that in the phonological utterance, for instance, *uniVERsity* becomes *university*, with no prominence.

Can you see that, logically, things could have been otherwise?

The common situation is for phonological words to have the same extension as lexical words. A revealing instantiation is provided by English compounds, where the prominence contours of the component (lexical) words are preserved:

> The common situation is for phonological words to have the same extension as lexical words

(61)   matérnity hòspital
defénce depàrtment
delívery vèhicle

These data suggest that the phonological word status of each of the compound's component words is maintained in English.

> Explain the logic of this conclusion.

Now consider Modern Greek:

(62)   a.   kúkla   b. spíti   c. kuklóspiti
            'doll'   'house'   'doll's house'

            psychí   pedí   psychopédi
            'spirit'   'child'   'adopted child'

            níchta   filakí   nichtofilakí
            'night'   'guard'   'night guard'

You can see that the stress patterns of the individual words are not preserved in Greek compounds, each of which has its own individual stress pattern, idiosyncratically. The obvious inference is that Modern Greek compounds constitute phonological words, in contrast with their English counterparts.

> Explain why we are drawing the inference that Modern Greek compounds are phonological words.

The difference between Modern Greek and English compounds illustrates the variability in size of the phonological word between languages. In section 16 we shall see that phonological words can also be smaller than lexical words.

15 Segmental Affiliation to the Phonological Word

At this point, we can make use of the phonological word to solve the problem that is still pending with respect to the affiliation of /θ/ in *depth*. Remember that we decided that the final /p/ of *deep* is licensed by extra-prosodicity ([diː<p>]) and attaches to the syllable node: [diː<p>]. A similar analysis of the /θ/ of *depth* is, however, not possible, for the simple reason that the sequence /pθ/ does not comply with Sonority Sequencing, a prerequisite for syllabic membership. As we have already mentioned, though, coronal obstruents can appear at the end of English words with no obvious limit: *depths*, *ropes*, *raked*, *text*, *texts*, and so on.

> Write down the (sequences of) word-final coronals that appear in these words. Think up two or three other words with longish such sequences.

Extra word-final coronal obstruents have often been interpreted as an "appendix". The question that obviously arises is what constituent they are appendices to, and the common answer is that they are appendices to the phonological word.

The appending of English extra word-final coronal obstruents directly to the phonological word obviously presupposes that the Phonological Word is not only a phonological domain, on a par with the Phonological Phrase, the Intonational Phrase and the Phonological Utterance, but also a phonological constituent, on a par with the foot and the syllable.

> Why do we need the assumption that the Phonological Word is both a phonological domain and a phonological constituent?

From this perspective, therefore, the phonological word has a dual identity: it is a member of both the phonological domain hierarchy and the phonological constituent hierarchy.

> What is the difference between the two hierarchies?

This conclusion does not seem unreasonable, given the similar dual status of the lexical word, of which the phonological word is the phonological correlate: the lexical word is both the largest morphological unit and the smallest syntactic unit.

> Explain the dual nature of the lexical word in your own words.

If we thus accept the phonological word as the highest phonological constituent, we can affiliate English word-final extra coronal obstruents directly to the phonological word node:

Coronal obstruents can appear at the end of English words with no obvious limit

We affiliate English word-final extra coronal obstruents and extrasyllabic word-initial s- directly to the phonological word node

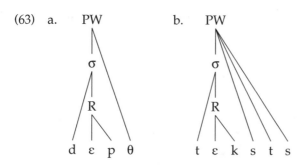

(63) a. PW   b. PW

Show how our account still leaves out a form like *twelfth(s)*. This form is, however, pronounced *twe*[lθ](*s*) in casual speech (check up on yourself and a few friends): is this casual pronunciation good or bad news for our proposal?

The approach can be extended to the also extrasyllabic word-initial *s-*, an issue pending from chapter 10 above:

(64)   PW

Opportunely, the configurations in (63) and (64) exemplify a violation of the Strict Layer Hypothesis, a possibility we referred to above.

Explain how the Strict Layer Hypothesis is violated in the configurations in (63) and (64).

The phonological word can be smaller than the lexical word

---

16 Small Phonological Words

We said above that the phonological word can be smaller than the lexical word. For example, in the Australian aboriginal language Yidin^y (referred to in chapter 12 in connection with stress), some suffixes which are an integral part of the lexical word can be shown to form phonological words of their own. For instance, [gumaːri]_{PW} [dagaːn^yy]_{PW} 'to become red' is one lexical word, formed on the stem *gumari* 'red' by double affixation (*-dagan-n^yy*). Although *gumaridagan^yy* is one lexical word, it exhibits (twice) the penultimate vowel lengthening typical of phonological words with an odd number of syllables (compare [gudaːga] 'dog-absolutive' with [gudagagu] 'dog-purposive').

> Make sure you understand the Yidin^y data. How do they bear on the issue of the relationship between the lexical word and the prosodic word?

The possibility of having phonological words smaller in size than lexical words provides a resolution to the bracketing paradoxes involving prefixes that we introduced in section 9 above. Consider, for instance, the case of *unhappier*.

> What is the problem with *unhappier*?

In order to account for the (apparently contradictory) facts, we can assume that the morphosemantic structure of this word is [[*unhappi*]_A*er*]_A – remember that *unhappier* means 'more unhappy'. Phonologically, however, the structure would be [*un*]_{PW} [*happier*]_{PW}, from a base [*un*]_{PW} [*happy*]_{PW}, where the second domain [*happy*]_{PW} does comply with the requirement of maximal bisyllabicity on *-er* suffixation (NB A = adjective):

(65)   A   Morphological structure

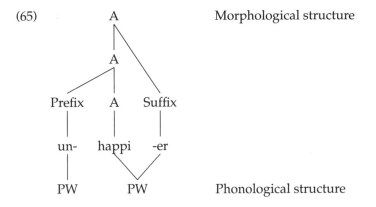

Phonological structure

The possibility of having phonological words smaller in size than lexical words provides a resolution to the bracketing paradoxes involving prefixes

Study the representation in (65). How come it is made up of two autonomous structures?

Phonological word status obviously carries certain implications, which must be fulfilled if the approach is to be substantiated. For instance, we know that phonological word status implies independent word stress. This prediction appears to be fulfilled in *un-*, which, on the one hand, clearly lies outside the stress domain of the main body of the lexical word *happier* (cf. *unháppy*, not **únhappy*), and, on the other, does appear to carry prominence of its own, in contrast to its synonym *in-*, which does not (cf. *ùnháppy* vs. *impóssible*).

Why does the putative stress of *un-* not undergo the rule of destressing in (20) of chapter 15? On the other hand, why does this stress never surface as primary?

Another prediction of the approach is that the *n* of *un-* will not syllabify with a following vowel in the stem, and this also seems correct, at least in slow speech: *un.able* seems a possible spontaneous pronunciation, whereas *in.active* does not.

Do you agree with our judgement?

Finally, Nasal Assimilation does not necessarily apply to the *n* of *un-*, although it does to the *n* of *in-*: *u[n]common* vs. *i[ŋ]competent*.

Many of the "bracketing paradoxes" of English and other languages can be resolved by the assumption that phonological domains are distinct from morphosemantic domains, but some problems remain

Again, do you agree? Check out your own pronunciation of these and similar words.

While many of the "bracketing paradoxes" of English and other languages may be resolved by the assumption that phonological domains are distinct from morphosemantic domains, some problems remain. For instance, in forms like *developmental, patentability, standardization*, and so on, a level-1 suffix (*-al* in *developmental*) is preceded by a level-2 suffix (*-ment*), contradicting the prediction of the affix ordering hypothesis, a keystone of Lexical Phonology. Notice in particular that *-ment* is non-cyclic, and *-al* is cyclic, as we know from the effects they have on the position of stress, among other things:

(66) [[[develop]$_c$ ment]$_{nc}$ al]$_c$

> Can you see any problem with the structure in (66)?

Paradoxes such as these led to the introduction of the LOOP in Lexical Phonology. The loop allows a form to be fed back into the *previous* level of derivation, in violation of the affix ordering hypothesis:

> The LOOP allows a form to be fed back into the *previous* level of derivation, in violation of the affix ordering hypothesis

> Why does the loop imply a relaxation of the affix ordering hypothesis?

(67) The loop:

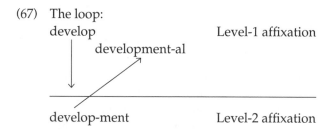

develop   Level-1 affixation

      development-al

develop-ment   Level-2 affixation

A reinterpretation of morphological constituency as a phonological domain will necessarily have -*mental* as a phonological word in *developmental*:

(68) (develop)$_{PW}$ (mental)$_{PW}$

As in the case of *unhappier* above, this phonological phrasing will not interfere with morphological constituency:

(69)   A   Morphological structure

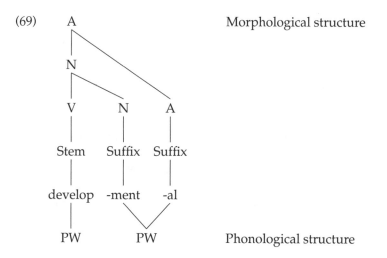

   N

 V   N   A

Stem   Suffix Suffix

develop -ment   -al

PW   PW   Phonological structure

In order to make -*ment* define a phonological word we must of course mark it as such in the lexicon, since we have said that phonological words are normally the result of a simple mapping from morphosyntactic words, and -*ment* is not a morphosyntactic word, but a suffix. In itself, this result is not outrageous, since we suggested a similar analysis for the prefix *un-* in English, also needed for a number of affixes in other languages. Some serious problems ensue, however. Consider first the fact that -*ment* systematically carries the main stress of *developméntal*. The problem is not how to get the stress on the *ment* of -*mental* (cf. the homophonous adjective *méntal*), but to have this stress as prominent over the stress in *devélop*: clearly, *developmental* would not constitute a word domain for End Stress [Right], since *(develop)*$_{PW}$ *(mental)*$_{PW}$ no longer makes up one phonological word. As a consequence, we would have to assume End Stress [Right] triggered by phrasal constituency, in the style of *time flies* in chapter 11 above; *developmental*, however, is clearly not a phrase, but, rather, a word, and we may have to stretch our conception of phrases quite a bit to fit it in. Even if we succeed, a serious problem remains. In particular, if -*ment* is a (lexical) phonological word, then it should also be so in *development*: *(develop)*$_{PW}$ *(ment)*$_{PW}$. Now, if *(ment)* is a phonological word here, then it should carry its own stress, as it does in *developmental*, and this stress ought to be prominent in the construction, again for the same reasons as in *developmental*, whatever these may be. The resulting stress contour, *developmént*, is, of course, incorrect, and the approach founders.

There are no doubt a number of ad hoc ways of repairing the damage (we could, for instance, stipulate that a monosyllabic suffix cannot surface as a phonological word, at least in English), but we shall not resort to these here. Instead, we will briefly refer to an alternative which does not make use of phonological constituency, but represents in effect a development of Lexical Phonology.

This alternative is simple in the extreme. All we have to do is take fully on board the fact that non-cyclic affixes do not necessarily occupy the outer morphological layer. We repeat the structure of *developmental* in (70):

(70) [[[develop]$_c$ ment]$_{nc}$ all]$_c$

Given this structure, the intermediate form *development* will be skipped by the cyclic stress rules of English, since cyclic rules can only apply in cyclic domains. The rules will, however, apply when the next cyclic layer, defined by -*al*, is reached, and the appropriate contour, *developméntal*, will be generated.

While this simple alternative does resolve the problems connected with *developmental* and similar forms, it obviously entails the official abandonment

We have to take fully on board the fact that non-cyclic affixes do not necessarily occupy the outer morphological layer of the affix ordering hypothesis, one of the foundation stones of Lexical Phonology.

C h a p t e r   S u m m a r y

In this chapter we showed large numbers of cases where suffixation fails to trigger the cyclic processes discussed in chapter 15 (vowel shortening and the relocation of main stress, which frequently falls outside the three-syllable window). All the cases alluded to involved a specific set of suffixes, all of which are ignored by these cyclic processes. This led to the observation that not only are rules designated to apply cyclically or non-cyclically, but there are also two classes of affix: those marked as "cyclic", whose affixation creates a domain for cyclic rule application, and those marked "non-cyclic", the affixation of which does not. We showed that some morphological operations seem to require the prior application of stress, and this insight led to the claim that, at the cyclic level, morphological operations and phonological processes are interleaved, each feeding on the other. The model which encapsulates this claim is known as "Lexical Phonology". The close affinity of the cyclic domains is expressed in the "Bracket Erasure Convention" which causes word-internal brackets to be erased at the end of each level, as a result of which no morphological information is available to non-cyclic processes. These processes affect the product of the cyclic block of rules. Confirmation of the interleaving of morphology and phonology seemed to be provided by the observation that the cyclic affixes tend to occur closer to the stem than the non-cyclic ones. We also showed that the properties of the two blocks of rules differ in a number of significant ways. Some of the early promise offered by the model of Lexical Phonology was, however, dashed by the occurrence of "ordering paradoxes", which do not lend themselves to resolution within the framework of the model. We made a number of suggestions for a solution to some of these cases, one of which was to treat phonological constituents (i.e. feet and syllables) as separate from phonological domains (mappings from morphological constituents, but not necessary identical to them). The largest of these domains is the phonological word, and, if we allow for mismatches between lexical and phonological words, we can explain some of the paradoxes earlier referred to by making the assumption that non-cyclic affixes can constitute separate phonological domains from the phonological word to which they are attached. Not all of the observed paradoxes were amenable to this solution, however, and we referred to a device known as the "loop", which allows for a form derived in the non-cyclic block to loop back into the cyclic block and be susceptible to rules applicable there. We showed that the word is not the only domain for the application of phonological rules, and offered definitions of the phonological phrase, the intonational phrase, and the phonological utterance. The bounds of the phonological phrase are largely determined by syntactic criteria, whereas the criteria for the determination of intonational phrases, which contain one or more phonological phrases, may be syntactic, semantic or even phonological in nature. A number of processes such as *r*-insertion and *t*-flapping are not constrained by such boundaries, since they are licensed by the phonological utterance, the largest phonological domain. Each phonological domain is made up of one or more phonological domains of the next smaller category, in compliance with the "Strict Layer Hypothesis".

Key Questions

1   What explanation can be advanced for violations of the two-mora restriction on rimes and of the three-syllable window?

2   What is the relationship between domains defined by affixes and the cyclic or non-cyclic status of rules?

3   List some cyclic and non-cyclic affixes.

4   What does infixation in English words tell us about the relationship between phonology and morphology?

5   Where does Bracket Erasure apply?

6   How do cyclic and non-cyclic affixes relate to their bases?

7   How does the Bracket Erasure Convention help to explain the contradictory behaviour of certain forms with regard to certain processes?

8   List some non-cyclic processes.

9   How are affixes ordered?

10   List the properties characteristic of rules applying in the cyclic and non-cyclic blocks.

11   Explain Structure Preservation.

12   How do we identify a Phonological Phrase? How does the Phonological Phrase relate to the syntactic phrase?

13   Name a phonological process whose application is confined to the Phonological Phrase.

14   What are the criteria for the delimitation of the Intonational Phrase?

15   Is the Intonational Phrase coextensive with any type of syntactic phrase?

16   Name a process of which the domain is the Phonological Utterance.

17   What does the Strict Layer Hypothesis state?

18   What are postlexical processes? Are they restricted in their properties as are lexical processes?

19   How is the Strict Layer Hypothesis violated by word-final coronals and word-initial *s*?

20   Suggest ways in which bracketing paradoxes can be resolved.

21   What is the loop?

F u r t h e r   P r a c t i c e

Dutch

The choice between the two denominal adjectival suffixes -*isch* and -*ief* in Dutch is not arbitrary. Examine the two sets of data in a. and b. and advance a hypothesis about what determines the choice of denominal suffix:

a. psychologíe   'psychology'   psychológisch   'psychological'
    hysteríe   'hysteria'   hystérisch   'hysterical'
    analogíe   'analogy'   analógisch   'analogical'
b. agréssie   'aggression'   agressíef   'aggressive'
    invéntie   'invention'   inventíef   'inventive'
    áctie   'action'   actíef   'active'

Do these data tell us anything about the relationship between morphology and phonology?

Maltese Arabic

In Maltese Arabic stress is either antepenultimate or penultimate, but the details are irrelevant to the present exercise. A further rule deletes an unstressed vowel in a word-internal open syllable. We illustrate the inter-action of these rules on the affixation of subject agreement in the paradigm of the verb *ḥataf* 'snatch' ("ḥ" stands for IPA [ħ], which represents a voiceless pharyngeal fricative)

a. /ḥataf-t/   [ḥtáft]   'I snatched'
    /ḥataf-na/   [ḥtáfna]   'we snatched'
    /ḥataf/   [ḥátaf]   'he snatched'
    /ḥataf-u/   [ḥátfu]   'she snatched'
    /ḥataf-it/   [ḥátfet]   'she snatched'

(i)   Show how this interaction of rules works in the examples in a.

Other morphemes, including object suffixes -*na* 'us', -*ik* 'you' (sg.), -*kum* 'you' (pl.) and -*ʃ* negative, can be added to the verb after the affixation of subject agreement, yielding examples such as:

b. [ḥàtáfna]   'he snatched us'
    [ḥàtáfʃ]   'he didn't snatch"
    [ḥàtfítkom]   'she snatched you' (pl.)
    [ḥátfek]   'he snatched you' (sg.)

(ii)   Assuming that there are two lexical levels involved, trace the derivations of the forms in b.

Polish

Consider the consonant clusters in word-initial position in Polish (the symbol [ć] stands for a prepalatal affricate and [ś] stands for a prepalatal fricative):

[fśc]iekly	'furious'	[bzd]ura	'nonsense'
[pʃtʃ]ola	'bee'	[fsp]anialy	'great'
[fst]yd	'shame'	[gʒb]iet	'back'
[lśn]ić	'shine'	[lgn]ǫć	'to stick'
[mdl]ić	'to feel seasick'	[mśc]ić się	'avenge'

(i)   Do these clusters present a problem for the Sonority Sequencing principle?
(ii)   If so, can the problem be resolved in the light of the discussion in section 15?
(iii) Assuming that Polish onsets (like English onsets) are maximally binary, say how the constraints on Polish onsets differ from those on English onsets.

Italian Raddoppiamento Sintattico

The Italian phenomenon known as Raddoppiamento Sintattico causes the lengthening of the word-initial consonant in the second in a sequence of two phonological words if the first word ends in a vowel bearing main stress. The process applies in the examples in a. but not those in b.

a.   Avrà [t:]rovato il pescecane   'He must have found the shark'
     La gabbia è [dʒ:]ià [k:]aduta   'The cage has already fallen'
     Perchè [k:]arlo non è venuto   'Why didn't Carlo come?'
     È appena passato con trè   'He has just passed by with
        [k:]ani   three dogs'
b.   Devi comprare delle mappe   'You must buy some very old
        di città [m]olto vecchie   city maps'
     La gabbia era dipinta di già   'The cage was already completely
        [k]ompletamente   painted'
     Che c'è un perchè [k]arlo lo sa   'Carlo knows that there is a reason'
     Ne aveva soltanto trè [d]i   'He had only three dachshunds'
        bassotti

Explain why RS occurs in a. but not in b.

French Liaison

The phenomenon of liaison occurring in French is illustrated in the following examples:

il est petit [ilepəti] 'he is small', *petit mec* [pətimɛk] 'small guy' vs. *petit enfant* [pətitãfã] 'small child'

In the last sentence, an otherwise latent word-final consonant (shown emboldened in the example) is attached to the initial vowel of the following word.

In the examples that follow, liaison occurs in a. (as marked by an under-scripted tie bar ‿) but not in b. (as indicated by double slashes //):

a. Ils sont‿arrivés   [ilsɔ̃tarive]   'They arrived'
    Des beaux‿italiens   [debozitaljẽ]   'Beautiful Italians'
    Ses anciens‿amis   [sezãsjẽzami]   'His former friends'
    Un savant‿anglais   [ẽsavãtãglɛ]   'A wise Englishman'
b. Ils sont arrivés // en retard   'They arrived late'
    Des maisons // italiennes   'Italian houses'
    Ses amis // anciens   'His ancient friends'
    Un savant // anglais   'An English scholar'

What is the domain in which liaison occurs?

Greek *s*-Voicing

In Greek *s* is voiced when it is followed by a voiced consonant, both inside words and across word boundaries, as the following examples illustrate: [kozmos] 'people', [θeliz na pas] 'Do you want to go?'. Consider the following examples and suggest what the domain for *s*-voicing is:

[o petroz ðen ine maθimenoz na troi axinuz me psomi]   'Petros is not used to eating sea urchins with bread'

[o anðras aftos, mu fenete, ine poli eksipnos]   'This man, it seems to me, is very bright'

[ekinos o anðras, martiz mu o θeos, ðen θa bi pote sto spiti mu]   'This man, God be my witness, will never enter my house'

CHAPTER SEVENTEEN

ASPECTS OF LEXICAL REPRESENTATION
UNDERSPECIFICATION, MARKEDNESS AND FEATURE GEOMETRY

Chapter Objectives

In this chapter you will learn about:
- How lexical underspecification can be called upon to explain underived forms apparently undergoing cyclic rules.
- Values predicted by universal principles.
- "Marked" and "unmarked" values on features.
- Unmarked values not being listed in the lexicon, but being supplied by redundancy rules.
- Theories of Underspecification, which hold that the fewer lexical features, the more highly valued the system.
- Problems with these theories.
- The organization of distinctive features into a hierarchical structure to reflect redundancy implications.
- The possibility that the binary notation contains a degree of redundancy.
- Eradicating such redundancies by means of monovalent features.

We now have a rich autosegmental structure of features, tones and timing slots or moras, augmented with syllables and metrical grids. We have shown a variety of processess applying on this structure in the appropriate phonological domains. For some of these processes, Turkish vowel harmony and Shona tone spread in particular, we assumed some of the feature specifications to be missing from the lexicon. In this chapter we explore further and formalize the lexical underspecification of features, with particular reference to the theories of Radical and Contrast-restricted Underspecification. The substance of underspecification is related to universal principles of markedness, by which certain feature values or combinations of feature values are preferred. The features themselves are organized in a geometry of feature dependencies, which has obvious repercussions for underspecification. Likewise, one of the two binary values of at least some features could in principle be redundant, and we examine some empirical evidence in this respect.

1 Effects of Strict Cyclicity

Let us consider the pairs in (1):

(1) a. gymnastics   b. gymnasium
         Caucasus   Caucasian
         Malthus   Malthusian
         fantasy   fantasia

The forms in (1a) and (1b) are obviously related, but they exhibit several phonological differences.

> Can you see what the phonological differences between (1a) and (1b) are?

Compare, for example, *Caucasus* with *Caucasian*. *Caucasus* has antepenultimate stress. Therefore, the *a* in the penult must be short underlyingly, as it is in the surface: if it were not lexically short, it would have attracted stress.

> Explain exactly how a long *a* in *Caucasus* would have attracted stress.

Moreover, the *s* that follows the *a* surfaces as voiceless: *Cauc*[əs]*us*. By contrast, in *Caucasian* the corresponding *a* is diphthongal in the surface, and the *s* voiced: *Cauc*[eɪz]*ian* (*Cauc*[eɪʒ]*ian* in many accents after palatalization of [z], as we will explain in section 11 below and in chapter 18). Similar observations apply to the other pairs in (1) (the [z] of *gymnasium* remains unpalatalized in all accents).

> Pause here and reassure yourself that you see all these patterns clearly.

We will discuss the mechanics of vowel lengthening in forms like those in (1b) in the next chapter, and will at this point focus exclusively on the alternation between voiceless and voiced *s*. Prerequisites for voicing in this set are the bimoraicity of the preceding vowel and the presence of a vocalic segment after the *s*, as we illustrate in (2):

(2) a. V:[z]V miser, magnesium, Pusey, cosy, posey, Moses, music
     b. V[s]V assembly, misogyny, pussy, russet, Russell, philosophy,
         potassium
     c. V:[s]C wastrel, pastry, maestro, Easter, acoustic, oestrogen

You will notice that, in order to voice, the *s* has to be preceded by a long
vowel or a diphthong and followed by a vowel. We formulate the rule of
s-Voicing in line with these facts in (3) (we omit the technical details of the
definition of *s* to keep matters simple):

> You may wish to provide the features defining *s* yourself, for
> practice.

(3) *s*-Voicing:

$$s \rightarrow [+voice] \: / \: [-cons] \: \underline{\quad} \: [-cons]$$

$$\mu \: \mu \qquad\qquad (\mu)$$

The forms in (4) look like straightforward exceptions to *s*-Voicing (the
spelling difference between *s* and *c* is irrelevant in the present context):

(4) basin, mason, isolate, Isocrates, isosceles, rhesus,
     Croesus, lucid, Lucy, license, recent, recess, decent

> Do the forms in (4) differ structurally from the ones in (1b)? How?

If you examine the forms in (4) more closely, you will notice an important
point of difference with their predecessors in (1b): in the forms in (1b), the
s occurs at the end of a morpheme, and the requisite following vowel in the
next morpheme (the suffix); by contrast, in the forms in (4) the *s* occurs in
the middle of a morpheme.

> Examine (4) and (1b) again to check on this.

The fact that there
are many more
exceptions
morpheme-
internally than
between mor-
phemes arouses
our suspicion that
there is something
in this distribu-
tional difference

We could of course dismiss this difference as irrelevant. On the other
hand, the fact that there are many more exceptions to *s*-Voicing morpheme-
internally than between morphemes arouses our suspicion that there is
something in this distributional difference. The rule can also fail to apply across

morphemes, as in *basic* or *facial* (with [ʃ] after palatalization, as we will explain in chapter 18), but the morpheme-internal cases are more numerous.

We will suggest that what is at work here is the Principle of Strict Cyclicity that we introduced in chapter 15, and now repeat in (5) as a reminder:

(5) Principle of Strict Cyclicity:
Structure-changing cyclic rules only apply in environments derived in that cycle, where "derived" = resulting from a morphological process, or, in some cases, from a phonological *change*

> In what way can the Principle of Strict Cyclicity account for failures to voice in (4)?

If *s*-Voicing is cyclic, it will systematically fail to apply in non-derived environments, such as those in (4) above. On the other hand, its failure to apply in some derived environments (*basic, facial*, etc.) can simply be attributed to the by now familiar fact that phonological rules (in particular, cyclic rules) can have lexical exceptions.

The failure of *s*-Voicing to apply in many non-derived environments is accounted for by declaring the rule cyclic

> Explain exactly what we mean by "lexical exceptions".

The cyclicity of *s*-Voicing is confirmed by the fact that it never applies in domains defined by suffixes that we know independently to be non-cyclic, even when its environment is met (remember that the spelling contrast *s* vs. *c* is inconsequential for our concerns):

The cyclicity of *s*-Voicing is confirmed by the fact that it never applies in domains defined by suffixes that we know independently to be non-cyclic

(6) mousy   placing   nicish   racist   racism
     pricy   splicing   loosish
     icy   voicing   sprucish
     juicy   sprucing
     saucy   piecing

> Remind yourself of other non-cyclic suffixes we introduced in the previous chapter. Why do we categorize all these suffixes as non-cyclic?

As we showed in chapter 16, cyclic rules may not apply in domains defined by non-cyclic affixes. Therefore, if *s*-Voicing is cyclic, its failure to apply in the forms in (6) will be entirely predictable.

2 Lexical Underspecification

In (2a) above, s-Voicing has apparently applied morpheme-internally, in contravention of the Principle of Strict Cyclicity in (5). We provide a few more such cases in (7):

(7)   raisin   reason
        season   Eisenhower
        poison   Susan
        laser   quasar
        Jesus   daisy
        Joseph   aphasia

The ensuing paradox poses an obvious challenge to the analysis we are proposing.

> Make sure you see the paradox brought on by the presence of [z] in (7) by stating it.

We shall get round this paradox through the introduction of underspecification in the lexical representations of the forms in (7). We made use of underspecification in our discussion of Turkish vowel harmony and Shona tone distribution, in chapters 6 and 14, respectively. In particular, we posited that the vowels of Turkish suffixes lack lexical information about their backness, and that Shona suffixes are lexically void of tonal information. In both cases, we obtained the surface representation by spreading the corresponding features from the root:

Apparent morpheme-internal applications of s-Voicing are accounted for through the postulation of underspecification in the corresponding lexical representations

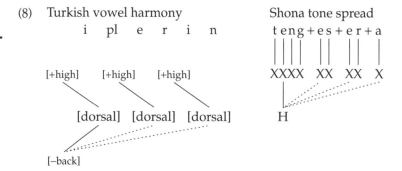

(8)   Turkish vowel harmony   Shona tone spread

We will now extend and generalize this approach in the context of a fully fledged THEORY OF UNDERSPECIFICATION, which we shall introduce.

Suppose that in forms like *raisin* in (7) the *s* contains no lexical information about [±voice], whereas in forms like *basin* in (4) it is marked [−voice]. What follows from this? Quite simply, our cyclic *s*-Voicing rule in (3) will be prevented from applying in *basin* and the like, as we already explained: if it did apply, it would infringe the Principle of Strict Cyclicity in (5), by changing structure in an environment which has not been derived in that cycle, indeed has not been derived at all.

> Check that you understand why *s*-Voicing will not apply to *basin* under our analysis.

By contrast, the application of *s*-Voicing in *raisin* and the like will not incur any such infringement of Strict Cyclicity, because, in the absence of lexical information for [±voice], *s*-Voicing will be creating structure rather than changing it. Creating structure is, of course, quite compatible with the Principle of Strict Cyclicity (PSC).

Creating structure is quite compatible with the Principle of Strict Cyclicity

> What exactly is the difference between the derivations of *raisin* and *basin*?

We illustrate the difference between *basin* and *raisin* in (9), where we italicize the lexical representation of *s* as an informal graphic reminder that its feature [±voice] is autosegmentalized:

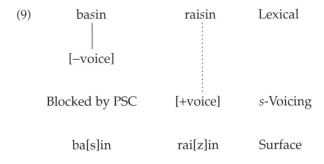

(9)   basin   raisin   Lexical

       [−voice]

       Blocked by PSC   [+voice]   *s*-Voicing

       ba[s]in   rai[z]in   Surface

> Why exactly does the Principle of Strict Cyclicity block *s*-Voicing in *basin*?

You can see that the value of [±voice] is missing from the lexical representation of *raisin*. This value is not supplied by spreading a neighbouring feature, as was the case in Turkish and Shona. Instead, it is supplied by the independently motivated rule of *s*-Voicing in (3) above. This approach thus achieves maximal simplicity: a single rule (naturally encapsulating a single process) accounts both for such alternations as in *Cauca*[s]*us* ~ *Cauca*[z]*ian* in (1), and for the phonotactic skewness of the two segments in the given environment, manifested in the numerical imbalance between forms like *ba*[s]*in* in (4), incompatible with *s*-Voicing, and forms like *rai*[z]*in* in (7), compatible with it.

> Explain what the difference is between phonological alternation and lexical distribution.

Clearly, the simplest situation is the one where the same rule is active both to change structure in derived environments and to supply structure in forms lexically empty for the relevant feature(s). Exceptions to rule application are possible, as we know, although by their very nature we expect them to be few. On the other hand, it is not unnatural for lexical items to be fully specified. Therefore, we shall not be unduly surprised at the existence of a substantial number of lexical forms contradicting a rule or process morpheme-internally, even though the forms compatible with it are of course still preferred, as they are formally simpler.

> Exceptions to rule application are possible, although by their very nature we expect them to be few. On the other hand, it is not unnatural for lexical items to be fully specified

> Explain in what way it is more natural for cyclic rules to be contradicted in underived forms than in derived forms.

3 Feature Transparency as Underspecification

Lexical underspecification has interesting consequences that go beyond phonotactics. We have already brought underspecification into our account of Turkish and Shona assimilation (see (8) above). However, in both these cases we could have assumed full lexical representations and a structure-changing assimilation rule: while the approach would have been more complex, it is technically feasible, because the assimilations in question take place across morphemes, and therefore they cannot be blocked by the Principle of Strict Cyclicity.

> Why exactly can't the Turkish and Shona cases be blocked by the Principle of Strict Cyclicity?

The case from Russian we will present next does require lexical underspecification.

In Russian, adjacent obstruents have the same value for voice, whether the cluster is word-internal or straddles two words. The occurrence of the alternations on the edge of morphemes leads to a construal of the phenomenon as right-to-left assimilation, as we illustrate in (10) and (11):

(10) a.   gorod-a   'town' (gen.)   b.   goro[t-k]-a   'little town'
           noʒ-a   'knife' (gen.)   no[ʃ-k]-a   'little knife'
           gotov-a   'ready' (fem.)   goto[f-k]-a   'preparation'
           arab-a   'Arab' (gen.)   ara[p-k]-a   'Arab' (fem. nom.)

(11) a.   ot ozera   'from a lake'   b.   ----------
           ot strasti   'from passion'   o[d]banka   'from a bank'
           ot Pragi   'from Prague'   o[d]grexa   'from a sin'
           ot ptits   'from birds'   o[d]bdenija   'from a vigil'

           ----------   bez ozera   'without a lake'
           be[s]strasti   'without passion'   bez banka   'without a bank'
           be[s]Pragi   'without Prague'   bez grexa   'without a sin'
           be[s]ptits   'without birds'   bez bdenija   'without a vigil'

> Why are we restricting assimilation as such to one column, in each of the cases of (11)?

The data in (12) show that sonorant consonants neither trigger (cf. (12a)), undergo (cf. (12b)) nor block (cf. (12c)) voice assimilation:

(12) a.   pesna   'song'   (NB not *pezna)
           tri   'three'   (NB not *dri)
           ot nravov   'from morals'   (NB not *od nravov)

      b.   on pojet   'he sings'   (*o[n̥] pojet]
           Mtsensk   'Mcensk'   (*[m̥]tsensk)
           mstitel'nost   'vindictiveness'   (*[m̥]stitel'nost)

      c.   o[d]mgli   'from fog'   (*ot mgli: cf. ot ozera in (11))
           o[d]lguni   'from the liar'   (*ot lguni)

> Go through these forms and check that you see the points we are making.

The data considered lead to the formulation of the Voice Assimilation rule in (13):

(13)   Russian Voice Assimilation:
       [−son] . . . [−son]

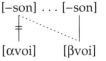

       [αvoi]   [βvoi]
       Condition: ". . ." does not include a syllable peak

In chapter 3 we said that sonorant consonants are normally voiced, and we would expect this also to be the case in Russian. If sonorant consonants are voiced, the Voice Assimilation rule in (13) ought to be blocked by intervening sonorant consonants.

> Why should Voice Assimilation (13) be blocked by intervening sonorant consonants?

In particular, the application of Voice Assimilation across sonorant consonants ought to cause association lines to be crossed, in contravention of No-Crossing of Lines, which we know is one of the basic principles of autosegmental phonology (see (17.3) in chapter 14 above):

> Before you read on, show how line crossing would occur.

(14)   −s +s −s   ("s" = sonorant)   i/z/ Mtsenska

       +v +v −v   ("v" = voice)   i[s] Mtsenska 'out of Mcensk'

In order for lines not to cross and the fricative in *iz* 'out of' still to devoice, we would obviously have to devoice the sonorant first, and only then spread [−voice] to the preceding obstruent:

(15)   −s +s −s   −s +s −s   i/z/ Mtsenska

       +v +v −v   →   +v   −v   i[s] *[m̥]tsenska

> Why is the output of (15) problematic?

The problem with the output of (15) is that it contains a voiceless sonorant, contrary to the universal tendency of sonorants to be voiced. The solution we shall now propose involves lexical underspecification.

> Can you anticipate this solution?

All we have to do in order to get both the facts and the representation right is to assume that sonorants do not have a value for voice specified in the lexicon. The TRANSPARENCY of Russian sonorants with respect to assimilation (that is, the fact that they behave as if they were not there) now follows automatically – they are indeed not there as far as [±voice] is concerned:

The transparency of Russian sonorants with respect to voice assimilation is explained if we assume that sonorants do not have a value for voice specified in the lexicon

(16)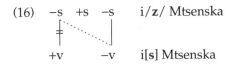

         −s   +s   −s   i/**z**/ Mtsenska

         +v   −v   i[**s**] Mtsenska

> Why does −v associate with −s, skipping +s, in (16)?

The representation in (16) makes clear why Russian sonorants cannot play any role in voicing assimilation: they are lexically unspecified for [±voice], and remain so throughout the derivation.

4 Underspecification and Markedness

We have just shown that Russian sonorants need to be underspecified for voice in the lexicon and throughout the derivation. In surface representation, however, we want them to be voiced, in line with most of the world's languages. The discussion in the previous section shows clearly that the surface voicing of sonorants cannot have originated in assimilation: so, where does it come from?

In chapter 14 we saw that, when there is no underlying tone to associate with a particular vowel in Shona and Tiv, a DEFAULT tone is supplied to fill in the gap.

> Explain to yourself the notion of "default" before you read on.

Similarly, it will be reasonable to provide [+voice] to lexically unspecified sonorants, as formulated in (17):

(17)   Sonorant Voicing Default (provisional formulation):
[+sonorant] → [+voice]

(17) does capture the essence of the process of sonorant voicing, but the formalization is ambiguous as between a REDUNDANCY RULE, which can only fill in a gap in the input representation, and an ordinary rule, which *changes* something in the input representation. The alternative formalism in (18) conveniently keeps redundancy rules visually separate from rules that change structure:

(18)   Sonorant Voicing Default (final formulation):

$$[\ ] \rightarrow [+\text{voice}] \ / \left[\begin{array}{c} \underline{} \\ +\text{sonorant} \end{array} \right]$$

The empty input matrix in (18) appropriately points to the lack of specification for [±voice], and therefore to the structure-building nature of the rule.

> Do you agree with our choice of formalism for redundancy rules?

Rule (18) gives obvious expression to the universal tendency of sonorants to be voiced. There are many other universal tendencies affecting many of the sounds of language. For instance, it was observed by Roman Jakobson, whom we have already cited in chapters 8 and 9, that the first vowel most children produce is [a]. Significantly, [a] is also the most common vowel in the inventories of the world's languages, and one of the most frequent vowels in lexical items. These facts suggest that [a] is the most UNMARKED vowel in language (equivalently, the least MARKED). For consonants, [p] and [t] are most unmarked, hence the frequency of such expressions as *papa* and *tata* in child language the world over (also *baba* and *dada*, with voicing, and *mama* and *nana*, with nasalization).

> Do our statements of the unmarkedness of [a], [p] and [t] agree with your own experience? Come up with a couple more words from (very early) child speech and see how these sounds fit in.

The observation
that the sounds
of language
are ranked on
grounds of
naturalness has
given rise to the
THEORY OF
MARKEDNESS

The observation that the sounds of language are ranked on grounds of naturalness has given rise to the THEORY OF MARKEDNESS. The term "markedness" means that some feature combinations, whether paradigmatic (that is, within the same segment) or syntagmatic (that is, across segments), are less natural than others, and therefore less likely to crop up in the world's languages. The combination [+sonorant, −voice], for instance, is marked paradigmatically, and the sequences [coronal] + [labial] or [coronal] + [dorsal] are marked syntagmatically.

> Say why each of the configurations we have just mentioned is marked.

The set of all natural, or unmarked, combinations of features makes up the NATURAL PHONOLOGY of language, that is, the phonology that is spontaneously present in children in the absence of marked input from the language of their environment.

> Do you understand what we are saying? From this perspective, can ordinary languages be considered phonologically deviant? Why?

The set of all natural, or UNMARKED, combinations of features makes up the NATURAL PHONOLOGY of language

We now provide a selection of the main universal MARKEDNESS STATEMENTS affecting segments paradigmatically. We formulate these statements as FILTERS or CONSTRAINTS prohibiting a particular feature or combination of features:

(19) Some markedness statements:
  I   Vowels:
    a. *[+high, +low]   (= Vowels cannot be high and low at the same time)
    b. *[−high, −low]   (= Vowels cannot be non-high and non-low at the same time)
    c. *[+low, −back]   (= Vowels cannot be low and front at the same time)
    d. *[+low, +round]   (= Vowels cannot be low and round at the same time)
    e. *[αround, −αback, −low] (= non-low vowels cannot have opposite values for roundness and backness)
    f. *[αATR, αlow]   (= Vowels cannot have the same value for lowness and ATRness)

> Read these constraints several times, thinking of examples, to ensure that you understand them and familiarize yourself with them.

II   Consonants:

g.	*[dorsal]$_P$	(= Consonants cannot be dorsal)
h.	*[labial]$_P$	(= Consonants cannot be labial)
i.	*[−anterior]	(= Consonants cannot be non-anterior)
j.	*[+distributed]	(= Consonants cannot be distributed)
k.	*[+lateral]	(= Consonants cannot be lateral)
l.	*[+round]	(= Consonants cannot be round)
m.	*[+continuant]	(= Consonants cannot be continuant)
n.	*[αcontinuant, −αstrident]	(= Consonants cannot have opposite values for continuancy and stridency)

> Again, read these constraints several times, thinking of examples to ensure understanding and familiarity.

III   Common to vowels and consonants:

o.	*[αconsonantal, αsonorant]	(= The values for consonantality and sonorancy cannot agree)
p.	*[αsonorant, −αvoice]	(= The values for sonorancy and voice cannot disagree)
q.	*[+nasal]	(= Segments cannot be nasal)
r.	*[+nasal, −sonorant]	(= Nasals cannot be obstruent)

> Once more, read these constraints several times, thinking of examples.

Each markedness constraint expresses a (usually relative) universal prohibition on feature occurrence or co-occurrence

---

Each of the constraints in (19) expresses a universal prohibition on feature occurrence or co-occurrence.

> What exactly does "universal prohibition on feature (co)occurrence" mean?

Most of the prohibitions in (19) are, however, relative: they only express a preferred tendency which individual languages respect to a greater or lesser extent, depending on their degree of markedness. Indeed, only the prohibitions in (19a) and (19r) are assumed to be inviolable, as a matter of sheer physics.

> Why are the prohibitions in (19a) and (19r) a matter of sheer physics?

The rule of Sonorant Voicing Default in (18), which we said above is ultimately responsible for the underspecification of the feature [±voice] in the underlying representation of Russian sonorants, is obviously related to the markedness statement (19p), according to which the values for sonorancy and voice cannot disagree: the implicational relation [+sonorant] → [+voice] that drives the default rule in (18) follows directly from constraint (19p).

> Justify the claim that rule (18) follows from statement (19p).

Indeed, each of the constraints in (19) automatically gives rise to one or more implicational statements, in accordance with the laws of logic. In particular, the logical expression ~[A & B] ("not 'A and B'") can readily be developed into A → ~B ("if A, then not B") and B → ~A ("if B, then not A").

> Make sure you understand these algebraic expressions. Then develop at least one constraint from each of the three groups in (19) into an implicational statement.

Each markedness constraint automatically gives rise to one or more implicational statements, in accordance with the laws of logic

To paraphrase from ordinary life, if we say that it cannot be day and night (simultaneously), we are effectively saying that if it is day, then it is not night, and if it is night, then it is not day. The same relations exist in the more abstract realm of distinctive features, as we have already seen in connection with sonorant voicing default, and as we will have the occasion to explore further in the next section.

5 The Theory of Radical Underspecification

While the idea of underspecification and the motivation behind it are fairly straightforward, its actual formal implementation has been an object of debate in the literature, and to a large extent the matter remains unsettled. Here we shall limit ourselves to a brief survey of the two main positions.

Suppose we take seriously the idea that economy is paramount in the evaluation of alternative phonological descriptions. This will mean that the simpler the description (that is, the fewer elements it contains), the more highly valued it will be. This perspective, therefore, validates our early proposal to leave English [z] lexically underspecified for voice in environments that match the *s*-Voicing rule: this saves on [+voice] entries, even allowing for "exceptions", which will be lexically encoded as [–voice], as we explained.

> **What exactly is the strategy we are proposing?**

If we take the idea of economy to its limit, we will want to save as many lexical features as is compatible with the differentiation of lexical entries. Obviously, we will have to draw the economy line at a point before the differences between lexemes are lost: in the extreme case, a lexical inventory with no feature specifications at all will fail to do the very job for which it is intended, namely, the differentiation of lexical entries.

> **Explain why a balance needs to be struck between lexical economy and lexical differentiation.**

The theory of RADICAL UNDER-SPECIFICATION takes the idea of lexical economy to its limit: we will want to save as many lexical features as is compatible with the differentiation of lexical entries

The theory of RADICAL UNDERSPECIFICATION takes this programme fully on board. We will present this theory through a hypothetical example: hypothetical examples have the advantage of simplicity relative to their real-world counterparts.

Suppose a language has the vowel inventory /i, e, a, o, u/, which we know is not at all unusual among the languages of the world. The full specification of these vowels requires information on the values they take for the features [±high], [±low], [±back], [±round] and [±ATR], as represented in the table in (20):

(20)

	i	e	a	o	u
High	+	–	–	–	+
Low	–	–	+	–	–
Back	–	–	+	+	+
Round	–	–	–	+	+
ATR	+	+	–	+	+

The universal markedness statements in (19) above allow us to cut down the amount of information in this table, as in (21):

(21)

	i	e	a	o	u
High	+	−		−	+
Low		−	+	−	
Back	−	−		+	+
Round					
ATR					

> Figure out on what basis the simplifications in (21) have been carried out.

The reason the simplifications in (21) are possible is that the empty cells can eventually be filled in by the effect of the implicational statements in (22), which are directly derived from the corresponding constraints in (19):

(22)   A set of default rules for vowels:

   a. $[\;] \rightarrow [-\text{high}] \;/\; \left[\underline{\quad\quad}\atop{+\text{low}}\right]$ $[\;] \rightarrow [-\text{low}] \;/\; \left[\underline{\quad\quad}\atop{+\text{high}}\right]$ (from (19a))

   c. $[\;] \rightarrow [+\text{back}] \;/\; \left[\underline{\quad\quad}\atop{+\text{low}}\right]$ (from (19c))

   d. $[\;] \rightarrow [-\text{round}] \;/\; \left[\underline{\quad\quad}\atop{+\text{low}}\right]$ (from (19d))

   e. $[\;] \rightarrow [\alpha\text{round}] \;/\; \left[\underline{\quad\quad}\atop{\alpha\text{back}\atop{-\text{low}}}\right]$ (from (19e))

   f. $[\;] \rightarrow [\alpha\text{ATR}] \;/\; \left[\underline{\quad\quad}\atop{-\alpha\text{low}}\right]$ (from (19f))

> Refer back to (19) to trace back each of the sources of the statements in (22), making sure you see the respective connections.

Constraint (19b), which disfavours mid vowels, is obviously not operative in this language, which does have /e/ and /o/. Notice, importantly, that the default rules in (22) incur no cost, since we are assuming that the markedness statements they interpret are part of universal grammar. The end result is, therefore, a considerable simplification of the lexical representation of all the vowels, as (21) attests.

> Are you clear that the rules in (22) simplify the vowels in (20)?

Radical Underspecification does not stop here in its endeavour to rid lexical representations of unnecessary clutter. In order to meet this goal fully, an imaginative step is taken next. Suppose that we take *all* feature values out of one of the vowels, say, /i/, for the sake of argument. The new, further simplified table will be as in (23):

	i	e	a	o	u
High		−		−	+
Low		−	+	−	
Back		−		+	+
Round					
ATR					

(23)

> Do you see what we have done in (23)? Explain it.

Following the logic of the strategy, we will have to admit that table (23) still contains too much information. Specifically, if the values [+high], [−low], [−back], [−round], and [−ATR] have been completely eliminated from the /i/ column on grounds of redundancy, logic dictates that they are also redundant everywhere else. We give the totally redundancy-free representation in (24), where, crucially, all the segments are still kept apart, since each pair is differentiated by the value of at least one of the features:

(24)

	i	e	a	o	u
High		−		−	
Low			+		
Back			+	+	
Round					
ATR					

> Again, can you see what we have done? Explain exactly how each pair of features is kept apart in (24).

Each feature value that is missing from the maximally underspecified lexical segment automatically gives rise to a COMPLEMENT RULE that eventually supplies the missing feature value

The underspecified entries in (24) correspond of course to lexical representation. At the surface, however, we are assuming that all the features need to be specified to enable segments to be realized phonetically. How can this be achieved if (24) contains a number of blanks? The answer is that each feature value that is missing from the maximally underspecified segment (here /i/) automatically gives rise to a COMPLEMENT RULE that eventually supplies the missing feature:

(25) Complement rules for maximally underspecified /i/:

[ ] → [+high]
[ ] → [–low]
[ ] → [–back]
[ ] → [–round]
[ ] → [+ATR]

> Explain how the complement rules in (25) are derived from the table in (24).

The application of the complement rules in (25) and the default rules in (22) will ensure that all the feature values are represented in the surface: the surface values will in fact be identical to the values in the table in (20) above.

> Explain how the application of the rules in (22) and (25) derives the feature values in (20).

Two questions remain outstanding. One concerns the timing of the application of redundancy rules, and we will provide the answer in the next section. The second question concerns the criterion for the selection of one segment as fully underspecified in the lexicon. In our present example, we simply chose /i/ at random, but clearly a principled criterion is required.

The solution provided by Radical Underspecification is grounded in one specific empirical fact: in many (perhaps all) languages, one of the segments in each major class behaves asymmetrically, in that it alone systematically appears in contexts of epenthesis, or in that it alone triggers, fails to trigger, or is pervasive in, certain rules. For example, in a vowel system like the one we have been discussing (similar in fact to the system of Japanese), [i] will systematically turn up as the epenthetic vowel, will be transparent to harmony, and so on.

In many (perhaps all) languages, one of the segments in each major class behaves asymmetrically: its selection as maximally underspecified follows automatically

> Explain why such asymmetries should turn up.

Among consonants, coronals have been found to exhibit such asymmetries in many languages, confirming the universal unmarked status given to them in (19).

> In what way does (19) give an unmarked status to coronals? Go back and check.

Once one segment in the relevant class singles itself out by such skewed behaviour, its selection as maximally underspecified follows automatically, both as a matter of theory-internal congruence and on account of the accuracy of the empirical predictions made by the model, in particular with regard to transparency or invisibility.

> Explain in your own words why the selection of the skewed segment as underspecified is required by the internal logic of the theory of Radical Underspecification. In what way does the model successfully account for transparency?

6 Problems for Radical Underspecification

There are a number of problems with Radical Underspecification

The data in (26), from the Australian aboriginal language Gooniyandi, prove problematic for the Radical Underspecification approach:

(26) a. duwu ~ ɖuwu   'cave'
          laɲgija ~ ḷaɲgija   'midday'

      b. ɖiṛipindi (*diṛipindi) 'he entered'
          dili (*ɖili)   'flame, light'

> What is notable about the pattern in (26a)?

(26a) shows that word-initial coronals are freely realized as [+anterior] ([d], [l]) or [−anterior] [ɖ], [ḷ]).

> What is notable about the pattern in (26b)?

(26b) shows that such free variation is suspended when the word-initial coronal is followed by another coronal in the same word – this second coronal transmits its value for [±anterior] to the word-initial coronal by assimilation:

(27)

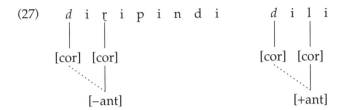

In (27) you can see that word-initial coronals are indeed lexically unspecified for [±anterior]. In the absence of a [±anterior] segment medially in the same word, such lack of specification gives rise to the phonetic fluctuation illustrated in (26a) – this obviously means that the markedness statement (19i) does not apply in Gooniyandi, and therefore that Gooniyandi lacks a default rule supplying a value for the feature [±anterior].

> Pause here and check that you understand the behaviour of Gooniyandi word-initial coronals, and how (19i) is suspended in this case.

Word-medially, no such fluctuation between anterior and non-anterior coronals exists. Indeed, we are seeing that the lexical [±anterior] value of Gooniyandi word-medial coronals is transmitted to their unspecified word-initial counterparts. The conclusion is obvious: Gooniyandi word-medial coronals are fully specified in the lexicon.

> Explain why we must assume that word-medial coronals are fully specified underlyingly in Gooniyandi.

This result contradicts the prediction of Radical Underspecification that one of the two complementary values ([+anterior] or [−anterior]) will be lexically empty, and subsequently filled by the corresponding complement rule, or by a default rule along the lines of (28), which interprets the markedness statement in (19i):

(28) $[\ ] \rightarrow [+\text{anterior}]/\begin{bmatrix} \underline{\qquad} \\ \text{coronal} \end{bmatrix}$

> How does (28) interpret (19i)? Why should one of the values of [±anterior] be absent from the lexicon?

There are other problems with Radical Underspecification. The default rule in (18), repeated now as (29), was pivotal in the analysis of the Russian voice assimilation process in section 3:

(29) $[\ ] \rightarrow [+\text{voice}] / \left[\begin{array}{c} \underline{\hspace{3cm}} \\ +\text{sonorant} \end{array} \right]$

We saw then that the existence of this rule allows sonorants to be lexically unspecified for [±voice], thereby failing to play a role in the process of regressive voice assimilation that affects obstruents. Crucially, however, in order for this to be so, we need to stipulate that the Russian rule of Voice Assimilation applies before the default rule in (29).

> Remind yourself why we need Voice Assimilation to precede (29).

This result is unsatisfactory for two reasons. First, it is conceptually undesirable to subject default rules, inspired in universal markedness statements, to language-specific ordering.

> Any suggestion as to why it is undesirable to order default rules extrinsically?

The Redundancy Rule Ordering Constraint predicts the ordering of a redundancy rule immediately before the first (ordinary) rule that refers to the output of the redundancy rule

---

Second, ordering Voice Assimilation before (29) is incompatible with the REDUNDANCY RULE ORDERING CONSTRAINT in (30). The Redundancy Rule Ordering Constraint is a universal principle of Radical Underspecification that predicts the ordering of redundancy rules, default rules included:

(30)   Redundancy Rule Ordering Constraint:
       A redundancy rule applies immediately before the first (ordinary) rule that refers to the output of the redundancy rule

> Say why ordering Voice Assimilation before the default rule in (29) is incompatible with the Redundancy Rule Ordering Constraint.

The ordering of Russian Voice Assimilation before (29) is incompatible with the Redundancy Rule Ordering Constraint in (30), because the Voice Assimilation rule in (13) above makes reference to [±voice], and therefore by the Redundancy Rule Ordering Constraint the redundancy rule in (29) must apply first. However, if (29) applies before Voice Assimilation (13), the account of assimilation we proposed above collapses:

> Before reading on, try and guess why applying voice default before voice assimilation subverts the analysis.

(31)   −s   +s   −s   i/**z**/ Mtsenska
       | | |
       +v   +v   −v   i*[**z**] Mtsenska

As shown in (31), the value [+voice] of /m/ now intervenes between the source and the putative target of Voice Assimilation, and consequently the process gets blocked (cf. also (15) above).

> Say exactly how Voice Assimilation gets blocked in (31).

Note that the motivation for the Redundancy Rule Ordering Constraint is overall very strong in the general context of Radical Underspecification Theory. In particular, the Redundancy Rule Ordering Constraint is needed to preserve feature binarity at the point where structure-changing rules apply: in the absence of the Redundancy Rule Ordering Constraint, feature binarity would be jeopardized by the use of underspecification, which effectively makes available a third value for features, [0F], beyond the two binary values [+F] and [−F] (the full demonstration of this point is rather technical, and best side-stepped in the present context).

The Redundancy Rule Ordering Constraint is needed to preserve feature binarity at the point where structure-changing rules apply

> See if you can explain why [0F] could be construed as a third feature value (we realize your task will not be easy, in the absence of the full argument in the text, but you can still usefully have a go at it).

A further problem area for Radical Underspecification concerns the identification of the maximally underspecified segment with the epenthetic segment. First, non-epenthetic null segments do exist: segments present in lexical representation (and thus not epenthetic) but still underspecified.

Explain the difference between null segments and epenthetic segments.

Indeed, we have seen that complete underspecification of one segment per class is basic to the Radical Underspecification machinery.

The mutual independence of the pattern of underlying underspecification and the choice of epenthetic segment is not only logical, but also backed by fact.

Do you need reminding of the difference between logical and empirical arguments?

For instance, in Basque (a non-Indo-European language of the corner of the Bay of Biscay) the genitive indefinite plural suffix is made up of an unspecified vowel followed by *n*: *-Vn*. We can reasonably assume that the quality of this vowel is unspecified because it is filled in by spreading from the adjacent vowel: *mendi* 'mountain' gives *mendiin* 'of mountains', *aśto* 'donkey' gives *aśtoon*, and so on. At the same time, Basque has an epenthetic vowel *e*, manifested in such forms as *giśonek* 'a man', from *giśon* 'man' + *k* (indefinite suffix): compare *mendik* 'a mountain', *aśtok* 'a donkey', etc., with no vowel. Clearly, this epenthetic *e* is distinct from the maximally underspecified vowel, the unspecified vowel of *-Vn*. Similarly, in Mohawk (a native language of North America), the epenthetic vowel *i* is distinct from its maximally unspecified vowel [ʌ̃], manifestly asymmetric with the remainder of the inventory /i, e, a, o, u/. And so on.

Next, some languages have more than one epenthetic segment in any one sound class: Hindi, for instance, the main language of India, has two epenthetic vowels: **i** before **s + obstruent** clusters, and schwa elsewhere.

Explain how having two epenthetic vowels creates a problem for Radical Underspecification.

Finally, in some languages one and the same surface segment can originate as lexically specified or as lexically underspecified, as attested by the behaviour of the segment. This is the case, for instance, with the Basque *e*: the *e* in *giśonek* is epenthetic, as we have just seen, but the *e* of the genitive plural definite *-en* is lexical. In particular, the *e* of *-en* triggers raising in a preceding vowel (*aśto* + *en* = *aśtuen* 'of the donkeys'), as do other vowels (*aśto* + *a* = *aśtua* 'donkey' (abs. sg.); *aśto* + *ok* = *aśtuok* 'donkey' (abs. pl. prox.)): if so, the *e* of *-en* cannot be underspecified.

> How can a segment be both lexically specified and underspecified? Isn't this a contradiction?

7 Contrast-Restricted Underspecification

In the face of all the difficulties we have just mentioned, it is obviously well worth exploring an alternative formalization of underspecification. One such alternative is based on the tenet that only features that implement lexical contrasts have both their values lexically specified in the relevant environment. For instance, in the Gooniyandi case discussed above, [±anterior] is lexically contrastive word-medially, and consequently it would need to be fully specified in this position. This prediction agrees with the facts, as we saw.

CONTRAST-RESTRICTED UNDERSPECIFICA-TION is based on the tenet that only features that implement lexical contrasts have both their values lexically specified in the relevant environment

> Explain the Gooniyandi pattern in your own words.

Similarly, [±voice] is lexically contrastive in Russian obstruents, but not in sonorants. Therefore, Russian sonorants can be left underspecified in the lexicon, but not so obstruents, again in agreement with the facts.

> Explain how the Russian situation fits in with the basic tenet of the underspecification alternative we are presenting.

The specification of both values of the same feature in the same environment undermines the basic tenet of Radical Underspecification that attainment of lexical economy is paramount.

> How exactly is the basic tenet of Radical Underspecification undermined by allowing both values of the same feature in the same environment?

In particular, while still favouring lexical economy (the values of features which are not contractive in the lexicon are still left underspecified, and filled in by the familiar default rules derived from the markedness statements), the alternative approach we are presenting gives priority to the explicit expression of lexical contrast over the attainment of radical lexical economy, supposedly on empirical grounds. This alternative approach to underspecification can transparently be referred to as CONTRAST-RESTRICTED UNDERSPECIFICATION, where the expression "contrast-restricted" must be interpreted as "restricted *by* contrast" – crucially, not "restricted *to* contrast", as the more common label CONTRASTIVE UNDERSPECIFICATION paradoxically appears to suggest. We spell out the basic principle of Contrast-restricted Underspecification in (32):

(32)   Contrast-Restricted Underspecification:
       Feature values are left unspecified in the lexicon if they are predictable from the pattern of distributional neutralization in the language

In Contrast-Restricted Underspecification feature values are left unspecified in the lexicon if they are predictable from the pattern of distributional neutralization in the language

> Study this definition until you are satisfied that you understand it fully.

We will see below that Contrast-restricted Underspecification is not empirically problem-free either. Before going into this matter, however, we need to be fully conversant with the way distinctive features are organized, and accordingly we turn to this matter in the next section.

8 Feature Dependencies

In chapter 4 we saw that the features [±distributed] and [±anterior] subclassify sounds which are [coronal] (that is, articulated with the blade of the tongue). It follows as a matter of logic that the two features in question will simply be absent from sounds which are exclusively [labial] or [dorsal].

> Why is it a matter of logic that [±distributed] and [±anterior] are irrelevant to labials and dorsals?

Similarly, the feature [±round] is restricted to [labial] sounds, and does not occur with sounds which are exclusively [coronal] or [dorsal]. Finally, [±high], [±low] and [±back] are restricted to [dorsal] segments, and will not turn up with sounds which are exclusively [labial] or [coronal].

> Why have we qualified the statements above with "exclusively"?

As we have been hinting, all these restrictions derive from the fact that the binary features in question introduce finer divisions in the class defined by the feature to which they are circumscribed: they define subsets within a set.

Dependent features define subsets within a set

> What exactly does "define subsets within a set" mean?

In chapters 4 and 6, we formalized the situation we are describing by means of feature dependencies:

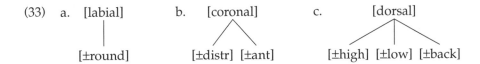

(33) a. [labial]   b. [coronal]   c.   [dorsal]

      [±round]   [±distr] [±ant]   [±high] [±low] [±back]

The linking lines in (33) are genuine autosegmental lines, denoting the simultaneous timing of the individual distinctive features.

> Do you see why the lines in (33) are lines of autosegmental association?

As we pointed out in chapter 4 and more than once since, this autosegmental formalism allows a very simple formalization of assimilation and dissimilation processes.

> Remind yourself of at least one such process, and of its mechanics.

9 Feature Geometry

There are other dependencies among features beyond the ones we have mentioned. Indeed, the full set of features makes up a web of dependencies, which we formalize in (34). This web of feature dependencies is conventionally referred to as FEATURE GEOMETRY:

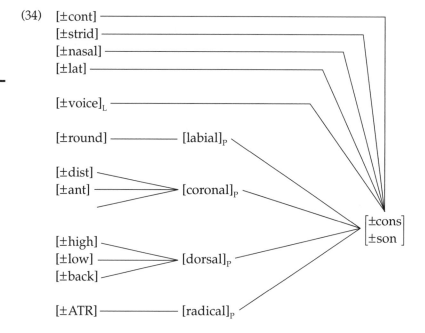

(34)

You can see in (34) that the root of the feature tree (rotated by 90 degrees from the more usual display to make it more manageable graphically) is made up of the conjunction of the features [±cons] and [±son]. These are the most fundamental of all features.

Check this out in (34).

The substantive claim behind the inclusion of [±cons] and [±son] in the tree root is that these two features do not exhibit autosegmental behaviour independently of the other features: when [±cons] and [±son] spread, for example, they drag along the remainder of the features (= total assimilation). This happens, for instance, with the English prefix *in-* before sonorants: *in-legal* → *illegal*, *in-regular* → *irregular*, but *in-ability*, *in-capable*, *im-pertinent*, and so on:

Why do these data illustrate total assimilation? NB here total assimilation needs to be followed by degemination, that is, the simplification of the cluster of identical consonants.

(35)   English total assimilation of nasals:

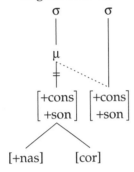

Say how the rule in (35) accounts for the relevant data, abstracting away subsequent degemination.

For convenience and for historical reasons, the root of the feature tree is some-times simply referred to as the ROOT, often abbreviated to R.

Among the features dependent on the root, some are direct dependents, and others indirect dependents, in that further dependents intervene between them and the root.

Enumerate one or two direct and indirect dependents from the root displayed in (34).

Once more you must bear in mind that the only motivating factor for the specific geometry in (34) is the autosegmental behaviour of each feature.

The motivating factor for the spe-cific geometry is the autosegmental behaviour of each feature

What exactly do we mean by the "autosegmental behaviour" of the feature?

So, the claim behind the direct dependency of [±cont], [±strid], [±nasal] and [±lat] on the root is literally that the root features [±cons, ±son] are the only features that are superordinate to [±cont], [±strid], [±nasal] and [±lat], which are otherwise independent.

> What exactly are [±cont], [±strid], [±nasal] and [±lat] independent of?

The situation is similar for [±voice] (in fact a shorthand for a set of other features, to be introduced in the next section), and for the place features [labial], [coronal], [dorsal] and [radical], each of them with its respective dependents, already commented on.

> Again, say what each of [labial], [coronal], [dorsal] and [radical] is independent of.

Notice the subscripts L (on [±voice]) and P (on the place features), which allow us to refer to the whole class thus designated: [. . .]$_P$ for the class of place features, and [. . .]$_L$ for the class of laryngeal features, at the moment only with one member. The label LARYNGEAL obviously means 'of the larynx', the space where the corresponding sound(s) are articulated.

> What exactly do the subscripts "$_P$" and "$_L$" signal?

Features sharing a given subscript exhibit parallel phonological behaviour

You will remember that the subscript formalism signals membership of a common class: features sharing a given subscript exhibit parallel phonological behaviour. For instance, we saw in chapter 4 that English consonants transmit their place of articulation feature, whichever this is, to a preceding coronal nasal.

> Jot down the English rule of place assimilation in nasals, going back to chapter 4 if you need reminding.

10 Class Nodes

For historical reasons, our subscripting practice is not common in the literature, which instead gives autosegmental representation to our subscripts in the form of CLASS NODES, as in (36), where we have emboldened the two class nodes to make them stand out visually:

(36)

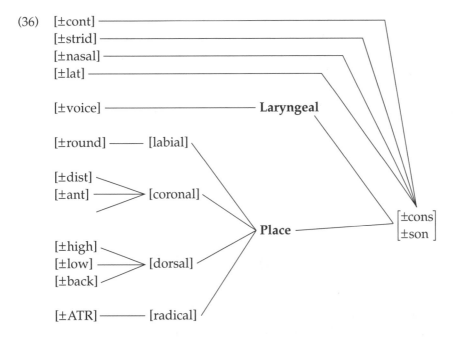

You will notice that we have not enclosed "Laryngeal" and "Place" in square brackets. This omission is quite deliberate, to signal that these labels do not correspond to distinctive features.

> Why don't the labels "Laryngeal" and "Place" correspond to distinctive features? What are they, then?

The intercalation of class node labels in what is otherwise a network of autosegmentalized features is conceptually a step of questionable legitimacy.

> Can you guess why?

In particular, the practice enshrined in (36) grants autosegmental status to "Laryngeal" and "Place". These, labels, however, have no individual reference, as we know. Instead, they define *classes* of individual features, a function which is arguably better reflected in the subscript notation.

> State clearly what the difference is between referring to an individual and defining a class.

"Laryngeal" and "Place" have no individual reference: they define *classes* of individual features

Be that as it may, the class node notation entails no loss of expressive power: nasal assimilation in (37a), for instance, is in all equivalent to our rule with subscript notation of chapter 4 above, repeated in (37b) to make comparison easy:

(37)   a. 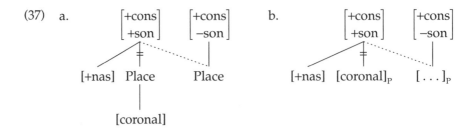   b.

Spell out the equivalence of the two notations in (37).

You can see that both notations capture the generalization that coronal nasals assimilate in place of articulation to the following obstruent irrespective of the place of articulation of this obstruent.

Throughout the book so far, we have been using the feature [±voice] to formalize the voiced or voiceless nature of segments, and indeed this is the only feature we included in the laryngeal class in (34) and (36) above. Besides voice, however, the larynx is responsible for the production of aspiration and glottalization. We give the features responsible for these various activities in (38), with their respective values:

Remind yourself of what aspiration and glottalization are, going back to chapters 1, 10 and 11 if necessary.

(38)

	Aspiration	*Glottalization*	*Voice*
[spread glottis]	+	−	
[constricted glottis]	−	+	
[stiff vocal folds]			−
[slack vocal folds]			+

The phonetic content of each of the four laryngeal features is expressed with reasonable transparency by the respective labels – for instance, SPREAD GLOTTIS means that the glottis is spread open, and so on. The full technicalities associated with these features are rather complex, and best left out of the present discussion. Just as a for instance, the exact implementation of voice is contingent on the specific type of segment, the values included in (38) only being valid for obstruents. There is also a connection between voicing and low tone, and between voicelessness and high tone. To keep matters simple, however, many authors, including ourselves, refer to voice activity with the relatively informal feature [±voice], instead of relying on the more complex set of features in (38).

There are four laryngeal features, but many authors refer to voice activity with the relatively informal feature [±voice]

> Have a good look at the table in (38), endeavouring to apprehend the general drift of the laryngeal features.

11 Relations between Vowels and Consonants

One important issue in feature geometry concerns the relationships between features for vowels and features for consonants. In particular, it is not uncommon in the languages of the world for the place of articulation of a consonant to be affected by the place of articulation of the following vowel. For instance, front high vowels often palatalize a preceding coronal consonant, as illustrated in (39) for English:

(39) impress → impre[ʃ]ion
      race   → ra[ʃ]ial
      right   → righ[ʧ]eous
      Christ   → Chris[ʧ]ian

It would obviously be desirable to express a process such as the one in (39) as assimilation. This goal is, however, unattainable in the context of the feature geometry in (36) above, where front high vowels are defined as [dorsal, +high, −back], while palatal consonants are [coronal, −anterior]: clearly, there is no formal connection between these two sets of features.

It is desirable to express the influence of the place of articulation of a vowel on the place of articulation of the preceding consonant as assimilation. This goal is achieved if vowels and consonants share the relevant set of features

> Verify the truth of our statement above by trying to formulate a palatalization rule using the geometry in (36).

The situation we just described could be interpreted as an indictment of the feature geometry in (36), and indeed an alternative is available in the literature, the relevant aspects of which are displayed in (40). As usual, different line heights are intended to suggest different tiers, each obviously defining a different plane:

(40)   Unified place features for consonants and vowels:

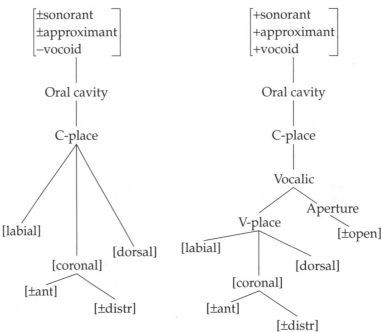

The key difference between the feature geometry in (40) and its predecessor in (34)/(36) lies in the fact that in (40) vowels and consonants share most of their features, assumed to receive a slightly different phonetic interpretation depending on whether they are dominated by the C-place or the V-place class node.

> Check the feature identity of vowels and consonants in (40). Why do you think the C-place node dominates the V-place node? Hint: think of secondary articulation, or of the frequent occurrence of vowel harmony.

The system in (40) includes a new feature [±open], to express degree of tongue height in vowels. This feature is assumed to be recursive, reflecting the open-ended nature of vowel height.

The various manifestations of [±open] are gathered under the class node Aperture

> Explain exactly what we mean by vowel height being open-ended.

The various manifestations of [±open] are gathered under the also new class node Aperture:

(41)   Vowel height under the class node Aperture:

/i, u/   /e, o/   /a/

Aperture   Aperture   Aperture

[–open]   \   [–open]   \   [+open]   \

          [–open]   [+open]   [+open]

> Study (41) for a minute, to make sure you understand it.

Notice the similarities between this proposal and the one based on the three quantum vowels that we discussed in chapter 8 in the context of the English Vowel Shift. In particular, [+open] in (41) could be claimed to correspond to <a> in the quantum vowel proposal, and [–open] to <i>.

> Explain the parallel between [+open] and <a>, and between [–open] and <i>. Make a proposal to formalize [ɛ] and [ɔ] in the framework in (41).

The existence of various alternative proposals for feature geometry is clear even from our brief exposé here. The question now is which of these alternatives is correct. The answer, unfortunately, is that the matter is still unresolved, since each of the models presented (and others we have ignored) has advantages and disadvantages. The issue of distinctive features is of course extremely complex, not least because it constitutes the interface of phonology with phonetics, and much more research is needed before the matter is settled.

12   Redundancies between Features

The existence of a feature geometry tree (in whatever incarnation) introduces an additional source of redundancy beyond those discussed earlier in the chapter.

There are redundancies in the feature geometry tree as a result of the feature dependencies

> Can you guess what this new type of redundancy is?

Think of the contrast between retroflex and non-retroflex coronals in Gooniyandi we came across in section 6: compare, for example, [d] vs. [ɖ] in *ḍiṛipindi* 'he entered'. We know that the two types of segment are distinguished by their opposed specification for [±anterior]: retroflexes are [–anterior] and non-retroflexes [+anterior]. These values need therefore to be specified in the lexicon for each of the respective segments. The question is, do we have to specify the rest of the feature geometry?

Do we have to specify the superordinate features?

The answer is contained in the feature geometry itself. You know, in particular, that the geometry contains lines linking some features, but not all of them. For instance, in the case of [d] and [ḍ] there is no need to specify [coronal] in the lexicon, for the simple reason that if a segment has a value for [±anterior] then it must of necessity be [coronal]. On the other hand, the presence of a value for [±anterior] says nothing about the possible value of, say, [±voice] or [±continuant].

Pause until you are sure you understand the point we are making.

The redundancies contained in the feature geometry tree in (36) above as a result of feature dependencies are now displayed in (42) ("⊃" = 'implies', and is thus equivalent to the "→" we have been using in default rules):

(42)   Feature geometry implicational redundancies:
      [±voice] ⊃ Laryngeal ⊃ [±consonant, ±sonorant]
      [±spread glottis] ⊃ Laryngeal ⊃ [±consonant, ±sonorant]
      [±constricted glottis] ⊃ Laryngeal ⊃ [±consonant, ±sonorant]
      [±stiff vocal folds] ⊃ Laryngeal ⊃ [±consonant, ±sonorant]
      [±slack vocal folds] ⊃ Laryngeal ⊃ [±consonant, ±sonorant]
      [±round] ⊃ [labial] ⊃ Place ⊃ [±consonant, ±sonorant]
      [±dist] ⊃ [coronal] ⊃ Place ⊃ [±consonant, ±sonorant]
      [±ant] ⊃ [coronal] ⊃ Place ⊃ [±consonant, ±sonorant]
      [±high] ⊃ [dorsal] ⊃ Place ⊃ [±consonant, ±sonorant]
      [±low] ⊃ [dorsal] ⊃ Place ⊃ [±consonant, ±sonorant]
      [±back] ⊃ [dorsal] ⊃ Place ⊃ [±consonant, ±sonorant]
      [±ATR] ⊃ [radical] ⊃ Place ⊃ [±consonant, ±sonorant]
      [±lat] ⊃ [±consonant, ±sonorant]
      [±nasal] ⊃ [±consonant, ±sonorant]
      [±continuant] ⊃ [±consonant, ±sonorant]
      [±strident] ⊃ [±consonant, ±sonorant]

The implications in (42) are of course simple reformulations of the tree in (36). Notice, in particular, that the set of implications in (42) includes class nodes (Laryngeal, Place) as well as features. From a more substantive perspective, however, class nodes are not *implied*, but, rather, *contained* in the relevant features, in a manner best expressed by our earlier subscript notation.

> Have a final think about the alternative formalizations of subscripts vs. class nodes.

The removal of class nodes from (42) would obviously reduce the implicational set to cases involving place features and to the across-the-board implication of the root features.

The implications in (42) (with or without the class nodes) are clearly different from the implications of the markedness relations discussed earlier.

> What is the basic difference between the implications in (42) and those arising from markedness filters?

In particular, the implications in (42) are implicit in the feature geometry tree, and therefore need no separate statement: we have only provided the statements in (42) to make the exposition clearer. By contrast, markedness statements must be specifically included in the grammar (ideally, in universal grammar).

> The implications in the feature geometry tree need no separate statement. By contrast, markedness statements must be specifically included in universal grammar

> Do you see why the implications in (42) need not be included in the grammar, but markedness statements do?

In addition, while feature geometry implications are inviolable by their very nature, most markedness implications are violable, as we know (the exception are cases considered of physical necessity, such as *[+high, +low] or *[+nasal, −sonorant]). All this points to a dichotomy between "hard" universals (inviolable) and "soft" universals (violable), the latter better formalized as parameters.

> While feature geometry implications are inviolable by their very nature, most markedness implications are violable

> Reflect briefly on the dichotomy between soft and hard universals.

13 Privative Features

A different type of implication (and thus of redundancy) is contained in the binary notation itself: [αF] automatically implies not [–αF], and conversely. Mathematically, if [αF] = ~[–αF], and [–αF] = ~[αF] ("~" is the logical symbol for "not"), it may be possible to dispense with α altogether and reduce the contrast to the presence of the unary feature [F] versus its absence.

> Explain these relations in your own words.

Empirically, the strongest case against binarity would come from the demonstration that one of the values of a feature plays no role in the phonological system

Empirically, the strongest case against binarity would come from the demonstration that one of the values of a feature plays no role in the phonological system. This seems to be the case to different degrees of likelihood for the settings [–nasal], [–round], and others.

Evidence against the existence of [–round] in the context of Contrast-restricted underspecification is available from the round harmony system of Khalkha Mongolian, a language already cited in connection with stress in chapter 13 above. Khalkha Mongolian reputedly possesses the relatively simple vowel system in (43) (there is some dispute as to the real phonetic substance of [y] and [ø] in Khalkha Mongolian, notwithstanding the phonetic symbols, which we will have to take at face value here):

> Remind yourself what [y] and [ø] stand for.

(43) i y   u
      e ø   o
          a

Rounding harmony in Khalkha Mongolian only affects non-high vowels: it does not affect [i, y, u]. The process involves rightward spread of the feature [labial] attached to [+round] from the initial vowel. In keeping with the phonetic symbols /y/, /ø/, we shall assume there is also [±back] harmony in this language, in a manner similar to Turkish:

(44)   sons-ogd-ox   'to be heard'
        ørg-øgd-øx   'to be raised'

        cf. nee-gd-ex   'to be opened'

Intervening high round vowels prevent the spread of [labial, +round] past them – more technically, high round vowels act as harmony BLOCKERS:

(45) boogd-uul-**a**x   'to hinder'

This state of affairs receives a straightforward formalization in our model of features:

(46)   b   oː   gd uː   l   a   x

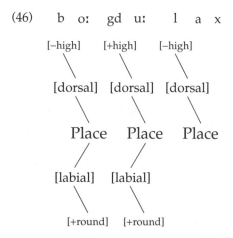

[−high]   [+high]   [−high]

[dorsal]   [dorsal]   [dorsal]

Place   Place   Place

[labial]   [labial]

[+round]   [+round]

The presence of the [+high] /uː/ between the source /oː/ and the possible target /a/ blocks the rightward spread of [labial, +round].

> Why doesn't [labial, +round] spread to the /a/ from the /uː/ in (46)?

Crucially, /i/ does not behave as a blocker:

(47) **oril-o**x   'to weep'
     oril-ogd-ox   'to be wept'

This outcome only makes sense if /i/ is unspecified for [labial], and hence for [−round], since otherwise [labial, −round] would interfere in the propagation of [labial, +round] in precisely the same way as [labial, +round] did in (46):

> Can you see how this would be the case?

(48)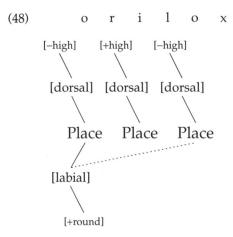

In the context of the theory of Contrast-restricted Underspecification, however, the underspecification of Khalkha Mongolian /i/ for [±round] is problematic. In particular, in the Khalkha Mongolian system, /i/ contrasts minimally with /y/ with regard to [±round], and therefore it ought to be fully specified for this feature in the lexicon.

> **What is the connection between contrasting minimally and being lexically specified?**

In turn, if /i/ is lexically [–round], it is by implication also [labial], since [±round] is a dependent of [labial]:

(49)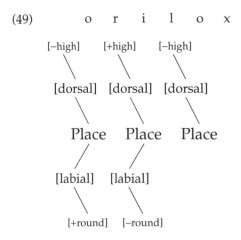

However, if /i/ is [labial, –round], [labial, +round] will not be able to spread from the *o* of the root to the underspecified *o* of the suffix, again for the simple reason that such spreading will violate the no-crossing constraint:

(50)

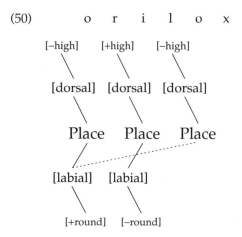

From all this we could of course conclude that Contrast-restricted Underspecification needs to be abandoned. However, we have seen above that Radical Underspecification, its main alternative, does not necessarily fare much better.

The Khalkha Mongolian problem is overcome if [round] is formalized as monovalent, that is, if the absence of rounding does not have a formal representation:

> Try this out for yourself before you read it in the text.

(51)

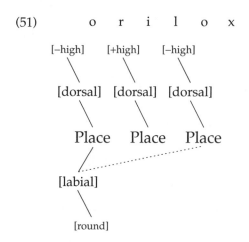

Similar arguments are being put forward in the literature for the monovalency of other distinctive features, although more work is necessary to dispel all doubts and allow wider acceptance across the field. For the time being, the question of how many features (if any) are monovalent must be added to the not inconsiderable list of issues in the area of distinctive features that still await a definitive solution.

Arguments are being put forward in the literature for the monovalency of other distinctive features, although more work is necessary to dispel all doubts

C h a p t e r   S u m m a r y

In this chapter we have further elaborated on the notion of underspecification – first encountered in chapter 6 in connection with Turkish vowel harmony, and then in chapter 14 in the context of Shona tones – in order to offer an explanation for the application of the English cyclic rule of intervocalic *s*-voicing to underived forms as well as the anticipated derived ones. We showed that the lexically unspecified values of features are frequently those which can be predicted by universal markedness principles. Unmarked features are those which are more natural, indeed unmarked feature combinations make up the natural phonology of the language: for instance, the feature [±voice] is unmarked for sonorants, since sonorants will naturally be voiced, and therefore it is rare for a language to present a contrast between voiced and voiceless sonorant sounds. We provided a list of such markedness statements, which, for the most part, encode universal preferences rather than inviolable constraints. We presented two theories of underspecification: Radical Underspecification and Contrast-restricted Underspecification. In the former theory, lexical economy is paramount. Lexical segments are left unspecified for those values which can be filled in, cost-free, by the default rules encoded in the universal markedness statements. In addition to this, certain sounds which occur in the inventory of the language will be left entirely unspecified in the lexicon, on the grounds that these sounds will emerge naturally through the application of the language-specific redundancy rules, in cases of epenthesis. We showed that this version of underspecification cannot always make the correct predictions, because languages violate universal markedness, or because of a contravention of the Redundancy Rule Ordering Constraint, or, finally, because the language allows a different epenthetic vowel (or consonant) to emerge in different contexts. The second theory of underspecification is Contrast-restricted Underspecification. This theory also favours lexical economy, and thus lexically non-contrastive feature values are still left unspecified, and then filled through the markedness statements. We showed that this theory is not without problems either. We presented two models of the organization of distinctive features and feature dependencies (introduced in chapters 4 and 6). One view of this organization, known as Feature Geometry, essentially has a common set of features for consonants and vowels, whilst the other model has a partially different set. Many feature redundancies are built into either model of Feature Geometry, and we listed these as a series of implications which can be read off the appropriate feature trees. Since these implications are implicit in the feature geometry tree, they are, by their very nature, inviolable and must be considered to be "hard" universals, in contrast to the violable, or "soft", universals, or parameters, expressed in the markedness statements. We pointed out that the binary notation itself contains a degree of redundancy, since [αF] necessarily implies not [−αF] and vice versa. We showed that some of the problems thrown up by the theories of underspecification discussed can be better dealt with by a theory that recognizes that at least some features are monovalent, only the presence of the feature having formal reality.

Key Questions

1 How can underspecification help to explain the fact that some cyclic rules apparently apply in underived contexts?

2 What is the difference between structure-changing and structure-building rules?

3 Why are some sounds transparent with respect to processes such as assimilation?

4 What is a "default rule"?

5 What is meant by marked and un-marked feature combinations?

6 What observation lies behind the Theory of Radical Underspecification?

7 What is the role of a complement rule? What does is complement?

8 What is the Redundancy Rule Ordering Constraint? Does it always apply unproblematically?

9 What is Contrast-restricted Underspecification? How does it differ from Radical Underspecification?

10 What motivates Feature Geometry?

11 "Laryngeal" and "Place" are class nodes: what does this signify?

12 How is a type of configuration in which vowels and consonants share a feature specification for place of articulation more revealing in some contexts?

13 How do the redundancies inherent in the Feature Geometry tree result?

14 On what grounds is it suggested that some features apart from place of articulation are in fact monovalent?

Further Practice

Bahasa Melayu/Indonesia Nasal Spread

The Austronesian language spoken in the states of Indonesia, Malaysia, Singapore and Brunei, and in some neighbouring areas, is known as Bahasa Indonesia in Indonesia, and as Bahasa Melayu elsewhere. In this language, the appearance of nasal vowels is totally predictable and non-distinctive. Nasalization spreads both within morphemes and across morpheme boundaries.

[mãkan]	'to eat'	[kəsamãʔãn]	'similarity'
[mãlam]	'night'	[kəmẽw̃ãhhãn]	'prosperity'
[tamãn]	'garden'	[kəmãtijan]	'death'
[nãẽʔ]	'to ascend'	[kəsənĩjãn]	'art'
[mãõt]	'died'	[mãŋãjã?]	'sift' (active)
[mũw̃ãt]	'fit'	[pəŋãjãʔãn]	'enriching'

(i)   State the formal mechanics of the spread of the nasal feature.

(ii)   Where and why does this spreading stop?

(iii)   Provide the nasalization patterns for the following forms:

pəŋawallan 'guarding'	mahal 'expensive'	məɲikot 'follow' (active)
majan 'stalk' (palm)	mewah 'luxury'	rambottan 'rambutan'
kənallan 'friend'	tanam 'to bury'	makannan 'food'

(iv)   What light do these data shed on the characterization of consonants for place of articulation?

Markedness

Each of the sets of sounds below would be an "unnatural" system for language. State which of the markedness statements are contravened in each case:

(i)   *Vowel system*
      i   u
      æ

(ii) *Vowel system*
      i   u
          ɒ

(iii) *Stop consonants*
      p   k
      b   g

(iv) *Fricatives*
      f   v
      θ   ð
      ʃ   ʒ

(v)   *Vowel system*
      y   ɯ
      ø   ɤ
      œ   ʌ

(vi) *Stop consonants*
      n   m   ŋ
      n̥   m̥   ŋ̥

(vii) *Consonant system*
      ɸ   f   s   x
      β   v   z   ɣ
              l

(viii) *Vowel system*
      e   o
      ɛ   ɔ
          a

Yoruba Vowel Assimilation

The oral vowel system of standard Yoruba is as listed below (the language also has three nasal vowels which we shall ignore for the purposes of this exercise):

```
i        u
e        o
ε        ɔ
    a
```

Work out the full feature specification for these vowels.

Vowel assimilation in Yoruba is illustrated in a. (tones are omitted):

a. owo+ade   →   owa ade   'Ade's money'
    owo+ojo   →   owo ojo   'Ojo's money'
    owo+ɔmɔ   →   owɔ ɔmɔ   'child's money'
    owo+εmu   →   owε εmu   'wine money'
    owo+epu   →   owe epu   'oil money'
    awɔ+ejo   →   awe ejo   'colour of a snake'
    ara+oke   →   aro oke   'northern Yoruba'
    εba+odo   →   εbo odo   'near the river'
    atɔ+oogun →   ato oogun   'medicine dispenser'
    ile+ayɔ   →   ila ayɔ   'Ayo's house'
    ara+εbun   →   arε εbun   'Ebun's body'
    ara+ejide →   are ejide   'Edjide's body'

(i)   Formalize the assimilation process.

Now consider the examples in b.:

b. ara+ilu   *ari ilu   'townsman'
    εru+igi   *εri igi   'bundle of wood'
    ile+iṣε   *ili iṣε   'office'

(ii)   Can you suggest any reason why assimilation does not occur in the cases in b.? What is there in the forms in b. that prevents them from undergoing assimilation?

(iii) How can a theory of underspecification help to account for the data above?

Japanese

In the native Yamato vocabulary of Japanese a combination of voiced obstruents within a root is avoided. Thus while such words as *buta* 'pig', *futa* 'lid' *fuda* 'sign' are acceptable, *buda* is not possible. This constraint, known as "Lyman's law", has the effect of undoing the effect of the pervasive rule of "Rendaku", which systematically voices the initial obstruent in the second component of a compound. The examples below illustrate the combined effects of these two processes:

a. iro 'coloured' + kami 'paper'   → irogami   'coloured paper'
    take 'bamboo' + sao 'pole'   → takezao   'bamboo pole'
    eda 'branch' + ke 'hair'   → edage   'split hair'
    zjuzu 'rosary' + tama 'beads'   → zjuzudama '(prayer) beads'

b. kita 'north' + kaze 'wind'   → kitakaze (*kitagaze)
                                                 'freezing north wind'
    ʃiro 'white' + tabi 'tabi'   → ʃirotabi (*ʃirodabi)   'white tabi'
    zjuzu 'rosary' +   → zjuzutunagi (*zyuzudunagi)
       tunagi 'sequence'   'roping together'
    taikutsu 'boredom' +   → taikutsuʃinogi (*taiuksuʒinogi)
       ʃinogi 'avoiding'   'time-killer'

Lyman's Law is clearly a dissimilation process. In the compounded forms in b. Lyman's Law has reversed any voicing effect that Rendaku might have had. Remember, however, that all sonorant consonants are inherently voiced. Notice that in a. there are examples where a voiced consonant does occur in the compounded form followed by a sonorant, but where the constraint of Lyman's Law is not applicable (*irogami, zjuzudama*).

(i)   Show how Lyman's Law works.
(ii)   Why does Lyman's Law not apply in *irogami* and *zjuzudama*?
(iii) Explain why it applies in *zjuzutunagi* and *taikutsuʃinogi*.

CHAPTER EIGHTEEN

RULES AND DERIVATIONS

C h a p t e r   O b j e c t i v e s

In this chapter you will learn about:
- How rules interact with each other in rule systems.
- Different possible types of rule ordering exemplified from English.
- How an overall order can be established even when two rules appear not to interact.
- The derivation of a large chunk of English lexical segmental phonology.
- The cyclic and non-cyclic status of these rules.

In the model we have been presenting throughout the book, alternants are related by means of rules which act on the lexical form, or on a representation ultimately derived from the lexical form. In particular, lexical forms are mapped onto surface forms in a series of steps, each defined by a rule: the sequence of representations thus obtained constitutes a "derivation". The action of a rule on a representation can have decisive effects on the applicability of some other rule, either by creating the input required for this rule or by destroying it. Rules can therefore interact with each other, and we need to monitor such interaction by ordering the rules precisely in the manner that will yield the desired output. In this chapter we study the mechanics of rule interaction and rule ordering making use of a substantial portion of the segmental rules of English, which accordingly we also survey. We pay close attention to the evidence that bears on the cyclic or non-cyclic status of the rules, and to the ensuing organization of the rules into blocks.

1 Rule Ordering: Feeding and Counterfeeding

In the previous chapter we considered alternations like those in (1), and accounted for them with the *s*-Voicing rule in (2) (as we said, in some accents some of the [z]s in (1) are only intermediate, and subsequently undergo palatalization):

(1) a. gymnastics   b. gymnasium
         Caucasus   Caucasian
         Malthus   Malthusian
         fantasy   fantasia

(2)   s → [+voice] / [−cons] ____ [−cons]

$$\overset{\displaystyle\bigwedge}{\mu\ \ \mu}\qquad\qquad\overset{\displaystyle\mid}{(\mu)}$$

> Remind yourself of the workings of this rule with the help of the data in (1).

We commented at the time that the long vowel that triggers *s*-Voicing in the set in (1b) cannot be lexical, for, if it were, the stress pattern of some of the forms in (1a) would have been different.

> Say what the stress pattern of *Caucasus* and *fantasy* would have been if the vowels in bold had been lexically long, and why.

Further examples of vowel lengthening, this time independent of *s*-Voicing, are provided in (3a). Notice once more that the corresponding vowels in the bases in (3b) are short:

(3) a. Canadian   b. Canada
         Jordanian   Jordan
         Mongolia   Mongol
         Arabia   Arab
         Babylonian   Babylon
         regalia   regal
         collegiate   college
         courageous   courage
         felonious   felon
         colonial   colony
         comedian   comedy
         Gregorian   Gregory

In (4) we formulate the rule responsible for the lengthening of the (crucially, non-high) vowel in (1b) and (3a). We shall refer to this rule as "*CiV*-Lengthening", for the simple reason that the lengthening in question takes place precisely in front of the sequence **consonant + i + vowel** (cf. *Bosnian*, *satin*, with no lengthening):

Explain exactly how these two words fail to meet the environment in question.

(4)   *CiV*-Lengthening:

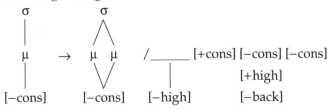

Condition: the contextual *i* is metrically weak

Before we proceed, we must say a word about the way we formalize distinctive features in this and other rules throughout this chapter. Features are of course organized autosegmentally, as we reiterated in chapter 17. To keep the representations free from unnecessary clutter, however, we do not include the feature geometry in our rules, except in cases where such geometry is directly relevant to the operation of the rule. Whenever possible, therefore, we adopt the practice of simply stacking up the features, with no indication of their position in the geometry.

You are obviously welcome to supply the missing geometry for the features involved in each of the rules.

Not unexpectedly, there are a number of exceptions to the rule of *CiV*-Lengthening in (4). Some are idiosyncratic:

(5)   Italian   centennial   rebellious   Maxwellian

Other exceptions are more systematic:

(6)   companion   battalion   medallion   rebellion   scullion

Quite simply, *CiV*-Lengthening does not take place in front of the suffix *-ion*.

Returning at this point to the data in (1), you will notice that *s*-Voicing requires the prior application of *CiV*-Lengthening in the relevant forms.

> Say why *CiV*-Lengthening needs to apply before *s*-Voicing in (1).

In particular, in order to undergo *s*-Voicing, the /s/ needs to be preceded by a long vowel, but there is no such vowel in the underlying representation of the forms in (1), as we have pointed out: *Cauc*/æ/*sus*, etc. Consequently, such forms would not be able to undergo *s*-Voicing if *CiV*-Lengthening had not applied first, as is substantiated by the forms in (7):

(7) hessian   massive   classic
     missile   passive   impressive

> Why exactly does *s*-Voicing not apply here? Why do the stressed vowels of these forms not lengthen?

In (8) we show that the application of *CiV*-Lengthening to forms like *Cauc*/æ/*sian* creates the appropriate environment for *s*-Voicing:

(8) *Cauc*/æ s/*ian*
           æː   *CiV*-Lengthening
           z   *s*-Voicing

The type of ordering illustrated in (8), where the first rule creates the input required by the second rule, is known as FEEDING ORDER, and the first rule is said to FEED the second.

> Explain exactly how *s*-Voicing is fed by *CiV*-Lengthening in (8).

The type of ordering where the first of two rules creates the input required by the second rule is known as FEEDING ORDER (the first rule FEEDS the second)

Clearly, the opposite ordering between the two rules we are discussing would not give the desired result:

(9) *Cauc*/æ s/*ian*
           NA   *s*-Voicing
           æː   *CiV*-Lengthening

> How come *s*-Voicing does not apply here, but *CiV*-Lengthening still does?

In (9), *s*-Voicing is prevented from applying because it has (mistakenly) been ordered before *CiV*-Lengthening: at the time *s*-Voicing is available in (9), the relevant contextual vowel is still short, and consequently *s*-Voicing cannot apply. This type of ordering, where the second of two rules would feed the first rule if the ordering were reversed, is referred to as COUNTERFEEDING ORDER (the first rule COUNTERFEEDS the second).

> Stop reading until you are sure you see the difference between the feeding and counterfeeding orderings. Explain it.

We will come across many instances of RULE ORDERING in the remainder of the chapter. Rule ordering is indeed one of the formal tools that characterize the model of phonology associated with *SPE*. The device of stipulating the order in which phonological rules apply is not, however, to the taste of all phonologists, and there have been through the years a number of attempts to remove it from the theory. Many rule orderings can indeed be removed from individual grammars, because they are either INTRINSIC ORDERINGS, that is, orderings that obtain even if the rules are allowed to apply unfettered, or UNIVERSAL ORDERINGS, that is, orderings that follow from some universal principle of rule interaction, such as the Elsewhere Condition.

> In what way does the Elsewhere Condition predict the ordering of rules?

The previous considerations notwithstanding, a core of recalcitrant cases remains which seems to require stipulative EXTRINSIC ORDERING, in English and in other languages.

> Go back to (8) and (9) and work out whether or not we need extrinsic ordering to bring about the correct order of application between *CiV*-Lengthening and *s*-Voicing.

A recent move from a novel, radical perspective to do away with rule ordering, indeed with rules and derivations themselves, will be presented in chapter 19.

The output of the derivation in (8) obviously needs some further processing: compare *Cauc*[æː]*sian* with the correct *Cauc*[eɪ]*sian*. Such processing is

---

The type of ordering where the second of two rules would feed the first rule if the ordering were reversed is known as COUNTERFEEDING ORDER (the first rule COUNTERFEEDS the second)

Many rule orderings are either INTRINSIC ORDERINGS or UNIVERSAL ORDERINGS, but a core of recalcitrant cases seems to require stipulative EXTRINSIC ORDERING

carried out by the rules of Vowel Shift, which we discussed in chapter 8 above, and Diphthongization, which we also mentioned then but did not formulate, in order to keep the presentation simple.

Jog your memory on these two processes and their motivation.

We formalize Diphthongization in (10):

(10)   Diphthongization:

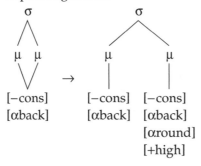

$$\begin{array}{c}[-\text{cons}] \\ [\alpha\text{back}]\end{array} \quad \rightarrow \quad \begin{array}{cc}[-\text{cons}] & [-\text{cons}] \\ [\alpha\text{back}] & [\alpha\text{back}] \\ & [\alpha\text{round}] \\ & [+\text{high}]\end{array}$$

Say exactly what segments are inserted by rule (10), and where.

The general effects of Diphthongization for the front vowels are specified in (11):

(11)   iː   →   ii
        eː   →   ei
        æː   →   æi

These outputs essentially match the phonetic realization (see chapter 7 above for more details), *Cauc*[eɪ]*sian* in the case at hand, after the laxing of the high vowel at the end of the diphthong.

What is the main difference between the outputs in (11) and the actual phonetic realizations? What variation can the high vowel /ii/ exhibit in the surface?

2 Bleeding and Counterbleeding

At this point, we must elucidate the ordering of the two additional rules we have just introduced, both with respect to each other and with respect to CiV-lengthening and s-Voicing.

Consider first the mutual ordering of Vowel Shift and Diphthongization. The order must be Vowel Shift > Diphthongization (the symbol ">" separates rules that are ordered; unordered rules are separated by a comma). The reason is that the application of Vowel Shift is restricted to (stressed) long vowels, as we specify in (12), which updates the formulation in (38) of chapter 8 above (notice that we have split the environment, to make the presentation clearer):

(12)   Vowel Shift:

$$[-\text{cons}] \rightarrow \left\{ \begin{array}{l} [-\alpha \text{high}] / [\underline{\quad}] \\ [\alpha \text{high}] \\ [-\text{low}] \\ \\ [-\beta \text{low}] / [\underline{\quad}] \\ [\beta \text{low}] \\ [-\text{high}] \end{array} \right\} / \underset{\sigma}{\overset{*\ *\ (*}{\underline{\quad}}}$$

We are now representing syllable structure under the line of the environment. Does this matter? Hint: autosegmental representations are multiplanar.

Now, as you can see in (10) above, Diphthongization destroys the bimoraicity of the input vowel, by robbing it of its second mora, which it associates with a (newly created) high vowel.

Go back to (10) and check that Diphthongization makes the input vowel monomoraic.

Obviously, if Diphthongization were allowed to apply before Vowel Shift, Vowel Shift would no longer be able to apply, because the vowel mentioned in the rule would not be long any more. We illustrate the situation in (13) with the /æː/ of *Caucasian*:

(13)   *Cauc*/æː/*sian*

        æɪ   Diphthongization

        NA   Vowel Shift

   *Cauc[æɪ]*sian*

> Can you see why Vowel Shift does not apply?

The situation where a rule removes material that would be necessary for the application of a subsequently ordered rule is referred to as BLEEDING ORDER (the first rule BLEEDS the second)

The situation where a rule removes material that would be necessary for the application of a subsequently ordered rule is referred to as BLEEDING ORDER, and the first rule is said to BLEED the second rule. Therefore, Diphthongization bleeds Vowel Shift in (13).

> What exactly is the difference between bleeding and feeding?

The correct order of application between Diphthongization and Vowel Shift is obviously the opposite of the one in (13): by giving the rules the opposite order, we prevent the unwanted bleeding from taking place.

> Reverse the ordering in (13) to see whether this works.

Reversing the order of two rules to prevent bleeding results in a COUNTERBLEEDING ORDER (the first rule now COUNTERBLEEDS the second)

Reversing the order of two rules to prevent bleeding results in a COUNTERBLEEDING ORDER (the first rule now COUNTERBLEEDS the second).

> What is the opposite of bleeding: counterbleeding or feeding? Correspondingly, what is the opposite of feeding: counterfeeding or bleeding? Say why in each case.

The (correct) counterbleeding order of Vowel Shift and Diphthongization is illustrated in (14):

(14)   *Cauc*/æː/*sian*

        eː   Vowel Shift

        eɪ   Diphthongization

   Cauc[eɪ]*sian*

It may be worth pointing out at this juncture that all the four possible rule ordering relations we have introduced (feeding, counterfeeding, bleeding, counterbleeding) are attested in the languages of the world, most often within the rule system of one and the same language.

> Define each of these four ordering relations, making sure you see the differences between them.

Consequently, you must not interpret the feeding and counterbleeding interactions between the English rules we have discussed as automatically correct, and the opposite orderings (counterfeeding and bleeding) as automatically incorrect. The orderings in question are indeed correct and incorrect, respectively, for the English data we have discussed, but the mutual ordering of any two rules in any one language must be established empirically, on the basis of the facts of the language, as indeed will be our practice throughout the chapter.

> Explain the point we are making in your own words.

Let us now scrutinize the interaction between Vowel Shift and *s*-Voicing.

> Make an educated guess about the interaction of Vowel Shift and *s*-Voicing.

In fact, *s*-Voicing and Vowel Shift are NON-INTERACTING, since the environments of both rules are met whatever the order of application:

(15)   a.   *Cauc*/æːs/*ian*   b.   *Cauc*/æːs/*ian*
                eː   Vowel Shift   z   *s*-Voicing
                 z   *s*-Voicing   eː   Vowel Shift

You can see that we obtain the correct output irrespective of the order in which the two rules are applied.

> Why exactly does the order between *s*-Voicing and Vowel Shift not matter to the output?

All four possible rule ordering relations (feeding, counterfeeding, bleeding, counterbleeding) are attested in the languages of the world

---

The mutual ordering of any two rules in any one language must be established empirically

3 Transitivity

If the orderings A > B and B > C can be established empirically, then it follows by TRANS-ITIVITY that A > C

Sometimes, two or more rules have to be left unordered because there is no evidence on the way they interact. More often than not, however, indirect evidence on their ordering can be gathered. In particular, if the orderings A > B and B > C can be established empirically, then it follows by TRANS-ITIVITY that A > C. We will now see that an argument of this kind can be used to order *s*-Voicing before Vowel Shift, as in (15b) above.

The argument comes from the existence of the rule of Velar Softening in English. Consider the alternations in (16), found in the "Latin" part of the English vocabulary:

(16) a. [k]   [s]   b. [g]   [dʒ]
          critical criticism   analogous   analogical
          classical classicist   pedagogue   pedagogic
          public   publicity   prodigal   prodigy
          medic   medicine   regal   regicide
          Catholic Catholicism   fungus   fungivorous

> State precisely what these alternations consist of.

In (16a), [k] alternates with [s], and in (16b) [g] alternates with [dʒ]. Phonetically, each of these alternations is somewhat idiosyncratic: there is not much in common between [k] and [s], or between [g] and [dʒ].

> Show this by breaking the segments down into their feature components.

What interests us here, however, is the environment. This is much more straightforward: /k/ and /g/ "soften" to [s] and [dʒ], respectively, before a front non-low vowel (also high in the data in (16), but this is irrelevant: *magnificent, maleficent,* etc.). The rule in (17) provides an adequate formalization of the situation. Note that angled brackets indicate a two-way implication, that is, here either [−voice] and [+continuant, +anterior], or neither:

Angled brackets indicate a two-way implication

> Explain the function of angled brackets in your own words.

(17) Velar Softening:

[–cont]		[+strid]	[–cons]
[+back]	→	[coronal] / ____	[–back]
<–voice>		<+cont>	[–low]
		<+ant>	

The restriction of the environment of Velar Softening to non-low vowels prevents the application of the rule in the set in (16a): /æ/ (cf. *criticality*) is a low vowel, and consequently it does not trigger Velar Softening.

Explain the relevance of *criticality* to our argument.

The data in (18) present a challenge to our account:

(18) a. criticize   b. medicate
         publicize   rusticate
         anglicize   implicate

Say exactly in what way the data in (18) challenge our account.

On the face of it, Velar Softening has overapplied in (18a) (cf. the low vowel [æ] in *critic*[æɪ]*se*), while in the forms in (18b) it has underapplied ([e] in *medic*[eɪ]*te* is not low).

Why should the lowness or non-lowness of the vowel matter to the application of Velar Softening?

The puzzle disappears if Velar Softening is ordered before Vowel Shift, so that we have Velar Softening counterbleeding Vowel Shift in the forms in (18a), and counterfeeding it in those in (18b): the contextual vowel for Velar Softening will be /iː/ and /æː/, respectively.

Provide the derivations of *criticize* and *medicate*.

Having established that Velar Softening precedes Vowel Shift, we shall now make a case for ordering Velar Softening after *s*-Voicing. If so, *s*-Voicing will precede Vowel Shift by transitivity.

> What ordering relation do *s*-Voicing and Velar Softening engage in, given the ordering *s*-Voicing > Velar Softening we are proposing?

Consider forms like those in (19):

(19)   a.   [s]   b.   [z]
           recite   resign
           recede   resist
           receive   design
           decide   reside

We shall analyse the forms in both sets in (19) as composed of a prefix (*re-*, *de-*) and a stem: *-cede* (cf. *recede*), *-sist* (cf. *resist*), and so on.

> The prefix *re-* in (19) is obviously different from the *re-* of *remarry* or *rehabilitate*: say why.

The fact that the forms in (19b) have undergone *s*-Voicing (*re*-[z]*ist* vs. *con*-[s]*ist*) suggests that the *e* of the prefix must be long, at least underlyingly.

> Why does the *e* of *re-*, *de-*, etc., need to be long in order for *s*-Voicing to apply? How can this *e* be long underlyingly if it surfaces as short?

The obvious problem with the analysis as it stands concerns the forms in (19a), which still fail to undergo *s*-Voicing, and will therefore have to be treated as exceptions.

> Check that *recite*, etc., need to be considered exceptions at this point.

While phonological rules often do have exceptions, we naturally want to minimize their number and integrate the corresponding data into the system as much as possible. In the present case, the stem of the forms in (19a) is spelled with an initial *c* (*re-cede*), whereas the stem of the forms in (19b) is spelled with *s* (*re-sist*). While spelling is, most emphatically, irrelevant to phonology, as we have been repeating ad nauseam throughout the book, in the present case the difference in spelling contains a useful clue: indeed, most of the literature assumes that forms like *recede* have an underlying /k/ (*re*/k/*ede*), and forms like *resist* an underlying /s/ (*re*/s/*ist*).

> Are we contradicting ourselves when we say that spelling is irrelevant to phonology but none the less contains a useful clue here?

The /s/ of *resist* will of course be voiced by *s*-Voicing (again, on the assumption that the vowel in the prefix *re-* in question is long at that stage). Velar Softening turns /k/s into [s]s, and therefore the /k/ of *re*/k/*ede* would also end up as [z] if the ordering were Velar Softening > *s*-Voicing, with Velar Softening feeding *s*-Voicing.

> Check with pencil and paper that the ordering Velar Softening > *s*-Voicing gives the wrong result for *recede*.

If we adopt the opposite, counterfeeding, order, however, the desired result will be achieved:

(20)   *re*/k/*ede*   *re*/s/*ist*
      NA   z   *s*-Voicing
       s   NA   Velar Softening
   re[s]*ede*   *re*[z]*ist*

> Compare this derivation to the one with Velar Softening > *s*-Voicing, focusing on the different effects of the feeding and counterfeeding orderings.

By this point, we have established the following orderings on empirical grounds:

(21)   Paired rule orderings:
     CiV-Lengthening > *s*-Voicing   (*Caucasian* vs. *hessian*)
     s-Voicing > Velar Softening   (*re*[s]*ede* vs. *re*[z]*ist*)
     Velar Softening > Vowel Shift   (*criticise* vs. *critical*)
     Vowel Shift > Diphthongization   (*Cauc*[eɪ]*sian* vs. *Cauc[æɪ]*sian*)

> Work out the type of ordering relation involved in each of these pairs.

By the (logical) principle of transitivity, we derive the overall ordering relations in (22):

> Explain exactly what transitivity is, and why it is logical.

(22)   Overall rule orderings:

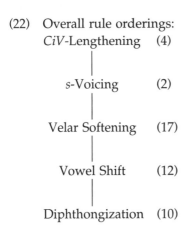

    CiV-Lengthening   (4)

        s-Voicing   (2)

    Velar Softening   (17)

    Vowel Shift   (12)

    Diphthongization   (10)

> Read this list carefully, making sure you see the effect of each rule on the input of the one that follows it. Give the full derivation of *fantasia* using these rules (NB one rule will not apply: which?).

You can see that we have now established that Vowel Shift must follow *s*-Voicing, even though there is no direct interaction between the two rules.

> Say what the bottom line of the argument for this ordering is.

4 Palatalization

We mentioned at the beginning of the chapter (and in chapter 17) that the [z] that is the output of *s*-Voicing is subject to palatalization in many words (in most accents). We illustrate such data again in (23):

(23)   Caucasian   Malthusian   fantasia

> Pronounce these words to verify whether or not you have a palatal.

Palatalization is in fact an extremely productive process in English. We provide further exemplification of the phenomenon in (24), this time independently of *s*-Voicing:

(24)   a.   [ʃ]   b.   [s]
        impression   impress
        obsession   obsess
        digression   digress
        racial   race
        official   office
        ferocious   ferocity
        efficacious   efficacy

        [ʒ]   [z]
        diffusion   diffuse
        confusion   confuse
        infusion   infuse
        erasure   erase
        incision   incisor
        vision   visor
        enclosure   enclose

> You should have a palatal in *all* the words in (24a).

Observation of the spelling of the alternants with the palatal reveals the sequence **i + vowel** after the segment that undergoes the palatalization.

> Check that this is the case in (24).

This orthographic *i* does not, however, have any correlate in the pronunciation (*impre[ʃə]n*, not **impre[ʃiə]n*, etc.).

> Verify this in your own pronunciation.

We could conclude from this fact that the *i* is purely a spelling matter, and therefore that there is no /ɪ/ present in the respective lexical representations. However, it is obvious that the suffix in the forms in (24a) does include /ɪ/ in non-palatalizing environments. Note that we are postulating /ɪ/, rather than /i/, on the grounds that the segment in question is short (although not necessarily lax in the cases where it does go through to the surface: this matter will be clarified below):

(25)   rebellion   rebellious   familiar   curious
        menial   Italian   centurion   imperial

Also, the palatalization of coronals before /ɪ/ is very natural, because both coronals and /ɪ/ are pronounced at the front of the mouth: indeed, /ɪ/ (like the other front vowels) is treated as [coronal] in the model of feature geometry we discussed in section 11 of the previous chapter.

> Pause and reflect on the articulatory connections between coronal consonants and front vowels.

Let us thus assume that there is indeed an /ɪ/ in the lexical representation of the suffixes in question, acting as the trigger of the palatalization process, which we formalize in (26) (we provide a choice between [–back] and [–anterior], a dependent of [coronal], with regard to the specification of /ɪ/, in line with the two alternative models of feature geometry we presented in chapter 17):

(26)   Palatalization:

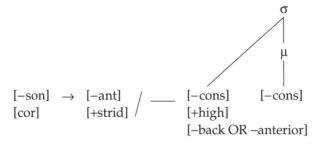

$$
\begin{array}{ccc}
\text{[–son]} & \rightarrow & \text{[–ant]} \\
\text{[cor]} & & \text{[+strid]}
\end{array}
\Big/ \underline{\quad}
\begin{array}{cc}
\text{[–cons]} & \text{[–cons]} \\
\text{[+high]} & \\
\text{[–back OR –anterior]} &
\end{array}
$$

Condition: σ immediately follows the syllable with the word's primary stress

> What does rule (26) predict about palatalization in such forms as *tune*, *attune* or *residue* in accents that admit [iu] in these environments? Hint: notice the condition.

Notice the direct affiliation of [−cons, +high, −back OR −anterior] to the σ node in (26), with no mora intervening. The non-moraicity of this vowel is therefore a precondition for the application of the rule, and corresponds to what much of the literature refers to by the label "glide". We have, however, raised problems with this notion in chapter 10, and we are now seeing that there is actually no need for it, since the same results can be achieved by reference to non-moraicity. In chapter 13 we suggested that vowels generally projected moras in the lexicon. What seems to be happening here is that the vowel /ɪ/ demorifies in the context **stressed syllable ___ vowel**. The application of this rule is, however, subject to idiolectal idiosyncrasies, and, in the absence of solid primary research, we shall not go any further into the matter. To maximize the clarity of the exposition, we shall transcribe such non-moraic [ɪ] as [j], following the practice we introduced in chapter 10. You must of course bear in mind that we are in no way implying a different segmental identity for [j]: it is identical to [ɪ] or [i], but it has no mora attached to it.

After Palatalization takes place (turning, for instance, *regre*[sj]*on* into *regre*[ʃj]*on*) the /j/ gets absorbed into the palatal.

> Would it be at all possible to relate the absorption of /j/ into the palatal to the OCP?

The rule in (27) formalizes the process:

(27) [j]-Deletion:

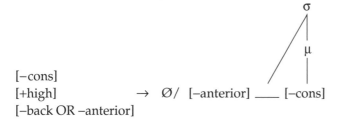

[−cons]
[+high]   →   Ø/ [−anterior] ___ [−cons]
[−back OR −anterior]

The rule of [j]-Deletion in (27) must obviously be ordered after Palatalization, a feeding relationship.

> Why do we need this ordering?

Where does Palatalization fit in the rule set in (22) above?

> Answer the question before you read on.

In fact, Palatalization must be ordered after Velar Softening, because of the progression *logi*/k/*ian* → *logi*[s]*ian* → *logi*[ʃ]*ian*. The /k/ of the initial form *logi*/k/*ian* is obviously justified by the base *logi*[k]. In order to end up as [ʃ], by Palatalization, /k/ must first be turned into [s] by Velar Softening, which thus feeds Palatalization:

(28)   *logi*/k/*ian*
　　　　　s　　　Velar Softening
　　　　　ʃ　　　Palatalization

Clearly, the opposite, counterfeeding ordering would not deliver the desired result.

> Show that the ordering Palatalization > Velar Softening doesn't work.

Turning now to Vowel Shift and Diphthongization, there is no evidence of their ordering with respect to Palatalization: these two rules and Palatalization seem to be non-interacting.

> Do some testing on our claim that neither Vowel Shift nor Diphthongization interacts with Palatalization.

The state of affairs we have established is set out in the augmented list of rule orderings in (29):

(29)   Overall rule orderings:

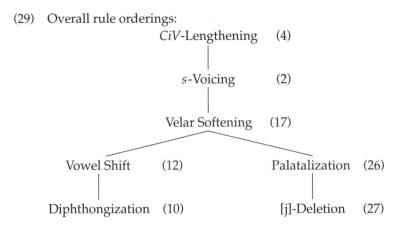

As you can see, the ordering branches after Velar Softening, one branch containing Vowel Shift > Diphthongization, and the other Palatalization > [j]-Deletion.

5 Further Twists

The forms in (30a) obviously do not undergo [j]-Deletion:

(30) a. artifi[ʃi]ality   b. artifi[ʃ]al
        presiden[ʃi]ality   presiden[ʃ]al
        confiden[ʃi]ality   confiden[ʃ]al

You will notice that /j/ has been deleted in the b. set in accordance with the rule of [j]-Deletion in (27). However, /j/ survives as [i] in the closely related a. set, which contains an additional cycle. The failure of [j]-Deletion to apply in the a. set is in fact systematic, and is caused by the presence of stress on the vowel that follows it. Accordingly, we formulate the corresponding rule of [j]-Morification in (31), where we use arrow heads to indicate prosodic projection:

(31)   [j]-Morification:

[−anterior] [+high]   [−cons]
   [−back OR −anterior]   (*
                            *)
                            *

> Check that you follow the data and see how the new rule accounts for them.

(31) needs to be ordered between Palatalization (26) and [j]-deletion (27).
    In the examples in (32), Palatalization applies as predicted, as does, subsequently, [j]-Deletion:

(32) Christian   question   digestion   (in most accents)
        bastion   celestial   bestial   (in some accents)

In particular, Palatalization turns the underlying /t/ (cf. *Christ*, etc.) into [ʧ] – *Canadian, comedian* and the like obviously have /i/, rather than /j/.

> Give the derivation of one of the words in (32).

Consider, however, the data in (33):

(33) Egyptian   exemption   deletion   extinction
      invention   torrential partial   contortion

      decision   exclusion   delusion   division
      allusion   explosion   erosion   invasion

Here, the palatal becomes fricative, rather than affricate, as it should on the basis of *Egypt, decide,* etc.

> Why should we expect an affricate here?

Simple application of Palatalization to the underlying stops would have produced the affricates [ʧ], [ʤ], respectively: compare the forms in (32) above. Clearly, then, there must be a further rule fricativizing the coronal stops in (33) before Palatalization comes into effect: *Egyp*/t/ → *Egyp*[s]*ian* → *Egyp*[ʃ]*ian.*

> Say exactly why we need this further rule turning coronal stops into fricatives.

The rule that turns coronal stops into fricatives is known as Spirantization, and we formulate it in (34):

(34) Spirantization:

$$
\begin{bmatrix} -son \\ +cor \end{bmatrix} \rightarrow \begin{bmatrix} +cont \\ +strid \end{bmatrix} \Big/ \begin{Bmatrix} +son \\ -cont \end{Bmatrix} \underline{\quad} \begin{bmatrix} -cons \\ +high \\ -back \end{bmatrix}
$$

$$
\qquad\qquad\qquad\quad \begin{bmatrix} -cons \\ +high \\ -back \end{bmatrix}
$$
Condition: [+high] does not support a stress bearer

> Explain the meaning of the braces in (34). Hint: [+son, −cont] segments do not block Spirantization (cf. *invent* → *invention*).

The condition on (34) limits the scope of the rule to cases where the high front vowel is directly attached to the syllable node (*Egyptian*), or where it is idiosyncratically outside metrical structure, in the suffix -*y* we discussed in chapter 15 (*presidency*).

> Explain the similarities and the differences between these two cases.

Just as desired, the [+son] or [−cont] disjunction in the environment excludes the cases in (32) above, where the preceding contextual segment is precisely [−son, +cont]: remember that we do not get *Chris[ʃ]ian*, etc.

The data in (35) appear to contradict the rule of Spirantization in (34):

(35) a. [ʧ]   b. [ʤ]
          conceptual   gradual
          eventual   residual
          habitual   individual
          virtuous   deciduous
          adventurous   arduous
          impetuous   incredulous

> Say in what way the data in (35) contradict Spirantization.

These and similar forms exhibit an affricate ([ʧ] or [ʤ]), even though the environment of Spirantization appears to be met, since the stop is followed by /i/ and is not preceded by a fricative.

> Followed by /i/?

The solution to this puzzle is found in the idiosyncrasy of the cluster [iu], to which we have already referred in chapter 10 above.

> Jog your memory on the status of [iu], going back to chapter 10 if necessary.

The [i] of [iu] is either not present in underlying representation or not incorporated into syllable structure until well into the derivation

What seems to be happening is that, at the point where Spirantization becomes operative, the [i] of [iu] is still not available, either because it is not present in underlying representation, being inserted subsequently by rule, or because, if it is present underlyingly, it has not yet been incorporated into syllable structure, and therefore is still not prosodically licensed.

> Explain the difference between these two alternatives in your own words. Which do you think is better?

Either way, forms like those in (35) only have /u/ visible at the point when Spirantization applies, and therefore the environment of the rule is not met.

> Make explicit why the environment of Spirantization is not met in (35).

Subsequently, [i] becomes available as [j] and triggers Palatalization. The order of these three rules is, therefore, Spirantization > [iu]-Formation (in some format we will not decide on) > Palatalization.

> Say why we need this order.

We now incorporate these rules, and their orderings, into the overall rule diagram:

(36)   Overall rule orderings:

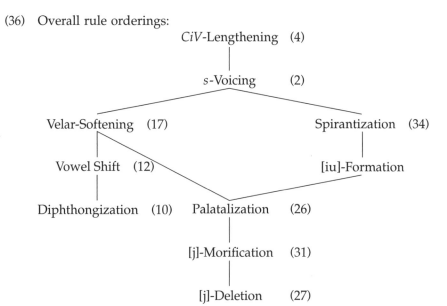

> Study this diagram very carefully, and justify the proposed orderings with some data.

You can see that Spirantization does not interact with Velar Softening. It must, however, follow *s*-Voicing, which counterfeeds it: the product of Spirantization is not subject to *s*-Voicing (cf. *promotion*). In turn, Palatalization is fed by [iu]-Formation (and indirectly by Spirantization) and by Velar Softening.

6 Vowel Length Alternations. Tensing

In chapter 15 we came across the shortening of vowels in forms like *depth* and *divinity* (compare *deep* and *divine*, respectively). We attributed this shortening to a tendency to favour a maximum of two moras per foot, which we formalized as the shortening rule repeated here as (37) (Σ = foot):

(37) Vowel Shortening:

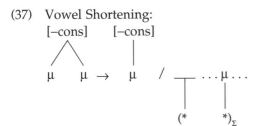

> Remind yourself of how the rule in (37) accounts for the shortening in *depth* and *divinity*.

The interaction of Vowel Shortening with *CiV*-Lengthening is a matter of some interest. Consider again the data in (3a) above, repeated here as (38):

(38) Canadian   collegiate
      Jordanian   courageous
      Mongolia   felonious
      Arabia   colonial
      Babylonian comedian
      regalia   Gregorian

These forms meet the conditions for both *CiV*-Lengthening (cf. /æniæ/ in *Jordanian*) and Vowel Shortening (cf. the trimoraic foot *(deɪ.nɪ)* also in *Jordanian*). The fact that *CiV*-Lengthening wins suggests the order Vowel

Shortening > *CiV*-Lengthening, with Vowel Shortening counterfeeding *CiV*-Lengthening:

> Check carefully that Vowel Shortening must counterfeed Vowel Lengthening.

(39) *Jord* /ænɪ/ *an*

      (* *)<*>   Stress

        *

      NA   Vowel Shortening

      æː   Vowel Lengthening

> Show that the reverse ordering of the rules in (39) would not work.

CiV-Lengthening is not the only rule that lengthens vowels in English. Consider the contrasts in (40):

(40) a. various   b. variety

       social   society

       notorious   notoriety

       simultaneous   simultaneity

       maniac   maniacal

> What exactly do the in contrasts in (40) consist of?

In the forms in column a., the *i* of the suffix must be underlyingly short, because it does not attract stress (*várious*, not *varíous*, etc.), thus justifying our decision to represent this vowel as /ɪ/. In b., however, the same underlying vowel turns up as long and shifted (and, of course, stressed).

> Do you see this in the data in (40b)? Why does /ɪ/ get the stress in *variety*?

The feature [±ATR] is lexically unspecified in English vowels

In order to explain these facts, we must consider the role of the feature [±ATR] in the English vowel system. Briefly, all lexical long non-low vowels end up as [+ATR], that is to say, they are all pronounced tense. The redundancy rule in (41) encapsulates this state of affairs:

(41)   [ ] → [+ATR] / ____
                [−cons]
                [−low]
                  /\
                 μ   μ

By contrast, lexical short vowels are in principle [−ATR]. This suggests the redundancy rule in (42), which complements (41):

(42)   [ ] → [−ATR] / ____
                [−cons]
                   |
                   μ

(41) applies across the board: there simply are no lax (= [−ATR]) phonologically long vowels in standard English.

> Have a quick think about this assertion to satisfy yourself of its veracity. How about the considerable surface length of the low front vowel in most accents, for instance: [æː]? Hint: look at the behaviour of this vowel *vis-à-vis* the phonological rules we have introduced.

By contrast, (42) is violated in the surface in several contexts. One such context is prevocalic position, since in most accents of English short vowels systematically surface as tense when they immediately precede another vowel:

(43)   menial   various   affiliate   toreador
       manual   graduate   tortuous   sensual

English short vowels systematically surface as tense when they immediately precede another vowel

> Do you have a prevocalic tense vowel in all these words?

The situation illustrated in (43) is expressed in the rule of Prevocalic Tensing in (44):

(44)   Prevocalic Tensing:
        [−cons] → [+ATR] / ____ [−cons]

As the result of this rule, the /ɪ/ of both *various* and *variety* will be tensed into [i]. We now want the [i] of *variety* (but not the [i] of *various*) to undergo

Vowel Shift and Diphthongization. How can this happen? The answer is in fact quite simple. First, Prevocalic Tensing must precede Vowel Shift, so as to feed it. Notice, however, that our formulation of Vowel Shift in (12) above requires length in the input vowel, not tenseness. This means that the feeding of Vowel Shift by Prevocalic Tensing is indirect: the vowel tensed by Prevocalic Tensing must first lengthen in *variety*, but, crucially, not in *various* (cf. **var[aɪ]ous*).

Say why the vowel must be lengthened in *variety*, but not in *various*.

Fortunately, the formal differentiation between these two vowels is quite straightforward: [i] carries stress in *variety*, but not in *various*.

Why does stress fall on a different vowel in *various* and *variety*?

Following these observations, we formulate the rule of Stressed Tense Vowel Lengthening as in (45):

(45)   Stressed Tense Vowel Lengthening:

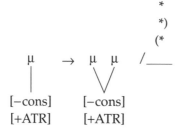

Show how this rule will give the result we are seeking.

The rule of Stressed Tense Vowel Lengthening in (45) feeds Vowel Shift, followed by Diphthongization, and the desired output *var[aɪ]ity* is obtained:

(46)   *var /ɪ/ i ty*
$$\text{* (* *)<*> \quad Stress}$$
$$*$$

    i   Prevocalic tensing
    iː   Stressed Tense Vowel Lengthening

æː   Vowel Shift

æɪ   Diphthongization

var[æɪ]*ity*

> ## List all the ordering relations that obtain in (46).

English non-low vowels also tense in word-final position, as demonstrated by the data in (47) (partly a selection from (25) in chapter 13 above):

English non-low vowels also tense in word-final position

(47) buffal**o**   pit**y**

       mosquit**o** jell**y**

       wind**ow**   yet**i**

       jujits**u**   wack**y**

       tof**u**   vanit**y**

       Kikuy**u**   hock**ey**

Of these, the front high vowel [i] remains short in many (albeit not all) accents, while its counterparts lengthen and/or undergo Diphthongization (but not Vowel Shift, because the vowel remains stressless):

(48) buffal[oʊ]   pit[i]

       mosquit[oʊ] jell[i]

       wind[oʊ]   yet[i]

       jujits[uː]   wack[i]

       tof[uː]   vanit[i]

       Kikuy[uː]   hock[i]

> ## Check your own pronunciation of the words in (48).

The desired results can be obtained either by subjecting non-low final vowels to a tensing rule and then lengthening them all but *i*, or by lengthening them all but *i* in the first place, and then tensing them. We leave it to the reader to work out the details of these alternative analyses, and to evaluate their respective merit.

> ## We would like to encourage you to take up this suggestion.

We wind up the section with an update of our overall list of rule orderings:

(49)   Overall rule orderings:

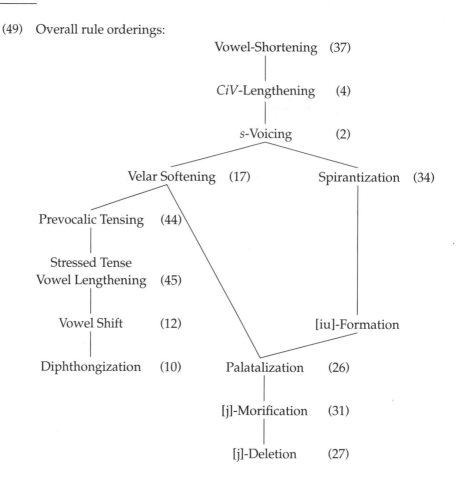

7 Cyclic Rules

By now, we have accumulated a sizeable number of rules related to the segmental patterns of English (we said at the beginning that we are deliberately keeping the focus of the chapter on segmental phonology). As we have been showing, these rules enter into specific ordering relations with each other.

In chapter 16 we explained that phonological rules affecting words are organized into (at least) two blocks, each with its own specific properties, and the most important of these properties is whether or not cyclic rules can apply.

> Jog your memory on the empirical motivation for the division into rule blocks.

In turn, cyclic rules obey the Principle of Strict Cyclicity, which you know blocks their application to any input that has not undergone some previous change in the same cycle.

The Principle of Strict Cyclicity restricts the application of cyclic rules to derived environments

> Remind yourself of the function and the mechanics of the strict cycle.

We will now set about establishing the cyclic or non-cyclic status of each of the rules in (49) above. We will conclude that the dividing line between the two blocks falls just after s-Voicing.

We shall first establish that s-Voicing is cyclic. In chapter 17 we argued that s-Voicing obeys the Principle of Strict Cyclicity.

> Do you remember what the evidence is of s-Voicing obeying the Principle of Strict Cyclicity?

In particular, a fairly substantial number of monomorphemic forms contradict the results of s-Voicing: *basin*, *mason*, and many others (cf. (4) in chapter 17). This is an awkward situation for a non-cyclic rule, which ought also to have voiced the s here, but is unproblematic for a cyclic rule, which has no power to change morpheme-internal structure.

> Make sure you see that the failure of s-Voicing to apply to *basin* is unproblematic in our account.

As you know, there are also some forms where s-Voicing fails to apply across morphemes (*facial* and a few others), but their number is much smaller.

> Explain how the Principle of Strict Cyclicity accounts for this imbalance.

As we explained at the time, this situation is easily accountable for if we leave the voice value of the anterior coronal strident (/s/, /z/) underspecified morpheme-internally, to allow s-Voicing to fill in the + value in a structure-building mode, thus bypassing the Principle of Strict Cyclicity.

> Why exactly is the Principle of Strict Cyclicity bypassed here?

On this analysis, the numerous monomorphemic exceptions are simply the result of a lexical specification [–voice].

> How does lexicalizing [–voice] account for words like *basin*?

On the other hand, the Principle of Strict Cyclicity does not block the rule across morphemes. As expected, the output [z] is present in all forms with cyclic suffixes but a handful of exceptions.

> Why doesn't the Principle of Strict Cyclicity block the rule across morphemes?

s-Voicing, however, systematically fails to apply in forms with non-cyclic suffixes. As we mentioned in the previous chapter, this is evidence that *s*-Voicing is cyclic.

Forms like *resist* in (19b) above present a problem for the cyclicity of *s*-Voicing. In particular, if the Principle of Strict Cyclicity restricts the application of cyclic rules to derived environments, the environment in which the /s/ becomes [z] should be derived in (19b) also. At first sight it is, since we have argued that such forms are made up of a prefix and a stem (*re-sist*, etc.). While this is true, there is evidence across languages that cyclic rules only apply within word domains, and *sist* and the other stems in (19b) are clearly not words.

Cyclic rules only apply within a word domain

> Say exactly what the problem is and propose a solution.

The solution to this conundrum involves leaving the relevant *s* in all such stems unspecified for [±voice] in the lexicon: the rule of *s*-Voicing will now apply without violating strict cyclicity.

> Why will *s*-Voicing not violate strict cyclicity now?

On the grounds discussed, we will assume the cyclic status of *s*-Voicing, with most of the literature.

If *s*-Voicing is cyclic, then all the rules ordered before it must also be cyclic, given the assumption we are operating under that cyclic rules and non-cyclic rules are organized in coherent blocks.

Check that you are absolutely clear about this.

Thus, in particular, *CiV*-Lengthening feeds *s*-Voicing, therefore preceding it in the ordering. Consequently, *CiV*-Lengthening must also be cyclic.

Explain the logic of this reasoning.

We are not aware of any evidence against the cyclicity of *CiV*-Lengthening.

Next, we have shown that Vowel Shortening must precede *CiV*-Lengthening, which it counterfeeds.

Show how *CiV*-Lengthening could logically have fed Vowel Shortening.

If Vowel Shortening precedes *CiV*-Lengthening, then Vowel Shortening must also be cyclic.

Say why.

In fact, in chapter 15 we presented independent evidence for the cyclicity of Vowel Shortening: its operation is restricted to cyclic domains, as attested by the contrast *div*[ɪ]*nity* vs. *div*[aɪ]*nishy*, a possible word.

In what way does *divinishy* attest to the cyclicity of Vowel Shortening?

A similar diagnostic ought to be applicable to *CiV*-Lengthening, but the test is made difficult by the shortage of suitable suffixes.

Make up a couple of hypothetical forms that would prove the point.

We have now established that *s*-Voicing and the two rules that precede it (Vowel Shortening > *CiV*-Lengthening) are cyclic. The next question is whether the two rules that follow *s*-Voicing in the ordering (Velar Softening and Spirantization, in the respective branches) are also cyclic.

Go back to (49) and check the position of these two rules.

If cyclic rules obey the Principle of Strict Cyclicity, as we are maintaining they do, then Velar Softening cannot be cyclic. The reason is that in forms like *re*/k/*ede*, etc., there has not been any previous change in the input, since the stems *cede*, etc., do not constitute cyclic domains, for the same reasons we argued for *sist* in *resist* above.

What are the reasons for *sist* not being a cyclic domain?

One obvious move forward is to declare Velar Softening non-cyclic, as indeed does most of the literature. An alternative would be to represent the forms in question with a lexical /s/, thus specified as [−voice]: a cyclic rule of Velar Softening would now be powerless to apply and voice the /s/, on account of the Principle of Strict Cyclicity. Be that as it may, we will assume with the bulk of the literature that Velar Softening is non-cyclic.

Turning now to Spirantization, it is clearly ordered after *s*-Voicing: *vacation* has [ʃ], rather than [ʒ].

Explain the relevance of the [ʃ] of *vacation* to the ordering *s*-Voicing > Spirantization we are proposing.

On the other hand, Spirantization must precede [iu]-formation, which it counterfeeds: *habitual* has [ʧ], not [ʃ].

Explain the bearing of *habitual* on the ordering Spirantization > [iu]-Formation.

It appears that [iu]-Formation must be non-cyclic, since it applies morpheme-internally with no need for a previous change: *cute*, *dispute*, etc., have [iu:], not [u:].

> Why does morpheme-internal application imply non-cyclic application? You should be absolutely clear on this by now.

If Spirantization precedes non-cyclic [iu]-Formation and follows cyclic s-Voicing, it could in principle be the last cyclic rule or the first non-cyclic rule.

> Say why Spirantization must be last or first in the respective blocks (that is, why it cannot be ordered in the middle of a block).

We are not aware of the existence of a clear argument either way. On the one hand, a number of forms, both derived and underived, fail to undergo Spirantization:

(50) a. Nadia, Tatiana, Katya, radio, patio, sodium, Arcadia
      b. Canadian, comedian, Ovidian, guardian, custodian

These forms could be taken as proof that Spirantization is cyclic: if it were non-cyclic, its application would not be constrained by strict cyclicity, and all the forms in (50) would be expected to undergo it. If Spirantization were cyclic, however, only the forms in (50b) would have to be marked as exceptions.

> Spell out why only the forms in (50b) have to be marked as exceptions if Spirantization were cyclic.

On the other hand, we could and shall assume that such forms as those in (50) simply fail to meet the environment of Spirantization, on account of the *i* of the environment being moraic, at least at the point where Spirantization applies.

> Explain this solution: why should the moraicity of the *i* matter?

In the absence of a clear empirical argument for the non-cyclic status of Spirantization, assumed in most of the literature, we shall fall back on the universal Principle of Late Block Rule Assignment:

(51)   Late Block Rule Assignment:
        Rules are assigned to the latest possible block in the absence of con-
        trary evidence

Following this principle, we shall assume with the rest of the literature
that Spirantization is ordered in the non-cyclic block, and therefore that it
is non-cyclic.

> How does this solution tally with the alternative pronunciations
> [ʃu] and [sju] in words like *issue* in some accents?

Having established that the dividing line between the cyclic and the
non-cyclic blocks falls immediately after *s*-Voicing, we make the identity of
the cyclic rules and their ordering explicit in (52):

(52)   Cyclic Block:

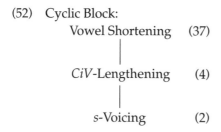

All the rules still to be discussed follow either Velar Softening (17) or
Spirantization (34), and therefore they must be non-cyclic, given the organization of the rules into coherent blocks.

> Remind yourself of which these rules are and how they are
> ordered.

8 Non-Cyclic Rules

In (49) Velar Softening is followed by Prevocalic Tensing > Stressed Tense
Vowel Lengthening > Vowel Shift > Diphthongization in one branch. Vowel
Shift must obviously follow Velar Softening, which counterbleeds or counter-
feeds it: *criticize* and *medicate*, respectively.

> Explain the relevance of data like *criticize* and *medicate* to the ordering of Vowel Shift.

If Velar Softening is non-cyclic, as we have suggested is the case, then by transitivity Vowel Shift must also be non-cyclic.

> Say why vowel shift must be non-cyclic.

Vowel Shift can be fed by the pair Prevocalic Tensing > Stressed Tense Vowel Lengthening, which must consequently precede it.

> Remind yourself of the facts that justify this ordering.

Prevocalic Tensing applies in defiance of the Principle of Strict Cyclicity (cf. *radio*, *patio*, etc.), and therefore it must be non-cyclic. If so, Stressed Tense Vowel Lengthening, which follows Prevocalic Tensing, must also be non-cyclic.

> Say exactly why Stressed Tense Vowel Lengthening must be non-cyclic.

Vowel Shift counterbleeds Diphthongization, which must therefore be ordered after it. Consequently, Diphthongization is also non-cyclic – there is indeed specific evidence that Diphthongization applies within morphemes, as also does Vowel Shift.

> Can you provide some evidence that both Diphthongization and Vowel Shift apply inside morphemes?

In the bottom branch of the non-cyclic block, Palatalization is fed by [iu]-Formation, which therefore precedes it. Accordingly, Palatalization is non-cyclic.

> Why exactly are we saying that Palatalization is non-cyclic?

Finally, Palatalization feeds [ɪ]-Deletion, which must consequently follow it, and thus also be non-cyclic.

> Why exactly is [ɪ]-Deletion non-cyclic?

Notice that Palatalization must also be part of the postlexical block, because it is applicable across words: *di*[ʤ]*ou?, go*[ʧ]*ou!, I mi*[ʃ]*you, do I plea*[ʒ]*ou?,* etc. We have already encountered rules assigned to both the cyclic and the non-cyclic blocks, and we must now extend the possibility of multiple block membership to the postlexical block. Multiple block membership is standardly constrained by the Stratum Contiguity Hypothesis of (53):

(53)   Stratum Contiguity Hypothesis:
         The strata a rule is assigned to must be contiguous

The strata a rule is assigned to must be contiguous

> Would the assigment of a rule to both the cyclic block and the postlexical block be consistent with the Stratum Contiguity Hypothesis?

We have now checked the status of all the rules in our list in (49) above with regard to cyclicity. In (53) we provide the full list of non-cyclic rules with their orderings, to complement the list of cyclic rules in (51):

(53)   Non-cyclic Block:

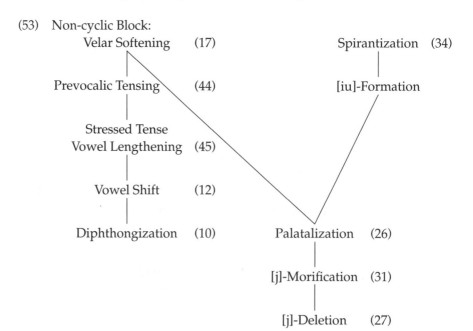

There are a number of segmental rules mentioned in previous chapters which we have omitted from the present discussion. Among these rules are Aspiration, Flapping, Glottalization, Sonorant Devoicing and *l*-Velarization.

> Remind yourself of the effect of each of these rules, and of the context in which we mentioned them.

These rules must be assumed to be postlexical (NB not just non-cyclic), for the simple reason that they possess all the properties that characterize postlexical rules: they are not structure-preserving (that is, they create segments which are not underlying), they have no exceptions, they apply in all types of word (not just in words which constitute "lexical categories"), they are not word-bounded, and so on (see chapter 16 above for a full list of properties of postlexical rules). We shall not explore the mutual ordering of these rules here, in order not to lengthen the chapter any further, but we warmly invite you to work out this ordering as an additional exercise.

Chapter Summary

This chapter has focused on derivations of lexical forms into surface forms and on the ordering of the corresponding rules, concentrating on the lexical rule system of English segmental phonology. Returning to an example we discussed in chapter 17, we showed that in alternations like *Caucasian ~ Caucasus* the rule of *CiV*-Lengthening has to be ordered before *s*-Voicing in order to create its required input. This is a "feeding order". Where a feeding ordering is reversed, the two rules stand in a "counterfeeding order". We used the rules of Vowel Shift and Diphthongization discussed in chapter 8 to illustrate two further types of rule interaction. In particular, we showed that, were Diphthongization to apply before Vowel Shift, Vowel Shift would be robbed of part of its input, a situation known as a "bleeding order". In reality, however, Vowel Shift "counterbleeds" Diphthongization. Although these four types of rule interaction are very widely attested in the languages of the world, there remain large numbers of cases where two rules are apparently non-interacting, since their environments are met whatever the ordering. Despite this, it is often possible to establish the place of two rules in a rule system by "transitivity", that is, through the relation of each of these rules to some third rule. Using transitivity we were indeed able to build up an order for a number of rules of English segmental phonology. We then set about assigning the rules discussed to the cyclic and non-cyclic lexical blocks we introduced in chapter 16. The status of a rule as cyclic implies its adherence to the Principle of Strict Cyclicity. Given block coherence, rules that precede a cyclic rule must be assumed also to be cyclic, and rules that follow a non-cyclic rule also non-cyclic. In the absence of concrete evidence, a rule is assigned to the later block by the principle of "Late Block Rule Assignment". Rules can be assigned to more than one block, provided they comply with the "Stratum Contiguity Hypothesis", which prohibits block skipping.

Key Questions

1 What is meant by "intrinsic" and "extrinsic" ordering of phonological rules?

2 Rules which stand in an Elsewhere relationship are said to be universally ordered: why?

3 What is meant by a feeding order and a counterfeeding order? Give an example of each.

4 What is meant by a bleeding order and a counterbleeding order? Give examples.

5 How does transitivity determine the overall order of rule application?

6 What do angled brackets in a rule indicate?

7 What restriction does the Principle of Strict Cyclicity impose on the application of cyclic rules?

8 How does the Principle of Late Block Rule Assignment help to determine the dividing line between the cyclic and non-cyclic blocks of rules?

9 What are the terms of the Stratum Contiguity Hypothesis?

Further Practice

Rule Ordering in Serbo-Croatian

Consider the following examples of adjectival and past participle paradigms from the South Slavic language Serbo-Croatian, spoken in much of the former Yugoslavia:

a.

Masc.	Fem.	Neut.	Pl.	
mlád	mladá	mladó	mladí	'young'
púst	pustá	pustó	pustí	'empty'
zelén	zelená	zelenó	zelení	'green'
ʧést	ʧestá	ʧestó	ʧestí	'frequent'

(i)   In the context of this evidence, how is main stress assigned in Serbo-Croatian?

Now consider the forms in b.:

b.   *Masc.*   *Fem.*   *Neut.*   *Pl.*
     debéo   debelá   debeló   debelí   'fat'
     vidéo   videlá   videló   videlí   'seen'
     béo   belá   beló   belí   'white'
     hodáo   hodalá   hodaló   hodalí   'walked'

(ii)   Account for the stem alternations in b. by means of a rule.
(iii)   How does this rule interact with the stress assignment procedure?

The forms in c. illustrate a further variation:

c.   *Masc.*   *Fem.*   *Neut.*   *Pl.*
     dóbar   dobrá   dobró   dobrí   'good'
     jásan   jasná   jasnó   jasní   'clear'
     sítan   sitná   sitnó   sitní   'tiny'
     óʃtar   oʃtrá   oʃtró   oʃtrí   'sharp'

(iv)   Account for the stem alternations in c. by means of a further rule.
(v)   How does this rule interact with either of those you have proposed so far?

Now consider the set of forms in d.:

d.   *Masc.*   *Fem.*   *Neut.*   *Pl.*
     podmúkao   podmuklá   podmukló   podmuklí   'treacherous'
     okrúgao   okruglá   okrugló   okruglí   'round'
     óbao   oblá   obló   oblí   'plump'
     pódao   podlá   podló   podlí   'base'

(vi)   What do the forms in d. tell us about the interaction of the rules you have proposed?

Rule Ordering in Tangale

Consider the following nominal paradigms from the Chadic language Tangale, spoken in Nigeria (tones omitted):

a.

Noun	Definite	Possessive 1sg.	Possessive 2sg.	Possessive 3sg.fem.	
loo	loo-i	loo-no	loo-go	loo-do	'meat'
bugat	bugat-i	bugad-no	bugat-ko	bugat-to	'window'
tugat	tugad-i	tugad-no	tugad-go	tugad-do	'berry'
aduk	aduk-i	adug-no	aduk-ko	aduk-to	'load'
kuluk	kulug-i	kulug-no	kulug-go	kulug-do	'harp'

(i)   What are the underlying forms of the nouns listed?
(ii)   Write rules to account for the stem-final voicing alternations.
(iii) Write a rule to account for the alternation in the 2sg. and 3sg.fem. possessive suffixes.

Now consider the noun paradigms in b.:

b.

Noun	Definite	Possessive 1sg.	Possessive 2sg.	Possessive 3sg.fem.	
wudo	wud-i	wud-no	wud-go	wud-do	'tooth'
lutu	lut-i	lut-no	lut-ko	lut-go	'bag'
taga	tag-i	tag-no	tag-go	tag-do	'shoe'
duka	duk-i	duk-no	duk-ko	duk-to	'salt'
ŋuli	ŋul-i	ŋul-no	ŋul-go	ŋul-do	'truth'

(iv)   What are the underlying forms of the nouns listed in b.?
(v)   What further rule operates on the noun paradigm shown in b.?
(vi)   How does this rule interact with those you proposed for a.?

The Elsewhere Condition

Western Finnish

In Western Finnish, word-final /k/ (synchronically justified in the grammar) is either assimilated to the word-initial consonant of a following word, or deleted before a pause or if the following word is vowel initial, as we can see in the examples below:

menek pois   →   menep pois   'go away'
menek alas   →   mene alas   'go down'
menek   →   mene   'go'

(i)   Write two rules to derive both these facts.
(ii)   Can the Elsewhere Condition prevent the incorrect deletion of the word final /k/ from *menek kotiin* ([menek kotiin], not *[mene kotiin])?

Lardil

In the Australian language Lardil the inflection marking future agreement on nouns in the accusative case is -uɽ [uɽ] (e.g. [ʈuŋal-uɽ] 'tree'). If the uninflected form is vowel-final then the [u] is deleted, as we show in column a., except if that final vowel is [i], in which case [w] is inserted between [i] and [u], as we show in column b.

a. wiʈe-ɽ   'inside'   b. kenʈi-wuɽ   'wife'
    mela-ɽ   'sea'   ɲiɲi-wuɽ   'skin'
    ŋuku-ɽ   'water'   tjimpi-wuɽ 'tail'

Demonstrate how an Elsewhere relationship between the rule of vowel deletion and [w] insertion can derive the forms above.

CHAPTER NINETEEN

CONSTRAINTS: OPTIMALITY THEORY

Chapter Objectives

In this chapter you will learn about:
- Markedness statements which impose constraints on possible phonologies.
- The violability of these constraints in Optimality Theory.
- The conflict between markedness constraints and faithfulness constraints.
- Ranking the constraints to obtain the optimal output.
- Examples of the type of constraint operative in language.
- Some specific rankings pertinent to English phonology.
- Cases which appear to call for extrinsic ordering overcome by "correspondence constraints".
- The interpretation of morphology, and of the interaction between morphology and phonology, in Optimality Theory.

The model of phonology we have presented throughout the book consists of several levels of representation related by context-sensitive rules. In particular, forms stored in the lexicon are mapped onto surface forms in a series of steps, each defined by a rule. The complete set of steps mapping a lexical form onto a surface form constitutes a derivation. The effects of the application of one rule can affect the subsequent application of some other rule, either by inducing it or by blocking it. Interaction between rules is regulated through extrinsic rule ordering, although some general principles that promote intrinsic rule ordering also exist. The two basic elements of this model can thus be summarized as follows: (i) there are two levels of representation, namely, the lexical level and the surface level; (ii) the mapping from the lexical level to the surface level is guided, and restrained, by rules. In the present chapter we will explore an alternative, though closely related, model. In particular, we will allow rules a completely free hand: it is in some way as if all rules of all languages applied in each and every possible context. The obviously wild output of this procedure is then filtered through a set of constraints, geared to excluding all the undesired outputs. Clearly, the target outputs vary from language to language: if they didn't, only one language would exist. Such language-specific targets are attained through the language-specific ranking of the crucially violable constraints, the substance of which is ideally conceived of as universal. This alternative model, still very much part of generative phonology, is known as OPTIMALITY THEORY, and it can be extended to morphology and even to syntax.

1 Naturalness of Phonological Inventory: Markedness

In chapter 17 we formalized markedness through the negative statements, or constraints, in (1):

(1)   Some markedness statements:

I   Vowels:

a.	*[+high, +low]	(= Vowels cannot be high and low at the same time)
b.	*[–high, –low]	(= Vowels cannot be non-high and non-low at the same time)
c.	*[+low, –back]	(= Vowels cannot be low and front at the same time)
d.	*[+low, +round]	(= Vowels cannot be low and round at the same time)
e.	*[αround, –αback, –low]	(= Non-low vowels cannot have opposite values for roundness and backness)
f.	*[αATR, αlow]	(= Vowels cannot have the same value for lowness and ATRness)

II   Consonants:

g.	*[dorsal]$_P$	(= Consonants cannot be dorsal)
h.	*[labial]$_P$	(= Consonants cannot be labial)
i.	*[–anterior]	(= Consonants cannot be non-anterior)
j.	*[+distributed]	(= Consonants cannot be distributed)
k.	*[+lateral]	(= Consonants cannot be lateral)
l.	*[+round]	(= Consonants cannot be round)
m.	*[+continuant]	(= Consonants cannot be continuant)
n.	*[αcontinuant, –αstrident]	(= Consonants cannot have opposite values for continuancy and stridency)

III   Common to consonants and vowels:

o.	*[αconsonantal, αsonorant]	(= The values for consonantality and sonorancy cannot agree)
p.	*[αsonorant, –αvoice]	(= The values for sonorancy and voice cannot disagree)
q.	*[+nasal]	(= Segments cannot be nasal)
r.	*[+nasal, –sonorant]	(= Nasals cannot be obstruent)

Taken literally, the constraints in (1) prohibit the occurrence of segments that contain any of the features or feature combinations they mention.

> Provide one prohibited segment for each of the constraints in (1), excepting (1a) and (1r).

The following is a selection of prohibited segments:

(2) I   Vowels:
    a.   Empty set
    b.   *e, *o
    c.   *æ
    d.   *Œ, *ɒ
    e.   *œ, *ø, *y, *ɯ, *ɤ, *ʌ
    f.   *ɪ, *ɛ, *ɐ, *ɔ, *ʊ

   II Consonants:
    g.   *k, *g
    h.   *p, *b, *f
    i.   *ʃ, *ʒ
    j.   *θ, *ð
    k.   *l
    l.   *kʷ
    m.   *f, *θ, *s, *ʃ, *h
    n.   *θ

   III Common to consonants and vowels:
    o.   *r, *l, *m, *n, *ŋ
    p.   *b, *v, *ð, *z, *ʒ, *l̩, *ạ
    q.   *m, *n, *ŋ, *ã, *õ
    r.   Empty set

It is obvious that, if all these predictions were fulfilled, the segmental inventory of natural languages would reduce to the vowels /a, i, u/ and the consonant /t/.

> State briefly why, if all the predictions in (2) were fulfilled, the segmental inventory of language would reduce to /a, i, u, t/.

This is not much material with which to build the tens of thousands of words usually present in any language.

> Why should words have to be built? Aren't they "given"?

As we pointed out in chapter 17, the constraints in (1a) and (1r) are taken to embody physical contradictions. All the other constraints in (1), however, rule out segments which do exist in at least some natural languages (some of them in many), at the underlying or surface levels. This means that these constraints are not to be interpreted literally, as absolute prohibitions on the segments they define.

> If these constraints do not express absolute prohibitions, what do they express?

Constraints (1b) to (1q) need instead to be interpreted as formal encapsulations of partial deviations from the simplest ideal, to which the various languages adhere to varying degrees. For instance, we saw that the most common vocalic system in the world's languages is /i, e, a, o, u/, and this set contains two violations of (1b). For consonants, practically all languages have bilabial stops (in violation of (1h)), most also have velar stops (in violation of (1g)), a majority has fricatives (in violation of (1m)) and nasals (in violation of (1q)), and so on.

Most markedness constraints are formal encapsulations of partial deviations from the simplest ideal

The real function of the constraints in question, therefore, is that of providing a formal measure of the "markedness" inherent in a system.

> Explain briefly what is meant by "markedness".

We achieved this goal in chapter 17 through a set of implicational statements, or REDUNDANCY RULES, directly derived from the negative statements or constraints in (1) in accordance with the general principles of logic (see (22) in chapter 17). These redundancy rules allow us to save on the corresponding lexical information: the less marked the system, the less information it will need in the lexicon. For instance, the low vowel /a/ will only be lexically marked as [+low], and the high vowels /i, u/ as [+high] and [αback] (− and +, respectively): in this way, there will be a direct correspondence between economy of lexical features and naturalness (= less markedness, formally).

We achieve a formal measure of the markedness inherent in a system through a set of REDUNDANCY RULES logically derived from the markedness constraints

> Stop here and explain the correlation between lexical economy and naturalness in your own words.

At this point we must ask why languages have segments which are unnatural, or, in less strong and more formal terms, marked. The answer is that there is an obvious correlation between segment markedness and the size of the system: the more marked the system, the more segments it will contain, assuming of course that the presence of a marked segment presupposes the presence of its unmarked counterpart(s). In turn, there is an obvious correlation between the size of the system and its encoding power: the more segments the system contains, the more lexical contrasts we can build without unduly lengthening the words.

There is an obvious correlation between segment markedness and the size of the system

> Substantiate the point we are making by constructing twenty words out of the radically impoverished segmental inventory /a, t/.

One plausible assumption in this connection is that, the younger we are, the greater the power the markedness constraints hold upon us. As we grow up, however, we become more capable of producing sounds which are less natural, hence the existence of many such sounds in most of the world's languages. Clearly, thus, the tension between the child's tendency towards naturalness and the almost certain presence of markedness in the language of the environment eventually resolves itself in favour of the language of the environment: sooner or later the child has to accept and learn the sounds contained in that language.

The younger we are, the greater the power the markedness constraints hold upon us

> What would happen to the language of the environment if the child did not learn all its sounds?

2 Constraint Ranking: Faithfulness

We shall now propose a formalization for the situation we have been describing. You will soon realise that this formalization is considerably simpler than the one embodied in the rule-and-derivation model we have been presenting up to this point. Indeed, the formalization we are about to introduce may well be the simplest one compatible with the phonology of natural languages.

> Is simplicity an important consideration in grammars? Why?

Suppose that we adopt the constraints in (1) above, and other similar ones, as the only formal devices responsible for the shape of surface representations. In particular, suppose that we do away with rules and derivations altogether. This is the essence of OPTIMALITY THEORY (OT), a novel development in generative phonology which we will be presenting in the remainder of the chapter. In the model we have sketched, the least marked vowel system /a, i, u/ will simply follow from the presence in the corresponding grammar of the constraints in (1b) to (1f) above, which we repeat here for your convenience:

Optimality Theory does away with rules and derivations

> Explain exactly how the /a, i, u/ system follows from (1b) to (1f).

(3) b. *[–high, –low]   (= Vowels cannot be non-high and non-low at the same time)

   c. *[+low, –back]   (= Vowels cannot be low and front at the same time)

   d. *[+low, +round]   (= Vowels cannot be low and round at the same time)

   e. *[αround, –αback, –low] (= Non-low vowels cannot have opposite values for roundness and backness)

   f. *[αATR, αlow]   (= Vowels cannot have the same value for lowness and ATRness)

How do these constraints bring about the desired state of affairs?

> Provide an answer to this question.

Quite simply, any vowel that is not one of /i, a, u/ will violate one of the constraints in (3), and therefore it will be ruled out by the system. Specifically, as we indicated in (2), /e, o/ violate (3b), /æ/ violates (3c), /ɒ/ violates (3d), /y, . . . / as well as /ɯ, . . . / violate (3e), and /ɪ, ʊ, . . . / violate (3f).

> Check on these violations if you have any doubts.

So, as we said then, the system as it stands will only allow /i, a, u/ through. Notice, crucially, that we are achieving this result exclusively through the medium of constraints, without any need for implicational statements, redundancy rules, derivations and the like.

> Explain exactly how /i, a, u/ are obtained just through the constraints.

The question that springs to mind immediately is: given this framework, how come languages do include (some of) the marked segments in their inventories? For instance, how can a language have /e, o/, in violation of (3b), /æ/, in violation of (3c), and so on? Obviously, unless the constraints are neutralized somehow, they will simply block the realization of any underlying form which is not compatible with them. If so, the surface representation will be as impoverished as it was at the child's initial stage.

> Why will the representation be thus impoverished?

Surface forms
must be
FAITHFUL to
the corresponding
lexical forms

The way Optimality Theory deals with this situation is as follows. Besides the markedness constraints in (1)/(3) above, the phonology is assumed to include the requirement, also formalized as a set of "constraints", that surface forms must be FAITHFUL to the corresponding lexical forms, that is, that surface forms must simply reproduce their lexical counterparts, with no change. Given this drive for faithfulness, a pronunciation of an underlying form /pɛn/ as [pin] (or [pan]), induced by the markedness constraint (1b)/(3b), will obviously be disallowed.

> Say exactly how the pronunciation of the underlying form /pɛn/ as [pin] is disallowed.

Or will it? Why isn't the conflict between the faithfulness constraint and the markedness constraint resolved in favour of the markedness constraint? This question constitutes in fact the nub of Optimality Theory. What we are witnessing is a tug of war between two constraints: if one wins, the other will automatically lose. This outcome contradicts our natural expectation that both constraints will be obeyed, the way rules are when their turn comes.

> Do you have a proposal to resolve the tug of war between the constraints?

The answer provided by Optimality Theory is, realistically, that the world is not totally harmonious: more often than not, in order to obey one constraint, another constraint needs to be disobeyed. Formally, the constraints are given a RANKING, the OT equivalent of the ordering of rules that we explored in depth in the preceding chapter. The consequence of mutually ranking two constraints is, of course, that the higher-ranked constraint will be complied with in preference to the lower-ranked constraint:

A higher-ranked constraint is complied with in preference to a lower-ranked constraint

(4)   Ranking metaprinciple:
      A higher-ranked constraint is complied with in preference to a lower-ranked constraint

In our /pɛn/ –/→ [pin] example, the ranking must therefore be IO-IDENT$_{\text{FEAT}}$ » MARKEDNESS (1b)/(3b). The constraint I[NPUT]O[UTPUT]-IDENT[ITY]$_{\text{FEAT[URE]}}$ embodies the specific requirement that surface features be faithful (= identical) to their underlying correspondents. In turn, "»" signals ranking between constraints, just as ">" signals ordering between rules. At the time the child still says [pin] (if that is indeed what the child says in this instance) we can assume that the ranking IO-IDENT$_{\text{FEAT}}$ » MARKEDNESS (1b)/(3b) still has not been established.

Why hasn't the ranking IO-IDENT$_{\text{FEAT}}$ » MARKEDNESS been established yet?

The difference between grammars is a function of differences in constraint rankings

At this time the markedness constraints (1b)/(3b) (and, undoubtedly, others) are still undominated, hence MARKEDNESS (1b)/(3b) » IO-IDENT$_{\text{FEAT}}$. What follows from this simple model is far-reaching: the difference between grammars, whether between child and adult grammar or between grammars of different languages, will be a function of differences in constraint rankings, the constraints themselves being universal. This is Optimality Theory in a nutshell.

Constraints are universal

Explain exactly in what way differences between grammars are a function of differences in the ranking of the constraints.

Constraint summary:
MARKEDNESS: Surface forms must be phonetically natural
IO-IDENT$_{\text{FEAT}}$: Surface features must be faithful to their underlying correspondents

3 Structural Constraints: Syllables

Let us now add to the edifice of Optimality Theory we are building. By now, we have encountered constraints of two kinds: faithfulness constraints, such as IO-IDENT$_{FEAT}$, and markedness constraints, inventoried in (1)/(3) above. Constraints therefore come in families (we will come across other faithfulness constraints besides IO-IDENT$_{FEAT}$ as we go along), each constraint family corresponding to one simple basic concept. For instance, each faithfulness constraint expresses one aspect of the requirement that surface forms must be faithful to the underlying form, all markedness constraints are embodiments of the tendency of language towards phonetic naturalness, and so on.

Constraints come in families, each constraint family corresponding to one simple basic concept

> Say what a constraint family is, in your own words.

Structural constraints are responsible for prosodic structure

The next constraint family we shall look at is made up of structural constraints. Structural constraints are the constraints behind such prosodic structures as syllables and metrical grids.

We know from chapter 9 that the most basic syllable is made up of a consonant and a vowel: CV. Of these two segments, the consonant makes up the syllable onset, and the vowel the nucleus. How can we obtain this state of affairs in our present, constraint-only system? The repertoire of constraints in Optimality Theory includes the set of structural constraints in (5):

(5) Syllable-structure constraints:
ONSET   = All syllables must have an onset
NUCLEUS   = All syllables must have a nucleus
NO-CODA   = Syllables must not have codas
*COMPLEX = Constituents must not be complex

> Say exactly how the simplest syllable is defined by precisely the constraints in (5).

Some of the constraints in (5) are stated positively, that is, as requirements, rather than as prohibitions. It is clear that the constraints in (5) will license precisely the structure we are aiming for: a simple onset followed by a simple nucleus. The table in (6) spells out how this is achieved, on the reasonable assumption that consonants go in the syllable margin, and vowels in the syllable nucleus, an assumption we formalize directly below. In (6) a tick (✓) indicates compliance with the corresponding constraint, and an asterisk (*) indicates a violation:

(6)

	CV	CCV	CVC	CVV	V	C
ONSET	✓	✓	✓	✓	*	✓
NUCLEUS	✓	✓	✓	✓	✓	*
NO-CODA	✓	✓	*	✓	✓	✓
*COMPLEX	✓	*	✓	*	✓	✓

It is clear from (6) that, given the proposed set of unranked constraints, the structure CV, made up of a simple onset and a simple nucleus, will emerge victorious.

> Spell out how CV emerges victorious.

Before testing out this model on the actual syllable structure of English, we must make formally explicit the reason why consonants go in the syllable margins, and vowels in the nucleus. You are already aware that this distribution is motivated by sonority, in particular by the fact that syllable peaks aim for maximum sonority: vowels of course have more sonority than consonants. In Optimality Theory, this situation is formalized by means of the two constraints in (7):

(7)   Sonority constraints:
*M/V = Vowels must not occupy the syllable margin
*N/C = Consonants must not occupy the syllable nucleus

> Specify the contribution of the two constraints in (7) to the selection of CV as the best syllable.

We illustrate the action of these two constraints in (8), where we revert to the non-moraic syllable formalism to keep in with the OT labelling of the relevant constraints (cf. ONSET, NUCLEUS, NO-CODA, etc.):

(8)

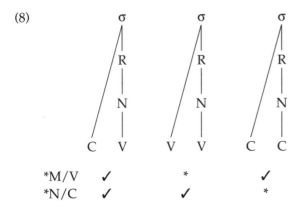

	CV	VV	CC
*M/V	✓	*	✓
*N/C	✓	✓	*

Out of the three possibilities, only CV does not incur a violation of *M/V or *N/C, and therefore CV is the best syllable.

Constraint summary:
ONSET   = All syllables must have an onset
NUCLEUS   = All syllables must have a nucleus
NO-CODA = Syllables must not have codas
*COMPLEX = Constituents must not be complex
*M/V   = Vowels must not occupy the syllable margin
*N/C   = Consonants must not occupy the syllable nucleus

---

4 The Generator. Tableaux

Before we proceed any further, we need to bring out an issue which is as yet only implicit: if the grammar only contains constraints, where do the different CANDIDATES that we are evaluating originate?

> Why is the origin of the candidates at all an issue?

This is of course a central question, because without candidates there would be no evaluation, and without evaluation the constraints would remain unenforced. The answer is that the model includes a further component, named GEN, for "generator", which randomly generates surface forms from each lexical representation, using only the most elementary principles of linguistic logic.

GEN randomly generates surface forms from each lexical representation

> Advance one or two outputs of GEN.

GEN will therefore produce a variety of syllabic parsings, a variety of associations between elements in different tiers (including features), and so on. For instance, given the sequence /hæpɪ/, we can assume that GEN will offer us the candidates in (9), at least:

(9)

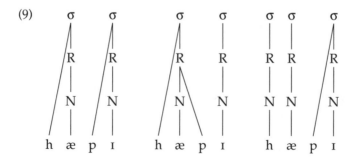

The job of the constraints, specifically ranked for each grammar, is the EVALUATION of these candidates, that is, the selection of one candidate as the most HARMONIC with respect to the grammar in question.

The job of the ranked constraints is the EVALUATION of candidates, one of which is selected as the most HARMONIC

> How will the candidate's harmony be established?

The candidate thus selected is the WINNER of the evaluation procedure. Accordingly, this candidate emerges as the surface representative of the corresponding underlying form.

The interaction between constraints and candidates is conventionally represented in tables with a special format, known as "tableaux" (singular: TABLEAU). In (10) we give the tableau for the syllabic structure of *happy*:

(10)

	Onset	Nucleus	No-coda	*Complex	*M/V	*N/C
a. ☞						
b.	*		*			
c.	**					*

You will notice in (10) that constraint violations are signalled with an asterisk in the appropriate box, while constraint compliances are simply left blank. You can also see that a tableau is simply a plotting of a set of candidates (usually listed in the left column) against the set of constraints (usually listed in the top row), with boxes in every intersection, in the style of a bar of chocolate. Unranked constraints are separated by a dotted line, the tableau equivalent of a comma in the text. The superiority of candidate (10a) (marked with a pointing hand as the winner) is clear at a glance: it is the only candidate which does not incur any violation of any constraint.

The visual advantages of tableaux are obvious. We could of course have included other candidates in (10) (and, correspondingly, in (9)), since, as we mentioned earlier, GEN knows few limits, if any, on the number of candidates it can produce. However, the common practice is, sensibly, to limit the selection of candidates to plausible forms. Similarly, only the constraints that are conceivably relevant to the phenomenon being examined are usually considered.

A tableau is a plotting of a set of candidates against the set of constraints

What exactly do we mean by "plausible candidates" and "relevant constraints"?

For your convenience, we end this section with a schematic summing up of the machinery of Optimality Theory we have introduced so far:

(11)   Optimality Theory machinery:

Device	*Function*
GEN(erator)	Generates candidates
Constraints	Reject candidates
Constraint rankings	Define specific grammars
Tableaux	Provide a visual representation of the process of evaluation of specific lexical forms by the ranked constraints

Ponder over this list until you feel comfortable with it.

5   Basic English Syllables

We will now put the machinery we have introduced to use to analyse English syllables. We shall enrich and refine this machinery as the need arises.

Consider first a simple and ordinary word like *egg*. This form violates Onset and No-Coda.

> Why does *egg* violate Onset and No-coda? How can these violations be remedied?

The violation of Onset could in principle be remedied by the insertion of a consonant in the onset position. Such insertion, or EPENTHESIS, is indeed the norm in some languages: for instance, Arabic epenthesizes [ʔ] when there is no lexical segment to occupy the onset position, as does German foot-initially. In English, however, the pronunciation [ɛg] prevails over its epenthesized alternative [ʔɛg], at least in ordinary speech.

> How can the prevalence of [ɛg] over [ʔɛg] be formalized in OT?

The prevalence of the pronunciation [ɛg] means that, in the case we are discussing, faithfulness to the lexical form takes priority over filling the onset. The (faithfulness) constraint that blocks epenthesis is known as Dep[ENDENCY] (Fill in early versions of Optimality Theory). Dep requires every surface segment to have a lexical correspondent, on which it therefore "depends".

> How exactly does Dep contribute to the selection of [ɛg] over [ʔɛg]?

Clearly, in order to get [ɛg] rather than *[ʔɛg] we need to rank Dep higher than Onset, as in (12). Higher ranking is represented in tableaux by means of a solid vertical line between the columns of the two relevant constraints:

(12)

/ɛg/	Dep	Onset
☞ ɛg		*
ʔɛg	*!	

You can see that the consequence of ranking Dep higher than Onset is the selection of [ɛg] over *[ʔɛg] as the surface form: [ɛg] obviously fares better than *[ʔɛg] with regard to the higher-ranked constraint Dep. Notice in particular that [ʔɛg] incurs a violation of Dep, while [ɛg] does not. The violation of the higher-ranked DEP by [?ɛg] is therefore a FATAL VIOLATION, and the evaluation need not be carried any further. This end-game situation is signalled by the exclamation mark after the asterisk in the DEP column and the shading of all the subsequent boxes, which are now irrelevant to the evaluation procedure: the violation of the lower-ranked constraint ONSET by the winning candidate [ɛg] in (12) is of no consequence.

> Say exactly why it is of no consequence.

Next, let us examine the violation of NO-CODA by [ɛg]. There are two obvious ways of circumventing this violation. First, we can epenthetize a final vowel, say, [ə], to create an additional syllable of which /g/ will be the onset: [ɛ.gə]. This result obviously does not match the data, and therefore we conclude that NO-CODA is also ranked lower than DEP (ONSET and NO-CODA are of course equally ranked, as indicated by the dotted line separating their respective columns):

(13)

/ɛg/	DEP	ONSET	NO-CODA
☞ ɛg		*	*
ɛgə	*!	*	

> How come [ɛg] beats [ɛgə] if each candidate scores the same number of violations?

In (13) it becomes clear that number of violations is irrelevant to the evaluation procedure: the two candidates in (13) tie in number of violations, but [ɛg] still wins. The decisive criterion is, obviously, compliance with the higher-ranked constraints, in line with the Ranking Metaprinciple in (4) above.

An alternative strategy to circumvent the violation of NO-CODA by /ɛg/ involves deleting /g/, to obtain the output form [ɛ]. This form may violate other constraints of English (in particular, it violates the constraint that words must contain at least one binary foot), but it manifestly does not violate NO-CODA. However, faithfulness prevails over structural perfection here too: you will recall from chapters 9, 10 and 16 that English does allow for codas. Formally, therefore, NO-CODA needs to be ranked lower than MAX[IMALITY] (PARSE in early Optimality Theory), the constraint responsible for the maximal mapping of underlying segments onto the surface:

(14)

/ɛg/	DEP	MAX	ONSET	NO-CODA
☞ ɛg			*	*
ɛgə	*!		*	
ɛ		*!	*	

You will notice that in (14) DEP and MAX are fatally violated by the losing candidates ([ɛgə] and [ɛ], respectively). Note that, because these two constraints are mutually unranked, the MAX box is not shaded, even though the preceding box contains a fatal violation.

Tableaux (12) to (14) obviously leave out many constraints.

> Any idea why we have left out these constraints?

Indeed, tableaux are routinely simplified in order to keep them within manageable spatial limits: the total number of constraints is very high, probably running into the hundreds, and the number of candidates is also very high, indeed infinite if epenthesis is given a free rein.

Tableaux are routinely simplified in order keep them within manageable spatial limits

> Why does the inclusion of epenthesis make the number of candidates infinite?

Granted all this, we now combine in (15) the tableaux in (12) and (14) (which subsumes (13)), for a more complete evaluation of [ɛg] and its competitors:

(15)

/ɛg/	DEP	MAX	ONSET	NO-CODA
☞ ɛg			*	*
ɛgə	*!		*	
ɛ		*!	*	
ʔɛg	*!			*

Tableau (15) makes clear why [ɛg] is selected over all its competitors: it fares best with regard to the highest-ranked constraints, DEP and MAX.

The constraint summary boxes include all the constraints mentioned in the text in the respective section. Newly introduced constraints are defined, but old constraints are simply listed. We strongly advise you to provide the definitions of these constraints for practice (check them up in the appropriate previous box if necessary).

Constraint summary:
ONSET
NO-CODA
DEP (formerly FILL)   = Every surface segment must have a lexical correspondent
MAX (formerly PARSE) = Underlying segments must be mapped onto the surface

6 Syllable Complexities

We have now analysed *egg* successfully. You know, however, that English syllables may include complex onsets and complex nuclei. We capture this legitimate complexity of English onsets and nuclei by ranking the structural constraint *COMPLEX lower than the faithfulness constraints DEP and MAX, as we illustrate with *clay* in (16):

(16)

/kleɪ/	DEP	MAX	ONSET	NO-CODA	*COMPLEX
☞ kleɪ					**
ke		*!*			
kle		*!			*
kə.leɪ	*!				*
kə.le	*!	*!			

Now, while *clay* is a legitimate English word, **lkay* obviously is not, even though it contains exactly the same segments.

Remind yourself of why **lkay* is not legitimate.

The reason for the difference between *clay* and **lkay* lies, of course, in the fact that **lkay* violates Sonority Sequencing, which we incorporate into our repertoire of constraints under the label Son[ority].

> Remind yourself of the role of Sonority Sequencing in syllabification.

The constraint Son must obviously be given a high ranking:

(17)

/lkeɪ/	Son	Dep	Max	Onset	No-Coda	*Complex
lkeɪ	*					**

Notice that the table in (17) does not constitute a tableau as such, because it carries out no evaluation. We have included it here simply to illustrate the high ranking of Son.

A real-life example of a Son violation is provided by the word *sky*. We obviously also want Son to prevent /sk/ from making up a complex onset. In chapter 16 we suggested that such a word-initial /s/ is salvaged from phonetic obliteration by direct affiliation to the Phonological Word (PW), skipping the σ node.

> Why should we expect the *s* to go to the σ node?

The affiliation of the word-initial /s/ to PW violates the Strict Layer Hypothesis in (58) of chapter 16, which we now incorporate into the OT model as the constraint SLH.

Sonority Sequencing and the Strict Layer Hypothesis are encapsulated in the constraints Son and SLH, respectively

> Remind yourself of the Strict Layer Hypothesis, and say why it gets violated in the case we are discussing.

SLH is obviously ranked lower than the faithfulness constraints Dep and Max:

> Why are we saying that SLH must be ranked lower?

(18)

/skaɪ/	Son	Dep	Max	Onset	No-Coda	*Complex	SLH
☞ PW / σ / R / N / s k a ɪ						*	*
σ / R / N / s k a ɪ	*!					**	

The inevitable violation of SLH by word-initial **s + obstruent** in English occurs because, as we mentioned in chapter 16, PW edges are endowed with special licensing powers, at least in English. Word-edge licensing also accounts for English extra word-final coronals, which we suggested in chapter 16 above also attach directly to the PW node (cf. *si*[ksθs]).

In chapters 10 and 16 we also saw that English allows one extra word-final consonant to be directly licensed by σ, provided Sonority Sequencing is complied with: *lame, lamp*.

> Why do we assume that the extra word-final consonant is licensed by σ, rather than by PW?

At present, the final *p* of *lamp* would be parsable in the coda, together with *m*, since we have ranked *Complex lower than Dep and Max, to allow for complex onsets. However, given the arguments in chapters 10 and 16, this parsing is undesirable.

Remind yourself of the arguments against parsing the *p* of *lamp* in the coda.

We shall resolve the tension between the need for a low ranking of *COM-PLEX for onsets, and the need for a high ranking for codas by the inclusion of a specific constraint *COMPLEX^{CODA}, over and above the general constraint *COMPLEX. *COMPLEX^{CODA} must obviously be ranked higher than DEP and MAX. By transitivity, it will also be ranked higher than *COMPLEX, indeed as follows independently from the Elsewhere Condition, renamed PĀṆINI'S THEOREM in Optimality Theory to honour its original discoverer:

In OT the Elsewhere Condition is renamed PĀṆINI'S THEOREM, to honour its original discoverer

With the help of pencil and paper, work out why Pāṇini's Theorem ranks *COMPLEX^{CODA} higher than *COMPLEX.

(19)

/lamp/	*COMPLEX^{CODA}	SON	DEP	MAX	ONSET	NO-CODA	*COMPLEX	SLH
☞ σ / R / N / l a m p						*	*	*
σ / R / N / l a m p	*!					*	*	

One last issue needs addressing before we close the discussion on syllables. In particular, the low ranking of *COMPLEX is consistent with the selection of both onsets and rimes with more than two elements, as in *[blju:] and [leɪm], respectively (complex codas are of course totally ruled out by *COMPLEX^{CODA}).

Explain exactly how we are dealing with complexity in the English onset and coda.

We clearly need an undominated constraint to rule out such configurations. Crucially, this constraint must outrank MAX, which would force any number of lexical segments through to the surface.

The constraint we are looking for is *COMPLEX&COMPLEX. This type of constraint differs from all our previous ones in that it contains a self-conjunction. Clearly, the self-conjunction of COMPLEX will rule out any constituent which includes more complexity than the minimal two-element one. A rime with a complex nucleus and a coda, for instance, will be complex twice over:

> A self-conjoined constraint rules out forms which incur more violations than the ones barred by the simple constraint

(20)

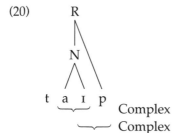

The configuration in (20) violates *COMPLEX&COMPLEX, and consequently it will be disallowed if this constraint is sufficiently high in the ranking: it is in fact undominated in English.

Work out how a ternary onset would also be complex twice over.

Constraint summary:

*COMPLEX

DEP

MAX

*COMPLEX^{CODA} = No complex codas

*COMPLEX&COMPLEX = No joint complexity

SLH   = Strict Layer Hypothesis

SON   = Sonority Sequencing

7 Basic Metrical Structure

We will now propose an interpretation of stress in terms of Optimality Theory. You know from chapter 13 above that in English verbs and primary adjectives stress is maximally penultimate.

Jog your memory on this matter if you need to.

In Optimality Theory, this pattern is formalized by means of the constraints V/μ, FOOT BINARITY, FOOT TYPE_TROCHEE and ALIGN-RIGHT, as we shall now explain.

V/μ demands that rime vowels be moraic. F[OO]T BIN[ARITY] requires feet to be strictly binary, either in terms of moras (in quantity-sensitive systems) or in terms of syllables (in quantity-insensitive systems). English is of course quantity-sensitive, and therefore all English feet will have to be bimoraic. F[OO]T TYPE_TROC[HEE] licenses left-headed feet ("trochees"), as against right-headed feet ("iambs"), which require the opposite setting, F[OO]T TYPE_IAMB. We illustrate the action of these three constraints in (21), before proceeding to discuss the fourth constraint we listed, ALIGN-RIGHT:

> FTBIN requires feet to be strictly binary

(21)	/develop/	V/μ	FTBIN	FT-TYPE_TROC
a.	* μ(μ μ) | | | develop			
b.	* (μ μ μ) | | | develop		*!	
c.	* μ (μ μ) | | | develop			*!
d.	* (μ μ)μ | | | develop			

You can see that candidates b. and c. are rejected, on account of their violation of FtBin and Ft-Type$_{TROC}$, respectively. By contrast, both candidate a. and candidate d. emerge unscathed. We know, however, that only candidate a. is legitimate. The necessary further selection is carried out by the constraint Align-Right, a member of the Align family. As suggested by the label, Align constraints regulate the spatial relation between two elements. In particular, Align implements either strict linearization, by requiring that two elements be sequentially abutting, or structural alignment, by requiring that the edges of two constituents in different structural levels be superimposed. In the case we are discussing, we want the right edge of the prosodic word to be superimposed on the right edge of a foot. We illustrate the situation in (22):

Align constraints implement either strict linearization (by requiring that two elements be sequentially abutting) or structural alignment (by requiring that the edges of two constituents in different structural levels be superimposed)

(22)

/develop/	V/μ	FtBin	Ft-Type$_{TROC}$	Align-Right
a. * μ (μ μ) ☞ ｜ ｜ ｜ develop				
b. * (μ μ)μ ｜ ｜ ｜ ｜ develop				*!

The desired result, *devélop*, has now been attained, as you can see.

Constraint summary:

Align-Right = The right edge of the prosodic word must be superimposed on the right edge of a foot

FtBin	= Feet must be strictly binary
Ft-Type$_{IAMB}$	= Feet must be right-headed ("iambs")
Ft-Type$_{TROC}$	= Feet must be left-headed ("trochees")
V/μ	= Rime vowels must be moraic

8 Extrametricality

You will recall that the stress pattern of English nouns is like the stress pattern of English verbs, with right extrametricality added. In Optimality Theory, right extrametricality is encoded in the constraint NON-FIN[ALITY], which keeps metrical structure away from the final edge of the phonological word:

Right extrametricality is encoded in the constraint NON-FINALITY

(23)

/America/	NON-FIN
a. * μ (μ μ)μ | | | | Americ a	
b. * μ μ(μ μ) | | | | Americ a	*!

The foot of candidate b. includes the mora on the right edge of the phonological word, and therefore it incurs a violation of NON-FIN. Candidate a. of course incurs a violation of ALIGN-RIGHT, which you know requires that the right edge of the phonological word be superimposed on the right edge of a foot. Indeed, the requirements of ALIGN-RIGHT and NON-FIN are mutually at odds, since the satisfaction of one of these constraints inevitably results in the violation of its counterpart.

> Explain exactly why NON-FIN and ALIGN-RIGHT are at odds with each other.

The existence of a conflict between the two constraints obviously means that for the set of English nouns and derived adjectives NON-FIN must outrank ALIGN-RIGHT:

(24)

/America/	NON-FIN	ALIGN-RIGHT
a. * μ (μ μ)μ | | | | Americ a ☞		*
b. * μ μ(μ μ) | | | | Amer ic a	*!	

For verbs and underived adjectives we need the opposite ranking – remember that we are assuming that all constraints are present in all grammars, although their ranking does of course vary from grammar to grammar:

> On what grounds are we assuming that all constraints are present in all grammars?

(25)

/develop/	ALIGN-RIGHT	NON-FIN
a. * μ(μ μ) | | | develop ☞		*
b. * (μ μ)μ | | | develop	*!	

The tableau in (26) incorporates the full set of constraints directly relevant to stress in nouns:

(26)

/America/	V/μ	FtBin	Ft-Type_TROC	Non-Fin	Align-Right
a. ☞ * μ (μ μ)μ Americ a					*
b. * μ μ(μ μ) Amer ic a				*!	
c. * (μ μ)μ μ America					**!
d. * μ (μ μ μ) America	*!			*!	
e. * μ (μ)μ μ Americ a	*!				**

You can see that the most harmonic candidate is, inevitably, a., which only incurs one violation of ALIGN-RIGHT. Notice in particular that candidate c. incurs two such violations, and, consequently, it is discarded.

Constraint summary:
ALIGN-RIGHT
FTBIN
FT-TYPE_TROC
V/μ
NON-FIN   = No metrical structure on the final edge of the phonological word

---

9 Quantity-Sensitivity

In chapter 13 we saw that a heavy syllable in the vicinity of the right edge attracts the stress: compare *agénda* with *América*, and *collápse* with *devélop*.

In OT, accenting of heavy syllables is encapsulated in a constraint labelled WEIGHT-TO-STRESS PRINCIPLE

The OT constraint responsible for this attraction is called the WEIGHT-TO-STRESS PRINCIPLE (WTS), and simply stipulates that a heavy syllable must carry stress. The application of WTS to *agenda* or *collapse* obviously presupposes the assessment of *gen* and *lapse* as heavy. We achieve this assessment through the OT equivalent of the Weight-by-Position principle projecting moras from coda consonants. Remember, however, that the word-final consonant does not project a mora: compare *collápse* with *devélop*, not **develóp*, because it has only one consonant on the right edge. This fact prompted the restriction of WEIGHT BY POSITION (WBP) to coda consonants immediately followed by another consonant (and preceded by a vowel) – in all other cases, mora provision is suppressed by the constraint *μ, a manifestation of the more general *STRUCTURE, which simply disfavours structure:

(27)

/develop/	V/μ	FtBin	Ft-Type$_{\text{TROC}}$	Align-Right	WTS	WBP	Non-Fin	*μ

a.   *
  μ(μ μ)
☞ | | |
  develop
							*	***

b. * (μ μ)μ | | | develop				*!				***
c. * (μ μ μ) | | | develop		*!					*	***
d. * μ μ(μμ) | | | | deve lop							*	****!
e. * μ(μ μ) | | | develop			*!				*	***

(28)

/collapse/	V/μ	FtBin	Ft-Type$_{TROC}$	Align-Right	WTS	WBP	Non-Fin	*μ
a. * μ (μμ) ☞ | || collapse							*	***
b. * (μ μ)μ | || colla pse				*!	*!			***
c. * (μ μμ) | || collapse		*!			*!		*	***
d. * (μ μ) | | collapse						*!	*	**
e. * (μ μ) | | collapse			*!			*!	*	**

The evaluation of *agenda* runs along similar lines to that of *collapse*, even though the consonant cluster is now word-internal. The ranking of Align-Right and Non-Fin is, of course, reversed, as we know is the case with all nouns:

(29)

/agenda/	V/μ	FtBin	Ft-Type_{TROC}	Non-Fin	WTS	WBP	Align-Right	*μ
a.　＊ 　μ(μμ)μ ☞ ┃┃┃┃ 　age nda							*	****
b. ＊ (μ μ)μ μ ┃┃┃┃ age nda					*!		**	****
c. ＊ (μ μμ)μ ┃┃┃┃ agenda		*!			*!		*	****

Constraint summary:
Align-Right
FtBin
Ft-Type_{TROC}
Non-Fin
V/μ
WBP   = Weight by Position
WTS   = Heavy syllables must carry stress
*μ   = No mora
*Structure = No structure

10 Secondary Footing

In chapter 15 we saw that in words like *pròsopopéia* the word-initial secondary stress is obtained by means of left-to-right (non-cyclic) footing. In OT, this requires the addition of a constraint Align-Left, yielding the opposite effect to Align-Right. In words like these, Align-Right therefore needs to be restricted to the head foot, and thus we recast it as Align-Right^{HEAD-FT}. Align-Right^{HEAD-FT} outranks the more general Align-Left by Pāṇini's Theorem, as we show in (30). To keep the tableau simple we omit those constraints which must be obvious by now:

(30)

/prosopopeia/	Non-Fin	WTS	WBP	Align-Right^HEAD-FT	Align-Left
a. ☞ (μ μ) μ(μμ)μ prosopopei a				*	***
b. (μ μ) μ(μμ)μ prosopopei a				**!**	***
c. μ(μ μ)(μμ)μ prosopopei a				*	****!

Words like *Epàminóndas*, with secondary stress in the second syllable, ostensibly require a constraint Non-Initial, mirroring Non-Fin, to ensure that the initial syllable is skipped.

Constraint summary:

Non-Fin

WBP

WTS

Align-Left   = Feet must be aligned with the word's left edge

Align-Right^HEAD-FT = The head foot must be aligned with the word's right edge

Non-Initial   = The word-initial syllable must not be metrified

---

11 Correspondence Constraints

In chapter 16 we presented evidence for the stratification of phonological rules. The resulting strata, or levels, are by definition mutually ordered. Ordering, whether of rules or of strata, is at odds with the common tenet of OT that constraints apply in parallel, with no intermediate stages between the lexical and the surface representations. We shall resolve this conflict by

Ordering, whether of rules or of strata, is at odds with the common tenet of OT that constraints apply in parallel

CORRESPON-
DENCE CON-
STRAINTS impose
correspondences
between surface
forms

introducing transderivational CORRESPONDENCE CONSTRAINTS, that is, constraints that impose correspondences between surface forms.

In the English of both New York and Philadelphia the low front lax vowel [æ] tenses to [Æ] in closed syllables, subject to additional requirements on the identity of the coda consonant, which are irrelevant for us here ([Æ] is our ad hoc phonetic symbol for a tense [æ]):

(31) a. [Æ]   b. [æ]
          man.   ma.nage
          can.did   ca.nnibal
          mas.ter   Ma.ssachusetts
          jam.   ja.nitor
          plant.   pla.net

This alternation permeates some derivational paradigms, as expected:

(32) a. [Æ]   b. [æ]
          class.   cla.ssic
          mass.   ma.ssive
          pass.   pa.ssive

In other forms, however, [æ] tenses even in ostensibly open syllables:

(33) a. [Æ]   b. [Æ]
          class.   cla.ssy
          mass.   ma.ssable
          pass.   pa.ssing

In (33b), the principle of Minimal Onset Satisfaction, now recast as the OT constraint ONSET, will parse the intervocalic consonant in the second syllable: *cla.ssy*, etc. Despite this, the [æ] tenses to [Æ], as shown.

By this stage you should have no difficulty in detecting a crucial difference between the forms in (32b) and those in (33b), over and above the difference in the quality of the vowel in question.

> Can you tell what this second difference between (32b) and (33b) is?

In particular, the derivatives in (32b) have suffixes that in chapter 16 we allotted to level 1, whereas the derivatives in (33b) have level-2 suffixes. Intuitively, this difference is responsible for the different fate of the vowel in the two sets. We will now propose an OT formalization for this intuition.

We will encapsulate the tensing of /æ/ in a constraint prohibiting the occurrence of [æ] in closed syllables: *[æc.]. We will assume that other constraints, which we will not include in the evaluation to keep the exposition simple, rule out undesired solutions to the problem input /æC./ – for instance, the deletion of the C (ruled out by a high ranking of MAX), the epenthesis of a vowel (ruled out by a high ranking of DEP), or the realization of the underlying /æ/ as a vowel other than [Æ] (ruled out by a high ranking of the relevant IO-IDENT$_{FEAT}$ constraints).

Explain how these constraints produce the results we seek.

The other constraints directly involved in the evaluation are *TENSE$_{LOW}$, which prohibits tense low vowels, and IO-IDENT$_{TENSE}$, which requires the surface realization of the underlying value for tense. We illustrate with *class* [klÆs] in (34):

(34) a.

/klæs/	*[æc.]	*TENSE$_{LOW}$	IO-IDENT$_{TENSE}$
klæs	*!		
☞ klÆs		*	*

b.

/klÆs/	*[æc.]	*TENSE$_{LOW}$	IO-IDENT$_{TENSE}$
klæs	*!		*
☞ klÆs		*	

You can see that the candidate with [Æ] is selected irrespective of whether we postulate /Æ/ or /æ/ underlyingly. For *classic*, with an open first syllable, the result will be the opposite one, correctly so:

(35) a.

/klæsɪk/	*[æc.]	*TENSE$_{LOW}$	IO-IDENT$_{TENSE}$
☞ klæ.sɪk			
klÆ.sɪk		*!	*

b.

/klÆsɪk/	*[æc.]	*TENSE$_{LOW}$	IO-IDENT$_{TENSE}$
☞ klæ.sɪk			*
klÆ.sɪk		*!	

If we apply the same procedure to *classy*, we will obviously obtain *cl[æ]ssy*, which is incorrect for the accents in question. As a consequence, we shall adopt a constraint BD-IDENT$_{\text{TENSE}}$ imposing identity in tenseness between the BASE *class* and its DERIVATIVE *classy*. Like the IO-IDENT constraints before, BD-IDENT$_{\text{TENSE}}$ presupposes a CORRESPONDENCE relation between two terms. Such constraints are accordingly categorized as CORRESPONDENCE CONSTRAINTS, and the branch of Optimality Theory that encompasses them is referred to as CORRESPONDENCE THEORY. Clearly, BD-IDENT$_{\text{TENSE}}$ must outrank all the other relevant conflicting constraints if the desired output is to be obtained. Against this background, the evaluation of *cl[Æ]ssy* goes as follows:

(36) a.

/klæsɪ/	BD-IDENT$_{\text{TENSE}}$	*TENSE$_{\text{LOW}}$	IO-IDENT$_{\text{TENSE}}$
klæ.sɪ	*!		
☞ klÆ.sɪ		*	*

b.

/klÆsɪ/	BD-IDENT$_{\text{TENSE}}$	*TENSE$_{\text{LOW}}$	IO-IDENT$_{\text{TENSE}}$
klæ.sɪ	*!		*
☞ klÆ.sɪ		*	

Because of the high ranking of BD-IDENT$_{\text{TENSE}}$, the output *cl[Æ]ssy* prevails, irrespective of the requirements of the other constraints.

> Make explicit in what way the prevalence of BD-IDENTITY yields [Æ] in *classy*. In particular, what does it presuppose?

The high ranking of BD-IDENT$_{\text{TENSE}}$ must obviously be confined to forms with level-2 suffixes, such as the *-y* of *classy*. In forms with level-1 suffixes, BD-IDENT$_{\text{TENSE}}$ must be outranked by *[æc.], TENSE$_{\text{LOW}}$ and IO-IDENT$_{\text{TENSE}}$, as you can verify by re-examining the tableau in (35) above. This means that the difference between strata needs to be maintained under OT, as it surely does under any theory, given the facts.

> Say in what ways the facts impose the difference between strata.

What will vary is the mode of implementation – by rule and affixation ordering in rule-and-derivation phonology, and by transderivational correspondence constraints and constraint ranking in OT. Notice that there is a close connection between both approaches, despite apparent disparities. Indeed, it is possible to mimic the correspondence formalism of OT in rule-and-derivation formalism by stipulating that in level 2 phonological segmental processes take place before affixation:

(37)   /klæs/   /klæs/   /klæs/

    Level 1:
    -ɪk suffixation   ---------   klæs-ɪk   ---------
    Syllabification   .klæs.   .klæ.sɪk.   .klæs.

    Level 2:
    æ-Tensing   Æ   NA   Æ
    -ɪ suffixation   ---------   ---------   .klÆs.ɪ.
    Resyllabification   NA   NA   .klÆ.sɪ.

                       [klÆs]   [klæsɪk]   [klÆsɪ]

> Study these derivations and state in what way they mimic the OT correspondence formalism.

You can see that æ-Tensing needs to be ordered in stratum 2. In particular, if it were ordered in stratum 1 it would be cyclic, and it would wrongly apply in forms with stratum-1 suffixes like *classic*. By contrast, by being ordered before affixation in stratum 2 it has precisely the desired effects.

Constraint summary:
*[æc.]   = No lax [æ] in closed syllables
BD-IDENT$_{TENSE}$ = Base-derivative faithfulness for tenseness
IO-IDENT$_{TENSE}$ = Input–output faithfulness for tenseness
*TENSE$_{LOW}$ = No tense low vowels

---

12 Cyclic Effects

In chapter 15 we presented some rather spectacular results of the cyclic application of rules in the tonal phonology of Tiv and in the metrical phonology of English. Correspondence constraints can also replicate the cycle of derivational phonology. Consider the words in (38), which supplement the ones we used in chapter 15 to justify the English stress cycle:

(38) a.   medícinal   b.   medìcinálity
           divísible   divìsibílity
           Napóleon   napòleónic
           persónify   persònificátion
           assímilable   assìmilabílity

You will notice once more that the secondary stress of the derivatives in b. falls on the syllable that bears the primary stress in their bases in a., rather than on the initial syllable predicted by the secondary stress procedure: compare *pròsopopéia* in section 10 above. We have of course come across other instances of secondary stress in the second syllable (cf. *Epàminóndas*), but, clearly, none of them is derivative the way those in (38) are.

> Can you propose a solution to the second-syllable secondary stress of the forms in (38b)?

The answer lies again in the correspondence constraint BD-IDENT, in this case referring to stress: BD-IDENT$_{\text{STRESS}}$. Clearly, this constraint must be ranked higher than the ALIGN-LEFT that yields initial stress in *pròsopopéia*:

(39)

/napoleonic/	ALIGN-RIGHT$^{\text{HEAD-FT}}$	BD-IDENT$_{\text{STRESS}}$	ALIGN-LEFT
a. * * * µ (µ µ)(µ µ) ☞ | | | | | napo le onic			****
b. * * * (µ µ) µ (µ µ) | | | | | napo le onic		*!	***

The confrontation between *napòleónic* and **nàpoleónic* is decided in favour of the former by BD-IDENT$_{\text{STRESS}}$, which is fatally violated by **nàpoleónic*.

Constraint summary:
ALIGN-LEFT
ALIGN-RIGHT$^{\text{HEAD-FT}}$
BD-IDENT$_{\text{STRESS}}$ = The stress of the base must be preserved in the derivative

13   Word Formation through Truncation

Correspondence constraints can also govern the phonology of word formation. An interesting example is provided by such word truncations as those
in (40):

Correspondence
constraints can
also govern the
phonology of
word formation

(40)   a.   Pamela   b.   Pam
            Janice   Jan
            cafeteria   caf
            Massachusetts   Mass

The relevant question is whether the vowel [æ] of the truncates will
undergo tensing to [Æ] in New York and Philadelphia.

> Make a guess as to whether the vowel in *Pam* undergoes
> tensing in New York and Philadelphia.

It obviously should on purely phonological grounds, since the constraint
*[æc.] rules out the non-tense vowel [æ] in closed syllables. In (40) and
similar cases, however, the vowel surfaces as lax: *P*[æ]*m*, etc.

> Suggest why the vowel in *Pam* surfaces as lax in New York
> and Philadelphia.

The reason is by now familiar: BD-IDENT$_{\text{TENSE}}$ outranks *[æc.]:

(41)

/pæm/	BD-IDENT$_{\text{TENSE}}$	*[æc.]	*TENSE$_{\text{LOW}}$	IO-IDENT$_{\text{TENSE}}$
☞ pæm.		*		
pÆm.	*!		*	*

The *a* of the base *Pamela* is of course non-tense, given the constraint
*TENSE$_{\text{LOW}}$ and the obvious irrelevance of *[æc.] here:

(42)   a.

/pæmela/	BD-IDENT$_{\text{TENSE}}$	*æc.	*TENSE$_{\text{LOW}}$	IO-IDENT$_{\text{TENSE}}$
☞ pæ.mela				
pÆ.mela			*!	*

b.

/pÆmela/	BD-IDENT$_{\text{TENSE}}$	*æc.	*TENSE$_{\text{LOW}}$	IO-IDENT$_{\text{TENSE}}$
☞ pæ.mela				*
pÆ.mela			*!	

You can see that the predominance of *TENSE$_{\text{LOW}}$ enforces a non-tense [æ] even when we hypothesize an underlying tense /Æ/. In turn, the [æ] of the base *Pamela* is transmitted to the truncate *Pam* by the ranking of the correspondence constraint BD-IDENT$_{\text{TENSE}}$ above the phonological constraint *[æc.].

Constraint summary:
*[æc.]
BD-IDENT$_{\text{TENSE}}$
IO-IDENT$_{\text{TENSE}}$
*TENSE$_{\text{LOW}}$

---

14 OT Morphology: English Plurals

The ALIGN constraint family can be used to get morphemes concatenated in the correct order

OT is also relevant to morphology. In particular, we shall now show that the ALIGN constraint family can be used to get morphemes concatenated in the correct order. Moreover, these constraints interact with phonological constraints in the selection of the correct candidate. It is currently being suggested that OT is also relevant to syntax, but this matter obviously falls beyond the scope of this book.

Orthographically, regular English plurals are formed from the singular by the addition of *-(e)s*. In particular, the forms in (43b) are well-formed plurals of the forms in (43a), but those in (43c) are not:

Morphological constraints interact with phonological constraints in the selection of the correct candidate

(43) a. map   b. maps   c. **s**map
         pod   pods   **s**pod**s**
         day   days   day
         ash   ashes   **s**ash
         coat   coats   coa**s**t

Is there a phonological motive for the ill-formedness of set c.?

Clearly, the reason for the ill-formedness of the pseudoplurals in (43c) is not phonological. Rather, it is a function of the suffixal status of the regular plural morpheme, orthographically *-(e)s*. Indeed, not only is *-(e)s* a suffix, but also it must be the right-most one:

(44) a.   action   b.   actions   c.   *actsion
            printer   printers   *printser
            cartoonist   cartoonists   *cartoonsist
            institution   institutions   *institutestion

> Explain how we have formed the plurals in (44).

Our formal arsenal already includes the resources we need to obtain the correct result, namely, the ALIGN family of constraints. In particular, the ALIGN family makes available the constraint in (45), among many others:

(45) ALIGN LEFT–RIGHT$_{\text{PLURAL–STEM}}$:
      The left edge of the plural morpheme /z/ must be aligned with the right edge of the stem

> Explain how the constraint in (45) imposes plural suffixation.

The inclusion of this constraint in the morphological grammar of English accounts for the well-formedness of the forms in the b. columns of (43) and (44), and the ill-formedness of their counterparts in the c. columns. This is thus a successful application of OT to morphology, if a particularly simple one. More complex cases of course exist, many of them in languages "exotic" to the English speaker: we shall not go into these here in order not to lengthen the exposition unduly (some such cases are included in the companion workbook, and you can check them out there).

To ease our way in, we have been using the orthographic representation -(e)s for the English plural morpheme, but by now you are fully aware that spelling is ultimately irrelevant to phonology. Consequently, we must now supply the proper phonological details of English plural formation.

> Can you venture some of the details of English plural formation before you read on?

The regular English plural morpheme has three allomorphs, as follows:

(46) English regular plural allomorphs:
      [z]:   day-s, pie-s, shampoo-s, piano-s, zebra-s
              road-s, leg-s, parcel-s, foundation-s, nerve-s
      [s]:   map-s, lot-s, obelisk-s, puff-s, birth-s
      [əz]:   ash-es, fortress-es, surprise-s, age-s, approach-es

We shall rationalize these allomorphs by adopting /z/ as the underlying representation, from which the two other forms will be derived by voice assimilation (-z → -s) and schwa epenthesis (-z → -əz), respectively. These two changes are phonetically grounded: voice assimilation comes about as a result of inertia of vocal fold activity (there is related discussion in chapter 2 above). In turn, the avoidance of a sibilant cluster, here resolved by the insertion of the maximally underspecified vowel [ə], follows from the difficulties associated with the articulation and perception of such clusters.

> "Sibilant" is an informal label for [coronal, +strident]. Make up a list of all the sibilants of English.

In rule-and-derivation phonology, we would need the two rules in (47) to obtain the surface forms. In (47a) we have abbreviated to z all the features of [z] other than [+voice], in order to keep the representation simple:

(47) a. Plural devoicing:

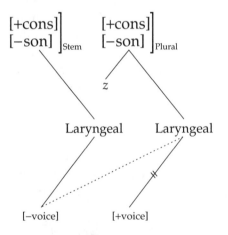

  b. Plural epenthesis:

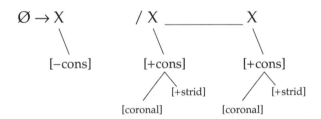

In (47b) the underspecification of the inserted vowel eventually leads to schwa, correctly so for many accents, although in some the plural vowel is [ɪ], an irrelevant matter here.

> Pronounce a few epenthetic plurals to find out if you have schwa.

The OT constraints equivalent to the rules in (47) are as in (48):

(48) a. VOICE HARMONY: *[αvoice] [−αvoice]
      b. OCP ON SIBILANTS: *[cor]   [cor]
                              [+strid] [+strid]

Obviously, additional constraints are needed if precisely the desired output is to be selected, rather than an output involving deletion of one of the two clashing segments, and so on. In particular, it is necessary to get violations of VOICE HARMONY in (48a) resolved by devoicing, rather than by epenthesis, which is only fallen back on to as a last resort. Accordingly, we shall introduce the faithfulness constraint ANCHOR-LEFT_PLURAL, which requires the left edge of the lexical plural morpheme to remain such in the surface. The remainder of the constraints and their rankings will simply be assumed:

> Propose a few of the missing constraints and their rankings.

(49) a.

/hɛd, z/	VOICE-HARM	OCP-SIB	ALIGN-RIGHT	ANCHOR-LEFT_PLURAL
☞ hɛdz				
hɛds	*!			
hɛdəz				*!

b.

/mæp, z/	VOICE-HARM	OCP-SIB	ALIGN-RIGHT	ANCHOR-LEFT_PLURAL
☞ mæps				
mæpz	*!			
mæpəz				*!

c.

/æʃ, z/	Voice-Harm	OCP-Sib	Align-Right	Anchor-Left$_{\text{PLURAL}}$
☞ æʃəz				*
æʃz	*!	*!		
æʃs		*!		
zæʃ			*!	

Constraint summary:

Align Left–Right$_{\text{PLURAL–STEM}}$ = Left edge of plural morpheme aligns with right edge of stem

Anchor-Left$_{\text{PLURAL}}$ = Surface left edge of plural morpheme corresponds to its lexical left edge

OCP on Sibilants = No adjacent sibilants

Voice Harmony = Uniform voice in consonant clusters

15 English Possessives and Correspondence Theory

The mechanics of the English possessive ('s) would seem to be similar to those of the plural:

(50) a. [z]:   Ted's, John's, Tony's, Gayle's
      b. [s]:   Pat's, Dick's, Ralph's, Math's
      c. [əz]: Rose's, Reg's, Maurice's, Thomas's

Indeed, the conditions on the distribution of the possessive allomorphs seem to be identical to those of their counterparts in the plural.

> Check that you see the parallel between the possessive and plural allomorphs.

The possessive of a form with the plural morpheme /-z/ is identical to the non-possessive plural

There is an interesting twist with the possessive of the plural, however. In particular, the possessive of a form with the plural morpheme /-z/ is identical to the non-possessive plural:

(51) a. the cats house here
      b. the cats' house is here

This situation is indeed peculiar on the strength of our constraints above, which would make us expect *catses*.

> Explain why our previous constraints would make us expect
> *catses for cats'.

The possessive marker 's of course cliticizes to phrases, not to nouns as such:

> How do we know that 's attaches to phrases?

(52)   the men who run's yellow jumper

Crucially, there is no incompatibility between the possessive and the plural:

(53)   children's, oxen's, mice's

If possessives could not be added to plurals, the forms in (53) would be ungrammatical, but clearly they are not.

All the facts considered reveal that the possessive marker -z cannot be added to the plural marker -z. In a rule-based approach, we would first have to allow the concatenation of both markers and then delete one. Alternatively, we could block the concatenation of one of the markers. Either way, the question arises as to which marker gets left out, and the answer has to be arbitrary, undesirably so.

> Why will the decision as to which marker to delete or to block
> be arbitrary?

The OT framework allows a more principled answer. All we have to do is adapt the ALIGN LEFT–RIGHT$_{\text{PLURAL-STEM}}$ of (45) above to possessives, as in (54):

(54)   ALIGN LEFT–RIGHT$_{\text{POSSESSIVE-STEM}}$:
       The left edge of the possessive morpheme -s must be aligned with the
       right edge of the stem

The crucial aspect of this constraint is that, like its counterpart for the plural, it enforces alignment of the possessive morpheme with the *stem*.

> What would be the obvious alternative to aligning the possessive
> suffix with the stem?

It is unusual for two morphemes competing for the same position both to get their way

The obvious consequence of this formulation is that both the plural and the possessive morphemes will be competing for the same position. What is unusual about this case is that they both get their way. Indeed, the machinery of Correspondence Theory is remarkably well suited to the attainment of this goal, as we now show for the form *cats'*. Note that the identity of each segment is made explicit in the representation as a subscript:

The machinery of Correspondence Theory is remarkably well suited to the attainment of this goal

(55)

$/k_1æ_2t_3, z_4, 'z_5/$	Voice-Harm	OCP-Sib	Align-Right	Anchor-Left$_{POSSESSIVE}$
☞ $k_1æ_2t_3s_{4,5}$				
$k_1æ_2t_3s_4s_5$		*!		
$k_1æ_2t_3s_4əz_5$			*!	*

You can see that in the winning candidate the noun's stem is aligned with both the plural morpheme (z_4) and the possessive morpheme (z_5). Therefore, the requirements of the two respective Align-Right constraints are complied with in this form.

Constraint summary:

OCP on Sibilants

Voice Harmony

Align Left–Right$_{POSSESSIVE–STEM}$ = The left edge of the possessive morpheme -*s* must be aligned with the right edge of the stem

Anchor-Left$_{POSSESSIVE}$ = Surface left edge of possessive morpheme corresponds to its lexical left edge

C h a p t e r   S u m m a r y

In this chapter we have introduced an alternative way of modelling the relationship between lexical forms and phonetic forms in generative phonology: Optimality Theory. Phonological naturalness is epitomized in part by the interpretation of the markedness statements in chapter 17 as a set of constraints on possible grammars, but these constraints may be violated in real languages. Whilst early child language violates few of the markedness constraints, on segmental structure or on syllable structure, adult language violates far more of them. As the child acquires the adult phonology, the conflict between the least marked segmental inventory and faithfulness to input forms is resolved in favour of faithfulness. The innovation of OT is to view grammars as a set of ranked violable constraints. These constraints are assumed to be universal, and the difference between child phonology and adult phonology, and between the grammars of different languages, now lies in differences in the ranking of the constraints. Given an input form, a generator, GEN, generates a list of candidates which are assessed by the constraints, the winning candidate being the one which violates not necessarily the fewest, but the lower-ranked constraints. The correct ranking produces the optimal, or most harmonic, form, while other rankings produce less harmonic ones. The constraint violations incurred by the rival candidates are displayed in a grid known as a "tableau". In the course of this chapter we have introduced a number of constraints from the universal set, and shown rankings which will ensure the correct output in a number of varying cases from the phonology of English, including syllable structure and metrical structure. We showed, for example, that faithfulness to input encoded through constraints against insertion (DEP) and deletion (MAX) of segments outranks the tendency to avoid syllable markedness as characterized by ONSET and NO-CODA. Alternations which call for stratal ordering of rules in a derivational model, apparently at odds with the parallel application of constraints in OT, are accounted for by transderivational correspondence constraints, which may impose identity requirements between a base and its derivatives. Constraints of this type, which can also be used to replicate the cycle in derivational phonology, are the hallmark of the branch of OT known as Correspondence Theory. OT is equally capable of accounting for morphological distribution, and we illustrated this with a discussion of English plural allomorphy. Correct placement of the morpheme is ensured by an ALIGN constraint, ALIGN LEFT-RIGHT PLURAL-STEM, which causes the left edge of the plural to align with the right edge of the stem. The selection of the correct plural allomorph is ensured by means of a voice harmony constraint and an OCP one. The English possessive is subject to the same conditions as the plural. In situations where a conflict between the plural and the possessive arises, Correspondence Theory allows for both morphemes to be aligned with the stem.

K e y   Q u e s t i o n s

1 What is the effect of faithfulness constraints outranking markedness ones?

2 List the constraints which exist on syllable markedness.

3 What is GEN?

4 The ranked constraints evaluate candidates: what for?

5 What is the effect of the MAX constraint?

6 What is the effect of the DEP constraint?

7 Under what name have you previously encountered Pāṇini's Theorem? What is its relevance in OT?

8 Outline the constraints relevant to basic metrical structure.

9 How is extrametricality incorporated into OT?

10 How is quantity-sensitivity incorporated into OT?

11 What are correspondence constraints? What function do they perform?

12 How do correspondence constraints replicate cyclic effects?

13 How can the ALIGN family of constraints ensure the correct order of morpheme concatenation?

F u r t h e r   P r a c t i c e

Syllable Structure in Urban Hijazi Arabic

Alternative candidates have been provided in the following data set from Urban Hijazi Arabic, spoken in Saudi Arabia:

mak.ta.bi	*ma.kV.ta.bi	'my office'
mak.ta.ba.ti	*mak.tab.at.i	'my library'
daħ.ra.dʒa.ti	*da.ħra.dʒa.ti	'my rolling'
ʃa.dʒa.ra.tu.hum	*ʃa.dʒa.ra.tu.hu.mV	'their tree'

(i) Work out the correct rankings for the following constraints, in order to produce the correct forms:

NO-CODA
ONSET
*COMPLEX
DEP

(ii) Show the effect of your rankings on *maktabati* and *daħradʒati*.

(iii) Can your constraint ranking account for:

faa.nuus   *fa.Ca.nu.Cus   *fa.nu   'a lantern'

(iv) Suggest further constraints to accommodate the additional data.

(v) How does your ranking need to be adjusted?

Stress in Latin

We repeat below the data from Latin which we provided earlier. Basing your analysis on the set of constraints outlined in the text, work out the constraint ranking which will yield the correct metrical structure for Latin:

amíːcus	'friend'		reféːcit	'set over' (3sg.perf)
agricoláːrum	'farmer' (gen.pl.)		agrícola	'farmer' (nom.sg.)
vólucres	'winged' (nom.l.)		pepérci	'spare' (1sg.perf)
símulaː	'snub nosed' (fem.)		magíster	'master'

Icelandic Deverbal Nouns

Syllable structure considerations dictate the choice of nominative singular allomorph in Icelandic, as we can see from the following alternations:

a. *Nom.sg.   Acc.sg.*
    dagur   dag   'day'
    bær   bæ   'farmhouse'
    læknir   lækni 'physician'

   Nom.sg.   Dat.sg.
    lifur   lifri   'liver'
    akur   agri   'field'
    hestur   hesti 'horse'

b. *Nom.sg.   Acc.sg.   Dat.pl.*
    lyfur   lyf   lyfjum   'medicine'
    bylur   byl   byljum   'snowstorm'

(i)   What are the two allomorphs?
(ii)   Give the constraint rankings for the constraints MAX, SON and DEP.

Deverbal action nouns in Icelandic are exceptions to the final cluster constraints, as we show in c.:

c. *Infinitive*   *Deverbal action noun*
    klifta   'climb'   klifr   'climbing'
    kumra 'bleat'   kumr   'bleating'
    grenja 'cry'   grenj   'crying'

(iii)   What further constraint interacts with those already proposed?
(iv)   Show the new rankings for the forms in c.

A ComPLEX COOP

LOOKING BACK AND MOVING ON

Chapter Objectives

In this chapter you will learn about:
- Further reading from the primary literature.
- Phonetics and its relationship with phonology.
- An introduction to the history of distinctive feature theory and autosegmental representation.
- The incorporation of syllable theory into the model.
- The analysis of stress and tone phenomena.
- The interaction between phonology, on the one hand, and morphology and syntax, on the other.
- Theories of markedness and underspecification of feature inventories.
- The mapping between lexical and surface forms.

So far in the text of the book, we have endeavoured not to burden the reader with contradictory or disparate information, and therefore we have tried to present a homogeneous picture of phonology as clear and free from debate as possible: quite obviously, it is more productive to direct all efforts to the acquisition of the basic tools of the phonological trade, not an easy task in itself, than to waste energy on internal disputes, arguably sterile at this preliminary stage. In aiming for this mode of presentation, we have deliberately modelled ourselves on the standard textbooks of the natural sciences, where concepts and formal apparatus have priority over the historic details of their elaboration. Of necessity, however, this approach involves a degree of oversimplification: behind the smooth, shiny surface lies the chaos of staggered discovery and intellectual debate, or even straight disagreement. The forceful arrival of Optimality Theory on the scene provides a pointed example of this internal strife. The dust will have to settle before we know with certainty the outcome of this particular contest, and in the meantime we have opted for the cautious strategy of presenting the body of phonology in as neutral, non-doctrinaire a manner as possible, with the aim of providing keen learners with the tool kit they need to achieve full participation in the subject. In this closing chapter, however, we turn the stone over and reveal some

amíːcus	'friend'		reféːcit	'set over' (3sg.perf)
agricoláːrum	'farmer' (gen.pl.)		agrícola	'farmer' (nom.sg.)
vólucres	'winged' (nom.l.)		pepérci	'spare' (1sg.perf)
símulaː	'snub nosed' (fem.)		magíster	'master'

Icelandic Deverbal Nouns

Syllable structure considerations dictate the choice of nominative singular allomorph in Icelandic, as we can see from the following alternations:

a. *Nom.sg.*   *Acc.sg.*

dagur	dag	'day'
bær	bæ	'farmhouse'
læknir	lækni	'physician'

Nom.sg.   *Dat.sg.*

lifur	lifri	'liver'
akur	agri	'field'
hestur	hesti	'horse'

b. *Nom.sg.*   *Acc.sg.*   *Dat.pl.*

lyfur	lyf	lyfjum	'medicine'
bylur	byl	byljum	'snowstorm'

(i)   What are the two allomorphs?

(ii)   Give the constraint rankings for the constraints MAX, SON and DEP.

Deverbal action nouns in Icelandic are exceptions to the final cluster constraints, as we show in c.:

c. *Infinitive*   *Deverbal action noun*

klifta	'climb'	klifr	'climbing'
kumra	'bleat'	kumr	'bleating'
grenja	'cry'	grenj	'crying'

(iii)   What further constraint interacts with those already proposed?

(iv)   Show the new rankings for the forms in c.

† Cₒₘₚₗₑₓᶜᵒᵒᵖ

LOOKING BACK AND MOVING ON

Chapter Objectives

In this chapter you will learn about:
- Further reading from the primary literature.
- Phonetics and its relationship with phonology.
- An introduction to the history of distinctive feature theory and autosegmental representation.
- The incorporation of syllable theory into the model.
- The analysis of stress and tone phenomena.
- The interaction between phonology, on the one hand, and morphology and syntax, on the other.
- Theories of markedness and underspecification of feature inventories.
- The mapping between lexical and surface forms.

So far in the text of the book, we have endeavoured not to burden the reader with contradictory or disparate information, and therefore we have tried to present a homogeneous picture of phonology as clear and free from debate as possible: quite obviously, it is more productive to direct all efforts to the acquisition of the basic tools of the phonological trade, not an easy task in itself, than to waste energy on internal disputes, arguably sterile at this preliminary stage. In aiming for this mode of presentation, we have deliberately modelled ourselves on the standard textbooks of the natural sciences, where concepts and formal apparatus have priority over the historic details of their elaboration. Of necessity, however, this approach involves a degree of oversimplification: behind the smooth, shiny surface lies the chaos of staggered discovery and intellectual debate, or even straight disagreement. The forceful arrival of Optimality Theory on the scene provides a pointed example of this internal strife. The dust will have to settle before we know with certainty the outcome of this particular contest, and in the meantime we have opted for the cautious strategy of presenting the body of phonology in as neutral, non-doctrinaire a manner as possible, with the aim of providing keen learners with the tool kit they need to achieve full participation in the subject. In this closing chapter, however, we turn the stone over and reveal some of the life teeming underneath. We also offer pointers to enable the reader to proceed beyond the necessarily limited confines of this book. For additional practice of the points raised throughout we recommend the exercises in the companion volume *A Workbook in Phonology*.

1 Phonetics

In chapters 1, 3, 5 and 7 we presented the phonetic matter we consider a necessary prerequisite to the study of phonology. In particular, we reviewed in some detail the mechanics of the articulation of obstruent and sonorant consonants, and of vowels. We paid special attention to the description of the sounds of English, in the belief that a good understanding of the mechanics of sound production needs to be rooted in one's own personal experience of the sound – we naturally assume that the reader of this book carries along a wealth of experience with the sounds of English. We have deliberately ignored the two other aspects of linguistic sound, acoustics and auditory phonetics, on account of the fact that it is perfectly possible to get into phonology without any previous grounding in these areas. Briefly here, ACOUSTIC PHONETICS is the branch of phonetics (and of physics) that investigates the patterns of vibration of molecules in the air caused by articulation. In turn, AUDITORY PHONETICS deals with the effects of these patterns on the human ear and with their subsequent reception and perception in the brain. You can find reasonably accessible information about acoustic phonetics in Denes and Pinson (1993), Fry (1979), and Kent and Read (1992), and more concise summaries in chapter 4 of Catford (1977), chapter 8 of Ladefoged (1993), chapter 3 of Borden et al. (1993), chapter 4 of Kenstowicz (1994a), and chapter 7 of J. Clark and Yallop (1995). Auditory phonetics is less well developed than its two counterparts, perhaps on account of the evasiveness of its subject matter. For an introduction, you can consult chapter 6 of Borden et al. (1993), chapter 4 of Kenstowicz (1994a), or chapter 7 of J. Clark and Yallop (1995).

There are a number of useful books on articulatory phonetics, and we have based our phonetic chapters on them: here and elsewhere, we could paraphrase Sir Isaac Newton and openly declare that we have stood on the shoulders of giants! The most recent such book is Ladefoged and Maddieson (1996). This is a thorough, rigorous survey of the sounds of the world's languages, including some likely to feel exotic to the exclusively English-speaking reader. The obvious predecessors are Ladefoged (1993) and Maddieson (1984). Ladefoged (1993) has been for some time, and arguably still is, the standard coursebook for phonetics (for articulatory phonetics, in particular), while Maddieson (1984) usefully surveys the sound inventories of 317 languages, carefully selected as representative of the approximately five thousand languages still spoken on the earth.

The most recent textbook on articulatory phonetics is Laver (1994). This is an extremely thorough survey of the production of speech sound, from respiration through phonation to the various articulations. It also deals with the temporal organization of speech, including its prosodic and metrical aspects. Unusually, but usefully, it frames the discussion in the wider context of human communication and linguistic variation. Also useful are Daniloff et al. (1980) and Catford (1977), the latter a bit of a classic. Catford (1988) presents the subject matter in the form of practical tasks. The physiology of speech production is surveyed in great detail in Hardcastle (1973). Hardcastle and Laver (1997) brings together a number of specialized papers on the central aspects of phonetics.

As we shall systematically do throughout this chapter, we will now provide specific references for the topics of the phonetics chapters in part I. Importantly, these sources will best be understood, and thus most profitably read, at this point in the exposition: it is most unlikely that any one of the sources we refer to keeps pace with the deliberately graded structure of our presentation in the corresponding chapters of this book. Also importantly, we do not attempt to provide an exhaustive bibliography on any topic, or even a complete list of major works on that area: our aim, as ever, is to help readers increase their knowledge, and accordingly we have been pedagogically selective in our choice of literature.

We start off with chapter 1. For useful discussion of the relationship between phonetics and phonology, and of the differences between the two disciplines, you can go to Pierrehumbert (1990, 1991), Diehl (1991b), chapter 2 of Laver (1994) and Ohala (1997). An overview of the physiology of articulation and the anatomy of the relevant organs, a bit technical, appears in Hardcastle (1973). The articulation of consonants, with special reference to English, is examined in chapter 3 of Ladefoged (1993). The articulation of fricatives is discussed in chapter 9 of Laver (1994). For a survey of actual fricative sounds, see chapter 5 of Ladefoged and Maddieson (1996). Chapter 7 of Ladefoged (1993) covers both place and manner of articulation. Place of articulation alone is reviewed in chapter 2 of Ladefoged and Maddieson (1996) and in chapter 8 of Catford (1977), who discusses manner of articulation in chapter 7. The principles and problems of phonetic transcription are examined in chapter 2 of Ladefoged (1993) and chapter 18 of Laver (1994). The phonetic symbols (standard and less standard) are reviewed and discussed individually in Pullum and Ladusaw (1986). The official guide to the IPA alphabet, International Phonetic Association (1949), is now out of print. A considerably revised edition is being prepared, and Nolan (1995) offers a comprehensive preview. Ladefoged (1990) comments on the then latest version of the IPA alphabet and reflects on the IPA transcription sytem in general. Ladefoged and Halle (1988) reassess the foundations of phonetic transcription and offers some suggestions for its improvement.

Voice production and phonation types are dealt with in chapter 6 of Catford (1977), chapter 6 of Ladefoged (1993), and chapter 7 of Laver (1994). Phonation types are typologically surveyed in chapter 3.1 of Ladefoged and Maddieson (1996). Stops are examined in chapter 8 of Laver (1994), and surveyed in chapter 3 of Ladefoged and Maddieson (1996). Finally, affricates and other multiple articulations are covered in detail in chapter 11 of Laver (1994), and surveyed in chapter 3.3 of Ladefoged and Maddieson (1996).

In chapter 3 we dealt with sonorant consonants: nasals, laterals and rhotics. A general discussion of sonorants, under the label "resonants", can be found in chapter 10 of Laver (1994). Ladefoged and Maddieson (1996) devotes three chapters to the typology of the specific sonorant classes: nasals in chapter 4, laterals in chapter 6, and rhotics in chapter 7.

In chapter 5 we discussed the articulation of vowels in the framework of Daniel Jones's cardinal vowels. Besides chapter 8 of D. Jones (1967), cardinal vowels are discussed in chapter 9 of Ladefoged (1993). They are usefully presented through exercises in chapter 8 of Catford (1988). A recording of the cardinal vowels by Daniel Jones is available from University College London. For a preliminary overview of vowel articulation you can go to chapter 4 of Ladefoged (1993). There are general discussions of vowels in the first half of chapter 10 of Laver (1994) and chapter 9 of Catford (1977), both with substantial reference to cardinal vowels. Chapter 9 of Ladefoged and Maddieson (1996) reviews the basic parameters relevant to vowels, with the appropriate cross-linguistic exemplification. For vowel typologies you can consult Crothers (1978) and Lass (1984). The topic of quantum vowels is a little technical, but a number of useful papers are collected in *Journal of Phonetics* 17, 1989, including an update of the theory by its originator, Kenneth Stevens: the quantum vowels were introduced in Stevens (1972).

In chapter 7 we reviewed the realization of English vowels in some detail. Wells (1982) gives a wealth of information on the English sounds of both standard and regional accents, with the emphasis on vowels: the three volumes respectively contain an introduction and general survey of English sounds, a discussion of the accents of the British Islands, and a discussion of English accents in the rest of the world. Some similar information can be found much abridged in Kreidler (1989, 1997). Specialized works on the vowel and consonant sounds of British English, RP in particular, are D. Jones's two manuals (1966, 1967) and the follow-up by Gimson (1994). There is a summary of RP sounds, aimed at foreign learners but useful generally as an introduction, in Roach (1991). Ramsaran (1990b) reviews the present state of RP. Classics on American English pronunciation, both general and regional, are Bronstein (1960), Kenyon (1935), Krapp (1969) and Thomas (1958). Labov (1994) comments on the pronunciation of many vowels in the US, but the context he is writing in (chain shifts and language change) does not make for easy identification of each individual vowel. For a handy comparison of some American vowel systems, including GA, you can check Moulton (1990). Canadian raising is specifically discussed in Chambers (1973). Burchfield (1994) contains specialized papers on the English of Australia (by G. Turner), New Zealand (by L. Bauer) and South Africa (by W. Branford). For the accents of New Zealand and South Africa, you can also consult Bauer (1986) and Lass (1990), respectively.

2 Foundations of Phonology

In the even-numbered chapters of part I (chapters 2, 4, 6 and 8) we presented the foundations of phonological theory, which the rest of the book elaborates on.

In Chapter 2 we introduced phonology, making use of some assimilation processes of English which are beyond the threshold of consciousness in most speakers. Processes like these are referred to in varying degree of detail in Wells (1982), Nespor and Vogel (1986), Kreidler (1989), chapter 8 of Giegerich (1992), Hawkins (1992), Ladefoged (1993) and Gimson (1994), and are conveniently brought together in chapter 6 of Spencer (1996). The existence of these assimilation processes led us to draw a distinction between the phonetic level of actual sound, and the phonological level of sound structure. The phonological level is rooted in Saussure's conception of language as a system of oppositions, and is kept in check by a principle of economy that we related to Occam's razor. Useful summaries of Saussure's doctrine from the perspective of phonology can be found in chapter 5 of Jakobson (1990) and in chapter 2 of S. Anderson (1985), the latter an excellent source of historical information on phonology. A recent edited and annotated English translation of Saussure's *Course* is R. Harris (1987). You will find a summary of Occam's philosophy, including his famous razor, in chapter 14 of B. Russell (1996).

In classical generative phonology the phonological and phonetic levels (relabelled lexical or underlying level and surface level, respectively) are related by means of phonological rules. For an early discussion of the role of rules in phonology, you can go to Halle (1962), although you should be warned that some of the features are now obsolete. Phonological rules include a focus, made up of the input sound to be changed and of its changed output, and a context or environment, made up of the constant surrounding sounds that condition the change. Each phonological rule effects one change in an input representation: a set of rules therefore carries out a sequence of changes, collectively known as a derivation. A particularly clear account of the mechanics and properties of rules and derivations appears in S. Anderson (1974). You can find an inventory of the formal machinery of early generative phonology in a ten-page appendix to chapter 8 of *SPE*.

In chapter 4 we broke down the phoneme into its primitive building blocks, the distinctive features. The concept of the phoneme is discussed in chapter 15 of Jakobson (1990), and its history is traced in S. Anderson (1985), chapters 3 and 4 in particular. For general discussion of distinctive features, you can consult chapter 5 of S. Anderson (1985), Clements (1992a), Halle (1983) and chapter 16 of Jakobson (1990) (also chapter 17, but this is more technical, and many of the features discussed in it have now been superseded). Halle and Clements (1983) and Halle (1991) are reader-friendly sources for a more or less contemporary inventory of features – references to more technical, up-to-date accounts framed in the theory of feature geometry are provided in section 7 below. Each distinctive feature captures one key aspect of the articulation of sound. It is normally related to the articulator actively involved in its production, and is usually given one of two values: positive if the aspect in question is activated, and negative if it isn't. This binarism permeates Jakobson's work (see the entry *binarism* in the index of Jakobson 1990), and is succintly defended in Halle (1957). In the *SPE* system all features are binary: features are discussed in chapter 7 of *SPE*. Subsequently, however, binarism came under attack from various directions. First, several alternative theories adopt feature unarism as one of their tenets: Dependency Phonology (J. Anderson and Ewen 1987, den Dicken and van der Hulst 1988, van der Hulst 1988, 1995), Government Phonology (Kaye et al. 1985, J. Harris and Lindsey 1995), Particle Phonology (Schane 1984). Second, major place of articulation features are now generally considered unary, on the grounds that the range of places of articulation is defined by the set of these features, rather than each individual place feature defining two existing opposites (Sagey 1986a, McCarthy 1988, Yip 1989a, Halle 1991, 1995). Last, a number of mainstream individual features are being argued by some to be "privative", that is, to have only the positive value, with particular reference to underspecification (Steriade 1995 offers a convenient summary). For the standard position on the matter of feature valency you can check Pulleyblank (1995). Place of articulation features are cumulative as a consequence of their monovalency, which originated in Sagey (1986a) (see also Halle 1991), and is forcefully argued for in McCarthy (1988). Trubetzkoy's distinction between binary and multiple oppositions is an obvious antecedent. Trubetzkoy's (1939) classic has been translated into English (1969), and is usefully discussed in Fischer-Jørgensen (1975). For specific arguments for binarity both in place features and in other features, see Lombardi (1996).

Distinctive features provide a formal characterization of the notion "natural class", that is, of the fact that phonological processes universally tend to affect specific families of segments, rather than random sets: formally, the segments in question share one or more distinctive features. The mutual interaction of features in rules is constrained by the autosegmental mode of representation: each feature occupies its own autonomous layer, or "tier", and is linked to other features by means of association lines. Autosegmental phonology was first fully articulated in Goldsmith (1976a). It is summarized in Goldsmith (1976b, 1979), and updated in Pulleyblank (1986a) and Goldsmith (1990). There is also a useful, if slightly dated, overview in the introduction of van der Hulst and Smith (1982b). Features that express multiple settings of one abstract parameter (for instance, place of articulation features) enjoy a high degree of functional unity, which we formalized by assigning a common subscript to the features in question, a notation akin to the one in Hayes (1990a) (commented on in Bird 1991), and, by extension, Halle (1995). The autonomy of some features is curtailed by their systematic formal attachment to some other specific feature, on which they are said to be dependent. Feature dependencies were officially introduced in mainstream generative phonology in Clements (1985), and have been adopted by most practitioners since (Sagey 1986a, McCarthy 1988, Odden 1991, Halle 1991, 1995, Clements and Hume 1995, Padgett 1995).

In chapter 6 we proposed a set of distinctive features for vowels and explored their empirical impact through the phenomena of back harmony, in Turkish, and umlaut, in German and also in English, where it is now reduced to the status of historical relic. The phonetic foundations of vowel features are presented in Lindau (1978) and Keating (1987). The standard generative account of Turkish vowel harmony is Clements and Sezer (1982). For German umlaut, see Lodge (1989) and the discussion in chapter 7.2 of Wiese (1996a). Aoki (1968), Ringen (1975), Halle and Vergnaud (1981) and van der Hulst and van de Weijer (1995) include useful typologies of vowel harmony. Clements (1977) pioneers the autosegmental treatment of the phenomenon. For vowel harmony in specific languages you can also consult Ringen (1975), Goldsmith (1985), Pulleyblank (1986b) and the papers in the second volume of van der Hulst and Smith (1988). Ringen and Vago (1995) scrutinize Hungarian vowel harmony in the context of Optimality Theory. Consonant harmony is relatively common in child speech (Vihman 1978), but rare in adult language (see Shaw 1991 for an overview).

In chapter 8 we applied the distinctive feature model to the analysis of the English Great Vowel Shift. The synchronic analysis of the Great Vowel Shift originated in *SPE*, and was updated in Halle and Mohanan (1985). Reference to history sheds useful light on the opaque set of contemporary vowel shift alternations, and you can go to Wolfe (1972) for a good historical account. Summary references to the phenomenon appear in C. Jones (1989), Lass (1984), Strang (1986) and Pyles and Algeo (1992). Wells (1982) also gives the essentials.

Our analysis of the Great Vowel Shift in chapter 8 was carried out in the context of the "timing tier" or "skeleton", an additional autosegmental tier formalizing the relative timing of segments: universally, vowels can be short or long, and consonants simple, geminate or affricate. The timing tier, or CV-tier, was introduced in Clements and Keyser (1983), and streamlined to an X-tier in Levin (1983), an unpublished but influential paper. The timing tier, or "skeleton", has been applied in the areas of compensatory lengthening and template-based morphology, the latter typical of, but not exclusive to, Semitic languages (see McCarthy 1981, 1984, McCarthy and Prince 1990, 1995). For premoraic treatments of compensatory lengthening, you can go to Ingria (1980) and Wetzels and Sezer (1986). Hayward (1988) puts up a defence of the timing tier in the context of four Ethiopian languages. We saw that the timing tier also allows a satisfactory analysis of affricates and of complex segments in general. The issue of the autosegmental representation of complex segments is examined in Sagey (1986b). For the specific case of affricates, see Hualde (1988) and Lombardi (1990). Yip (1989b) purposely relates contour tones to affricates.

3 Syllables

In chapter 9 we introduced the notion of the "syllable", the architecture of which we discussed both from a general perspective and in the context of English. In chapter 10 we specifically explored the syllable structure of English, which we saw exhibits a considerable amount of complexity.

We started chapter 9 with the observation that young children systematically simplify the sound input they receive, aiming for the core syllable CV in their own output. The child data we provided at the beginning of chapter 9 are from Vihman (1996 ["Timmy", on pp. 258–60]), a valuable survey of child phonology. A CV output also pervades the adaptation of English loans by Japanese adult speakers, as explained in detail in Lovins (1975) – both Shibatani (1990) and Tsujimura (1996) refer to the matter briefly, summarized usefully in Kimura (1996). Itô and Mester (1995, 1996a) explore Japanese loan phonology in the context of the overall structure of the Japanese vocabulary. The omnipresence of the core syllable was noticed by Jakobson (see Jakobson 1941, and chapter 18 of Jakobson 1990). The alternation of a consonant (with low sonority) with a vowel (with high sonority) of course best embodies the regular alternation of sonority that constitutes speech: Öhman (1966). Other phonetic arguments for the core syllable are provided in Ohala and Kawasaki (1984). The core syllable can be altered minimally by deleting the onset or adding a coda, the latter making up a rime with the nucleus: much of the syllable typology of the world's languages can be reduced to this basic inventory. Syllable typologies are to be found in Clements and Keyser (1983) and Blevins (1995). Pike and Pike (1947), Hockett (1956), Hooper (1972, 1976) and Vennemann (1972) have fairly pretheoretical discussions of the structure of the syllable and its motivation.

The anchoring of syllable structure on the skeleton is justified in Clements and Keyser (1983) and in Levin (1985). For the X-bar notation in syntax you can check Kornai and Pullum (1990), or Cook and Newson (1996) for a less technical summary. Borowsky (1986) argues for a two-timing-unit maximum in English onsets and nuclei. In essence, syllables are mountains of sonority. The sonority hierarchy is discussed in various guises in Saussure (1916), Hankamer and Aissen (1974), Hooper (1976: chapters 10 and 11), Selkirk (1984a), Clements (1991) and Rice (1992), among many others. The sonority relations between the segments of any one syllable are governed by the principle of Sonority Sequencing (Selkirk 1984a) and the Minimal Sonority Distance parameter (Steriade 1982).

In chapter 10 we gave data hinting at the existence of complex codas in English. The matter, however, is less clear cut than for onsets and nuclei: for discussion, see Selkirk (1982), Borowsky (1986) and J. Harris (1994). In chapters 15 and 16 we essentially followed the analyses of Myers (1987b) and Borowksy (1989): we return to this issue in section 7 below. The identification of syllable nuclei with vowels and of syllable margins with consonants, while generally sound, was found to leak in both directions. First, sonorant consonants can be compelled by sonority sequencing to become nuclei. Bell (1978) provides a universal typology of syllabic consonants, and Rubach (1990) gives a particularly enlightening discussion of the German case. For English, reference to the matter is made in Mohanan (1985) and Borowsky (1993). Second, high vowels are allowed in the onset in English (see again Mohanan 1985), and quite generally cross-linguistically. In complex onsets, the onset parsing of high vowels is substantiated by OCP effects (see J. Harris 1994 for a brief discussion). However, Selkirk (1982) and Steriade (1994) prefer an analysis in terms of single segments. The OCP disfavours the inclusion of similar segments in the same subsyllabic constituent: for discussion of the OCP, see McCarthy (1986), Odden (1986) and Yip (1988). The syllabification of intervocalic consonants is governed by the principle of Minimal Onset Satisfaction (see Roca 1994) – known variously as the Maximal Onset Satisfaction Principle (Selkirk 1982), the CV rule (Steriade 1982), etc. – and by the Onset Maximization Parameter (Roca 1994). Some French data discussed in the text demonstrate the separate identity of the Maximal Onset Satisfaction Principle and the Onset Maximization Parameter, not always explicit in the literature: the Maximal Onset Satisfaction Principle is stronger than the Onset Maximization Parameter (for French data, see Tranel 1995). Allophony provides support for many of the syllabification principles we have presented, which we showed interact in interesting ways. We have already referred to Wells (1982), Nespor and Vogel (1986), Kreidler (1989), chapter 8 of Giegerich (1992), Hawkins (1992), Ladefoged (1993), Gimson (1994), and Spencer's (1996) summary, in connection with English allophonic processes. Kahn (1976) offers a particularly thorough review of English stop allophones, and Gussenhoven (1986) is also worth consulting. The idiosyncratic behaviour of *s* in English is discussed in Selkirk (1982) and, in a different theoretical framework, in Kaye (1992).

4 Stress

In chapters 11 to 13 we dealt with the phenomenon of stress. The first complete generative treatment of stress is found in *SPE*. Hyman (1977a) gathers an interesting collection of papers on the topic. Van der Hulst (in press *a*) focuses on the stress and tone patterns of European languages, but also contains useful general papers, among them an overview of stress by van der Hulst (chapter 1) and a survey of the word prosodic systems of European languages by van der Hulst, Hendriks and van de Weijer (chapter 7). Kager (1995) is an excellent, very clear overview of the vicissitudes of metrical theory from its inception to the date of publication.

While the intuition that certain syllables are "stressed" is probably available to all speakers of stress languages, the nature of stress itself is much less obvious. A particularly useful window on stress is the phenomenon of stress movement, which we surveyed in chapter 11 for English. Differences in stress placement are often reducible to differences in syntactic category or syntactic constituency. For noun vs. verb stress, you can check sections 1.1 and 1.2 of chapter 7 in Halle and Vergnaud (1987a), and for compound vs. phrase stress section 1 in chapter 2 of *SPE* (in a now superseded formalism), and sections 9.1 and 9.3 in chapter 7 of Halle and Vergnaud (1987a). For a discussion of English compounds, you can go to Lieber (1989), and Downing (1977), and to Selkirk (1984b) for a summary. Meaning has no part in regular stress assignment, besides cases of marked focus: discussion on the role of focus in stress can be found in Selkirk (1984b) and Ladd (1997). Stress is a manifestation of rhythm, more basic than poetic rhythm: for rhythm in verse you can refer to Kiparsky (1977), Attridge (1982, 1989) and the papers in Kiparsky and Youmans (1989). The idea of relating stress to rhythm is developed in Liberman (1975) and Liberman and Prince (1977).

We adopted the metrical grid as a formal device for the representation of stress: Prince (1983) is probably the best source for acquiring familiarity with the grid. The metrical grid allows a simple account of apparent anomalies in the distribution of stress. In particular, English disfavours stress clash, a clashing asterisk retracting to the position marked by the nearest asterisk in the line below: Prince (1983), 7.9.2 in Halle and Vergnaud (1987a) and Hayes (1995). Gussenhoven (1991) offers a deletion alternative to asterisk movement. Retraction takes place both across and within words. Some retraction failures are accountable for by the ban imposed by the Continuous Column Constraint on gaps in metrical columns (Hayes 1995). In German, asterisks can move forward, as well as retract, to avoid clash: see the summary in Wiese (1996a). Besides asterisk movement, rhythm can also induce asterisk insertion (Selkirk 1984b). Nespor and Vogel (1989) review the phenomenon in a number of languages, including English. General discussion of English linguistic rhythm appears in Abercrombie (1967) and in Liberman and Prince (1977). Nespor (1990a, 1990b) provides useful discussion of the dichotomy stress rhythm vs. syllable rhythm. The repercussions of metrical structure on such segmental phenomena as vowel reduction and consonant allophony contribute additional evidence for stress and its distribution: see Sainz (1992) for vowel reduction, and Gimson (1994), Kahn (1976) and Gussenhoven (1986) for English stop allophony.

Metrical structure can be minimally reduced by systematically disregarding the metrical element on the edge, a device known as "extrametricality" (Liberman and Prince 1977, Hayes 1979, 1980, 1982, 1995, Halle and Vergnaud 1987a, Archangeli 1988a, Roca 1988, 1992). The edge requirement is encapsulated in the Peripherality Condition. Prince and Smolensky (1993) provide a very useful critical overview of the properties of extrametricality. The interaction of overlapping rules is subject to the Elsewhere Condition: Kiparsky (1973), Koutsoudas et al. (1974) and Iverson and Wheeler (1988). For a brief discussion of French stress, see Tranel (1987). The metrical patterns of English are developed in Hayes (1980, 1982), Prince (1983) and Halle and Vergnaud (1987a, 1987b), among other sources. Kager (1989) provides a valuable critical evaluation. The metrical foot as the basic unit of rhythm is elaborated in Liberman and Prince (1977), Selkirk (1980), Hayes (1980, 1995) and Halle and Vergnaud (1987a). For iteration in English stress, see Prince (1983) and Selkirk (1980, 1984b). Metrical parameters are examined in Hayes (1980), Prince (1983), Halle and Vergnaud (1987a) and Dresher and Kaye (1990). For the stress patterns of Polish and Macedonian, see Franks (1985 and 1987, respectively), and also Dogil (1998) for Polish. Aklan, Maranungku and Yidin[y] are discussed in Hayes (1980), and Winnebago in K. Hale and White Eagle (1980) and Halle and Idsardi (1995). Line conflation is specifically justified in Halle (1990), while the opposing iterativeness parameter is defended in Blevins (1990). Hayes (1995) formulates the Faithfulness Condition, building on Halle and Vergnaud (1987a). For the so-called "Duke of York Gambit", see Pullum (1976).

The effects of syllable weight on stress are taken account of in *SPE*, but their distinct formalization in terms of moras begins with Hyman (1985). The Free Element Condition, formulated in Prince (1985), captures the idea that stress rules are structure-building, in the sense of Kiparsky (1982, 1985). Degenerate feet are paid special attention in Hayes (1995). The effects of final consonants on English stress are carefully reviewed in Ross (1972) in an *SPE* framework. Final vowel lengthening was introduced in *SPE*. Hyman's (1985) moraic formalization of syllable structure is modified in Hayes (1989a), who also formulates Weight by Position. For a comparison between moras and skeletal slots see Broselow (1995), and Rubach (1993) with specific reference to Slovak. The model in Hayes (1995) is grounded in the empirical asymmetries in the distribution of foot types, underpinned by the perceptual findings reported in Woodrow (1951). Kager (1993) favours a No-Lapse Constraint over the Iambic-Trochaic Law. The unbounded feet of Khalkha Mongolian are discussed in Hayes (1980), Halle and Vergnaud (1987a) and Halle and Idsardi (1995), and the Selkup data are taken from Halle and Clements (1983). Irregular stress is formalized as accent in Halle and Vergnaud (1987a) and Halle (1990). Sanskrit stress is discussed in Kiparsky and Halle (1977), and summarized in Halle and Mohanan (1985) and Halle and Vergnaud (1987a, 1987b). Halle and Idsardi (1995) develop the theory of Halle and Vergnaud (1987a) in suggestive ways.

5 Tone

In chapter 14 we presented three linguistic functions of pitch: intonation, pitch accent and tone. Variations in pitch result from variations in the frequency of vibration of the vocal folds. Vocal fold vibration is an aerodynamic effect induced by the outgoing air on a given vocal fold configuration. Phonologically, high pitch can contrast with low pitch, and mid pitch with both (Ladefoged 1993). Such units of pitch contrast are referred to as "tones". The difference between intonation, pitch accent and tone languages hinges on the pattern of association of the tones to the segmental material, and on the function of the tones in the system. In particular, in intonation strings of tones making up "tunes" associate to certain segments in a certain domain (probably the "intonational phrase", but see section 7 below) to express functional or attitudinal meanings: whether the utterance is a statement or a question, whether the speaker is enthusiastic or reserved about it, and so on. Bolinger (1989) provides an accessible overview. In pitch accent languages, a constant, meaningless tune (or a restricted set of tunes) associates to the segmental material algorithmically. Finally, in tone languages tone differentiates words or expresses morphological functions: in the former case, different words (with a different meaning, for instance) which are segmentally identical are kept apart by their tonal shape; in the latter, morphological functions like tense in verbs or plurality in nouns are expressed by a change in tone, rather than by affixation. The lexical function of tone prevails throughout South East Asian languages, while the morphological function is common in African languages. Yip (1995) and Odden (1995) provide excellent overviews of Asian and African tones, respectively.

We illustrated intonation with English. We saw that each intonational tune is composed of a string of tones, divided into boundary tones, word tones (one of them dominant) and a phrasal tone (Pierrehumbert 1980, Ladd 1997). For pitch accent we focused on Japanese. Japanese words can be accented (with a mark on one of the syllables) or unaccented, idiosyncratically. Accented syllables attract the dominant tone of a fixed, meaningless tonal melody, the remainder of the tones being associated to the remaining syllables in a predetermined manner (Haraguchi 1977). In words with no accented syllable the dominant tone associates to the word-final syllable. Chinese provides the prototypical example of a lexical tonal language: segmentally homophonous words can have different lexical tones. In the last two sections of the chapter we illustrated the mechanics of tone in African languages. The autosegmental approach to phonology was in fact developed in connection with African tones, and we scrutinized the basic principles of autosegmental association in this context. Many of the principles originally proposed (Goldsmith 1976a) have subsequently been found not to be universal (Pulleyblank 1986a). We showed that the most resilient of these principles, the No-Crossing of Lines Constraint, is in fact derivable from the logic of the geometry: see Sagey (1988), followed up by Hammond (1988) and, in a different context, Bagemihl (1989). Coleman and Local (1991) offer criticism of the constraint.

Bolinger (1986) provides a painless introduction to the phenomenon of intonation – also, more concisely, the introduction and chapter 1 of Bolinger (1972). Chapter 1 of Ladd (1997) is very useful, although a little less beginner-friendly – in particular, it offers a critical overview of the main models of intonation available. For a basic intonational typology, see Bolinger (1978). For the mechanics of voice production, see chapter 7.4 of Laver (1994), and for the use of pitch in intonation, chapter 15 of Ladefoged (1993). The autosegmental analysis of intonation started with Liberman (1975) and came of age with Pierrehumbert (1980), otherwise a little technical. Useful summaries appear in Ladd (1992), Pierrehumbert and Hirschberg (1990) (commented on in Hobbs 1990), and, of course, Ladd (1997). The connection between intonation and primary stress in English is spelled out in Hayes (1995). Cruttenden (1986) is a good source for pre-Pierrehumbert intonation from the particular perspective of the so-called "British school". For the tones of English, you can also look at Leben (1976) and Goldsmith (1981). M. Beckman and Pierrehumbert (1986) is a ground-breaking comparison of English and Japanese intonation, in the footsteps of M. Beckman's (1986) investigation of stress and accent, but again most of it is rather technical. An oft-cited study of tone is Pike (1948). Fromkin (1978) is a most useful early generative collection. It includes, among others, chapters by Ohala on the phonetic production of tone, Leben on the representation of tone, S. Anderson on tone features, McCawley on what constitutes a tone language, and Schuh on the types of rule that affect tone.

For an early autosegmental investigation of Chinese tone you must go to Yip (1980). More recent discussion appears in Duanmu (1990) and Bao (1990), the latter from a general theoretical perspective. The specific issue of contour tones is addressed in Yip (1989b) and Duanmu (1994). The introduction of van der Hulst and Smith (1988) reviews the typology of pitch accent systems. The autosegmental analysis of Japanese pitch accent began with McCawley (1977) and Haraguchi (1977). The next important study was Poser (1984), followed by Pierrehumbert and Beckman (1988). There are convenient summaries in Shibatani (1990) and Tsujimura (1996). M. Clark (1987) attempts an analysis of Japanese as a tone language. Kubozono (1993) includes several experimentally based studies of various aspects of Tokyo Japanese pitch. In the European area, the classical study of Swedish pitch accent is Bruce (1977). For Serbo-Croatian you can look at Inkelas and Zec (1988), and for Lithuanian at Blevins (1993). Hualde (1991a, 1998) examines several aspects of Basque pitch-accent. Clements and Goldsmith (1984) is an important early collection on African tones. The Mende data are discussed in Leben (1978). The original principles of autosegmental association are presented and justified in Goldsmith (1976a). For Shona tonology, you can see Odden (1981) and Myers (1987a). Pulleyblank (1986a) updates the general theory and discusses such central phenomena as floating tones and downstep, much of it in the context of Tiv tonology. For the non-universality of tonal association conventions see also Hyman and Ngunga (1994), and for Meeussen's law Goldsmith (1984). Tone features are discussed in Yip (1980, 1989b), Pulleyblank (1986a), Snider (1988, 1990), Bao (1990) and Duanmu (1990), among others. For the role of accent in African tonal systems, see Goldsmith (1987) and Hyman (1978, 1989).

6   The Interaction between Morphology and Phonology

In chapters 15 and 16 we carried out a systematic investigation of the influence of grammar, morphology in particular, on phonology. Chapter 15 focused on the cycle and chapter 16 on the layering of phonology. The common thread is the delimitation of the domains in which any one phonological rule applies. Our first approximation was to identify these domains with grammatical constituents: syntactic at the phrasal level and morphological inside the word. However, we eventually saw that this approach runs into problems, and in the second part of chapter 16 we explored the construction of specifically phonological domains on grammatical constituents, to allow for mismatches.

In our investigation of stress in chapter 11 we came across the phenomenon of stress retraction in English phrases under conditions of clash. In chapter 15 we saw that the correct results follow if we build the grid in tandem with the grammatical constituency of the phrase, a cyclic mode of construction (Prince 1983, Selkirk 1984b, Halle and Vergnaud 1987a, Hayes 1984, 1995). Cyclicity also governs tone association in many languages, and we illustrated the particular case of Tiv (Pulleyblank 1986a). More recently, however, there has been a turn away from the cycle: see Cole and Coleman (1992), for instance, in a Declarative Phonology framework. Hyman (1994) presents data supportive of the cycle from the Bantu language Cibemba. For an overall discussion of these and other issues related to the cycle, you can go to Cole (1995).

In chapter 15 we completed the picture of English word stress that we started putting together in chapter 12, and investigated the mechanics of English secondary stress in some detail. First, we showed the need to reapply the footing procedure in a non-cyclic mode, that is to say, in the maximal word domain (Halle and Vergnaud 1987a, 1987b). We suggested that this non-cyclic reapplication of footing builds feet from left to right, the opposite direction of its cyclic counterpart (Halle and Kenstowicz 1991), hence our dubbing non-cyclic footing "refooting". Refooting is followed by destressing, a specifically non-cyclic procedure which deletes a mono-moraic degenerate foot that immediately precedes a foot head: cf. Halle and Vergnaud's (1987a) construct "stress well". Next comes a non-cyclic reapplication of accenting, rendered necessary by the destructive action of conflation at the end of each cycle: heavy syllables tend to have some degree of surface stress, whether or not they carry the word's main stress (Halle and Kenstowicz 1991). Non-cyclic accenting is subject to a fair bit of lexical exceptionality, in direct contrast to cyclic accenting, which is prac-tically exceptionless – this skewedness runs in the wrong direction (it is non-cyclic rules that tend to be exceptionless), possibly revealing a weak-ness in the analysis. One further rule retracts primary stress from the word's last syllable. We provisionally assimilated this rule to the Rhythm Rule that effects retraction under clash (Halle and Vergnaud 1987a), and ordered it last in the sequence of non-cyclic stress rules. We went on to demon-strate the cyclicity of the rules responsible for the assignment of word-primary stress: the primary stress of words embedded in larger words tends to surface (as secondary) irrespective of rhythm (*SPE*, Halle and Vergnaud 1987a, Hammond 1989, Halle and Kenstowicz 1991). In order to account for this situation, we preserved internal primary stresses on independent planes, eventually copying them onto the plane of the largest domain to provide accentual sites for secondary stresses, over and above the rhythmic secondary stresses assigned by the non-cyclic stress algorithm. This pro-cedure is justified and explained in Halle and Vergnaud (1987a), and sum-marized in Kager (1995). An early discussion of the stress cycle in languages other than English is to be found in Brame (1974). Sainz (1992) is an attempt to dispense with the English stress cycle altogether, while both Hargus (1993) and Inkelas (1993) argue for maintaining the relationship between phonological rule application and morphological formation.

We investigated English vowel shortening also in chapter 15. The Great Vowel Shift alternations we discussed in chapter 8 are anchored in a length contrast: the lexical long vowel only shortens in the longer alternant, and in chapter 15 we attributed this shortening to a pressure for bimoraic feet, which we formalized as a rule of Vowel Shortening (Borowsky 1986, 1989, Myers 1987b, Halle and Vergnaud 1987a, Rubach 1996). We observed that Vowel Shortening fails to apply in a number of forms. Some of these forms are straightforward exceptions, but others simply fall under the remit of the Principle of Strict Cyclicity, which limits the application of cyclic rules to domains derived in their cycle: lexical material can therefore remain unaffected by cyclic rules. The idea of the strict cycle was introduced in phonology in Kean (1974) and was further developed in Mascaró (1976). For additional discussion of the strict cycle you can go to Kiparsky (1982, 1985, 1993), Hualde (1989), and Poser (1993). Cole (1995) offers a convenient summary. Vowel Shortening is also active in the word-final syllable, for the same reason as word-internally: preference for bimoraic feet. Rubach (1984a) is one of the earliest global applications of the theory of the cycle to one language (Polish), and Rubach (1984b) accounts for the segmental rules of English in a similar mould.

In chapter 16 we accounted for the imperviousness of some affixes to cyclic rules by dividing affixes idiosyncratically into two sets, namely, the set of affixes which define a domain where cyclic rules apply and the set of affixes which do not define such a domain: cyclic rules can therefore skip some morphological structure, typically the outer layers. The observation that the linear order of affixes determines their behaviour with respect to cyclic rules is akin to Siegel's (1974) "Ordering Hypothesis". Affixation processes can be sensitive to non-lexical phonological properties of the input: cf. McCarthy's (1982) discussion of English expletive infixation, for instance. If the properties in question are non-lexical, then they must be derived; if they are derived, then some phonological rules must precede some affixation: in a nutshell, morphology and phonology are interleaved, not segregated. The model of Lexical Phonology integrates this interleaving with the Ordering Hypothesis. Lexical Phonology developed in the early 1980s in such work as Kiparsky (1982, 1983, 1985) and Mohanan (1986), following on from Siegel (1974), Allen (1978) and Pesetzky (1979), among others. A useful collection of articles on the Lexical Phonology of the 1980s appeared in *Phonology Yearbook* 2 (1985), Kaisse and Shaw's opening paper conveniently summarizing the model. Hargus and Kaisse (1993) took further stock at a time when Lexical Phonology was no longer in the limelight. Of particular theoretical interest in this new collection are the papers by Kiparsky, on the relationship between Strict Cyclicity and the derived status of the environment, by Borowsky, on the ordering of morphology and phonology in level 2, and by Odden, on the general interaction between morphology and phonology. The introduction by Kaisse and Hargus evaluates the evolution of Lexical Phonology and maps out its present and its possible future. Inkelas and Zec (1990), a sister collection, investigates the relationship between phonology and syntax. It contains, among others, papers by Hayes on precompiled phonology, by Kaisse on the properties of post-lexical rules, by Nespor on the separation of prosody and rhythm, by Rice on the prediction of rule domains in the phrasal phonology, by Vogel and Kenesei on the influence of syntax and semantics on phonology, and by Zec and Inkelas on prosodically constrained syntax. Szpyra (1992) is a critical evaluation of the theory of cyclic and lexical phonology in the context of Polish and English, and Mohanan (1995) takes a fresh look at the overall organization of the grammar. Pulleyblank (1986a) uses Lexical Phonology to analyse tone association in several African languages. The most complete treatment of English phonology in a Lexical Phonology framework is probably Borowsky (1986), akin to Rubach (1984a) for Polish. Rubach (1985) focuses on the distinction between lexical and postlexical rules, and Rubach (1990) applies the theory to a set of puzzling data concerning the voice value of word-final obstruents in German. For a recent evaluation of the theoretical apparatus of Lexical Phonology, you can go to Odden (1993), and for a state-of-the-art overview to Booij (1994).

7 Phonological Domains

In chapter 16 we argued for licensing the English word-final consonant directly from the syllable node, to account for the fact that the maximally bimoraic rime can be followed by an extra consonant word-finally, only subject to Sonority Sequencing (Selkirk 1982, 1984a, Myers 1987b, Borowsky 1989). On addition of a consonantal suffix (-[θ] to *deep*, for instance), the formerly word-final consonant is pushed into the rime, where it takes over one of the moras of the vowel, thus shortened: *dep*[θ] (cf. Myers 1987b). This shortening does not take place before some suffixes (consider *deepness*, for instance), and we resolved this paradox through a three-fold strategy: (i) we allotted the -[θ] suffix to level 1, and both the -*ness* suffix and the rule of Stray Erasure to level 2; (ii) we made the licensing of the word-final consonant contingent on adjacency to a morphological right bracket (the analysis in Borowsky 1993 is, in essence, equivalent); (iii) we adopted the convention of deleting word-internal morphological brackets at the end of each level – Mohanan (1986) discusses the rationale for bracket erasure in Lexical Phonology. Following this procedure, the] at the end of *deep* will license the *p* in level 2 even after the non-cyclic -*ness* is suffixed, also in level 2. Not so, however, for the *p* in *dep*[θ], which will get deleted by the Bracket Erasure Convention at the end of level 1. Therefore, in level 2 the two forms will be represented *[[deep]ness]* and *[dep[θ]]*, respectively. As a consequence, level-2 Stray Erasure will have no effect on the *p* of *deepness*; by contrast, it would have deleted the *p* of *depth* if this *p* had not become licensed by one of the vowel's two moras. Many English processes similarly exhibiting paradoxical behaviour are brought to rule once the proposed machinery is in place, the retraction of primary stress from the word-final syllable among them: Borowsky (1993) provides a good survey. While most of the data can indeed be accounted for in this way, a non-negligible set of bracketing paradoxes remains where the bracketing provided by the morphology and the semantics is at odds with the bracketing required by the phonology, as usefully summarized in Spencer (1990). Marantz (1988) and Sproat (1988) propose a mapping of morphological structure onto phonological structure as a solution. Also problematic is the fact that most of the affix combinations predicted by the model fail to materialize (Fabb 1988). All these difficulties obviously weaken the approach, pointing at the illegitimacy of identifying phonological domains with grammatical constituency (Inkelas 1989, 1993).

There is strong evidence that in phrasal domains phonological rules do not act directly on the domains defined by the syntax, but, rather, on phonological domains built parasitically on syntactic constituency: Selkirk (1981, 1986, 1990), Nespor and Vogel (1986) and Hayes (1989b); a direct-syntax approach is advocated in Kaisse (1985). One such phonological domain, the Phonological Phrase, constrains the application of clash-driven asterisk retraction in English (Nespor and Vogel 1986). The next higher domain, the Intonational Phrase, is usually construed as the domain of intonational association (Selkirk 1984b, Nespor and Vogel 1986), albeit not uncontroversially (Gussenhoven 1990, Gussenhoven and Rietveld 1992). The Intonational phrase can also constrain the application of phonological rules (Selkirk 1984b, Nespor and Vogel 1986, Rice 1987, Vogel and Kenesei 1990), and we mentioned the rule of place of assimilation of nasals in English in this connection. The largest phonological domain, the Phonological Utterance, does not just correspond to a speech utterance, but is also defined on specific, if varied, criteria. Phonological domains (often referred to as "prosodic domains" in the literature) are expected to comply with the Strict Layer Hypothesis (SLH), which conceives of each phonological domain as made up of one or more occurrences of the phonological domain immediately lower in the hierarchy, with no material left out (Selkirk 1984b, 1990). Selkirk (1996) decomposes the SLH into a set of four more basic constraints. Phrasal phonological domains provide the bounds for the application of the so-called postlexical rules of Lexical Phonology. The postlexical component is specifically investigated in Booij and Rubach (1987) and Iverson (1993), among others. The Phonological Word normally corresponds to the morphosyntactic word, but can be larger or smaller. The Clitic Group, made up of a Phonological Word and one or more clitics attached to it (Nespor and Vogel 1986), is not universally accepted (see Booij 1996).

Below the word, we drew a distinction between phonological domains and phonological constituents. In particular, we argued that prosodic elements such as syllables and feet constitute phonological constituents, while phonological domains are the result of a (frequently vacuous) mapping from morphological structure, parallelling the mapping of syntactic structure onto phrasal phonological domains (Inkelas 1989, 1993). From this perspective, the Phonological Word must be deemed to enjoy dual status, as a phonological constituent (dominating the foot and the syllable) and as a phonological domain (dominated by the Phonological Phrase, or maybe the Clitic Group). The availability of the Phonological Word (PW) as a phonological constituent makes possible the direct licensing from the PW node of such word-peripheral extra segmental material as the word-initial *s-* or (any number of) word-final coronal obstruents in English (see Borowsky 1986; also Rubach and Booij 1990a for Polish).

The model we have outlined achieves a welcome integration between Lexical Phonology and the "Prosodic Phonology" of most of the literature. Prosodic Phonology (our "phonological domains") must of course not be confused with the Prosodic Morphology developed in the work of McCarthy and Prince, and of which McCarthy and Prince (1995) provides a convenient summary. For the relationship between Lexical Phonology and Prosodic Phonology you can check, Booij and Rubach (1984), Booij (1988) and Booij and Lieber (1993). One pending problem concerns the bracketing paradoxes we mentioned above. In Lexical Phonology, Mohanan's (1986) looping back into a previous level (see also Halle and Mohanan 1985) looks suspiciously like an admission of defeat. An alternative made available by the autonomy of phonological domains involves the elevation of some affixes to the rank of phonological words (Booij and Lieber 1993), but some forms seemingly remain intractable. One solution involves interspersing non-cyclic affixes among the cyclic affixes, then allowing cyclic rules to skip non-cyclic domains (Halle and Vergnaud 1987a). However, this strategy entails the abandonment of the Ordering Hypothesis, perhaps the very heart of Lexical Phonology. As we said above, Marantz (1988) and Sproat (1988) advocate a rebracketing strategy to overcome this.

8 Aspects of Lexical Representation

The Principle of Strict Cyclicity that we presented in chapter 15 restricts the application of the cyclic rule of *s*-Voicing to derived environments. In chapter 17 we came across exceptions to this prediction, but this is of course to be expected with any phonological rule. More challenging is the fact that *s*-Voicing appears to have applied morpheme-internally in a majority of monomorphemic forms, contrary to the ruling of the Principle of Strict

Cyclicity. The answer is that the lexical forms in question do not have a lexical value for [±voice], and therefore s-Voicing can fill in the gap without contravening Strict Cyclicity. Monomorphemic forms where the s does not voice include the lexical specification [–voice], which blocks s-Voicing by Strict Cyclicity (Kiparsky 1982, 1985). This model automatically accounts for the transparency of some segments to some assimilation processes: these segments are in effect not there when the assimilation takes place, since the relevant feature is unspecified. A case in point is the regressive assimilation of voice in Russian obstruents, in which sonorants play no role (Halle and Vergnaud 1981, Hayes 1984, Kiparsky 1985).

Underspecification interprets natural values as literally "unmarked" in the lexicon: they are simply left out of lexical representation. Jakobson (1941) is the obvious precursor of this view. The natural values of the distinctive features are inventoried in a set of universal markedness statements, which give rise to a set of implicational relationships deriving some feature values from others (*SPE*, Kean 1975, Calabrese 1995). Stampe's (1969) Natural Phonology addresses the acquisition of phonology from a markedness perspective: see Donegan and Stampe (1979) for a convenient summary.

The formal implementation of underspecification has given rise to several theories, of which in chapter 17 we presented Radical Underspecification and Contrast-restricted Underspecification. Radical Underspecification aims for maximal ("radical") economy of lexical inventory (Archangeli 1984b, 1988). To achieve this aim, one of the segments in each class (for instance, one of the vowels) is assumed not to have feature values in the lexicon: such a segment is maximally underspecified. The identity of the maximally underspecified segment must be determined language by language: it is based on such language-specific facts as the asymmetric behaviour of the segment with respect to some phonological rules, its status as the epenthetic vowel of the language, and so on. The feature values omitted from the maximally underspecified segment are also omitted from all the other segments in the class. This language-specific underspecification adds to the general underspecification derivable from markedness, and obviously results in a drastic simplification of lexical entries, the overt goal of Radical Underspecification. Each feature value missing from the maximally underspecified segment gives rise to a "complement rule" that eventually supplies the value in question. Whether supplied by a complement rule or by a markedness statement, underspecified values must be filled in before they are appealed to in a feature-changing rule, an ordering convention known as the "Redundancy Rule Ordering Constraint". However, ongoing research on actual phonetic implementation is casting doubt on the adequacy of feature filling by phonological redundancy rule, since the phonetic value of underspecified segments often seems to originate in interpolation: see Keating (1984, 1988, 1990) and Pierrehumbert and Beckman (1988), for instance.

For successful applications of the theory of Radical Underspecification you can consult Pulleyblank (1986b, 1988a, 1988b), Abaglo and Archangeli (1989), and Archangeli and Pulleyblank (1989), among others. The predictions of this theory do not always come true, however (Steriade 1995, Hualde 1991a, 1991b), and the theory of Contrast-restricted Underspecification has been brought in (Steriade 1987, 1995, Christdas 1988, Clements 1988). Contrast-restricted Underspecification restricts underspecification to those values that do not contrast in a particular environment. Contrast-restricted underspecification is not trouble-free either. One move to preserve the validity of the theory involves the formalization of (some) distinctive features as unary: the standard negative value would simply correspond to the absence of the feature. Indeed, in chapter 17 we showed that a principled analysis of Khalkha Mongolian backness harmony in the context of Contrast-restricted Underspecification points to a unary feature [round] (Steriade 1987, 1995). For evaluation of the two theories of underspecification, you can go to Archangeli (1988b) and Steriade (1995), while Mohanan (1991) and Myers (1991) take a general stand against underspecification as such. Archangeli and Pulleyblank (1994) develops Radical Underspecification into Combinatorial Specification.

Another major theme in chapter 17 concerned the organization of features: see Broe (1992) for a particularly clear overview. First, we reminded ourselves of the fact that many features are linked in a relationship of dependency, extended by many to class nodes (Clements 1985, Sagey 1986a, McCarthy 1988, Halle 1991, Padgett 1995), a formal equivalent of our subscript notation (cf. Hayes 1990a and Halle 1995). The global network of features is commonly referred to as "Feature Geometry". There are several versions of the feature geometry, with a shared basic structure, but differing in some of the details. The root of the feature geometry tree is assumed by most to be composed of the features [±consonantal] and [±sonorant] (McCarthy 1988), although Kaisse (1992) argues for the independence of [±consonantal], and Hume and Odden (1996) against the very existence of the feature. The idea underlying feature geometry is that associations between features are restricted in the ways encoded in the geometry. Clements (1991) and Clements and Hume (1995) advance a feature geometry common to both consonants and vowels, simply augmented for vowels with the class node "Aperture" and its dependent feature [±open]. Halle and Stevens (1971) and Ladefoged (1973) scrutinize the laryngeal features responsible for voicing, aspiration, glottalization, and so on. The feature geometry tree naturally implies a specific set of redundancies between features: a feature lower in the tree automatically presupposes all the higher features (and class nodes) along its path to the root. Stevens et al. (1987) and Stevens and Keyser (1989) put forward the notion of "enhancement" to justify the frequent co-occurrence of some feature values – [+round] with [+back], for instance.

9 Derivational Theory

In chapter 18 we reviewed rule ordering, one of the trademarks of *SPE*-based phonology, anticipated in Bloomfield (1939). In particular, the lexical and surface levels of representation are assumed to be mediated by an open number of sequential levels, each mapped onto the next by means of a rule. This sequential set of levels mapping the lexical representation of any one form onto its surface representation constitutes a derivation: see S. Anderson (1974) for a particularly lucid presentation. The ordering of the rules, that is, the fact that rule X applies before rule Y, can be automatic: given an input A, rule X (but not rule Y) can and will apply, to yield B; in turn, Y (but not X) can and will apply to B, to yield C; and so on. The situation just described, where rule application is only driven by the substance of the input, is known as "intrinsic ordering". Very often, however, an intrinsic order of application yields incorrect results, and outside intervention (by the linguist or, more to the point, by the learner) is necessary. In this case, we talk about "extrinsic ordering", and we say that the rules in question are extrinsically ordered. Extrinsic ordering by definition disrupts intrinsic ordering: if it didn't, it would be redundant. Rule ordering is discussed in chapter 8.3 of *SPE*. Chafe (1968) defends persistent rule application, as does Myers (1991) in a more modern context. For specialized treatment of the issues of rule ordering see Iverson (1974), and for useful general discussion Booij (1981). Opposition to extrinsic rule ordering has been a recurring theme through the years, and several proposals have been made to dispense with it. Some ordering can indeed be attributed to universal principles: *SPE*'s disjunctive ordering, Kiparsky's (1973) Elsewhere Condition, Archangeli's (1984) Redundancy Rule Ordering Constraint, and so on. Other authors have attempted to extend free ordering beyond areas regulated by such principles: see Koutsoudas et al. (1974), Hooper (1976), Koutsoudas (1980). The main aspects of this debate and other issues concerning rule ordering are summarized in Iverson (1995).

The application of a rule X to an input A can affect the potential of some other rule, Y, to apply. Thus, it is possible that, while the conditions for the application of Y are not met in A (simply because A does not include the environment required for the application of Y), such conditions are met after X has changed A into B: B does include the environment required by Y. In a case like this we say that X and Y stand in a feeding relation, and that X feeds Y (in reality, though, it is the application of X to A that feeds Y). If we invert the order of the two rules, the relation becomes one of counterfeeding, the reverse of feeding: X would feed Y if it were ordered prior to it, as we have just seen. The establishment of counterfeeding orderings obviously requires outside intervention: if the rules were left to their own devices, X would apply to A (because it can), but not to Y (because it can't); in turn, after X has produced B from A, Y will apply to B (again, simply because it can); and so on. Actual examples of these ordering relations in chapter 18 are the English rules of *CiV*-Lengthening and *s*-Voicing for feeding (*CiV*-Lengthening > *s*-Voicing), and Spirantization and [iu]-Formation for counterfeeding (Spirantization > [iu]-Formation). Defenders of free ordering face the challenge of reinterpreting counterfeeding orderings, to achieve the same result without extrinsic ordering. One obvious strategy involves enriching the environment of the rule we want to prevent from applying to the initial input (Koutsoudas et al. 1974): if we enrich the environment of rule Y in our abstract example, so that it is no longer met in A, there will be no need to order Y after X.

Counterfeeding must not be confused with bleeding – all the concepts we are discussing, and their labelling, originate in Kiparsky (1968): see S. Anderson (1974) and chapter 5 of Hooper (1976) for particular, clear illustrations. In counterfeeding, an ordering Y > X prevents X from feeding Y, that is, it blocks the creation of forms to which Y would be applicable: at the time Y is called up (crucially, before X) such forms are simply not available. They will of course become available after the application of X, but by this time Y will no longer be applicable, because of the ordering: the turn of Y has gone, so to speak. Bleeding is different. In bleeding, the application of a rule X to an input A actually removes some material required for the application of another rule Y, ordered after X. In this case, we say that X bleeds Y. Clearly, if we invert the ordering (Y > X, rather than X > Y), bleeding will no longer take place, and Y will be able to apply to A (whatever X does next is immaterial). In cases like these we talk about a counterbleeding order, and say that Y counterbleeds X. Counterbleeding, therefore, simply means 'the opposite of bleeding', in the way that counterfeeding means 'the opposite of feeding'. You can now see that bleeding is not the same as counterfeeding: counterfeeding does not remove anything from the input (the input simply fails to meet the environment of the next rule), but bleeding does, by definition. If bleeding is not the same as counterfeeding, then counterbleeding cannot be the same as feeding, and indeed it isn't – feeding creates the environment required by the next rule, but counterbleeding does not create anything: it simply prevents destruction. The rules in chapter 18 also provide examples of these additional relationships: [j]-Morification > [j]-Deletion for bleeding, and Palatalization > [j]-Morification for counterbleeding. As with counterfeeding, a bleeding relation can only be established on the basis of extrinsic ordering. Without this outside intervention, rules will apply whenever their environment is met: if rule Y has its environment met in a form A (although it wouldn't if rule X had applied first), it will simply apply to it, in a counterbleeding order.

Rules in a system do not necessarily affect each other: rules can be non-interacting. However, the effects of transitivity often impose a specific ordering even between non-interacting rules. Thus, suppose that we can establish empirically that rule X precedes rule Y in the ordering, and that rule Y precedes rule Z. If so, by the principles of logic X must also precede Z. For notice what would happen if it did not. In this case, we would have the following ordering relations: on the one hand, Z > X (ex hypothesi), and on the other X > Y > Z (empirically). But these two orderings are contradictory, because if X > Y > Z, then we cannot in the same breath hypothesize that Z > X, the opposite order. This is precisely what we mean by "transitivity": if X > Y, and Y > Z, then of necessity X > Z. Transitivity is therefore a matter of logic, once we assume, as practically everybody else does, that the order of rules is fixed once and for all for each system: each two rules can only have one ordering (in S. Anderson's 1974 "local ordering", however, the ordering of rules need not be constant across derivations). In chapter 18 we showed that Vowel Shift follows s-Voicing (s-Voicing > Vowel Shift), even though there is no direct interaction between these two rules: s-Voicing must precede Velar Softening (s-Voicing > Velar Softening), and Velar Softening must precede Vowel Shift (Velar Softening > Vowel Shift); therefore, by transitivity, s-Voicing precedes Vowel Shift (s-Voicing > . . . > Vowel Shift). The interaction between these and other rules of English is examined in detail in Rubach (1984b), Halle and Mohanan (1985) and Borowsky (1986), among others. Jensen (1993) provides a convenient summary of these and other matters of English phonology. As we said above, rule ordering is part and parcel of the model of phonology that stemmed from *SPE*, even though there have been several attempts through the years to remove it from the theory. Indeed, extrinsic rule ordering has proved one of the most resilient aspects of *SPE*-inspired phonology: see Bromberger and Halle (1989) for a recent statement, and Kaye (1990), Klausenberger (1990) and Hyman (1993) for alternative views. However, recent developments departing from *SPE* in significant ways can, and do, dispense with rule ordering. Of course, this outcome presupposes the abandonment of derivations, which in turn entails narrowing the distance between the lexical and the surface representation, either because these two representations are related directly, as is the case in Optimality Theory (Prince and Smolenky 1993), or because there are no such two representations in the first place: only surface representation, as in Declarative Phonology (see Scobbie 1993, Bird 1995 and Coleman 1998) and in some versions of Correspondence Theory, a development in Optimality Theory which we will present in the next section (see Burzio 1996, 1997a, for an insightful defence of this position).

In chapter 18 we exemplified and justified rule ordering with a range of English segmental rules: Vowel Shortening, *CiV*-Lengthening, *s*-Voicing, Velar Softening, Spirantization, [iu]-Formation, Palatalization, [j]-Morification, [j]-Deletion, Prevocalic Tensing, Stressed Tense Vowel Lengthening, Vowel Shift and Diphthongization (cf. Rubach 1984b, Borowsky 1986, Halle and Mohanan 1985, Jensen 1993). Of these, Vowel Shortening, *CiV*-Lengthening and *s*-Voicing are cyclic, that is, apply stepwise in each morphological constituent, from smallest to largest. If they are cyclic, then they must obey the Principle of Strict Cyclicity, and therefore they can only apply in derived environments (Kean 1974, Mascaró 1976, Kiparsky 1982, 1985, 1993; see Cole 1995 for a convenient summary). Indeed, arguments advanced for the cyclicity of a given rule often rely on its behaviour with regard to Strict Cyclicity. In the absence of empirical arguments for the cyclicity or otherwise of a rule (either from direct empirical considerations, or indirectly via Strict Cyclicity), the Principle of Late Block Rule Assignment (Halle and Mohanan 1985) assigns the rule to the latest possible stratum. All the other English rules just mentioned have been assigned to the non-cyclic lexical stratum, mostly on empirical considerations, but on the strength of the Principle of Late Block Rule Assignment in the case of Spirantization. In addition to lexical rules, languages have postlexical rules, subject to a number of properties that we listed in (59) in chapter 16. At the end of chapter 18 we mentioned a few postlexical rules of English, but did not go into details (for discussion of English postlexical rules see Rubach 1985, Booij and Rubach 1987). Rules can be assigned to more than one stratum (Halle and Mohanan 1985, Kiparsky 1985). When this happens, the strata in question must be contiguous, in keeping with the Stratum Contiguity Hypothesis, referred to in the literature as the Stratum Continuity Hypothesis, perhaps a less transparent label (see Mohanan 1986).

10 Optimality Theory

In chapter 19 we explained how the markedness constraints introduced in chapter 17 can be brought to bear on the simplifications typical of the language of young children. From this perspective, the task of the language-learning child would be to achieve faithfulness to the adult output by suppressing the effect of the markedness constraints (cf. Stampe 1972). One simple way of modelling this situation consists in also formalizing faithfulness as a constraint (a set of constraints, in fact), ranked *vis-à-vis* the markedness constraints. Assuming that, in case of conflict between two constraints, the higher-ranked constraint prevails, we can naturally construe the child's phonology as involving a higher ranking of the markedness constraints, and the adult's phonology as involving a higher ranking of the faithfulness constraints (Gnanadesikan 1995, Smolensky 1996, Tesar and Smolensky 1998; but see M. Hale and Reiss 1997). Similarly, differences between the phonologies of different languages can be attributed to differences in the respective ranking of the constraints: the constraints themselves are conceived of as universal, simply the incarnation of natural tendencies, as proposed in Prince and Smolensky (1993) and elaborated on in Hayes (1996) and Myers (1997), among others (Archangeli and Pulleyblank 1994 is an obvious antecedent). The model just outlined is known as Optimality Theory (OT). One major innovation of Optimality Theory is, obviously, the reduction of the derivation to a direct mapping of the underlying form onto the surface form. The main body of OT is laid out in Prince and Smolenky (1993). For (updated) summaries you can consult Archangeli (1997) and Sherrard (1997), and for a textbook presentation Kager (in press).

The technical apparatus of Optimality Theory is conceptually very simple. As in more traditional forms of generative phonology, surface alternations are regarded as arising from a shared lexical representation. OT lexical forms and surface forms are in effect related by rules, again as in traditional generative phonology. The difference is that in traditional generative phonology the rules are tailor-made to the requirements of the particular language, as we have seen throughout the book. In Optimality Theory, by contrast, the rules are universal and act freely on the lexical form to change it into an infinite number of surface forms, not just one as in traditional generative phonology. Moreover, because of their universal and automatic nature, rules have remained unformalized in the OT literature: they are tucked away in the GEN component of the model, effectively a black box closed to the observer (see Bromberger and Halle's 1997 assessment of Tesar 1995a, 1995b; Norton 1998 argues that GEN is redundant). The wild output of GEN obviously requires drastic cleaning up if the correct output form is to be obtained: indeed, all the surface forms generated by GEN but one need to be thrown out. This result is achieved by the filtering action of the ranked constraints. In the body of the book we have also encountered constraints as part of the traditional theory, where they are needed for exactly the same reason as they are needed in OT: to correct mismatches between rule outputs and actual forms. There are two main differences between the two theories with regard to the role of constraints, however. First, in traditional theory the constraints are few and far between, because the rules themselves are shaped in such a way that they usually generate the correct output. By contrast, in OT, rules (= GEN) act wildly and generate incalculable garbage: in principle, an infinite number of candidates. Consequently, in OT the main burden of selecting the appropriate surface form rests on the constraints. The second difference is that in traditional theory constraints are inviolable, in a manner similar to the general laws of physics. By contrast, in Optimality Theory constraints are freely violable, and indeed for any particular form most constraints will be violated. The reason constraints can be (and often are) violated is that, as in real everyday life, obedience to superiors is more important than obedience to inferiors: indeed, obedience to inferiors is rather a contradiction in terms! This means that the guiding principle of the procedure evaluating the adequacy of candidates will be the maximization of obedience to the higher constraints: first the constraints ranked highest, then the constraints ranked next highest, and so on in ordered steps. The evaluation procedure (EVAL) is made visually explicit in tableaux where the ranked constraints are plotted against a list of plausible candidates: constraint violations are marked with an asterisk in the corresponding box of the tableau. The optimal candidate will be the candidate which best complies with the constraints, in the manner just explained. Notice, importantly, that the optimal candidate (which must obviously correspond to the surface form) need not be the ideal candidate in the sense of complying with all the constraints: in evaluating candidates, again as in real life, best does not necessarily mean perfect. This point is forcefully made in McCarthy and Prince (1994), who label this misconception "the fallacy of perfection". McCarthy and Prince (1994) also demonstrate that the effect of lower-ranked constraints is not necessarily lost for ever: lower constraints become relevant whenever their higher-ranked counterparts are inactive, a phenomenon McCarthy and Prince refer to as "the emergence of the unmarked".

Constraints come in families, and in chapter 19 we examined a number of these, illustrating their operation with data usually drawn from English. We have already mentioned two such families: the family of markedness constraints and the family of faithfulness constraints. In essence, markedness constraints derive the most natural phonetic forms, if left unimpeded: Golston (1996) indeed identifies (non-natural) lexical representations with markedness violations. Faithfulness constraints account for the fact that the phonologies of natural languages need not coincide with the most natural phonology: less natural forms can make their way into the language, and then be respected as a result of pressure from the faithfulness constraints. We mentioned MAX and DEP as the two central faithfulness constraints, forbidding the alteration of lexical forms by deletion and insertion, respectively (McCarthy and Prince 1996). Identity of segmental material between the two levels of representation is captured by a set of IDENT constraints, in the obvious way (McCarthy and Prince 1996: McCarthy and Prince (in press) is a more accessible version of this paper). Another constraint family contains the constraints responsible for the prosodic structures we discussed in part II of the book: syllabic and metrical structure in particular (Kenstowicz 1994b, 1995, are reasonable introductions to the application of OT in the respective areas). The syllable constraints are geared to the selection of the optimal syllable, CV, by imposing a nucleus (NUC) and an onset (ONSET), ruling out a coda (NO-CODA) and any type of complex constituent (*COMPLEX), allotting vowels to the nucleus (*M/V) and consonants to the margins (*N/C), and enforcing the correct sonority profile (SON). Prince and Smolensky (1993) give a good rundown of the OT syllabification procedure. Many of the constraints (but not all) are of course violated in the phonologies of real languages, among them English, as we would expect they would be. Clements (1997) applies the procedure to Berber, a language notorious for its liberality with regard to the sonority threshold of the nucleus, and Rubach (1997) to Polish, famous for its consonant clusters. The constraints responsible for metrical structure include FTBIN (to enforce foot binarity), FT-TYPE (to select between trochees and iambs), and NON-FIN (to implement extrametricality). Quantity-sensitivity results from the action of the constraints WTS (Weight-to-Stress Principle) and WBP (Weight by Position). For surveys of metrical constraints, you can consult Hammond (1997a) and Roca and Al-Ageli (in press), the latter cross-comparing OT constraints with the parameters of classical metrical theory.

Particularly active in OT analyses is the ALIGN family of constraints, developed in McCarthy and Prince (1993a) (see also McCarthy and Prince 1993b). As we explained in chapter 19, ALIGN is brought in to enforce either abuttedness between two constituents in the same level or superimposition of the edges of two constituents, possibly of different grammatical types, in different levels. Among the effects derived from ALIGN are the enhancement of the first or the last of the word's feet (similarly to Prince and Smolensky's 1993 EDGEMOST), the directionality of iteration (Mester and Padgett 1994; cf. Itô 1986, 1989), and the formal reduction of some of the syllabification constraints (Itô and Mester 1994). Functionally related to ALIGN are CONTIGUITY and ANCHOR. CONTIGUITY (Kenstowicz 1994b) requires abuttedness of elements (segments, syllables, feet), thus blocking epenthesis and/or deletion, to this extent replicating the effect of DEP and MAX string-internally. ANCHOR establishes correspondences between peripheral elements, and effectively subsumes ALIGN (McCarthy and Prince 1996). At a more general level, the Strict Layer Hypothesis translates into the constraint SLH (Rubach 1997), decomposed in Selkirk (1996) into four more specific constraints, each dealing with a specific aspect of the SLH, as we have already mentioned. The Elsewhere Condition is recast under the label "Pāṇini's Theorem", interpreted as a principle governing constraint ranking (Prince and Smolensky 1993).

The version of Optimality Theory currently predominant, "Correspondence Theory" (McCarthy and Prince 1996), increases the scope and number of correspondence constraints. Paramount among these are surface-to-surface corresponding constraints, that simply relate surface forms, in a manner unacceptable to standard generative phonology (the via rules in Hooper 1976 can perhaps be considered a precedent). In chapter 19 we showed how these correspondence constraints can replicate the effects of both the cycle and level ordering in traditional theory: see Kenstowicz (1995), McCarthy

(1995), Benua (1996, 1997) and Burzio (1997b). While level ordering also implies constraint reranking, this not an outrageous outcome, given the very nature of the strata. More worrying is perhaps the use of constraint reranking in cases like English noun and verb stress. Constraint reranking is problematic because of learnability. In particular, a model where the substance of constraints is universal and the ranking between constraints is learnt once and for all for each language meets a reasonable level of plausibility (Tesar and Smolensky 1993, 1998; Pulleyblank and Turkel 1997). However, if we allow the ranking of the constraints to be specific to word classes within a language (Cohn and McCarthy 1994), perhaps even to individual words themselves (Hammond 1997b), the learnability of the system obviously becomes problematic.

At the end of chapter 19 we examined the applicability of OT to morphology (cf. McCarthy and Prince 1993b, 1996): to the processes of regular plural formation and possessive suffixation in English, to be more precise. We saw that the model is indeed successful in predicting both the correct order of concatenation of the morpheme and the selection of its correct allophonic shape (see K. Russell 1997 for specific discussion). Particularly interesting is the interaction between the plural -s and the possessive -'s, which Correspondence Theory allows us to construe as simple allophone overlap. Some puzzling facts of the phonology of English truncates (the apparent overapplication of the rule of [æ]-Tensing, in particular) are also resolved satisfactorily when correspondence constraints are brought into the picture, provided that we also allow for constraint reranking (Benua 1996).

Two areas are clearly problematic to Optimality Theory. The first such area concerns the possible need for rules of a traditional kind outside GEN (McCarthy 1993). Halle and Idsardi (1997) view this development as a direct indictment of OT, but Blevins (1997) argues that rules can be integrated into OT without damaging it. The second problematic area concerns the treatment of opaque surface forms. Idsardi (1997), Noyer (1997) and Paradis (1997) interpret the existence of such forms as support for traditional derivations. Booij (1997) and Rubach (1997) accommodate such data into OT theory by appealing to level ordering and by augmenting Optimality Theory into Derivational Optimality Theory, respectively. McCarthy's (1998) "Sympathy Theory" proposes to solve this problem by designating a (possibly) dominated constraint as the "selector". The selector selects a specific candidate as the "object of sympathy": it is the best of the candidates that comply with the selector. The overall winner (which must of course match the surface form) is then the candidate that best corresponds with the object of sympathy. For further discussion of Sympathy Theory, you can go to Itô and Mester (1996b).

In addition to the regular publication outlets, there are several collections where you can find out more about Optimality Theory, chiefly among them J. Beckman et al. (1996) and Roca (1997), the latter deliberately aimed at comparing OT with derivational theory. Most usefully also, many OT practitioners make their unpublished papers or dissertations available on the World Wide Web, in the so-called Rutger's Optimality Archive (ROA). At the time of writing there are 286 such papers available, and the number is growing steadily. You can download the files freely at the following address:

http://ruccs.rutgers.edu/roa.html

We have now reached the end of this book. Assuming you have read the text carefully and thoughtfully, and worked through the various exercises we have proposed, you are now in a position to tackle the primary literature of generative phonology. However, some of this literature is not immediately transparent, even to the connoisseur, and you may wish to ease your way in by first looking into such advanced distillations of the subject as Roca (1994) and Kenstowicz (1994a), most profitably in this order (Kenstowicz 1994a is reviewed in *Lingua* 96, 1995, 189–95 [J. Szpyra] and *Phonology* 12, 1995, 131–4 [D.A. Dinnsen] and Roca 1994 in *Journal of Linguistics* 32, 1996, 534–6 [J. Durand] and *Phonology* 13, 1996, 433–8 [T.A. Hall]).

Chapter Summary

The purpose of this final chapter has been to remind readers of the topics covered in the book and to direct them to the texts which have informed and inspired us. Our overall aim throughout has been to guide the learner step by step, from the basic constructs of phonetic and phonological analysis through to very advanced concepts and the most up-to-date version of phonological theory. In the first section of the chapter, we concentrated on articulatory phonetics, but also referred to some works which open the gate to the fields of acoustic and auditory phonetics. The second section was mainly concerned with distinctive features, and with the autosegmental approach that allows such features freedom of action: both feature theory and autosegmental formalism are fundamental to the edifice of phonology as currently construed. An additional building block in this edifice is the syllable, and in the third section we reminded ourselves of syllable theory and of the role of sonority in syllabification. Syllables are of course part of the prosodic structure of language. A higher prosodic constituent, the foot, leads us into metrical structure, the subject matter of section 4. The weight of the rime is often criterial in the calculation of stress patterns, and we presented mora theory as an alternative to the skeleton or timing tier. In section 5 we turned our attention to tone. In stress languages like English the modulation of pitch in the form of intonation may change the pragmatic force of an utterance, but it leaves its essential meaning and its grammatical categorization unaffected. Intonation also provides additional evidence for the reality of stress. In other languages, tone may have a lexical or a morphological function, while in yet another class of languages ("pitch-accent languages") words are automatically assigned a fixed tonal melody. In section 6 we summarized the relationship between phonology and morphology. In particular, we looked at the cycle and at the interleaving of morphology and phonology, encapsulated in the model of "Lexical Phonology". Various problems with Lexical Phonology, among them the notorious "bracketing paradoxes", led us to explore an alternative in section 7, making use of specifically phonological domains. Such domains are quite obviously needed above the word in order to account for the relationship between phonology and syntax, and their general principles can profitably be extended to the word and below. In section 8 we saw that the incorporation into the theory of a set of universal markedness statements considerably reduces the burden on lexical specification: maximal language-specific lexical economy is indeed the aim of underspecification theory. We also completed the analysis of distinctive features in the context of the theory of "feature geometry", which incorporates universal dependencies between features, and we broached the issue of feature monovalency. Sections 9 and 10 presented two radically different approaches to the mapping of lexical forms onto surface forms, respectively favouring rules and derivations, and surface constraints. In particular, in section 9 we reviewed the derivational approach traditional in generative phonology, and explored the different ordering relations between rules, with detailed reference to English. In section 10, we surveyed Optimality Theory, where surface forms are selected by a set of ranked constraints: the constraints are assumed to be universal, with idiosyncratic rankings of them making up the different phonologies of the different languages.

Key Questions

1 What is meant by "articulation"? How does articulation relate to acoustics and to perception?

2 Explain why some distinctive features have binary values, whereas others are unary.

3 Describe the role of sonority in syllabification.

4 List the parameters available to languages in the determination of stress patterns.

5 List the different ways in which the modulation of pitch known as "tone" is used in the languages of the world.

6 How does the Principle of Strict Cyclicity regulate the interaction between phonology and morphology?

7 The application of phonological processes is frequently restricted to particular domains, apparently defined by morphological and

syntactic criteria. List the domains discussed and say how they are defined.

8   Underlying forms do not need to be marked for some feature values. How is the realization of these values in the surface forms eventually arrived at?

9   What types of relationship can exist between pairs of extrinsically ordered rules?

10   In OT, what is an "optimal" candidate? How is it chosen?

F u r t h e r   P r a c t i c e

In chapter 19 we discussed transderivational correspondence constraints relating a base form with its derivative. Correspondence Theory was initially conceived as an answer to the problems characterizing the relationship between base and reduplicant in cases of reduplication. Such a relationship gives rise to three different patterns, known as "overapplication", "underapplication" and "normal application":

(i)   overapplication involves a situation where, in the interest of preserving a phonological match between the base and the reduplicant, some phonological processes apply to both base and reduplicant, although the triggering condition is only found in one of them;

(ii)   underapplication obtains when one or other of the reduplicative partners *fails* to undergo some phonological process, again in the interest of a phonological match, even though the triggering condition is present in that partner;

(iii)   under normal application the phonology takes precedence over the identity relationship, which is sacrificed in the interests of the phonological process(es).

The family of IDENT correspondence constraints we introduced in chapter 19 will therefore need to be extended to include BR–IDENT [base–reduplicant identity].

Bahasa Melayu/Indonesia (1)

In Bahasa Melayu/Indonesia, the prefixation of a stem with an initial voiceless obstruent by a nasal-final prefix causes the nasal to coalesce with the obstruent, which leaves its place behind (e.g. məN+potoŋ → məmotoŋ, for "N" = nasal consonant unspecified for place). In reduplication cases the active voice morpheme *məN* may be preposed or it may be interposed, as we show in a. and b. below:

a. *Preposed prefix /məN+base+reduplicant/*
    potoŋ   məmotoŋ-monoŋ   'cut' (intensive, repetitive)
    tulis   mənulis-nulis   'write' (intensive, repetitive)
    kira   məɲira-ɲira   'guess' (intensive, repetitive)

b. *Interposed prefix /base+məN+reduplicant/*
    pukul   pukul-məmukul   'hit' (reciprocal)
    tari   tari-mənari   'dance' (reciprocal)

(i)   The two data sets above show examples of two types of application we referred to above: which are they?

(ii) Provide a suitable set of candidates for evaluation for each of the cases illustrated, and show how different rankings of the same constraints can yield the two types of application in a. and b. (For convenience, the nasal coalescence process can be covered by a general constraint labelled PHON-CONS [phonotactic constraints].)

Bahasa Melayu/Indonesia (2)

In Bahasa Melayu/Indonesia there is a prohibition against final /r/. The effects of this are the following:

Absolute root final /r/ is deleted and the preceding vowel is lengthened (/kotor/ → [kotoː] 'dirty')

Where the root is followed by a vowel initial suffix, /r/ geminates (/kotor+an/ → [kotorran])

Where an /r/-final prefix precedes a vowel initial root, /r/ is deleted (/bər+kərdʒə/ → [bəkərdʒə] 'work').

Consider the following set of forms which show underapplication in reduplication:

Root		Bare root	Affixed root
/bəsar/	'big'	[bəsaː-bəsaː]	[bəsar-bəsarran]
/saior/	'vegetable'	[sajoː-sajoː]	[sajor-sajorran]
/tabor/	'spread'	[taboː-taboː]	[tabor-taborran]

Taking into account the fact that /r/-gemination is prompted by a constraint against onsetless syllables, work out a suitable constraint ranking for the affixed root set. (Hint: your constraint set may need to include an ANCHOR constraint (see chapter 19, section 14) in order to exclude some apparently well-motivated candidates.)

Japanese

The consequence of the rule of Voiced Velar Nasalization (VVN) in conservative Tokyo speech is that the voiced dorsal stop [g] and the dorsal nasal [ŋ] appear in complementary distribution: [g] only occurs word-initially and [ŋ] only word-internally ([geta] *[ŋeta] 'clogs' vs. *[kagi] [kaŋi] 'key'). This distribution extends to compounds formed with "bound" roots (roots which cannot occur independently), yielding such alternations as *gai+dʒiN* 'foreigner' vs. *koku+ŋai* 'abroad'. We can therefore posit the following constraints, which we offer in a shorthand (but we hope transparent) form:

*[ŋ   =   No dorsal nasal in prosodic word-initial position
*g   =   No voiced dorsal

In ordinary compounds VVN is optional:

a. geta   'clogs'   niwa+g/ŋeta   'garden clogs'
    gara   'pattern'   ʃima+g/ŋara   'striped pattern'
    gei   'craft, art'   ʃirooto+g/ŋei   'amateur's skill'

A pervasive process in Japanese compounding is Rendaku (see the exercise in chapter 17). The effect of Rendaku is to voice the initial obstruent in the second element of a compound (e.g. *ama* 'nun' + *tera* 'temple' → *amadera* 'nunnery'). Unlike the situation with compounds of the type shown in a., when [g] would result from the operation of Rendaku it is obligatorily pronounced as [ŋ]:

b. kutʃi 'mouth'   doku+ŋutʃi   'abusive language'
    kuni   'country'   juki+ŋuni   'snow country'
    kami   'paper'   ori+ŋami   'origami paper'

In order to account for these facts we need to add some additional constraints to our pair above:

IDENT$_{SS}$ = Surface-to-surface identity (segmental identity between a bound stem and its free form)
IDENT$_{LS}$ = Lexical-to-surface identity (segmental identity between a lexical and surface form for [nasal])
RENDAKU

Show the appropriate rankings for *niwa-geta*, *niwa-ŋeta* and *doku-ŋutʃi*, bearing in mind that optionality of surface forms must be the result of free constraint rankings.

Axininca Campa

In the Arawakan language Axininca Campa, spoken in Peru, a hiatus at a V + V juncture is disallowed, leading to the epenthesis of [t]:

/i-N-koma-i/	iŋ.ko.ma.ti	'he will paddle'
/i-N-koma-aa-i/	iŋ.ko.ma.taa.ti	'he will paddle again'
/i-N-koma-ako-i/	iŋ.ko.ma.ta.ko.ti	'he will paddle for'
/i-N-ʧʰik-i/	iɲ.ʧʰi.ki	'he will cut'
/i-N-ʧʰik-aa-i/	iɲ.ʧʰi.kaa.ti	'he will cut again'
/i-N-ʧʰik-ako-i/	iɲ.ʧʰi.ka.ko.ti	'he will cut for'

Notice that although epenthesis seems to be prompted by an ONSET constraint, this does not affect initial vowels, nor is there coalescence between adjacent vowels of stem and affix. Notice also that there is a phonotactic constraint on codas: in this position the language only permits nasals homorganic to a following stop or affricate. This constraint can be labelled CODA COND[ITION].

Show how the constraints indicated above interact with the two following alignment constraints:

ALIGN-LEFT = Align(Stem, L, PrWd, L)
ALIGN-RIGHT = Align(Stem, R, σ, R)

REFERENCES

(ROA = Rutgers Optimality Archive; see page 659.)

Abaglo, P. and Archangeli, D. 1989: Language-particular underspecification: Gengbe /e/ and Yoruba /i/, *Linguistic Inquiry* 20, 457–80.

Abercrombie, D. 1967: *Elements of General Phonetics*. Edinburgh: Edinburgh University Press.

Allen M. 1978: Morphological investigations. PhD, University of Conneticut.

Anderson, J. and Ewen, C. 1987: *Principles of Dependency Phonology*. Cambridge: Cambridge University Press.

Anderson, S. 1974: *The Organization of Phonology*. New York: Academic Press.

Anderson, S. 1978: Tone features. In Fromkin (1978), 133–75.

Anderson, S. 1985: *Phonology in the Twentieth Century*. Chicago: University of Chicago Press.

Aoki, H. 1968: Toward a typology of vowel harmony. *International Journal of American Linguistics* 34, 142–5.

Archangeli, D. 1984: Underspecification in Yawelmani phonology and morphology. PhD, MIT. Published by Garland, New York, 1988.

Archangeli, D. 1988a: Extrametricality in Yawelmani. *The Linguistic Review* 4, 101–20.

Archangeli, D. 1988b: Aspects of underspecification theory. *Phonology* 5, 183–207.

Archangeli, D. 1997: Optimality theory: an introduction to linguistics in the 1990s. In Archangeli and Langendoen (1997), 1–32.

Archangeli, D. and Langendoen, T. (eds) 1997: *Optimality Theory: An Overview*. Oxford: Blackwell.

Archangeli, D. and Pulleyblank, D. 1989: Yoruba vowel harmony. *Linguistic Inquiry* 20, 173–217.

Archangeli, D. and Pulleyblank, D. 1994: *Grounded Phonology*. Cambridge, MA: MIT Press.

Aronoff, M. and Oehrle, R. (eds) 1984: *Language Sound Structure*. Cambridge MA: MIT Press.

Attridge, D. 1982: *The Rhythms of English Poetry*. London: Longman.

Attridge, D. 1989: Linguistic theory and literary criticism: *The Rhythms of English Poetry* revisited. In Kiparsky and Youmans (1989), 183–99.

Bagemihl, B. 1989: The Crossing Constraint and 'backwards "languages" '. *Natural Language and Linguistic Theory* 7, 481–549.

Bao, Z. 1990: On the nature of tone. PhD, MIT.

Bauer, L. 1986: Notes on New Zealand English phonetics and phonology. *English World Wide* 7, 225–58.

Bauer, L. 1994: English in New Zealand. In Burchfield (1994), 382–429.

Beckman, J., Walsh Dickey, L. and Urbanczyk, S. (eds) 1996: *Papers in Optimality Theory. University of Massachusetts Occasional Papers in Linguistics* 18. Graduate Linguistic Student Association.

Beckman, M. 1986: *Stress and Non-Stress Accent*. Dordrecht: Foris.

Beckman, M. and Pierrehumbert, J. 1986: Intonational structure in English and Japanese. *Phonology Yearbook* 3, 255–309.

Bell, A. 1978: Syllabic consonants. In Greenberg (1978), 153–201.

Benua, L. 1996: Identity effects in morphological truncation. In Beckman et al. (1996), 77–136.

Benua, L. 1997: Transderivational identity: phonological relations between words. PhD, University of Massachusetts at Amherst.

Bird, S. 1991: Feature structures and indices. *Phonology* 8, 137–44.

Bird, S. 1995: *Computational Phonology: A Constraint-based Approach*. Cambridge: Cambridge University Press.

Blevins, J. 1990: Alternatives to exhaustivity and conflation in metrical theory. MS, University of Texas at Austin.

Blevins, J. 1993: A tonal analysis of Lithuanian nominal accent. *Language* 69, 237–73.

Blevins, J. 1995: The syllable in phonological theory. In Goldsmith (1995), 206–44.

Blevins, J. 1997: Rules in Optimality Theory: two case studies. In Roca (1997), 227–60.

Bloomfield, L. 1939: Menomini morphophonemics. *Travaux du Cercle Linguistique de Prague* 8, 105–15.

Bolinger, D. (ed.) 1972: *Intonation*. Harmondsworth: Penguin.

Bolinger, D. 1978: Intonation across languages. In Greenberg (1978), 471–524.

Bolinger, D. 1986: *Intonation and its Parts: Melody in Spoken English*. London: Edward Arnold.

Bolinger, D. 1989: *Intonation and its Uses*. London: Edward Arnold.

Booij, G. 1981: Rule ordering, rule application, and the organization of grammars. In W.U. Dressler (ed.), *Phonologica 1980*, Innsbruck: Institut für Sprachwissenschaft, 45–56.

Booij, G. 1988: On the relation between lexical and prosodic phonology. In P.M. Bertinetto and M. Loporcaro (eds), *Certamen Phonologicum: Papers from the 1987 Cortona Phonology Meeting*, Turin: Rosenberg and Sellier, 63–76.

Booij, G. 1994: Lexical Phonology: a review. *Lingua e Stile* 29, 525–55.

Booij, G. 1996: Cliticisation as prosodic integration. *The Linguistic Review* 13, 219–42.

Booij, G. 1997: Non-derivational phonology meets lexical phonology. In Roca (1997), 261–88.

Booij, G. and Lieber, R. 1993: On the simultaneity of morphological and prosodic structure. In Hargus and Kaisse (1993), 23–44.

Booij, G. and Rubach, J. 1984: Morphological and prosodic domains in Lexical Phonology. *Phonology Yearbook* 1, 1–27.

Booij, G. and Rubach, J. 1987: Postcyclic versus postlexical rules in Lexical Phonology. *Linguistic Inquiry* 18, 1–44.

Borden, G., Harris, K. and Raphael, L. 1993 [1980]: *Speech Science Primer*. Baltimore and London: Williams and Wilkins.

Borowsky, T. 1986: Topics in the lexical phonology of English. PhD, University of Massachusetts at Amherst. Circulated by the Graduate Linguistic Student Association. Published by Garland, New York, 1990.

Borowsky, T. 1987: Antigemination in English phonology. *Linguistic Inquiry* 16, 671–8.

Borowsky, T. 1989: Structure preservation and the syllable coda in English. *Natural Language and Linguistic Theory* 7, 145–66.

Borowsky, T. 1993: On the word level. In Hargus and Kaisse (1993), 199–234.

Brame, M. 1974: The cycle in phonology: stress in Palestinian, Maltese and Spanish. *Linguistic Inquiry* 5, 39–60.

Branford, W. 1994: English in South Africa. In Burchfield (1994), 430–96.

Broe, M. 1992: An introduction to feature geometry. In Docherty and Ladd (1992), 149–65.

Bromberger, S. and Halle, M. 1989: Why phonology is different. *Linguistic Inquiry* 20, 51–70.

Bromberger, S. and Halle, M. 1997: The contents of phonological signs: a comparison between their use in derivational theories and in optimality theories. In Roca (1997), 93–123.

Bronstein, A.J. 1960: *The Pronunciation of American English*. New York: Appelton-Century-Crofts.

Broselow, E. 1995: Skeletal positions and moras. In Goldsmith (1995), 175–205.

Bruce, G. 1977: *Swedish Word Accents in Sentence Perspective*. Lund: Gleerup.

Burchfield, R. (ed.) 1994: *The Cambridge History of the English Language*, vol. 5: *English in Britain and Overseas: Origins and Development*. Cambridge: Cambridge University Press.

Burzio, L. 1996: Surface constraints versus underlying representations. In Durand and Katamba (1996), 123–41.

Burzio, L. 1997a: Strength in numbers. *University of Maryland Working Papers in Linguistics* 5, 29–52.

Burzio, L. 1997b: Cycles, non-derived-environment blocking, and correspondence. MS, Department of Cognitive Science, Johns Hopkins University.

Calabrese, A. 1995: A constraint-based theory of phonological markedness and simplification procedures. *Linguistic Inquiry* 26, 373–463.

Catford, J.C. 1977: *Fundamental Problems in Phonetics*. Edinburgh: Edinburgh University Press.

Catford, J.C. 1988: *A Practical Introduction to Phonetics*. Oxford: Oxford University Press.

Chafe, W. 1968: The ordering of phonological rules. *International Journal of American Linguistics* 24, 115–36.

Chambers, J. 1973: Canadian raising. *Canadian Journal of Linguistics* 18, 113–35.

Chomsky, N. and Halle, M. 1968: *The Sound Pattern of English*. New York: Harper and Row.

Christdas, P. 1988: The phonology and morphology of Tamil. PhD, Cornell University.

Clark, J. and Yallop, C. 1995 [1990]: *An Introduction to Phonetics and Phonology*. Oxford: Blackwell.

Clark, M. 1987: *Japanese as a Tone Language*. Dordrecht: Foris.

Clements, G.N. 1977: The autosegmental treatment of vowel harmony. In W. Dressler and O. Pfeiffer (eds), *Phonologica 1976*, Innsbruck: Innsbrucker Beiträger zur Sprachwissenschaft, 111–19.

Clements, G.N. 1983: The hierarchical representation of tone. In I.R. Dihoff (ed.), *Current Approaches to African Linguistics*, vol. 1, Dordrecht: Foris, 145–76.

Clements, G.N. 1985: The geometry of phonological features. *Phonology Yearbook* 2, 225–52.

Clements, G.N. 1988: Toward a substantive theory of feature specification. *North Eastern Linguistic Society* 18, 79–93.

Clements, G.N. 1991: Place of articulation in consonants and vowels: a unified theory. *Working Papers of the Cornell Phonetics Laboratory* 5, 77–123.

Clements, G.N. 1992a: Phonological primes: features or gestures? *Phonetica* 49, 181–93.

Clements, G.N. 1992b: The sonority cycle and syllable organization. In W. Dressler, H. Luschützky, O. Pfeiffer and J. Rennison (eds), *Phonologica 1988*, Cambridge: Cambridge University Press, 63–76.

Clements, G.N. 1997: Berber syllabification: derivations or constraints? In Roca (1997), 289–330.

Clements, G.N. and Goldsmith, J. 1984: *Autosegmental Studies in Bantu Tone*. Dordrecht: Foris.

Clements, G.N. and Hume, E. 1995: The internal organisation of speech sounds. In Goldsmith (1995), 245–306.

Clements, G.N. and Keyser, S.J. 1983: *CV Phonology: A Generative Theory of the Syllable*. Cambridge, MA: MIT Press.

Clements, G.N. and Sezer, E. 1982: Vowel consonant and disharmony in Turkish. In van der Hulst and Smith (1982), part 2, 213–55.

Cohen, P.R., Morgan, J. and Pollack, M.E. (eds), 1990: *Intentions in Communication*. Cambridge, MA: MIT Press.

Cohn, A. and McCarthy, J. 1994: Alignment and parallelism in Indonesian phonology. MS, Cornell University and University of Massachusetts at Amherst. ROA-25.

Cole, J. 1995: The cycle in phonology. In Goldsmith (1995), 70–113.

Cole, J. and Coleman, J. 1992: No need for cyclicity in generative grammar. *Chicago Linguistic Society* 28, vol. 2: *The Parasession on the Cycle in Linguistic Theory*, 36–50.

Cole, J. and Kisseberth, C. 1994: *Perspectives in Phonology*. Stanford: CSLI Publications.

Coleman, J. 1998: *Phonological Representations*. Cambridge: Cambridge University Press.

Coleman, J. and Local, J. 1991: The "No crossing constraint" in autosegmental phonology. *Linguistics and Philosophy* 14, 295–338.

Cook, V. and Newson, M. 1996: *Chomsky's Universal Grammar*. Oxford: Blackwell.

Crothers, J. 1978: Typology and universals in vowel systems. In Greenberg (1978), 93–152.

Cruttenden, A. 1986: *Intonation*. Cambridge: Cambridge University Press.

Daniloff, R., Schuckers, G. and Feth, L. 1980: *The Physiology of Speech and Hearing. An Introduction*. Englewood Cliffs, NJ: Prentice-Hall.

Denes, P. and Pinson, E. 1993 [1973]: *The Speech Chain*. Garden City, NY: Freeman.

Diehl, R. (ed.) 1991a: *On the Relationship between Phonetics and Phonology*. Special issue of *Phonetica* 48.2–4.

Diehl, R. 1991b: The role of phonetics within the study of language. In Diehl (1991a), 120–34.

Dinnsen, D. 1979: *Current Approaches to Phonological Theory*. Bloomington, IN: Indiana University Press.

Docherty, G. and Ladd, R. (eds) 1992: *Papers in Laboratory Phonology*, II: *Gesture, Segment, Prosody*. Cambridge: Cambridge University Press.

Dogil, G. 1998: Slavic languages. In van der Hulst [in press *a*], ch. 11.1.

Donegan, P. and Stampe, D. 1979: The study of natural phonology. In Dinnsen (1979), 126–73.

Downing, P. 1977: On the creation and use of English compound nouns. *Language* 53, 810–42.

Dresher, E. and Kaye, J. 1990: A computational learning model for metrical phonology. *Cognition* 34, 137–95.

Duanmu, S. 1990: A formal study of syllable, tone, stress and domain in Chinese languages. PhD, MIT.

Duanmu, S. 1994: Against contour tone units. *Linguistic Inquiry* 25, 555–608.

Durand, J. and Katamba, F. (eds) 1995: *Frontiers of Phonology*. London and New York: Longman.

Durand, J. and Laks, B. (eds) 1996: *Current Trends in Phonology: Models and Methods*. Salford: University of Salford Press.

Fabb, N. 1988: English suffixation is constrained only by selectional restrictions. *Natural Language and Linguistic Theory* 6, 527–39.

Fischer-Jørgensen, E. 1975: *Trends in Phonological Theory. A Historical Introduction*. Copenhagen: Akademisk Forlag.

Franks, S. 1985: Extrametricality and stress in Polish. *Linguistic Inquiry* 16, 144–51.

Franks, S. 1987: Regular and irregular stress in Macedonian. *International Journal of Slavic Linguistics and Poetics* 1, 227–40.

Fromkin, V. (ed.) 1978: *Tone: A Linguistic Survey*. New York: Academic Press.

Fry, D. 1979: *The Physics of Speech*. Cambridge: Cambridge University Press.

Giegerich, H. 1992: *English Phonology*. Cambridge: Cambridge University Press.

Gimson, A. 1994 [1970]: *An Introduction to the Pronunciation of English* [revised by A. Cruttenden]. London: Edward Arnold.

Gnanadesikan, A. 1995: Markedness and faithfulness conditions in child phonology. MS, University of Massachusetts at Amherst. ROA-106.

Goldsmith, J. 1976a: Autosegmental phonology. PhD, MIT. Circulated by the Indiana University Linguistics Club. Published by Garland, New York, 1979.

Goldsmith, J. 1976b: An overview of autosegmental phonology. *Linguistic Analysis* 2, 23–68.

Goldsmith, J. 1979: The aims of autosegmental phonology. In Dinnsen (1979), 202–22.

Goldsmith, J. 1981: English as a tone language. In D. Goyvaerts (1981), *Phonology in the 1980's*, Ghent: Story-Scientia, 287–308.

Goldsmith, J. 1984: Meeussen's rule. In Aronoff and Oehrle (1984), 245–59.

Goldsmith, J. 1985: Vowel harmony in Khalkha Mongolian, Yata, Finnish and Hungarian. *Phonology Yearbook* 2, 251–75.

Goldsmith, J. 1987: Tone and accent and getting the two together. *Berkeley Linguistic Society* 13, 88–104.

Goldsmith, J. 1990: *Autosegmental and Metrical Phonology*. Oxford: Blackwell.

Goldsmith, J. (ed.) 1995: *The Handbook of Phonological Theory*. Oxford: Blackwell.

Golston, C. 1996: Direct Optimality Theory: representation as pure markedness. *Language* 72, 713–48.

Greenberg, J. (ed.) 1978: *Universals of Human Language*, vol. 2: *Phonology*. Stanford: Stanford University Press.

Gussenhoven, C. 1986: English plosive allophones and ambisyllabicity. *Gramma* 10, 119–41.

Gussenhoven, C. 1990: Tonal association domains and the prosodic hierarchy in English. In Ramsaran (1990a), 27–37.

Gussenhoven 1991: The English rhythm rule as an accent deletion rule. *Phonology* 8, 1–35.

Gussenhoven, C. and Rietveld, A. 1992: Intonation contours, prosodic structure and preboundary lengthening. *Journal of Phonetics* 20, 283–303.

Hale, K. and White Eagle, J. 1980: A preliminary metrical account of Winnebago accent. *International Journal of American Linguistics* 46, 117–32.

Hale, M. and Reiss, C. 1997: Formal and empirical arguments concerning phonological acquisition. MS, Concordia University, Montreal. ROA-233. [To appear in *Linguistic Inquiry*.]

Halle, M. 1957: In defense of the number two. In E. Pulgram (ed.), *Studies Presented to Joshua Whatmough*, The Hague: Mouton, 65–72.

Halle, M. 1962: Phonology in generative grammar. *Word* 18, 54–72.

Halle, M. 1983: On distinctive features and their articulatory implementation. *Natural Language and Linguistic Theory* 1, 91–105.

Halle, M. 1990: Respecting metrical structure. *Natural Language and Linguistic Theory* 8, 149–76.

Halle, M. 1991: Phonological features. In W. Bright (ed.), *International Encyclopedia of Linguistics*, Oxford: Oxford University Press, 207–12.

Halle, M. 1995: Feature geometry and feature spreading. *Linguistic Inquiry* 26, 1–46.

Halle, M. and Clements, G.N. 1983: *Problem Book in Phonology*. Cambridge, MA: MIT Press.

Halle, M. and Idsardi, W. 1995: General properties of stress and metrical structure. In Goldsmith (1995), 403–43.

Halle, M. and Idsardi, W. 1997: *r*, hypercorrection, and the Elsewhere Condition. In Roca (1997), 331–48.

Halle, M. and Kenstowicz, M. 1991: The Free Element Condition and cyclic versus noncyclic stress. *Linguistic Inquiry* 22, 457–501.

Halle, M. and Mohanan, K.P. 1985: Segmental phonology of Modern English. *Linguistic Inquiry* 16, 57–116.

Halle, M. and Stevens, K. 1971: A note on laryngeal features. *MIT Quarterly Progress Report* 11, Research Laboratory of Electronics, MIT, 198–213.

Halle, M. and Vergnaud, J.-R. 1981: Harmony processes. In W. Klein and W. Levelt (eds), *Crossing the Boundaries in Linguistics*, Dordrecht: Reidel, 1–22.

Halle, M. and Vergnaud, J.-R. 1987a: *An Essay on Stress*. Cambridge, MA: MIT Press.

Halle, M. and Vergnaud, J.-R. 1987b: Stress and the cycle. *Linguistic Inquiry* 18, 45–84.

Hammond, M. 1988: On deriving the Well-Formedness Condition. *Linguistic Inquiry* 19, 467–99.

Hammond, M. 1989: Cyclic stress and accent in English. *West Coast Conference on Formal Linguistics* 8, 139–53.

Hammond, M. 1997a: Optimality Theory and prosody. In Archangeli and Langendoen (1997), 33–58.

Hammond, M. 1997b: Underlying representations in Optimality Theory. In Roca (1997), 349–65.

Hammond, M. and Noonan M. (eds) 1988: *Theoretical Morphology*. San Diego, CA: Academic Press.

Hankamer, J. and Aissen, J. 1974: The sonority hierarchy. *Chicago Linguistic Society* 10: *Parasession on Natural Phonology*, 131–45.

Haraguchi, S. 1977: *The Tone Pattern of Japanese: An Autosegmental Theory of Tone*. Tokyo: Kaitakusha.

Hardcastle, W. 1973: *Physiology of Speech Production: An Introduction for Speech Scientists*. London: Academic Press.

Hardcastle, W. and Laver, J. (eds) 1997: *The Handbook of the Phonetic Sciences*. Oxford: Blackwell.

Hargus, S. 1993: Modelling the phonology–morphology interface. In Hargus and Kaisse (1993), 45–74.

Hargus, S. and Kaisse, E. (eds) 1993: *Studies in Lexical Phonology*. San Diego, CA: Academic Press.

Harris, J. 1994: *English Sound Structure*. Oxford: Blackwell.

Harris, J. and Lindsey, G. 1995: The elements of phonological representation. In Durand and Katamba (1995), 34–79.

Harris, R. 1987: *Reading Saussure*. La Salle, IL: Open Court.

Hawkins, P. 1992: *Introducing Phonology*. London: Routledge.

Hayes, B. 1979: Extrametricality. *MIT Working Papers in Linguistics* 1, 77–86.

Hayes, B. 1980: A metrical theory of stress rules. PhD, MIT. Circulated by the Indiana University Linguistics Club, 1981. Published by Garland, New York, 1985.

Hayes, B. 1982: Extrametricality and English stress. *Linguistic Inquiry* 13, 227–76.

Hayes, B. 1984: The phonology of rhythm in English. *Linguistic Inquiry* 15, 33–74.

Hayes, B. 1989a: Compensatory lengthening in moraic phonology. *Linguistic Inquiry* 20, 253–306.

Hayes, B. 1989b: The prosodic hierarchy in meter. In Kiparsky and Youmans (1989), 201–60.

Hayes, B. 1990a: Diphthongization and coindexing. *Phonology* 7, 31–71.

Hayes, B. 1990b: Precompiled phrasal phonology. In Inkelas and Zec (1990), 85–108.

Hayes, B. 1995: *Metrical Stress Theory: Principles and Case Studies*. Chicago: University of Chicago Press.

Hayes, B. 1996: Phonetically-driven phonology: the role of Optimality Theory and inductive grounding. MS, University of California, Los Angeles. ROA-158.

Hayward, R. 1988: In defence of the skeletal tier. *Studies in African Linguistics* 19, 131–72.

Hobbs, J. 1990: The Pierrehumbert–Hirschberg theory of intonational meaning made simple: comments on Pierrehumbert and Hirschberg. In Cohen et al. (1990), 313–23.

Hockett, C. 1956: *A Manual of Phonology*. Baltimore, MD: Waverly Press.

Hooper, J. 1972: The syllable in phonological theory. *Language* 48, 525–40.

Hooper, J. 1976: *An Introduction to Natural Generative Phonology*. New York: Academic Press.

Hualde, J.I. 1988: Affricates are not contour segments. *West Coast Conference on Formal Linguistics* 7, 143–57.

Hualde, J.I. 1989: The strict cycle condition and noncyclic rules. *Linguistic Inquiry* 20, 675–80.

Hualde, J.I. 1991a: *Basque Phonology*. London: Routledge.

Hualde, J.I. 1991b: Unspecified and unmarked vowels. *Linguistic Inquiry* 22, 205–9.

Hualde, J.I. 1998: Basque accentuation. In van der Hulst [in press *a*], ch. 14.

Hulst, H. van der 1988: Atoms of segmental structure: components, gestures, and dependency. *Phonology* 6, 253–84.

Hulst, H. van der 1995: Radical CV Phonology: the categorial gesture. In Durand and Katamba (1995), 80–116.

Hulst, H. van der (ed.) [in press *a*]: *Word Prosodic Systems in the Languages of Europe*. Berlin: Mouton de Gruyter.

Hulst, H. van der [in press *b*]: Word accent. In van der Hulst [in press *a*], ch. 1.

Hulst, H. van der and Smith, N. 1982a: Prosodic domains and opaque segments in autosegmental theory. In van der Hulst and Smith (1982b), part 2, 311–36.

Hulst, H. van der and Smith, N. (eds) 1982b: *The Structure of Phonological Representations*. Dordrecht: Foris.

Hulst, H. van der and Smith, N. (eds) 1988: *Features, Segmental Structure, and Harmony Processes*. Dordrecht: Foris.

Hulst, H. van der and Weijer, J. van de 1995: Vowel harmony. In Goldsmith (1995), 495–534.

Hulst, H. van der, Hendriks, B. and Weijer, J. van de [in press]: A survey of word prosodic systems of European languages. In van der Hulst [in press *a*], ch. 7.

Hume, E. and Odden, D. 1996: Reconsidering [consonantal]. *Phonology* 13, 345–76.

Hyman, L. (ed.) 1977a: *Studies in Stress and Accent*. Special issue of *Southern California Occasional Papers in Linguistics* 4, Department of Linguistics, University of Southern California.

Hyman, L. 1977b: On the nature of linguistics stress. In Hyman (1977a), 37–82.

Hyman, L. 1978: Tone and/or accent. In D.J. Napoli (ed.), *Elements of Tone, Stress, and Intonation*, Washington, DC: Georgetown University Press, 1–20.

Hyman, L. 1985: *A Theory of Phonological Weight*. Dordrecht: Foris.

Hyman, L. 1989: Accent in Bantu: a reappraisal. *Studies in the Linguistic Sciences* 19, 111–28.

Hyman, L. 1993: Problems for rule ordering in phonology: two Bantu cases. In J. Goldsmith (ed.), *The Last Phonological Rule*, Chicago: University of Chicago Press, 195–222.

Hyman, L. 1994: Cyclic phonology and morphology in Cibemba. In Cole and Kisserberth (1994), 81–112.

Hyman, L. and Ngunga, A. 1994: On the non-universality of tonal association 'conventions': evidence from Ciyao. *Phonology* 11, 25–68.

Idsardi, W. 1997: Phonological derivations and historical changes in Hebrew spirantisations. In Roca (1997), 367–92.

Ingria, R. 1980: Compensatory lengthening as a metrical phenomenon. *Linguistic Inquiry* 11, 465–95.

Inkelas, S. 1989: Prosodic constituency in the lexicon. PhD, Stanford University. Published by Garland, New York, 1990.

Inkelas, S. 1993: Deriving cyclicity. In Hargus and Kaisse (1993), 75–110.

Inkelas, S. and Zec, D. 1988: Serbo-Croatian pitch accent: the interactions of tone, stress, and intonation. *Language* 64, 227–48.

Inkelas, S. and Zec, D. 1990: *The Phonology–Syntax Connection*. Chicago: University of Chicago Press.

International Phonetic Association. 1949: *The Principles of the International Phonetic Association*. International Phonetic Association.

Itô, J. 1986: Syllable theory in prosodic phonology. PhD, University of Massachusetts at Amherst. Circulated by the Graduate Linguistic Student Association. Published by Garland, New York, 1988.

Itô, J. 1989: A prosodic theory of epenthesis. *Natural Language and Linguistic Theory* 7, 217–60.

Itô, J. and Mester, A. 1994: Reflections on CodaCon and Alignment. *Phonology at Santa Cruz*, iii, 27–46.

Itô, J. and Mester, A. 1995: Japanese phonology. In Goldsmith (1995), 817–38.

Itô, J. and Mester, A. 1996a: The core–periphery structure of the lexicon and constraints on reranking. In J. Beckman et al. (1996), 181–210.

Itô, J. and Mester, A. 1996b: Sympathy theory and German truncations. *University of Maryland Working Papers in Linguistics* 5, 117–38. ROA-211.

Iverson, G. 1974: Ordering constraints in phonology. PhD, University of Minnesota.

Iverson, G. 1993: (Post)lexical rule application. In Hargus and Kaisse (1993), 255–75.

Iverson, G. 1995: Rule ordering. In Goldsmith (1995), 609–14.

Iverson, G. and Wheeler, D. 1988: Blocking and the Elsewhere Condition. In Hammond and Noonan (1998), 325–38.

Jakobson, R. 1941: *Kindersprache, Aphasie und allgemeine Lautgesetze*. Translation: A.R. Keiler, *Child Language, Aphasia and Phonological Universals*, The Hague: Mouton, 1968. Also in *Selected Writings*, vol. 1. The Hague: Mouton, 328–401.

Jakobson, R. 1990: *On Language*. Cambridge, MA: Harvard University Press.

Jensen, J. 1993: *English Phonology*. Amsterdam: Benjamins.

Jones, C. 1989: *A History of English Phonology*. London: Longman.

Jones, D. 1966 [1909]: *The Pronunciation of English*. Cambridge: Cambridge University Press.

Jones, D. 1967 [1918]: *An Outline of English Phonetics*. Cambridge: Heffer.

Kager, R. 1989: A metrical theory of stress and destressing in English and Dutch. PhD, University of Utrecht. Published by ICG Printing, Dordrecht, 1989.

Kager, R. 1993: Alternatives to the iambic-trochaic law. *Natural Language and Linguistic Theory* 11, 381–432.

Kager, R. 1995: The metrical theory of word stress. In Goldsmith (1995), 367–402.

Kager, R. [in press]: *Optimality Theory: A Textbook*. Cambridge: Cambridge University Press.

Kahn, D. 1976: Syllable-based generalizations in English phonology. PhD, MIT. Circulated by the Indiana University Linguistics Club. Published by Garland, New York, 1980.

Kaisse, E. 1985: *Connected Speech: The Interaction of Syntax and Phonology*. New York: Academic Press.

Kaisse, E. 1990: Toward a typology of postlexical rules. In Inkelas and Zec (1990), 127–43.

Kaisse, E. 1992: Can [consonantal] spread? *Language* 68, 313–32.

Kaisse, E. and Hargus, S. 1993: Introduction. In Hargus and Kaisse (1993), 1–19.

Kaisse, E. and Shaw, P. 1985: On the theory of lexical phonology. *Phonology Yearbook* 2, 1–30.

Kaye, J. 1990: What ever happened to dialect B? In Mascaró and Nespor (1990), 259–63.

Kaye, J. 1992: Do you believe in magic? The story of s + C sequences. *SOAS Working Papers in Linguistics and Phonetics* 2, 293–313.

Kaye, J., Lowenstamm, J. and Vergnaud, J.-R. 1985: The internal structure of phonological elements: a theory of charm and government. *Phonology Yearbook* 2, 305–28.

Kean, M.-L. 1974: The strict cycle in phonology. *Linguistic Inquiry* 5, 179–203.

Kean, M.-L. 1975: The theory of markedness in generative grammar. PhD, MIT. Circulated by the Indiana University Linguistics Club.

Keating, P. 1984: Phonetic and phonological representation of stop consonant voicing. *Language* 60, 286–319.

Keating, P. 1987: Survey of phonological features. *UCLA Working Papers in Phonetics* 66, 124–50. Circulated by the Indiana University Linguistics Club.

Keating, P. 1988: Underspecification in phonetics. *Phonology* 5, 275–92.

Keating, P. 1990: Phonetic representation in a generative grammar. *Journal of Phonetics* 18, 321–34.

Kenstowicz, M. 1994a: *Phonology in Generative Grammar*. Oxford: Blackwell.

Kenstowicz, M. 1994b: Syllabification in Chuckchee: a constraint based analysis. *Formal Linguistics Society of the Midwest* 4, 160–81. ROA-30.

Kenstowicz, M. 1995: Cyclic *vs.* non-cyclic constraint evaluation. *Phonology* 12, 397–436.

Kenstowicz, M. 1996: Base-identity and uniform exponence: alternatives to cyclicity. In Durand and Laks (1996), vol. 1, 365–95.

Kent, R. and Read, C. 1992: *The Acoustic Analysis of Speech*. San Diego, CA: Singular Publishing Group.

Kenyon, J.S. 1935 [1924]: *American Pronunciation*. Ann Arbor, MI: George Wahr.

Kimura, A. 1996: A phonological analysis of English loanwords in Japanese. Masters, University of Essex.

Kingston, J. and Beckman, M. (eds) 1990: *Papers in Laboratory Phonology I: Between the Grammar and Physics of Speech*. Cambridge: Cambridge University Press.

Kiparsky, P. 1968: Linguistic universals and linguistic change. In E. Bach and R. Harms (eds), *Universals in Linguistic Theory*, New York: Holt, Rinehart and Winston, 170–202.

Kiparsky, P. 1973: "Elsewhere" in phonology. In S. Anderson and P. Kiparsky (eds), *A Festschrift for Morris Halle*, New York: Holt, Rinehart and Winston, 93–106.

Kiparsky, P. 1977: The rhythmic structure of English verse. *Linguistic Inquiry* 8, 189–247.

Kiparsky, P. 1982: Lexical morphology and phonology. In I.-S. Yang (ed.), *Linguistics in the Morning Calm*, Seoul: Hanshin Publishing, 3–91.

Kiparsky, P. 1983: Word formation and the lexicon. In *Proceedings of the 1982 Mid-America Linguistics Conference*, 3–29.

Kiparsky, P. 1985: Some consequences of lexical phonology. *Phonology Yearbook* 2, 85–138.

Kiparsky, P. 1993: Blocking in non-derived environments. In Hargus and Kaisse (1993), 277–313.

Kiparsky, P. and Halle, M. 1977: Towards a reconstruction of the Indo-European accent. In Hyman (1977a), 209–38.

Kiparsky, P. and Youmans, G. (eds) 1989: *Rhythm and Meter*. San Diego: Academic Press. [Review: Hammond, M. 1992: *Phonology* 9, 358–62.]

Klausenberger, J. 1990: Topic . . . Comment. *Natural Language and Linguistic Theory* 8, 621–3.

Kornai A. and Pullum, G. 1990: The X-bar theory of phrase structure. *Language* 66, 24–50.

Koutsoudas, A. 1980: The question of rule ordering: some common fallacies. *Journal of Linguistics* 16, 19–35.

Koutsoudas, A., Sanders, G. and Noll, C. 1974: On the application of phonological rules. *Language* 50, 1–28.

Krapp, G. 1969 [1919]: *The Pronunciation of Standard English in America*. New York: Ams Press.

Kreidler, C. 1989: *The Pronunciation of English*. Oxford: Blackwell.

Kreidler, C. 1997: *Describing Spoken English*. London: Routledge.

Kubozono, H. 1993: *The Organization of Japanese Prosody*. Tokyo: Kurosio.

Labov, W. 1994: *Principles of Linguistic Change: Internal Factors*. Oxford: Blackwell.

Ladd, R. 1992: An introduction to intonational phonology. In Docherty and Ladd (1992), 321–34.

Ladd, R. 1997: *Intonational Phonology*. Cambridge: Cambridge University Press.

Ladefoged, P. 1973: The features of the larynx. *Journal of Phonetics* 1, 73–83.

Ladefoged, P. 1990: Some reflections on the IPA. *Journal of Phonetics* 18, 335–46.

Ladefoged, P. 1993 [1975]: *A Course in Phonetics*. Fort Worth, TX: Harcourt Brace Jovanovitch.

Ladefoged, P. and Halle, M. 1988: Some major features of the International Phonetic Alphabet. *Language* 64, 577–82.

Ladefoged, P. and Maddieson, I. 1996: *The Sounds of the World's Languages*. Oxford: Blackwell.

Lass, R. 1984: *Phonology: An Introduction to Basic Concepts*. Cambridge: Cambridge University Press.

Lass, R. 1990: A 'standard' South African vowel system. In Ramsaran (1990a), 272–85.

Laver, J. 1994: *Principles of Phonetics*. Cambridge: Cambridge University Press.

Leben, W. 1976: The tones in English intonation. *Linguistic Analysis* 2, 69–107.

Leben, W. 1978: The representation of tone. In Fromkin (1978), 177–219.

Levin, J. 1983: Reduplication and prosodic structure. MS, MIT.

Levin, J. 1985: A metrical theory of syllabicity. PhD, MIT.

Liberman, M. 1975: The intonational system of English. PhD, MIT. Circulated by the Indiana University Linguistics Club. Published by Garland, New York, 1980.

Liberman, M. and Prince, A. 1977: On stress and linguistic rhythm. *Linguistic Inquiry* 8, 249–336.

Lieber, R. 1989: Argument linking and compounds in English. *Linguistic Inquiry* 14, 251–85.

Lindau, M. 1978: Vowel features. *Language* 54, 541–63.

Lodge, K. 1989: A non-segmental account of German umlaut: diachronic and synchronic perspectives. *Linguistische Berichte* 124, 470–91.

Lombardi, L. 1990: The nonlinear organization of the affricate. *Natural Language and Linguistic Theory* 8, 375–425.

Lombardi, L. 1996: Postlexical rules and the status of privative features. *Phonology* 13, 1–38.

Lovins, J. 1975: Loanwords and the phonological structure of Japanese. PhD, University of Chicago. Circulated by the Indiana University Linguistics Club.

McCarthy, J. 1981: A prosodic theory of non-concatenative phonology. *Linguistic Inquiry* 12, 443–66.

McCarthy, J. 1982: Prosodic structure and expletive infixation. *Language* 58, 574–90.

McCarthy, J. 1984: Prosodic structure in morphology. In Aronoff and Oehrle (1984), 299–317.

McCarthy, J. 1986: OCP effects: gemination and antigemination. *Linguistic Inquiry* 17, 207–63.

McCarthy, J. 1988: Feature geometry and dependency: a review. *Phonetica* 43, 84–108.

McCarthy, J. 1993: A surface case of constraint violation. In Paradis and LaCharité (1993), 169–95.

McCarthy, J. 1995: Extensions of faithfulness: Rotuman revisited. MS, University of Massachusetts at Amherst. ROA-110.

McCarthy, J. 1998: Sympathy and phonological opacity. ROA-252.

McCarthy, J. and Prince, A. 1990: Foot and word in prosodic morphology: the Arabic broken plural. *Natural Language and Linguistic Theory* 8, 209–83.

McCarthy, J. and Prince, A. 1993a: Generalized alignment. *Yearbook in Morphology 1993*. Dordrecht: Kluwer, 79–153.

McCarthy, J. and Prince, A. 1993b: Prosodic morphology I. Constraint interaction and satisfaction. MS, University of Massachusetts at Amherst and Rutgers University.

McCarthy, J. and Prince, A. 1994: The emergence of the unmarked: optimality in prosodic morphology. *North Eastern Linguistic Society* 24, 333–79.

McCarthy, J. and Prince, A. 1995: Prosodic morphology. In Goldsmith (1995), 318–66.

McCarthy, J. and Prince, A. 1996: Faithfulness and reduplicative identity. In J. Beckman et al. (1996), 249–384.

McCarthy, J. and Prince, A. [in press]: Faithfulness and identity in Prosodic Morphology. In R. Kager, H. van der Hulst and W. Zonneveld [in press]: *The Prosody–Morphology Interface*. Cambridge: Cambridge University Press. ROA-216.

McCawley, J. 1977: Accent in Japanese. In Hyman (1977a), 261–302.

Maddieson, I. 1984: *Patterns of Sounds*. Cambridge: Cambridge University Press.

Marantz, A. 1988: Clitics, morphological merger, and the mapping of phonological structure. In Hammond and Noonan (1988), 253–70.

Mascaró, J. 1976: Catalan phonology and the phonological cycle. PhD, MIT. Circulated by the Indiana University Linguistics Club.

Mascaró, J. and Nespor, M. (eds) 1990: *Grammar in Progress. Glow Essays for Henk van Riemsdijk*. Dordrecht: Foris.

Mester, A. and Padgett, J. 1994: Directional syllabification in generalized alignment. *Phonology at Santa Cruz*, iii, 79–87. ROA-1.

Mohanan, K.P. 1985: Syllable structure and lexical structure in English. *Phonology Yearbook* 2, 139–55.

Mohanan, K.P. 1986: *The Theory of Lexical Phonology*. Dordrecht: Foris.

Mohanan, K.P. 1991: On the basis of Radical Underspecification. *Natural Language and Linguistic Theory* 9, 285–325.

Mohanan, K.P. 1995: The organization of grammar. In Goldsmith (1995), 24–69.

Moulton, W. 1990: Some vowel systems in American English. In Ramsaran (1990a), 119–36.

Myers, S. 1987a: Tone and the structure of words in Shona. PhD, University of Massachusetts at Amherst. Circulated by the Graduate Linguistic Student Association.

Myers, S. 1987b: Vowel shortening in English. *Natural Language and Linguistic Theory* 5, 485–518.

Myers, S. 1991: Persistent rules. *Linguistic Inquiry* 22, 315–44.

Myers, S. 1997: Expressing phonetic naturalness in phonology. In Roca (1997), 123–52.

Nespor, M. 1990a: On the rhythm parameter in phonology. In I. Roca (ed.), *Logical Issues in Language Acquisition*, Dordrecht: Foris, 157–75.

Nespor, M. 1990b: On the separation of prosodic and rhythmic phonology. In Inkelas and Zec (1990), 243–58.

Nespor, M. and Vogel, I. 1986: *Prosodic Phonology*. Dordrecht: Foris.

Nespor, M. and Vogel, I. 1989: On clashes and lapses. *Phonology* 6, 69–116.

Nolan, F. 1995: Preview of the IPA handbook. *Journal of the International Phonetic Association* 25, 1–33.

Norton, R. 1998: Optimality Theory without Gen. *Essex Graduate Student Papers in Language and Linguistics* 2, 19–30.

Noyer, R. 1997: Attic Greek accentuation and intermediate derivational representations. In Roca (1997), 501–27.

Odden, D. 1981: Problems in tone assignment in Shona. PhD, University of Illinois.

Odden, D. 1986: On the Obligatory Contour Principle. *Language* 62, 353–83.

Odden, D. 1991: Vowel geometry. *Phonology* 8, 261–89.

Odden, D. 1993: Interaction between modules in Lexical Phonology. In Hargus and Kaisse (1993), 259–77.

Odden, D. 1995: Tone: African languages. In Goldsmith (1995), 444–75.

Ohala, J. 1978: Production of tone. In Fromkin (1978), 5–39.

Ohala, J. 1997: The relation between phonetics and phonology. In Hardcastle and Laver (1997), 674–94.

Ohala, J. and Kawasaki, H. 1984: Prosodic phonology and phonetics. *Phonology Yearbook* 1, 113–27.

Öhman, S. 1966: Coarticulation in CVC utterances: spectrographic measurements. *Journal of the Acoustic Society of America* 66, 1691–1702.

Padgett, J. 1995: *Stricture in Feature Geometry*. Stanford, CA: CSLI Publications.

Paradis, C. 1988: On constraints and repair strategies. *The Linguistic Review* 6, 71–97.

Paradis, C. 1997: Non-transparent constraint effects in Gere: from cycles to derivations. In Roca (1997), 529–50.

Paradis, C. and LaCharité, D. (eds) 1993: *Constraint Based Theories in Multilinear Phonology*. Special issue of the *Canadian Journal of Linguistics* 38 (2).

Pesetzky, D. 1979: Russian morphology and lexical theory. MS, MIT.

Pierrehumbert, J. 1980: The phonetics and phonology of English intonation. PhD, MIT.

Pierrehumbert, J. 1990: Phonological and phonetic representation. *Journal of Phonetics* 18, 375–94.

Pierrehumbert, J. 1991: The whole theory of sound structure. In Diehl (1991a), 223–32.

Pierrehumbert, J. and Beckman, M. 1988: *Japanese Tone Structure*. Cambridge, MA: MIT Press.

Pierrehumbert, J. and Hirschberg, J. 1990: The meaning of intonational contours in the interpretation of discourse. In Cohen et al. (1990), 271–311.

Pike, K. 1948: *Tone Languages*. Ann Arbor, MI: University of Michigan Press.

Pike, K. and Pike, E. 1947: Immediate constituents of Mazatec syllables. *International Journal of American Linguistics* 13, 78–91.

Poser, W. 1984: The phonetics and phonology of tone and intonation in Japanese. PhD, MIT.

Poser, W. 1993: Are Strict Cycle effects derivable? In Hargus and Keisse (1993), 315–21.

Prince, A. 1983: Relating to the grid. *Linguistic Inquiry* 14, 19–100.

Prince, A. 1985: Improving tree theory. *Berkeley Linguistic Society* 11, 471–90.

Prince, A. and Smolensky, P. 1993: Optimality Theory: Constraint Interaction in generative grammar. MS, Rutgers University and University of Colorado.

Pulleyblank, D. 1986a: *Tone in Lexical Phonology*. Dordrecht: Reidel.

Pulleyblank, D. 1986b: Underspecification and low vowel harmony in Yoruba. *Studies in African Linguistics* 17, 119–53.

Pulleyblank, D. 1988a: Underspecification, the feature hierarchy and Tiv vowels. *Phonology* 5, 299–326.

Pulleyblank, D. 1988b: Vocalic underspecification in Yoruba. *Linguistic Inquiry* 19, 233–70.

Pulleyblank, D. 1996: Feature geometry and underspecification. In Durand and Katamba (1996), 3–33.

Pulleyblank, D. 1997: Optimality Theory and features. In Archangeli and Langendoen (1997), 59–101.

Pulleyblank, D. and Turkel, W. 1997: Gradient retreat. In Roca (1997), 153–93.

Pullum, G. 1976: The Duke of York gambit. *Journal of Linguistics* 12, 83–103.

Pullum, G. and Ladusaw, W. 1986: *Phonetic Symbol Guide*. Chicago: University of Chicago Press.

Pyles, T. and Algeo, J. 1992 [1978]: *The Origins and Development of the English Language*. New York: Harcourt Brace Jovanovich.

Ramsaran, S. (ed.) 1990a: *Studies in the Pronunciation of English*. London and New York: Routledge.

Ramsaran, S. 1990b: RP: fact and fiction. In Ramsaran (1990a), 178–90.

Rice, K. 1987: The function of structure preservation: derived environments. *North Eastern Linguistic Society* 17, 501–20.

Rice, K. 1990: Predicting rule domains in the phrasal phonology. In Inkelas and Zec (1990), 289–312.

Rice, K. 1992: On deriving sonority: a structural account of sonority relationships. *Phonology* 9, 61–99.

Ringen, C. 1975: Vowel Harmony: theoretical implications, PhD, Indiana University. Published by Garland, New York, 1988.

Ringen, C. and Vago, R. 1995: A constraint-based analysis of Hungarian vowel harmony. In I. Kenesei (ed.), *Approaches to Hungarian*. vol. 5: *Levels and structures*, Szeged: JATE, 309–19.

Roach, P. 1991 [1983]: *English Phonetics and Phonology*. Cambridge: Cambridge University Press.

Roca, I. 1988: Theoretical implications of Spanish word stress. *Linguistic Iinquiry* 19, 393–423.

Roca, I. 1992: Constraining extrametricality. In W. Dressler, H. Luschützky, O. Pfeiffer and J. Rennison (eds), *Phonologica 1988*, Cambridge: Cambridge University Press, 239–48.

Roca, I. 1994: *Generative Phonology*. London: Routledge.

Roca, I. (ed.) 1997: *Derivations and Constraints in Phonology*. Oxford: Clarendon Press.

Roca, I. and Al-Ageli, H. [in press]: Optimal metrics. In J.S. Hannah and M. Davenport (eds), *Proceedings of the 1994 Durham Phonology Conference*.

Ross, J. 1972: A reanalysis of English word stress. In M. Brame (ed.), *Contributions to Generative Phonology*, Austin and London: University of Texas Press, 229–323.

Rubach, J. 1984a: *Cyclic and Lexical Phonology: The Structure of Polish*. Dordrecht: Foris.

Rubach, J. 1984b: Segmental rules of English and cyclic phonology. *Language* 60, 21–54.

Rubach, J. 1985: Lexical Phonology: lexical and postlexical derivations. *Phonology Yearbook* 2, 157–72.

Rubach, J. 1990: Final devoicing and lexical syllabification in German. *Linguistic Inquiry* 21, 79–94.

Rubach, J. 1993: Skeletal versus moraic representations in Slovak. *Natural Language and Linguistic Theory* 11, 625–53.

Rubach, J. 1996: Shortening and ambisyllabicity in English. *Phonology* 13, 197–237.

Rubach, J. 1997: Extrasyllabic consonants in Polish: Derivational Optimality Theory. In Roca (1997), 551–81.

Rubach, J. and Booij, G. 1990a: Edge of constituents effect in Polish. *Natural Language and Linguistic Theory* 8, 427–64.

Rubach, J. and Booij, G. 1990b: Syllable structure assignment in Polish. *Phonology* 7, 121–58.

Russell, B. 1996 [1946]: *History of Western Philosophy*. London: Routledge.

Russell, K. 1997: Optimality Theory and morphology. In Archangeli and Langendoen (1997), 102–33.

Sagey, E. 1986a: The representation of features and relations in nonlinear phonology. PhD, MIT.

Sagey, E. 1986b: On the representation of complex segments in Kinyarwanda. In Wetzels and Sezer (1986), 251–95.

Sagey, E. 1988: On the ill-formedness of crossing association lines. *Linguistic Inquiry* 19, 109–18.

Sainz, S. 1992: A noncyclic approach to English word stress. *Chicago Linguistic Society* 28, vol. 2: *The Parasession on the Cycle in Linguistic Theory*, 263–76.

Saussure, F. de 1916: *Cours de Linguistique Générale*. Paris: Payot. Translation: W. Baskin, *Course in General Linguistics*, New York: Philosophical Library, 1959. *See also* Harris, R. (1987).

Schane, S. 1984: The fundamentals of Particle Phonology. *Phonology* 1, 129–55.

Schuh, R.G. 1978: Tone rules. In Fromkin (1978), 221–56.

Scobbie, J.M. 1993: Constraint violation from the viewpoint of Declarative Phonology. In Paradis and LaCharité (1993), 155–67.

Selkirk, E. 1980: The role of prosodic categories in English word stress. *Linguistic Inquiry* 11, 563–605.

Selkirk, E. 1981: On prosodic structure and its relationship to syntactic structure. In T. Fretheim (ed.), *Nordic Prosody, II*, Trondheim: Tapir, 111–40.

Selkirk, E. 1982: Syllables. In van der Hulst and Smith (1982b), part 2, 337–83.

Selkirk, E. 1984a: On the major class features and syllable theory. In Aronoff and Oehrle (1984), 107–36.

Selkirk, E. 1984b: *Phonology and Syntax: The Relation between Sound and Structure*. Cambride, MA: MIT Press.

Selkirk, E. 1986: On derived domains in sentence phonology. *Phonology Yearbook* 3, 371–405.

Selkirk, E. 1990: On the nature of prosodic constituency. In Kingston and Beckman (1990), 179–200.

Selkirk, E. 1996: The prosodic structure of function words. In J. Beckman et al. (1996), 439–70.

Shaw, P. 1991: Consonant harmony systems: the special status of Coronal Harmony. In C. Paradis and J.-F. Prunet (eds), *The Special Status of Coronals*, San Diego, CA: Academic Press, 125–57.

Sherrard, N. 1997: Questions of priorities: an introductory overview of Optimality Theory in phonology. In Roca (1997), 43–89.

Shibatani, M. 1990: *The Languages of Japan*. Cambridge: Cambridge University Press.

Siegel, D. 1974: Topics in English morphology. PhD, MIT. Published by Garland, New York, 1979.

Smolensky, P. 1996: On the comprehension/production dilemma in child language. *Linguistic Inquiry* 27, 720–31.

Snider, K. 1988: Towards the representation of tone. In van der Hulst and Smith (1988b), part 1, 237–67.

Snider, K. 1990: Tonal upstep in Krachi: evidence for a register tier. *Language* 66, 453–74.

SPE, see Chomsky and Halle (1968).

Spencer, A. 1990: *Morphological Theory*. Oxford: Blackwell.

Spencer, A. 1996: *Phonology: Theory and Description*. Oxford: Blackwell.

Sproat, R. 1988: Bracketing paradoxes, cliticization, and other topics. In M. Everaert, A. Evers, R. Huybregts and M. Trommelen (eds), *Morphology and Modularity*, Dordrecht: Foris, 339–60.

Stampe, D. 1969: The acquisition of phonetic representation. *Chicago Linguistic Society* 5, 443–54.

Stampe, D. 1972: How I spent my summer vacation. A dissertation on natural phonology. PhD, University of Chicago. Published by Garland, New York, 1980.

Steriade, D. 1982: Greek prosodies and the nature of syllabification. PhD, MIT. Published by Garland, New York, 1991.

Steriade, D. 1987: Redundant values. *Chicago Linguistic Society* 23, 339–62.

Steriade, D. 1994: Complex onsets as simple segments. In Cole and Kisseberth (1994), 203–91.

Steriade, D. 1995: Underspecification and markedness. In Goldsmith (1995), 114–74.

Stevens, K. 1972: The quantal nature of speech: evidence from articulatory–acoustic data. In E.E. David and P.B. Denes (eds), *Human Communication: A Unified View*, London: Academic Press, 51–66.

Stevens, K. 1989: On the quantal nature of speech. *Journal of Phonetics* 17, 3–46.

Stevens, K. and Keyser, S.J. 1989: Primary features and their enhancement in consonants. *Language* 65, 81–106.

Stevens, K., Keyser, S.J. and Kawasaki, H. 1987: Toward a phonetic and phonological theory of redundant features. In J. Perkell and D.H. Klatt (eds), *Symposium on Invariance and Variability*, Hillsdale, NJ: Lawrence Erlbaum, 426–49.

Strang, B. 1986 [1970]: *A History of English*. London: Routledge.

Szpyra, J. 1992: *The Phonology–Morphology Interface: Cycles, Levels and Words*. London: Croom Helm.

Tesar, B. 1995a: Computing optimal forms in Optimality Theory. Technical Report CU-CS-763–95, Feb. 1995, Department of Computer Science, University of Colorado at Boulder. ROA-52.

Tesar, B. 1995b: Computational Optimality Theory. PhD, University of Colorado. ROA-90.

Tesar, B. and Smolensky, P. 1993: The learnability of Optimality Theory. An algorithm and some basic complexity results. MS, University of Colorado at Boulder. ROA-2.

Tesar, B. and Smolensky, P. 1998: Learnability in Optimality Theory. *Linguistic Inquiry* 29, 229–68. [Longer version in ROA-156.]

Thomas, C.K. 1958 [1947]: *The Phonetics of American English*. New York: Ronald.

Tranel, B. 1987: *The Sounds of French*. Cambridge: Cambridge University Press.

Tranel, B. 1995: Current issues in French phonology: liaison and position theories. In Goldsmith (1995), 798–816.

Trubetzkoy, N.S. 1939: *Grundzüge der Phonologie*. Güttingen: Vandenhoeck and Ruprecht. Translation: C.A.M. Baltaxe, *Principles of Phonology*, Berkeley, CA: University of California Press, 1969.

Tsujimura, N. 1996: *An Introduction to Japanese Linguistics*. Oxford: Blackwell.

Turner, G. 1994: English in Australia. In Burchfield (1994), 277–327.

Vennemann, T. 1972: On the theory of syllabic phonology. *Linguistische Berichte* 18, 1–18.

Vihman, M. 1978: Consonant harmony: its scope and function in child language. In Greenberg (1978), 281–334.

Vihman, M. 1996: *Phonological Development. The Origins of Language in the Child*. Oxford: Blackwell.

Vogel, I. and Kenesei, I. 1990: Syntax and semantics in phonology. In Inkelas and Zec (1990), 339–63.

Wells, J. 1982: *Accents of English*. 3 volumes. Cambridge: Cambridge University Press.

Wetzels, L. and Sezer, E. (eds) 1986: *Studies in Compensatory Lengthening*. Dordrecht: Foris.

Wiese, R. 1996a: *The Phonology of German*. Oxford: Clarendon Press.

Wiese, R. 1996b: Phonological vs. morphological rules: on German umlaut and ablaut. *Journal of Linguistics* 32, 113–35.

Wolfe, P. 1972: *Linguistic Change and the Great Vowel Shift in English*. Berkeley, CA: University of California Press.

Woodrow, H. 1951: Time perception. In S. Stevens (ed.), *Handbook of Experimental Psychology*, New York: Wiley, 1234–6.

Yip, M. 1980: The tonal phonology of Chinese. PhD, MIT. Circulated by the Indiana University Linguistics Club.

Yip, M. 1988: The Obligatory Contour Principle and phonological rules: a loss of identity. *Linguistic Inquiry* 19, 65–100.

Yip, M. 1989a: Feature geometry and cooccurrence restrictions. *Phonology* 6, 349–74.

Yip, M. 1989b: Contour tones. *Phonology* 6, 149–74.

Yip, M. 1995: Tone in East Asian languages. In Goldsmith (1995), 476–94.

Zec, D. and Inkelas, S. 1990: Prosodically constrained syntax. In Inkelas and Zec (1990), 365–78.

GLOSSARY

The purpose of this glossary is to provide the reader with a quick look-up facility. As might be expected, it must be interpreted in conjunction with the text. (For a more general list of phonological and phonetic terms, we recommend R.L. Trask, *A Dictionary of Phonetics and Phonology*, London: Routledge, 1996.)

ACCENT: (1) Each of the ways of pronouncing a language, characteristic of a geographical area, a social group, or even a single individual. (2) In metrical theory, the projection of the baseline asterisks of heavy rimes onto line 1 in the grid. *See also* Pitch Accent, Phrase Accent, Standard Accent.

ACCENTED TONE: *See* Dominant Tone.

ACOUSTIC PHONETICS: The branch of phonetics (and of physics) that investigates the patterns of vibration of molecules in the air produced as a result of the articulation. *See* Articulatory Phonetics, Auditory Phonetics.

ACTIVE ARTICULATOR: The articulator that moves as opposed to the static, or "passive", articulator. *See* Passive Articulator.

AD HOC: An expression applied to an unmotivated analysis, driven only by the need to get the right result. Similar to brute force.

ADVANCED ARTICULATION: An articulation made slightly more towards the front of the mouth than the reference point. *Cf.* Retracted.

ADVANCED TONGUE ROOT (ATR): A distinctive feature ([±ATR]) dependent on [radical] and implemented by drawing the root of the tongue forward, to enlarge the pharyngeal cavity, often also resulting in a raising of the body of the tongue.

AFFIX: A morpheme that needs to be attached to a base.

AFFIX ORDERING HYPOTHESIS: The hypothesis inherent to Lexical Phonology that affixes are attached to the base in a specific order, which is fixed for each affix and has phonological consequences.

AFFRICATE: A complex consonant made up of a stop gesture and a fricative gesture made in rapid succession, without changing the position of the articulators.

ALGORITHM: A word designating a self-contained procedure, such that each step automatically leads to the next, ultimately reaching the output.

ALIGN: In OT, a family of constraints which regulate the spatial relation between two elements, either by requiring that they be sequentially abutting, or by requiring that the edges of two constituents in different structural levels be superimposed.

ALLOMORPH: A contextual variant of a morpheme.

ALLOMORPHY: The situation in which a morpheme has several allomorphs.

ALLOPHONE: A contextual variant of a phoneme.

ALLOPHONY: The situation in which a phoneme has several allophones.

ALTERNANT: A form that partakes in an alternation.

ALTERNATION: A phenomenon involving a systematic difference in sound between two or more allomorphs.

ALVEOLAR: A sound articulated on the (upper) tooth ridge.

ALVEOLAR TRILL: A consonantal sound that involves the vibration of the tip of the tongue against the upper tooth ridge.

ANCHOR: In OT, a constraint that enforces correspondence between edge elements.

ANTERIOR: A binary distinctive feature which is dependent on [coronal] and distinguishes an articulation in the alveolar or dental areas ([+anterior]) from an articulation in the postalveolar or palatal areas ([−anterior]).

APERTURE: A class node pertinent to vowels in a model of feature geometry aiming for a uniform place of articulation specification for consonants and vowels.

APICAL: An articulatory gesture made with just the tip of the tongue.

APPENDIX: Said of consonants occurring on the edge of the word which do not fit into the canonical structure: the assumption is that such consonants are affiliated to a higher constituent.

APPROXIMANT: A term applied to sounds that are continuant and frictionless.

ARTICULATORS: The organs that make contact to produce linguistic sound.

ARTICULATORY PHONETICS: The branch of phonetics which is concerned with the production of sound.

ASH: The name conventionally given to the symbol [æ], generally assigned to a raised version of cardinal vowel no. 4, but identified with cardinal vowel no. 4 itself in this book.

ASPIRATION: The period between the release of the closure of a consonant and the start of vocal fold activity for the vowel that follows it. Aspiration can be felt physically as a puff of air.

ASSIMILATION: A term used in phonology to designate the "contamination" of a sound by another (usually adjacent) sound, formalized as feature spreading in autosegmental phonology.

ASSOCIATION CONVENTION: A principle of autosegmental phonology by which autosegments (particularly tones) associate to their bearers one-to-one from left to right.

ATR: *See* Advanced Tongue Root.

AUDITORY PHONETICS: The branch of phonetics that deals with the effects of acoustic patterns on the human ear and with their subsequent reception and perception in the brain.

AUTOSEGMENT: A unit of phonological structure in autosegmental phonology.

AUTOSEGMENTAL PHONOLOGY: An approach to phonology where each feature or structural element is granted autonomy of action.

BABBLING: A stage in developmental phonology in which the child combines consonants and vowels into recognizable words, at around six or nine months of age. *Cf.* Cooing, Vocal Play.

BACK: A binary distinctive feature which is dependent on [dorsal] and whose positive value is characterized by a retraction of the body of the tongue.

BASE: (1) The core, irreducible form of a word, to which affixes are added. (2) In reduplication, the word which is reproduced (wholly or partly) in the reduplicant.

BBC ENGLISH: The standard form of English traditionally used in the British media, in particular the BBC, and characterized by an RP-type accent.

BILABIAL: A sound articulated with both lips.

BILABIAL TRILL: A trill made by the vibration of both lips, used more or less unconsciously by English speakers to indicate cold.

BINARISM: A type of formalism which involves the characterization of a feature as + or −, corresponding respectively to the presence or the absence of the property encapsulated in the feature.

BINARY FOOT: A foot with only two elements. Cf. Unbounded Foot.

BLADE: The most mobile and versatile part of the tongue, that sticks out most easily, located behind the tip. Cf. Body, Root, Tip.

BLEEDING ORDER: A situation in which a rule removes material that would be necessary for the application of a subsequently ordered rule.

BLOCKER: In harmony systems, an element which stands in the way of the propagation of the harmonizing feature.

BODY: The section of the tongue behind the blade, more massive and less mobile than the blade. Cf. Blade, Root, Tip.

BOUNDARY TONE: In an intonational melody, the tones associated to elements on the edge of the intonational domain. Cf. Phrase Tone, Word Tone.

BRACKET ERASURE CONVENTION: A convention of Lexical Phonology according to which domain-internal morphological brackets are erased (= become invisible = become inaccessible) at the end of each block or level.

BREAKING: A label which is sometimes used to indicate the unfolding of a vowel into a diphthong.

BROAD TRANSCRIPTION: A phonetic transcription which is phonemically oriented. Cf. Narrow Transcription.

BRUTE FORCE: An expression which suggests forcing an analysis to fit the data. Similar to ad hoc.

C: A symbol that informally stands for a consonant, that is, a segment defined as [+consonantal]. Cf. V.

C-PLACE: A class node for consonants in a theory of feature geometry favouring a uniform set of place features for consonants and vowels. Cf. V-Place.

CANDIDATE: In OT, each of the forms competing for victory in the evaluation by the ranked constraints.

CARDINAL VOWELS: A set of vowels proposed by Daniel Jones as reference points for the description of the vowels of the world's languages.

CASE: The form of a word expressing a specific syntactic or semantic function.

CATEGORY: The lexical class in which a word belongs according to morphological, syntactic or semantic criteria.

CENTRALIZATION: The articulation of a usually front or back vowel sound in the centre of the vowel space, or near it.

CENTRING DIPHTHONG: A diphthong the second phase of which is articulated in the central area of the vowel space, usually in the area of the schwa.

CLASS: *See* Level.

CLASS NODE: A node in the tree of the feature geometry which defines a functional class of features, rather than a distinctive feature as such, therefore an alternative to the subscript notation.

CLITIC: A small, stressless function word which prosodically cannot stand by itself, but must lean on a host.

CLOSED SYLLABLE: Said of a syllable with a coda. *Cf.* Open Syllable.

COARTICULATION: A term by which phoneticians express essentially what phonologists refer to as "assimilation". More precisely, it refers to the fact that articulatory planning is not segment-sized, but may include a whole string of segments, which are accordingly brought closer in their articulation.

CODA: The consonant that follows the nucleus, and that joins it to make up the rime.

COMBINATORIAL SPECIFICATION: A development of Radical Underspecification that builds on the notion of "F-element" (a valued feature or a class node) and its status with regard to association (associated or unassociated).

COMPENSATORY LENGTHENING: A phenomenon involving the lengthening of a segment as the result of the deletion of its neighbouring segment.

COMPETENCE: The language system that underlies actual performance, and which must be assumed to be permanently present in the brain, in some form. *Cf.* Performance.

COMPLEMENT: In syntax, the material that follows the head of a phrase in languages like English, to make up a constituent with the head. *Cf.* Specifier.

COMPLEMENT RULE: In Radical Underspecification, the redundancy rules which by convention fill in the values of the distinctive features that define the maximally underspecified segment.

COMPLEMENTARITY: The property characterizing binary features, such that when one of the values of the feature is present, the other value must of necessity be absent.

COMPLEMENTARY DISTRIBUTION: The non-overlapping distribution of two allophones of one phoneme.

COMPOUND: A type of word created by combining other words, such as the English nouns *greenhorn* and *greenhouse*, which contrast with the phrases *green horn* and *green house*, and with the non-compound words *greenish* and *greenness*.

COMPOUND STRESS: The stress pattern assigned to compounds, which in English usually involves greater prominence in the first member of the pair.

CONSONANT: A sound produced with an obstruction to the airflow. *Cf.* Vowel.

CONSONANTAL: The distinctive feature differentiating consonants characterized by a drastic constriction somewhere along the centre of the oral passage ([+consonantal]), from sounds which do not have such a constriction ([−consonantal]).

CONSTITUENT: An element or string of elements which fulfil a particular structural role together, as is the case with the consonant(s) that make up the onset, or the feet that make up a phonological word.

CONSTRAINT: An injunction in the grammar regulating the shape of a form.

CONSTRAINT FAMILY: In OT, a group of constraints that express one single basic concept; for instance, faithfulness to the underlying form, or alignment of constituents.

CONSTRAINT RANKING: In OT, the hierarchization of the power of constraints, somewhat reminiscent of the ordering of the rules in rule-based phonology.

CONSTRAINT VIOLATION: In OT, the disobedience of a constraint by a candidate, usually signalled by an asterisk (*) in the corresponding box.

CONSTRICTED GLOTTIS: The gesture of bringing the vocal folds together, responsible for glottalization of sounds, and expressed by a positive specification of the distinctive feature thus named.

CONTENT WORD: *See* Lexical Word.

CONTEXT: *See* Environment.

CONTINUANT: A binary distinctive feature expressing the state of the oral channel during the production of the sound: for [+continuant] sounds the channel remains unobstructed and allows the air to escape freely.

CONTINUOUS COLUMN CONSTRAINT: A constraint in metrical theory to the effect that the columns of the metrical grid must be continuous, without lines being skipped.

CONTRAST-RESTRICTED UNDERSPECIFICATION: A theory of underspecification in which only non-contrastive segments (in a particular context) can be left unspecified (in that context). *Cf.* Radical Underspecification.

CONTRASTIVE STRESS: The prominence assigned to a syllable or a word to make it stand in opposition to some other syllable or word, either syntagmatically or paradigmatically.

CONTRASTIVE UNDERSPECIFICATION: Another name for Contrast-restricted Underspecification, used by its proponents.

COOING: An early stage in the development of phonology characterized by the production of contented vocalizations by the infant. *Cf.* Babbling, Vocal Play.

CORE SYLLABLE: The most basic and most common syllable, made up of a simple nucleus preceded by a simple onset.

CORONAL: A unary distinctive feature expressing movement of the blade of the tongue.

CORRESPONDENCE CONSTRAINTS: In OT, a type of constraint that imposes some form of identity between two representations.

CORRESPONDENCE THEORY: In OT, the subtheory that countenances correspondence constraints.

COUNTERBLEEDING ORDER: An ordering relation between two rules such that, if the order were reversed, a bleeding relation would be created.

COUNTERFEEDING ORDER: An ordering relation between two rules such that, if the order were reversed, a feeding relation would be created.

CV-TIER: Another name for the skeleton, suggestive of its composition as a string of Cs and Vs in early autosegmental theory.

CYCLE: A mode of rule application in which the rule applies to the smallest constituent of a form first, and then to successively larger constituents, rather than directly and exclusively to the full form.

CYCLIC DOMAIN: A domain which only allows the application of cyclic rules.

CYCLIC RULE: A rule that applies in accordance with the dictates of the cycle. *Cf.* Non-Cyclic Rule.

DEFAULT RULE: A redundancy rule that supplies the missing value of a feature in a given language, usually thought of as selected by UG.

"DEFECTIVE" *r*: A sound produced by drawing the inside of the lower lip, onto the edge of the upper teeth further back than for [f] or [v], and not quite close enough to cause friction.

DEGEMINATION: The simplification of a geminate.

DEGENERATE FOOT: A foot that has its growth stunted, and therefore only has one syllable.

DENTAL: A consonant that involves an articulation on the teeth.

DEP[ENDENCY]: In OT, the (faithfulness) constraint that blocks epenthesis by requiring every surface segment to have a lexical correspondent, on which it therefore "depends". *See also* Fill.

DERIVATION: The mapping of a lexical form onto its correspondent surface form in a series of steps, each defined by a rule.

DERIVATIVE: A composite form which has been derived from a base, usually by affixation.

DIACRITIC: A mark added to a phonetic symbol to implement a slight modification in the reference of the symbol.

DIALECT: A variant of a language used by a geographical or social section of its speakers.

DIPHTHONG: A complex vowel of non-steady quality, made up of two phases.

DIPHTHONGIZATION: The act of a vowel becoming a diphthong, a very common tendency of many vowels in many accents of English.

DISHARMONY: The failure of some segment to harmonize in a harmony system.

DISTINCTIVE FEATURES: A standard set of parameters which together define the segments of languages, each distinctive feature encapsulating a particular aspect of language sound. Most distinctive features tend to be considered binary, with the positive value indicating that the property named by the label is present, and the negative value indicating that it is not.

DISTRIBUTED: A binary distinctive feature which is dependent on [coronal] and refers to the length of the blade area involved in the articulation: [+distributed] indicates a long area, and [–distributed] a short area.

DISTRIBUTION: The pattern of occurrence of sounds in the forms of any given language, determined by the environment.

DOMAIN: An array of elements under a common scope.

DOMINANT TONE: The tone of a tonal melody that associates to the stressed syllable. It is commonly known as "accented tone".

DORSAL: A unary distinctive feature that refers to activity of the body of the tongue.

DOWNSTEP: A term that refers to a resetting of the tone register to a lower level. Downstep is usually thought of as triggered by a preceding floating L.

DOWNSTEPPED TONE: A tone that is pronounced at a lower pitch level than it otherwise would, as a result of downstep.

DRAG CHAIN: A type of serial sound change, particularly common in vowel systems, which involves the shifting of sounds into positions vacated by other sounds which have previously shifted. It is also known as a "pull chain".

EDGEMOST: In early OT, a constraint that controlled the positition of stress on the edge of a domain. It was superseded by ALIGN.

ELSEWHERE CONDITION: A universal principle governing the interaction of two overlapping rules, whereby the more restricted rule (with the more detailed environment) is tried out first; if it fails to apply, the more general rule (with the fewer qualifications) will apply instead.

ENCLITIC: A clitic that follows its host. *Cf.* Proclitic.

END STRESS: A process that involves the projection of an edge asterisk, particularly frequent in languages.

ENHANCEMENT: The reinforcement of acoustic differences between segments by means of additional articulations, which explains the frequency of some feature co-occurrences (for instance, [+round] with [+back]).

ENVIRONMENT: The phonological frame in which a given phonological phenomenon takes place, also referred to as "context". *Cf.* Focus.

EPENTHESIS: A word used to refer to the insertion of a segment.

EVALUATION: In OT, the examination of the candidates to select one as the most harmonic with respect to the ranked constraints.

EXTRAMETRICALITY: The exclusion of a designated peripheral element from the computations in the metrical grid.

EXTRAPROSODICITY: A generalization of extrametricality to formalize the special licensing powers exhibited by the edges of words, which allow an element on the word edge to be excluded from some process.

EXTRASYLLABICITY: A term sometimes used to refer to syllabic underparsing, particularly common on word edges, where it can perhaps be subsumed under extraprosodicity.

EXTRINSIC ORDERING: The stipulative order of rules, to prevent their free application. It is one of the devices associated with the model of phonology propounded in *SPE*.

FACTORING OUT: The elimination of redundancy in formal expressions by reducing common elements to a single statement.

FAITHFULNESS: In OT, the requirement that surface forms must replicate their corresponding lexical forms.

FAITHFULNESS CONDITION: In metrical theory, the requirement that each grid constituent have a head and each head have a domain.

FAITHFULNESS CONSTRAINTS: The family of constraints that enforce faithfulness in OT.

FATAL VIOLATION: In OT, a violation that disqualifies a candidate *vis-à-vis* some other candidate. It is conventionally signalled by an exclamation mark ("!") after the corresponding asterisk, with the boxes that follow in the tableau usually shaded to indicate their irrelevance.

FEATURE DEPENDENCY: The fixed connection of some distinctive feature to some other feature, determined by UG – for instance, [±round] is thought to be a dependent of [labial].

FEATURE GEOMETRY: The full web of feature dependencies, connected to the skeleton by means of the root.

FEATURE VALENCY: The number of values that a distinctive feature allows for, often one (for monovalent or unary features) or two (for binary features).

FEEDING ORDER: An ordering relation between two rules such that the first rule creates the input required by the second.

FILL: In OT, the predecessor of DEP to prevent epenthesis. The label appears to be a misnomer, meaning as it does an injunction not to fill.

FILTER: Another name for constraint in rule-and-derivation theory (NB not used in OT).

FLAP: A type of consonant characterized by the brevity of the contact between the articulators: the active articulator simply taps the passive articulator on its way to its rest position, as in the typical American *t* in *waiting*. *See also* Tap.

FLOATING: Said of an autosegment which is unassociated.

FLOATING TONE: A tone which is not associated to any melody or skeletal slot.

FOCUS: In a rule, the element that undergoes the change. *Cf.* Environment.

FOOT: A metrical constituent typically made up of two moras or syllables (binary foot), in quantity-sensitive systems, or of several syllables (unbounded foot), in quantity-insensitive systems. The head is placed on either the left or the right edge of the foot.

FOOTING: The construction of feet in a given domain.

FORMALISM: A system of notation which is as concise as is compatible with full explicitness, and which usually makes use of symbols.

FREE ELEMENT CONDITION: In metrical theory, the requirement that only metrically free elements may undergo metrical construction.

FRICATIVE: A consonant sound that involves friction noise made by the air escaping through a narrow obstacle. *Cf.* Stop.

FRONTING: The articulation in the front of the mouth of a sound which is typically pronounced further back.

FUNCTION WORD: A word which is defined by its grammatical function, such as *the* in English. *Cf.* Lexical Word.

GA: *See* General American.

GEMINATE: A segment, particularly a consonant, which occurs twice in succession. True geminates are formalized autosegmentally as one single melody associated to two skeletal slots.

GEMINATION: The act of a single segment becoming a geminate.

GEN: In OT, a label standing for "generator", the function that randomly generates surface forms from each lexical representation, using only the most elementary principles of linguistic logic.

GENERAL AMERICAN (GA): A pronunciation of English common in North America, characterized by lacking any obvious regional traits. Also referred to as Network English.

GENITIVE: The case used to indicate possession.

GLIDE: A label often given to non-syllabic vowels in the literature. It is a moot point whether "glides" do constitute an independent class of sounds in some languages.

GLOTTAL: A type of sound made by the intervention of the vocal folds.

GLOTTAL FRICATIVE: A sound made by the vocal folds narrowing the glottis, as in the English *h* of *hot*.

GLOTTAL STOP: A sound made by the vocal folds coming together to close the glottis, thus causing a momentary interruption to the airstream; the glottal closure is then released suddenly, exactly as happens with the remainder of the stops. *Cf.* Slack Vocal Folds, Spread Glottis, Stiff Vocal Folds.

GLOTTALIZATION: The addition of a glottal gesture to another sound.

GLOTTALLING: The substitution of a glottal sound for a sound of another type, as in the Cockney pronunciation of *cutting* as *cu*[?]*ing*.

GLOTTIS: The space surrounded by the vocal folds.

GRAMMATICAL WORD: *See* Function Word.

GREAT VOWEL SHIFT: A far-reaching chain of changes in the vowel system of English which eventually yielded [aɪ], [iː] and [eɪ], at the front, and [aʊ], [uː] and [oʊ], at the back.

GREEK LETTER VARIABLES: A set of variables available in the standard formalism of generative phonology, such that the value of each variable (α, β, γ, etc.) can be arbitrarily set as + or −, independently of the value assigned to the other variables.

H: A shortand for a high tone. *Cf.* M, L.

HARD PALATE: The front and mid parts of the palate, supported by a bony structure. *Cf.* Soft Palate.

HARD UNIVERSALS: Universals which are inviolable, best formalized as principles. *Cf.* Soft Universals.

HARMONY: (1) A situation where a designated feature has the same value throughout a given domain, as happens with [±back] in Turkish. (2) In OT, the property of a candidate of complying with the (ranked) constraints.

HEAD: In a constituent, the most important element of that constituent, indeed the core element: without the head the constituent would simply not exist. *See also* Faithfulness Condition.

HEAVY SYLLABLE: A syllable whose rime contains either a long nucleus or a coda. *Cf.* Light Syllable.

HIATUS: The allocation of two adjacent vowels to two different syllables.

HIGH: (1) A tone characterized by a relatively high pitch. *Cf.* Mid, Low. (2) A binary distinctive feature, a dependent of [dorsal], whose positive value is characterized by a raising of the body of the tongue.

HOMORGANIC: Made at the same place.

HOST: The word that supports a clitic.

HYPER-RHOTICITY: A phenomenon involving the pronunciation of *r* in forms and environments where there is no reason to pronounce it, as in the pronunciation *china*[ɹ] for *china*.

HYPOTHESIS: A term used to refer to an idea that explains some body of data.

IAMB: A classical word for a right-headed (binary) foot. *Cf.* Trochee.

IAMBIC–TROCHAIC LAW: The observation that elements of uneven intensity (and even duration) tend to pair up as left-headed feet (= trochees), and elements of uneven duration (and even intensity) as right-headed feet (= iambs).

IDIOLECT: The specific manner of speaking of an individual speaker.

INFIX: An affix that neither precedes nor follows the stem, in the way that prefixes or suffixes do, but is inserted in the middle of the stem. *Cf.* Prefix, Suffix.

INTERDENTAL: A consonant articulated (with the tip of the tongue) between the teeth.

INTERNATIONAL PHONETIC ASSOCIATION (IPA): An association founded in 1886 to foster the phonetic transcription of languages.

INTERPOLATION: The phenomenon by which a particular phonetic gesture bridges over a segment or stretch of segments lacking it, as when the pitch of the left tone changes gradually into the pitch of the right tone over a tonally empty space.

INTONATION: A phenomenon that involves the modulation of pitch over phrasal domains for functional or attitudinal purposes.

INTONATIONAL PHRASE: A phonological domain traditionally identified with the domain of association of the intonational melodies to the segmental material.

INTRINSIC ORDERING: The ordering between two rules that obtains when the rules are allowed to apply freely.

INTRUSIVE *r*: An expression referring to pronouncing an *r* between a non-high vowel and a following vowel in the next word or morpheme even though the *r* does not appear in the spelling. *Cf.* Linking *r*.

IPA: Acronym of International Phonetic Association.

IPA ALPHABET: The alphabet of phonetic symbols promoted by the IPA.

ITERATIVE: A word used in linguistics to indicate repetitive application within the same domain. *Cf.* Cyclic Rule.

ITERATIVENESS: In metrical theory, a parameter that controls the repetition of footing.

L: A shorthand for a low tone. *Cf.* H, M.

LABIAL: A sound that involves lip action in its articulation.

LABIODENTAL: A consonant made with the lower lip and the upper teeth.

LAMINAL: An articulatory gesture involving the full blade of the tongue.

LANDING SITE: In metrical theory, the asterisk that provides the stopping point for an asterisk that undergoes movement in the grid's next higher line.

LANGUAGE ACQUISITION DEVICE: A device which we assume the human brain is innately in possession of, and that allows it to acquire language spontaneously in childhood.

LARYNGEAL: An adjective meaning 'of the larynx'.

LARYNX: A cylindrical frame made up of cartilage which sits on the top of the trachea, and which can visibly protrude as the Adam's apple, particularly in males.

LATERALITY: A term that refers to the lowering of the sides of the tongue.

LATERALS: A type of consonant characterized by the lowering of one or both sides of the tongue, but not the front, to allow the air to flow out at the sides.

LEARNABILITY: The question of how humans (specifically, children) manage to work out and learn the grammars of languages, their phonologies included.

LEFT-HEADED: Applied to a constituent which has its head on the left edge. *Cf.* Right-Headed.

LEVEL: In Lexical Phonology, each of the blocks holding together a cluster of morphological and phonological rules, also referred to as class or stratum.

LEXICAL CATEGORY: An expression referring to words which have full semantic meaning, like *cup* or *table*, as opposed to words which chiefly perform a grammatical function ("grammatical" or "function" words).

LEXICAL ENTRY: A unit in the lexicon containing all the information relevant to sound, meaning and grammar that needs to be memorized.

LEXICAL ITEM: An item which is contained as an entry in the lexicon.

LEXICAL LEVEL: In Lexical Phonology, the level or levels confined to word and subword domains. *Cf.* Postlexical Level.

LEXICAL PHONOLOGY: A model of the interaction of phonology and morphology based on the clustering of phonological rules and morphological processes into levels or strata, hence the alternative labels of Level-Ordered Phonology or Stratal Phonology. The strata are typically classified as lexical and postlexical, and the lexical strata as cyclic and non-cyclic.

LEXICAL REPRESENTATION: The phonological information contained in a lexical item, also referred to as underlying representation.

LEXICAL RULES: In Lexical Phonology, the rules which apply at a lexical level. *Cf.* Postlexical Rules.

LEXICAL STRATUM: *See* Lexical Level.

LEXICAL WORD: A word which has full conceptual meaning, listed in the lexicon. *Cf.* Function Word.

LEXICALLY SELECT: An expression used to signify that an affix cannot be attached freely to just any base, but, rather, the information as to what bases the affix attaches to is an integral part of its lexical entry.

LEXICON: The set of all forms making up the vocabulary of a language.

LIGHT SYLLABLE: A syllable with neither a branching nucleus nor a coda. *Cf.* Heavy Syllable.

LICENSING: A relational property which allows an element to surface.

LICENSER: The element (melodic or structural) which licenses some other element.

LINE CONFLATION: In metrical theory, the deletion of line 1 from the grid to dispose of all the feet but the one bearing the main stress.

LINGUISTIC SIGN: For Saussure, the basic element of language, made up of the arbitrary conjunction of a signifier and a signified.

LINGUISTICS: The analytic study of language.

LINGUO-: A prefix signifying 'tongue', from the Latin *lingua*.

LINKING *r*: An expression referring to pronouncing an *r* between a non-high vowel and a following vowel in the next word, in accents where that *r* is not pronounced when the word is said in isolation, even though it appears in the spelling. *Cf.* Intrusive *r*.

LIQUIDS: A type of consonant that has one part of the oral channel blocked during its production, while another part remains unobstructed and allows the air to escape freely.

LOOP: A device allowed in some types of Lexical Phonology, whereby a form is fed back into the previous level.

LOW: (1) A tone characterized by a relatively low pitch. *Cf.* High, Mid. (2) A binary distinctive feature, a dependent of [dorsal], whose positive value is characterized by a lowering of the body of the tongue.

M: A shorthand for a mid tone. *Cf.* H, L.

MANNER OF ARTICULATION: The parameter that defines the degree of constriction present in the articulation of a sound.

MAPPING: The transformation of one level of representation into the next one. *Cf.* Projection.

MARKED: A label given to sounds or structures which are 'more complex', 'less expected', 'less natural', and the like. *Cf.* Unmarked.

MARKEDNESS: Nominalization of "marked", a concept that inspires the Theory of Markedness.

MARKEDNESS CONSTRAINTS: In OT, the family of constraints that express the universal tendencies exhibited in the constitution of segments.

MARKEDNESS STATEMENTS: The filters or constraints that make up the theory of markedness, prohibiting a particular feature or a combination of features.

MAXIMAL ONSET PARAMETER: *See* Onset Maximization.

MAX[IMALITY]: In OT, the constraint responsible for the maximal mapping of underlying forms onto the surface. *See also* Parse.

MEDIAN LINE: The line made by the intersection of the median plane with the anatomical structures.

MEDIAN PLANE: The vertical plane that cuts the human body into two symmetrical halves, one to the left and one to the right.

MELODY: A generic label used in autosegmental phonology to refer to quality, that is, phonetic substance, as against quantity, that is, length. A synonym for "segment".

METRICAL: The adjective corresponding to "meter", which suggests measurement, as is characteristic of rhythm.

METRICAL GRID: A formal object made out of marks (conventionally written as asterisks) organized in rows intersecting with a series of columns, in the style of a grid, and used to represent prominence relations.

MID: A tone pronounced at a pitch intermediate between H and L, and transcribed as M. In a handful of languages, the mid tone is split into a high mid and a mid proper. *Cf.* High, Low.

MIDDLE ENGLISH: The English that resulted from the mixture of the purely Germanic Old English with the Norman French of the conquerors, and which became Modern English towards the end of the fifteenth century.

MINIMAL ONSET SATISFACTION: The principle that all syllables in a given domain need to have an onset before codas are allowed.

MINIMAL PAIR: Any pair of words that differ by just one sound in the same position.

MINIMAL SONORITY DISTANCE: A parameter that regulates the configuration of complex syllable constituents (notably onsets) by imposing a minimal distance in sonority between the component segments.

MODEL: A word that refers to a scientific idealization of reality.

MODERN ENGLISH: The form of English that emerged from Middle English towards the end of the fifteenth century.

MONOPHTHONG: A vowel which is pronounced with the same quality all through. *Cf.* Diphthong.

MONOVALENT: Another word for "unary" as referred to features. Derived from "valency".

MORA: Traditionally, a basic unit of classic versification, also used in the phonological analysis of Japanese. Now also an alternative to skeletal slots, conventionally represented by the Greek letter "μ" ("mu" [mju] in English).

MORPHEME: A minimal unit of grammatical function.

NARROW TRANSCRIPTION: A phonetic transcription which is phonetically oriented, rather than phonemically. *Cf.* Broad Transcription.

NASAL CAVITY: The cavity which is situated above the oral cavity, and opens up to the outside environment through the nostrils.

NASAL SOUND: A sound characterized by the use of the nasal cavity as an additional resonating chamber, a situation achieved by lowering the velum, to allow the air into the nasal cavity. *Cf.* Oral Sound.

NATURAL CLASS: Each of the families of segments which universally tend to be affected by the same phonological processes. A natural class is formally defined by a shared feature or set of features.

NATURAL PHONOLOGY: The phonology that is spontaneously present in children in the absence of influence from marked input from the language of the environment.

NETWORK ENGLISH: *See* General American.

NEUTRALIZATION: The suspension of a contrast in a certain context.

NO-CROSSING CONSTRAINT: In autosegmental phonology, the requirement that association lines do not cross.

NON-CYCLIC AFFIXES: Affixes which do not define a domain compatible with cyclic rules.

NON-CYCLIC RULE: A rule that only applies once, at the level of the largest constituent. *Cf.* Cyclic Rule.

NON-INTERACTING: Said of two rules that have no influence on each other, and therefore can apply in either order, without the results being affected.

NON-RHOTIC: An accent which does not have rhoticity.

NUCLEAR TONE: In a tune, the sequence last word tone + phrase tone + boundary tone, that carries the main load of the tune.

NUCLEUS: The most sonorous element of the syllable, typically a vowel.

OBLIGATORY ARGUMENT: In syntax, a word whose meaning is integrated in the meaning of the verb in a particularly close manner.

OBLIGATORY CONTOUR PRINCIPLE (OCP): The tendency to disallow adjacent similar elements from all tiers but the skeleton, within a common domain or constituent.

OBSTRUENT: A type of sound characterized by the presence of a radical obstruction to the airflow in the oral cavity.

OCCAM'S RAZOR: The methodological principle in science that entities must not be multiplied beyond necessity.

OCP: *See* Obligatory Contour Principle.

OLD ENGLISH: The purely Germanic form of English that eventually merged with Norman French to give way to Middle English.

ONSET: The constituent that starts the syllable, and precedes the rime. *Cf.* Rime.

ONSET FIRST PRINCIPLE: The principle that onset formation takes precedence over coda formation.

ONSET MAXIMIZATION: The principle that onsets must be fully formed, in accordance with the principles of the language, before coda formation is carried out with the remnant.

OPAQUE VOWEL: In vowel harmony, a vowel prespecified for the harmonizing feature, which starts off a new harmony domain. *Cf.* Transparency.

OPEN: A binary distinctive feature expressing degree of tongue height in vowels in an approach to feature geometry that aims for a uniform place specification of consonants and vowels. The feature [±open] is assumed to be recursive, to reflect the open-ended nature of vowel height.

OPEN SYLLABLE: A syllable with no coda. *Cf.* Closed Syllable.

OPTIMALITY THEORY (OT): A development in generative phonology that restricts phonological grammars to a set of (violable) ranked constraints. The constraints evaluate a potentially infinite range of candidates generated by a universal function named GEN, to find the most harmonic one.

ORAL CAVITY: The cavity inside the mouth, where most language sounds are produced. *Cf.* Nasal Cavity.

ORAL SOUND: A sound produced with no air coming out through the nose, as a result of the raising of the soft palate. *Cf.* Nasal Sound.

ORDERING HYPOTHESIS: *See* Affix Ordering Hypothesis.

ORDERING PARADOXES: In Lexical Phonology, combinations of affixes which are predicted to be illegitimate but which do occur.

ORTHOGRAPHY: The spelling system.

OT: *See* Optimality Theory.

PALATAL: A term referring to sounds articulated on the hard palate.

PALATE: The dome of the oral cavity, commonly referred to as "the roof of the mouth".

PALATOALVEOLAR: A class of sounds so called because their place of articulation straddles the palate and the tooth ridge or "alveoli".

PĀṆINI'S THEOREM: In OT, the Elsewhere Condition as applied to constraint interaction, renamed thus to honour its original discoverer.

PARADIGMATIC: Said of a relation between two elements such that they can both (potentially) occupy the same position in the string. *Cf.* Syntagmatic.

PARALINGUISTIC: Interacting with language without being part of it.

PARAMETER: A criterion for classification.

PARAMETER SETTING: The assignment of a specific value to a parameter out of the range of values it allows.

PARENT NODE: The parent node of a node is the node that immediately dominates it. Also called "mother node".

PARSE: In early OT, a constraint enforcing the mapping of underlying elements onto the surface. *See also* Max.

PARSING: A term which denotes allotment of elements to constituents.

PASSIVE ARTICULATOR: The inert articulator. *Cf.* Active Articulator.

PATH: A direct route from a subordinate feature to its superordinate feature along a feature geometry web.

PERFORMANCE: Language as it occurs in the real world. *Cf.* Competence.

PERIPHERALITY CONDITION: A condition on extrametricality (or extraprosodicity, in general) to the effect that it can only affect elements on the edge of the domain.

PHARYNX: The backmost part of the mouth, immediately above the larynx.

PHONEME: A unit of explicit sound contrast.

PHONETIC LEVEL: The last level of a derivation, corresponding to the phonological surface representation.

PHONETIC REPRESENTATION: The level of representation that corresponds to the way an utterance is heard or said.

PHONETIC TRANSCRIPTION: A representation of phonetic sound by means of phonetic symbols, such as those of the IPA.

PHONETICS: The discipline concerned with the analysis of actual language sound: its articulation by a speaker, its acoustic patterns in the air, and the perception of these patterns by a hearer.

PHONOLOGICAL CONSTITUENT: A constituent in the phonology.

PHONOLOGICAL DOMAIN: The spatial bounds within which certain phonological rules apply.

PHONOLOGICAL PHRASE (PP): A phonological domain essentially made up of a lexical head and its specifier.

PHONOLOGICAL UTTERANCE (PU): The largest phonological domain, roughly corresponding to a speaker's utterance.

PHONOLOGICAL WORD (PW): A phonological domain and a phonological constituent that usually corresponds to a morphosyntactic word.

PHONOLOGY: The discipline concerned with the study of linguistically significant sound patterns, that is, with the organization of the sounds of speech.

PHONOTACTIC CONSTRAINTS: Restrictions on the patterning of sounds in the words of any given language.

PHRASAL STRESS: The patterns of stress assigned to phrases.

PHRASE: A string of words obeying syntactic requirements.

PHRASE ACCENT: *See* Phrase Tone.

PHRASE TONE: In an intonational melody, the tone that closely follows the last word tone, just before the right boundary tone. *Cf.* Boundary Tone, Word Tone.

PITCH ACCENT: *See* Word Tone.

PITCH ACCENT LANGUAGE: A language where a fixed tonal melody is associated with each word.

PLACE OF ARTICULATION: The spot in the vocal tract where the sound is articulated.

PLURAL: A morphosemantic category denoting more than one referent.

POSTLEXICAL LEVEL: In Lexical Phonology, a level or stratum which is not word-bound, as opposed to a lexical level, which is. *Cf.* Lexical Level.

POSTLEXICAL RULES: In lexical phonology, the rules which apply at a postlexical level. *Cf.* Lexical Rules.

PP: *See* Phonological Phrase.

PREFIX: An anteposed affix. *Cf.* Infix, Suffix.

PRESPECIFICATION: Specified in the lexicon, contrary to expectation. *Cf.* Underspecification.

PRIMARY ARTICULATION: The main articulation in segments with a complex articulation. It is located along the median plane of the vocal tract. *Cf.* Secondary Articulation.

PRIMARY ARTICULATOR: The articulator responsible for the sound's primary articulation.

PRIMARY CARDINAL VOWELS: The eight basic cardinal vowels, unrounded at the front and rounded at the back, except for [ɑ]. *Cf.* Secondary Cardinal Vowels.

PRIMARY STRESS: The strongest stress in a particular domain, usually the word.

PRINCIPLE OF LATE BLOCK RULE ASSIGNMENT: In Lexical Phonology, the postulate that rules are assigned to the latest possible block in the absence of contrary evidence.

PRINCIPLE OF STRICT CYCLICITY: The principle which restricts the application of structure-changing cyclic rules to environments derived in that cycle, where "derived" = resulting from a morphological process or, in some cases, from a phonological change.

PRIVATIVE FEATURE: A monovalent feature, with only the positive value.

PROCLITIC: A clitic that precedes its host. *Cf.* Enclitic.

PRODUCTIVE: Said of a process which can be applied freely to form new material.

PROGRESSIVE ASSIMILATION: Assimilation to the preceding segment, which thus "progresses". *Cf.* Regressive Assimilation.

PROJECTION: The operation by which an element replicates itself at a higher level of structure. *Cf.* Mapping.

PROPOSITION: A word used to refer to the logical content of utterances.

PROSODIC DOMAIN: An expression commonly used for "phonological domain".

PROSODIC HIERARCHY: The hierarchy made up of the ranked prosodic domains.

PROSODIC PHONOLOGY: An ambiguous expression, used to refer both to the theory of phonological domains and to the theory of phonological constituents.

PROSODIC STRUCTURE: Abstract structure over and above the structure that corresponds to the linear arrangement of segments and to the relations between the features inside the segments.

PU: *See* Phonological Utterance.

PULL CHAIN: *See* Drag Chain.

PW: *See* Phonological Word.

QUALITY: The substance of a segment, particularly a vowel.

QUANTITY: The length of a segment, autosegmentally formalized by its number of skeletal associations.

QUANTUM VOWELS: The vowels [a], [i] and [u], each of which can be articulated over a reasonably broad space with minimal effect on perception.

QUANTITY-INSENSITIVE: Said of stress systems that do not require accenting of heavy syllables.

QUANTITY-SENSITIVE: Said of stress systems that require accenting of heavy syllables.

R-COLOURED: An expression that refers to an [ɹ]-type quality superimposed on a vowel, usually achieved by curling up the tip of the tongue, in a gesture of retroflection.

RADICAL: A unary feature that refers to the root of the tongue and dominates [±ATR].

RADICAL UNDERSPECIFICATION: A theory of underspecification that aims for maximal lexical simplicity, which it achieves by leaving all the feature values defining one segment (in a class) unspecified in every language. *Cf.* Contrast-restricted Underspecification.

RANKING METAPRINCIPLE: In OT, the requirement that a higher-ranked constraint be complied with in preference to a lower-ranked constraint.

RECEIVED PRONUNCIATION: *See* RP.

RECURSIVENESS: The application of a process to its own output.

REDUNDANCY: A term applied to information which is predictable.

REDUNDANCY RULE: A structure-building rule that fills in a gap in an underspecified input.

REDUNDANCY RULE ORDERING CONSTRAINT: In Radical Underspecification, the requirement that a redundancy rule apply before the first (ordinary) rule that refers to the output value provided by the redundancy rule.

REDUPLICANT: In reduplication, the affixal copy of the base.

REDUPLICATION: A process of word formation which consists in copying the whole or part of a word in a prefixal, infixal or suffixal position.

REGRESSIVE ASSIMILATION: Assimilation to the following segment, which thus "regresses". *Cf.* Progressive Assimilation.

RESONATING CHAMBER: An enclosed space where sound gets enhanced at certain acoustic frequencies.

RETRACTED: Said of a sound when it is pronounced at a place of articulation more towards the back of the mouth than is usually the case. *Cf.* Advanced Articulation.

RETROFLECTION: The action of curling back the blade of the tongue.

RETROFLEX: A sound produced with retroflection.

RHOTIC: An accent which exhibits rhoticity.

RHOTICITY: A term referring to the systematic occurrence of the sound represented by *r*, whereas in non-rhotic accents *r* only occurs before vowels.

RHOTICS: A general term to designate a class of sounds that are phonologically "*r*-like" in some way: the members of this class do not necessarily have much in common with each other phonetically.

RHYMING: A device used in versification involving identical rimes.

RHYTHM: A pattern of repetition of certain prominent elements.

RIGHT-HEADED: Applied to a constituent which has its head on the right edge. *Cf.* Left-Headed.

RIME: An immediate constituent of the syllable placed after the onset and made up of the nucleus and the coda. *Cf.* Onset.

ROLLED *r*: An alveolar trill.

ROOT: (1) The base of the word, to which affixes can be added. (2) The topmost superordinate node in the feature geometry, currently conceived of as made up of the features [±consonantal, ±sonorant]. (3) The section of the tongue behind the body, mainly tucked away in the pharynx. *Cf.* Blade, Body, Tip.

ROUND: A binary feature dependent on [labial] whose positive value involves a rounding of the lips.

RP: A shorthand for "Received Pronunciation", a term that refers to an accent of English traditionally associated with the English upper middle classes and their "preparatory" and "public" schools.

RULE: The formal statement of a mapping between an input and an output representation.

RULE ORDERING: The strategy of applying rules sequentially, rather than simultaneously. The order of the rules can be intrinsic or extrinsic.

SCHWA [ʃwɑ]: A central mid vowel, represented as an inverted "e" ([ə]) in the IPA alphabet.

SECONDARY ARTICULATION: In segments with a complex articulation, the subsidiary articulation. *Cf.* Primary Articulation.

SECONDARY CARDINAL VOWELS: The set of eight cardinal vowels produced by deliberately reversing the normal action of the lips. *Cf.* Primary Cardinal Vowels.

SECONDARY STRESS: A peak of prominence lower than the one corresponding to the primary stress.

SEGMENT: A cluster of distinctive feature values associated with one root in the feature geometry.

SELF-CONJUNCTION: In OT, a special type of constraint consisting of a constraint conjoined to itself.

SEMANTIC OPACITY: The opposite of semantic transparency.

SEMANTIC TRANSPARENCY: The situation where the meaning of a word or expression is equal to the sum of the meanings of each of its parts. *Cf.* Semantic Opacity.

SEMANTICS: The branch of linguistics that studies the meaning of words and linguistic expressions.

SIBILANT: An informal label for a segment which is [coronal, +strident].

SIBLING NODES: Nodes which are immediately dominated by the same parent node. Also known as "sister nodes".

SIGNIFIED: In Saussurian linguistics, the characteristic meaning of each linguistic sign.

SIGNIFIER: In Saussurian linguistics, the characteristic sound of each linguistic sign.

SKELETAL SLOTS: Each of the elements that make up the skeleton, also referred to as timing units.

SKELETON: The central tier in the autosegmental model of phonology, from which all autosegmental planes fan out, with the exception of those that house dependent features.

SLACK VOCAL FOLDS: One of the four features concerning the state of the vocal folds, specifically referring to their lax condition. The value [+SlackVF] is responsible for both voice and high pitch. *Cf.* Glottal Stop, Spread Glottis, Stiff Vocal Folds.

SOFT PALATE: The soft area at the back of the palate. *Cf.* Hard Palate.

SOFT UNIVERSALS: Universals which are violable, best formalized as parameters. *Cf.* Hard Universals.

SONORANTS: Sounds where the pressure of the air behind the constriction is the same as the pressure of the ambient air. Sonorancy is formalized by means of the binary distinctive feature [±sonorant]. *Cf.* Obstruent.

SONORITY: The amount of sound present in each segment.

SONORITY HIERARCHY: *See* Sonority Scale.

SONORITY SCALE: A universal ranking of segments according to the amount of sonority each carries.

SONORITY SEQUENCING: The property of the sonority profile of the syllable, involving rising until the sonority peaks, and then falling.

SPECIFIER: In syntax, the material that precedes the head in languages like English, and which makes up a phrase with the head and the complement. *Cf.* Complement.

SPELLING: The way words are conventionally written down in any one language, in principle totally irrelevant to phonology.

SPREAD GLOTTIS: One of the four distinctive features concerning the state of the vocal folds. The positive value [+SG] is responsible for aspiration. *Cf.* Glottal Stop, Slack Vocal Folds, Stiff Vocal Folds.

STANDARD ACCENT: Said of an accent with high social prestige, favoured by the organs of social power, such as the media.

STEM: The basic part of a word, essentially equivalent to the root.

STIFF VOCAL FOLDS: One of the four features concerning the state of the vocal folds, specifically referring to their tense condition. The value [+StiffVF] is responsible for both voicelessness and low pitch. *Cf.* Glottal Stop, Slack Vocal Folds, Spread Glottis.

STOP: A consonantal sound produced by blocking the airflow for a fraction of a second, and then abruptly releasing the closure to allow the air to rush out.

STRATAL PHONOLOGY: *See* Lexical Phonology.

STRATUM: *See* Level.

STRATUM CONTIGUITY HYPOTHESIS: The principle by which the strata a rule is assigned to must be contiguous.

STRATUM CONTINUITY HYPOTHESIS: Another name for the Stratum Contiguity Hypothesis, common in the literature.

STRAY ERASURE: The rule or convention that deletes material which is not prosodically licensed.

STRESS: The prominence with which certain syllables are pronounced, usually materialized as greater loudness, greater length, greater precision, or association with the word tone.

STRESS-AND-INTONATION LANGUAGES: Languages in which certain tone combinations, or tunes, provide the functional or attitudinal meaning of utterances.

STRESS CLASH: The situation that obtains between two asterisks in any grid line when they are adjacent and there is no asterisk in between the corresponding pair of asterisks in the line immediately below.

STRICT CYCLICITY: *See* Principle of Strict Cyclicity.

STRIDENT: A binary distinctive feature whose positive value is characterized acoustically as involving high energy at the higher frequencies.

STRONG VERB: A verb which is conjugated by means of vowel alternations in the stem, rather than through the more common affixation.

STRUCTURAL CONSTRAINTS: In OT, the family of constraints expressing the universally favoured structures for syllables, feet, and so on.

STRUCTURE-BUILDING RULES: Rules which add structure to the input. *Cf.* Structure-Changing Rules.

STRUCTURE-CHANGING RULES: Rules which change some of the structure of the input. *Cf.* Structure-Building Rules.

STRUCTURE PRESERVATION: The property of some phonological rules of being strictly respectful of the basic structural properties of the language, such as the identity of lexical segments or the core syllable structure.

SUFFIX: A morpheme concatenated to the right of some base. *Cf.* Prefix, Infix.

SUPRASEGMENTAL: Literally 'above the segment' (*cf.* Latin *supra* 'above'), it is referred to phenomena such as stress, tone and length, not unambiguously.

SURFACE LEVEL: *See* Phonetic Level.

SURFACE REPRESENTATION: *See* Phonetic Representation.

SYLLABLE: A prosodic constituent made up of segments abstractly connected in sonority clusters.

SYLLABLE WEIGHT: The property of syllables of being light or heavy.

SYNONYMS: Words which have the same meaning but sound different.

SYNTAGMATIC: Said of a linear relation between two elements. *Cf.* Paradigmatic.

SYNTAX: The principles that govern the way that words are strung together.

TABLEAU: In OT, the visual representation of the evaluation of the candidates by the ranked constraints, in the form of a grid.

TAP: A type of consonant similar, but supposedly not identical, to a flap.

TAUTO-: A prefix which signifies 'same'.

THEORY OF MARKEDNESS: The theory made up of the set of markedness statements and of the implications that logically follow from them.

THREE-SYLLABLE WINDOW: The property of word stress of not occurring beyond one of the three peripheral syllables.

TIMING TIER: Another word for the skeleton.

TIP: The frontmost point of the tongue. *Cf.* Blade, Body, Root.

TONE: A phonological element realized by a certain relative pitch.

TONE LANGUAGES: Languages where lexical entries can be differentiated by tones.

TONE TIER: The tier that houses the tones.

TOOTH RIDGE: The edge of the palate from which the teeth stem out.

TOTAL ASSIMILATION: Assimilation in all features, resulting in two segments becoming identical.

TRACHEA: The windpipe that links the lungs to the mouth.

TRANSDERIVATIONAL CORRESPONDENCE CONSTRAINTS: In OT, the constraints that impose correspondences between surface forms.

TRANSITIVITY: A logical property of ordered rules, such that A > B and B > C implies A > C.

TRANSPARENCY: The failure of a segment to interfere with the spread of harmony or assimilation, as if it were not there. *Cf.* Opaque Vowel.

TREE: A visual representation of a network of hierarchical relations.

TRILL: A type of consonant articulated at various places in the vocal cavity making use of a mechanism similar to voice, to take advantage of the Bernoulli effect. *See* Voice.

TROCHEE: A classical word used to refer to a left-headed (binary) foot. *Cf.* Iamb.

TUNE: A melody made up of a string of tones.

UG: *See* Universal Grammar.

UMLAUT: Fronting of a vowel induced by assimilation to the front quality of a following vowel.

UNARY: Said of features with only one value.

UNBOUNDED FOOT: A foot with any number of elements in the baseline. *Cf.* Binary Foot.

UNDERLYING LEVEL: The level that contains underlying representations.

UNDERLYING REPRESENTATION: An expression usually used interchangeably with "lexical representation". Strictly speaking, however, "lexical representation" specifically relates to the lexicon, whereas "underlying representation" refers to the starting line of a derivation.

UNDERSPECIFICATION: The omission of feature specifications in lexical representation. *See* Prespecification.

UNIVERSAL GRAMMAR (UG): The set of principles for language that all humans are supposed to be endowed with innately.

UNMARKED: A label given to sounds or structures which are 'less complex', 'more expected', 'more natural', and the like. *Cf.* Marked.

UVULA: The fleshy appendage found dangling down at the end of the soft palate.

UVULAR FRICATIVE: A fricative consonant articulated at the uvula.

UVULAR TRILL: A consonantal sound produced with a vibrating uvula, in a manner reminiscent of gargling.

V: A symbol that informally stands for a vowel. *Cf.* C.

V-PLACE: A class-node for vowels which depends on the C-Place class-node in a theory of feature geometry favouring a uniform set of place features for consonants and vowels. *Cf.* C-Place.

VACUOUS APPLICATION: Said of rules whose application does not change anything.

VALENCY: The number of values that can be assigned to a particular feature – features can mainly be monovalent or unary, binary, ternary, or multivalent or n-ary.

VELAR: Said of sounds made at the soft palate.

VELUM: The anatomical word for the soft palate, derived from the Latin *velum* 'veil'.

VOCAL CORDS: Another way of referring to the vocal folds. It is a somewhat misleading expression anatomically.

VOCAL FOLDS: The two bands of muscular tissue which stretch across the larynx.

VOCAL PLAY: A stage in developmental phonology during which the child experiments with a multitude of possibilities of what might be construed as consonant articulations, at around four or six months. *Cf.* Babbling, Cooing.

VOCAL TRACT: The tube(s) channelling the airflow responsible for the production of speech. The term is often restricted in use to the section above the larynx.

VOICE: The technical term used in phonetics to refer to the vibration of the vocal folds, by the so-called "Bernoulli effect", as a result of the rapid stream of air flowing through.

VOICE ONSET TIME: The time span between the release of the closure for a stop and the start of the vibration of the vocal folds for the following vowel.

VOICED: Said of a sound which is pronounced with simultaneous voicing.

VOICELESS: Said of a sound pronounced without voice.

VOWEL: A sound produced without obstructing the airflow, and formalized as [–consonantal]. *Cf.* Consonant.

VOWEL TRIANGLE: The triangle made up of the three most basic, or "quantum", vowels ([i], [a], [u]), or, by extension, of the five most common vowels ([i], [e], [a], [o], [u]).

VOWEL REDUCTION: A phenomenon whereby the range of vowels available in a language diminishes in certain contexts, typically involving the absence of stress. It is not uncommon for reduced vowels to be realized as schwa.

WBP: *See* Weight by Position.

WEIGHT: *See* Syllable Weight.

WEIGHT BY POSITION (WBP): A procedure involving the structural projection of a mora from a coda consonant, as is the case with /n/ in *agenda*.

WELL-FORMEDNESS CONDITION: A principle of early autosegmental phonology formulated in connection with African tone languages. It required that at each stage in the derivation all syllables be associated with at least one tone, and all tones be associated with at least one syllable.

WORD TONE: In an intonational melody, the tones which are associated with the stressed syllable of each word. Commonly referred to as "pitch accent". *Cf.* Boundary Tone, Phrase Tone.

X: Each of the elements that make up the "timing tier", meant to be units of (abstract) phonological timing.

X-TIER: Another word for the skeleton, connotative of the X elements that make it up. Historically, the X-tier is the successor to the CV-tier.

INDEX OF LANGUAGES

INDEX OF NAMES

INDEX OF SUBJECTS